Exams with S Chand

Exams with S Chand helps you with :

- **Exam-Relevant Updates First**
  Get timely updates on SSC, UPSC, Banking, Railway, CUET, NDA & other competitive exams — all in one place.
- **Trusted Preparation with S Chand Books**
  Learn from India's most trusted academic publisher, recommended by toppers and educators nationwide.
- **Smart Study Tips & Exam Hacks**
  Practical shortcuts, strategy tips, and last-minute revision tricks to boost accuracy and confidence.
- **PYQs, MCQs & Concept Clarity**
  Access previous year questions, concept explanations, and practice insights aligned with latest exam patterns.
- **Guidance by Experts & Faculties**
  Content curated with insights from experienced teachers, authors and subject experts.
- **Student-Centric & Easy to Understand**
  Simple explanations, bilingual content, and visual learning to suit every aspirant.

 https://www.instagram.com/examswithschand/
 https://www.youtube.com/@ExamswithSChand1
 https://www.facebook.com/examswithschand/
 https://linktr.ee/examswithschand
 t.me/exams_withschand

Tenth Edition 2026-27

INDIAN ECONOMY

(GENERAL STUDIES – UPSC CIVIL SERVICES EXAMINATION)

"In this age of information overload, this book presents the most precise as well as comprehensive, relevant and analytical content"

VIVEK SINGH

S Chand And Company Limited
(ISO 9001 Certified Company)

S Chand And Company Limited

(ISO 9001 Certified Company)

Head Office: D-92, Sector–2, Noida 201301, U.P. (India), Ph. 91-120-4682700

Registered Office: A-27, 2nd Floor, Mohan Co-operative Industrial Estate, New Delhi – 110 044

Phone: 011-49731800

www.schandpublishing.com; e-mail: info@schandpublishing.com

Marketing Offices:

Chennai : Ph: 23632120, chennai@schandpublishing.com

Guwahati : Ph: 2738811, 2735640 guwahati@schandpublishing.com

Hyderabad : Ph: 40186018, hyderabad@schandpublishing.com

Jalandhar : Ph: 4645630, jalandhar@schandpublishing.com

Kolkata : Ph: 23357458, 23353914, kolkata@schandpublishing.com

Lucknow : Ph: 4003633, lucknow@schandpublishing.com

Mumbai : Ph: 25000297, mumbai@schandpublishing.com

Patna : Ph: 4011400, patna@schandpublishing.com

First Edition 2024
Revised Edition 2025
Ninth Edition 2025
Tenth Edition 2026

ISBN: 978-93-7359-700-3 **Product Code:** H1IEG47ECON10ENAJ26O

PRINTED IN INDIA

By Shrinath Prints N Packing, C-60,61, Delhi Pin -110020 and Published by S Chand And Company Limited, A-27, 2nd Floor, Mohan Co-operative Industrial Estate, New Delhi – 110 044

Preface To The Revised Edition

This book on Indian Economy will serve as a comprehensive guide for aspirants preparing for the UPSC Civil Services Examination, covering both the Preliminary and Main sections of General Studies Paper III, with a specific focus on economic development. It includes the latest Budget 2026-27 and Economic Survey 2025-26, ensuring that the content is not only relevant but also up-to-date. The book is structured to provide a balanced mix of static and conceptual topics alongside current economic issues, aiming to facilitate a deep understanding of the subject matter. Emphasis has been placed on conceptual clarity, which is supported by diagrams, graphs, flowcharts, and numerous examples to enhance the learning experience.

In addition to covering the UPSC syllabus, this book is thoroughly updated with the latest economic data and government schemes. It includes previous years' UPSC Preliminary and Main exam questions to provide a clear understanding of the examination pattern and question trends. Economic terms are compiled at the end of the book for easy reference, and important keywords are highlighted in bold for quick revision. The book also maps the UPSC (CSE) syllabus with relevant chapters and extends its coverage to the State PSC exams, and the syllabi of RBI, NABARD, and SEBI, making it a valuable resource for a wide range of competitive examinations.

For all the latest economy related updates, you can join author's telegram channel: "Economy by Vivek Singh" (https://t.me/VivekSingh_Economy) or you can mail at viveksingheconomy@gmail.com

Vivek Singh

INDIAN ECONOMY – UPSC (CSE) SYLLABUS and Mapping of Chapters

Preliminary Exam Syllabus:

- Economic and Social Development-Sustainable Development, Poverty, Inclusion, Demographics, Social Sector Initiatives, etc. *[Chapters 1, 2 and 4 covers the major syllabus but you need to read rest of the chapters also.]*

Main Exam Syllabus:

- Indian Economy and issues relating to planning, mobilization, of resources, growth, development and employment *[Chapter 6, 7 & 8]*
- Inclusive growth and issues arising from it *[Chapter 8]*
- Government Budgeting *[Chapter 4]*
- Major crops-cropping patterns in various parts of the country, - different types of irrigation and irrigation systems storage, transport and marketing of agricultural produce and issues and related constraints; e-technology in the aid of farmers *[Chapter 10 & 11]*
- Issues related to direct and indirect farm subsidies and minimum support prices; Public Distribution System- objectives, functioning, limitations, revamping; issues of buffer stocks and food security; Technology missions; economics of animal-rearing *[Chapter 9, 10 & 11]*
- Food processing and related industries in India- scope' and significance, location, upstream and downstream requirements, supply chain management *[Chapter 12]*
- Land reforms in India *[Chapter 5]*
- Effects of liberalization on the economy, changes in industrial policy and their effects on industrial growth *[Chapter 6 and 7]*
- Infrastructure: Energy, Ports, Roads, Airports, Railways etc. *[Chapter 14]*
- Investment models *[Chapter 14]*

CONTENTS

1 Fundamentals of Macro Economy

1.1 Introduction

Economics is the study of how societies use scarce resources to produce valuable goods and services and distribute them among different individuals. Certain European and North American countries are very rich (per person income is high which leads to higher living standard) while countries in Africa and Latin America are poor. Have you ever thought of the basic reason behind it? Even if the African countries are very rich in mineral resources like coal, iron ore, other metals, they are quite poor, while if you see Japan, it has very fewer natural resources but it has high per capita income. The basic reason behind this difference in the standard of living of these countries is that the government and the people in these developed/rich countries have **efficiently exploited the limited resources** of land, labour and capital for the betterment and development of its people.

Economics is divided into two major subfields: Microeconomics and Macroeconomics.

Microeconomics is the study of decisions that people and businesses (*individual economic agents*) make regarding the allocation of resources and prices of goods and services. For example, the study of what mix of products an individual purchase with a given amount of money is part of microeconomic study. Microeconomics would look at how a particular company whether small or big can maximize its production and capacity so that it can lower prices and better compete with its competitors in its industry.

Macroeconomics, on the other hand, is the study of the **national economy as a whole.** Macroeconomics examines a wide variety of areas such as how total investment and consumption in the economy are determined, how central banks manage money and interest rates, what causes international financial crises, how an increase/ decrease in net exports would affect a nation's capital account and why some nations grow rapidly while others stagnate. The study of variables at the country level such as Gross Domestic Product (GDP) and how it is affected by the changes in the unemployment rate, interest rate and price levels is part of the macroeconomic study.

The UPSC syllabus is about macro economy, which is concerned with the overall performance of the economy.

1.2 Economic Organization (the three problems)

Every human society - whether it is an advanced industrial nation, a centrally planned economy, or an isolated tribal nation – must confront and resolve three fundamental economic problems. Every society must have a way of determining what commodities are to be produced, how these goods are made, and for whom they are produced. Indeed, these three fundamental questions of economic organization - **what, how, and for whom** - are as crucial today as they were at the dawn of human civilization. Let's look more closely at them:

What commodities are to be produced and in what quantity? A society must determine how much of each of the many possible goods and services it will make and when they will be produced. Will we produce pizzas or shirts today? A few high-quality shirts or many cheap shirts? Will we use scarce resources to produce many consumption goods (like pizzas)? Or will we produce fewer consumption goods and more capital goods (like pizza making machines), which will boost production and consumption tomorrow?

How are the goods to be produced? A society must determine who will do the production, with what resources, and what production techniques they will use. Who does the farming and who teaches? Is electricity generated from oil, from coal, or from the sun? Will factories be run by people or robots?

For whom are the goods to be produced? Who gets to eat the fruit of economic activity? Is the distribution of income and wealth fair and equitable? How is the national product divided among different households? Are many people poor and a few rich? Does high income go to teachers or athletes or autoworkers or capitalists? Will society provide minimal consumption to the poor, or must people work if they are to eat?

1.3 Economic Systems

What are the different ways in which a society can answer the questions of what, how, and for whom? Different societies are organized through alternative economic systems, and economics studies the various mechanisms that a society can use to allocate its scarce resources.

We generally distinguish two fundamentally different ways of organizing an economy. At one extreme, government makes most economic decisions, with those on top of the hierarchy giving economic commands to those further down the ladder. At the other extreme, decisions are made in markets, where individuals or enterprises voluntarily agree to exchange goods and services, usually through payments of money. Let's briefly examine each of these two forms of economic organization.

In the United States, and increasingly around the world, most economic questions are settled by the market mechanism. Hence their economic systems are called market economies. A **market economy** is one in which individuals and private firms make the major decisions about production and consumption. A system of prices, of markets, of profits and losses, of incentives and rewards determines what, how and for whom. Firms produce the commodities that yield the highest profits (the *what*) by the techniques of production that are least costly (the *how*). Consumption is determined by individuals' decisions about how to spend the wages and property incomes generated by their labour and property ownership (the *for whom*). The extreme case of a market economy, in which the government keeps its hands-off economic decisions, is called a **laissez-faire** economy.

By contrast, a **command economy** is one in which the government makes all important decisions about production and distribution. In a command economy, such as one which operated in the Soviet Union during most of the twentieth century, the government owns most of the means of production (land and capital); it also owns and directs the operations of enterprises in most industries: it is the employer of most of the workers and tells them how to do their jobs; and it decides how the output of the society is to be divided among different people. In short, in a command economy, the government answers the major economic questions of what, how and for whom, through its ownership of resources and its powers to enforce decisions.

No contemporary society falls completely into either of these polar categories. Rather, all societies are **mixed economies**, with elements of market and command both. Today most of the decisions in the developed and developing economies are made in the market place. But the government also plays an important role in overseeing the functioning of the market; governments pass laws that regulate economic life, produce goods, educational and police services. Most societies today operate as mixed economies.

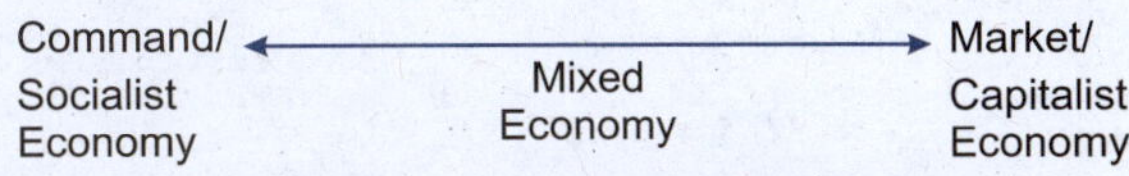

1.4 Four Sectors of Economy

From the economic point of view, a mixed economy is divided into four sectors.

1. Private Sector:

All the **enterprises** owned by the private individuals or group of individuals belong to the private sector. The private sector consists of companies/firms/enterprises in India which are not owned by the government.

2. Government Sector:

This sector includes public administration, police, defence, framing of laws and enforcing them. Apart from imposing taxes and spending money on various infrastructure and healthcare services and education etc., government also undertakes production activity through its companies like Coal India Ltd. (CIL), National Thermal Power Corporation (NTPC) etc. So, all the companies owned by the Central or State Governments i.e. Public Sector Undertakings (PSUs) also belong to the government sector.

3. Household Sector:

A group of persons who normally live together and take food from a common kitchen constitutes a household. The size of a household is the total number of persons in the household. We should always remember that households consist of people. These people work in firms as workers and earn wages. They are the ones who work in the government departments and earn salaries and they are the owners of firms and earn profits. So, **all the human beings (population) belong to household sector**.

Suppose a person named "John" works in "Coal India Ltd. (CIL)" which is a government company then John belongs to the household sector and the company CIL belongs to the government sector.

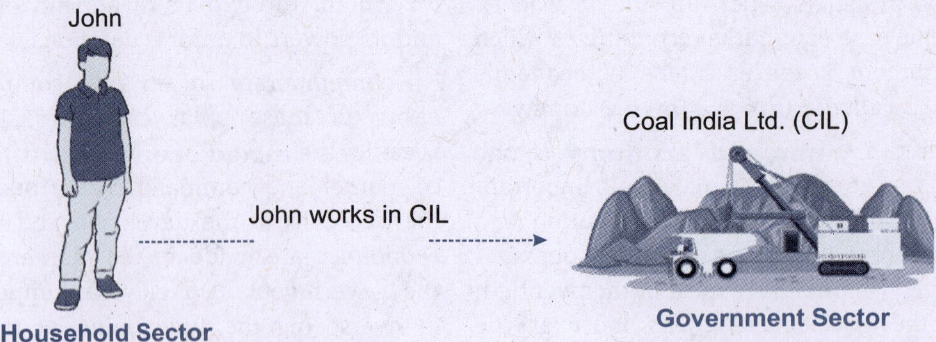

Reliance Industries Ltd. (RIL) is owned by Mukesh Ambani but Mukesh Ambani belongs to the household sector and the "RIL" (which is a passive object and on whose name all the business is being carried out) belongs to the private sector.

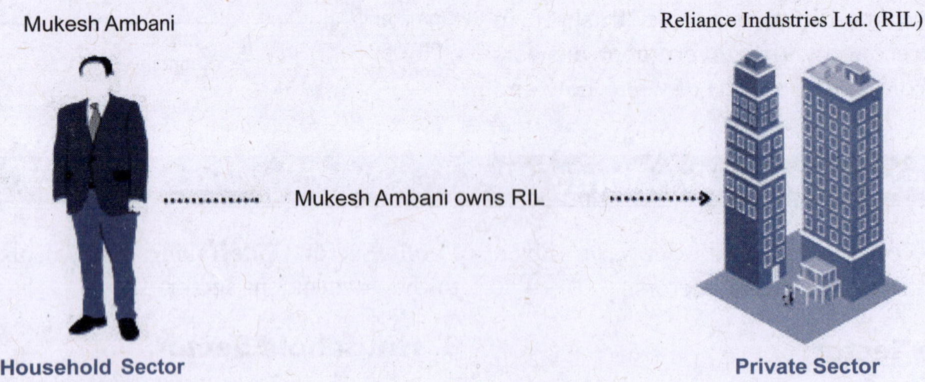

4. External Sector:

This sector consists of the exports and imports of goods and services flowing into the country or out of the country. It also includes the financial flows from and into the domestic country.

Let us understand in detail the private sector first.

1.5 Private Sector

All the firms or enterprises owned by private individuals or entrepreneurs belong to private sector and their basic function is production of output i.e. goods and services. To produce output, any enterprise will require certain inputs. An enterprise may require one input or it may require hundreds of inputs to produce the desired output. All the inputs that an enterprise may require are broadly divided into four categories i.e. entrepreneur, capital, natural resources and labour.

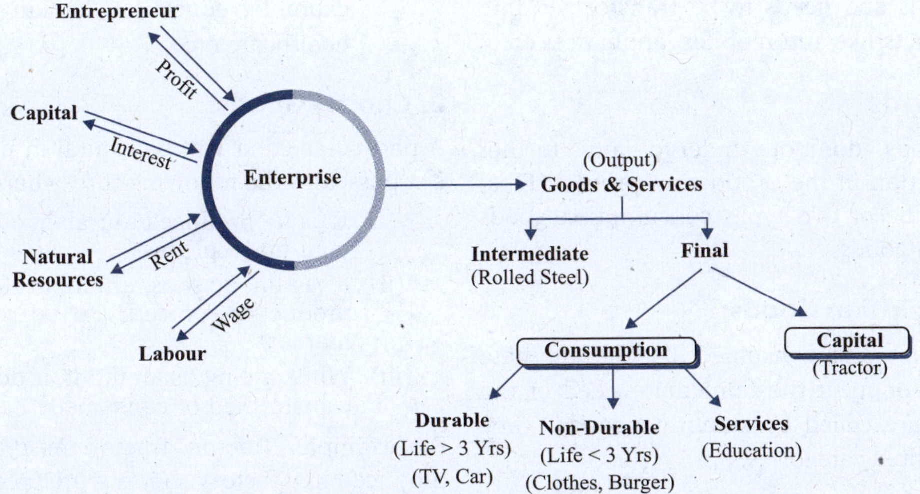

Figure: The four factors/inputs of production combining together to produce output and the classification of output (goods and services) into consumption and capital goods.

The four inputs that an enterprise requires to produce output (goods and services) are called the four "factors of production" or the "inputs of production". These four factors of production are the following (as shown in the figure):

1. Entrepreneur:

The person who takes the risk and starts a new business. This person takes the risk to bring in capital, labour and natural resources together in the form of an enterprise and in return expects "**Profit**". *The entrepreneur is a human being and he belongs to the household sector.*

2. Capital:

In today's world, capital can be physical, financial or intellectual. But from an economic point of view, only the physical capital goods are considered as capital. So, capital includes the building, machinery, equipment etc. The return for the capital is called "**Interest**".

3. Natural Resources:

Natural resources include land and raw materials which are naturally available and are not produced through man-made processes. The return for the natural resources is called "**Rent**".

4. Labour:

It is the human labour which may be physical or mental i.e., it can be unskilled, semi-skilled or skilled. When a human being provides his labour to the enterprise, in return he/she expects "**wages**". *The labour (who is providing the labour services) is a human being and belongs to the household sector.*

1.6 Types of Goods

Intermediate Goods

These are semi-finished goods which have been produced by a process but cannot be used as it is and need to go through further production process to be converted into a final good. For example, steel sheets. The steel sheets cannot be used as it is and needs to be transformed into final products like automobiles, appliances etc.

Final Goods

These goods do not undergo any further transformation in the production process. Final goods can be of two types consumption goods and capital goods.

1. Consumption Goods:

Goods which are consumed by the ultimate consumers or meet the immediate need of the consumer are called consumption goods. They can be of three categories.

(i) Durable Consumption Goods: Consumption goods which do not get exhausted immediately but last over a period of time are called consumer durables. Life of consumer durables is generally more than 3 years. For examples home appliances, consumer electronics, furniture etc.

(ii) Non-Durable Consumption Goods: Consumption goods which get consumed immediately and whose life is generally less than 3 years. For example, cosmetics, food, fuel, paper, clothing etc.

(iii) Services: Services are intangibles and are a kind of consumption goods only, as, it is consumed immediately. For example, education, banking, telecom, healthcare etc.

2. Capital Goods:

A particular good will be capital in nature only if it possesses the following three characteristics:

(i) It is a produced durable output of a man-made process

(ii) It again acts as an input for further production process (to be sold in the market)

(iii) While acting as an input, it does not get transformed or consumed

For example, Tractor. Tractor must have been produced in a factory so it is a produced durable output. Tractor again acts as an input in the production of agricultural products like wheat and rice. And while acting as an input it does not get transformed and remains as it is. *(Wear and tear of tractor happens over a long period of time but we cannot say that the tractor is getting transformed or consumed)*

In strict sense, the economists consider only the physical capital as the capital but in today's world, intangible capital is increasingly becoming important. So, capital can be divided into three categories:

(i) Physical Capital (capital goods)

(ii) Financial Capital (money)

(iii) Intellectual Capital (patents, copyrights etc.)

Consumption and Capital Goods

A particular good can be consumption as well as capital good. For example, washing machine. When a person is using washing machine at his home for washing of his own clothes then it will act as consumption good. But if the same washing machine is purchased by a businessman for providing laundry services, then it is acting as a capital good. Because in the latter case, washing machine is being used to produce washed clothes for the market and not for own consumption. So, whether a good is consumption or capital also depends on the purpose for which it is being used.

If a good is being used to produce some other goods/services to be sold in the market then it will be a capital good. For example, when we purchase a car for our home then it is consumption good but when "Ola Cabs" purchase a car to provide transportation services for the market then the car becomes a capital good.

Intermediate and Final good

A particular good can be final as well as intermediate. For example, "tea leaves". When a person is purchasing the "tea leaves" for his home consumption purpose then the "tea leaves" will be a final good. But when a tea seller is purchasing the "tea leaves" to prepare "tea" and sell it in the market then "tea leaves" is intermediate good and the "tea" is the final good. The distinguishing characteristic whether a good is final or intermediate is "the last transaction in the market". In case of tea seller, the last transaction in the market is of tea, so "tea" is final good. But in case of the person purchasing tea leaves for home purpose, "tea leaves" is the last transacted good in the market, so "tea leaves" will be final good.

1.7 Investment

That part of the final output which comprises of physical capital goods is called gross investment. So, investment in a country is not measured as money put in a business or any economic activity but it is basically that portion of the final output (GDP) which consists of capital goods.

Consider the following diagram:

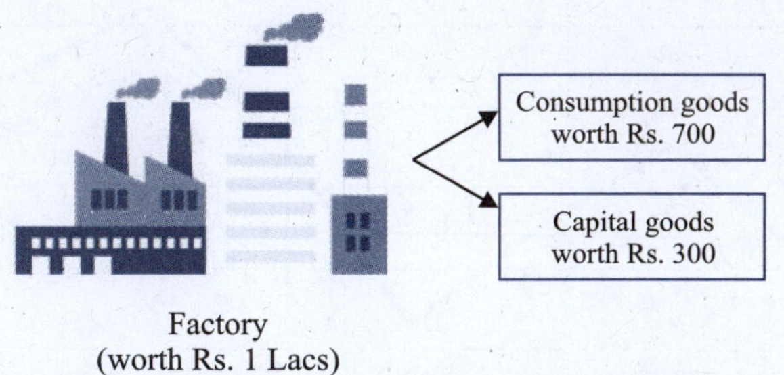

Suppose there is only one factory (capital good) in a country, which is worth Rs. one lakh and is producing consumption goods worth Rs. 700 and capital goods worth Rs. 300 in a particular year (say 2019-20) in an economy. This means that the GDP in 2019-20 will be Rs. 1000 (which is the total production of both consumption and capital goods) and the gross investment in the economy will be Rs. 300 or (Rs. 300/Rs. 1000) 30%, as investment is measured as the percentage of **output** which consists of capital goods.

In the above example, if the country imports capital goods worth Rs. 100 in the year 2019-20 then the gross investment will be Rs. 300 + Rs. 100 i.e. Rs. 400 and investment percent will be Rs. 400/ Rs. 1000 = 40%. This is because Rs. 400 worth of capital goods is getting added in the economy. But if we also export capital goods worth Rs. 40 then the gross investment will be Rs. 300 + (Rs. 100 - Rs. 40) i.e. Rs. 360 and investment percent will be 36%. Investment in the economy is also called Gross Capital Formation.

Gross Capital Formation = Gross Fixed Capital Formation (machinery + equipment + new construction + intellectual property) + Net acquisition of valuable Metals like gold, silver, platinum, gems and stones + Change in stock/inventory

Now when the factory runs for a year then wear and tear happens in the factory which is called depreciation. Depreciation is also defined as consumption of physical capital. In the above example Rupees one lakh worth of capital goods produce Rs. 700 consumption goods and Rs. 300 capital goods, but during this production process suppose there is wear and tear of Rs. 50 in the factory. This implies that to produce Rs. 700 of consumption goods and Rs. 300 of capital goods there is a loss of Rs. 50 of capital goods in the economy i.e. net production of capital goods (investment) in the economy is Rs. 300 minus Rs. 50.

Net Investment = Gross Investment – Depreciation
= Rs. 300 – Rs. 50 = Rs. 250

The chart represents gross fixed capital formation (investment) of India in the last few years:

2016-17	2017-18	2018-19	2019-20	2020-21	2021-22	2022-23	2023-24	2024-25	2025-26
28.20%	28.20%	29.50%	28.50%	27.30%	29.60%	31.20%	30.40%	29.90%	30.00%

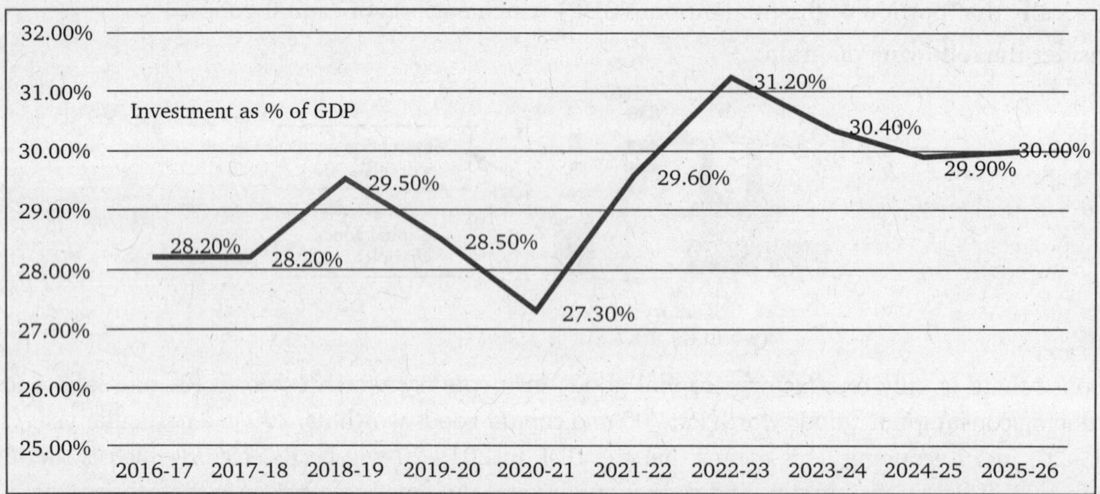

1.8 Circular Flow

For simplicity, let us assume that as of now there is no government and external sector and only the private sector and the household sector are present in the economy.

Case I

Assume that the household sector is not saving anything and hence all the goods and services produced by the private sector will be consumed by the household sector. (First A step will happen then B then C and then D)

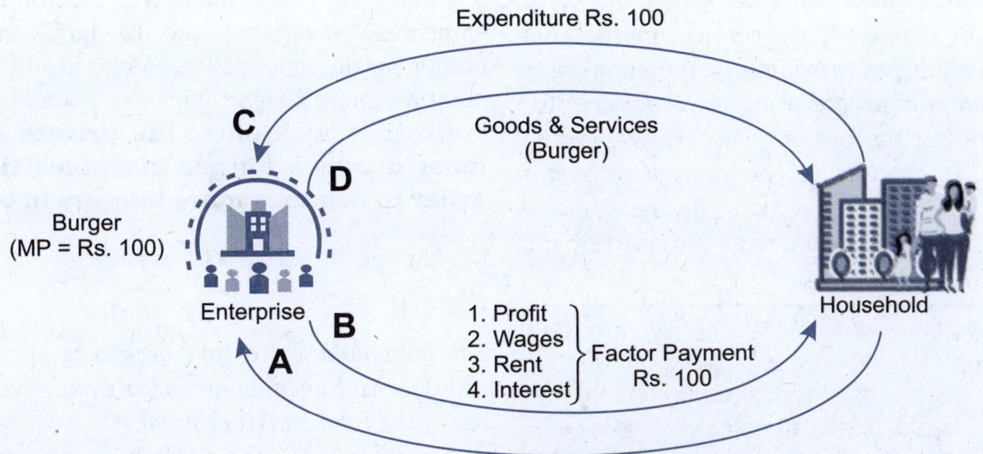

Suppose the enterprise produces the burgers as it is demanded by the people in the household sector. To produce the burger the enterprise will require certain inputs like entrepreneur (the owner of the enterprise), the capital (the machine to produce burger), the natural resources (land & water and other intermediate goods wheat, salt etc.) and labourers. The entrepreneur and the labourer belong to the household sector. Suppose the capital and the natural resources are also being provided by some individuals who belong to the household sector. So, **all these four factor services** (entrepreneur, capital, natural resources and labour) **are being provided by the individuals belonging to the household sector** and which has been represented in the above figure by arrow A.

By using these inputs, suppose the enterprise produces a burger which it wants to sell in **the market for Rs. 100** (Market Price = Rs. 100). Since the burger is sold in the market for Rs. 100, the whole amount of Rs. 100 generated from sale of the burger **will be distributed among the people who are providing the four factor services** i.e., entrepreneurship, labour, capital and natural resources. **Since the burger is being produced with the contribution of these four factors (inputs), the Rs. 100 generated by selling it in the market will ultimately be distributed** (by arrow B) **among these four service providers** as profit (say Rs. 40), wages (Rs. 10), rent (Rs. 20) and interest (Rs. 30) and will go to the household sector. **Hence, interest, rent, wages and profit must add up to the value of the product produced i.e., Rs. 100.**

The household sector will now spend this Rs. 100 (by arrow C) to purchase the burger worth Rs. 100 produced by the enterprise and the enterprise will return (by arrow D) the burger of Rs. 100 to the household sector. The amount of money representing the aggregate (total) value of goods and services is moving in a circular way and hence it represents the **circular flow of income** in the economy.

The two arrows on the top (C & D) represent the goods and services market – the arrow C represents the flow of payments for the goods and services, the arrow D represents the flow of goods and services to the household sector. The two arrows on the bottom (A & B) of the diagram similarly represent the factors of production market. The arrow A going from the households to the firms symbolises the services market that the households are providing to the enterprises and the enterprises are using these services for manufacturing the output. The arrow B going from the enterprises to the household sector represents the payments made by the firms to the households for the services provided by the household sector.

The value of the burger i.e., Rs. 100 is called the Gross Domestic Product (GDP) of the country for that year. Since the amount of money representing the aggregate value of goods and services, is moving in circular way, if we want to estimate the aggregate value of goods and services (GDP) produced during a year, we can measure the annual value of flows at any of the lines indicated in the diagram. For example, if we measure the GDP by the aggregate value of spending that the firms receive for the final goods and services which they produce (by line C) then this method is called the expenditure method.

If we measure the flow at D by measuring the aggregate value of final goods and services produced by all the firms, then it is called product method (value added). If we measure the total factor payments at B then it is called the income method. Thus, we can measure the aggregate output (GDP) in three ways.

In the above case, the households were producing the burger and purchasing the same burger from the enterprise and consuming it. They were spending all their income earned during the production process on the purchase of goods and services. They were not saving at all. **In such a situation, the production in the economy will remain stagnant i.e.** they will produce the same one burger worth Rs.100 each year and consume.

Now, suppose the households want to increase their consumption of burgers. But this will be possible only when the private sector i.e. the enterprises produce more burgers. And the burger production can be increased only when there are more burger machines (capital goods) in the economy. **Hence, the private sector must produce burger machines first in order to produce more burgers in future.**

Let us see how this is possible.

Case II

The household sector now decides to spend only Rs.70 for its consumption purpose and save Rs. 30 out of the total Rs. 100 earned.

The household sector will be providing the same factor services (their value of work done is same i.e. Rs. 100) and the enterprise will be producing goods in total worth Rs. 100 only but now the enterprise will produce burger worth Rs. 70 (because now the household sector wants to consume burgers worth Rs. 70 only) and other goods worth Rs. 30. **By arrow B the enterprise will return Rs. 100 as factor payments to the household sector**. The household sector will spend Rs. 70 through arrow C and the enterprise will return the burger worth Rs. 70 to the household sector through arrow D. This burger will be consumed by the household sector.

Now there is Rs. 30 savings left with the household sector (which they may deposit in a financial institution like banks) and there is Rs. 30 (capital goods) lying with the enterprises. The other enterprises present in the private sector will borrow Rs. 30 (which the household sector has saved in banks) from banks and will purchase the Rs. 30 capital goods from the enterprises. *The Rs. 30 goods produced by the enterprises will be capital good in nature and not a consumption good as it has been produced for the private sector (and not for the household sector).* This Rs. 30 of capital goods (which may be burger machines) will help in increasing the production of burgers in future years.

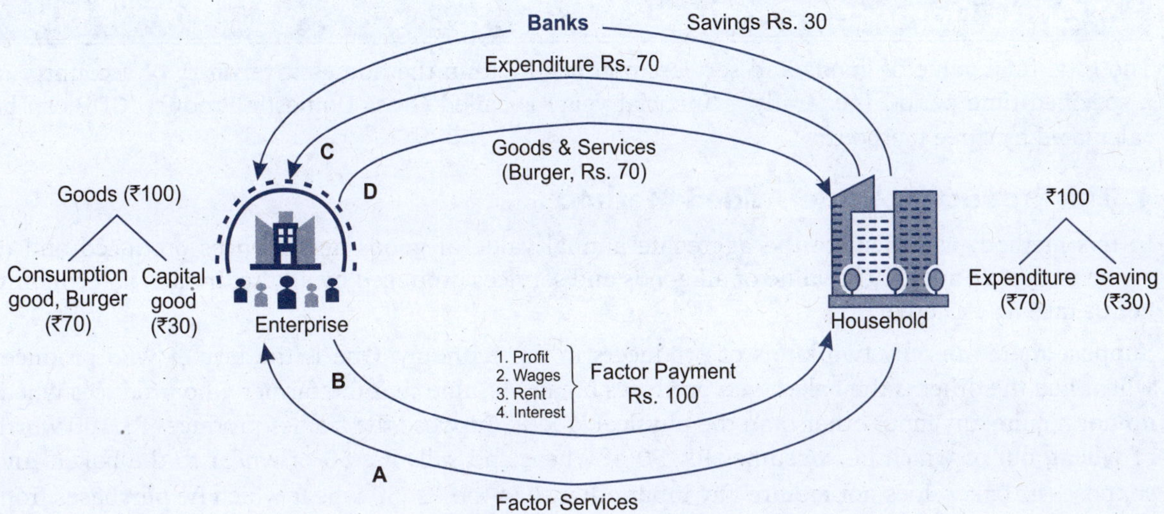

So, if the household sector will save Rs. 30, then the same value of capital goods will be produced in the economy. **If the household sector buys only Rs. 60 consumption goods and saves Rs. 40 then the enterprises will produce Rs. 60 consumption goods for the household sector and the rest Rs. 40 goods they will produce for the private sector which will be capital goods.** This implies that, savings is equal to the production of capital goods in the economy *(when there is no government and external sector)*. So, if an economy wants to produce more capital goods, then it will have to save more also. Greater the saving in the economy, greater will be the production of capital goods. As we know, that portion of the final output which comprises of capital goods is also called investment, hence savings will be equal to investment and higher the savings, higher will be the investment.

This shows that if an economy wants to produce more goods and services in future years then it must produce capital goods (i.e., investment) first, which in turn implies that the economy should save more. Higher the savings, higher will be the capital goods produced in the economy which will propel the economy on a higher growth path.

When India got independence, our economy was producing 95% consumption goods and 5% capital goods i.e., savings was only 5%. At that time, we wanted to increase the output of the economy to serve millions of starving populations and hence we started saving more. More savings led to an increase in production of capital goods in the economy which further increased the production of goods and services. In 2019-20, India's savings was around 28% of the GDP which means India was producing around 72% consumption goods and 28% capital goods i.e., investment. China has consistently been able to produce more than 40% capital goods out of the total output (GDP) of their economy which has propelled China into the fastest growing economies of the world.

1.9 Gross Domestic Product

The total final value of goods and services produced within the domestic territory of a country in a specified time period (generally a financial year) is called Gross Domestic Product. GDP can be calculated by three methods:

1. The Product or Value-Added Method

In this method, we calculate the aggregate annual value of goods and services produced and to arrive at this we add up the value of all goods and services produced by all the firms in an economy. Let us take an example:

Suppose there are only two kinds of producers in the economy. One is the farmer who produces wheat and the other is the baker who produces bread. Assume that the farmer who produces wheat do not require any input other than the physical labour. Suppose the farmer produces Rs.100 worth of wheat, out of which he consumes Rs. 50 of wheat and sells Rs. 50 of wheat to the baker. And suppose the baker does not require any input other than the Rs. 50 wheat which he purchases from the farmer. The baker uses this Rs. 50 of wheat completely and produces bread worth Rs. 200.

Farmer	:	Rs. 50	+	Rs. 50 (consumed)	= Rs. 100 wheat produced
		↓			
Baker	:	Purchase	+	Value Addition	= Rs. 200 bread produced

The farmer has produced Rs. 100 of wheat for which it did not need assistance of any inputs. Therefore, the entire Rs. 100 is rightfully the contribution or the value addition of the farmer. But the Rs 200 bread produced by the baker is not entirely his own contribution because to produce this bread the baker has purchased wheat from the farmer worth Rs. 50. So the value added by the baker will be equal to the value of production of the firm (baker) – value of intermediate goods used by the firm.

Since, there are only two firms in the economy, one is baker and the other is farmer, to calculate the GDP we will add value addition by both these firms.

GDP = Value addition by Baker + Value addition by Farmer
= (Rs. 200 – Rs. 50) + (Rs. 100)
= Rs. 150 + Rs. 100
= Rs. 250

Value addition by the farmer is Rs. 100. Value addition does not depend on whether the farmer is selling the wheat in the market or consuming himself. *Value addition is basically "the value/price that somebody's work will fetch in the market" and it includes profit also.*

By the standard definition, GDP should be equal to the final value of all goods and services produced in the economy. So, we can cross check the above example.

GDP = Final value of all goods produced
= Final value of wheat + Final value of bread
= Rs. 50 + Rs. 200
= Rs. 250 *(which is same as above calculated from the value-added method)*

Out of the Rs. 100 wheat produced by the farmer, only Rs 50 wheat consumed by the farmer is final good. The wheat that the farmer sold to the baker worth Rs. 50 is an intermediate good and not final good.

2. Expenditure Method

An alternative way to calculate GDP is by looking at the expenditure side of all the sectors. Whatever goods and services are produced in the economy are ultimately purchased by the four sectors of the economy i.e. household sector, government sector, private sector and external sector. So, if we add the expenditures done by these four sectors on the purchase of final goods and services produced by the firms within the domestic territory then it shall be equal to the GDP of the country.

- The household sector spends only on the consumption goods (denoted by C')
- The private sector spends only on capital goods (investment) barring some exceptions when firms buy consumables to treat their guest or for their employees (denoted by I')
- The Govt. sector purchases both capital and consumption goods (denoted by G')
- The external sector also purchases both consumption and capital goods from our economy which is basically called the exports from India (denoted by X).

$$
\begin{aligned}
GDP &= C' + I' + G' + X \\
&= C - C_m + I - I_m + G - G_m + X \\
&= C + I + G + X - (C_m + I_m + G_m) \\
&= C + I + G + X - M \\
GDP &= C + I + G + X - M
\end{aligned}
$$

C', I' and G' are all expenditure on **domestically produced** final goods as we are trying to calculate GDP. And C, I and G are expenditure by the three sectors **on domestic and imported both** final goods.

- Since C' is expenditure of household sector on **domestically** produced consumption goods, so this can also be written as expenditure on domestic and imported both consumption goods (C) - expenditure on imported consumption goods (C_m) i.e. $C - C_m$
- Similarly, $I - I_m$ will represent the expenditure by private sector on **domestically** produced capital goods i.e. investment expenditure; and
- $G - G_m$ will represent the expenditure by government sector on **domestically** produced consumption and capital goods.
- And $C_m + I_m + G_m$ represents the total imports by the country combining the household, private and government sector.

The above formula of GDP can also be written as:

GDP = Private consumption (C) + Private investment (I) + Government Investment and Consumption (G) + exports (X) – imports (M)

GDP = [Private consumption + Government consumption] + [Private investment + Government investment] + Exports – Imports

GDP = Total consumption + Total Investment + Exports – Imports

In GDP, the major component is private consumption which is around 60% of GDP, Government consumption is around 12%, total investment is around 32% and exports minus imports is around -4%.

When, the government and the external sector are present in the economy, then the savings and investment may vary but an increase in savings generally leads to an increase in the investments and the circular flow will always hold true.

Whatever income households receive, either they spend it for consumption or save it (S) or pay taxes (T). So,

$$GDP = C + S + T$$
$$C + I + G + X - M = C + S + T$$
$$I + G + X - M = S + T$$
$$\mathbf{(I - S) + (G - T) = M - X}$$

If there is no govt. and no external sector then, $G = T = M = X = 0$ and hence, $\mathbf{I = S}$

3. Income Method

It has already been stated in the beginning that the sum of the final goods produced in the economy must be equal to the income received by all the four factors of production *i.e.*, wages, rents, interests and profits. This follows from the simple idea that the revenues earned by all the firms put together must be distributed to those who has contributed in the production process which are basically the four factors of production entrepreneurship, labour, capital and natural resources.

GDP = Profit earned by all the firms + Interest received by all the capital deployed + Rent received for the natural resources + Wages earned by all the labourers

GDP = Profit + Interest + Rent + Wages

The concept of domestic territory (economic territory) is different from the geographical or political territory of a country. Domestic territory of a country includes the following:

- *Political frontiers of the country including its territorial waters.*
- *Ships, and aircrafts operated by the residents of the country between two or more countries for example, Air India's services between different countries.*
- *Fishing vessels, oil and natural gas rigs and loating platforms operated by the residents of the country in the international waters or engaged in extraction in areas where the country has exclusive rights of operation.*
- *Embassies, consulates and military establishments of the country located in other countries, for example, Indian embassy in U.S.A., Japan etc. It excludes all embassies, consulates and military establishments of other countries and offices of international organizations located in India.*

Thus, domestic territory may be defined as the political frontiers of the country including its territorial waters, ships, aircrafts, fishing vessels operated by the residents of the country, embassies and consulates located abroad etc.

1.10 GDP Calculation Methodology by NSO

NSO calculates GDP by Value Added Method and Expenditure Method both. Under Value Added Method, it calculates the value addition done by various economic activities viz:

- Agriculture, Forestry and Fishing
- Mining and Quarrying
- Manufacturing
- Electricity, Gas, water supply and other utility services Construction
- Trade, Hotels and transport, and communication and services related to broadcasting
- Financial, Insurance, real estate and professional services
- Public administration and defence and other services

Under Expenditure Method, it adds up the various components of expenditure viz:

- Private (Final) Consumption Expenditure *(it is basically household expenditure) [60%]*
- Government (Final) Consumption Expenditure [12%]
- Gross Fixed Capital Formation (Investment expenditure of private and Govt.) [32%]
- Net of Exports and Imports [–4%]

Though GDP measured from either side should be equal, since reliable data is not available for private consumption expenditure, there is always a difference in the two ways of measuring GDP. The difference is usually put as "discrepancies" in the expenditure approach of measuring GDP.

GDP of India = All States Gross Domestic Product (SGDP) + Output from Centre specific activities like Railways, Defence, Central Highways etc. + Embassies located in other countries + Fishing vessels, oil and natural gas rigs, floating platforms etc. operated by the residents of the country in the international waters.

1.11 Macroeconomic Variables

Gross Domestic Product (GDP) measures the aggregate/total production of final goods and services taking place within the domestic territory of the country during a year. But it may be possible that the foreign nationals working within India have contributed in that GDP production.

So, now we are interested in measuring the output/earnings made by Indian residents only whether in India or abroad which is termed as Gross National Product (GNP). GNP is that income or product which accrues to the economic agents who are **residents** of the country. *(i.e., income earned by the Non-Resident Indians (NRIs) will not be part of India's GNP).*

To calculate GNP, we add the factor income of Indians from abroad in GDP and subtract the contribution of foreigners in India's GDP.

Gross National Product (GNP)

= GDP + Factor income earned by the domestic factors of production employed in the rest of the world – Factor income earned by the factors of production of the rest of the world employed in the domestic economy

GNP = GDP + Net factor income from abroad (NFIA)

Factor income is basically the income earned by the four factors of production i.e., profit, rent, interest and wages but it does not include the transfer payments. Hence, GNP is the sum of ***GDP*** *and* ***factor income*** *and it does not include transfer payments (free money) received from the rest of the world (for example remittances).*

National Disposable Income = National Income + Transfer payments from rest of the world

The figure below presents a diagrammatic representation of the relations between the various macroeconomic variables.

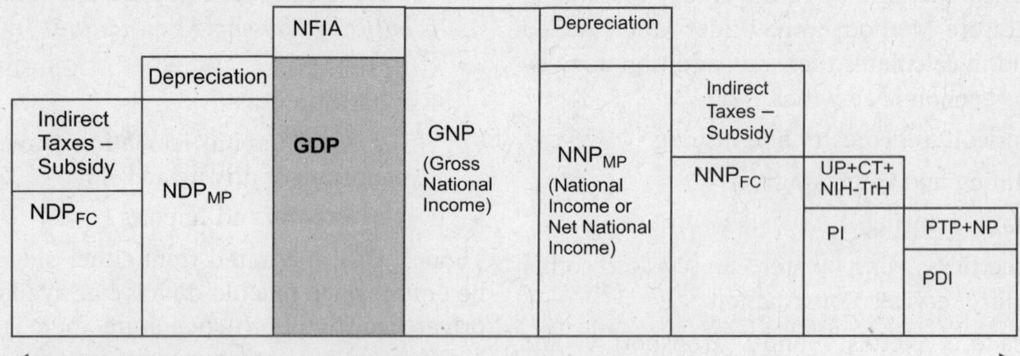

Gross Domestic Product (GDP) + NFIA = Gross National Product (GNP)

Gross Domestic Product (GDP) – Depreciation = Net Domestic Product (NDP)

Gross National Product (GNP) – Depreciation = Net National Product (NNP)

"Gross National Product (GNP) is also called Gross National Income; and Net National Product (NNP) is also called Net National Income or just National Income."

Let us try to understand the Factor Cost and Market Prices

Suppose few people produced a burger and they wanted to sell it in the market at Rs. 100 i.e. they want Rs. 100 for their effort in the production of burger. This means that the total factor cost of the burger which is equal to profit plus interest plus rent plus wages shall be equal to Rs. 100. So in this case GDP at Factor Cost will be equal to Rs. 100.

But when they went to the market to sell the burger, government imposed an indirect tax of Rs. 10 on the burger. So now they will have to sell the burger in the market at a price of Rs.110, so that they can fetch Rs. 110 from the market out of which they will keep Rs. 100 for themselves (factor cost) and Rs. 10 will be given to the government as tax.

So, Market Price = Factor Cost + Indirect Tax

= Rs. 100 + Rs. 10

= Rs. 110

Similarly, if government gives subsidies, Market Price = Factor Cost – Subsidies

Hence, Market Price = Factor Cost + (Indirect Taxes- Subsidies)

Let us take another example of value-added method.

Suppose there is a farmer who sold wheat in Rs. 100 which then was purchased by ITC which converted wheat into flour (Aashirwaad atta) and sold it in Rs. 500 to a restaurant. The restaurant converted flour into chapati and sold the chapati in Rs. 1000 to a customer in the restaurant. The customer in total paid Rs. 1100 (i.e. Rs. 1000 plus 10% tax)

If we have to calculate GDP at market price, first we will calculate Gross Value Addition (GVA) at factor cost/basic prices and then separately add the taxes-subsidies.

$GDP_{MP} = GVA_{\text{factor cost/basic prices}}$

$+ \text{Indirect taxes} - \text{Subsidies}$

GVA by farmer (agriculture sector) = Rs. 100

GVA by ITC (Industrial sector) = Rs. 500 – Rs. 100 = Rs. 400

GVA by Restaurant (Service sector) = Rs. 1000 – Rs. 500 = Rs. 500

$GVA_{\text{factor cost/basic prices}}$ = Rs. 100 + Rs. 400 + Rs. 500 = Rs. 1000

Indirect taxes – subsidy = Rs. 100

GDP_{MP} = Rs. 1100

Actually, there is a slight difference between $GVA_{\text{basic prices}}$ and $GVA_{\text{factor cost}}$.

$GVA_{\text{basic prices}} = GVA_{\text{factor cost}}$ + *Production Taxes – Production subsidies*

$GDP_{MP} = GVA_{\text{basic prices}}$ + *product taxes – Product subsidies*

Land revenue is a kind of production tax and railway subsidies are a kind of production subsidies. Production taxes and production subsidies are independent of the volume of actual production. Production taxes – Production subsidies are negligible as compared to other parameters, so we can ignore it and hence for all practical purposes, we can say that

$$GVA_{\text{basic prices}} = GVA_{\text{factor cost}}$$

In India (since January 2015 onwards) we calculate GDP at Market Prices rather than at Factor Cost. The way we are calculating GDP at MP and FC, similarly, NDP can also be calculated at MP and FC and GNP and NNP can also be measured at MP and FC.

Let us understand Personal Income (PI) and Personal Disposable Income (PDI)

That part of NNP (FC) which is received by households is called Personal Income (PI). So, we need to subtract those items which are part of NNP (FC) but does not go to households.

- The first such item is Undistributed Profits (UP). Profit is earned by private and government enterprises and some part of it remains with them and is not distributed among the factors of production which is called UP. Undistributed profit does not accrue to the households.
- Similarly, Corporate Tax, which is imposed on the earnings made by the firms, will also have to be deducted from the NNP (FC), since it does not accrue to the households.
- Households do receive interest payments from private enterprises and government on past loans advanced by them. And households may have to pay interests to the firms and the government as well, in case they had borrowed money from either. So, we have to deduct the net interests paid by the households to the firms and government (NIH).
- Households receive transfer payments from government and firms (for example pensions, scholarship, prizes etc.) which have to be added to calculate the Personal Income of the households.

Thus, Personal Income (PI) = NNP (FC) – Undistributed profits (UP) – Corporate Tax (CT) – Net interest payments made by households (NIH) + Transfer payments to the households from the government and firms (TrH)

However, even Personal Income (PI) is not the income over which the households have complete say. They have to pay taxes from PI. If we deduct the Personal Income Tax payments and Non-tax Payments (such as fines) from PI, we obtain what is known as the Personal Disposable Income (PDI).

Thus, Personal Disposable Income (PDI) = Personal Income (PI) – Personal tax payments (PTP) – Non-tax payments (NP)

Personal Disposable Income belongs to the households out of which some part they may consume and the rest they can save.

Per capita GDP:

If the population of the country in any particular year say 2020-21 is P and the GDP is Y then per capita (i.e. per person) GDP will be Y/P. Now, if the population growth of our country is say 1% (in 2021-22) and GDP growth of the country is say 8% (in 2021-22) then per capita GDP in 2021-22 will be (1.08 Y)/ (1.01 P) = 1.069 Y/P. Hence, in percentage terms per capita GDP **growth** in 2021-22 will be 6.9%.

Year	2020-21		2021-22
GDP	Y		1.08 Y
Population	P		1.01 P
Per capita GDP	Y/P		1.08 Y/ 1.01 P
Per capita GDP Growth		1.08/1.01 (=6.9%)	

1.12 Nominal and Real GDP

Real GDP growth measures growth in **quantity** only and nominal GDP measures growth in **value** (which includes quantity and prices both).

Now, suppose an economy produces wheat and rice. The quantities produced and the market price is given in the table.

	2022-23	2023-24	2024-25	2025-26
Wheat	*10kg × Rs. 10/kg*	*11kg × Rs. 10.5/kg*	*12kg × Rs. 11/kg*	*12.5kg × Rs. 12/kg*
Rice	*8kg × Rs. 12/kg*	*9kg × Rs. 12.5/kg*	*10kg × Rs. 13/kg*	*10.5 kg × Rs. 13.5/kg*
Nominal GDP	*10×10 + 8×12 = Rs. 196*	11×10.5+ 9×12.5 = Rs. 228	12×11 + 10×13 = Rs. 262	12.5×12+10.5×13.5 = Rs. 291.75
To calculate Real GDP, we take the price of any year as constant and declare it as a base year. So, suppose we declare 2022-23 as base year then we will take price of wheat as Rs. 10/kg and price of rice as Rs. 12/kg as constant in all the subsequent years to calculate the real GDP in the following years.				
Real GDP	*10×**10** + 8×**12** = Rs. 196*	*11×**10** + 9×**12** = Rs. 218*	*12×**10** + 10×**12** = Rs. 240*	*12.5×**10** + 10.5×**12** = Rs. 251*

National Statistical Office (NSO) under the Ministry of Statistics and Programme Implementation (MoSPI) has revised the base year for calculation of GDP to 2022-23. So, if we want to calculate India's Real GDP for 2025-26, we will have to take the quantities produced in 2025-26 and the prices of 2022-23 (base year). And if we want to calculate the Nominal GDP of 2025-26 then we will have to take the quantities produced in 2025-26 and the market prices of the same year i.e., 2025-26.

Before 2015, NSO was not using market prices to calculate GDP, rather it was using Factor Cost i.e., Market Price excluding indirect taxes and subsidies. Now, as per the global best practices and the IMF's World Economic Outlook projections based on GDP at market prices, India has changed its methodology of GDP calculation at market prices.

In India, **economic growth** is measured by **real GDP** i.e., GDP at **constant** Market Prices.

Consider the above table once again.

	2022-23		2023-24		2024-25		2025-26
Nominal GDP	Rs. 196		Rs. 228		Rs. 262		Rs. 291.75
Change in Nominal GDP		*16.3%*		*14.9%*		*11.4%*	
Real GDP	Rs. 196		Rs. 218		Rs. 240		Rs. 251
Change in Real GDP		*11.2%*		*10.1%*		*4.6%*	

So, economic growth from 2022-23 to 2023-24 will be measured by change in Real GDP (and not nominal GDP) which is 11.2 %

In the above example, Real GDP is steadily/consistently increasing from 2022-23 to 2025-26 but "change in real GDP" is decreasing from 11.2% to 4.6%. (And same is true for nominal GDP also). Above is a case of economic growth as **real GDP** is increasing.

As per the latest estimates released by NSO, the GDP of India at current market prices (nominal) is around **Rs. 345 lakh crores** for 2025-26 as against Rs. 318 lakh crores in 2024-25 showing a (nominal) growth of 8.6 percent.

The GNP of India at current market prices (nominal) is around **Rs. 341 lakh crores** for 2025-26.

GDP of India at constant market prices (2022-23) in the year 2025-26 is around Rs. 323 lakh crores as against Rs. 300 lakh crores in 2024-25, showing a growth of 7.6 percent.

The following chart represents Real GDP growth rate of India in the last few years:

2016-17	2017-18	2018-19	2019-20	2020-21	2021-22	2022-23	2023-24	2024-25	2025-26
8.30%	6.80%	6.50%	3.90%	-5.80%	9.10%	7.60%	9.20%	6.50%	7.60%

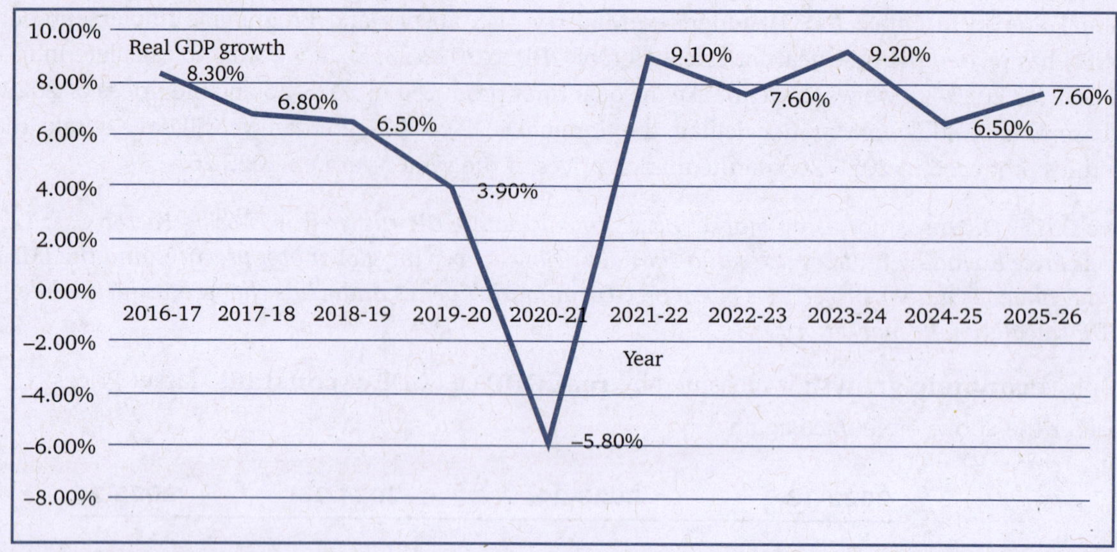

1.13 Productivity, Capital Output Ratio and ICOR

First let us develop the general concept of average productivity and marginal productivity.

1 Acre Land
5 Labourers
2 Tonnes production

If one acre of land produces 2 Tonnes of food-grains, then;

Productivity of Land

$$= \frac{\text{Output}}{\text{Input (land)}} = \frac{\text{2 Tonnes}}{\text{1 acre}} = \text{2 Tonnes/acre}$$

Productivity of Labour

$$= \frac{\text{Output}}{\text{Input (labour)}} = \frac{\text{2 Tonnes}}{\text{5 labourers}}$$

$= 0.4$ Tonne/ labour

The above two are basically **average** productivity.

If by adding one extra labour, production increases by 0.2 tonne, then

Marginal *productivity of labour*

$$= \frac{\textit{change in output}}{\textit{change in labour}} = \frac{\textit{0.2 tonne}}{\textit{1 labour}}$$

= 0.2 tonne/labour

Similarly, we can calculate productivity of capital

$$= \frac{\text{Output}}{\text{Capital}}$$

Higher is the productivity of capital, it is good for the economy.

The inverse of "productivity of capital" is Capital/Output ratio.

Capital output ratio is the ratio of capital to output. It measures how much of capital is required per unit of output. So, if more capital is required per unit of output, then the capital is less efficient. Hence, it also measures (average) efficiency of capital (but it is inverse of productivity/efficiency).

$$\text{Capital Output Ratio} = \frac{\text{Capital}}{\text{Output}}$$

Higher the capital/output ratio, it is bad for economy. If Capital/Output ratio is 3/1, that means Rs. 1 unit of output is produced from Rs.3 units of capital. And if Capital/Output ratio is 4/1, that means to produce Rs. 1 unit of output, Rs. 4 units of capital is required. So, 3/1 is better than 4/1 for the economy.

We measured capital/output ratio because we are ***not*** *interested in measuring the productivity of capital rather, we want to know that in India how much (average) capital is required to produce one unit (Rupee one) of output /GDP.*

Our target variable is "output/GDP" and we are always interested in knowing that if we have to produce one unit of output then how much capital will be required.

So, now we are more interested in knowing that how much **new/additional** capital (in value/rupee) will be required to increase the output by **one more unit** (in rupee). This is because whenever a new government comes, it tries to attract new investment and hence it is more interested in knowing that if it has to increase the GDP by **one additional unit** then how much **additional capital** will be required. And for that we have another term called **Incremental Capital Output Ratio (ICOR)**. *(Our target variable is GDP/Output, so we/Govt. is always interested in knowing that how much extra capital will be required to produce one extra unit of output rather than the other way around).*

Incremental Capital Output Ratio (ICOR) is defined as how much **additional** capital will be required to produce one **additional** unit of output.

$$\text{ICOR} = \frac{\text{change in capital}}{\text{change in output}}$$

$$= \frac{(\text{change in capital/GDP})}{(\text{change in output/GDP})}$$

$$= \frac{\text{investment \% in GDP}}{\text{\% change in GDP}}$$

ICOR represents how efficiently the **new/additional capital** is being used in a country to produce output.

If ICOR of India = 5, that means India requires Rs. 5 value of extra capital goods to produce Rs. 1 of additional output.

Investment % in GDP = "ICOR" × "% change in GDP"

From the above formula, if our ICOR is 5 and we want economic growth of 8% then we will have to do 40% investment. But if somehow, we are able to reduce our ICOR to 4 (by making ourselves more efficient) then we can achieve the same 8% economic growth with just 32% of investment.

The incremental capital output ratio is a catch-all expression. **It depends upon a multiple number of factors such as governance, quality of labour which again depends on education and skill development levels, and technology etc.** For example, if the labour is not skilled and he is not able to use the machines properly then our output produced will be less and our ICOR will increase even if there is no problem with the machine/capital.

1.14 Potential GDP

Potential GDP is the real value of goods and services that can be produced when a country's factors of production are fully employed. It is the maximum sustainable level of output that an economy can produce. When an economy is operating at its potential (trend), there are high levels of utilization of the labour force and the capital stock.

Potential output is determined by the economy's productive capacity which depends upon the inputs available (capital, land, labour etc.) and the economy's technological efficiency. Potential GDP tends to grow slowly because inputs like labour and capital and the level of technology changes quite slowly over time.

Potential GDP growth also changes slowly with time depending on various factors like political set up, governance, infrastructure, health and education of the people, utilization of capital etc. As per economic survey 2015-16, the potential GDP growth of our country is between 8% to 10%.

Actual GDP is subject to business cycle swings i.e. the cycles of upturn and downturn. During downturn, the actual GDP falls below the potential level and during upturn, the actual GDP rises above the potential GDP level.

Technically, a recession is defined as (at least) two consecutive quarters of negative economic growth as measured by a country's real GDP. A recession is a period of significant decline in total output, income and employment, usually lasting from 6 months to 18 months and marked by widespread contractions in many sectors of the economy. A severe and protracted recession is called depression.

Economic (growth) slowdown is generally considered as the phase when GDP growth rate of the economy is declining but it may still be positive.

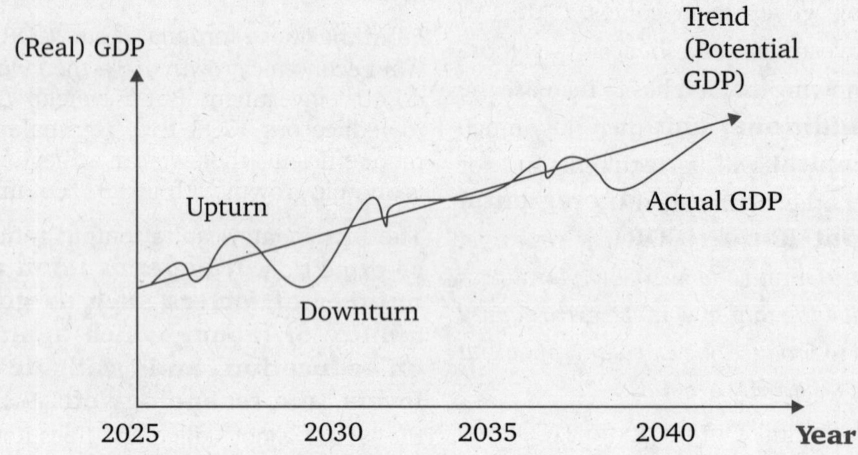

Let us take an example to understand recession.

Year	2023		2024		2025		2026
Real GDP	*Rs.100*		*Rs.108*		*Rs.112*		*Rs.115*
Real GDP growth		*8%*		*3.7%*		*2.7%*	

In the above example, the country is not going through any recession as real GDP (output) of the economy is still increasing even if the growth rate of GDP is decreasing. The recession occurs when the growth rate of GDP becomes negative or output starts decreasing. The above is a case of economic (growth) slowdown and not recession.

India has faced recession five times in 1957-58 (-1.2%) [Drought], 1965-66 (-3.66%) [drought/war], 1972-73 (-0.32%) [drought/Oil crisis] and 1979-80 (-5.2%) [Drought/political instability] and 2020-21 (-6.6%) [Covid-19].

1.15 Nominal, PPP and Real Exchange Rates

1. Nominal Exchange Rate (NER)

NER = Price of one currency in terms of another currency.

For example, if we can purchase one dollar by paying rupees 80 in the market, that means NER is: $1 = Rs. 80

Now this exchange rate can also be written as Rs. 80/$ **or** $.0125/Rs. But the standard followed is 'abroad' with respect to 'domestic'. So, we will use the standard format:

So, $1 = Rs. 80, means NER is **"$.0125 per Rs"**.

The NER depends on the market forces of demand and supply. If more and more people are purchasing dollars in the exchange market, then the demand of dollar increases and dollar will become stronger or appreciate. But if more and more tourists are coming to India and are converting their dollars and demanding rupees then rupee will appreciate.

2. Purchasing Power Parity (PPP) Exchange Rate

Suppose NER is $1 = Rs.80 and India and US produce just one burger each which are exactly same in quantity and quality.

	India	US
And, Burger Price is	Rs. 40	$1

PPP exchange rate means that if $1 can purchase one burger in US then that same burger can be purchased in how many rupees in India.

To calculate PPP exchange rate in the above case, we just need to compare the prices of the burger in both the countries.

In the above case, by comparing the prices of burger in India and US, we get, $1 = Rs. 40. So, $1 = Rs. 40 is the PPP exchange rate (or it can also be written as **$ .025/Rs**). This implies that whatever Rs. 40 can purchase in India, the same item/items can be purchased in US in $1 i.e., purchasing power of Rs. 40 in India is equal to purchasing power of $1 in US. Or we can also say that purchasing power of $.025 in US is equal to purchasing power of Rs. 1 in India, so PPP exchange rate is $.025 per Rs.

So, PPP exchange rate is: $ 1 = Rs. 40

i.e. $ (1/40) per Rs

i.e. $ 0.025 per Rs

So, PPP exchange rate can be derived as = Abroad Price/Domestic Price

(We can write it as domestic price/abroad price also, but standard is abroad/domestic).

Above example was a case of just one product. But, if both the countries are producing several commodities then to calculate PPP exchange rate, consider the same basket of commodities which are produced in both the countries and compare the prices, whatever we will get that will be PPP exchange rate.

For example, consider the following:

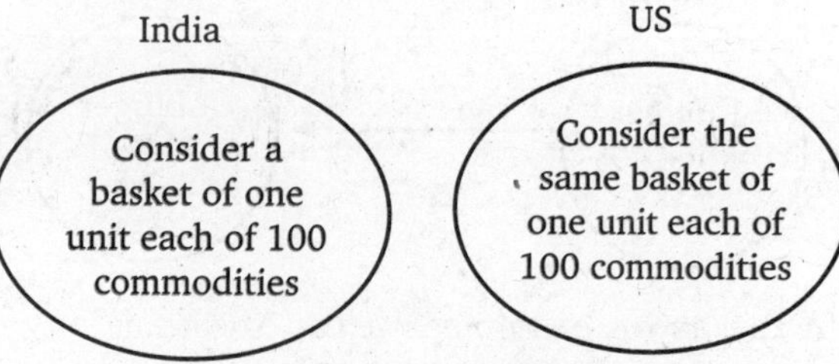

Suppose the price of the basket of commodities in India is Rs 2000 and the price of the same basket of commodities in US is $100. This means that purchasing power of Rs. 2000 in India is same as purchasing power of $100 in US.

So, PPP exchange rate will be \$ 100 = Rs. 2000

i.e. \$1 = Rs. 20

i.e. \$.05 per Rs. (Abroad Price/Domestic Price)

This means that whatever we can purchase in Rs. 1 in India, the same items can be purchased in \$.05 in US.

If the inflation rate is different in both the countries then PPP exchange rate will change with time. But if both countries have same rate of inflation or zero inflation then PPP exchange rates will remain constant.

When Nominal Exchange Rate becomes equal to PPP exchange rate, we say that the currencies of the two countries are at purchasing power parity.

As per IMF "The purchasing power parity between two countries is the rate at which the currency of one country needs to be converted into that of a second country to ensure that a given amount of the first country's currency will purchase the same volume of goods and services in the second country as it does in the first."

3. Real Exchange Rate (RER)

Consider the above example of burger:

NER: \$1 = Rs. 80 (\$.0125/Rs.)

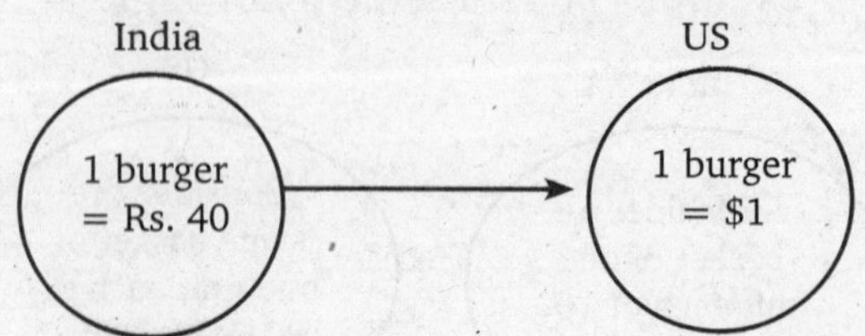

In the above example, we can see that burger is costing \$1 in US while in India burger can be purchased in Rs. 40 or \$0.5. So, we can say that Indian burgers are cheaper or Indian burgers are more competitive and hence in the above case India will export burgers while US will import burgers.

So, let us calculate trade competitiveness i.e., which country's trade is more competitive?

Trade competitiveness will depend on three parameters:

- Price of burger in India (Domestic Price)
- Price of burger in US (Abroad Price)
- Nominal Exchange Rate (NER)

As we are following the standard 'Abroad with respect to domestic', so we will calculate trade competitiveness of US with respect to India.

Trade competitiveness of US w.r.t. India

$\propto$ Price of burger in India

$\propto$ 1/Price of burger in US

$\propto$ Nominal Exchange Rate

So, Trade competitiveness of US w.r.t. India

$$= \frac{\text{Domestic Price} \times \text{Nominal Exchange Rate}}{\text{Abroad price}}$$

$$= \frac{\text{Nominal Exchange Rate}}{(\text{Abroad price/ Domestic price})}$$

$$= \frac{\text{NER}}{\text{PPP}} = \frac{\text{Rs. } 40 \times \$\,.0125/\text{Rs.}}{\$1} = 1/2$$

And this is also called 'Real Exchange Rate' (RER) i.e., RER = NER/PPP (US w.r.t. India)

- ❖ Trade competitiveness of US w.r.t. India is ½ (<1), this means that US products are less competitive as compared to India which also means that "in any amount of money, whatever we can purchase from India, we will be able to purchase only half of the items from US".
- ❖ If this ½ will start increasing, this means that US trade competitiveness is increasing (but may be less than India) and once it reaches to 1 then it means that both the countries trade is equally competitive i.e. in any amount of money, we will be able to purchase the same (quantity of) products from India and US and trade may stop.

- If trade competitiveness of US w.r.t. India is 2 (>1), this means that US products are twice competitive as compared to India which means that in any amount of money if we are able to purchase certain items from India, then in the same money we will be able to purchase twice the number of items in US.
- And one thing we need to understand that if some currency is appreciating then it means that its value is increasing and it will be costlier to purchase that currency and hence its costlier to purchase the goods from that country (by purchasing that country's currency) and then we say that that country's trade is becoming less competitive. *So, when a currency appreciates (either in real or nominal terms) then it means that its trade is becoming less competitive.*
- In the case of NER, if the exchange rate is $.0125/Rupee and if its value is increasing to $.025/Rupee that means we are getting more dollars per rupee and hence we say that rupee is appreciating and this means that rupee trade is becoming less competitive.
- In the same way, if the value of ½ (abroad w.r.t. domestic) in case of real exchange rate is increasing that means rupee is appreciating and since rupee is appreciating, so Indian trade is becoming less competitive or US trade is becoming more competitive.
- Now if we want to create an index of real exchange rate and represent the value ½ with 100, then if ½ is increasing *(Refer the figure below)* that means the real index number 100 will increase, and we will say that rupee is appreciating (in real terms) and rupee (Indian) trade is becoming less competitive.
- And if ½ is decreasing then the number 100 will decrease *(Refer the figure below)* which will mean that rupee is depreciating in real terms and hence (Indian) exports will become more competitive. So, real exchange rate tells about the trade competitiveness and it already includes the effect of nominal exchange rate.
- *If India wants to measure its export competitiveness with respect to its trading partners with just one parameter, then it calculates Real Effective Exchange Rate (REER) which is a weighted average (with respect to trade value) of the Real Exchange Rates of its trading partners. Similarly, if India wants to calculate its nominal exchange rate with respect to a group of other countries, then it can calculate Nominal Effective Exchange Rate (NEER).*
- When Real Exchange Rate = 1, Nominal Exchange Rate = PPP Exchange rate, and we say that **the currencies are at purchasing power parity**. This means that goods cost the same in two countries when measured in the same currency.
- From the figure below we can see that from Dec 2017 to Oct 2018, the index value is decreasing that means rupee has depreciated in both REER and NEER terms that means 'trading partners' trade has become less competitive and India's trade has become more competitive. And from Oct 2018 to January 2019, rupee has appreciated in both REER and NEER terms.

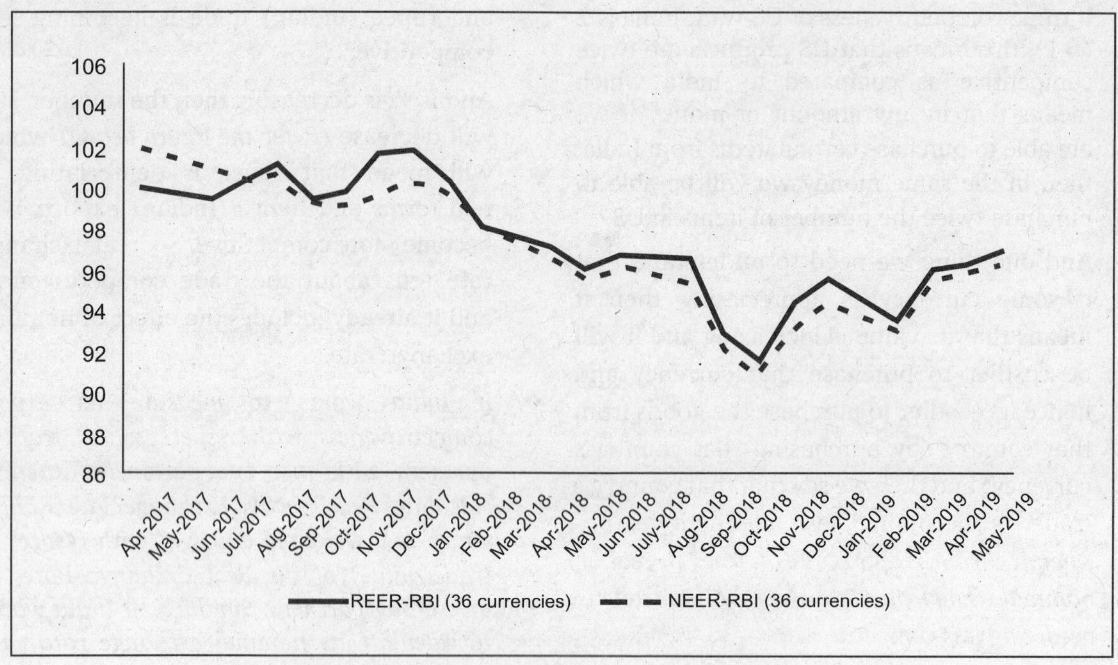

Figure: Movement of Indices in REER and NEER (2017-18 = 100)

1.16 GDP, Welfare, Development and Human Capital

GDP measures the total market value of goods and services produced in an economy in a year. It does not claim to measure welfare or well-being or inequality or happiness.

An economy can have rising levels of inequality, falling levels of democratic norms, falling levels of civil liberties, increasing air and water pollution, worsening gender equality etc. and still have rising levels of GDP. The question is: Does the existence of any (or all) of these ills imply that GDP is a faulty measure of "the total market value of all final goods and services"? The answer is: No.

The GDP is a simple measure and criticizing it by judging it based on social or moral norms would be completely missing the point of using GDP.

It is true that GDP often fails to account for all the things that bring down our welfare and diminish our well-being. For instance, damage done by the use of fossil fuels. But then GDP often doesn't adequately account for all the welfare gains as well.

As far as the broader question of people's well-being is concerned, of course, GDP is inadequate but again, that is by design. GDP does not include its **distribution, externalities** and **activities at home**. In other words, if one wants to know about the distribution of wealth, state of air pollution, or even happiness, then one would need to map other measures.

There is no simple way of representing every aspect of well-being in a single number in the way GDP describes market economic output. This has led to GDP being used as a **proxy** for the welfare of the people, but GDP was not designed for this task. That is why we need to complement GDP with a broader set of indicators that would reflect the distribution of well-being in society and its sustainability across its social, economic, and environmental dimensions.

It is true that solely focusing on GDP can lead to policies that are blind to people's broader well-being, but it is also true that it is difficult to find a worthy replacement of GDP. So, instead of pulling down GDP, it is better to look at a broader set of variables to get a more nuanced understanding of people's well-being.

Economic Development: Economic development is a broader concept than economic growth (GDP). Development reflects social and economic progress and requires economic growth. Economic growth is a vital and necessary condition for development, but it is not a sufficient condition as it cannot guarantee development.

Development focuses on the improvement of the overall well-being of the people in terms of increase in per capita income, better health and education facilities, better infrastructure, reduction in poverty, generation of employment etc.

Obstacles to development include poverty, lack of economic opportunities, corruption, poor governance, lack of education and lack of health.

Human Capital:

Just as a country can turn physical resources like land into physical capital like factories, similarly, it can also turn human resources like students into human capital like engineers and doctors. Societies need sufficient human capital in the first place – in the form of competent people who have themselves been educated and trained as professors and other professionals. In other words, we need good human capital to produce other human capital. Sources of human capital formation is investments in education, health, on-the-job training etc.

Human capital considers education and health as a means to increase labour productivity. Human capital treats human beings as a **means to an end**; the end being the increase in productivity.

Human development is based on the idea that education and health are **integral** to human well-being because only when people have the ability to read and write and the ability to lead a long and healthy life, they will be able to make other choices which they value.

The causality between human capital and economic/income growth flows in either direction:

- Higher income ⟶ Building of high level of human capital
- High level of human capital ⟶ Growth of income

Green GDP:

Ecosystem resources such as mineral deposits, water resources, soil nutrients, fossil fuels etc. are capital assets but traditional national accounts do not include measures of the depletion of these resources. This means a country could cut its forests to set up a factory and deplete its fisheries, and which would ultimately show only as a positive gain in GDP without registering the corresponding decline in assets. This is where Green GDP comes into play. The green GDP is the measurement of GDP growth with the environmental consequences of that growth factored in. Green GDP accounts for the monetized loss of biodiversity, costs caused by climate change etc. Green GDP is the index of the economic growth of a particular country which enshrines the environment consequences of the economic activities. It is a measure of how a country is prepared for sustainable development.

1.17 World Bank & IMF Classification of Countries

World Bank classifies the world's economies based on estimates of gross national income (GNI) per capita based on nominal exchange rate. The GNI per capita estimates are also used as input to the World Bank's operational classification of economies that determines lending eligibility. As per the 2026 data, the following is the classification of world economies:

Group	Sub-group	GNI per capita
➤ High Income		$13935 < GNI per capita
➤ Middle Income	Upper Middle	$4496 <= GNI per capita < = $13935
	Lower Middle	$1136 <= GNI per capita < = $4495
➤ Low Income		GNI per capita < = $1135

India belongs to the "Lower Middle" group as its GNI per capita is $2850 (Rs. 2.40 lakhs) in terms of nominal exchange rate. As per the PPP exchange rate, India's GNI per capita is approx. $9500.

The World Economic Outlook (WEO, **IMF**) classifies the world into two major groups:

- Advanced economies
- Emerging market and developing economies

This above classification is based on three parameters:

- Per capita income (using PPP exchange rate)
- Export dirversification
- Degree of integration into the global financial system

1.18 Inflation Indices

An index is a number designed to measure the relative change in the level of an activity/ phenomenon from time to time. An index is used to measure the changes in various fields like stock market, wages, prices etc. An inflation index is a tool used to measure the rate of inflation in an economy.

To measure the price rise in the economy, an inflation index is chosen for a particular year as the base year. Generally, the index is taken as 100 in the base year. In the next year when the inflation in the economy increases, then this index is also increased proportionally based on the data collected from the field.

Suppose, for example, we assume inflation index as 100 in the year 2010 (base year). We need to keep in mind that 100 is just a representation of the price level in the year 2010 and not the average price and we can start this number even from 1000 or 100,000 also, it will not matter. If the inflation in the economy increases by 10% in the year 2011 then this index number of 100 is moved up to 110. If the inflation in the economy is 5% in the year 2012 then this index number moves to 115.5 and so on.

An index can be designed to measure the price increase of a particular commodity or average price increase of a basket of commodities. Since the variation in prices of different commodities may be different, we take the weighted average increase in the prices of a basket of commodities to measure the inflation.

In India, we predominantly use the following indices to measure the average price increase for a basket of commodities.

1. Consumer Price Index (CPI):

CPI measures the change in prices paid by the ultimate consumers in the retail market. Since different class of consumers' consumption pattern varies, there can be difference in the price increase in the basket of commodities consumed by one class of people from the other class/group. So, in India we have several CPI indices for different category/class of people:

- **CPI - Industrial Workers (CPI -IW):** This index measures the change in price of commodity basket consumed by the industrial workers
- **CPI - Agricultural Labourers (CPI -AL):** This index measures the change in price of commodity basket consumed by the agricultural labourers
- **CPI - Rural Labourers:** This index measures the change in price of commodity basket consumed by the rural labourers

These indices are published monthly by Labour Bureau under Ministry of Labour and Employment for all India as well as States and Union Territories.

Since the above three indices covered only a segment of the population, and not the overall nation, so we have designed three more indices of CPI:

➢ **CPI - Rural:** This index measures the change in price of commodity basket consumed by rural population

➢ **CPI - Urban:** This index measures the change in price of commodity basket consumed by urban population

➢ **CPI - Combined:** It is computed by combining CPI Rural and CPI Urban Index

The base year for the above three indices has been revised to 2024 (using Household Consumption Expenditure Survey 2023-24). The item basket and the corresponding weights are based on Household Consumption Expenditure Survey 2023-24. There are 308 goods items and 50 services items in the revised CPI resulting in total 358 items in the CPI basket.

Key enhancements in the revised CPI Index (with base year 2024=100)

- First-time inclusion of rural house rent for improving coverage of rural housing consumption
- Strengthened representation of modern consumption items such as online media services and fuels (CNG/PNG)
- Improved coverage of data available on digital and administrative sources, including telephone charges, rail fare, air fare, fuel, postal charges and online media and streaming services (OTT subscriptions).

The weights in the CPI basket for different items are assigned based on the expenditure made by the retail people on those items. And these weights are assigned once during the base year and then it remains fixed till the base year gets revised. These indices are published monthly by National Statistical Office (NSO) for all India as well as States and Union Territories.

As per the new CPI series, 'Food and beverages' have the highest weight of 36.75% in CPI Combined, 41.98% in CPI Rural and 30.25% in CPI Urban. Hence any fluctuation in food items impacts the CPI in a major way. Second highest weight is of housing, water, electricity, gas and other fuels (17.67%) in CPI Combined. CPI **includes** the impact of indirect taxes.

Consumer Food Price Index (CFPI): CFPI measures the change in retail prices of food items consumed by the population. It is also released monthly for rural, urban and combined (all India basis).

2. Wholesale Price Index (WPI):

WPI measures the change in prices in the wholesale market, where goods are traded in bulk. It is published monthly by Office of Economic Advisor, Department for Promotion of Industry and Internal Trade (DPIIT) under Ministry of Commerce and Industry.

While the CPI-based retail inflation looks at the price which the consumer pays to buy the goods and services, the WPI tracks prices which the producer gets at the wholesale, or factory gate/mandi levels.

Between the wholesale price and the retail price, the difference essentially is the former only tracks basic prices devoid of transportation cost, indirect taxes and the retail margin etc. WPI includes the price change of goods only and not services because services are not traded in wholesale markets.

WPI commodities are divided into three major groups:

	Primary Articles *(Like agriculture commodities and minerals)*	**Fuel and Power**	**Manufactured Products**
Weight	22.62%	13.15%	64.23%

There are around 697 items in the WPI basket and their weights are assigned based on the "Domestic production of that item plus Net imports" which is also called "Net traded value". And this weight is kept constant till we revise the base year and start a new series. The present base year for WPI is 2011-12.

The weight of food articles in WPI is 24.4%

3. GDP Deflator:

To understand GDP Deflator, consider an example where India is producing 10kg of wheat at the market price of Rs. 10 in 2023 and 11kg of wheat at Rs. 10.5 in 2024.

	2023	2024
Wheat	10kg × Rs. 10	11kg × Rs. 10.5

If we want to know the inflation from 2023 to 2024 then we can see that it is 5% (Rs. 10 to Rs. 10.5). But inflation can be calculated in another way also by keeping the quantity constant in both the years.

In the above example,

Nominal GDP of 2024

$$= 11\text{kg} \times \text{Rs. } 10.5$$
$$= \text{Rs } 115.5$$

and, Real GDP of 2024

$$= 11\text{kg} \times \text{Rs. } 10$$
$$= \text{Rs } 110$$

If we divide Nominal GDP of 2024 by Real GDP of 2024, then what we get is the change in price because in Nominal GDP and Real GDP of 2024, the quantity is same/constant *i.e.,* 11kg.

So, Change in price from 2023 to 2024

$$= \frac{\text{Nomina l GDP of 2024}}{\text{Real GDP of 2024}}$$

$$= \frac{11\text{ kg} \times \text{Rs. } 10.5}{11\text{ kg} \times \text{Rs. } 10} = \frac{\text{Rs } 115.5}{\text{Rs. } 110} = \frac{1.05}{1}$$

This means that the prices have increased by 1.05 times from 2023 to 2024 i.e. inflation is 5%. And this ratio of Nominal GDP/ Real GDP is called the **"GDP deflator";**

$$\text{So, GDP Deflator} = \frac{\text{Nominal GDP}}{\text{Real GDP}}$$

GDP deflator is published by NSO quarterly.

National income aggregates are estimated at current and constant prices. Under the production (value added) approach of calculation of GDP:

- For some activities, estimates are prepared at current prices and the constant price estimates are derived using a suitable price indicator
- For some activities, estimates are prepared at constant prices and the current price estimates are derived using a suitable price indicator
- For some other activities, volumes are estimated independently

The price indicator used to convert from current/constant price to constant/current price is generally WPI or CPI (at aggregate or disaggregated level) or it can be a mix of both.

Estimates of all activities are aggregated to arrive at GVA estimates at both constant and current price separately and adjusted for taxes less subsidies to arrive at GDP at market prices.
The ratio of current to constant price estimate (of GDP or GVA) thus derived is the implicit GDP or GVA price deflator, reflecting overall inflation in all goods and services produced in the economy. [Source: RBI]

The following are some basic differences in CPI, WPI and GDP deflator:

- In wholesale market services are not traded, so WPI does not include the inflation in services, while CPI and GDP deflator capture inflation in services also.
- The goods purchased by consumers in the retail market do not represent all the goods produced in the country (like inputs, intermediates and capital goods are purchased by the companies), so CPI does not include these items but WPI takes into account of all such goods.
- CPI and WPI include prices of goods produced domestically and imported both but GDP deflator does not include prices of imported goods.
- The weights are constant in CPI and WPI index (till base year gets revised), but they differ according to production level of each good and services in GDP deflator.

PREVIOUS YEARS' QUESTIONS

Prelim Questions

1. A rapid increase in the rate of inflation is sometimes attributed to the "base effect". What is "base effect"? **[2011]**
   (a) It is the impact of drastic deficiency in supply due to failure of crops
   (b) It is the impact of the surge in demand due to rapid economic growth
   (c) It is the impact of the price levels of previous year on the calculation of inflation rate
   (d) None of the statements (a), (b) and (c) given above is correct in this context

2. A "closed economy" is an economy in which **[2011]**
   (a) The money supply is fully controlled
   (b) Deficit financing takes place
   (c) Only exports take place
   (d) Neither exports nor imports take place

3. In the context of Indian economy, consider the following statements: **[2011]**
   (i) The growth rate of GDP has steadily increased in the last five years
   (ii) The growth rate in per capita income has steadily increased in the last five years

   Which of the following statements given above is/are correct?
   (a) (i) only (b) (ii) only
   (c) Both (i) & (ii) (d) Neither (i) nor (ii)

4. Economic growth in country X will necessarily have to occur if **[2013]**
   (a) There is technical progress in the world economy
   (b) There is population growth in X
   (c) There is capital formation in X
   (d) The volume of trade grows in world economy

5. Which of the following brings out the "Consumer Price Index Number for Industrial Workers"? **[2015]**
   (a) The Reserve Bank of India
   (b) The Department of Economic Affairs
   (c) The Labour Bureau
   (d) The Department of Personnel and Training

6. Increase in absolute and per capita real GNP do not connote a higher level of economic development, if **[2018]**
   (a) industrial output fails to keep pace with agricultural output.
   (b) agricultural output fails to keep pace with industrial output.
   (c) poverty and unemployment increase.
   (d) imports grow faster than exports.

7. Despite being a high saving economy, capital formation may not result in significant increase in output due to **[2018]**
   (a) weak administrative machinery
   (b) illiteracy
   (c) high population density
   (d) high capital-output ratio

8. Consider the following statements **[2019]**
   (i) Purchasing Power Parity (PPP) exchange rates are calculated by comparing the prices of the same basket of goods and services in different countries

(ii) In terms of PPP dollars, India is the sixth largest economy in the world

Which of the statements given above is / are correct?

(a) (i) only
(b) (i) & (ii) only
(c) Both (i) & (ii)
(d) Neither (i) nor (ii)

9. Consider the following statements: **[2020]**

1. The weight age of food in Consumer Price Index (CPI) is higher than that in Wholesale Price Index (WPI).
2. The WPI does not capture changes in the prices of services, which CPI does.
3. Reserve Bank of India has now adopted WPI as its key measure of inflation and to decide on changing the key policy rates.

Which of the statements given above is/are correct?

(a) 1 and 2 only
(b) 2 only
(c) 3 only
(d) 1, 2 and 3

10. Other things remaining unchanged, market demand for a good might increase if: **[2021]**

(i) price of its substitute increases
(ii) price of its complement increases
(iii) the good is an inferior good and income of the consumers increases
(iv) its price falls

Which of the above statements are correct?

(a) (i) & (iv) only
(b) (ii), (iii) & (iv) only
(c) (i), (iii) & (iv) only
(d) (i), (ii) & (iii) only

11. With reference to the Indian economy, consider the following statements: **[2022]**

1. An increase in Nominal Effective Exchange Rate (NEER) indicates the appreciation of rupee.
2. An increase in the Real Effective Exchange Rate (REER) indicates an improvement in trade competitiveness.
3. An increasing trend in domestic inflation relative to inflation in other countries is likely to cause an increasing divergence between NEER and REER.

Which of the above statements are correct?

(a) 1 and 2 only (b) 2 and 3 only
(c) 1 and 3 only (d) 1, 2 and 3

12. With reference to physical capital in Indian economy, consider the following pairs: **[2024]**

Items	Category
1. Farmer's plough	Working capital
2. Computer	Fixed capital
3. Yarn used by the weaver	Fixed capital
4. Petrol	Working capital

How many of the above pairs are correctly matched?

(a) Only one (b) Only two
(c) Only three (d) All four

ANSWERS

1. (c) 2. (d) 3. (d) 4. (c) 5. (c) 6. (c) 7. (d) 8. (a) 9. (a) 10. (a)
11. (c) 12. (b)

Main Questions

1. Define potential GDP and explain its determinants. What are the factors that have been inhibiting India from realizing its potential GDP? **[2020]**

2. Explain the difference between computing methodology of India's Gross Domestic Product (GDP) before the year 2015 and after the year 2015. **[2021]**

3. Do you agree that the Indian economy has recently experienced V-shaped recovery? Give reasons in support of your answer. **[2021]**

2

Money and Banking : Part-I

2.1 Introduction

In earlier times, economic transactions used to happen as barter exchanges i.e., one commodity is exchanged for the other commodity. But for barter exchanges to happen there must be **double coincidence of wants** i.e., there should be diametrically opposite demand of the two parties doing the exchange. Consider, for example, an individual has a surplus of rice which he wishes to exchange for wheat. If he is not lucky enough, he may not be able to find another person who has the diametrically opposite demand for rice with a surplus of wheat to offer in exchange. The process can become very cumbersome in case of a large economy. To smoothen the transaction, an intermediate "commodity" is necessary which is acceptable to both the parties. The individuals can then sell their produce for this commodity and use this commodity to purchase the other goods that they need. Now what should be the characteristics of this commodity?

Suppose this intermediate "commodity" is decided to be "iron" or "water". Then in such a case, if water and iron are easily/freely available in the country, then a person who has produced rice with so much of effort would never be willing to exchange his rice in return for iron or water as he can easily/freely get iron and water in the economy. That means the intermediate "commodity" should be such that it is very limited in supply and difficult to get. So, we decided this intermediate "commodity" as gold or silver as both were very limited in supply and started buying and selling of goods in exchange of gold and silver. Such a commodity is called money. This system of gold and silver continued for a long time.

But there were problems associated with this also. Suppose there is a country (economy) where people are buying and selling goods and services with the help of the gold coins. If the production of goods and services (GDP) is increasing every year then the country may require more gold coins for transaction of the increased goods and services. If the supply of gold coins is not keeping pace with the increase in goods and services then there could again be problems in transaction process. And the other problem associated with this system was, every time a person is purchasing a commodity, he needs to carry the physical gold with him.

Now, suppose there is a person X in the economy whom everybody used to trust. One day an individual say A deposited his physical gold with the person X and he issued the individual A, a paper slip with his signature and the amount of gold written on that slip (suppose 1 milligram). When this person A went to the market to purchase goods worth 1 milligram (mg) of gold from a person B, then rather than offering 1 mg of gold, A offered the paper slip to B that X had signed. B willingly accepted that paper slip from A as B also knew and trusted that person X, and had trust that whenever he will go to X and offer him the paper slip, he will get 1 mg of gold. In the same way, everybody in the economy deposited their gold with the trustworthy person X and in return got paper slips and started buying and selling goods with these paper slips. These paper slips became the currency "Rupee" and X is the RBI.

Still, **if the production of goods and services is increasing every year, then we require more rupees** and if we do not have gold how will we get the rupee? In such a situation, RBI used to issue the paper slips without the deposition of physical gold (but by keeping some other assets). So, if the production of goods and services (i.e., the output) is increasing in the economy, then RBI can issue more Rupee currency notes (by accepting some other assets like government securities, foreign currency) to facilitate transaction in the economy.

The logic is if RBI is issuing the currency notes, then it must be backed by some asset physical or financial (may not necessarily gold).

Now we have a huge population and if all the people are going to transact with RBI asking for Rupee notes or deposition of gold then it will be very difficult for RBI to manage them. So, a layer of commercial banks was created between RBI and the public.

People (Served by Banks)

Commercial Banks (Served by RBI)

RBI

In any particular year, suppose there is some level of output/GDP and some level of money supply in the economy. Now, next year, RBI tries to increase the money supply in the economy based on two factors; one is the expected real GDP growth and the other is the level of inflation (that RBI wants to maintain/target in the economy). So, basically money supply is increased proportional to the expected nominal GDP.

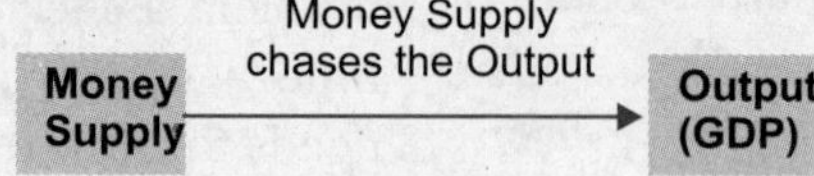

Money supply chases the output and inflation will depend on the proportion of output (GDP) and money supply. The following scenarios are possible:

- If money supply is increased while output decreases or remains constant, then prices may go up
- If money supply is decreased while output increases or remains constant, then prices may come down
- If money supply remains constant and output decreases, then prices may go up
- If money supply remains constant and output increases, then prices may come down

2.2 Functions of Money

Money plays three important roles/functions in the economy.

(i) Money acts as a medium of exchange. Facilitation of exchanges/transactions is the most important role of money.

(ii) Money also acts as a convenient unit of account. This means that the value of all goods and services can be expressed in monetary units. When we say that the value of a book is Rs. 300, we mean that the book can be exchanged for 300 units of money, where the unit is rupee in this case. So, the value of all goods and services can be expressed in rupee terms.

(iii) Money acts as a *store of value*. This means that wealth can be stored in the form of money for future use. Money is not perishable and its storage costs are also considerably lower and are acceptable to everyone at any point of time. It may be noted that any asset other than money can also act as a store of value *i.e.*, gold, property etc. However, they may not be easily convertible to other commodities and do not have universal acceptability. In case the prices are rising steeply then the purchasing power of money erodes and the "store of value" function of money gets compromised as money starts losing its value.

2.3 Exchange Rate Systems

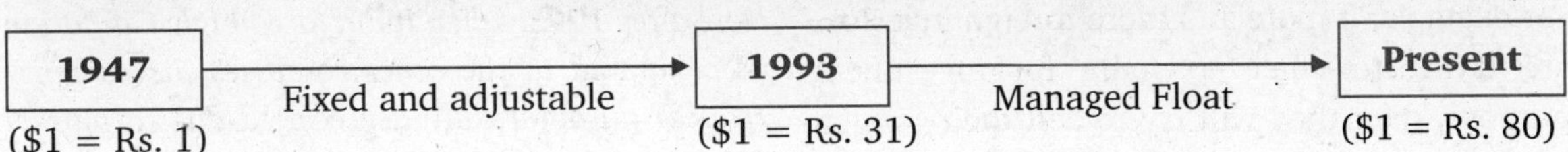

Before 1993

Since independence and till 1993, India used to fix its exchange rate with respect to dollar and other major currencies and depending on economic situation, whenever required it used to adjust or devalue and revalue the rupee. This is called "Fixed and Adjustable" exchange rate system.

In 1947, the nominal exchange rate was \$1 = Rs. 1, but due to continued adverse Balance of Payment (BoP) situation and relatively higher inflation in India as compared to other major trading partners, we used to devalue the rupee because of which it reached to \$1 = Rs. 31 by 1993. *(A country goes for devaluation of its currency to correct its adverse Balance of Payment situation so that its exports get cheaper and import becomes costlier)*. Let us understand with an example:

Suppose the Nominal Exchange Rate is:

\$1 = Rs. 20

	India	US
Burger Price	Rs. 10	\$1

In this case US will import the burgers from India as in \$1 they will get Rs. 20 and in Rs. 20 they will get 2 burgers in India, so India will export burgers to US.

But if due to inflation the burger price in India becomes Rs. 20 then exports from India will stop (i.e., inflation in India is making its exports less competitive).

But in that situation when price has increased to Rs. 20, if RBI devalues the exchange rate to $1 = Rs. 30 then again exports from India will start. Because now foreigners will get Rs. 30 in $1 and in Rs. 30 they will get one and a half burger in India.

Hence, to increase its exports and improve the balance of payment situation, India consistently devalued its currency till 1993.

After 1993

After 1993, RBI left the rupee to the market forces of demand and supply i.e., floating exchange rate. Floating exchange rate implies that its value will depend/float as per the market forces of demand and supply of the currency in the market and the Central bank of the country will not manipulate it.

For example, if more and more foreign investors are trying to come to India for investment purpose, then they will try to sell their foreign currency and purchase rupees as they can invest in India in Indian Rupee only. As they will try to purchase more and more Indian Rupees the demand of Rupees will increase and it will appreciate. If the opposite happens and investors start leaving India then they will sell their investments in India in Rupee and purchase the foreign currency which will lead to increase in demand of foreign currency and the Rupee will start depreciating.

Let us take another example to understand why Rupee depreciated against Dollar continuously after 1993:

Suppose the Nominal Exchange Rate is :

$1 = Rs. 40

	India	US
Burger Price	Rs. 20	$1

In this case, US will import the burgers from India as in $1 they will get Rs. 40 and in Rs. 40 they will get 2 burgers in India, so India will export burgers to US.

But if due to inflation the burger price in India has started increasing and becomes Rs. 30 then exports from India will start declining which in another way implies that demand for rupees will start declining. The decline in rupee demand will depreciate the rupee exchange rate and it may move to $1 = Rs. 50 which again will push the export of burgers from India as US people will get more burgers at $1 = Rs. 50 exchange rates than $1 = Rs. 40.

So, when our exchange rate was fixed and adjustable (before 1993) and there was comparatively high inflation in India or BoP issues, then RBI used to devalue rupee to make our exports competitive. Now after 1993, when India faced higher inflation as compared to the other countries, its currency (rupee) automatically depreciated due to market forces of demand and supply.

Floating exchange rates are of two types:

- Free Float: Under this system, the Central bank of the country never intervenes in the foreign exchange market and the currency price is totally left to the demand and supply forces i.e. market forces. For example, US, Japan and some European countries.
- Managed Float: Under this system, the Central bank sometimes intervenes in the market to buy and sell foreign currencies in case the domestic currency becomes very volatile. For example, Indian Rupee is **managed float**. So, if the Rupee has become very volatile and is depreciating against dollar then, RBI starts selling dollars in the market from its foreign exchange reserves to check the appreciation

of dollar and keep the rupee stable and prevent its depreciation. In case of India, RBI intervenes in the foreign exchange market generally indirectly through select public sector banks (these banks, in turn, buy or sell on behalf of RBI in the market) to contain volatility in the rupee and not to set any price band.

2.4 Securities

Securities are financial instruments (receipts/ slips) which promises return (payment) in future and which are tradable. For example, suppose somebody deposited Rs. 1 lakh in his account and got an account statement/pass book. The person who is holding the account statement will receive interest in future but he is not allowed to sell this paper (account statement) in the market. Hence the account statement is not considered as a security in a strict sense. Securities can be broadly categorized into two categories viz. equity and debt.

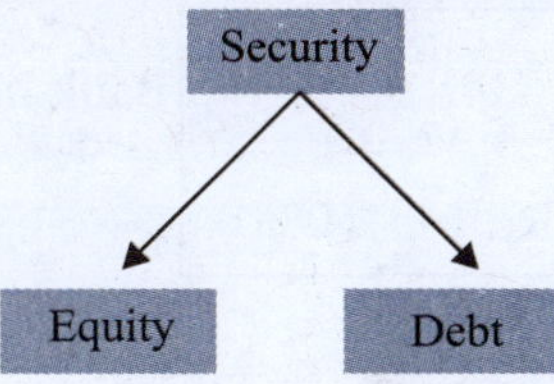

1. Equity security (stock/shares) represents ownership held by shareholders (owners) in a company/corporation. Holders of equity security receive **profit**/dividend and capital gains (share price appreciation). Equity securities entitle the holder to some control of the company on a proportionate basis i.e., the equity holders get voting rights and thus some control of the business.
2. Debt security represents money that is borrowed and must be repaid with terms that define the amount borrowed, interest rate and maturity date. Holders of debt security receive **interest** and repayment of the principal.

The entity (company) that issues the securities is known as the issuer of security.

Whenever a person invests (puts money) in a company/ project, then this investment can be done broadly in two ways.

1. By purchase of **equity securities**. In this case the investor puts the money in the company and gets a share in the ownership of the company. In this case the person does not get any fixed return but receives profit/ dividend based on the performance of the company. This is the form of purchase of equity securities of the company by the investor.
2. By purchase of **debt securities.** In this case, the investor puts the money in the company at a fix interest rate for a specific period of time and receives interest (regularly) and principal back at the end of maturity period. This is the form of purchase of debt securities of the company by the investor.

To understand securities in a better way, let us take an example of a newly registered company "XYZ Private Limited". The company maintains its account in the form of a balance sheet (shown below) and the assets and liabilities of the company in the balance sheet are always equal. Initially the company does not have any money/capital and has an account opened in a particular bank to keep its money.

The owner/entrepreneur initially puts up some money say Rs. 1 crore in the company (which will be deposited in the company's account) and the company in return issues him an 'ownership document'/ share. The cash in the account of the company will be an asset for the company as the company can do anything with that cash of Rs. 1 crore. Against this amount the company will be issuing a document to the owner which will represent 100% ownership in the company, and will be represented on the liability side of the company as a statement "owner's money" or "shareholders money". The ownership document or the share is asset for the owner but will act as liability for the company. This transaction will look like the following:

"XYZ Pvt. Ltd."

Asset	Liability
Cash = Rs. 1 cr	Owner's Money = Rs. 1 cr
Rs. 1 cr	Rs. 1 cr

If the company is expanding its business and wants more funds then it may approach a bank. Suppose the bank gave loan to the company worth Rs. 2 crores. The cash that the company got will be an asset for the company but the company will have to sign a "loan document" representing Rs. 2 crore loan to the company and this loan document will be a liability for the company (represented on the liability side as Bank Loan) and asset for the Bank. This transaction will look like:

"XYZ Pvt. Ltd."

Asset	Liability
Cash = Rs. 1 cr Cash = Rs. 2 cr	Owner's Money = Rs. 1 cr
	Bank Loan = Rs. 2 cr
Rs. 3 cr	Rs. 3 cr

If the company wants more funds, then it may approach the individual people i.e. retail market to put in money into the company at a **particular/fixed interest rate** (similar to the way people put money in banks). Suppose the company approached 1 lakh individuals who could invest Rs. 100 each (total = Rs. 1 crore) for 5 years in the company at a fixed interest rate of 10% *(just assume that banks were offering 9% interest rate, so company offered 1% more)*. People have decided to put money in the company rather than banks as the company was offering higher interest rate as compared to the banks. This transaction will increase the assets of the company by Rs. 1 crore and the liabilities of the company will also increase by 1 crore. The company will issue paper "slips" worth Rs. 100 to the individuals which will be assets for the individuals but will act as liability for the company.

The slips will look like.

"Slips"

XYZ Pvt. Ltd.	
Value = Rs. 100 Time = 5 years Interest Rate = 10%	Bank Interest Rate = 9%

Now, after some time, if the banks increase their interest rate to 12% due to changes in the economic conditions, then the people holding the "slips" will try to get rid of the slips as the slip is offering them just 10% interest rate. But if they would go in the market to sell the slips, nobody would be willing to purchase these slips in the market at Rs. 100 because why anybody will purchase the slips at 10% interest rate if they can deposit Rs. 100 in banks and can earn 12% interest rate. So, the slip holders will offer the slips at a discounted/lower price if they want it to be sold in the market. But what shall be that lesser price.

Anybody will be willing to purchase the slips

if they can earn higher interest rate on slips as compared to what is being offered in the market i.e., 12%. Suppose a purchaser purchases this slip in Rs. 80 from the market. Let us see his earning or interest rate.

Money spent by the purchaser in purchasing the slip = Rs. 80

Annual interest received by the purchaser

= Rs. 10 (10% of Rs 100)

Effective Interest rate earned by the purchaser

= Rs. 10/Rs. 80 = 12.5%

Hence the purchaser will purchase this slip in Rs. 80 as he is getting a higher return *(which is also called yield)* of 12.5% as compared to the bank interest rate of 12%. Why the person who had initially purchased the slip will sell the slip in Rs. 80? Because he thinks that if the bank interest rate rises further to say 13% or 14%, nobody would be willing to purchase the slip even in Rs. 80. *(All trading activity happens based on future projections)*. These slips are called **bonds**. So, bonds prices in the market decrease when the bank interest rate rises. And the bonds prices in the market increase when the bank interest rate falls. The company's balance sheet will look like:

"XYZ Pvt. Ltd."

Asset	Liability
Cash = Rs. 1 cr Cash = Rs. 2 cr Cash = Rs. 1 cr	Owner's Money = Rs. 1 cr Bank Loan = Rs. 2 cr Bonds = Rs. 1 cr
Rs. 4 cr	Rs. 4 cr

If the company converts its cash to purchase building and machinery then the balance sheet will look like:

"XYZ Pvt. Ltd."

Asset	Liability
Building 1 = Rs. 1 cr Building 2 = Rs. 2 cr Machinery 1 = Rs. 1 cr	Owner's Money = Rs. 1 cr Bank Loan = Rs. 2 cr Bonds = Rs. 1 cr
Rs. 4 cr	Rs. 4 cr

Now, suppose the company is making profit and more and more people want to invest in the company and become owners. Let us assume that one lakh people invested Rs. 100 each (total Rs. 1 crore) to become owners in the company and the company purchased machinery with this Rs. 1 crore cash. The balance sheet will look like:

"XYZ Pvt. Ltd."

Asset	Liability
Building1 = Rs. 1 cr Building2 = Rs. 2 cr Machinery1 = Rs. 1 cr Machinery2 = Rs. 1 cr	Owner's Money = Rs. 1 cr Owner's Money = Rs. 1 cr Bank Loan = Rs. 2 cr Bonds = Rs. 1 cr
Rs. 5 cr	Rs. 5 cr

Now the value of the owners in the company will be Rs. 2 crore representing 100% ownership. And the new owners would like to hold the ownership/share document in proportion to their ownership. So, the ownership document that the initial entrepreneur was holding (whose value has now become Rs. 2 crore) will be divided into two lakh pieces.

So now, 100% ownership = Rs. 2 crore

= 2 lakh shares × Value of each share

Hence, value of each share = Rs. 100

The entrepreneur will be holding 50% ownership and one lakh shares of Rs. 100 each.

And the new one lakh owners will be holding combined 50% ownership with one share each worth Rs. 100.

Now, if the company's assets increase either by increase in the valuation of the building or because the company is making profit then the value of each share will increase. For example, if the company makes Rs. 2 crore of profit, then this profit will be company's assets (deposited in company's account) and the value of two lakh shares will become Rs. 4 crores, so the share price will increase to Rs. 200 per share. Hence company's share price increases with increase in **profit**. The balance sheet will look like:

"XYZ Pvt. Ltd."

Asset	Liability	
Building 1 = Rs. 1 cr Building 2 = Rs. 2 cr Machinery 1 = Rs. 1 cr Machinery 2 = Rs. 1 cr Cash (from profit) = Rs. 2 cr	Shareholder's Money = Rs. 4 cr *(Two lakh shares × Rs. 200 each)*	**Equity**
	Bank Loan = Rs. 2 cr Bonds = Rs. 1 cr	**Debt**
Rs. 7 cr	Rs. 7 cr	

In the above example, investors are investing/putting money in the company in the following two ways:

- at a particular/fixed interest rate and gets the **debt security**
- at profit or loss and becomes owner and gets **equity security**

So, against the total assets, the company issues either debt or equity securities to the investors and the same are represented in the company's account book on the liability side.

2.5 Government Securities

- A Government Security (G-Sec) is a tradable instrument issued by the Central Government or the State Governments. G-Secs carry practically no risk of default and, hence, are called risk-free gilt-edged instruments. Govt. issues only debt securities.
- G-Secs are issued through auctions conducted by RBI. Auctions are conducted on the electronic platform called the E-Kuber, the Core Banking Solution (CBS) platform of RBI. So, basically e-Kuber is a platform where primary market transaction happens.
- Commercial banks, scheduled UCBs, Primary Dealers, insurance companies and provident funds, who maintain funds account (current account) and securities accounts with RBI, are members of this electronic platform. All members of E-Kuber can place their bids in the auction through this electronic platform.
- There is an active secondary market in G-Secs and Negotiated Dealing System-Order Matching (NDS-OM) is such a market/platform. Stock exchanges are also a secondary market for government securities.

There are four kinds of government securities.

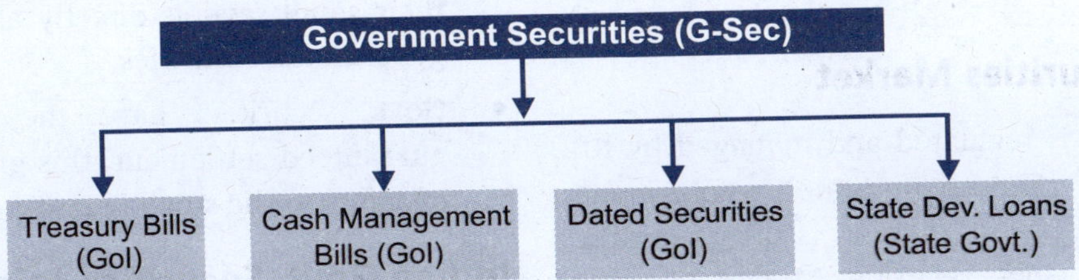

1. **Treasury bills or T-bills:** These are short term debt instruments issued by the Government of India for a maturity of less than one year. Treasury bills are zero coupon securities and pay no interest. Instead, they are issued at a discount and redeemed at the face value at maturity. For example, a 91-day Treasury bill of ₹100/- (face value) may be issued at say ₹ 98.20, that is, at a discount of say, ₹1.80 and would be redeemed at the face value of ₹100/-. (Treasury bills are traded in money market).
2. **Cash Management Bills (CMB):** In 2010, Government of India, in consultation with RBI introduced a new short-term instrument, known as Cash Management Bills (CMBs), to meet the temporary mismatches in the cash flow of the Government of India. The CMBs have the generic character of T-bills but are issued for maturities less than 91 days and are traded in money market.
3. **Dated Securities:** These are basically long-term securities issued by the Central Govt. and generally have a tenor of 5 years to 50 years. They can be of different categories:
    - **Fixed rate bonds:** Interest rate is fixed till maturity.
    - **Floating rate bonds:** The interest/ coupon rate is not fixed and can be linked to the yield of Treasury bills
    - **Inflation indexed bonds:** Interest and principal both are protected against inflation and can be linked with any inflation index like CPI or WPI. Every year principal is increased by the inflation index and the interest is offered on the increased principle.
    - **Special Securities:** Under the market borrowing program, the Government of India also issues, from time to time, special securities to entities like Oil Marketing Companies, Fertilizer Companies, the Food Corporation of India, etc. (popularly called oil bonds, fertiliser bonds and food bonds respectively) as compensation to these companies in lieu of cash subsidies.
    - **Bank recapitalization bonds:** Government of India has also issued Bank Recapitalisation Bonds to specific Public Sector Banks in 2018. (Discussed in detail in bank recapitalization)
    - **Sovereign gold bonds (SGB):** SGBs are unique instruments, prices of which are linked to commodity price viz Gold. SGBs are also budgeted in lieu of market borrowing.
4. **State Development Loans (SDL):** When States want money, they issue long term bonds or dated securities of more than one year maturity which are called SDLs.

All the above four types of Govt. securities qualify for SLR.

Govt. Securities Market

This market is regulated and managed by RBI. When Govt. (Central or State) wants money, RBI raises money for them by issuing securities/ bonds in the Govt. Securities Market. First time the securities are issued in the Govt. Securities Market (basically primary market transaction) and then secondary market transactions happen. All the four types of Govt. securities i.e., "Cash Management Bills", "Treasury Bills", "Dated Securities" and "State Development Loans" are traded in the Govt. Securities Market. "Treasury Bills", "Dated Securities" and "State Development Loans" are also traded in Capital Market like BSE/NSE.

Retail Direct Scheme (of RBI)

- Retail individual investors will be able to open a Retail Direct Gilt (RDG) Account with the RBI.
- Retail individual investors will be able to purchase Govt. securities in the primary market directly as well as in the secondary market. [But still, they cannot participate in the competitive bidding process].
- Retail investors can purchase Central Government Securities (Treasury Bills and Dated Securities), State Govt. Securities (State Development Loans) and Sovereign Gold Bonds.
- This scheme will expand investment opportunities in the country and ensure easier access to capital markets with simple and secure mechanism.
- The scheme will give strength to the inclusion of everyone in the economy as it will bring in the middle class, employees, small businessmen and senior citizens with their small savings directly and securely in government securities.
- Govt. securities have the provision of guaranteed settlement; this gives assurance of safety to the small investors.

Indian Govt. Securities Joining Global Bond Index

- JP Morgan and Bloomberg has included Govt. of India bonds/securities in their 'Global Bond Index'. This will enable Govt. of India to access foreign debt capital easily.
- A 'bond index' includes bonds of different entities like different corporations and Governments.
- An investor can invest either in the bonds of a single institution/company/government or they can invest in a "Bond Index (fund)" where the money will be put in bonds of various institutions/Governments proportionately as per the weights of the different bonds in the "Bond Index".
- If a foreign investor wants to purchase Govt. of India bonds, then they need approval of SEBI. But if foreign investors are investing through bond index (fund) then every foreign investor does not require SEBI approval, rather, only the (JP Morgan) bond index (fund) will require SEBI approval as a foreign portfolio investor (FPI).
- This could lead to billions of dollars worth of inflows into India's rupee-denominated government debt.
- Everything else remaining same, an incremental source of demand from foreign investors will bring down the government cost of borrowing and will free up the liquidity for domestic financers to deploy

in more productive assets. This will also result in increase in liquidity in Indian Govt. securities.

- But it could also expose the country to a greater degree of exchange rate risk and potentially lead to volatility in the rupee if external conditions were to turn adverse.
- Earlier there was a cap/ceiling as to how much non-residents (foreign) investors can invest in bonds in India. But inclusion of Govt. securities in the Global Bond Index requires this cap to be removed. So, RBI in March 2020 removed this cap for investments by non-residents (NRIs, FPIs) in Govt. securities under 'Fully Accessible Route'. There is a plan to remove the limit on corporate debt/bond too.
- The Financial Markets Regulation department of RBI will handle the listing of Govt. of India securities in the Global Bond Market on the international platform "Euroclear".

2.6 Corporate Bond Market in India

The existence of a deep and liquid corporate debt/bond market has the capability to make India less vulnerable, especially to volatile capital flows. For, a reasonably well-developed bond market could supplement the banking system in meeting the requirements of the corporate sector for long term capital investment and asset creation. It could provide a stable source of finance; especially when the equity/share market is volatile and resource requirements of the corporate entities are large. The development of a corporate bond market has now become crucial especially, in view of the need for raising large amount of resources for infrastructure development in the country during the next couple of years.

Following are the factors responsible for the slow growth of corporate bond market in India.

- There are only a few corporate entities which are capable of meeting investor requirements in terms of transparency and governance standards. This has resulted in a yawning gap between demand for and supply of corporate bonds in India. Corporate governance and disclosure standards available do not provide enough confidence to investors to go in for investments in bonds unlike banks.
- Public offering of bonds (the process) being expensive, time consuming and procedure oriented, corporates have been finding it easier to either borrow from banks or make a private placement (to few select investors rather than to general public/investor) of their bonds.
- Non-availability of bankruptcy laws to ensure investor protection has also contributed towards slow development of the corporate bond market *(with the coming of IBC 2016 this challenge has now been resolved)*.
- Building the infrastructure required for a well-developed bond market is subject to significant time and resource costs which India has not put till now.

Efforts are being made by the Government to create a vibrant, dynamic, and deep corporate debt/bond market in the country. The following are few steps in this direction.

- Government, in consultation with RBI, has raised the Foreign Portfolio Investors (FPI) ceiling limit to 15% from the present 9% in corporate bonds. This means that whatever value of total corporate bonds are outstanding (presently issued), 15% could be held by FPIs.

- Government is framing an investor charter that would focus on the rights and responsibilities of investors and a grievance redressal mechanism. The investor charter will not only help bring in more transparency in the investment process but will also encourage investors to invest with better knowledge.
- Govt. has announced in the budget 2021-22 regarding creation of a 'backstop facility'. [A backstop is a financial arrangement that creates a secondary source of funds in case the primary source is not enough to meet current needs. It can also be thought of as an insurance policy that covers the inadequacy of a source of funds]. 'Backstop facility' would purchase the bond/debt papers (of investors) which are of investment grade (investment grade securities mean which has relatively better credit rating and less risky. Opposite of investment grade is junk grade) both in stressed and in normal times, which will help in the development of the bond market.

2.7 Financial Markets

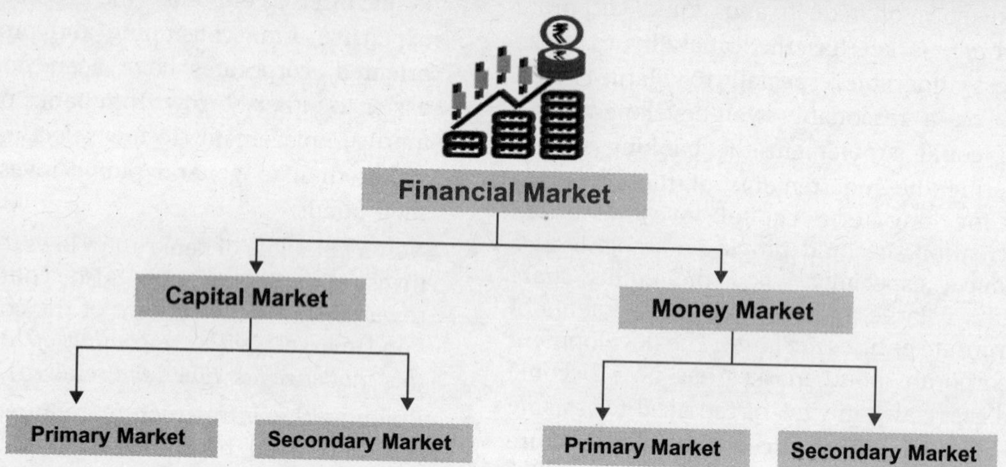

A **financial market** is a market that brings buyers and sellers together to trade in financial securities or assets such as stocks, bonds, derivatives, currencies etc. Financial markets are broadly of two types.

1. Capital Market

Financial markets for buying and selling **debt and equity** securities. In this market, (generally) securities of medium and long term of more than one year are bought and sold. Capital markets are of two types:

(i) Primary Market: It refers to the financial market where securities are created. It is in this market that companies sell new shares and bonds for the first time (Initial Public Offering, IPO). In this market transaction is between the issuer (company) of security and the investor. In the securities example earlier, the market in which the company issued bonds for the first time to one lakh investors is the primary market.

(ii) Secondary Market: Once the securities have been issued by the issuer in the primary market, it gets traded in the secondary market among the investors. In this market, investors trade the previously issued securities among themselves without the involvement of the issuer of security (company). Example, Bombay Stock Exchange. In the securities example, the market in which the investors started buying and selling the bonds among themselves is a secondary market.

2. Money Market

A segment of the financial market in which financial instruments with **high liquidity** and very short maturities (**less than one year**) are traded. Money market instruments are basically **debt instruments** and include Call/Notice money, Repos, Treasury Bills, Cash Management Bills, Commercial Paper, Certificate of Deposits and Collateralized Borrowing and Lending Obligations (CBLO). The players who can trade in the money market are financial institutions, commercial banks, central banks and highly rated corporates. These markets are less risky. Money Market transactions can also be classified as primary and secondary.

- Call/Notice Money: In call money, funds are transacted for overnight basis and under notice money, funds are transacted for the period between 2 days and 14 days. These are unsecured instruments. Participants include Commercial and Cooperative Banks, Primary Dealers (PDs), development finance institutions, insurance companies and select mutual funds.
- **Certificate of Deposits (CD):** CDs are negotiable/tradable, unsecured money market instruments issued mostly by Scheduled Commercial Banks for a maturity period up to one year against funds deposited at the bank.
- **Commercial Paper (CP):** CP is an unsecured money market instrument issued in the form of a promissory note (promise to pay in future). The maturity of a CP shall be between seven days to one year. NBFCs, development financial institutions (like NABARD, SIDBI etc.), cooperative societies, Govt. entities (PSUs) and other companies can issue CP to raise money in the money market.

2.8 Types of Company

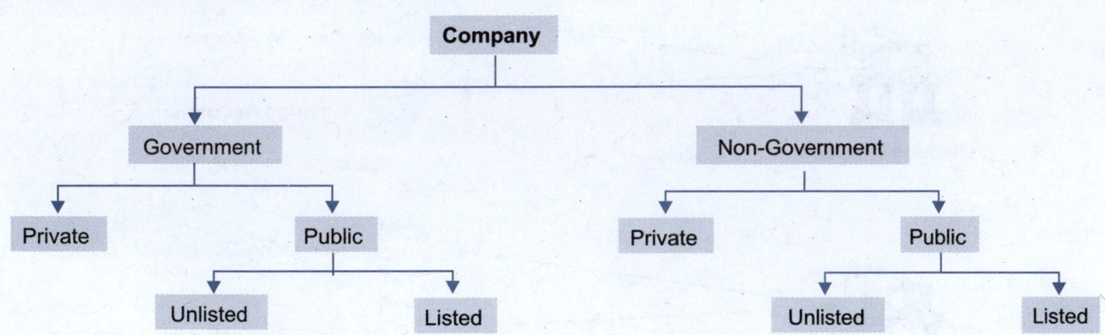

- **Government company** means any company in which not less than 51% shares are held by the Central government or by any state government or governments or partly by the Central government and partly by one or more state governments and includes subsidiary company of a government company.
- **Non-government companies** are those which are not government companies and defined as those companies where government ownership is less than 49% and majority of the ownership lies with private individuals/companies.
- **A private company** or close corporation is a company where the number of members is limited to 200 and there is restriction on the transfer of shares. The shares are not available to the general public but rather, owned and exchanged privately. (*The private word here does not refer to private ownership rather it tells about whether the shares of the company can be bought/sold publicly or not*).
- **Publicly Company** is a company which is not private.
- **Unlisted Public Company** means a public company whose securities are not traded on any stock exchange.
- **Listed Public company** means a company which has any of its securities (shares/ bonds) are listed on any recognized stock exchange. But in India, listed is used in reference to shares/equity securities.

A private company might become a publicly listed company by conducting an initial public offering (IPO), under which the company offers its **shares** for the first time to the general public through a stock exchange for trading purpose.

2.9 Accounts and Deposits

If someone has got money, then it can be kept in the banking system in mainly two ways viz. demand form i.e., demand deposits and time form i.e., time deposits or term deposits. In case someone wants to deposit money in demand form, then two kinds of accounts can be opened viz. Current Account and Savings Account. And in case someone wants to deposit money in time form then again two kinds of account can be opened viz. Fixed Deposit Account and Recurring Deposit Account.

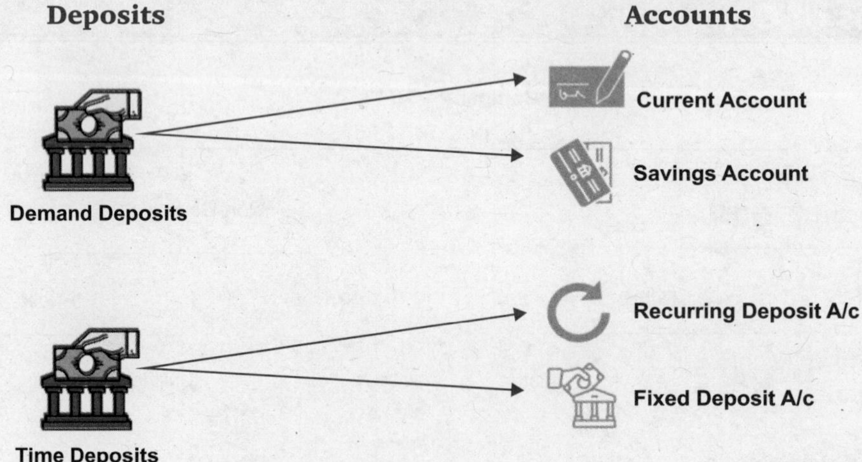

Types of Deposits

1. **Demand Deposit:** Funds held in demand deposits can be withdrawn at any time on demand without any advance notice to the depository institution. Demand deposits can be demanded by an account holder any time and there is no fixed term of maturity for demand deposits. Banks issue cheques on this kind of deposits and cheques can be drawn on these deposits and hence demand deposits are also called cheque-able deposits.
2. **Time Deposit:** Funds held in time deposits can be withdrawn only by giving an advance notice to the depository institution. The deposits are held for a specified time period or maturity. Banks do not issue cheques on this kind of deposits and are hence non cheque-able deposits. These are also called term deposits.

Types of Accounts

1. **Current Account:** It is always a demand deposit A/c and the bank is obliged to pay the money on demand. There is no limit on number of transactions and value of transactions and these are the most liquid deposits. Current account is used mainly for business purpose/ companies and never used for saving purpose. No interest is paid by banks on these accounts and the banks charge certain service charge on these accounts. Banks provide convenient operational facilities on these accounts and also issue chequebooks.
2. **Savings Account:** This account is mainly for individuals. These are also demand deposits but there are restrictions on the number of transactions and the value of transactions during a specified period. Banks generally prescribe minimum balances in the accounts in order to offset the cost of maintaining and servicing such deposits. The deposits in these accounts earn interest.
3. **Recurring Deposit Account:** These are term deposits which are suitable for people who do not have lump sum amount of savings but are ready to save small amount every month or quarterly or half yearly. Such deposits earn interest on the amount already deposited as applicable to fixed deposits. It is best suited for child's education or marriage purpose. Maturity is generally between 6 months to 10 years.
4. **Fixed Deposit Account:** These are term deposits with tenure varying from 7 days to 10 years. These deposits are for fixed term but can be withdrawn prematurely by giving an advance notice to the bank and some penalty.

The different types of accounts which can be maintained by an NRI/PIO (*An NRI is a person resident outside India, who is a citizen of India or is a person of Indian origin*) in India are:

1. Foreign Currency Non-Resident (FCNR) Account: This account can be maintained in any freely convertible **foreign** currency but only in the form of term deposits. The interest and principal are non-taxable and freely repatriable.
2. Non-Resident External (NRE) Account: This account can be maintained in **Rupee** in the form of Current, Savings, Recurring or Fixed Deposit. The interest and principal are non-taxable and freely repatriable.
3. Non-Resident Ordinary (NRO) Account: This account can be maintained in **Rupee** in the form of Current, Savings, Recurring or Fixed Deposit. Principal and Interest are taxable and has restricted repatriability. Income earned from Indian sources like rent, dividend, pension can be deposited only in this account.

2.10 Money Supply

In an economy, money consists of mainly **currency notes**, **coins** and **deposits** of public in banks. In India, coins and currency notes are **issued** for circulation by the Reserve Bank of India (RBI), which is the monetary authority (or Central Bank) in India. One-rupee note and all coins and subsidiary coins, the magnitude of which is relatively small, are minted/printed by the Government of India, while all the other currency notes are printed by the RBI. All the currency notes and coins are put into **circulation only through the RBI**, which is the **sole authority for the issue of currency and coins** in India.

The One Rupee note is signed by the finance secretary (and printed by Govt.) as a testimony that it is the base unit of the currency system.

Coins and One Rupee note are minted/printed by the government of India and hence constitute the liability of Government of India. As part of the circulation process, RBI buys the one rupee note and minted coins from the Government of India and hence the coins and one rupee note come and sit under the asset section of RBI's balance sheet.

All banknotes (except one rupee note) issued by RBI are ***backed*** *by assets such as gold, Government Securities and Foreign Currency Assets, as defined in Section 33 of RBI Act, 1934.*

"I promise to pay the bearer the sum of Rupees ..." denotes the obligation on the part of the RBI towards the holder of the banknote that the RBI is liable to pay the value of banknote. This liability of RBI is further **guaranteed** by Government of India as per Section 26 of the RBI Act, 1934.

The value of the currency notes and coins is derived from the guarantee provided by the Central Government on these items. Every currency note bears on its face a promise from the RBI that if someone produces the note to RBI or any other commercial bank, RBI will be responsible for giving the person purchasing power/value equal to the value printed on the note. The same is also true for coins. **Currency notes and coins do not have intrinsic value** i.e., the piece of paper in case of rupee note or the iron in case of coin does not have the value of the material but it derives its value from the promise of RBI. Currency notes and coins are therefore called **fiat money**. They are also called **legal tenders** as they cannot be refused by any citizen of the country for payment/ discharge of debt *(For example: Is an autowallah obliged to accept your currency note for a ride? Not necessarily! If you are yet to get into the auto, the autowallah can turn you down despite it being a legal tender. But once you make the trip, and you have incurred a debt, he cannot refuse to take your currency note.)*. But cheques can be refused by anyone as a payment mode and are hence not legal tenders.

Currency = Notes + Coins

Currency in Circulation = Currency with the **Public** + Currency with the **banks**

The total stock of money in circulation among the **public** at a particular point of time is called **money supply**. So, **money supply** is **money of the public either in cash form or in deposit form**. RBI publishes figures for four alternative measures of money supply. They are as follows:

M1 = Currency with Public + Demand deposits of public with banks + *[*Other deposits with RBI]*

M2 = M1 + Savings Deposits with Post Office Savings Bank

M3 = M1 + Time deposits of public with banks

M4 = M3 + Total deposits with Post Office Savings Bank

*[*Other deposits with RBI include deposit from foreign central banks, multilateral institutions, financial institutions etc. For practical purposes this can be ignored]*

Only deposits of public (including businesses) held by the banks are part of money supply and inter-bank deposits are excluded. Cash reserves of the commercial banks are not treated as a component of money supply, because cash held by the creators/suppliers of money (**RBI, Government and Banks**) is never treated as a component of money supply.

M1 is the most liquid and M4 is the least liquid. M1 and M2 are called narrow money and M3 and M4 are called broad money. M3 is the most commonly used measure of money supply and is also called "**aggregate monetary resources**".

The numbering from 1 to 4 is in decreasing order of liquidity.

(Now mostly M1 and M3 terms are used by RBI)

2.11 Money Circulation

Now we will try to understand how money circulates between individuals/public, banks and RBI. Suppose an individual possesses physical gold worth Rs. 500. He deposits this physical gold with RBI and RBI issues him currency note worth Rs. 500. *(Alternatively, it can also be said that, RBI purchased Rs. 500 gold from the market and issued Rs. 500 note to the public/ individual)*. It can be represented as following.

Individual

☺

Rs. 500 Note

Commercial Bank

Assets	**Liability**

RBI

Assets	**Liability**
Gold = Rs. 500	Currency held by Public = Rs. 500
Rs. 500	Rs. 500

Money Supply = Rs. 500

Suppose the individual thinks that he requires only Rs. 200 for his cash transactions and deposits Rs.300 in bank for safety purpose and to earn interest. This can be represented as following.

Individual

Rs. 200 Note
+
Rs. 300 in A/c

Commercial Bank

Assets	Liability
Vault Cash = Rs. 300	Deposits of Public = Rs. 300
Rs. 300	Rs. 300

RBI

Assets	Liability
Gold = Rs. 500	Currency held by Public = Rs. 200 Vault Cash held by banks = Rs. 300
Rs. 500	Rs. 500

Money Supply = Rs. 500

Suppose the bank requires only Rs. 100 to meet the day-to-day cash demands of the public then it can deposit the rest Rs. 200 with RBI. This can be represented as.

Individual

Rs. 200 Note
+
Rs. 300 in A/c

Commercial Bank

Assets	Liability
Vault Cash = Rs. 100 Deposits with RBI = Rs. 200	Deposits of Public = Rs. 300
Rs. 300	Rs. 300

RBI

Assets	Liability
Gold = Rs. 500	Currency held by Public = Rs. 200 Vault Cash held by banks = Rs. 100 Deposits of bank = Rs. 200
Rs. 500	Rs. 500

Money Supply = Rs. 500

Monetary Base = Currency held by public + currency held by banks + deposits of bank with RBI + [*Other deposits with RBI] = Rs. 200 + Rs. 100 + Rs. 200 = Rs. 500.

*[*Other deposits with RBI include deposit from foreign central banks, multilateral institutions, financial institutions etc. For practical purposes this can be ignored]*

'Monetary Base' is also called 'High Powered Money' or 'Reserve Money' or 'Base Money' or 'Central Bank Money' or 'M0'.

Monetary base and money supply are two different terms.

Suppose govt. collects Rs. 50 as tax from the individual and keeps this money with RBI then 'money supply' as well as 'monetary base' both will reduce: This can be represented as.

Individual

Rs. 150 Note + Rs. 300 in A/c

Commercial Bank

Assets	Liability
Vault Cash = Rs. 100 Deposits with RBI = Rs. 200	Deposits of Public = Rs. 300
Rs. 300	Rs. 300

RBI

Assets	Liability
Gold = Rs. 500	Currency held by Public = Rs. 150 Vault Cash held by banks = Rs. 100 Deposits of bank = Rs. 200 Deposits of Govt. (Treasury Deposits) = Rs. 50
Rs. 500	Rs. 500

Money Supply = Rs. 450

Monetary Base = Rs. 150 + Rs. 100 + Rs. 200 = Rs. 450.

The RBI may sell some part of its gold assets to purchase foreign exchange reserves or government securities. This can be represented as.

Individual

Rs. 150 Note + Rs. 300 in A/c

Commercial Bank

Assets	Liability
Vault Cash = Rs. 100 Deposits with RBI = Rs. 200	Deposits of Public = Rs. 300
Rs. 300	Rs. 300

RBI

Assets	Liability
Gold = Rs. 100 Foreign Exchange Reserve = Rs 200 Govt. Securities = Rs. 200	Currency held by Public = Rs. 150 Vault Cash held by banks = Rs. 100 Deposits of bank = Rs. 200 Deposits of Govt. (Treasury Deposits) = Rs. 50
Rs. 500	Rs. 500

Money Supply = Rs. 450

Monetary Base = Rs. 450

DEMONETIZATION

On November 8, 2016, the Central Government demonetized the Rs. 500 and Rs. 1000 currency notes which constituted 86% of the cash/currency in circulation. This was done as per the RBI Act 1934 which says that "on recommendation of the Central Board of RBI, the Central Government may, declare that any series of bank notes of any denomination shall cease to be legal tender".

Demonetization led to the reduction in RBI's liability to the extent the old notes were not returned to the banking system. And hence in turn it led to the transfer of wealth from holders of illicit black money to the public sector.

Impact of Demonetization in the Short Run:

On liquidity

- Demonetization led to liquidity (effective cash in circulation) crunch as the old Rs. 1000 and Rs. 500 notes could not be used for transaction purpose and there was restriction on withdrawal of new currency notes
- In the banking system, demonetization led to increase in liquidity (here liquidity means deposits with the banks) which has resulted in decreased market interest rates

On Money Supply

- Economists define money supply as broad measures that encompasses both cash and bank deposits, because these are very close substitutes. A key aspect of the Nov. 8 demonetization, however, is that the convertibility between cash and bank deposits was impeded. Cash could not be easily deposited into bank accounts, while withdrawals were subject to strict limits. So, we can say that demonetization led to reduction in money supply in the economy

On GDP

- An aggregate demand shock, because demonetization reduced the supply of money and affected private wealth (especially of those holding unaccounted money and owning real estate)
- An aggregate supply shock to the extent that cash was a necessary input for economic activity (for example agricultural producers required cash to pay labour)

2.12 Money Creation

- Currency Deposit Ratio (cdr) $= \dfrac{\text{Currency held by Public}}{\text{Deposits of public in banks}}$

  $= 1$ *(assumption)*

cdr equal to 1 means whenever an individual gets some amount of cash say Rs. 100, then he will keep Rs. 50 as cash and Rs. 50 as deposit in banks, so that the ratio of cash in hand and deposits in banks is Rs.50/Rs.50 = 1.

- Reserve Deposit Ratio (rdr) $= \dfrac{\text{Reserves of Banks}}{\text{Deposits of public in banks}}$

  $= 0.2(20\%)$ (*assumption*)

rdr equals to 0.2 or 20% means whenever an individual deposits certain sum of money say Rs.100 with the bank, the bank will have to keep Rs. 20 as reserve money and the rest Rs. 80 they can lend to someone else. Banks can keep the reserves either with themselves (SLR) or with RBI (CRR). So, rdr is sum of CRR and SLR.

Now we will understand the mechanism of money creation by monetary authority i.e. RBI.

Suppose RBI wishes to increase the money supply in the economy. Let us assume that RBI purchases some assets, say, government bonds or gold worth Rs. H from the market and in turn issues the currency note worth Rs. H to that person (P1). So, in this situation, money supply is H and monetary base is also H.

Now, since we have assumed that cdr is 1 in the economy, the first person (P1) will keep half of the money as cash and half he will deposit with the bank. And if the bank kept all the deposited money in cash form in its vault, then the money supply will be H.

	Currency with Public	Vault Cash	Deposits of Public	Total Money Supply
P1	H/2	H/2 ←	—H/2	H

But since rdr is 20%, the bank will keep only 20% of the deposited money in its vaults as cash (reserve money) and the rest it will lend to some other person (P2). So, now the first person has money H (H/2 as cash and H/2 in the deposit form) and the second person (P2) has money 0.8 (H/2) i.e. 0.4 H. So, the total money supply in the economy increases from H to H + 0.4H = **1.4H**. This has been possible because banks have been given the liberty to keep only a fraction of the deposited money as reserve in their vaults and the rest they can lend to others. *(This is called "fractional reserve banking")*. So, additional money is getting created through **fractional reserve banking**. This has been represented in the following table:

	Currency with Public	Vault Cash	Deposits of Public	Total Money Supply
P1	H/2	0.2 (H/2) ←	H/2	H
P2	0.8 (H/2) ←	money creation		

Now the person P2 will again keep only half of the money which he has got from the bank in cash form and the rest he will deposit with the bank. The bank will again keep only 20% of the deposited money as reserve in its vault and the rest it will lend to a third person (P3). The third person P3 will again keep only half of the money which he has got from the bank in cash form and the rest he will deposit with the bank and this process will go on endlessly in the economy. This is represented in the following table:

	Currency with Public	Vault Cash	Deposits of Public	Money Supply
P1	H/2	0.2 (H/2) ←	H/2	H
P2	1/2(0.8 (H/2))	0.2/2 (0.8 (H/2)) ←	1/2(0.8 (H/2))	0.8 (H/2)
P3	0.8/2 (0.8 (H/2))	.	.	.
P4	.	.	.	.
.	.	.	.	.
Sum	1/2 (5H/3)	0.2/2 (5H/3)	1/2 (5H/3)	**5H/3**

Now, Money Supply= 5H/3

And, Monetary Base= H

$$\text{Money Multiplier} = \frac{\text{Money Supply (M3)}}{\text{Monetary Base (M0)}} = \frac{(5H/3)}{H} = 5/3$$

So, with H monetary base and H money supply initially, the RBI has been able to increase/create the money supply to 5H/3 through fractional reserve banking. So, money supply is now 5/3 times of the monetary base, hence the money multiplier is 5/3.

The value of the money multiplier depends on two variables:

- currency-deposit ratio (cdr); and
- reserves-deposit ratio (rdr) which is equal to required reserves plus excess reserves

While currency deposit ratio depends on the behaviour of the public, the reserve deposit ratio depends on RBI regulations on CRR and SLR. So, money multiplier can also be defined as:

Money multiplier = (1+ cdr)/(cdr+rdr)

= (1+1)/(1+0.2)

= 2/1.2 = 20/12 = 5/3

2.13 Monetary Policy

Monetary Policy is the process by which monetary authority (RBI) of a country controls the creation and supply of money in the economy.

Over time, the objectives of monetary policy in India have evolved to include maintaining price stability, ensuring adequate flow of credit to productive sectors of the economy for supporting economic growth and achieving financial stability. Based on its assessment of macroeconomic and financial conditions, RBI takes the call on the stance of monetary policy and monetary measures. RBI issues monetary policy statements which reflect the changing circumstances and priorities of the RBI and the thrust of the policy measures for the future.

The monetary policy framework in India, as it is today, has evolved over the years. A new **"Monetary Policy Framework"** Agreement was signed between the Government of India and RBI in Feb 2015. As per the new monetary policy framework agreement, following are the important points: -

- The objective of the monetary policy is to primarily maintain **price stability**, while keeping in mind the objective of growth.
- The monetary policy framework is operated by RBI.
- The inflation target is 4% with a band of +/– 2%.
- The inflation target is decided by the Government of India in consultation with RBI. The central government has notified the above inflation target for the period till March 31, 2026. The RBI Act 1934 provides for the inflation target to be set by the government of India, in consultation with the Reserve Bank, once in every five years.
- The inflation is the "**Consumer Price Index (CPI) – Combined**" published by Ministry of Statistics and Programme Implementation (NSO).
- The RBI shall be seen to have failed to meet the Target if inflation is more than 6% or less than 2% for three consecutive quarters.
- In case RBI fails to meet the target, it will have to give a written report to Government of India explaining the reasons of failure, remedial actions to be taken and an estimated time period within which the Target would be achieved *(RBI has failed in achieving the target once in 2022)*.

The Government of India constituted **"Monetary Policy Committee" (MPC)** in September 2016 which now determines the Policy (Repo) Rate required to achieve the inflation target.

- RBI should organize at least four meetings of Monetary Policy Committee (MPC) in a year. Presently RBI conducts the meetings of MPC 6 times a year i.e., bi-monthly. But there can be "Off-cycle" meeting of MPC as well if the situation warrants.
- MPC has 6 members, three from RBI (including the RBI Governor) and 3 appointed by the Government of India. All the members have one vote and in the event of equality of votes, the Governor gets a second or casting vote.
- The decision of the MPC is **binding** on RBI. MPC has the authority to decide the repo rate only and not reverse repo, CRR, SLR etc.

There are two components in the MPC framework: Inflation and the requirements of growth in mind. The decisions of MPC are based on these two twin objectives, with primacy being given to price stability. Currency market fluctuations, depreciation or appreciation of the rupee is not a factor for consideration for the MPC. And for dealing with those situations, RBI has other instruments which are deployed as per the requirement.

The following are the major instruments/ tools that RBI uses for conducting its monetary policy:

1. **Repo Rate:** The interest rate at which the Reserve Bank provides liquidity under the liquidity adjustment facility (LAF) to all LAF participants against the collateral of government and other approved securities.

   Repo Rate is also called the "Policy Rate".

2. **Reverse Repo Rate:** The interest rate at which the Reserve Bank absorbs liquidity, from banks against the collateral of eligible government securities under the LAF.

3. **Standing Deposit Facility (SDF):** Introduced in April 2022 by an amendment in RBI Act 1934. The following are its important features:
   - Banks can deposit any amount for overnight (in future it can be for longer tenure also) with RBI at repo rate – 0.25% (it may change)
   - As there is no binding collateral constraint on RBI under SDF, it will strengthen the operating framework of monetary policy
   - The SDF is also a financial stability tool in addition to its role in liquidity management.
   - *SDF will be at the discretion of banks and will be available on all days of the week, throughout the year unlike repo and reverse repo which are available at the discretion of RBI.*

4. **Marginal Standing Facility (MSF):** It is a facility introduced in 2011, under which scheduled commercial banks can borrow additional amount of overnight money (over and above what is available to them through repo rate) from the Reserve Bank at their own discretion **by dipping into their SLR portfolio up to a limit** (2% of NDTL) at a penal rate of interest. This provides a safety valve against unanticipated liquidity shocks to the banking system.

   When banks take loan from RBI at Repo rate, banks need to keep Govt. Securities with RBI, but this security is in addition to the requirement under SLR. Banks cannot keep SLR securities to avail loan from RBI at Repo Rate.

   ***But under MSF**, banks can borrow from RBI by dipping into the SLR reserve. This means that the banks can keep 2% of the SLR securities with RBI (i.e., the SLR can go down up to 2% of NDTL below the normal SLR requirement) and can borrow cash from RBI. This is called Marginal Standing Facility (MSF).*

   MSF Rate= Repo Rate + 0.25%

5. **Bank Rate :** It is the standard rate at which the Reserve Bank is prepared to buy debt instruments. On introduction of LAF, the Reserve Bank has discontinued this operation. As a result, the Bank Rate became dormant as an instrument of monetary management. It is now aligned to MSF rate and used for calculating penalty on default in the cash reserve ratio (CRR) and the statutory liquidity ratio (SLR). For example, the current penal rate on shortfall in reserves is Bank Rate plus 3 percent.

   Bank Rate= MSF Rate

6. **Liquidity Adjustment Facility (LAF):**

   The LAF refers to the RBI's operations through which it injects/absorbs liquidity into/from the banking system. It consists of overnight as well as term repo/reverse repos (fixed as well as variable rates), SDF and MSF.

   Apart from LAF, instruments of liquidity management include outright open market operations (OMOs), forex swaps and market stabilization scheme (MSS).

   The aim of term repo is to help develop the inter-bank term money market, which in turn can set market-based benchmarks for pricing of loans and deposits, and hence improve transmission of monetary policy. The Reserve Bank also conducts variable interest rate **reverse repo auctions**, as necessitated under the market conditions.

- **Long Term Repo Operation (LTRO):** RBI lends to banks @repo rate only up to a limit of bank's NDTL for overnight. RBI from time to time, on its own discretion, also lends for long term **at** or **above** the repo rate. In case RBI wants to lend above repo rate then the interest rate is decided by **auction** i.e., if banks want more money, the interest rate will go higher, if few banks are competing for RBIs money, then interest rate may be less but it is above the repo rate. This is called **"long term repo operation (LTRO)"** which means RBI gives money for a fixed long term. The LTRO is generally at above the repo rate decided by the auction but it can be at repo rate also. (Collateral of government security is required but may not be 100%).
- Similarly, **variable long-term reverse repo auctions** are also done where bids should be below the repo rate and above the reverse repo rate.
- **Targeted LTRO** (TLTRO) is done targeting specific sectors where RBI provides funds for specific sectors through banks.

7. **LAF Corridor:** The MSF rate and reverse repo rate determines the policy/LAF corridor for the daily movement in the 'weighted average call money rate' (explained later).

With the introduction of Standing Deposit Facility (SDF), the policy/LAF corridor has changed and now it is SDF and MSF where SDF is the floor and MSF is the upper end with the policy repo rate in the middle of the corridor.

8. **Reserve Requirements (Fractional Reserve Banking):**

- **Cash Reserve Ratio (CRR)** The amount of cash that the scheduled commercial banks are required to maintain with RBI with respect to their NDTL (on a fortnightly basis) is called CRR. *"In terms of Section 42(1) of the RBI Act, 1934 the Reserve Bank, having regard to the needs of securing the monetary stability in the country, prescribes the CRR for SCBs without any floor or ceiling rate".*
- Statutory Liquidity Ratio (SLR) The amount of reserves that the scheduled commercial banks are required to maintain with themselves on a daily basis in safe and liquid assets such as government securities, gold and cash with respect to their NDTL is called SLR. Excess CRR balances are also treated as liquid assets for the purpose of SLR i.e., SLR can be maintained as cash balance with RBI. Scheduled Commercial Banks are required to maintain SLR as per the Banking Regulation Act 1949. The ceiling on SLR is 40%.

Deposits of public are the liability of banks. The public's demand deposits are demand liability of the bank and time deposits are time liability of the banks and the total demand and time deposits of the public is called 'Net Demand and Time Liabilities (NDTL)' of the banks.

The CRR and SLR enable RBI to control the amount of money that banks can create and make public deposits safe and liquid.

It ensures that banks have a safe cushion of assets to draw on when account holders want to be paid. In absence of the CRR and SLR requirements, to make more profits bank may lend most of the deposits and if there is a sudden rush to withdraw, banks will struggle to meet the repayments.

All Commercial and Cooperative Banks (either scheduled or non-scheduled) are required to maintain CRR and SLR. For scheduled banks, the maintenance of CRR is governed through The Reserve Bank of India Act 1934 and for Non-Scheduled banks CRR is governed through Banking Regulation Act 1949. Banking Regulation Act 1949 (Section 24) governs maintenance of SLR for all banks (scheduled and non-scheduled) commercial and cooperative.

9. **Open Market Operations (OMO):** Sale or purchase of government securities by RBI in the open market (secondary market) to banks/financial institutions for absorption and injection of durable liquidity in the economy is called open market operations. If the inflation in the economy is high then, to control the inflation RBI reduces the money supply by selling government securities. And if RBI wants to increase the money supply then it buys government securities from the banks/financial institutions and pays them money in exchange of government securities which ultimately increases the money supply in the economy.

   There are two types of Open Market Operations (OMOs).

   - Outright OMOs: They are permanent in nature. When the central bank buys/sells these securities, it is without any promise to sell/buy them later.
   - LAF OMOs: This is a type of operation in which when the central bank buys/sells the securities, the agreement also has specification about the date and price of resale/repurchase of this security. This type of agreement is called a repurchase agreement or repo.

10. **Market Stabilization Scheme (MSS)/ Sterilization:** Many developing countries have reaped handsome rewards from surging capital inflows in recent years. This is widely regarded as a very welcome phenomenon, raising levels of investment and encouraging economic growth. But surging capital inflows can also lead to destabilizing side effects, including a tendency for the local currency to appreciate, undermining the competitiveness of export industries, and potentially giving rise to inflation. Why inflation? When foreign investors bring foreign currency/ dollars, ultimately this dollar comes to RBI and new money/currency is given by RBI to the investors which increase money supply (and monetary base) in the economy without a corresponding increase in production: too much money begins to chase too few goods and services resulting in inflation.

    To ease the threat of currency appreciation or inflation, central banks often attempt what is known as the "**sterilization**" of capital flows. In a successful sterilization operation, the domestic component of the monetary base/ money supply is reduced to offset the inflow of capital, at least temporarily. In theory, this can be achieved by encouraging private investment overseas, or allowing foreigners to borrow from the local market. But the classical form of sterilization, however, has been through the use of **open market operations** , that is, selling Treasury bills and other securities by RBI to reduce the domestic component of the monetary base/ money supply.

[*Reverse repos and outright Open market operation sales demanded the availability of adequate stock of Govt. securities with the RBI, which became a constraining factor in sterilization operations as the volume of capital inflows expanded. Moreover, reverse repo operations involved sterilisation costs, impacting the profit of the RBI, with implications for RBI's operational independence. Using the LAF as an instrument of sterilisation tended to erode its utility as a day-to-day liquidity adjustment tool operating at the margin. It was in this context that the RBI introduced Market Stabilisation Scheme (MSS) in 2004.*]

MSS is an instrument of sterilization, which empowered the RBI to **issue** Government Treasury Bills and medium duration dated securities for the purpose of liquidity absorption. This instrument of monetary management was introduced in 2004 to absorb surplus liquidity of a **more enduring nature** arising from large capital inflows. The scheme worked by impounding/taking the proceeds of auctions of Treasury bills and dated Government securities in a separate identifiable MSS cash account maintained and operated by the RBI. At the same time, interest payments have to be given to the institutions who buy the Market Stabilization Bonds (MSB) (the Treasury bills and dated securities of Govt). Here, for the interest payment, the government allocates money from its budget to the RBI. This expenditure to service interest payment for MSBs is called *carrying cost*. The amounts credited into the MSS cash account by selling MSBs were appropriated only for the purpose of redemption/buy back of the Treasury Bills/dated securities issued under the MSS. *The introduction of MSS succeeded broadly in restoring the LAF to its intended function of daily liquidity management.*

Monetary policy can be either **expansionary** or **contractionary.** Expansionary monetary policy increases the supply of money whereas contractionary policy reduces the money supply. Expansionary policy is also called 'Dovish' or 'Accommodative' or 'Easy Money Policy'. Contractionary policy is also called 'Hawkish' or 'Tight Money Policy' or 'Restrictive Policy.

2.14 Indian Financial System

The following are important points regarding the Indian Financial System (refer the Figure):

1. The financial institutions in India are broadly divided into two categories viz. Banks and Non-Banking Financial Institutions (NBFI). The basic difference between a Bank and a NBFI is **Banks accept demand deposits** and NBFIs do not accept demand deposits. Banks issue cheques but NBFIs cannot issue cheques drawn on itself.

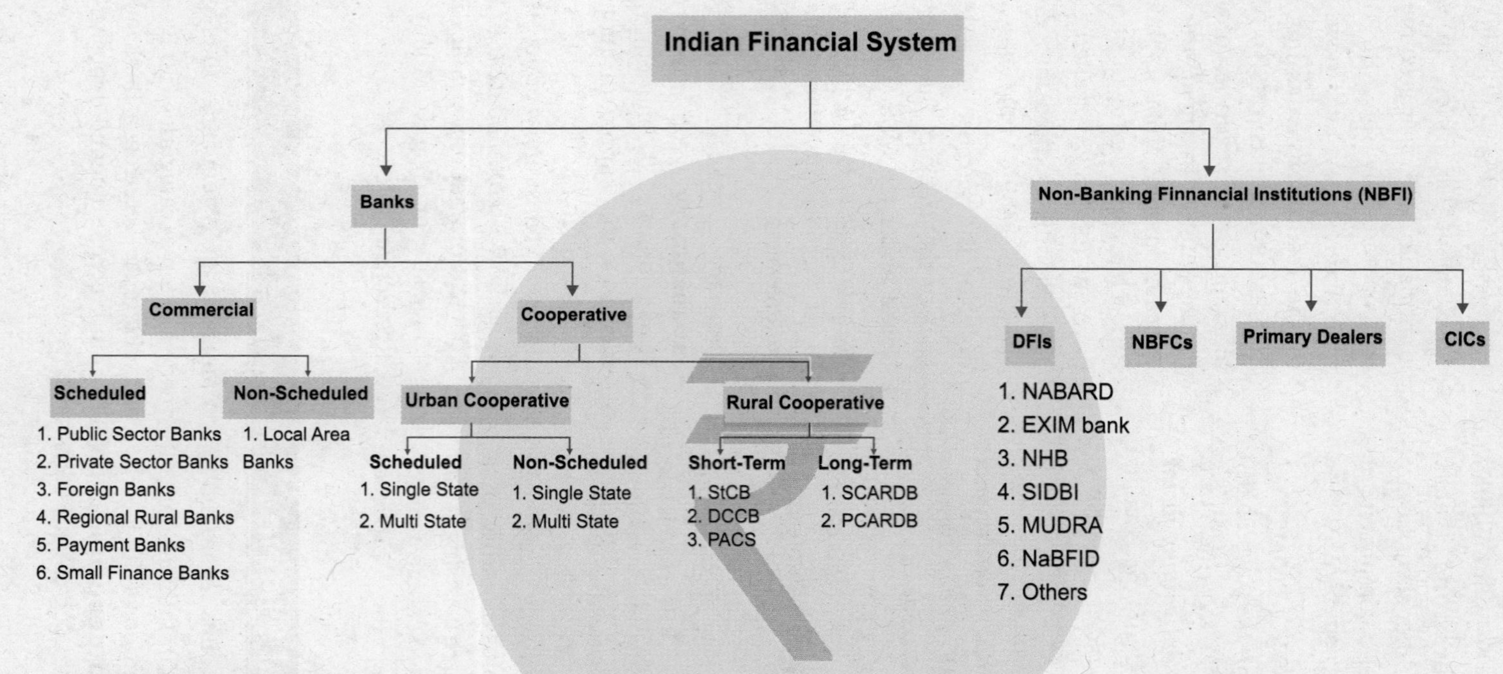

1. StCB : State Co-operative Bank
2.DCCB : District Central Co-operative Bank
3. PACS : Primary Agricultural Credit Society
4. SCARDB : State Co-operative Agriculture and Rural Development Bank
5. PCARDB : Primary Co-operative Agricultural and Rural Development Bank
6. DFIs : Development Financial Institutions also called All India Financial Institutions (AIFIs)
7. CICs : Credit Information Companies

2. Banks are classified into **commercial** and **cooperative**. Commercial banks operate on the commercial (profit) principles while the basis of operation for cooperative banks is on cooperative lines i.e., service to its members and the society. Cooperative banks provide a higher rate of interest on deposits as compared to commercial banks.

3. Commercial banks are of two categories viz. scheduled commercial banks and non-scheduled commercial banks. A scheduled bank is so called because it has been included in the second schedule of the RBI Act 1934. The other conditions for a scheduled bank are it must be a corporation and the Paid-up share capital should be at least Rs. 500 crores. The difference between scheduled and non-scheduled banks is the type of banking activity that they are allowed to carry out in India. A Non-Scheduled bank can carry out limited operations, for example, non-scheduled banks are not allowed to deal in Foreign Exchange. Non-Scheduled banks need to maintain reserve requirements (as per the Banking Regulation Act 1949) but may not be with RBI. Scheduled Banks are required to maintain reserve requirements with RBI as per the RBI Act 1934.

4. Co-operative Banks: The Co-operative banks are of two categories viz. Urban Co-operative banks (UCB) and Rural Co-operative banks.
   - The Urban Co-operative banks (UCB) (also called **Primary Co-operative** Banks) are located in urban and semi urban areas and were traditionally centred around communities, localities work place groups. They essentially lent to small borrowers and businesses. Today, their scope of operations has widened considerably.
   - UCBs are again classified into Scheduled and Non-scheduled categories, which are then further classified into single state and multi state. Single State UCBs are registered as cooperative societies under the provisions of the State Government Cooperative Societies Act and are regulated by the Registrar of Cooperative Societies (RCS) of State concerned. Multi-State UCBs are registered as cooperative societies under the provisions of Multi-State Cooperative Societies Act, 2002 and are regulated by the Central Registrar of Cooperative Societies (CRCS).
   - The rural co-operative credit system in India is primarily mandated to ensure flow of credit to the agriculture sector. It comprises short-term and long-term co-operative credit structures. The short-term co-operative credit structure operates with a three-tier system – **State Cooperative Banks (StCBs)** at the **State level**, (District) Central Cooperative Banks (**DCCBs**) at the **district level** and **Primary Agricultural Credit Societies (PACS)** at the **village level**. A PACS is organized at the grass roots level of a village or a group of small villages. It is this basic unit which deals directly with the rural (agricultural) borrowers, gives them loans and collects repayments of loans given **PACS are outside the purview of the Banking Regulation Act, 1949 and hence not regulated by RBI**. StCBs/DCCBs are registered under the provisions of State Cooperative Societies Act of the State concerned and comes under the **dual regulation of State governments and RBI**. All Rural Cooperative Banks are supervised by

NABARD (RBI delegated its supervisory power) and Registrar of Cooperative Societies of State.

Though the Banking Regulation Act came into force in 1949, the banking laws were made applicable to cooperative societies only in 1966 through an amendment to the Banking Regulation Act, 1949. Since then, there is '**duality of control**' over cooperative banks (urban and rural both) between the State Registrar of Cooperative Societies/Central Registrar of Cooperative Societies and the RBI. RBI regulates and supervises the banking functions and amalgamation and liquidation of UCBs/StCB/DCCB through the Banking regulation Act, 1949 and the non-banking aspects like registration, management, administration and recruitment are regulated and supervised by the State/ Central Governments.

RBI approval is required for appointment of Chairman/Whole-time Director/ Managing Director/CEO in case of all Primary/Urban Cooperative Banks (UCBs) with deposit size of ₹100 crore and above. In public interest and to protect the interest of the depositors, if required, RBI can ***supersede*** *the Board of multi state Urban/Primary Cooperative Banks.*

PACS and long-term credit co-operatives (SCARDB and PCARDB) **are outside the purview** of the **Banking Regulation Act, 1949** and are hence not regulated and supervised by the RBI. NABARD conducts voluntary inspection of SCARDBs, apex-level co-operative societies and federations.

- With prior approval of RBI, cooperative banks can issue (either through public or private placement) equity shares and bonds or unsecured debentures or any other security with maturity of not less than 10 years.

5. Public Sector Banks: Banks owned by the Central or State governments having more than 51% ownership with the government. For example, SBI and its associates, Punjab National Bank, Bank of India etc. Nationalized Banks (private banks taken over by government) which were nationalized in 1969 and 1980's are also public sector banks as government owns more than 51% in these banks.
6. Private Sector Banks: Banks owned by private individuals for example ICICI bank, Axis Bank etc.
7. Foreign Banks: Banks established in India but owned by foreign entity/ies for example Citi Bank. These are basically private banks only owned by foreign entities.
8. Regional Rural Banks (RRB) were established in 1975 under the provisions of the Regional Rural Banks Act, 1976 with a view to developing the rural economy by providing, for the purpose of development of agriculture, trade, commerce, industry and other productive activities in the rural areas, credit and other facilities, particularly to small and marginal farmers, agricultural labourers, artisans and small entrepreneurs. RRBs are owned by the Central government, concerned State government and the sponsor bank in proportion of 50:15:35 *(each RRB is sponsored by a particular bank)*. RRBs need to provide 75% of the lending to priority sectors. RRBs are under the supervision of NABARD. In order to improve operational viability of Regional Rural Banks (RRBs) and to take advantage of economies of scale, Government of India initiated structural consolidation of RRBs in FY 2005-06. From 196 in 2005-06, number of RRBs has been reduced to 28. As per 'One Sate One RRB' norm, RRBs have been consolidated and now there are 28 RRBs (26 in states and 2 in UTs)

9. Payment Banks:

- In August 2015, RBI granted license to 11 applicants for Payment Banks.
- RBI has put a cap of Rs. 2 lakhs on deposits that payment banks can receive from individual customers. This restriction will allow only those companies to seek for payment bank licenses who are really interested in targeting the poor. Hence, the main target for payment banks will be migrant labourers, self-employed, low-income households etc. as they will offer low-cost savings accounts and remittance services so that those who now transact only in cash can take their first step into the formal banking system *(payment banks* **will not be allowed to lend and issue credit cards**. *Payment banks will accept only demand deposits i.e., only savings account and current account facility will be available).*
- The payment banks will be cashing in on mobile technology and applications to cater to the various services they will be offering and with the use of technology they can be cost efficient.
- Payment banks will be acting as add-on to the already established banks, rather than their competitors.

10. Small Finance Banks:

- In Sept. 2015, RBI granted license to 10 applicants for Small Finance Banks which is a step in the direction of furthering the financial inclusion.
- The small finance banks shall primarily undertake basic banking activities of acceptance of deposits and lending to unserved and underserved sections including small business units, small and marginal farmers, micro and small industries and unorganized sector entities.
- There will not be any restriction in the area of operations of small finance banks.
- The small finance banks will be required to extend 75% of its total credit to the sectors eligible for classification as priority sector lending (PSL) by the RBI.
- At least 50% of its loan portfolio should constitute loans of up to Rs 25 lakhs
- Both payment banks and small finance banks are niche or **differentiated banks** i.e., specialized in certain banking functions and not universal.

11. Local Area Banks (LAB) were set up as per a Government of India Scheme announced in 1996. The intention of the government was to set up new private local banks with jurisdiction over two or three contiguous districts. The objective of establishing the local area banks was to enable mobilization of the rural savings by local institutions and make them available for investments in local areas. There are only four Local Area Banks in India which exist in the form of Non-Scheduled banks, one such example is Coastal Local Area Bank in Vijayawada, Andhra Pradesh.

12. All India Financial Institutions (AIFIs), Non-Banking Financial Companies (NBFCs) and Primary Dealers (PDs) form three important segments of the Non-Banking Financial Institutions (NBFIs) sector in India that are regulated and supervised by the RBI. Credit Information Companies (CIC) are also a category of Non-banking financial institutions regulated by RBI.

13. AIFIs constitute institutional mechanism entrusted with providing sector-specific long-term financing. Currently, there are four AIFIs also called Development Financial Institutions (DFIs) regulated and supervised by the RBI.

14. NABARD:
    - NABARD was established in 1982 under the provisions of National Bank for Agriculture and Rural Development Act 1981.
    - NABARD provides credit for the promotion of agriculture, small scale industries, cottage and village industries, handicrafts and other rural crafts and other allied economic activities in rural areas.
    - NABARD acts as coordinator/supervisor in the operations of rural credit institutions like RRBs and Rural Cooperative Banks *(RBI has delegated its supervisory powers in case of rural sector to NABARD while retaining its regulatory powers)*.
    - NABARD assists in policy formulation of Govt. of India, RBI and State Governments on matters related to agricultural credit and rural development.
    - Offers training and research facilities for banks, cooperatives and organizations in matters relating to rural development.
    - It does not extend direct credit at individual level but extends indirect financial assistance by way of refinance *(NABARD finances those institutions which provide financial assistance to rural sector)*. NABARD provides direct finance to **institutions** as may be approved by the Central government.
15. National Housing Bank (NHB):
    - NHB was set up in 1988 under the National Housing Bank Act, 1987.
    - NHB operates as a principal agency to promote housing finance institutions both at local & regional levels and to provide financial and other support to such institutions.
    - It does not extend direct credit at individual level but extends indirect financial assistance by way of refinance *(i.e., NHB finances those institutions which provide finance to individual borrowers, builders etc.)*
16. EXIM Bank
    - EXIM bank was established in 1982 under the Export Import bank of India Act 1981.
    - The objective of EXIM bank is to provide financial assistance to exporters and importers, and function as the principal financial institution for coordinating the working of institutions engaged in financing export and import of goods and services with a view to promoting the country's international trade.
    - EXIM bank also extends loans to overseas financial institutions, regional development banks, sovereign governments and other entities overseas, to enable buyers in those countries to import goods and services from India. It extends loan on its own and also at the order and with the support of Government of India.
    - It provides both direct financial assistance to exporters/importers and indirect financial assistance by way of refinance.
17. Small Industries Development Bank of India (SIDBI):
    - SIDBI was established in 1990 under the provisions of Small Industries Development of India Act 1989
    - SIDBI acts as the principal financial institution for the promotion, financing and development of the Micro, Small and Medium Enterprise (MSME) sector and for co-ordination of the functions of the institutions engaged in similar activities

- SIDBI mainly extends indirect financial assistance (by way of refinance) to financial institutions for onward lending to MSMEs.

18. MUDRA Bank:

- MUDRA (Micro Units Development and Refinance Agency Ltd.) is a financial institution set up by Govt. of India for development and refinancing micro unit enterprises. Pending enactment of an act for MUDRA Bank, a Non-Banking Finance Company as MUDRA Ltd has been set up as a subsidiary of SIDBI.
- The purpose of MUDRA is to provide funding to the **non-corporate** (**informal sector**) small business sector such as small manufacturing units, shopkeepers, fruits and vegetable sellers, hair salons, beauty parlours, truck operators, hawkers, artisans in rural and urban areas with financing requirements of up to Rs 10 lakhs.
- MUDRA would be responsible for **refinancing** all Last Mile Financiers such as Micro Financial Institutions, NBFCs, Societies, Trusts, Companies, Co-operative Societies, SFBs, Scheduled Commercial Banks and RRBs which are in the business of lending to micro/ small business entities engaged in manufacturing, trading and services activities *(Refinancing means MUDRA loans will be available through Banks/ NBFCs/MFIs and not direct lending)*.
- MUDRA loans are available in three categories. For small business, loans up to Rs. 50,000/- is available under the 'Shishu' category, beyond Rs. 50,000 and up to Rs. 5 lakhs under the 'Kishor' category and between Rs. 5 lakhs to Rs. 10 lakhs under the 'Tarun' category. These products have been designed to cater to the customers operating at the lower end of the enterprise spectrum. A new category 'Tarun Plus' has been launched for loans above Rs. 10 lakh and up to Rs. 20 lakh and would be available to entrepreneurs who have availed and successfully repaid previous loans under the Tarun category.

19. Recently, Govt. has set up a DFI named **National Bank for Financing Infrastructure and Development (NaBFID)** with Rs. 20,000 crores. Presently Govt. holds 100% equity but later on it will reduce its stake/ownership to 26%.

20. Non-Banking Financial Companies (NBFCs):

- An NBFC is a company registered under the Companies Act, 1956/2013 engaged in the business of loans and advances, acquisition of shares/stocks/ bonds/ debentures/ securities issued by Government or local authority or other marketable securities of a like nature, leasing, hire-purchase, insurance business, chit business but does not include any institution whose principal business is that of agriculture activity, industrial activity, purchase or sale of any goods (other than securities) or providing any services and sale/ purchase/construction of immovable property. NBFCs are mainly private sector institutions.
- As per the RBI Act 1934, no NBFC can carry business without obtaining a certificate of registration from RBI. However, in terms of powers given to the RBI, to remove dual regulation, certain categories of NBFCs which are regulated by other regulators are exempted from the requirement of registration with RBI for example:

- ❖ Venture Capital Fund, Merchant Banking Companies, Stock broking companies registered with SEBI,
- ❖ Insurance Company holding a valid certificate of registration issued by IRDA,
- ❖ Nidhi Companies registered under Company's Act and regulated by Ministry of Corporate Affairs
- ❖ Chit companies as defined in the Chit Funds Act, 1982 and regulated by respective State governments

- NBFC- MFIs means a non-deposit taking NBFC which has a minimum of 75 percent of its total assets deployed towards "microfinance loans".

Microfinance (micro + finance) is provision of financial services to poor and low-income households. These financial services include small loans/credit, savings, insurance, funds transfer/remittance facilities etc. Microfinance is an economic tool designed to promote financial inclusion which enables the poor and low-income households to come out of poverty, increase their income levels and improve overall living standards.

A **microfinance loan** (Micro-credit) is defined as a collateral-free loan given to a household having annual household income up to Rs. 3,00,000. For this purpose, the household shall mean an individual family unit, i.e., husband, wife and their unmarried children. All collateral-free loans, irrespective of end use and mode (either through physical or digital channels), provided to low-income households, i.e., households having annual income up to Rs. 3,00,000, shall be considered as microfinance loans. The Banks/NBFCs should clearly mention a ceiling on the interest rate and all other charges applicable to the microfinance loans.

Microfinance loan/credit (one of the services under microfinance) is delivered through a variety of institutional channels viz. commercial & cooperative banks, NBFCs, NBFC-MFIs etc.

- **Peer to Peer (P2P) Lender :** *P2P intermediaries are new class of NBFCs that provide the platform which pairs borrowers and individual lenders. With P2P lending, borrowers take loans from individual investors who are willing to lend their own money for an agreed interest rate. The profile of a borrower is usually displayed on a P2P online platform where investors can reassess these profiles to determine whether they want to risk lending money to a borrower. The repayments are also made through the NBFC-P2P which processes and forwards the payments to the lenders who invested in the loan. P2P lending is also called social lending or crowd lending.*

RBI Guidelines Regarding P2P Lending

- Fund transfer between the participants on the P2P Lending Platform shall be through escrow account (a temporary pass-through account held by a third party during the process of a transaction between two parties) mechanisms operated by the NBFC-P2P. All fund transfers shall be through and from bank accounts and cash transaction is strictly prohibited.
- NBFC – P2P shall:
  - o act as an intermediary providing an online marketplace or platform to the participants involved in Peer-to-Peer lending;
  - o not raise deposits and not lend on its own

- o not provide any credit guarantee
- o not facilitate or permit any secured lending linked to its platform
- o undertake due diligence on the participants;
- o undertake credit assessment and risk profiling of the borrowers and disclose the same to their prospective lenders;
- o require prior and explicit consent of the participant to access its credit information;
- o undertake documentation of loan agreements and other related documents;
- o provide assistance in disbursement and repayments of loan amount;
- o render services for recovery of loans originated on the platform.

21. **Primary dealers (PDs):** Primary dealers are registered entities with the RBI who have the license to purchase and sell government securities. PDs buy government securities directly from the government in the primary market (RBI issues these government securities on behalf of the government), aiming to resell them to other buyers in the secondary market. Hence, they play a crucial role in fostering both the primary and secondary government securities markets. As on 30th June 2015, there are seven standalone PDs and thirteen banks authorized to undertake PD business departmentally.

22. **Credit Information Companies (CIC):** A CIC is an independent organization that signs up banks, NBFCs and financial institutions as its members and aggregates data and identity information for individual consumers and businesses from its members. CICs inform banks whether a prospective borrower is creditworthy or not based on his past payment track record. The quality of information defines the ability of lenders to evaluate risk and of consumers to obtain credit at competitive rates. The CICs are regulated and licensed by RBI as per the Credit Information Companies (Regulation) Act 2005. Currently there are four CICs operating in India viz. TransUnion Credit Information Bureau of India Limited (CIBIL), Equifax, Experian and High Mark Credit Information Services.

2.15 RBI and its Functions

The Reserve Bank of India is the central bank of the country. Central banks are a relatively recent innovation and most central banks, as we know them today, were established around the early twentieth century.

The Reserve Bank of India was set up on the basis of the recommendations of the Hilton Young Commission. The Reserve Bank of India Act, 1934 provides the statutory basis of the functioning of the Bank, which commenced operations on April 1, 1935.

The Bank began its operations by taking over from the Government the functions so far being performed by the Controller of Currency and from the Imperial Bank of India, the management of Government accounts and public debt. The Reserve Bank, which was originally set up as a shareholder's/private bank, was nationalised in 1949.

An interesting feature of the Reserve Bank of India was that at its very inception, the Reserve Bank was seen as playing a special role in the context of development, especially Agriculture.

When India commenced its plan endeavours, the development role of the Reserve Bank came into focus, especially in the sixties when the Reserve Bank, in many ways, pioneered the concept and practise of using finance to catalyse development. The Reserve Bank was also instrumental in institutional development and helped set up institutions like the Deposit Insurance and Credit Guarantee Corporation of India, the Unit Trust of India, the Industrial Development Bank of India, the National Bank of Agriculture and Rural Development, the Discount and Finance House of India etc. to build the financial infrastructure of the country.

With liberalisation, the Bank's focus has shifted back to core central banking functions like Monetary Policy, Bank Supervision and Regulation and Overseeing the Payments System and onto developing the financial markets.

The objective of RBI is *"to regulate the issue of Bank notes and keeping of reserves with a view to securing* ***monetary stability*** *in India and generally to operate the currency and credit system of the country to its advantage; to have a modern monetary policy framework to meet the challenge of an increasingly complex economy, to maintain* ***price stability*** *while keeping in mind the objective of growth; to maintain* ***macroeconomic stability and financial stability."***

The RBI affairs are governed by a central board of directors (Maximum 21 in number including the governor and four deputy governors who are also on the central board) who are appointed by the government of India in keeping with the Reserve Bank of India Act 1934 for a period of 4 years. RBI is the Central Bank of India and is also called the Monetary Authority of India.

The following are the various functions of RBI:

1. **Monetary Management/Authority**

   The most important function of central banks is formulation and execution of monetary policy *(discussed in detail in the monetary policy topic)* to *regulate the issue of RBI notes and the keeping of reserves with a view to securing monetary stability in India and generally to operate the currency and credit system of the country to its advantage.*

2. **Regulation and Supervision of the Banking and Non-Banking Financial Institutions**

   The objective of this function is to protect the interest of depositors through an effective prudential regulatory framework for orderly development and conduct of banking operations and liquidity and solvency of banks and to maintain overall financial stability through various policy measures. RBI derives these powers from the RBI Act 1934 and the Banking Regulation Act 1949. RBI's regulatory and supervisory functions extend not only to the Indian banking system but also to the Non-Banking Financial Institutions.

   The following are various functions of RBI regarding commercial banks, cooperative banks, regional rural banks, Financial Institutions, NBFCs, Primary Dealers, CICs etc:

Commercial Banks

- A license is required from RBI to commence banking operations, opening of new bank branches and closing of branches or change in the location of existing branches. RBI regulates merger, amalgamation and winding up of banks. *(For shifting, merger and closure of urban branches, now no approval is required).*

- RBI issues various guidelines for directors of banks and also has powers to appoint additional directors on the board of a banking company. Commercial Banks (except PSBs) need prior approval of RBI for appointment/ re-appointment/termination of Chairman, Whole-time Directors, Managing Director and CEO. RBI can appoint additional directors in commercial banks (except PSBs). RBI in consultation with Central Govt., can supersede the Board of Directors of Commercial Banks (except PSBs).
- Public Sector Banks (PSBs) are under dual regulation of Central Govt. and RBI. RBI's powers are curtailed regarding PSBs, where RBI cannot remove directors and management, cannot supersede banks board and does not have the power to force a merger or trigger liquidation. Also, PSBs banking activity does not require license from RBI and hence RBI cannot revoke license of PSBs.
- RBI regulates the banks to maintain certain reserves in the form of CRR and SLR
- The interest rate on most of the categories of deposits and lending have been deregulated and are largely determined by banks but RBI regulates the interest rate on NRI deposits, export credits (loans) and a few other categories.
- RBI prescribes prudential norms to be followed by banks in several areas of their operations. Some of the prudential norms are asset classification, income recognition, provisioning, capital adequacy etc. *(no need to go in detail about these norms)*
- To prevent money laundering through the banking system, banks are required to carry out Know Your Customer (KYC) exercise for all their customers to establish their identity and report suspicious transactions to authorities.
- RBI has set up (100% subsidiary) Deposit Insurance and Credit Guarantee Corporation (DICGC) to protect the interest of small depositors in case of bank **failures/bankruptcy**. The DICGC provides insurance cover to all eligible bank depositors up to Rs. 5 lakhs (principal and interest combined) per depositor per bank. DICGC charges premium from banks to provide insurance. If one person has different accounts in a bank like savings, fixed, recurring and current, does not matter, his total insurance cover is max five lakhs rupees. But if one person has account in different banks, then he is separately covered five lakhs rupees in each bank. All commercial banks including branches of foreign banks and UCBs/StCBs/DCCBs are covered except deposits of foreign governments, deposits of central and state governments, and inter-bank deposits.
- Even if a bank has not gone bankrupt but is **not doing well and** RBI has imposed moratorium/restrictions on withdrawal of deposits to improve the condition of the bank, then in that case also DICGC will have to pay to depositors Rs. 5 lakhs (maximum, depending on what is in your account) within 90 days. This was a major issues for depositors as in the last few years several banks had cases related to fraud and were not doing well and RBI imposed moratorium/restrictions on public deposit withdrawal. *(It was done by amending the DICGC Act in 2021).*

- The RBI has permitted banks to undertake para-banking (non-traditional banking) activities such as mutual fund business, insurance business, venture capital etc.

Cooperative Banks

- Cooperative Banks are under dual regulation of RBI and Government. Banking related functions are regulated by RBI and management related functions are regulated by respective State governments or Central government, as the case may be.

Financial Institutions, NBFCs, Primary Dealers and Credit Information Companies (CIC)

- The four All India Financial Institutions – NABARD, NHB, EXIM Bank and SIDBI are under full-fledged regulation and supervision of the RBI. NBFCs, Primary Dealers and CICs are also under the regulation and supervision of RBI.

RBI regulates Banks and NBFCs both but till July 2019 RBI had the powers to supersede the Board of Banks only (in case of any mismanagement/ default) and not NBFCs. In July 2019, RBI Act 1934 was amended to allow RBI to supersede the Board of NBFCs also (and appoint administrator) in public interest.

3. **Regulation of Foreign Exchange Market, Govt. Securities Market and Money Market**

   Foreign Exchange Market: For a long time, foreign exchange in India was treated as a controlled commodity because of its limited availability. The early stages of foreign exchange management in the country focused on control of foreign exchange by regulating the demand due to limited supply of foreign exchange for which the statutory powers were provided by the Foreign Exchange Regulation Act (FERA), 1973. Prompted by the liberalization measures introduced since 1991 and developments in the external sector such as substantial increase in foreign exchange reserves, growth in foreign trade, liberalization of Indian investments abroad and participation of foreign institutional investors in Indian stock market, the Foreign Exchange Management Act (FEMA) was enacted in 1999 to replace the FERA 1973 with effect from June 2000. So now, RBI oversees the foreign exchange market in India and supervises and regulates it through the provisions of the FEMA Act 1999.

   Government securities market, which trades securities issued by the Central and State Governments are regulated by the RBI for which RBI derives its powers from the RBI Act 1934.

   Money Market (explained in financial markets topic), which trades short term and highly liquid debt securities are also regulated by the RBI for which RBI derives its powers from the RBI Act 1934.

4. **Management of Foreign Exchange Reserves**

   The foreign exchange reserves include foreign currency assets (FCA), Special Drawing Rights (SDRs) and gold. The RBI, as the custodian of the country's foreign exchange reserves, is vested with the responsibility of managing their investment. The legal provisions governing management of foreign exchange reserves are laid down in the RBI Act 1934. The RBI Act permits the RBI to invest these reserves in the following types of instruments:

   - Deposits with Bank for International Settlement and other central banks.
   - Deposits with foreign commercial banks.

- Debt instruments representing sovereign or sovereign guaranteed liability.
- Other instruments as approved by the Central Board of the RBI.

The basic parameters of the RBI's policies for foreign exchange reserves management are safety, liquidity and returns. RBI used to traditionally asses the reserves adequacy in terms of import cover but now it also looks at the type of external shocks to which the economy is potentially vulnerable. The objective is to ensure that the quantum of reserves is in line with the growth potential of the economy, the size of capital flows and national security requirements.

5. **Current Account and Capital Account management**

RBI manages the current account and capital account which has been explained in detail under the balance of payment topic.

6. **Banker to Central and State governments**

- As a banker to the government, RBI receives and pays money on behalf of the various Government departments. As it has offices in only 27 locations, the RBI appoints other banks to act as its agents (Agent Banks) for undertaking the banking business on behalf of the governments.

  Earlier Scheduled Public Sector banks and only few large private sector banks were allowed to take up Government related business like collection of taxes, pension payments and small savings schemes like PPF, Kisan Vikas Patra, Sukanya Samridhi Yojana etc.But this embargo on private sector banks has been lifted and now all public and private sector Scheduled Commercial Banks can act as Agent Banks of RBI.

- RBI maintains the account for the central and state government funds like Consolidated Fund, Contingency Fund and Public Account.
- RBI also provides "Ways and Means Advances" (WMA) – it is a temporary loan facility to the centre and state/UT governments as a banker to government.

  The WMA scheme is designed to meet temporary mismatches in the receipts and payments of the government. This facility can be availed by the government if it needs immediate cash from the RBI. The WMA is a loan facility from the RBI for 90 days which implies that the government has to vacate the facility after 90 days. Interest rate for WMA is currently charged at the repo rate. The limits for WMA are mutually decided by the RBI and the Government of India. WMA is just a loan paper and is **non-tradable** (T-bills, Dated Securities, SDL and Cash Management Bills are tradable). WMAs are not used to fund Fiscal deficit.

- Besides it arranges for investments of surplus cash balances of the Governments as a portfolio manager.
- The RBI also acts as advisor to the Government, whenever called upon to do so, on monetary and banking related matters.

7. **Debt Manager of Central and State governments**

The RBI manages the public debt and issues new loans on behalf of the Central and State Governments. The RBI's debt management policy aims at minimising the cost of borrowing, reducing risk, smoothening the maturity structure of debt.

8. **Banker to Banks**

- RBI enables banks to open their (current) accounts with RBI for maintenance of statutory reserve requirements (CRR and SLR).
- RBI acts as a common banker for different banks to enable settlement of interbank transfer of funds.
- RBI provides short term loans and advances to banks for specific purposes.
- RBI acts as lender of last resort.
  - ❖ RBI comes to the rescue of a bank that is solvent (has not gone bankrupt) but faces temporary liquidity (funds) problems by supplying it with much needed funds against good collateral at a penal rate of interest. RBI provides this emergency liquidity assistance only if the troubled financial institution has exhausted all the resources it can obtain from the market and from the RBI's regular liquidity facilities like LAF, MSF etc. RBI extends this facility to protect the interest of the depositors of the bank and to prevent possible failure of a bank, which in turn may also affect other banks and institutions and can have an adverse impact on macroeconomic and financial stability.
  - ❖ **Bank Run** is a situation that occurs when everybody wants to take money out of one's bank account before the bank runs out of reserves. As more and more people withdraw their funds, the probability of default increases, thereby prompting more people to withdraw their deposits. In extreme cases, the bank's reserves may not be sufficient to cover the withdrawals. A bank run is typically the result of panic which can ultimately lead to default. In such a situation, the RBI stands by the commercial banks as a guarantor and extends loans to ensure the solvency of the banks. *(Solvency is the ability of a company to meet its long-term financial obligations which is essential to staying in business)*. This system of guarantee assures individual account holders that their banks will be able to pay their money back in case of a crisis and there is no need to panic thus avoiding bank runs. This role of RBI is also called 'lender of last resort'.

9. **Issuer of Currency**

- The RBI, along with the government of India, is responsible for the design, production and overall management of the nation's currency, with the goal of ensuring an adequate supply of clean and genuine notes. In consultation with the government, the RBI routinely addresses security issues and targets ways to enhance security features to reduce the risk of counterfeiting of currency notes.
- The RBI carries out the currency management function through its department of currency management (Mumbai), 19 Issue Offices located across the country and a currency chest at its Kochi branch. To facilitate the distribution of notes and rupee coins across the country, the RBI has authorized selected branches of banks to

establish currency chests *(currency chests are storehouses where bank notes and rupee coins are stocked on behalf of RBI)*.

10. **Oversight of payment and settlement systems**

The central bank of any country is usually the driving force in the development of national payment systems. The Reserve Bank of India (RBI) as the central bank of India has been playing this developmental role and has taken several initiatives for Safe, Secure, Sound, Efficient, Accessible and Authorised payment systems in the country.

In India, the payment and settlement systems are regulated by the Payment and Settlement Systems Act, 2007 (PSS Act). In terms of Section 4 of the PSS Act, no person other than RBI can commence or operate a payment system in India unless authorised by RBI.

For many years in India, banks have been the traditional gateway to extend payment systems. Over a period of time, given the demand for varied payment services and in keeping with the fast pace of technological changes, non-bank entities have also been permitted access to the payment space. These non-banks are co-operating, as well as, competing with banks, either as **technology service providers** to banks or by **directly providing retail electronic payment services**. It may be noted that licensed banks also need to obtain specific permission from RBI for setting up and operating a **payment system**. This is because banking function is different and operating a "payment system" (which facilitates payment from one entity to other) is different.

The Reserve Bank has since authorised various types of payment system operators, some of which are mentioned below:

(i) Financial Market Infrastructure (Clearing Corporation of India)

(ii) Retail Payment (National Payment Corporation of India)

(iii) Card Payment Network (MaserCard, VISA)

(iv) Prepaid Instruments (AmazonPay)

(v) Cross Border Money Transfer (UAE Exchange Centre)

National Payments Corporation of India (NPCI) is a **non-bank payment system operator** authorized by RBI to operate the following payment systems under the PSS Act 2007.

- National Financial Switch
- Immediate Payment System (IMPS)
- Unified Payments Interface (UPI)
- Aadhar Enabled Payment System (AEPS)
- Rupay Cards
- National Automatic Clearing House (ACH)
- Linking of ATMs across India (some other operators are also involved)
- National Electronic Toll collection (It provides an electronic payment facility to customer to make the payments at national, state and city toll plazas by identifying the vehicle uniquely through a FASTag)

NPCI is a 'Not for Profit' company where 51% stake is owned by public sector banks.

11. **Developmental Role**

RBI's developmental role includes ensuring credit to productive sectors of the economy, creating institutions to build financial infrastructure and expanding access to affordable financial services. The following schemes come under the developmental role of RBI:

(i) Priority Sector Lending:

Priority sectors refer to those sectors of the economy which may not get timely and adequate credit in the absence of this special scheme. **Priority sector guidelines do not lay down any preferential rate of interest for priority sector loans.** Typically, these are small value loans to those sectors of the society/economy that impact large segments of the population and weaker sections, and to the sectors which are employment intensive such as agriculture and small enterprises.

Banks having any shortfall in lending to priority sector are allocated amounts for contribution to the Rural Infrastructure Development Fund (RIDF) established with NABARD and other Funds with NABARD/ NHB/SIDBI/ MUDRA Ltd.

Commercial Banks including foreign banks	Regional Rural Banks	Small Finance Banks	Payment Banks	Urban (Primary) Cooperative Banks	Rural Cooperative Banks
40%	75%	60%	They do not give credit	75%	*As such no guideline may be because they already focus in rural areas.*

Priority Sectors are:

1. Agriculture:
    - Loans to Individual farmers and Farmer Producer Organisations
    - Includes crop loans, machinery loans for all kinds of agri and allied activities
    - Loans for food and agro-processing activities are also included under Agriculture
    - Loans for installation of solar plants and for solarisation of grid connected pumps
    - Setting up Compressed Bio gas plants
2. MSME
3. Export
4. Education
5. Housing
6. Renewable energy
7. Social Infrastructure
    - Setting up schools, drinking water facilities, sanitation facilities, healthcare facilities
8. Others
    - Distressed persons for prepayment of loan borrowed from money lenders
    - Start-ups (loans up to Rs. 50 crores)
9. Weaker Sections
    - Small and marginal farmers, artisans, village and cottage industries, SC/ST, SHG, Persons with disabilities, minority communities etc.

New Models Implemented to Meet Priority Sector Lending (PSL) Targets

1. On-lending model

Onward lending by registered Non-Banking Finance Companies (NBFCs) including Micro Finance Institutions (MFI) for the various priority sectors will be considered as Priority Sector Lending.

RBI has done the above changes in order to boost credit to the needy segment of borrowers. Under the revised **on-lending model**, banks can classify only the fresh loans sanctioned by NBFCs out of bank borrowing as priority sector lending. Bank credit to NBFCs for 'On-Lending' will be allowed up to a limit of five percent of individual bank's total priority sector lending on an ongoing basis.

2. Higher weights for Incremental Priority Sector Credit in 'Identified Districts'

As per RBI "To address regional disparities in the flow of priority sector credit at the district level, it has been decided to rank districts on the basis of per capita credit flow to priority sector and build an incentive framework for districts with comparatively lower flow of credit and a dis-incentive framework for districts with comparatively higher flow of priority sector credit. Accordingly, from FY 2021-22 onwards, a higher weight (125%) would be assigned to the incremental priority sector credit in the identified districts where the credit flow is comparatively lower (per capita PSL less than ₹6000), and a lower weight (90%) would be assigned for incremental priority sector credit in the identified districts where the credit flow is comparatively higher (per capita PSL greater than ₹25,000)." RBI has given the list of different categories of districts.

Explanation:

Suppose a Bank gave total credit of Rs. 100. So it has to give Rs. 40 to the priority sectors.

But, suppose, the bank gave only Rs. 32 loan to a district where per capita PSL credit is less than Rs. 6000 then its weight is 125%, which basically means it will be counted as Rs. 32 * 1.25 = Rs. 40 And hence it will be assumed that the bank has met the PSL criteria of 40%.

Similarly, if the bank is giving credit to higher per capita credit districts then it will have to give more than 40% of the credit to priority sectors because weightage is 90% only.

And this will be applicable for the new (incremental) loans given from 1st April 2021 onwards. A very innovative way of inclusive growth/development. This step of RBI will make growth inclusive across geography also, which was earlier focussing only on sectors.

3. Co-Lending Model by Banks and NBFCs

*RBI in **Nov 2020** issued guidelines regarding Co-Lending (or Co-origination) by Banks and NBFCs for lending to priority sector. Earlier (in 2018) RBI had released guidelines for co-origination of loans which now stands replaced by the Co-lending guidelines.*

1. The Co-lending of loans provides a unique opportunity for formal lenders to come together and share their **synergies** to create a winning proposition for all the stakeholders. It enables **banks** and Non-Banking Finance Companies (**NBFCs**)to enter into an arrangement where the risks and rewards are shared by all parties to the co-lending agreement throughout the lifecycle of the loan, as per a pre-decided ratio.

2. NBFCs often face challenges in getting cheaper access to funds for lending purposes, which in turn results into higher interest rates for their borrowers and hence less demand for their loans; whereas large commercial banks find it difficult and expensive to extend their reach to certain locations, where the NBFCs have a stronger presence. Co-lending helps in bridging these gaps.
3. The co-lending model empowers multiple stakeholders of the lending ecosystem. While NBFCs can leverage their strong presence in local markets, commercial banks have the cheap availability of funds for credit disbursal. Another advantage of this partnership is that NBFCs have mastered the art of assessing the creditworthiness of certain niche customer segments, which the banks have been ignoring, primarily due to differences in their core target segment and credit risk management approach.

   The NBFCs use a number of innovative mechanisms for credit risk assessment including usage of non-traditional sources of data, observing an individual's modus operandi and cash-flow at work, building customized scorecards, etc. for both small-ticket retail & MSME segment. This is a big pie for banks to look forward to.
4. But while the present RBI guidelines highlight co-lending as an initiative to propel priority sector lending, the model has a much broader potential to go beyond just lending to the priority sectors.
5. *Example/Explanation:*
   - Total Loan given to a customer (the customer will not know separate amounts) = Rs. 50 lakhs.
   - NBFC gave Rs. 10 lakhs @ 10% (which will be on NBFC account books).
   - Bank gave Rs. 40 lakhs @8% (which will be on Bank's account books).
   - So, the customer will see that he has got loan of Rs. 50 lakhs @ **8.4%** (10% of Rs. 10 lakhs = Rs. 1 lakh.And 8% of Rs. 40 lakhs = Rs. 3.2 lakh. So, total interest = Rs. 4.2 lakh/year on Rs. 50 lakh loan. So, effective interest rate will be (Rs. 4.2 lakh/ Rs. 50 lakhs) * 100% = **8.4%**).
   - The banks can claim priority sector status in respect of their share of credit i.e., Rs. 40 lacs.
6. In Co-Lending, banks are permitted to co-lend with all registered NBFCs based on a prior agreement. **Co-lending enables both the partners to price their portions of the loan as they want.** The co-lending banks will take their share of the individual loans (on a back-to-back basis) in their account books. However, NBFCs shall be required to retain a minimum **of 20 per cent** share of the individual loans on their books.

(ii) Lead Bank Scheme

The Lead Bank Scheme was introduced by RBI in December 1969. The Scheme aims at coordinating the activities of banks and other developmental agencies through various fora in order to achieve the objective of enhancing the flow of bank finance to priority sector and other sectors and to promote banks' role in overall development of the rural sector. For coordinating the activities in the district, a particular bank is assigned the lead bank responsibility of the district which leads the consortium of all banks and other agencies in the area. The lead bank is expected to assume leadership role for coordinating the efforts of the credit institutions and Government in matters of local development and are entrusted with the responsibility of identifying growth centres, assessing deposit potential and credit gaps and evolving a coordinated approach for credit deployment in each district.

A High-Level Committee in 2009 noted that the Scheme has been useful in achieving its original objectives of improvement in branch expansion, deposit mobilisation and lending to the priority sectors, especially in rural/semi urban areas. The Lead Bank Scheme (LBS) has been extended to the districts in the metropolitan areas thus bringing the entire country under the fold of the Lead Bank Scheme.

Lead Bank Scheme is administered by the RBI since 1969. The assignment of lead bank responsibility to designated banks in every district is done by RBI following a detailed procedure formulated for this purpose. As on June 30, 2017, 25 public sector banks and one private sector bank have been assigned lead bank responsibility in 706 districts of the country.

(iii) Kisan Credit Cards (KCC):

KCC scheme was introduced in the year 1998-99 to enable the farmers to purchase agricultural inputs and draw cash for their production needs. The scheme was later on revised to cover long term loan as well as working capital (day to day activity) loan for agriculture and allied activities and a reasonable component for consumption needs. The scheme is an innovative credit delivery mechanism to meet the credit requirements of the farmers in a timely and hassle-free manner.

The scheme is under implementation in the entire country by the vast institutional credit framework involving Commercial Banks, RRBs, Small Finance Banks and Cooperatives and has received wide acceptability amongst bankers and farmers. Under the scheme, the limits are fixed on the basis of operational land holding, cropping pattern and scales of finance. The interest rate is as per the RBI guidelines.

Kisan Credit Card Scheme aims at providing adequate and timely credit support from the formal banking system under a single window to the farmers for their following needs:

Short-Term loan

- To meet the credit requirements for cultivation of crops
- Post-harvest expenses
- Produce Marketing loan
- Consumption requirements of farmer household
- Working capital for maintenance of farm assets and activities allied to agriculture, like dairy animals, inland fishery etc.

Long-Term loan

- Investment (long term) credit requirement for agriculture and allied activities like pump sets, sprayers, dairy animals etc.

The following people are eligible for this scheme:

- All Farmers – Individuals / Joint borrowers who are owner cultivators
- Tenant Farmers, Oral Lessees & Share Croppers
- Self-Help Groups or Joint Liability Groups of Farmers

To ensure that the farmers pay a minimal interest rate to the banks, the Government of India has introduced the Modified Interest Subvention Scheme (ISS), to provide short-term credit to farmers at subsidised interest rates. Under this scheme, short-term agriculture loan up to ₹5 lakh is available at 7 per cent per annum to farmers engaged in Agriculture and other Allied activities, including Animal Husbandry, Dairying, Poultry, Fisheries etc. An additional 3 per cent subvention (Prompt Repayment Incentive) is also given to the farmers for prompt and timely repayment of loans. Therefore, if a farmer repays his loan on time, he gets credit at 4 per cent per annum. Assuming a benchmark loan rate of 9%, those farmers who make timely repayment gets a subsidy of around 5% (9%-4%). The scheme is implemented through public and private sector banks and RRBs and Cooperatives.

The long-term loan limit is based on the proposed investment and the bank's perception on the repaying capacity of the farmer. The short-term loan limit plus the estimated long-term loan requirement will be the Maximum Permissible Limit (MPL) and is to be treated as the Kisan Credit Card limit.

12. **Consumer education and protection**

Consumer education and protection is an integral component of RBI's full-service central banking functions. The Consumer Education and Protection Department (CEPD), set up in 2006 as Customer Service Department (CSD), frames policy guidelines for consumer protection and oversees the functioning of the 22 Offices of RBI Ombudsman and 30 Consumer Education and Protection Cells.

13. **Fintech**

To keep pace with the dynamically changing landscape, Reserve Bank has been making conscious efforts to facilitate innovation in Fintech sector, for the larger public good. Accordingly, a Fintech Department was setup in January 2022 with a view to give greater focus to the Fintech sector, facilitate innovation and to keep pace with the dynamically changing financial landscape. All matters related to the facilitation of constructive innovations and incubations in the Fintech sector, which may have wider implications for the financial sector/ markets and falling under the purview of the Bank, is being dealt with by the Fintech Department.

14. **Policy Research and Data Dissemination**

RBI has over time established a sound and rich tradition of policy-oriented research and an effective mechanism for disseminating data and information. The research undertaken at the RBI revolves around issues and problems arising in the current environment at national and international levels, which have critical implications for the Indian economy.

The RBI disseminates data and information regularly in the form of several publications, press releases and through its website. India is a signatory of the **Special Data Dissemination Standards (SDDS)** as defined by the IMF for the purpose of releasing data.

RBI is under legal obligation to publish two reports every year:

- *Annual Report* (as per RBI Act 1934)
- *Report on Trend and Progress of Banking in India* (As per Banking Regulation Act 1949)

Besides, there are periodical statements on monetary policy, official press releases and speeches and interviews given by the top management which articulate the RBI's assessment of the economy and its policies.

RBI conducts quarterly 'Consumer Confidence Survey' in which RBI collects responses on household's perceptions and expectations on the general economic situation, the employment scenario, the overall price situation and their own income and spending.

RBI conducts 'Inflation Expectation Survey' of households on quarterly basis wherein RBI gauges the household's expectation regarding inflation for the three months ahead and one-year ahead period. These surveys are used for monetary policy purpose.

2.16 RBI's Sources of Income and Economic Capital Framework

The following are the various sources of income of RBI:

- **Seigniorage:** Seigniorage refers to the **profit from money creation** and, thus, is a way for governments to generate revenue without levying conventional taxes. Seigniorage is the profit that accrues to the central banks in the following ways:
    - While issuing currency, the reserves/ backup that the RBI keeps with itself, these reserves give RBI interest Income on the total amount of currency in circulation (minus cost of printing currency)
    - Interest accruing from bank balances with central banks arises from funds banks have to hold with the central banks to meet their reserve requirements (CRR), either as interest-free balances or at below market interest rates.
    - The inflation tax concept which is measured as the product of the inflation rate and the monetary base. (Because of inflation the currency note that the public is holding loses value which reduces the liability of RBI)
- The Foreign Currency Assets (FCA) are around 90% of the Forex reserves. This FCA RBI has invested in US govt. bonds and it earns interest on that. It has also deposited some FCA with other Central Banks. (an example of seigniorage)
- When RBI purchase Indian Govt. bonds from the OMO, then it earns interest on the holding of govt bonds/securities (an example of seigniorage)
- Lending at Repo rate to banks
- RBI acts as 'Debt Manager' of Central Govt and State Govt for which it gets commission/ income.
- RBI acts as 'portfolio manager' to invest surplus cash balance of Central govt. and State Govt.

Economic capital is a measure of risk in terms of capital. More specifically, it's the amount of capital that a company (usually in financial services) needs to ensure that it stays **solvent** (opposite of bankrupt) given its risk profile. Economic capital is calculated internally by the company and it is the amount of capital that the firm should have to support any risks that it takes.

As per RBI Act 1934, Section 47, there are two clear objectives for the Economic Capital Framework (ECF).

- First, the RBI as a macroeconomic institution has the responsibility to fight any crisis in the financial system and to handle such a crisis, the RBI should have adequate funds attached under the capital reserve.
- And, second is transferring the remaining part of the net income to the government.

Accordingly, RBI has developed an Economic Capital Framework (ECF) for determining the allocation of funds to its **capital reserves** so that any risk contingency can be met and as well as to transfer the profit of the RBI to the government.

The process of adding funds to the capital reserve is a yearly one where the RBI allots money out of its net income to the capital reserve. How much funds shall be added to the capital reserve each year depends upon the risky situation in the financial system and the economy. After allotting money to the capital reserve, the remaining net income of the RBI is transferred to the government as profit (RBI is a 100% subsidiary of Government of India, so every year it transfers its profit/dividend to Govt. of India).

RBI's Board has revised the Economic Capital Framework (ECF). As per the new ECF, RBI will keep a Contingency Risk Buffer (CRB) in the range of 4.5% to 7.5% of the balance sheet (assets/liabilities). The purpose of the Contingency Risk Buffer (CRB) is:

- Buffer for Monetary Risk
- Buffer for Financial Stability Risk
- Buffer for Credit Risk
- Buffer for Operational Risk

Following is the graph showing the RBI surplus transfer to the Govt. in the last 10 years:

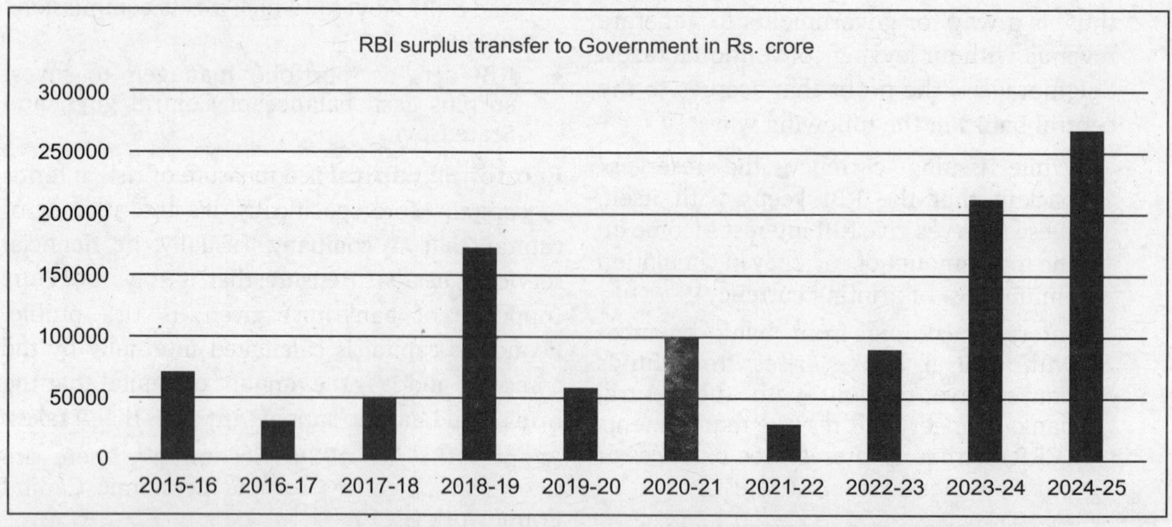

2.17 Crypto Currency and Central Bank Digital Currency (CBDC)

What are Crypto Currencies?

- Crypto currencies are a kind of assets like gold, silver on which Govt. does not have any control. As you may not be able to purchase vegetables in the market by paying in gold, in the same way you may not be able to purchase through crypto currencies too, but you can purchase through Rupee. So, in that sense crypto currencies are not a "currency" (the word is a misnomer). Gold/Crypto currencies are generally not accepted in transactions (they are not legal tender) but these are assets. As people can accept any commodity with another if they want to like in a "Barter System", in the same way people may accept even these crypto currencies and gold also for any transaction purpose because as such they are not prohibited and it is not illegal to transact in crypto currencies or gold.

- Crypto currencies are not issued by Government or RBI but rather encryption techniques are used to both create and control the number of units and verify its exchange. With crypto currencies, a chain of private computers - a network - is constantly working towards authenticating the transactions by solving complex cryptographic puzzles. For solving the puzzles, these systems are rewarded with crypto currencies. This process is called mining. At the backend of these transactions is technology called blockchain.
- Crypto currencies derive their value as they can be mined/generated only in limited numbers. The willingness of people to hold/possess it impacts the price of the crypto currency (asset) in the same way as the gold price gets impacted.
- They are neither legal tenders nor fiat currency.
- Any income from transfer of any virtual digital asset (cryptos) is taxed at the rate of 30 per cent. In order to capture the transaction details, TDS of 1% is deducted on payment made in relation to transfer of virtual digital asset.

What is Central Bank Digital Currencies (e-Rupee)?

- e-Rupee is a legal tender issued by a central bank in a digital form. It is the same as a fiat currency and is no different from cash and is exchangeable one-to-one with the fiat currency (bank notes/cash) at par. Only its form is different i.e., digital.
- RBI recently launched e-Rupee on pilot basis for Wholesale and retail markets.
- RBI Act 1934 has been amended to include e-rupee in 'bank note' and now it's a legal tender.

Why RBI launched e-Rupee?

- Many Central Banks are worried that the widespread adoption of these independent crypto currencies could weaken their control over the financial system. This could cause financial instability especially because crypto currencies do not have the legal or the regulatory safeguard that the Central Bank money does, so why not issue a digital currency of their own.
- Central banks seek to meet the public's need for digital currencies, manifested in the increasing use of private virtual currencies, and thereby avoid the more damaging consequences of such private currencies.
- Central banks, faced with dwindling usage of paper currency, seek to popularize a more acceptable electronic form of currency like e-rupee.

How will e-Rupee work?

- e-rupee will not replace cash rather it will complement it.
- It will be issued in the same denominations that paper currency and coins are currently issued.
- e-rupee will be distributed through intermediaries i.e., banks and it can be converted to other forms of money like deposits with bank.
- If I am holding cash and making payment to someone then it does not require any kind of settlement with a third party and the RBI's liability moves from me to the other person, whom I have paid. But when I make payment through cheque/card then it requires inter-bank settlement (through RBI in case of different banks). e-rupee would just be like cash, and I can make payment to

anyone through the e-Rupee and the RBI's liability will move to the other person. And the requirement of inter-bank settlement would disappear.

- Transactions can be both person to person and person to merchant (payments to merchants can be made using QR Codes).
- Users will be able to transact with e-rupee through a digital wallet offered by the participating banks and stored on mobile phones and other devices.
- Just like we withdraw cash from our bank deposits in the same way we can transfer our bank deposits to a CBDC wallet and this transaction is recorded in Core Banking Solution (CBS) of the bank.
- But when transactions are made from one CBDC wallet to another CBDC wallet then this transaction is not recorded in the CBS of the bank and remains anonymous. This is just like a person is paying cash to a grocery shop. It does not have any trail. And hence it does not come under tax net. Transaction anonymity is key to building customer confidence in using the CBDC for daily purpose.
- e-Rupee will be a bearer instrument i.e., whoever is holding the e-Rupee will be assumed to be the owner at any given point of time.
- e-rupee will not earn any interest like cash.

Advantages of CBDC

- Unlike our savings in commercial banks which rely on the bank's promise to fulfil, CBDCs are recognized by law and backed by Central Bank which cannot go bankrupt. For example, if a commercial bank collapses, then our savings could potentially be wiped out, but this would not be the case with CBDCs, which we can hold on to our own in digital form and could be as trusted as cash.
- CBDCs would be as convenient as payment apps and it also benefits from the same blockchain technology (Distributed Ledger Technology) which supports crypto currency.
- Payments would be faster and easier without any delay as there is no settlement issue
- Legal tender-based payment which will be efficient, trusted and regulated.
- Higher seigniorage due to lower cost of printing, transportation/distribution and storing paper currency.
- Introduction of CBDC would lead to a more robust, efficient, trusted, regulated and legal tender-based payments option.
- e-rupee would offer features of physical cash like trust, safety and settlement facility

Risks associated with CBDC

- In an extreme situation such as after a financial crash, if depositors/savers would shift their savings from bank accounts to CBDCs (with just a mouse click) then banks could have a problem of funding which might have an effect on financing the whole economy.
- CBDC ecosystems may be at similar risk for cyber-attacks as the current payment systems are exposed to. In countries like India with lower financial literacy levels, the increase in digital payment related frauds may also spread to CBDCs.

2.18 Base Rate, MCLR and External Benchmark Rate

First let us understand the link between deposit rate and lending rate:

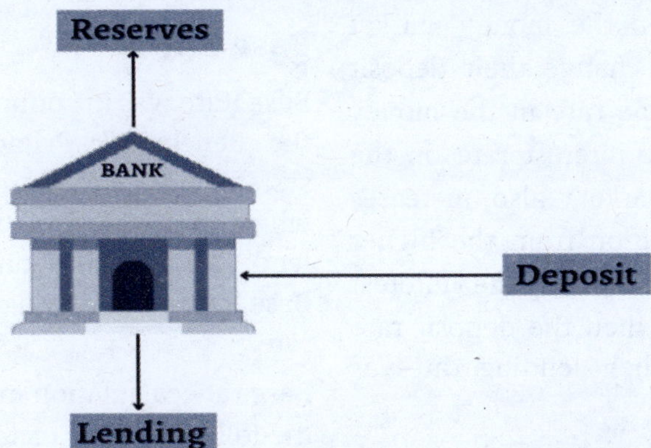

If banks are getting deposits of Rs. 1 lakh at 8% interest rate from the public then for banks the cost of Rs. 1 lakh money is 8% (i.e., also called cost of deposits or cost of funds) and banks will not be able to lend this money at less than 8% interest rate as banks will incur losses. If banks are required to keep 20% of the public's deposit as reserves with themselves or RBI on which banks are not earning interest then it will be an extra cost for banks. So, in such a situation the banks will be able to lend only Rs. 80,000 in the market.But they need to pay the depositor 8% on Rs. 1 lakh i.e., Rs. 8000. Now to earn Rs. 8000 the banks will have to lend the Rs. 80,000 in the market at 10% interest rate. But in lending and deposit, the banks incur operational costs. Therefore, at what rate banks will lend will depend on the cost of deposits (deposit rate), the cost of keeping reserves, the operational cost of banks and the profit that the banks want to earn. And all these costs may be different for different banks hence the lending rates of banks differ.

Transmission of Repo Rate into Lending Rate

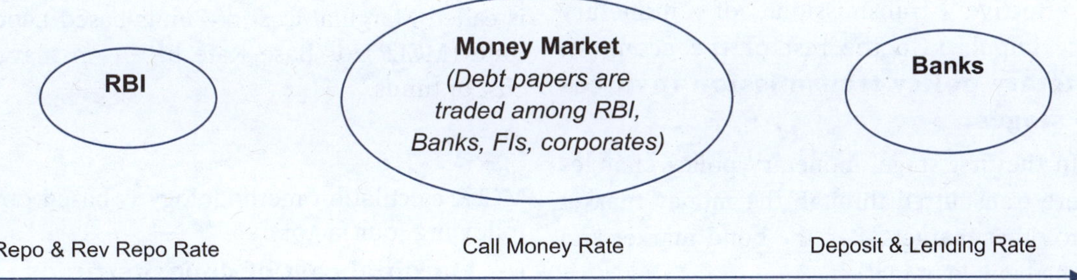

When RBI changes the repo rate, reverse repo rate automatically changes (reverse repo rate = repo rate – 0.25%). This means that the rate at which banks earn interest by keeping their excess funds with RBI changes. This also impacts the rate at which money (debt papers) is being traded in the money market i.e., "call money rate". This is because if a bank can earn interest rate equal to "reverse repo rate" by keeping its funds with RBI which is totally risk free then they will charge higher interest rate for funds lent in the money market. When the rate in the money market changes then banks also change their deposit rates. This is because if the rate in the money market increases then the interest rate on the bonds (in the capital market) also increases and banks facing competition from the higher interest rate on bonds increase the interest rate for depositors. And when the deposit rate changes, banks change their lending rates as already explained before.

[*In short, Repo rate changes transmit through the money market to the entire financial system, which, in turn, influences aggregate demand – a key determinant of inflation and growth. The Monetary Policy Framework aims at setting the policy (repo) rate based on an assessment of the current and evolving macroeconomic situation. Once the repo rate is announced, the operating framework designed by the Reserve Bank envisages liquidity management on a day-to-day basis through appropriate actions, which aim at* ***anchoring the operating target – the weighted average call rate/ money market rate*** *– around the repo rate.*]

Financial markets play a critical role in effective transmission of monetary policy impulses to the rest of the economy. **Monetary policy transmission involves two stages:**

- In the first stage, monetary policy changes are transmitted through the money market to other markets, i.e., the bond market and the bank loan market.
- The second stage involves the propagation of monetary policy impulses from the financial market to the real economy - by influencing spending decisions of individuals and firms.

Within the financial system, money market is central to monetary operations conducted by the central bank.

Base Rate

Base Rate was introduced in July 2010 replacing the Benchmark Prime Lending Rate (BPLR) system. Base Rate is the minimum rate below which Scheduled Commercial Banks cannot lend. RBI publishes guidelines for calculation of Base Rate and every bank calculates its own base rate.

Base rate calculation methodology was based on the following four factors:

- **(Average) Cost of deposits/funds** (interest rate that bank offers to its depositors)
- Cost of maintaining CRR and SLR (if the banks are required to keep higher reserves like CRR and SLR, then they will be able to lend less money & will have to charge higher interest rate)
- Operational Costs of Banks
- Return/profit on Net worth (investment)

From 1st April 2016, RBI introduced a new methodology for calculation of the Base Rates based on marginal cost of funds rather than average cost of funds. This new methodology is called Marginal Cost of Funds based Lending Rate (MCLR) or Base Rate based on marginal cost of funds.

MCLR

MCLR calculation methodology is based on the following four factors:

- **Marginal cost of deposits/funds**
- Cost of maintaining reserves (CRR)
- Operational Costs of Banks
- Tenor Premium (based on the time period for which loan is given)

The basic difference between the previous Base Rate and the MCLR based rate is the change of calculation of cost of deposits from **average** to **marginal**. The banks shall review and publish their MCLR every month.

Let us understand the difference between Base Rate and MCLR in detail:

Explanation of the working of Base Rate and MCLR

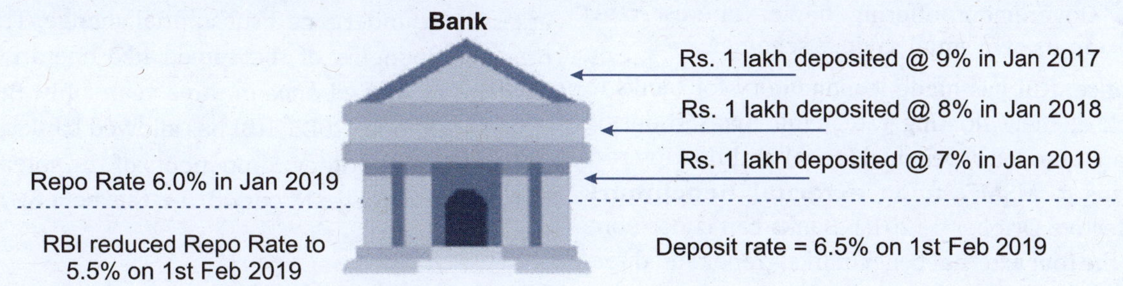

Suppose RBI's repo rate was 6.0% in January 2019 and the bank had accepted the deposits at different rates in the past totalling Rs. 3 lakhs @ 9%, 8% and 7% interest rate. The average costs of deposit/funds for the banks were 8% and suppose the bank's lending rate was 9.5% *(calculated using average cost of deposit method)* in January 2019.

Now suppose, RBI reduces its repo rate to 5.5% on 1st Feb 2019 and the bank reduced its deposit rate to 6.5%. But the bank is still paying 8% deposit rate on an average to its previous depositors and the banks' cost of funds (for the past accumulated deposits) has not reduced even if it has reduced the deposit rate for the new depositors to 6.5%. That is why banks generally do not reduce their lending rates to the new borrowers even if they have reduced their deposit rates for the new depositors. So, there used to be slow transmission from repo rate to lending rate.

As per the MCLR methodology, the banks must link their lending rates with the marginal/additional cost of deposits i.e., the rate at which they are receiving the new deposits i.e. in the above case 6.5%. So, in this situation whenever RBI reduces the repo rate, banks reduce their deposit rate and since the lending rate is linked to the new deposit rate, they reduce the lending rate also. Hence, because of linking the lending rate with marginal cost of deposits, there will be fast transmission of repo rate into lending rate *(better monetary policy transmission)*. It will also help improve the transparency in the methodology followed by banks for determining the lending rates. The MCLR methodology will help ensure availability of bank credit at interest rates which are fair to the borrowers as well as banks.

Every Bank calculates its own MCLR rate based on cost of deposits, operational costs, reserve requirements and tenor premium. So MCLR (or Base Rate) is an "**internal benchmark**" which varies from bank to bank. Banks link their lending rate with MCLR.

But, the transmission of policy (repo) rate changes to the lending rate of banks under the

MCLR framework has not been satisfactory due the various reasons like:

- Banks fearing that they will lose depositors/ customers if they will reduce the deposit rate first, and since deposit rate was not reduced, MCLR (or base rate) was also not coming down.
- Government offering higher interest rates on its own small savings schemes

Hence, RBI has made it mandatory for banks to link all new floating rate retail loans (housing loan, auto loan, personal loans) and floating rate loans to MSMEs to an **external benchmark** effective October 1, 2019. Banks can choose one of the four external benchmarks – repo rate, three-month treasury bill yield, six-month treasury bill yield or any other benchmark interest rate published by Financial Benchmarks India Pvt. Ltd. *Banks are not mandated to link their deposit rates with an external benchmark rate.*

Now, suppose Axis Bank links its loan rates as per the following:

Home Loan= repo rate + 3%

(3% is called the Spread)

Education Loan= repo rate + 4%

Personal Loan= repo rate + 5%

Here, all the loans are linked to repo rate, which is an **external benchmark**, on which Axis Bank do not have any control. So, the moment RBI changes the repo rate, it will automatically be transmitted to the lending rates (for the new borrowers) at the same moment *(Even if the bank links the lending rate with Treasury bill yield; when RBI changes repo rate, the T-bill yield also changes in the market immediately)*. The purpose of linking the lending rate with an external benchmark is faster transmission of repo rate into lending rate and this mechanism is more transparent also. Adopting of multiple benchmarks by the same bank is not allowed within a loan category.

Banks are free to decide the components of spread and the amount of spread. But in general, the **spread** consists of credit risk premium, business strategy, operational costs of banks etc. While the banks are free to decide on the spread over the external benchmark, credit risk premium can change only when borrower's credit assessment undergoes a substantial change. The other components of the spread like operating cost can be altered once in three years only. But from 1st October 2025, RBI has allowed banks to reduce even the other components of the spread before the three-year period for the benefit of the borrowers.

RBI has mandated **banks** to link the lending rate with an "**anchor rate**" like MCLR or some external benchmark rate. But there is no mandate for NBFCs to link their lending rates.

***[Students always ask that when a Question says "**interest rate** or **market interest rate**", then what should we consider it, whether **deposit** or **lending rate or something else**???*

So, the answer is: "Interest rate or Market Interest rate" is the rate at which money is available in the market. Now, the rate at which money is available to banks (from public) is called the deposit rate and the rate at which money is available to the public/companies (from banks) is called the lending rate. So "interest rate" is a general term which could mean either lending rate or deposit rate depending on the context.

Now, if the question says just "interest rate", you could assume anything either deposit rate or lending rate and your answer will not get impacted.If the question requires a specify rate, then it will be mentioned in the question whether they mean deposit or lending rate.]

2.19 BASEL Norms

Banks accept deposit from the general public and they also raise capital from the financial markets through debt and equity. Banks then lend this money to different category of borrowers having different risk profile. The lending activity exposes banks to different kinds of risks which in many cases lead to the failure of banks and loss of depositor's wealth. Basel norms are provisions to tackle this risk of bank failures and to maintain a sound financial system in the economy.

Basel, a city in Switzerland, is the headquarters of Bank for International Settlement (BIS), which fosters co-operation among Central Banks with a common goal of financial stability and common standards of banking regulations. Every two months BIS hosts a meeting of the governor and senior officials of central banks of member countries. Currently there are 28 member nations in the committee. Basel guidelines refer to broad supervisory standards formulated by this group of central banks – called the Basel Committee on Banking Supervision (BCBS). The set of agreement by the BCBS, which mainly focuses on risks to banks and the financial system are called **Basel accord**. The purpose of the accord is to ensure that financial institutions have enough capital on account to meet obligations and absorb unexpected losses. India has accepted Basel accords for the banking system.

Basel I: In 1988, BCBS introduced capital measurement system called Basel capital accord, also called as Basel I. It focused almost entirely on credit risk *(the risk that some of its borrowers may not repay the loan and it varies from borrower to borrower)*. It defined capital and structure of risk weights for banks. The minimum capital requirement was fixed at 8% of risk weighted assets. Risk weighted assets means assets with different risk profiles. For example, an asset backed by collateral would carry lesser risks as compared to personal loans, which have no collateral. India adopted Basel I guidelines in 1999.

Basel II: In June 2004, Basel II guidelines were published by BCBS, which were considered to be the refined and reformed versions of Basel I accord. The guidelines were based on three parameters, which the committee calls as pillars:

- Capital Adequacy Requirements: Banks should maintain a minimum capital adequacy requirement of 8% of risk assets
- Supervisory Review: According to this, banks were needed to develop and use better risk management techniques in monitoring and managing all the three types of risks that a bank faces, viz. credit, market and operational risks
- Market Discipline: This needs increased disclosure requirements. Banks need to mandatorily disclose their CAR, risk exposure, etc to the central bank. Basel II norms in India and overseas are yet to be fully implemented.

Basel III: In 2010, Basel III guidelines were released. These guidelines were introduced in response to the financial crisis of 2008. A need was felt to further strengthen the system as banks in the developed economies were under-capitalized, over-leveraged (high debt) and had a greater reliance on short-term funding. Also, the quantity and quality of capital under Basel II were deemed insufficient to contain any further risk. Basel III norms aim at making most banking activities such as their trading book activities more capital-intensive. The guidelines aim to promote a more resilient banking system by focusing on four vital banking parameters viz. capital, leverage/debt, funding and liquidity.

The main objectives of Basel III are:

- Improve the banking sector's ability to absorb shocks arising from financial and economic stress
- Improve risk management and governance
- Strengthen banks' transparency and disclosure

Explanation: To understand Basel norms in a better way, let us understand the capital and risk weighted assets of banks i.e., Capital to Risk Weighted Asset Ratio (CRAR) or Capital Adequacy Ratio.

Bank 1

Assets	Liability
Personal Loan = 1 cr Project Loan against some collateral = 3 cr	Owners Money = 1 cr Deposit of Public = 3 cr
Rs. 4 crores	Rs. 4 crores

Bank 2

Assets	Liability
Personal Loan = 3 cr Project Loan against some collateral = 1 cr	Owners Money = 1 cr Deposit of Public = 3 cr
Rs. 4 crores	Rs. 4 crores

Above is balance sheet of two banks where the owners of banks have put in Rs. 1 crore each (which is considered as capital of bank) and public has deposited Rs. 3 crores in each of the banks which is reflected on the liability side. This Rs. 4 crores of funds (from the owners and depositors) have been given as loan by the banks.

Bank 1 has given personal loan of Rs. 1 crore and loan against some collateral/security of Rs 3 crore. And Bank 2 has given personal loan of Rs. 3 crore and loan against some collateral/security of Rs 1 crore.

RBI specifies the risk weights of various kinds of assets depending on their risk profile. Just assume that personal loan has risk weight of 100% and loan against collateral has risk weight of 50%. Now let us calculate the Capital to Risk Weighted Asset Ratio (CRAR) of each Bank.

CRAR (Bank 1) = 1/(1*1 + 3*0.5)
= 1/2.5 = 0.4

CRAR (Bank 2) = 1/(3*1 + 1*0.5)
= 1/3.5 = 0.3

Since CRAR of Bank 1 is higher, it implies that the depositor's money is safer in Bank1 as compared to Bank 2. Hence, *higher the capital to risk weighted asset ratio (CRAR), higher is the safety of bank deposits.*

Even without calculating the CRAR ratio, we can compare the safety of depositor's money in Bank1 and Bank 2. If we just look at the two bank's balance sheet then we can see that if the personal loan in both the banks become NPA then in case of Bank1 there are other assets from which the depositor's money can be returned but in case of Bank 2 the depositors will not be able to get their full money back.

To make banks safer, banks should have higher CRAR and to increase the CRAR the capital of the banks must be increased. **Capital is a combination of equity, equity-like instruments and bonds.** As per the international (Basel III) norms, the minimum capital required is 10.5% which includes 2.5% capital conservation buffer (which is nothing but just additional capital). In India RBI has kept Capital Adequacy Requirement of 11.5% (including 2.5% capital conservation buffer).

Tier 1 Capital (*Equity and Equity like capital*)	= 7%
Tier 2 Capital (*Bonds*)	= 2%
Capital Conservation Buffer (*Equity capital*)	= 2.5%
Minimum Total capital requirement	= 11.5%

Scheduled Commercial Banks have achieved the minimum Basel III capital requirement.

The higher the capital is above the regulatory minimum, the greater the freedom banks have to make loans. The closer bank capital is to the minimum, the less inclined banks are to lend. If capital falls below the regulatory minimum, banks cannot lend or face restrictions on lending. When loans go bad and turn into non-performing assets (NPAs) banks have to make provisions for potential losses *(i.e., banks are required to keep certain funds in reserve which they can't lend and is called provisioning against NPAs)*. This tends to erode bank capital and put brakes on loan growth. That is why Central Govt. **recapitalised PSBs** so as to infuse funds to increase the capital adequacy ratio.

Government recapitalized of PSBs in the following two ways:

- First it is putting capital into the PSBs from budgetary resources.
- Second is through **recapitalization bonds** in which Govt. issues bonds to PSBs and gets cash from the PSBs and then this cash Govt. again puts into the PSBs as equity capital *(a technical process)*.

2.20 Unified Lending Interface (ULI)

Developed by Reserve Bank Innovation Hub, a wholly owned subsidiary of RBI. ULI is a platform that facilitates the seamless flow of a customer's digitized financial and non-financial data from multiple data service providers to lenders, making credit appraisal seamless and frictionless for a diverse range of borrowers. This platform facilitates seamless and consent-based flow of digital information, including even land records of various States. This will also bring down the time taken for credit appraisal, especially for smaller and rural borrowers without any credit history. The ULI architecture has common and standardised Application Programming Interfaces (APIs) designed for a 'plug and play' approach to ensure digital access to information from diverse sources. This will reduce the complexity of multiple technical integrations besides enabling borrowers to get the benefit of seamless delivery of credit and quicker turnaround time without requiring extensive and time-consuming documentation.

Example, for a dairy farmer seeking a loan, the lender (bank/NBFC) can find data from the milk cooperative to know about cash flows; land ownership status from land records of States; and insights into his financial condition through farming patterns. So, what was once a blind spot for the lender would turn into a visible customer to do business with. With the help of ULI, the lenders can immediately know the income of the loan applicant and credit eligibility. Thus, decision making would be automated and loans could be sanctioned and disbursed within minutes.

2.21 Prompt Corrective Action (PCA)

RBI, under its supervisory framework, uses various measures/tools to maintain sound financial health of banks. Under Prompt Corrective Action (PCA) framework, RBI has specified certain regulatory trigger points in terms of three parameters, i.e., **capital** (Capital Adequacy Ratio), **Asset Quality** (NPA) and **Leverage** (equity capital/total assets). Once banks hit certain level of threshold in terms of these three parameters, RBI initiates certain structured and discretionary actions.

Once RBI puts a bank under PCA framework then RBI can take the following actions:

- RBI can put restrictions on branch expansion, distributing dividends, capping compensation and fees of management and directors.
- In extreme cases, banks may be stopped from lending and there can be a cap on lending to specific sectors/entities.
- May increase the provisioning requirement for banks
- Further, RBI may take steps to bring in new management/Board, appoint consultants for business/organizational structuring, take steps to change ownership, can also take steps to merge the bank and can supersede the bank board.

Under PCA framework, RBI's objective is to facilitate the banks to take corrective measures including those prescribed by the RBI, in a timely manner, in order to restore their financial health. The framework also provides an opportunity to the RBI to pay focused attention on such banks by engaging with the management more closely in those areas. The PCA framework is, thus, intended to encourage banks to eschew certain riskier activities and focus on conserving capital so that their balance sheets can become stronger. The RBI has clarified that the PCA framework is not intended to constrain normal operations of the banks for the general public like lending and depositing.

This PCA framework is applicable to scheduled commercial banks excluding Regional Rural Banks, Payment Banks and Small Finance Banks.

Since a lot of urban-cooperative banks (UCBs) were also facing issues, RBI has brought in PCA framework for all UCBs also. The three parameters based on which the PCA framework will be invoked are:

1. Capital Adequacy Ratio (CAR)
2. NPA level
3. Two consecutive years loss

Once the UCBs above three parameters deteriorate beyond a certain level then RBI will take supervisory actions which may be related to Governance / Strategy / Business or even cancellation of banking license too.

RBI has brought in PCA for Non-Banking Finance Companies (NBFC) also.

2.22 Systemically Important Financial Institutions

Few **Financial Institutions** (Banks and NBFCs) assume systemic importance due to their size, cross-jurisdictional activities, complexity, lack of substitutability and interconnectedness. The disorderly failure of these financial institutions has the propensity to cause significant disruption to the essential services provided by these institutions, and in turn, to the overall economic activity.

These financial institutions are considered Systemically Important **Banks** (SIBs) or Systemically Important **NBFCs** as their continued functioning is critical for the uninterrupted availability of financial services to the real economy. They are also called "**Too Big to Fail**" which means they are so big/important that the Government/economy can't afford their failure.

Such a perception and the expectation of government support (sometimes govt. come to the rescue as they don't want these institutions to fail because of their importance) may increase risk taking, reduce market discipline, create competitive distortions and increase the possibility of distress in futures. **These institutions are also subjected to additional regulatory/supervisory measures like capital requirements**.

Banks are regulated by RBI and NBFCs are regulated by RBI/SEBI/IRDA. So, all these regulatory bodies declare Systemically Important Institutions.

- RBI declares those banks which has asset size of more than 2% of GDP as Domestically Systemically Important Banks. It declares the list of DSIB annually and right now SBI, HDFC & ICICI are classified as DSIB.
- Similarly, RBI also declares Domestic Systemically Important NBFCs if their asset size is more than Rs. 500 crores.
- Similarly, IRDAI also declares Domestic Systemically Important Insurers (D-SII) based on value of assets under management and premium underwritten (received). For 2020-21, IRDAI has declared LIC/GIC/NIAC as D-SII.
- Similarly, SEBI also declares Domestically Systemically Important Financial Market Infrastructure (FMI) like commodity exchanges MCX/NCDEX.

2.23 Foreign Investment

- Foreign Investment means any investment made by a 'person' resident outside India in '**capital instruments**' of an Indian company. Person means foreign individuals, NRIs, companies etc.
- 'Capital Instruments' means **equity shares**, **debentures** (fully, compulsorily and mandatorily convertible debentures), **preference shares** (fully, compulsorily and mandatorily convertible preference shares) and **share warrants** issued by the Indian company.
    - Equity shares: Equity shares represent ownership of the company and voting rights.
    - Preference shares (fully, compulsorily and mandatorily convertible preference shares): They have preferential rights over dividend and to repayment of the capital in the case of a winding-up of the company. They must be converted into (common) equity shares after some time.
    - Debentures (fully, compulsorily and mandatorily convertible debentures): They are like bonds but must be converted into equity shares after some time.
    - Share Warrants: Share warrant is a document issued by the company to the investor that gives the warrant holder (investor) a right to subscribe to equity shares of the company at a predetermined

price on or after a pre-determined time period. The warrant holder is given a right but not an obligation to subscribe equity shares. If the warrant holder does not exercise his option to subscribe to equity shares, then the initial amount (some percent of the total amount paid by the warrant holder to purchase the warrant) paid stands forfeited.

- Foreign investment can be broadly classified into two ways:

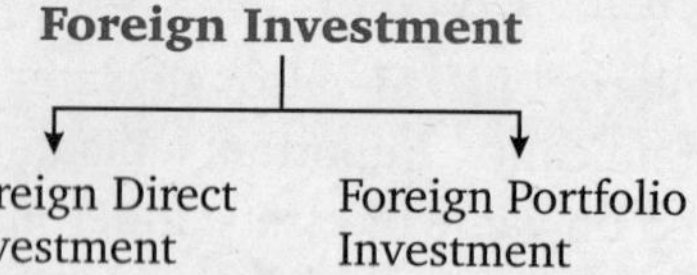

- Foreign Direct Investment (FDI) is the investment through '**capital instruments**' by a person resident outside India:
  - In an unlisted Indian company; or
  - In 10 percent or more of the equity capital of a listed Indian company.
- Foreign Portfolio Investment (FPI) is any investment made by a person resident outside India in '**capital instruments**' where such investment is less than 10 percent of the equity capital of a listed Indian company.
- Foreign Portfolio Investors (FPIs) can also invest in Central and State Government securities/bonds and corporate bonds and are treated as debt.
- Foreign Direct Investment can come through two routes viz. automatic and government approval route. More than 95% of the FDI comes in India through the "Automatic Route" where no government approval is required and are subject to only sectoral laws. Certain sectors that are still under "Government approval route" are scrutinised and cleared by the respective departments and ministries.
- In respect of applications in which there is a doubt about the Administrative Ministry/ Department concerned, DPIIT shall identify the Administrative Ministry/Department where the application will be processed. In respect of proposals where the respective department/ ministry proposes to reject the proposals or in cases where conditions for approval are stipulated in addition to the conditions laid down in the FDI policy or sectoral laws/regulations, concurrence of DPIIT shall compulsorily be sought by the said Ministry. The Department for Promotion of Industry and Internal Trade (DPIIT), Ministry of Commerce and Industry sets the rules for foreign investment and makes policy pronouncements on FDI through various Press Releases.
- As per the regulations under Foreign Exchange Management Act (FEMA) 1999, an Indian company receiving FDI/FPI does not require any prior approval of RBI at any stage. It is only required to report the capital inflow and subsequently the issue of shares to the RBI in prescribed formats. FPIs require SEBI approval/license.
- Foreign Portfolio Investors (FPIs) are institutions incorporated outside India and include mutual fund, insurance company, pension fund, banks, NRIs etc. registered with SEBI.
- A single foreign portfolio investor can invest maximum up to 10% in an Indian company and all FPIs on aggregate basis can maximum invest up to the sectoral cap/ statutory ceiling as applicable for that sector under foreign investment. Government now specifies composite cap/ ceiling for foreign investors (rather than separate limits for FDI and FPI) in various sectors under which all kinds of foreign investments are allowed.

- An investor may be allowed to invest below the 10 percent threshold and this can be treated as FDI subject to the condition that the FDI stake is raised to 10 percent or beyond within one year from the date of the first purchase. The obligation to do so will fall on the company. If the stake is not raised to 10% or above, then the investment shall be treated as portfolio investment.
- In case an existing FDI falls to a level below 10 percent, it can continue to be treated as FDI, without an obligation to restore it to 10% or more. **Once an FDI always an FDI.**
- In a particular company, an investor can hold the investments either under the FPI route or under the FDI route, but not both.
- We have already provided above the definition of FDI and FPI very clearly but there are some other general differences between FDI and FPI that are mentioned below:

Foreign Direct Investment (FDI)	Foreign Portfolio Investment (FPI)
It happens generally through off-market transaction or primary market.	Generally, through secondary market but can happen through primary market as well.
Generally new shares are issued and the capital comes to the company through which the company invests in new factory, machines etc.	Generally, only the owners change hands and new capital does not come to the company.
The foreign investor appoints Board of Directors and get involved in the decision making (active management) of the company by purchase of large shareholdings.	Foreign investors generally do not get involved in the management of the company and purchase minority stakes.
Foreign investors try to make the company profitable through their decision making and target the profit of the company.	Foreign investors target the share price of the company and derive their gain from change of share prices.
FDI investors look for higher nominal growth in the economy. This is because share prices follow nominal growth trend.	FPI debt investors look for higher interest rate and FPI equity investors look for higher nominal growth in the economy.
It is sector specific. For example, a steel company in US will invest only in a steel company in India and try to make that company profitable through their management and get a share of the profit.	It is in general capital market. For example, a foreign investor is not particular about any sector and is willing to invest in any sector/ company which gives a chance of share price appreciation.
It is a long-term investment as to turn the company profitable, the foreign investor needs to get invested for a long time.	It is generally short-term investment.
Generally, there is a lock in period and during this period the foreign investor cannot sell his investment and hence it is quite stable.	There is no lock in period and the foreign investor can return any time by selling his investment. It results in exchange rate volatility.
It can happen in three ways viz. by purchase of shares, by forming a Joint Venture company or by establishing a subsidiary company.	It happens through purchase of shares.

Overseas Direct Investment (ODI)

An Indian company investing (any percentage of shares) in an unlisted foreign entity or investing 10% or more in a foreign listed entity or investing less than 10% but having management control is considered as ODI. ODI is opposite of FDI.

Overseas Portfolio Investment (OPI)

Investment other than ODI in a foreign entity is called OPI. It is the opposite of FPI.

Current Facts Regarding FDI

- Gross FDI flow in India was around $80.6 billion in 2024-25.
- Top 3 countries from which India got the maximum FDI inflow are Singapore (30%) Mauritius (17%), and United States (11%).
- Top 3 States receiving highest FDI Equity Inflow during FY 2024-25 are Maharashtra (39%), Karnataka (13%), an Delhi (12%).
- Top 3 sectors receiving highest FDI Inflow during FY 2024-25 are Services Sector (Finance, Banking, Insurance etc.), Computer Software & Hardware.

The following are few other ways which are used to raise finance from abroad:

❖ **Global Depository Receipt (GDR)/ American Depository Receipt (ADR):**

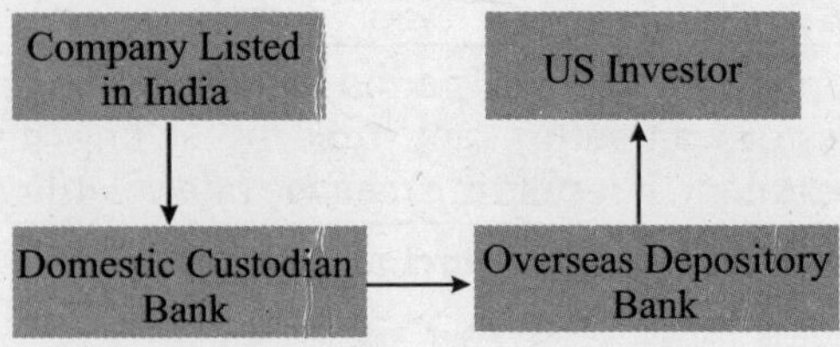

- Through ADRs, US investors buy shares of companies based outside US (i.e. India).
- ADRs exist because many companies (outside US) do not want to bother with the expense and hassle of directly listing their shares on US stock exchanges.
- An ADR is a share (security) issued by the Overseas Depository Bank to the US investor. It represents one or more shares of Indian company held by the Overseas Depository Bank with the Domestic Custodian Bank.
- It may be possible that for every 10 shares held, one ADR is created by the Overseas Depository Bank and accordingly prices will get adjusted. These ADRs will be listed and traded in US.
- The company in India can be either a government company or a private company.

Debt Instruments

❖ **External Commercial Borrowing (ECB):** ECBs are commercial **loans/ debt** raised by 'resident' entities from 'non-resident' entities. It can be in foreign currency or Indian rupee denominated. ECBs include bank loans, bonds, debentures, preference shares (other than fully and compulsorily convertible instruments), trade credits, Foreign Currency Convertible Bonds (FCCB), Financial Lease.

Masala Bonds are a kind of ECB where the bonds are issued outside India but denominated in Indian Rupees, rather than the local currency. Masala is an Indian word and it means spices. Unlike dollar bonds, where the borrower takes the currency risk, Masala bond makes the investors bear the currency risk.

ECB	MASALA Bonds
$1 = Rs. 70 (2019)	
$1 Bond was issued to foreign investor and the borrower (Indian company) got $1 for one year. Money is raised in foreign currency and the borrower issued Dollar denominated bond to the foreign investor.	Rs. 70 Bond was issued to foreign investor and the borrower (Indian company) got $1(Dollar equivalent of Rs. 70 is $1) for one year. (Since, the Indian rupee has limited convertibility, so money is raised in dollar only). Money is raised in foreign currency but the borrower issued Rupee denominated bond to the foreign investor.
$1= Rs. 80(2020)	
In 2020, the borrower needs to return $1 to the foreign investor and for that he will have to spend Rs. 80 to get $1. The conversion/exchange risk is of the borrower (Indian company).	In 2020, the borrower needs to return dollar equivalent of Rs. 70 (Rs.70/Rs.80* $1 = $0.875) to the foreign investor rather than $1. So, basically the conversion/exchange risk is borne by the foreign investor.

ECB falls under two routes: Automatic Route and Approval Route. Under 'Automatic Route' no approval is required. RBI has set up an Empowered Committee to consider proposals coming under the 'Approval Route'.

2.24 Currency Swap and Forex Swap

Currency Swap Agreement between Two Countries

The currency swap agreement between two countries is entered between the Central Banks of the two countries. One country exchanges its national currency for that of another or even a third one. Let us understand this with example.

India and Japan signed currency swap agreement in 2018 worth $ 75 billion. As per the arrangement India can/will get Yen (or dollars) from Japan worth max $ 75 billion and Japan will get equivalent Indian Rupees as per the market exchange rate at the time of transaction. The exchange will be reversed after an agreed period using the same exchange rate as per in the first transaction.

Whatever amount of dollars India will take from Japan, India will have to pay interest on that amount and whatever Rupee Japan will take from India, Japan will have to pay interest on that (depending on some benchmark rate). So, a bilateral currency swap is a kind of **open-ended credit line** from one country to another at a fixed exchange rate. So, India got dollars from Japan and Japan may or may not take Rupees from India. As India would be paying interest on the dollars taken from Japan, so it does not matter whether Japan took rupees from India or not. And that is why this currency swap is also called **open-ended credit line facility**.

This currency swap arrangement will allow the Indian central bank to draw up to $75 billion worth of yen or dollars **as a loan** from the Japanese government whenever it needs this money. The RBI can either sell these dollars (or yen) to importers to settle their bills or to borrowers to pay off their foreign loans. The RBI can just keep these dollars with itself also to shore up its own foreign exchange reserves and defend the rupee.

Actually, the rupee was falling against the dollar because of its widening current account deficit. This led to importers upping their demand for dollars far beyond what exporters bring into the country leading to further depreciation of rupee. If RBI would have gone to the market to purchase these dollars (by selling rupees) then it would have further depreciated the rupee. So, currency swap is a kind **of out of market transaction**.

Even if RBI has amassed dollars, having a $75-billion loan-on-demand (as and when need arises) from Japan gives the RBI an additional buffer to fall back on, should it need extra dollars. Hence, this currency swap agreement **will bring in greater stability to foreign exchange and capital markets in India**.

These swap operations carry **no exchange rate or other market risks, as transaction terms are set in advance**. The absence of an exchange rate risk is the major benefit of such a facility. This facility provides the country, which is getting the dollars, with the flexibility to use these reserves at any time in order to maintain an appropriate level of balance of payments or short-term liquidity.

In July 2020, India and Sri Lanka signed a currency swap agreement worth $ 400 million in which India will give dollars to Sri Lanka and in return India will get 'Sri Lankan Rupee'. The RBI also offers similar swap lines to central banks in the SAARC region within a total corpus of $2 billion. Under the framework for 2019-22, the RBI will continue to offer a swap arrangement within the overall corpus of $2 billion.

Forex Swap Agreement

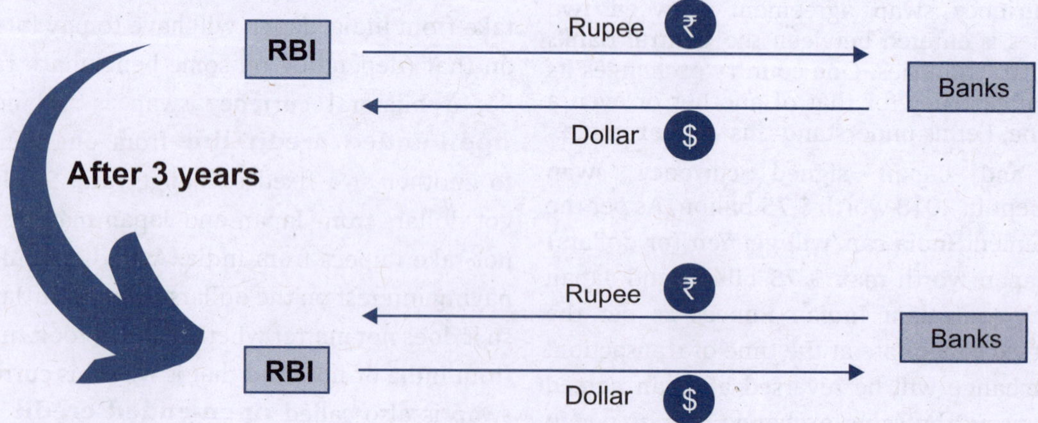

Under forex swap, RBI will buy dollars (say $ 1 billion) from Bank and give them Indian rupees Rs. 70 billion (at the rate $1 = Rs. 70). After the swap period is over (3 years), RBI will give back the $1 billion and will ask rupees from banks. The bank which will promise to pay **maximum premium above Rs. 70** will be selected by RBI for the swap deal. For example, Bank A said Rs 0.50 per dollar, Bank B said Rs 0.40 per dollar and Bank C said Rs 0.75 per dollar then, Bank C will be selected to do the swap agreement and Bank C will have to offer Rs. 70.75 billion (Rs. 70.75/ dollar) after 3 years to RBI.

RBI in March 2019, did forex swap to increase (rupee) liquidity/money supply in the economy because RBI had already exhausted much of the open market operation limit. And RBI was not willing to further buy the government securities to inject money in the economy. This swap deal leads to better transmission into the lending rate also.

It can be the other way around also like RBI selling dollars first and then purchasing later.

Alternative Investment Funds (AIF)

AIF means any fund established in India which is a privately pooled investment vehicle which collects funds from sophisticated investors, whether Indian or foreign, for investing it in accordance with a defined investment policy for the benefit of its investors. Generally, institutions and HNIs invest in AIFs as substantial investments are required.

An AIF is a special investment category that doesn't fall into the conventional investment categories like stocks, bonds and mutual funds.

AIFs include Angel Funds, Venture Capital Funds, SME Funds, Social Venture Funds, Infrastructure Funds, Real Estate Funds, Private Equity Funds, Debt Funds, Hedge Funds, Derivatives etc.

These investment vehicles adhere to the SEBI (Alternative Investment Funds) Regulations, 2012. AIFs can be formed as a company, Limited Liability Partnership (LLP), trust, etc.

2.25 Balance of Payment (BoP)

BoP systematically summarizes the economic transactions of a country (individuals, businesses, Governments) with the rest of the world for a given period of time specifically for a financial year. BoP is transaction between residents of a country with the rest of the world. So, BoP of India will record all transactions which happen between the Indian residents (individuals, companies, governments etc.) and non-residents/ foreigners/ foreign entities. RBI is responsible for preparing BoP and it shall be consistent with the BoP manual of International Monetary Fund (IMF).

(Money flowing in the country is taken as + and money going out of the country is taken as negative). For example, when India exports something it earns foreign currency and is taken as positive in BoP record and when India imports something, we need to pay in foreign currency and money goes out of the country and is taken as negative.

BoP has two main components viz. current account and capital account.

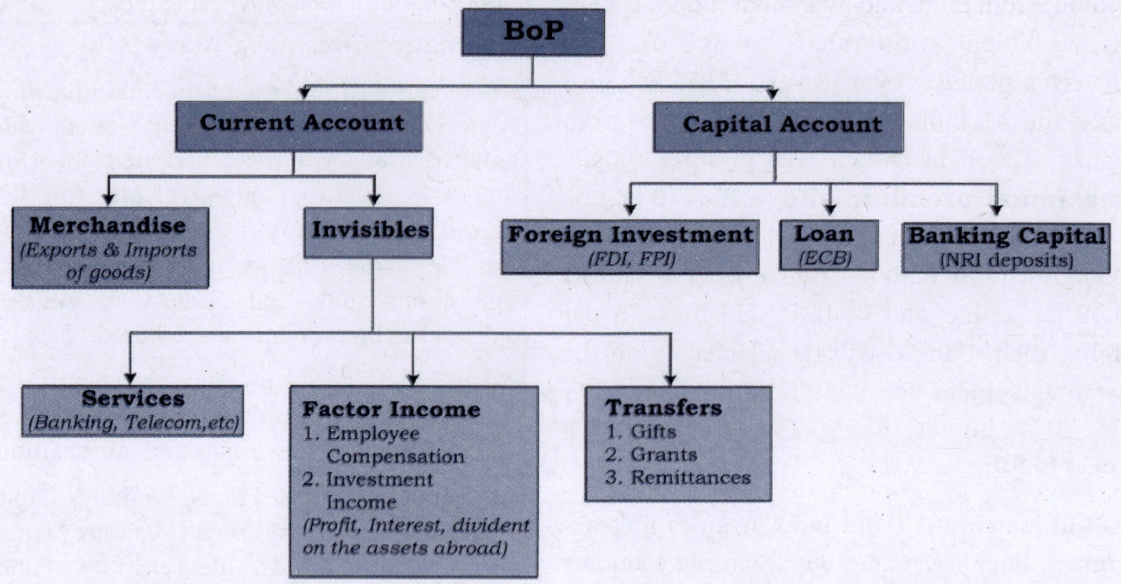

Current Account: Current account deals in those transactions which do not alter Indian residents' assets or liabilities, including contingent liabilities, outside India and foreign resident's assets or liabilities inside India. Current account comprises of visible trade (export and import of goods), invisible trade (export and import of services), unilateral transfers and investment income (income earned from factors of production such as land, foreign shares, loans etc.).

Capital Account: This account is a record of the inflows and outflows of capital that directly affect a country's foreign assets and liabilities. Capital account transactions are those transactions which alter Indian residents' assets or liabilities, including contingent liabilities, outside India and foreign resident's assets or liabilities inside India. It comprises of foreign investments like FDI and FPI, Loans by companies and governments and banking capital such as NRI deposits.

Explanation: When a person is purchasing shares abroad, it comes under capital account as it is a change in assets. But when the person will receive dividend from the shares then it comes under current account as it is not changing the assets. In the same way when we are taking loan from an international agency then it comes under capital and financial account as it is creating liability. But when we are paying interest on this loan then it comes under current account as interest payment is not reducing previous liabilities. Similarly, if we are receiving gifts or grants or remittances then it is not creating any obligation or liability for future and hence will come under current account.

Let us consider an example to understand BoP in a better way:

As on 31.03.22 Forex	01.04.2022 – 31.03.2023	As on 31.03.23 Forex
$ 650 Billion	1. Current A/c balance = $ – 100 billion 2. Capital A/c balance = $ + 150 billion Balance of Payment = $ + 50 billion Increase in Reserves = $ 50 billion	$ 700 Billion

Assume that on 31st March 2022, RBI was having foreign exchange reserve (Forex) of $ 650 billion. Suppose, in the FY 2022-23, there was deficit in current account balance of $ 100 billion and a surplus in capital account balance of $ 150 billion. So, the overall balance of payment will be + $ 50 billion in the FY 2022-23. Since we have earned net foreign exchange worth $ 50 billion in the FY 2022-23, so our foreign exchange reserves will increase at the end of the financial year to $ 700 billion.

Current A/c + Capital A/c = Overall balance of payment = Change in Forex Reserves

The balance of payment surplus or deficit is obtained after adding the current account and capital account balance which is then added or subtracted from the forex reserves.

Actually, there may be some changes in the Forex reserves because of valuation effect i.e., appreciation/depreciation of the US Dollar and the change in price of the gold. This also has an impact on the Forex reserves in addition to Current A/C and Capital A/c transactions.

[*Recently RBI has brought in new format (as per the guidelines of IMF) for Balance of Payment under which Capital Account has been redefined as 'Capital and financial Account' with a distinction between Capital Account Transactions and Financial Account Transactions. FDI, FPI, Forex Reserves etc. have been made a part of the Financial A/c Transactions. As such, I don't think that we need to go into those minute details of the new format*].

Whether our forex reserves are adequacy or not may depend on:

1. **Import Cover:** Presently India's Forex reserves are around $720 billion and our monthly imports are around $80 billion, which means that if we do not earn additional Forex then this $720 billion will be sufficient for the next 9 months of import. Thus, we say that our present Forex reserves provide import cover for 9 months. Forex reserves are also measured in terms of import cover.

2. **Net International Investment Position (NIIP):** NIIP measures the difference between our Residents (includes individual, companies, Government) stock of foreign assets and foreigner's (non-residents) stock of our nation's asset.

   Our nations stock of foreign assets includes Overseas Direct Investment (ODI), Forex Reserves; and foreigner's stock of our nation's asset includes FDI, FPI, ADR/GDR, ECB etc.

   NIIP position as on end June 2025 was -$300 billion which is equivalent to around 8% of GDP. This means that on a net basis there is a claim of $300 billion on India of non-residents.

Remittances

Balance of Payment (BoP) records all transactions which happen between **'Indian Residents'** and **'Foreigners or Non-Resident Indians (NRI)'**. NRI (in context of BoP) means a person who has gone abroad for more than one year and has plans to stay abroad. Now, when a person goes to Gulf region generally for more than one year he becomes an NRI and then whatever he (NRI) sends money to his family here in India is counted in BoP. Now, try to understand that this transaction between the 'NRI' and 'his family in India' will get recorded in BoP as this transaction is between 'Indian Resident (his family in India)' and 'NRI'. And this transaction between **'Indian Resident** (his family in India)' and **'NRI'** is for **free** which means the 'Indian Resident (his family in India)' did not do anything for the 'NRI' but 'NRI' gave money to 'Indian Resident (his family in India)' for **free**. This is called Remittance under BoP in Current Account. But whatever the 'employer' pays to the 'NRI' person will not be counted in BoP because both are Foreigners/NRIs.

Another case:

If I have gone to US for two months (that means I am still Indian Resident) and if I earn something there and then send to my family in India then the transaction between **"Me (in US)"** and **"my family in India"** will not be recorded in BoP because both the parties in the transaction "Me (in US)" and "my family in India" are Indian residents. BUT whichever company (say X) paid me in US that transaction will be recorded in India's BoP. This is because the transaction is between **"Me (in US)** [an Indian Resident]" and **"Company X** [Foreigner]". And this transaction is not for free, as I worked and then the company X paid to me. So, this is called **'Factor Income'** under BoP (Current Account).

India is the largest recipient of remittances (private transfers) in the world and last year in 2022 it received around $100 billion in remittances. The largest sources of remittances for India comes from Gulf Cooperation Council (GCC) Countries and the US, UK. Kerala is one of the largest recipients of remittances in India. The top five recipient countries are India, Mexico, China, Philippines and Egypt.

Current Account Convertibility

- RBI allows full conversion of Rupee into foreign currencies and foreign currencies into Rupee (at market price i.e., Nominal Exchange Rate) for any transactions under current account of BoP. This is called *"rupee is fully convertible at current account"*.
- So, suppose someone wants to import commodities worth $10 billion in India then RBI will convert that many Rupees into $10 billion without any restriction for import purpose. As a part of the economic reforms initiated in 1991 rupee was made fully convertible at current account in 1993.

Capital Account Convertibility:

- RBI does not allow full conversion of Rupee into foreign currencies and foreign currencies into Rupee for transactions falling under capital account of BoP. There are restrictions/limits imposed by the RBI and government on the value of transactions that anybody can do under capital account. This is called *"rupee is partially convertible at capital account"*.
- There are restrictions on how much ECB can be raised in a particular year, there are restrictions on how much foreign investors can invest in Government securities, there are restriction on how much individuals/companies can do capital account kind of transactions etc.
- Capital account convertibility leads to free exchange of currency at market rates and an unrestricted mobility of capital. It is beneficial for a country because it increases inflow of foreign investment. But the flip side is that it

could destabilize an economy due to massive capital flows in and out of the country.

- Rupee will move to full capital account convertibility once the macroeconomic parameters like current account deficit, fiscal deficit, external debt, inflation become stable at low range and there is resilience to absorb shocks related to capital outflows.
- Since capital convertibility is risky and makes foreign exchange rate more volatile, it is introduced only sometime after the introduction of convertibility on current account when exchange rate of currency of a country is relatively stable, deficit in balance of payments is well under control and enough foreign exchange reserves are available with the Central Bank.
- Moving in the direction of allowing full capital account convertibility, in March 2020 RBI introduced 'Fully Accessible Route (FAR)' under which it removed the cap/ceiling and allowed full non-resident (foreign) investors investments in Government securities. There is a plan to remove the limit on corporate debt too.

There is no international authority which directs that trade between two countries should happen only with some specific currencies. Any two countries are free to transact with any currency if they are willing.

Generally, any country will accept that currency for its trade (exports), if that currency is not losing value (less inflation) and it is stable and it is freely convertible in other currencies.

Internationalization of Rupee

- An international currency is one that is freely available to non-residents, essentially to settle cross-border transactions. It is a process that involves increasing use of the local (rupee) currency in cross-border transactions i.e., international markets.
- In this process first current account transactions are allowed and then capital account transactions between resident Indians and non-Resident Indians. The last step is use of rupee for transactions between non-residents.
- Internationalization of a currency is an expression of external credibility in the currency as well as in the economy.
- All truly international currencies belong to large, advanced economies. And their use for international transactions confers substantial economic privileges to the host countries. The privileges/advantages include:
  - Immunity from BoP crises as the country can pay for its external deficits with its own currency
  - The dominance of its financial institutions, markets and policies in the global economy
  - Increased bargaining power of domestic business adding weight to the economy and enhancing the country's global stature and respect
  - Protection for its businesses from currency risk
  - Seigniorage that accrues to it
  - Reduces the need for holding foreign exchange reserves
  - Reducing dependence on foreign currency which makes the country less vulnerable to external shocks.
- All of the above privileges flow from its status as the preeminent reserve currency.
- Clearly, very few countries can enjoy such privileges at any given point of time in history. And the preconditions - size of the economy and a dominant share of global GDP, globally dominant businesses, extraordinary military capabilities etc. limit the prospects of owning an international currency to any but the largest few economies.

- The preconditions for owning an international currency are - size of the economy and a dominant share of global GDP, globally dominant businesses, extraordinary military capabilities etc. And these preconditions limit the prospects of owning an international currency to only few largest economies.
- Hence internationalization of rupee cannot just be achieved by financial regulation alone.

Liberalized Remittance Scheme (LRS)

- Under LRS, all resident individuals (in India) can freely (without seeking specific approvals) remit/ send $250,000 overseas every financial year for a permissible set of current or capital account transactions. Remittances are permitted for overseas education, travel, medical treatment and purchase of shares and property, apart from maintenance of relatives living abroad, gifting and donations. Individuals can also open, maintain and hold foreign currency accounts with overseas banks for carrying out transactions.
- The LRS represents India's baby steps towards dismantling controls on foreign exchange movements in and out of the country. It has allowed large numbers of Indians to study abroad and diversify their portfolios from purely desi stocks and property.
- Ideally speaking, capital controls in any form have no place in a liberalized economy. But for India, which is heavily dependent on imports of critical goods and perpetually spends more foreign exchange than it earns, it is difficult to free up remittances because of the havoc this can wreak on exchange rates.
- The LRS gives you the freedom to put your money to work anywhere in the world. Until India is ready to free all capital controls, the LRS remains the most viable way for individuals to legally remit money overseas.

2.26 GIFT (Gujarat International Financial Tech) City

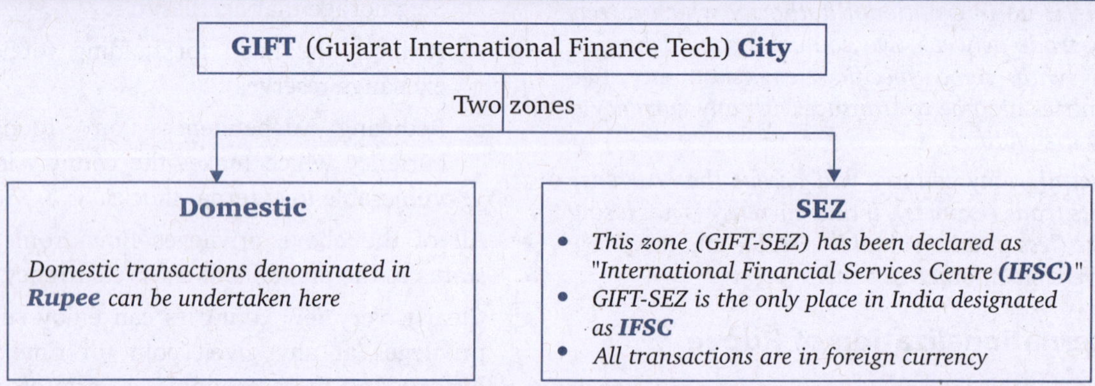

- GIFT City has two zones, one is "Domestic" and the other is "SEZ".
- GIFT SEZ is India's first International Financial Services Centre (IFSC) set up under Special Economic Zones Act, 2005.
- An **IFSC** is a jurisdiction that provides financial services to non-residents and residents, to the extent permissible under the current regulations, in any currency except Indian Rupee.

- Units (entities) related to Banking, Insurance and Capital Markets are considered as IFSC units and hence Banks, Insurers and Capital Market related companies can set up their units in the IFSC (GIFT-SEZ).
- The IFSC in GIFT-City seeks to bring to the Indian shores, those financial services transactions that are currently carried outside India by overseas financial institutions and overseas branches/subsidiaries of Indian financial institutions to a centre which has been designated for all practical purposes as a location having the same eco system as their present offshore location (like London, Singapore etc.), which is physically on Indian soil.
- IFSC (GIFT-SEZ) is the only place in India which allows offshore transactions (i.e., it is treated as outside India transactions)
- IFSC is deemed to be a foreign territory and entities approved as IFSC unit are treated as non-resident in India. Therefore, RBI ODI (Overseas Direct Investment, which means investments outside India) Rules are applicable on investments in IFSC. Accordingly, Indian parties are allowed under Automatic route to make investment in IFSC entities and that shall be treated as **ODI**.
- Individual person resident in India is allowed to invest up to USD 2, 50,000 per financial year under Liberalized Remittance Scheme (LRS) outside India or in **IFSC.**
- Bombay Stock Exchange (BSE) has established its subsidiary in IFSC called India International Exchange **(India-INX)** and National Stock Exchange has established NSE International Exchange (**NSE-IX**) where any **foreign company** or **Indian company** can list its securities (shares/bonds/derivatives). For example, a US based company can list its shares on India INX (various tax incentives are given like no STT, not LTCG, MAT just 9%) and the securities can be purchased by anyone from **outside India or from India** through ODI route up to a limit.

International Financial Services Centres Authority (IFSCA)

- The International Financial Services Centres Authority (IFSCA) was established in April, 2020 under the International Financial Services Centres Authority Act, 2019. It is headquartered at GIFT City, Gandhinagar in Gujarat.
- IFSCA is a unified authority for the development and regulation of financial products, financial services and financial institutions in the International Financial Services Centre(s) (IFSC) in India. Prior to the establishment of IFSCA, the domestic financial regulators, namely, RBI, SEBI, PFRDA and IRDAI regulated the business in IFSC.
- As the dynamic nature of business in the IFSCs requires a high degree of inter-regulatory coordination within the financial sector, the IFSCA has been established as a unified regulator with a holistic vision in order to promote ease of doing business in IFSC and provide world class regulatory environment.
- The main objective of the IFSCA is to develop a strong global connect and focus on the needs of the Indian economy as well as to serve as an international financial platform for the entire region and the global economy as a whole.

2.27 Liquidity Trap

Nominal Interest Rate (Deposit Rate) = Inflation + Real Interest Rate

Nominal interest rate is the interest rate offered by banks on your deposits. People will be willing to keep money in bank deposits only if banks are offering interest rate higher than the inflation rate prevailing in the economy. Suppose inflation in the economy is 6% then nobody will keep money in bank deposits at less than 6% interest rate. Because at this rate effective earning for the individual will be either zero ore negative. Until and unless banks offer higher deposit rates than the inflation rate, nobody will keep money in banks. This rate in addition to the inflation is called real interest rate as it is the real or effective earning for depositors.

For example, if inflation rate is 6% in the economy and banks are offering 8% on their deposits, this implies real interest rate of 2%. That means, effectively the earning or return for the depositors is 2%.Consider an example:

Nominal Interest Rate (Deposit Rate)	= Inflation	+	Real Interest Rate
8%	= 6%	+	2%
6%	= 4%	+	2%
4%	= 2%	+	2%
2%	= 0%	+	2%
0%	= –2%	+	2%

Suppose the economy is in recession/slowdown and the inflation/prices are falling as shown above. To pull the economy out of recession i.e. to stimulate the economy, the Central Bank may reduce the repo rate to increase the supply of money and to push demand. When the repo rate is reduced, the banks will reduce the deposit rates and lending rate. But if the demand in the economy is not increasing, then Central Bank may further reduce the repo rate to increase the money supply and demand. But if still the economy is not pulled out of recession/slowdown and the demand is not increasing, then Central Bank may keep on reducing the repo rate and the banks will keep on reducing their deposit and l ending rates. The Central Bank will keep on reducing the repo rate till the repo rate (almost) touches zero. At this point, the banks deposit rate and lending rate will also reach almost zero. The Central Bank cannot reduce the repo rate beyond zero and similarly banks also cannot reduce their deposit and lending rate beyond zero *(practically the lower limit on repo rate, lending rate or deposit rates are zero)*. The Central Bank cannot stimulate the economy beyond this point and it is trapped in a quagmire called the Liquidity Trap. At this point the government should use its fiscal tools to pull the economy out of recession/slowdown.

In case of liquidity trap, people keep their funds in normal savings account (demand deposits) and do not want to lock their investment in fixed deposits at a very low interest rate. They hope that in future the interest in the market will rise and then they will invest in bonds or fixed deposits.

It is called a 'trap' because if investors hold on to cash (or in demand form) instead of spending or investing it because they expect the economy to be weak, the economy will stay weak. Additionally, it is a 'trap' because the central bank cannot lower the interest below zero to stimulate lending or spending.

2.28 Inflation

The rate at which general level of prices of goods and services rises and subsequently purchasing power falls is called inflation. Depending on the level of severity, it can be classified into three categories.

1. **Low Inflation:** Prices that rise slowly and predictably and the rate is in single digit annually. In case of low inflation, people are willing to save money and put in bank deposits. People are willing to sign long term contracts (linked with inflation index) in money terms because they are confident that the relative prices of goods and services they buy and sell will not get too far out of line.
2. **Galloping Inflation:** Inflation in double digit or triple digit range of 20, 100 or 200 percent per year is called galloping inflation or very high inflation. It is found in countries suffering from weak governments, war or revolution. In this case people will hoard goods, buy houses and never ever lend money at low nominal interest rates. People are not willing to deposit money in banks as banks offer less nominal interest rate (deposit rate) as compared to the inflation rate prevailing in the economy. Businessmen are also not willing to invest as the lending rates are high and demand declines.
3. **Hyper Inflation:** Prices rise over a million percent per year and relative prices become highly unstable. In early 1920's, Germany could not raise taxes and used monetary printing press to pay the government bills. People used to carry money in bags to purchase goods. In USSR in 1991 when prices were freed from the government controls, prices rose by 4,00,000 percent in next five years.

There are mainly two causes of inflation:

1. **Demand Pull Inflation:** Demand-pull inflation occurs when there is an increase in aggregate demand, categorized by the four sectors of the economy: households, private, governments and foreign buyers. When these four sectors concurrently want to purchase more output than the economy can produce, then it leads to increase in prices. This excessive demand, also referred to as "too much money chasing too few goods", usually occurs in an expanding economy. Demand pull inflation may be caused due to over expansion of the money supply, government reducing tax and spending more etc.
2. **Cost Push or Supply Shock Inflation:** Cost-push inflation basically means that prices have been "pushed up" by increase in costs of any of the four factors of production (labour, capital, land or entrepreneurship) or there is a supply shortage which allows the producer to raise prices. Inflation occurs because of increase in cost of inputs rather than because of increase in demand. Cost push inflation may be caused due to wage inflation (overall increase in the cost of goods due to rise in wages), monopoly situation, natural disasters, devaluation of exchange rates (leads to inflation in imported products) etc.

Deflation: A general decline in prices, often caused by a reduction in the supply of money. Deflation can also be caused by a decrease in government, personal or investment spending. The opposite of inflation, deflation is bad because of the following reason:

When prices start falling i.e., there is deflation, people become less willing to spend and postpone their purchase decisions. This is because when prices are falling, just sitting on cash becomes an investment with a positive real yield. This decreases the demand in the economy and prices fall further and economy slows down. People are less willing to borrow also even for a productive investment because it has to be repaid in rupees that are worth more than the rupees borrowed. Deflation thus increases unemployment since there is a lower level of demand in the economy, which may also lead to an economic depression.

Disinflation: Disinflation is the slowing down in the rate of inflation. It means there is inflation in the economy but the inflation percentage is decreasing and is positive. For example, let us consider the prices of onions:

	2013		2014		2015		2016
Prices:	Rs. 10/kg		Rs. 11/kg		Rs. 12/kg		Rs. 12.5/kg
Inflation:		10%		9%		4.2%	

So, in the above example, **prices are rising** but the "**rate of change of prices**" i.e. inflation is decreasing. So, it is a case of disinflation not deflation.

In case of recession (or slowdown), generally demand starts decreasing first (which can be because of any reason) and then companies reduce their production resulting in overall contraction in output and then we say that there is recession. So, in case of economic recession, there should not be high inflation as the **demand reduces first** and then the output/supply reduces.

In exceptional cases, recession (or slowdown) can be triggered by supply side factors like drought or Lockdown (of factories in case of Covid-19), in which case the inflation may be high. But it will be for short span of time as the resulting loss of jobs will lead to reduction in demand and decrease in inflation.

2.29 Phillips Curve

An economic concept developed by A. W. Phillips, which states that inflation and unemployment have a stable and inverse relationship which means that higher the inflation rate in the economy, lower will be the unemployment rate, and vice-versa.

According to the Phillips curve, the lower an economy's rate of unemployment, the more rapidly wages paid to labour increase in that economy and hence higher the inflation in the economy. The theory states that economic growth leads to more jobs (and higher inflation) and less unemployment.

However, the original concept has been somewhat disproven empirically due to the occurrence of **stagflation** in the 1970s, when there were high levels of both inflation and unemployment. The implications of the Phillips curve are true only in the short term.

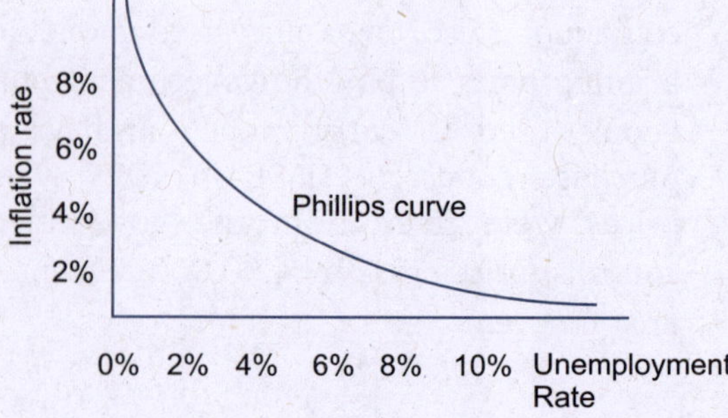

PREVIOUS YEARS' QUESTIONS

Prelim Questions

1. Consider the following actions which the Government can take: **[2011]**

   (i) Devaluing the domestic currency

   (ii) Reduction in the export subsidy

   (iii) Adopting suitable policies which attract greater FDI and more funds from FIIs

   Which of the above action/actions can help in reducing the current account deficit?

   (a) (i) & (ii) (b) (ii) & (iii)

   (c) (iii) only (d) (i) & (iii)

2. Microfinance is the provision of financial services to people of low-income groups. This includes both the consumers and the self-employed. Services rendered under microfinance is/are: **[2011]**

   (i) Credit facilities

   (ii) Savings facilities

   (iii) Insurance facilities

   (iv) Fund transfer facilities

   Select the correct answer using the codes given below the lists:

   (a) (i) only (b) (i) & (iv) only

   (c) (ii) & (iii) only (d) (i), (ii), (iii) & (iv)

3. Economic growth is usually coupled with **[2011]**

   (a) Deflation (b) Inflation

   (c) Stagflation (d) Hyperinflation

4. The balance of payments of a country is a systematic record of **[2013]**

   (a) all import and export transactions of a country during a given period of time, normally a year

   (b) goods exported from a country during a year

   (c) economic transaction between the government of one country to another

   (d) capital movements from one country to another

5. The Reserve Bank of India regulates the commercial banks in matters of **[2013]**

   (i) Liquidity of assets

   (ii) Branch expansion

   (iii) Merger of banks

   (iv) Winding-up of banks

   Select the correct answer using the codes given below.

   (a) (i) & (iv) only

   (b) (ii), (iii) & (iv) only

   (c) (i), (ii) & (iii) only

   (d) (i), (ii), (iii) & (iv)

6. In India, deficit financing is used for raising resources for **[2013]**

   (a) Economic development

   (b) Redemption of public debt

   (c) Adjusting the balance of payments

   (d) Reducing the foreign debt

7. Which of the following constitute Capital Account? **[2013]**

   (i) Foreign Loans

   (ii) Foreign Direct Investment

   (iii) Private Remittances

   (iv) Portfolio Investment

   Select the correct answer using the codes given below.

   (a) (i), (ii) & (iii) (b) (i), (ii) & (iv)

   (c) (ii), (iii) & (iv) (d) (i), (iii) & (iv)

8. Disguised unemployment generally means **[2013]**

(a) Large number of people remain unemployed
(b) Alternative employment is not available
(c) Marginal productivity of labour is zero
(d) Productivity of workers is low

9. Consider the following students: **[2013]**
(i) Inflation benefits the debtors
(ii) Inflation benefits the bondholders
Which of the statements given above are correct?
(a) (i) only (b) (ii) only
(c) Both (i) & (ii) (d) Neither (i) nor (ii)

10. A rise in general level of prices may be caused by **[2013]**
(i) An increase in the money supply
(ii) A decrease in the aggregate level of output
(iii) An increase in the effective demand
Select the correct answer using the codes given below:
(a) (i) only
(b) (i) & (ii) only
(c) (ii) & (iii) only
(d) (i), (ii) & (iii)

11. Which of the following is likely to be the most inflationary in its effect? **[2013]**
(a) Repayment of public debt
(b) Borrowing from the public to finance a budget deficit
(c) Borrowing from banks to finance a budget deficit
(d) Creating new money to finance a budget deficit

12. Supply of money remaining the same when there is an increase in demand for money, there will be **[2013]**
(a) A fall in the level of prices
(b) An increase in the rate of interest
(c) A decrease in the rate of interest
(d) An increase in the level of income and employment

13. With reference to Balance of Payments, which of the following constitutes/constitute the Current Account? **[2014]**
(i) Balance of trade
(ii) Foreign assets
(iii) Balance of invisibles
(iv) Special Drawing Rights
Select the correct answer using the code given below.
(a) (i) only (b) (ii) & (iii) only
(c) (i) & (iii) only (d) (i), (ii) & (iv)

14. What does venture capital mean? **[2014]**
(a) A short-term capital provided to industries
(b) A long-term start-up capital provided to new entrepreneurs
(c) Funds provided to industries at times of incurring losses
(d) Funds provided for replacement and renovation of industries

15. In the context of Indian economy, which of the following is/are the purpose/purposes of "Statutory Reserve Requirements"? **[2014]**
(i) To enable the Central Bank to control the amount of advances the banks can create
(ii) To make the people's deposits with banks safe and liquid
(iii) To prevent the commercial banks from making excessive profits
(iv) To force the banks to have sufficient vault cash to meet their day-to-day requirements
Select the correct answer using the code given below.
(a) (i) only
(b) (i) & (ii) only
(c) (ii) & (iii) only
(d) (i), (ii), (iii) & (iv) only

16. If the interest rate is decreased in an economy, it will **[2014]**

(a) Decrease the consumption expenditure in the economy

(b) Increase the tax collection of the Government

(c) Increase the investment expenditure in the economy

(d) Increase the total savings in the economy

17. With reference to Indian economy, consider the following: **[2015]**

(i) Bank rate

(ii) Open market operations

(iii) Public debt

(iv) Public Revenue

Which of the above is/are component/ components of Monetary Policy?

(a) (i) only (b) (ii), (iii) & (iv) only

(c) (i) & (ii) only (d) (i), (iii) & (iv) only

18. The problem of international liquidity is related to the non-availability of **[2015]**

(a) Goods and services

(b) Gold and silver

(c) Dollars and other hard currencies

(d) Exportable surplus

19. There has been a persistent deficit budget year after year. Which of the following actions can be taken by the Government to reduce the deficit? **[2015]**

(i) Reducing revenue expenditure

(ii) Introducing new welfare schemes

(iii) Rationalizing subsidies

(iv) Expanding industries

Select the correct answer using the code given below.

(a) (i) & (iii) only

(b) (ii) & (iii) only

(c) (i) only

(d) (i), (ii), (iii) & (iv) only

20. When the Reserve Bank of India reduces Statutory Liquidity Ratio by 50 basis points, which of the following is likely to happen? **[2015]**

(a) India's GDP growth rate increases drastically

(b) Foreign Institutional Investors may bring more capital into our country

(c) Scheduled Commercial Banks may cut their lending rates

(d) It may drastically reduce the liquidity to the banking system

21. Convertibility of rupee implies **[2015]**

(a) Being able to convert rupee notes into gold

(b) Allowing the value of rupee to be fixed my market forces

(c) Freely permitting the conversion of rupee to other currencies and vice versa

(d) Developing an international market for currencies in India

22. With reference to 'IFC Masala Bonds', sometimes seen in the news, which of the statements given below is/are correct? **[2016]**

(i) The International Finance Corporation, which offers these bonds, is an arm of the World Bank

(ii) They are the rupee-denominated bonds and are a source of debt financing for the public and private sector

Select the correct answer using the code given below

(a) (i) only (b) (ii) only

(c) Both (i) & (ii) (d) Neither (i) nor (ii)

23. The term 'Core Banking Solutions' is sometimes seen in the news. Which of the following statements best describes/ describe this term? **[2016]**

(i) It is a networking of a bank's branches which enables customers to operate their accounts from any branch of the bank on its network regardless of where they open their accounts.

(ii) It is an effort to increase RBI's control over commercial banks through computerization.

(iii) It is a detailed procedure by which a bank with huge non-performing assets is taken over by another bank

Select the correct answer using the code given below.

(a) (i) only (b) (ii) & (iii) only
(c) (i) & (iii) only (d) (i), (ii) & (iii)

24. What is/are the purpose/purposes of the 'Marginal Cost of Funds based Lending Rate (MCLR)' announced by RBI? **[2016]**

(i) These guidelines help improve the transparency in the methodology followed by banks for determining the interest rates on advances.

(ii) These guidelines help ensure availability of bank credit at interest rates which are fair to the borrowers as well as the banks.

Select the correct answer using the code given below.

(a) (i) only (b) (ii) only
(c) Both (i) & (ii) (d) Neither (i) nor (ii)

25. With reference to 'Bitcoins', sometimes seen in the news, which of the following statements is/are correct? **[2016]**

(i) Bitcoins are tracked by the Central Banks of the countries.

(ii) Anyone with a Bitcoin address can send and receive Bitcoins from anyone else with a Bitcoin address.

(iii) Online payments can be sent without either side knowing the identity of the other.

Select the correct answer using the code given below.

(a) (i) & (ii) only (b) (ii) & (iii) only
(c) (iii) only (d) (i), (ii) & (iii)

26. Pradhan Mantri MUDRA Yojana is aimed at **[2016]**

(a) Bringing the small entrepreneurs into frmal financial system
(b) Providing loans to poor farmers for cultivating particular crops
(c) Providing pension to old and destitute persons
(d) Funding the voluntary organizations involved in the promotion of skill development and employment generation

27. What is /are the purpose/ purposes of Government's Sovereign Gold Bond Scheme' and 'Gold Monetization Scheme'? **[2016]**

(i) To bring the idle gold lying with Indian households into the economy

(ii) To promote FDI in the gold and jewellery sector

(iii) To reduce India's dependence on gold imports

Select the correct answer using the code given below.

(a) (i) only (b) (ii) & (iii) only
(c) (i) & (iii) only (d) (i), (ii) & (iii)

28. Consider the following statements: **[2017]**

(i) National Payments Corporation of India helps in promoting financial inclusion in the country.

(ii) NPCI has launched RuPay, a card payment scheme.

Which of the statements given above is/are correct?

(a) (i) only (b) (ii) only
(c) Both (i) & (ii) (d) Neither (i) nor (ii)

29. What is the purpose of setting up of Small Finance Banks (SFBs) in India? **[2017]**

(i) To supply credit to small business units

(ii) To supply credit to small and marginal farmers

(iii) To encourage young entrepreneurs to set up business particularly in rural areas.

Select the correct answer using the code given below:

(a) (i) & (ii) only (b) (ii) & (iii) only
(c) (i) & (iii) only (d) (i), (ii) & (iii)

30. Which one of the following best describes the term "Merchant Discount Rate" sometimes seen in news? **[2018]**

(a) The incentive given by a bank to a merchant for accepting payments through debit cards pertaining to that bank.

(b) The amount paid back by banks to their customers when they use debit cards for financial transactions for purchasing goods or services.

(c) The charge to a merchant by a bank for accepting payments from his customers through the bank's debit cards.

(d) The incentive given by the Government, to merchants for promoting digital payments by their customers through Point of Sale (PoS) machines and debit cards.

31. Which one of the following statements correctly describes the meaning of legal tender money? **[2018]**

(a) The money which is tendered in courts of law to defray the fee of legal cases

(b) The money which a creditor is under compulsion to accept in settlement of his claims

(c) The bank money in the form of cheques, drafts, bills of exchange, etc.

(d) The metallic money in circulation in a country

32. Consider the following statements: **[2018]**

(i) The Reserve Bank of India manages and services Government of India Securities but not any State Government Securities.

(ii) Treasury bills are issued by the Government of India and there are no treasury bills issued by the State Governments.

(iii) Treasury bills offer are issued at a discount from the par value.

Which of the statements given above is/are correct?

(a) (i) & (ii) only (b) (iii) only
(c) (ii) & (iii) only (d) (i), (ii) & (iii)

33. Consider the following statements: **[2018]**

(i) Capital Adequacy Ratio (CAR) is the amount that banks have to maintain in the form of their own funds to offset any loss that banks incur if the account-holders fail to repay dues.

(ii) CAR is decided by each individual bank.

Which of the statements given above is/are correct?

(a) (i) only (b) (ii) only
(c) Both (i) & (ii) (d) Neither (i) nor (ii)

34. Which of the following is not included in the assets of a commercial bank in India? **[2019]**

(a) Advances
(b) Deposits
(c) nvestments
(d) oney at call and short notice

35. In the context of India, which of the following factors is/are contributor/ contributors to reducing the risk of a currency crisis? **[2019]**

(i) The foreign currency earnings of India's IT sector

(ii) Increasing the government expenditure

(iii) Remittances from Indians abroad

Select the correct answer using the code given below.

(a) (i) only (b) (i) & (iii) only
(c) (ii) only (d) (i), (ii) & (iii)

36. Which one of the following is not the most likely measure the Government/RBI takes to stop the slide of Indian rupee? **[2019]**

(a) Curbing imports of non-essential goods- and promoting exports
(b) Encouraging Indian borrowers to issue rupee denominated Masala Bonds
(c) Easing conditions relating to external commercial borrowing
(d) Following an expansionary monetary policy

37. The money multiplier in an economy increases with which one of the following? **[2019]**

(a) Increase in the cash reserve ratio
(b) Increase in the banking habit of the population
(c) Increase in the statutory liquidity ratio
(d) Increase in the population of the country

38. If another global financial crisis happens in the near future, which of the following actions/policies are most likely to give some immunity to India? **[2020]**

1. Not depending on short-term foreign borrowings
2. Opening up to more foreign banks
3. Maintaining full capital account convertibility

Select the correct answer using the code given below:

(a) 1 only (b) 1 and 2 only
(c) 3 only (d) 1, 2 and 3

39. If you withdraw Rs. 1,00,000 in cash from your demand deposit account at your bank, the immediate effect on aggregate money supply in the economy will be **[2020]**

(a) To reduce it by Rs. 1,00,000
(b) To increase it by Rs. 1,00,000
(c) To increase it by more than Rs. 1,00,000
(d) To leave it unchanged

40. Under the Kisan Credit Card Scheme, short-term credit support is given to farmers for which of the following purposes? **[2020]**

1. Working capital for maintenance of farm assets
2. Purchase of combine harvesters, tractors and mini trucks
3. Consumption requirements of farm households
4. Post-harvest expenses
5. Construction of family house and setting up of village cold storage facility

Select the correct answer using the code given below:

(a) 1, 2 and 5 only
(b) 1, 3 and 4 only
(c) 2, 3, 4 and 5 only
(d) 1, 2, 3, 4 and 5

41. With reference to the Indian economy, consider the following statements: **[2020]**

1. 'Commercial Paper' is a short-term unsecured promissory note
2. 'Certificate of Deposit' is a long-term instrument issued by the RBI to a corporation
3. 'Call money' is a short-term finance used for interbank transactions.
4. 'Zero coupon Bonds' are the interest-bearing short-term bonds issued by the Scheduled Commercial Banks to corporations

Which of the statements given above is/ are correct?

(a) 1 and 2 only (b) 4 only
(c) 1 and 3 only (d) 2, 3 and 4 only

42. With reference to Foreign Direct Investment in India, which of the following is considered its major characteristics? **[2020]**

(a) It is the investment through capital instruments essentially in a listed company

(b) It is a largely non-debt creating capital flow

(c) It is the investment which involves debt-servicing

(d) It is the investment made by foreign institutional investors in the Government securities

43. Consider the following statements: **[2021]**

(i) The Governor of the Reserve Bank of India (RBI) is appointed by the Central Government.

(ii) Certain provisions in the Constitution of India give the Central Government the right to issue directions to the RBI in public interest.

(iii) The Governor of the RBI draws his power from the RBI Act.

Which of the above statements are correct?

(a) (i) & (ii) only

(b) (ii) & (iii) only

(c) (i) & (iii) only

(d) All of the above

44. With reference to 'Urban Cooperative Banks' in India, consider the following statements : **[2021]**

(i) They are supervised and regulated by local boards set up by the State Governments.

(ii) They can issue equity shares and preference shares

(iii) They were brought under the purview of the Banking Regulation Act, 1949 through an Amendment in 1966.

Which of the statements given above is/are correct?

(a) (i) only (b) (ii) & (iii) only

(c) (i) & (iii) only (d) All of the above

45. Indian Government Bond Yields are influenced by which of the following? **[2021]**

(i) Actions of the United States Federal Reserve

(ii) Actions of the Reserve Bank of India

(iii) Inflation and short-term interest rates

Select the correct answer using the code given below.

(a) (i) & (ii) only (b) (ii) only

(c) (iii) only (d) All of the above

46. Consider the following: **[2021]**

(i) Foreign currency convertible bonds

(ii) Foreign institutional investment with certain conditions

(iii) Global depository receipts

(iv) Non-resident external deposits

Which of the above can be included in Foreign Direct Investments?

(a) (i), (ii) & (iii) only

(b) (iii) only

(c) (ii) & (iv) only

(d) (i) & (iv) only

47. The effect of devaluation of a currency is that it necessarily **[2021]**

(i) improves the competitiveness of the domestic exports in the foreign markets

(ii) increases the foreign value of domestic currency

(iii) improves the trade balance

Which of the above statements is/are correct?

(a) (i) only (b) (i) & (ii) only

(c) (iii) only (d) (ii) & (iii) only

48. With reference to Indian economy, demand-pull inflation can be caused / increased by which of the following? **[2021]**

(i) Expansionary policies

(ii) Fiscal stimulus

(iii) Inflation-indexing wages

(iv) Higher purchasing power

(v) Rising interest rates

Select the correct answer using the code given below.

(a) (i), (ii) & (iv) only

(b) (iii), (iv) & (v) only

(c) (i), (ii), (iii) & (v) only

(d) All of the above

49. With reference to the Indian economy, consider the following statements: **[2022]**

1. If the inflation is too high, Reserve Bank of India (RBI) is likely to buy government securities.
2. If the rupee is rapidly depreciating, RBI is likely to sell dollars in the market.
3. If interest rates in the USA or European Union were to fall, that is likely to induce RBI to buy dollars.

Which of the statements given above are correct?

(a) 1 and 2 only (b) 2 and 3 only

(c) 1 and 3 only (d) 1, 2 and 3

50. With reference to the Indian economy, what are the advantages of "Inflation-Indexed Bonds (IIBs)"? **[2022]**

1. Government can reduce the coupon rates on its borrowing by way of IIBs.
2. IIBs provide protection to the investors from uncertainty regarding inflation.
3. The interest received as well as capital gains on IIBs are not taxable.

Which of the statements given above are correct?

(a) 1 and 2 only (b) 2 and 3 only

(c) 1 and 3 only (d) 1, 2 and 3

51. With reference to Convertible Bonds, consider the following statements: **[2022]**

1. As there is an option to exchange the bond for equity, Convertible Bonds pay a lower rate of interest.
2. The option to convert to equity affords the bondholder a degree of indexation to rising consumer prices.

Which of the statements given above is/are correct?

(a) 1 only (b) 2 only

(c) Both 1 and 2 (d) Neither 1 nor 2

52. Consider the following statements: **[2023]**

Statement – I: In the post-pandemic recent past, many Central Banks worldwide had carried out interest rate hike.

Statement – II: Central Banks generally assume that they have the ability to counteract the rising consumer prices via monetary policy means.

Which one of the following is correct in respect of the above statements?

(a) Both Statement-I and Statement-II are correct and Statement-II is the correct explanation for Statement-I

(b) Both Statement-I and Statements-II is are correct and Statement-II is not the correct explanation for Statement-II

(c) Statement-I is correct but Statement-II is incorrect

(d) Statement-I is incorrect but Statement-II is correct

53. Which one of the following activities of the Reserve Bank of India is considered to be part of 'sterilization'? **[2023]**

(a) Conducting 'Open Market Operations'

(b) Oversight of settlement and payment systems

(c) Debt and cash management for the Central and State Governments

(d) Regulating the functions of Non-banking Financial Institutions

54. Consider the following markets:

1. Government Bond Market
2. Call Money Market
3. Treasury Bill Market
4. Stock Market

How many of the above are included in capital markets?

(a) Only one (b) Only two

(c) Only three (d) All four

55. With reference to Central Bank digital currencies, consider the following statements: **[2023]**

1. It is possible to make payments in a digital currency without using US dollar or SWIFT system.
2. A digital currency can be distributed with condition programmed into it such as a time- frame for spending it.

Which of the statements given above is/are correct?

(a) 1 only (b) 2 only

(c) Both 1 and 2 (d) Neither 1 nor 2

56. Consider the following statements: **[2024]**

Statement-I: If the United States of America (USA) were to default on its debt, holders of US Treasury Bonds will not be able to exercise their claims to receive payment.

Statement-II: The USA Government debt is not backed by any hard assets, but only by the faith of the Government.

Which one of the following is correct in respect of the above statements?

(a) Both Statement- I and Statement-II are correct and Statement-II explains Statement -I.

(b) Both statesment-I and Statement II are correct but statement-II does not explain statement-I.

(c) Statement-I is correct, but statement-II is incorrect

(d) Statement-I is incorrect, but Statement II is correct.

57. Consider the following statements: **[2024]**

Statement-I: Syndicated lending spreads the risk of borrower default across multiple lenders.

Statement-II: The syndicated loan can be a fixed amount/lump sum of funds, but cannot be a credit line.

Which one of the following is correct in respect of the above statements?

(a) Both Statement-I and Statement-II are correct and Statement-II explains Statement-I.

(b) Both Statement-I and Statement-II are correct, but Statement-II does not explain Statement-I

(c) Statement-I is correct, but Statement-II is incorrect

(d) Statement-I is incorrect, but Statement-II is correct

58. Consider the following statements in respect of the digital rupee: **[2024]**

1. It is a sovereign currency issued by the Reserve Bank of India (RBI) in alignment with its monetary policy.
2. It appears as a liability on the RBI's balance sheet.
3. It is insured against inflation by its very design.
4. It is freely convertible against commercial bank money and cash.

Which of the statements given above are correct?

(a) 1 and 2 only (b) 1 and 3 only
(c) 2 and 4 only (d) 1, 2 and 4

59. Consider the following statements: **[2024]**

1. In India, Non-Banking Financial Companies can access the Liquidity Adjustment Facility window of the Reserve Bank of India.
2. In India, Foreign Institutional Investors (can) hold the Government Securities (G-Secs).
3. In India, Stock Exchanges can offer separate trading platforms for debts.

Which of the statements given above is/are correct?

(a) 1 and 2 only
(b) 3 only
(c) 1, 2 and 3
(d) 2 and 3 only

60. In India, which of the following can trade in Corporate Bonds and Government Securities? **[2024]**

1. Insurance Companies
2. Pension Funds
3. Retail Investors

Select the correct answer using the code given below:

(a) 1 and 2 only
(b) 2 and 3 only
(c) 1 and 3 only
(d) 1, 2 and 3

61. "Consider the following: **[2024]**

1. Exchange-Traded Funds (ETF)
2. Motor vehicles
3. Currency swap

Which of the above is/are considered financial instruments?

(a) 1 only (b) 2 and 3 only
(c) 1, 2 and 3 (d) 1 and 3 only

62. With reference to the rule/rules imposed by the Reserve Bank of India while treating foreign banks, consider the following statements: **[2024]**

1. There is no minimum capital requirement for wholly owned banking subsidiaries in India.
2. For wholly owned banking subsidiaries in India, at least 50% of the board members should be Indian nationals.

Which of the statements given above is/are correct?

(a) 1 only (b) 2 only
(c) Both 1 and 2 (d) Neither 1 nor 2

63. With reference to the Indian economy, "Collateral Borrowing and Lending Obligations" are the instruments of: **[2024]**

(a) Bond market (b) Forex market
(c) Money market (d) Stock market

64. With reference to investments, consider the following: **[2025]**

1. Bonds
2. Hedge funds
3. Stocks
4. Venture Capital

How many of the above are treated as Alternative Investment Funds?

(a) Only one (b) Only two
(c) Only three (d) All the four

65. Which of the following are the sources of income for Reserve Bank of India? **[2025]**

1. Buying and selling Government bonds
2. Buying and selling foreign currency
3. Pension fund management
4. Lending to private companies
5. Printing and distributing currency notes

Select the correct answer using the code given below:

(a) 1 and 2 only (b) 2, 3 & 4 only
(c) 1, 3, 4 & 5 only (d) 1, 2 & 5 only

66. Consider the following statements:

Statement 1: As regards returns from an investment in a company, generally, bondholders are considered to be relatively at lower risk than stockholders.

Statement 2: Bondholders are lenders to a company whereas stockholders are its owners.

Statement 3: For repayment purposes, bond- holders are prioritized over stockholders by a company.

Which one of the following is correct in respect of the above statements?

(a) Both statement 2 and statement 3 are correct and both of them explain statement 1
(b) Both statement 1 and statement 2 are correct and statement 1 explains statement 2
(c) Only one of the statements 2 and 3 is correct and that explains statement 1
(d) Neither statement 2 nor statement 3 is correct

ANSWERS

1. (d)	2. (d)	3. (b)	4. (a)	5. (d)	6. (a)	7. (b)	8. (c)	9. (a)	10. (d)
11. (d)	12. (b)	13. (c)	14. (b)	15. (a)	16. (c)	17. (c)	18. (c)	19. (a)	20. (c)
21. (c)	22. (c)	23. (a)	24. (c)	25. (b)	26. (a)	27. (c)	28.(c)	29. (a)	30. (c)
31. (b)	32. (c)	33. (a)	34. (b)	35. (b)	36. (d)	37. (b)	38. (a)	39. (d)	40. (b)
41. (c)	42. (b)	43. (c)	44. (b)	45. (d)	46. (a)	47. (a)	48. (a)	49. (b)	50. (a)
51. (c)	52. (a)	53. (a)	54. (b)	55. (c)	56. (d)	57. (c)	58. (d)	59. (d)	60. (d)
61. (d)	62. (b)	63. (c)	64. (b)	65. (d)	66. (a)				

Main Questions

1. How would the recent phenomena of protectionism and currency manipulations in world trade affect macroeconomic stability of India? **[2018]**

2. Do you agree with the view that steady GDP growth and low inflation have left the Indian economy in good shape? Give reasons in support of your arguments. **[2019]**

◈◈◈

3

Money and Banking : Part-II

3.1 History of Indian Banking and Reforms

Modern banking in India began in the 18th Century, with the founding of the English Agency Houses in Calcutta and Bombay. Then in the first half of the 19th Century three presidency banks viz. Bank of Bengal (1806), Bank of Bombay (1840) and Bank of Madras (1843) were established. After the introduction of limited liability in 1860, private and foreign banks entered into the market. The beginning of 20th century saw the introduction of Joint stock banks. In 1921, the three presidency banks were merged to create Imperial Bank of India. Imperial Bank of India performed all the normal functions which a commercial bank was expected to perform. In the absence of any Central Bank in India till 1935, the Imperial Bank of India also performed a number of functions which are normally carried out by a Central Bank.

At the time of Independence in 1947, the banking system in India was fairly well developed with over 600 commercial banks operating in the country. However soon after independence, the view that the banks from the colonial heritage were biased in favour of working capital loans for trade and large firms and against extending credit to small scale enterprises, agriculture and commoners, gained prominence. To ensure better coverage of banking needs of larger parts of economy and the rural constituencies, the Government of India acquired the Imperial bank (through RBI) which was established in 1921 and transformed it into the State Bank of India (SBI) with effect from 1955.

Despite the progress in 1950s and 1960s, it was felt that the creation of SBI was not far reaching enough since the banking needs of small-scale industries and the agricultural structure was still not covered sufficiently. This was partially due to the existing close ties commercial and industry houses maintained with the established commercial banks, which give them an advantage in obtaining credit. Additionally, there was a perception that banks should play a more prominent role in India's development strategy by mobilizing resources for sectors that were seen as crucial for economic expansion. As a result, the policy of social control over banks was announced. Its aim was to cause changes in the management and distribution of credit by commercial banks.

The post war development strategy was in many ways a socialist one and Indian Government felt that banks in private hands didn't lend enough to those who needed it most. In July 1969, the Government nationalized all 14 banks whose nationwise deposits were greater than Rs. 50 crores. The bank nationalization in July 1969 with its objective to 'Control the commanding heights of the economy and to meet progressively the needs of development of the economy in conformity with the national policy and objectives' served to intensify the social objective of ensuring that financial intermediaries fully met the credit demands for the productive purposes. Two significant purposes of nationalization were rapid branch expansion and channelling of credit according to the plan priorities.

The Indian banking system progressed by leaps and bounds after Nationalization and bank branches expanded rapidly both in rural and urban areas. There was a rapid growth in deposits mobilized by the banks, besides credit expansions, especially in the areas designated as priority sector. After nationalization, the breadth and scope of Indian banking sector expanded at a rate perhaps unmatched by any other country. In April 1980, the government undertook a second round of nationalization, placing under government control the six private banks whose nationwide deposits were above Rs. 200 crores, which increased the public sector bank's share of deposits to 92%. The second wave of nationalizations occurred because control over the banking system became increasingly more important as a means to ensure priority sector lending reach the poor through a widening branch network and to fund rising government deficits. In addition to the nationalization of banks, the priority sector lending targets raised to 40% from 33.3%. Besides the establishment of priority sector credits and nationalization of banks, the government took further control over banks funds by raising the statutory liquidity ratio (SLR) and the cash reserve ratio (CRR). From a level of 2% for the CRR and 25% for the SLR in 1960, both witnessed a steep increase until 1991 to 15% and 38.5% respectively.

In the period of 1969 to 1991, bank branches increased a lot but banks remained unprofitable, inefficient, and unsound owing to their poor lending strategy and lack of internal risk management under government ownership.

The major factors that contributed to deteriorating bank performance included:

- Too stringent regulatory requirements of CRR and SLR that required banks to hold a certain amount in government and eligible securities
- Low interest rates charged on government bonds as compared to commercial advances
- Directed and concessional lending
- Administrated interest rates, and
- Lack of competition

These factors not only reduced incentives to operate properly, but also undermined regulators incentives to prevent banks from taking risks. While government involvement in the financial sector can be justified at the initial stage of economic development, the prolonged presence of excessively large public sector banks often results in inefficient resource allocation and concentration of power in a few banks. The policies that were supposed to promote a more equal distribution of funds, also lead to inefficiencies in the Indian banking system.

India's banking system until 1991 was an integral part of the government's spending policy. Through the directed credit rules and the statutory pre-emptions, it was a captive source of funds for the fiscal deficit and the key industries. Through the CRR and the SLR, more than 50% of the savings had either to be deposited with the RBI or used to buy government security. Of the remaining savings, 40% had to be directed to priority sectors that were defined by the government. Besides these restrictions on the use of funds, the government had also control over the prices of the funds, that is, the interest rates on saving and loans. Like the overall economy, the Indian banking sector had severe structural problems by the end of 1980s. The major of those problems were unprofitability, inefficiency and financial unsoundness. By international standards, the Indian banks were, even despite a rapid growth of deposits, extremely unprofitable. Despite the impressive progress made by the banks in the two decades following nationalization, the excessive controls enforced on them by the government fostered certain rigidities and inefficiencies in the commercial banking system. This not only hindered their development but also eroded their profitability.

The need to correct the defects of financial sector was felt during the 1991 crisis. Hence, a high-level committee was constituted under the chairmanship of Shri. M. Narasimhan (Committee on Financial System or Narasimhan Committee - I) to review the progress and working of the Indian financial sector and to suggest measures to reform it. **The following were some of the recommendations of the committee:**

- Statutory Liquidity Ratio (SLR) should be based on prudential requirement for banks and not viewed as a major instrument for financing government budget. SLR should be brought down to 25%.
- Interest rates should be deregulated gradually and with the deregulation of interest rates, the RBI should resort more to open market operations (buying and selling securities) than changing Cash Reserve Ratio (CRR) to control the secondary expansion of credit.
- Interest rates on SLR investments should be market related while that on CRR should be broadly related to banks' cost of deposits.
- The directed credit programme (requirements to lend certain minimum amount to specific sectors at specified/ concessional rates of interest) should be phased out/redefined.
- Create a level playing field between the public sector, private sector and foreign sector banks.
- An Asset Reconstruction Company (ARC) should be established which could take over from banks and financial institutions a portion of the bad and doubtful debts at an appropriate discount and the ARC should be provided with special powers of recovery.
- Select few large banks which could become international in character and eight to ten national level banks with a network of branches throughout the country.
- The duality of control over the banking system between the RBI and the Ministry of Finance should end, and RBI should be the primary agency for the regulation of the banking system.

The Government of India felt towards the end of 1997 that the time was ripe to look ahead and chart the reforms necessary in the years ahead so that India's banking system can become stronger and better equipped to compete effectively in a fast-changing international economic environment. Another committee specifically called Committee on banking Sector Reforms was accordingly constituted in 1997 under the chairmanship of the same M. Narasimhan (Narasimhan Committee - II). Following were the major recommendations of Narasimhan Committee - II:

- **Autonomy in Banking:** Greater autonomy was proposed for the public sector banks in order for them to function with equivalent professionalism as their international counterparts. For this the panel recommended that recruitment procedures, training and remuneration policies of public sector banks be brought in line with the best-market-practices. Secondly, the committee recommended GOI equity in nationalized banks be reduced to 33% for increased autonomy.

- **Stronger Banking System:** The committee recommended for merger of large Indian banks to make them strong enough for supporting international trade.
- **Capital Adequacy Norms:** In order to improve the inherent strength of the Indian banking system the committee recommended that the Government should raise the prescribed capital adequacy norms. This would also improve their risk-taking ability.
- **Reform in the role of RBI:** The committee recommended that the Reserve Bank as a regulator of the monetary system should not be the owner of a bank in view of a possible conflict of interest. Pursuant to the recommendations, RBI has transferred its shareholdings of public banks like SBI, NHB and NABARD to government of India.

Most of the reforms as recommended by the two committees have now been implemented.

The "Committee on Comprehensive Financial Services for Small Businesses and Low-Income Households" was set up by the RBI in Sep. 2013 under the chairman **Nachiket Mor**. The committee gave its report in January 2014, of which some of the recommendations are listed below:

- Each Indian resident, above the age of 18 years, would have an individual, full service, safe and secure bank account.
- Aadhaar should be the prime driver towards rapid expansion in the number of bank accounts
- Every resident in India should be within a fifteen-minute walking distance of a payment access point.
- Each low-income household and small business would have access to providers that can offer them suitable investment and deposit products. Such services must be available to them at reasonable charges.

P J NAYAK Committee

Public Sector Banks (PSBs) has been established through the "State Bank of India Act 1955" and "The banking companies (acquisition and transfer of undertakings) act, 1970" also referred as Bank Nationalization Act.

These Acts require Govt. of India to have majority shareholding and voting power in the PSBs and this empowers the Govt. to appoint Board of Directors and involve in the decision making of the PSBs. It leads to governance issues as the people appointed on the board of these PSBs are not that qualified for their job but are close to Govt. Through this, Govt. starts manipulating the decisions which lead to various kinds of frauds and corruption.

In January 2014, P J Nayak committee was constituted, for review of governance of boards of banks in India (which submitted its report in May 2014) to examine the working of banks' boards, review RBI guidelines on bank ownership and representation in the board, and investigate possible conflicts of interest in the board representation. **The following were the main recommendations:**

- Government should setup a Bank Investment Company (BIC), under Companies act, 2013. Govt. should transfer its present ownership in PSBs to BIC and all the PSBs will be incorporated as subsidiaries of BIC and will be registered under the Companies Act 2013. And the PSBs will become limited companies for example "State Bank of India" will become "State Bank of India Limited". (This limited means now if the State Bank of India Limited will become bankrupt then Govt. of India/BIC will not be liable and may not have to put funds from their own resources to protect SBI limited). Government should reduce its stake in PSBs (through BIC) to less than 50%.

- The BIC will become a holding company which will be owned by Govt. of India. BIC will have the voting powers to appoint Board of directors and other policy decisions of the banks. Government will sign shareholding agreement with BIC, promising its autonomy. This means that even if the Govt. will be majority shareholders in BIC, but it will not intervene in its working and BIC will select banks directors and top management. (And if required to preserve the autonomy of BIC, Govt. may reduce its ownership to less than 50% in BIC).
- But since repealing of the Acts (1955, 1970) and establishment of BIC will take time, so for the time being Govt. can establish Banks Board Bureau (BBB) through an executive order and BBB will select and appoint directors/top management in public sector banks and other public sector financial institutions like NABARD/SIDBI/LIC etc. And once BIC is set up, BBB will be dissolved.

In line with the recommendations of the P J Nayak committee and with a view to improve the Governance of Public Sector Banks (PSBs), the GoI appointed an autonomous **Banks Board Bureau (BBB)** but it was later on replaced by **Financial Services Institutions Bureau** (FSIB) from 1st July 2022. **The following are the functions of the FSIB:**

- To recommend persons for appointment as whole-time directors (WTDs) and non-executive chairpersons (NECs) on the Boards of Directors in Public Sector Banks, financial institutions and Public Sector Insurers (hereinafter referred to as "PSBs", "FIs" and "PSIs" respectively.
- To advise the Government on matters relating to appointments, transfer or extension of term of office and termination of services of the said directors.
- To advise the Government on the desired management structure at the Board level for PSBs, FIs and PSIs.
- To advise the Government on a suitable performance appraisal system for WTDs and NECs in PSBs, FIs and PSIs.
- To build a databank containing data related to the performance of PSBs, FIs and PSIs.
- To advise the Government on formulation and enforcement of a code of conduct and ethics for whole-time directors in PSBs, FIs and PSIs.
- To advise the Government on evolving suitable training and development programmes for management personnel in PSBs, FIs and PSIs.
- To help PSBs, FIs and PSIs in terms of developing business strategies and capital raising plan etc.
- To carry out such process and draw up a panel for consideration of competent authority for any other bank, financial institution or insurer for which the Government makes a reference.

(FIs are basically public sector financial institutions like NABARD, NHB, SIDBI, EXIM, MUDRA etc.)

3.2 Relationship between RBI and Government of India

Reserve Bank of India

[*As per the RBI Act, the Central Board is made up of the following members (21): Governor, four Deputy Governors, Four Directors (one each from the four regional boards of the RBI), 10 directors to be nominated by the Centre, and two government officials, also to be nominated by the Centre*].

The relationship between the Board and the Governor is not comparable to a corporate set-up where the managing director (the corporate equivalent of the Governor) reports to the board and draws his powers from it. While a managing director is an agent of the board in a company, in the RBI, the Governor is not. He draws his powers from the RBI Act and not from the Central Board. He is appointed by the Prime Minister in consultation with the finance minister. The RBI Board has no say whatsoever in his appointment. In a company, the board of directors chooses one of its own to be appointed as the managing director. In the RBI, the Governor secures board membership only after he is appointed to the post. It is, thus, wrong to compare a corporate board to the RBI's and suggest that the Governor is subservient to it.

In RBI, policy decisions are taken by the Governor with its 4 deputy governors and the (Central) Board is just engaged in providing a broader vision to the RBI. RBI Board has always functioned in an advisory role with the understanding that the Governor would consider its advice while making policy decisions. In other words, there is mutual respect between the Board and the Governor, with both operating in a spirit of accommodation.

Relationship between Centre (GoI) and RBI

Centre (GoI) and RBI both has their task cut out but they work in close coordination. But in case of a fundamental disagreement between the Centre and the Governor (RBI management), where they are unable to arrive at a common ground, then Centre has the upper hand and can use **Section 7** of the RBI Act to give written direction to RBI and in that case RBI decision making will pass on to the RBI (Central) Board and then RBI Governor will have no say. *Section 7 has never been unleashed in the 90 year existence of RBI. It is not as if there have not been any disagreements between RBI Governors and governments before this but, things did not reach the brink and were sorted out quietly behind the scenes. Centre also understands that using Sections 7 will necessarily come with a price and will set a bad precedent.*

RBI has been kept at arm's length from the Centre and bestowed with a certain independence. That is because the Centre is the spender and the RBI is the creator of money, and there has to be a natural separation between the two. The Centre arming itself with powers to run the RBI runs afoul of this precept.

But there is also a clear reason why, even while it is conceded that control of the nation's currency should be with an independent authority removed from the sway of elected representatives, the RBI Act has the veto option to the Government in the form of Section 7. And that's because it is not the technocrats and economists sitting in Mumbai's Mint Street who carry the can for the policies they frame; it is the rulers in Delhi who do. Ultimately, it is the elected representative ruling the country who is answerable to the citizen every five years. The representative cannot split hairs before the voter while explaining the economy's performance — he has to own up for everything, including the RBI's actions, as his own.

In a democracy, it is unthinkable that we will have an institution that is so autonomous that it is not answerable to the people. The risk of such an institution is that it will impose its preferences on society against the latter's will, which is undemocratic.

Seen from this perspective, the limits to the RBI's autonomy will be clear. It is autonomous and accountable to the people ultimately, through the government. The onus is thus on responsible behaviour by both sides. There is enough creative tension between the two built into the system. The Governor has to be conscious of the limits to his autonomy at all times, and the government has to consider the advice coming from Mint Street in all seriousness.

Interpretation of RBI Act Regarding its Autonomy by Previous Governors

- **Dr. Manmohan Singh:** The dynamic between the RBI and the government is one of give and take but if the finance minister insists on a certain course of action, his view need to prevail and the governor may not refuse, unless he is willing to quit his job. The governor of the Reserve Bank is not superior to the finance minister.
- **Bimal Jalan:** RBI is accountable to the government and should make policies within the framework set by the government.
- **D. Subbarao:** RBI does not have the absolute autonomy but it is autonomous within the framework of RBI Act 1934. The existence of Section 7 in the RBI Act, even if it has never been used till now, proves that the RBI is not fully autonomous. The fact that it has never been used is testimony to the sense of responsibility that the government and the central bank have displayed. The Central Bank is autonomous within the limits set by the government and its extent depends on the subject and the context.
- **Y. V. Reddy:** RBI is independent, but within the limits set by the government. I believe that, in operational issues, RBI has total freedom. But, in case of policy related matters, RBI should prior consult with the mandarins in the Finance ministry. It is important to have continuous and sustained dialogue, and an atmosphere of give and take is much needed.

3.3 Should Large Corporate be Allowed to Open their Own Banks?

Background

Even after three decades of liberalization and rapid growth, "the total balance sheet of banks in India still constitutes less than 70% of the GDP, which is much less compared to global peers" such as China, where this ratio is closer to 175%. Further, domestic bank credit to the private sector is just 50% of GDP when in economies such as China, Japan, the US and Korea it is upwards of 150%.

The Indian economy, especially the private sector, needs money (credit) to grow. Far from being able to extend credit, the government-owned banks are struggling to contain their NPAs. Government finances were already strained before the Covid crisis. With growth faltering, revenues have plummeted and the government has limited ability to push for growth through the public sector banks. Large corporates, with deep pockets, are the ones with the financial resources to fund India's future growth. But choosing this option is not without serious risks, of which some are mentioned below:

1. **Conflict of Interest (technically it is inter-connected lending):** Inter-connected lending refers to a situation where the promoter/owner of the bank is also a borrower and, as such, it is possible for a promoter to channel the depositors' money into their own group companies. So corporate houses can easily turn banks into a source of funds for their own businesses and ensure that funds are directed to their cronies (and at more relaxed terms and conditions which will increase the cost for

other borrowers). They can use banks to provide finance to customers and suppliers of their businesses. Adding a bank to a corporate house thus means an increase in concentration of economic power.

2. Even if we equip RBI with legal framework to deal with inter-connected lending, RBI can only react to interconnected lending ex-post, that is, after substantial exposure to the entities of the corporate house has happened. It is unlikely to be able to prevent such exposure. Corporate houses are adept at routing funds through a maze of entities/ subsidiaries in India and abroad. Tracing interconnected lending will be a challenge. Monitoring of transactions of corporate houses will require the cooperation of various law enforcement agencies. Corporate houses can use their political clout to thwart such cooperation.
3. Even if RBI gets hold on to interconnected lending, how is the RBI to react? Any action that the RBI may take in response could cause a flight of deposits from the bank concerned and precipitate its failure. The challenges posed by interconnected lending are truly formidable.
4. The recent episodes in ICICI Bank, Yes Bank, DHFL etc. were all examples of inter-connected lending. The so-called **ever-greening of loans** (where one loan after another is extended to enable the borrower to pay back the previous one) is often the starting point of such lending.
5. Banks owned by corporate houses will be exposed to the risks of the non-bank entities of the group. If the non-bank entities get into trouble, sentiment about the bank owned by the corporate house is bound to be impacted and the depositors will have to be protected through the use of public safety net.
6. Unlike an NBFC (many of which are backed by large corporates), a bank accepts deposits from common public and that is what makes this riskier.

Hence, it is prudent to keep the class of borrowers (big corporates) separate from the class of lenders (banks). But if in case large corporates and industrial houses has to be allowed as promoters of banks then this should be done only after the strengthening the supervisory mechanism for large conglomerates.

3.4 Financial Stability and Development Council (FSDC)

With a view to strengthening and institutionalizing the mechanism for maintaining financial stability, enhancing inter-regulatory coordination and promoting financial sector development, the Financial Stability and Development Council (FSDC) was set up by the Government of India as the apex level forum in December 2010. FSDC is not a statutory body and was set up through a gazette notification.

The Chairman of the Council is the finance minister and its members include the heads of financial sector Regulators (RBI, SEBI, PFRDA, IRDA), Chairperson of Insolvency and Bankruptcy Board of India (IBBI), Chief Economic Advisor and secretaries from ministry of finance, ministry of Information Technology and ministry of Corporate Affairs. The Council can also invite experts to its meeting if required.

Without prejudice to the autonomy of regulators, FSDC shall deal with issues relating to:

- Financial stability
- Financial sector development
- Inter-regulatory coordination
- Financial literacy

- Financial Inclusion
- Macro prudential supervision of the economy including the functioning of large financial conglomerates
- Coordinating India's international interface with financial sector bodies like Financial Action Task Force (FATF), Financial Stability Board (FSB), and any such body as may be decided by the finance minister from time to time
- Any other matter relating to the financial sector stability and development referred to by a member/Chairperson and considered prudent by the Council/Chairperson.

3.5 Development Financial Institutions (DFIs)

An efficient and robust financial system acts as a powerful engine of economic development by mobilizing resources and allocating the same to their productive uses. In a developing country, however, financial sectors are usually incomplete in as much as they lack a full range of markets and institutions that meet all the financing needs of the economy. For example, there is generally a lack of availability of **long-term finance** for infrastructure and industry, finance for agriculture and small and medium enterprises (SME) development and financial products for certain sections of the people. The role of development finance is to identify the gaps in institutions and markets in a country's financial sector and act as a **'gap-filler'**. The principal motivation for developmental finance is, therefore, to make up for the failure of financial markets and institutions to provide certain kinds of finance to certain kinds of economic agents and sectors. The failure may arise because the expected return to the provider of finance is lower than the market-related return (notwithstanding the higher social return) or the credit risk involved cannot be covered by high-risk premium as economic activity to be financed becomes unviable at such risk-based price.

The vehicle for extending development finance is called development financial institution (DFI) or development bank. The following are the important features of DFIs:

- A DFI is defined as "an institution promoted or assisted by Government mainly to provide development finance to one or more sectors or sub-sectors of the economy.
- The institution distinguishes itself by a judicious balance between commercial norms of operation, as adopted by any private financial institution, and developmental obligations;
- It emphasizes the "project approach" - meaning the viability of the project to be financed – against the "collateral approach";
- Apart from provision of long-term loans, equity capital, guarantees and underwriting functions, a development bank normally is also expected to upgrade the managerial and the other operational pre-requisites of the assisted projects.
- Its insurance against default is the integrity, competence and resourcefulness of the management, the commercial and technical viability of the project and above all the speed of implementation and efficiency of operations of the assisted projects.
- Its relationship with its clients is of a continuing nature and of being a "partner" in the project than that of a mere "financier".

Thus, the basic emphasis of a DFI is on long-term finance and on assistance for activities or sectors of the economy where the risks may be higher than that the ordinary financial system is willing to bear. DFIs may also play a large role in stimulating equity and debt markets by (i) selling their own stocks and bonds; (ii) helping the assisted enterprises float or place their securities and (iii) selling from their own portfolio of investments.

The success of various DFIs across the world provided strong impetus for creation of DFIs in India after independence, in the context of the felt need for raising the investment rate. RBI was entrusted with the task of developing an appropriate financial architecture through institution building so as to mobilize and direct resources to preferred sectors as per the (Five Year) Plan priorities. While the reach of the banking system was expanded to mobilize resources and extend working capital finance on an ever-increasing scale, to different sectors of the economy, the DFIs were established mainly to cater to the demand for long-term finance by the industrial sector. The first DFI established in India in 1948 was Industrial Finance Corporation of India (**IFCI**) followed by setting up of State Financial Corporations (SFCs) at the State level after passing of the SFCs Act, 1951.

Besides IFCI and SFCs, in the early phase of planned economic development in India, a number of other financial institutions were set up, which included the following. ICICI Ltd. was set up in 1955, LIC in 1956, Refinance Corporation for Industries Ltd. in 1958 (later taken over by IDBI), Agriculture Refinance Corporation (precursor of ARDC and NABARD) in 1963, UTI and IDBI in 1964, Rural Electrification Corporation Ltd. and HUDCO Ltd. in 1969-70, Industrial Reconstruction Corporation of India Ltd. (precursor of IIBI Ltd.) in 1971 and GIC in 1972. NABARD, NHB, SIDBI, EXIM bank are also treated as development financial institutions. As such, the term "DFI" is not standardized in any statute.

3.6 Categorization of Loans

(No need to go in detail on this topic, just have a look on the terms which will help you in understanding other topics)

Loans and advances given by banks are 'assets' for them (the "loan document" signed by the borrower and kept with banks is an asset for the bank as based on this loan document the bank receives principal and interest back). Depending on the performance of such loans (i.e. whether banks are receiving interest & principal or not) they are classified as per the norms provided by RBI. The RBI's classification of assets is aimed to bring transparency and consistency in the accounts.

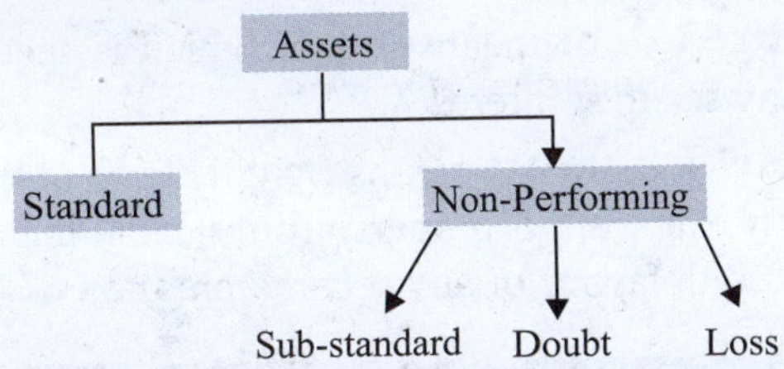

There are different criteria for different types of loans (assets) for standard and non performing classification, and there is no need to go into detail. But generally non-performing assets (NPA) are those assets for which interest and/or principal have remained overdue for a period of more than 90 days.

Restructured asset or loan are that assets which got an extended repayment period, reduced interest rate, converting a part of the loan into equity, providing additional financing, or some combination of these measures. Hence, under restructuring a bad loan is modified as a new loan (standard). A restructured loan also indicates bad asset quality of banks. This is because a restructured loan was a past NPA and it has been modified into a new loan.

Write-off: It is an accounting term. It means that the lender doesn't count the money you owe them as an asset of the company anymore and it removes it from the balance sheet. The banks write-off loan when they are sure that they won't be able to recover the money and they reduce the value of the loan/asset to zero. They're required to write off certain bad loans so as not to mislead investors. But you still owe the money.

Default means non-payment of debt when whole or any part or instalment of the amount of debt has become due and payable and is not repaid by the debtor.

Stressed assets = NPAs + Restructured loans + Written off assets

Secured debt means a debt which is secured by any security interest.

Security interest means right, title or interest of any kind, upon property (physical/financial) created in favour of any secured creditor.

Secured Creditor means any bank or financial institution holding any right, title or interest upon any physical or financial (tangible or intangible) asset.

Security agreement means an agreement, instrument or any other document or arrangement under which **security interest** is created **in favour of** the **secured creditor** including the creation of mortgage by deposit of title deeds with the secured creditor.

Secured asset means the **property** (physical like house or financial like shares) on which **security interest** is created.

Asset Reconstruction Company (ARC): A company registered with RBI (and regulated by RBI) for the purpose of carrying on the business of asset reconstruction or securitization.

Asset reconstruction means acquisition by an ARC of any **right** or **interest** of any bank or financial institution in any **debt/loan/advance** for the purpose of realisation/recovery of such debt.

Securitization: Acquisition of financial assets (debt or security interest) by an ARC from any financial institution for the purpose of converting such assets into marketable securities. It refers to conversion of illiquid assets into liquid assets.

ARCs can purchase both the **rights/interest** (asset reconstruction) in a debt or the **debt** itself (for the purpose of securitization).

3.7 SARFAESI Act 2002

The Securitization and Reconstruction of Financial Assets and Enforcement of Securities Interest Act 2002 (SARFAESI Act 2002)

Earlier, the banks and financial institutions in India did not have power to take possession of securities and sell them in case of a loan default (rather they had to enforce their security interests through the court process, which was extremely time consuming). This had resulted in slow pace of recovery of defaulting loans and mounting levels of non-performing assets of banks and financial institutions. Narasimham Committee I and II constituted by the Central Government for the purpose of examining banking sector reforms had considered the need for changes in the legal system in respect of these areas. These Committees, inter alia, suggested enactment of a new legislation for securitization and empowering banks and financial institutions to take possession of the securities and to sell them without the intervention of the court. Acting on these suggestions, the Securitization and Reconstruction of Financial Assets and Enforcement of Security Interest Act, 2002 was enacted to regulate securitization and reconstruction of financial assets and enforcement of security interest.

The SARFAESI Act sanctions three processes to recover Non-Performing Assets as follows:

1. Security Enforcement **without court's intervention**: As per the Act, the financial institutions are entitled to issue notice to the defaulting loan takers as well as guarantors, asking them to clear the sum in arrears within 60 days from the date of issuing the notice. If the defaulter fails to act in accordance with the notice, the bank is entitled to enforce security interest (i.e., the act allows banks and financial institutions to sell the "security interest" in case the debt/ loan is secured and it has become non performing).
2. Asset reconstruction: It means acquisition by an ARC of any **right** or **interest** of any bank or financial institution in any **debt/loan/advance** for the purpose of realisation/recovery of such debt.
3. Securitization: Acquisition of financial assets (loans) by an ARC from any financial institution for the purpose of converting such assets into marketable securities.

The provisions have enabled banks and financial institutions to improve recovery by exercising powers to take possession of securities, sell them and reduce nonperforming assets by adopting measures for recovery and reconstruction.

3.8 NPA Crisis and Bad Bank

Credit led boom of the 2000 decade followed by the Global Financial Crisis of 2008 and then domestic issues in the UPA-II regime (2009-2014) resulted in huge NPAs in the economy. When the NPA's started surfacing in the post 2013 period because of the RBI's strict supervision then various measures/schemes were announced by RBI to resolve the NPA mess and IBC 2016 was also enacted. But every default cannot go to NCLT under IBC, so the Economic Survey in 2017 suggested for a different approach to set up a centralized public sector asset reconstruction company to resolve the NPA mess.

And due to Covid-19, which is once in a century crisis, the problem of NPA is expected to aggravate, and the establishment of a bad bank is now more pertinent to handle the stressed asset crisis.

Accordingly, Govt. of India created a 'Bad Bank' named 'National Asset Reconstruction Company Ltd.' (NARCL) in 2021 which is basically an 'Asset Reconstruction Company' (ARC). NARCL will be 51% owned by Public Sector Banks and financial institutions, and the remaining 49% stake will be held by private sector lenders. NARCL is "Government Company", "Public Company" and "Unlisted Company". Another entity, India Debt Resolution Company (IDRCL), has also been set up which is a 'Non-Govt.' Company.

NARCL and IDRCL will together act as bad bank. NARCL will first purchase the bad loans from commercial banks and then IDRCL will try to sell out the bad loans and recover money. A two-entity structure has been created for operational and governance purpose.

Let us understand with an example. Suppose SBI had earlier given loan worth Rs. 1000 crore and it turned into NPA. So, SBI would sell this NPA to the bad bank for recovery and would rather focus on its banking business.

So, Bad bank will purchase this NPA from SBI but not in Rs. 1000 crore. The bad bank will try to estimate how much money it would actually be able to recover from the NPA and accordingly it would quote a price for it. If SBI also agrees then, SBI will sell this NPA/bad loan (paper) to bad bank, let us say in Rs. 300 crores. But the bad bank will not immediately pay in cash Rs. 300 crores to SBI. Rather, the bad bank will pay just 15% of the agreed amount (of the Rs. 300 crore) i,e. Rs. 45 crores in cash and the rest 85% i.e., Rs. 255 crores in securities (a kind of debt paper), which will be paid once the bad bank recovers the money by resolution or liquidation of the bad asset.

But what if the bad bank in future is unable to sell the bad loan or sells the bad loan at a loss (i.e., at less than Rs. 300 crore) and is not able to pay Rs. 255 crores to SBI. So, Govt. of India has agreed to provide "Government Guarantee" on the securities that will be issued by the bad bank.

A bad bank conveys the impression that it will function as a bank but has bad assets (NPAs) to start with. Technically, a bad bank is an asset reconstruction company (ARC) or an asset management company that takes over the bad loans of commercial banks, manages them and finally recovers the money over a period of time. The bad bank is not involved in lending and taking deposits, but helps commercial banks clean up their balance sheets and resolve bad loans. The bad bank concept is in some ways similar to an Asset Reconstruction Companies (ARC) but is funded by the government initially, with banks and other investors co-investing in due course. The presence of the government is seen as a means to speed up the clean-up process.

Bad bank will lead to freeing of the commercial bank's capital which will lead to further lending and will promote investment and growth in the economy. And Bad Banks will have experts which will try to recover/resolve the NPAs (bad loans) that it has acquired from all the banks. This will clean up the bank's balance sheet but mere transferring the NPAs to bad bank will not reduce the overall NPA in the economy which will have to be taken care of by the bad bank.

3.9 RBI Circular (June 2019) on Resolution of NPAs

Once a borrower is reported to be in default, lenders should start a review of the borrower account within 30 days of the default. "During this review period of thirty days, lenders may decide on the resolution strategy, including the nature of the resolution plan (RP), the approach for implementation of the RP.

If the RP is to be implemented, lenders have been asked to enter into an inter-creditor agreement (ICA), within the review period, to provide for ground rules for finalization and implementation of the RP. The ICA shall provide that any decision agreed by lenders representing 75% by value of total outstanding credit facilities and 60% of lenders by number shall be binding upon all the lenders. The RP will have to be implemented within 180 days from the end of review period.

There is a disincentive for banks if they delay implementing a viable resolution plan. In case the plan is not implemented within 180 days from the end of review period, banks have to make additional provision of 20% and another 15% if the plan is not implemented within 365 days from the start of the review period.

The additional provisions would be reversed if resolution is pursued under IBC Code. Half of the additional provisions could be reversed on filing of insolvency application and the remaining additional provisions may be reversed once case is admitted for insolvency proceedings. This has been done so that more lenders move to IBC Code.

The new guidelines are applicable to Scheduled Commercial Banks (excluding RRBs), Small Finance Banks, Non-Banking Financial Companies (NBFCs) and Development Financial Institutions like NABARD, SIDBI, EXIM Bank and NHB.

Amendments done in 2017 in Banking Regulation Act 1949 (regarding resolution of NPAs):

- The Central Government may, by order, authorize RBI to issue directions to any banking company to initiate insolvency resolution process in respect of a default, under the provisions of Insolvency and Bankruptcy Code 2016
- RBI may from time-to-time issue directions to any banking company for resolution of stressed assets

As per Supreme Court judgement dated 2nd April 2019, "RBI can only direct banking institutions to move under the IBC Code 2016 if there is a central government authorization and it should be in respect of specific defaults. Thus, any directions which are in respect of debtors in general, would-be ultra vires Section 35AA of Banking Regulation Act 1949".

3.10 Insolvency and Bankruptcy Code 2016

Insolvency is a situation when an individual or a company is unable to pay its debt while bankruptcy is a legal procedure for liquidating (winding up) a business (or property owned by an individual) which cannot fully pay its debts out of its current assets.

Before the IBC code, there were multiple overlapping laws and adjudicating forums in India like Company Law Boards, Debt Recovery Tribunal, SARFAESI Act 2002, Sick Industrial Companies (Special Provisions) Act, 1985 and the winding up provisions of the Companies Act, 1956 etc. dealing with financial failure of companies and individuals leading to significant delays in winding up a company. The legal and institutional framework did not help lenders in effective and timely recovery or restructuring of defaulted assets and caused undue strain on the Indian credit system. Recognizing that reforms in the bankruptcy and insolvency regime were critical for improving the business environment and alleviating distressed credit markets, the Government enacted the Insolvency and Bankruptcy Code in **May 2016**, making it easier to wind up a failing business and recover debts.

The Code makes a significant departure from the earlier resolution regime by shifting the responsibility on the creditor to initiate the insolvency resolution process against the corporate debtor. Under the previous legal framework, the primary onus to initiate a resolution process lied with the debtor, and creditor may pursue separate actions for recovery, security enforcement and debt restructuring.

Procedure: Under the IBC code, a creditor (financial or operational) or the corporate debtor may initiate corporate insolvency resolution process in case a default is committed by corporate debtor worth more than Rs. 1 crore. An application can be made before the National Company Law Tribunal (NCLT) for initiating the resolution process. The creditor needs to give demand notice of 10 days to corporate debtor before approaching the NCLT. If corporate debtor fails to repay dues to the creditor or fails to show any existing dispute or arbitration, then the creditor can approach NCLT. Upon admission of application by NCLT, corporate insolvency process shall be completed within 180 days (in complex cases it can be extended to 90 days) during which time NCLT hears the proposals for revival and decide on the future course of action. *[The corporate insolvency resolution process should be completed within 330 days if there are any legal proceedings involved but in case of exceptional cases (tardy legal proceedings) it can be extended even beyond 330 days].*

NCLT appoints the Insolvency Professionals (IP) upon confirmation by the Insolvency and Bankruptcy Board (IBB). NCLT causes public announcement to be made of the initiation of corporate insolvency process and calls for submission of claims by any other creditors. After receiving claims pursuant to public announcement, IP constitutes the creditors' committee called **Committee of Creditors (CoC)** constituting all creditors (first interim IPs are appointed and when the CoC approves, then the IPs are confirmed as **Resolution Professionals**). Resolution Professionals shall submit the insolvency resolution plan before the creditors' committee for its approval. The CoC has to then take decisions regarding insolvency resolution by a 66% majority voting (by value). The **resolution plan** could either be a **revised repayment plan** (which is essentially a reorganization plan through debt restructuring, sale of assets, merger, takeover of the company etc.) for the company, or **liquidation of the assets** of the company. The resolution plan will be sent to NCLT for final approval, and implemented once approved. If no decision is made during the resolution process or **CoC** fails to approve the resolution plan then the debtor's assets will be **liquidated** to repay the debt.

The IBC process flowchart

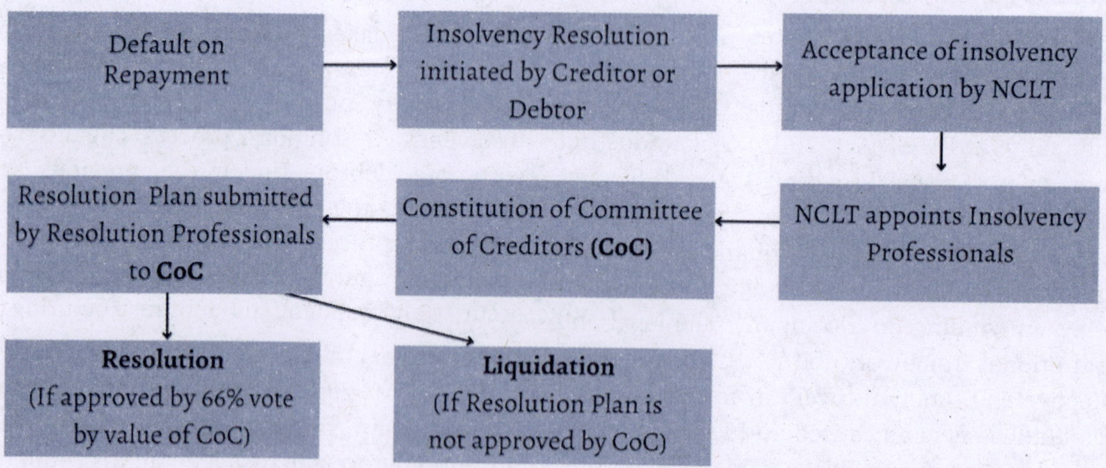

*[The Resolution Plan is submitted by interested resolution applicants who can participate in the resolution process and submit 'resolution plans', which are basically instruments for taking over the corporate debtor, paying the dues of its creditors and undertaking its revival and turn-around. The Resolution plan is placed for consideration before the Committee of Creditors ("**CoC**") by the Resolution professionals. If **Resolution** happens that means the company will exist and continue its business and **Liquidation** means company's assets will be sold and the company will cease to exist].*

[Committee of Creditors (CoC) consists of only financial creditors (like banks, NBFCs etc.). But the proceeds/money from the resolution process is shared by the financial and operational creditors both. Only CoC will decide how the resolution proceeds will be shared among financial and operational creditors and NCLT will not have any say. NCLT cannot interfere in the merits of the commercial decision taken by the CoC but a "limited judicial review" is possible to see that the CoC had taken into account, inter alia, the fact that the interest of all stakeholders, including operational creditors had been taken care of. A Financial creditor, operational creditor, or a corporate debtor (who has borrowed money) anyone can initiate insolvency proceedings upon any default made by the corporate debtor.]

The objective of the new law is to promote entrepreneurship, availability of credit, and balance the interests of all stakeholders by consolidating and amending the laws relating to reorganization and insolvency resolution of companies and individuals in a time bound manner and for maximization of value of assets. Some business ventures will always fail, but they will be handled rapidly and swiftly. Entrepreneurs and lenders will be able to move on, instead of being bogged down with decisions taken in the past.

The Code has four pillars of institutional infrastructure which is its most innovative feature and are as following: -

1. The first pillar of institutional infrastructure is a class of regulated persons, the 'Insolvency Professionals'. They would play a key role in the efficient working of the bankruptcy process. They would be regulated by 'Insolvency Professional Agencies'.
2. The second pillar is a new industry of 'Information Utilities'. These would store facts about lenders and terms of lending in electronic databases. This would eliminate delays and disputes about facts when default does take place.
3. The third pillar is adjudication. The National Company Law Tribunal (NCLT) will adjudicate cases related to insolvency of companies and Debt Recovery Tribunal (DRTs) will do the same for individual insolvencies. These institutions, along with their Appellate bodies, viz. National Company Law Appellate Tribunal (NCLAT) and Debt Recovery Appellate Tribunal (DRAT) will help in better functioning of the bankruptcy process.
4. The fourth pillar is a regulator viz., 'The Insolvency and Bankruptcy Board (IBB) of India'. This body will have regulatory over-sight over the Insolvency Professional, Insolvency Professional agencies and information utilities.

The code also protects workers (paying their salaries for up to 24 months will get first priority in case of liquidation of assets) in case of insolvency and disqualifies anyone declared bankrupt from holding any public office.

The Insolvency and Bankruptcy Code (IBC) 2016 was not applicable for Financial Service Providers (FSP) like Commercial, Co-operative and Regional Rural Banks, NBFCs, Insurance Companies, Pension Funds, Securities Market Players etc.

But, as there were a lot NBFCs like IL&FS, DHFL etc. facing crisis, Ministry of Corporate Affairs, Govt. of India, on **15th Nov. 2019**, notified section 227 of IBC 2016 (only temporary arrangement) to enable the resolution of NBFCs (Financial Service Providers) regulated by RBI, through NCLT under IBC. As per Section 227 of IBC 2016:

"Notwithstanding anything to the contrary examined in this Code or any other law for the time being in force, the Central Government may, if it considers necessary, in consultation with the appropriate financial sector regulators, notify financial service providers or categories of financial service providers for the purpose of their insolvency and liquidation proceedings, which may be conducted under this Code….."

Ministry of Corporate Affairs, using the powers under section 227, consulted the regulator i.e., RBI and notified that those NBFCs with asset size of more than Rs. 500 crores can be brought under IBC code for resolution. The insolvency for Financial Service Provider (NBFCs) can be initiated only on an application by the regulator (RBI). This is not applicable in other company cases where in case of default, either the creditor or the debtor (company), anyone can move for resolution under IBC 2016. DHFL was the first NBFC to be referred to NCLT under section 227 of IBC 2016.

Government is working on a new framework/law to handle insolvencies of Financial Service Providers (FSP) like Commercial, Co-operative and Regional Rural Banks, NBFCs, Insurance Companies, Pension Funds, Securities Market Players etc. This new framework/law will be on the lines of Financial Resolution and Deposit Insurance (FRDI) Bill, which Govt. had planned to introduce in 2018 but did not do so because of the protests regarding the controversial "Bail-in" clause.

Important Features of the Code

- Time bound and market linked resolution of stressed assets.
- During the resolution process, management of the company passes on to resolution professionals who will prevent any siphoning off funds or manipulation by debtors.
- IBC tries for maximization of value of assets by prioritizing **resolution** (where the company will continue to function) rather than **liquidation** (company cease to exist and assets are sold in the market). Some business ventures will always fail, but they will be handled rapidly and swiftly which will promote entrepreneurship, availability of credit, and balance the interests of all stakeholders.
- The code makes it easier to exit or attempt revival of a business, thereby improving the NPA scenario for the financial services sector. Entrepreneurs and lenders will be able to move on, instead of being bogged down with decisions taken in the past.
- The IBC has provided a major stimulus to ease of doing business, enhanced investor confidence and has given a boost to both foreign and domestic investors as they now look at India as an attractive investment destination.
- The implementation of IBC has helped in pushing economic growth higher by a

few percentage points by saving various companies from premature death.

- The success of the IBC is not just in numbers, rather its performance lies in the behavioural change of the companies (debtors). Credible threat of the IBC process that a company may change hands has changed the behaviour of the debtors. Thousands of debtors are settling defaults in early stages of the life cycle of a distressed asset.

Challenges

- Out of all the cases admitted to NCLT under IBC, only around 15% ended in Resolution and rest went for Liquidation
- Very few benches of NCLT to admit the insolvency cases, resulting in delay in resolution
- Cross border insolvency has not yet been implemented

Comment

The code aims at early identification of financial failure and maximizing the asset value of insolvent firms. The Code is thus a comprehensive and systemic reform, which will give a quantum leap to the functioning of the credit/bond market. It would take India from among relatively weak insolvency regimes to becoming one of the world's best insolvency regimes giving a big boost to ease of doing business in India.

IBC 2016 was amended in 2021 to introduce a **"Pre-Pack" scheme for MSMEs**.

✓ If an MSME has defaulted and the default is of less than Rs. 1 crore then "Pre-Pack" scheme can be used. Under this scheme the previous promoters and the creditors will take up a resolution plan to NCLT for approval rather than resolution plan suggested by outsiders through open bidding process in which case the company may go to new owners. And during this resolution process, the management of the firm (MSME) will remain with the original promoters. [Under normal IBC proceedings, the management control of the firm passes on to Resolution Professionals]

✓ If the resolution plan does not offer full recovery for operational creditors, then an open bidding process for submission of resolution plan can be conducted in which there will be chances that the company (MSME) may go to some other new owners and this will force the original promoters to compensate the operational creditors. This is called "Swiss Challenge".

Following are differences between Pre-Pack and Corporate Insolvency Resolution Process:

Pre-Packaged Insolvency Resolution Process (PIRP)	Corporate Insolvency Resolution Process (CIRP)
Only corporate debtors can initiate PIRP	Corporate debtors or creditors anyone can initiate CIRP
The owner of the distressed company (debtor) submits the resolution plan	Public bidding process happens wherein anyone can submit the resolution plan
Existing management retains control of the distressed firm under PIRP	Management of the distressed firm is passed on to 'Resolution Professionals' in CIRP
Applicable for defaults of less than Rs. 1 crore	Applicable for defaults of more than Rs. 1 crore.
Should be completed in 120 days	Should be completed in 180 days

4

Government Budgeting

4.1 Introduction

Budget is an estimate of income and expenditure for a future period of time. The estimated receipts and expenditure of the government of India in respect of each financial year is called the budget of GoI. Article 265 of the Constitution provides that no tax shall be levied or collected except by authority of law. And as per Article 266 no expenditure can be incurred except with the authorization of the legislature. Government takes the approval of the parliament for the taxes/receipts through the Finance Bill and the approval for the expenditures through the Appropriation Bill.

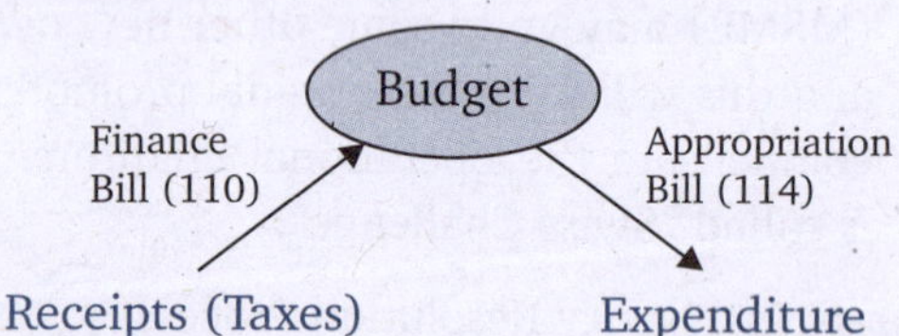

Budget is prepared by the Budget Division, Department of Economic Affairs, Ministry of Finance. The Article 112 specifies that the President shall, in respect of every financial year, cause to be laid before both the houses of the parliament, the Annual Financial Statement (Budget) of estimated receipts and expenditures of the government in respect of every financial year from 1st April to 31st March. Every budget gives three sets of figures. For example, the budget (Annual Financial Statement) presented in Feb 2023 for the year 2023-24 will contain the following figures:

- Budget Estimate (BE) for the next FY 2023-24
- Budget and Revised Estimate (RE) for the current FY 2022-23
- Actual figures for the preceding FY 2021-22

There can be three kinds of Budget (based on time period) presented by the government:

1. **Full Budget:** It contains the government's estimate for expenditure and receipts for the entire financial year.
2. **Interim Budget:** During an election year, the ruling government may present an interim budget which is a complete set of accounts, including both expenditure and receipts but only for a part of the year. An Interim Budget gives the complete financial statement, very similar to a full Budget. When the new government will be formed, it shall prepare the full budget. There is no such constitutional obligation to prepare an interim budget, it is just an unwritten convention that political parties have developed.
3. **Vote-on-Account:** [Article 116] If the budget has not been passed and the

government needs money to carry on its normal activities, then to overcome such difficulty, the Constitution has authorized the Lok Sabha to make any grant in advance in respect to the estimated expenditure (through Appropriation bill) for a part of the financial year, pending the completion of the procedure for the voting of the demand for grants and the enactment of the Appropriation bill in accordance with Article 114. This provision is known as the 'vote on account'. 'Vote on Account' deals only with the expenditure side of the government's budget. Through 'Vote on Account', the government obtains the vote of the Parliament for a sum sufficient to incur expenditure on various items for a part of the year. Normally, the 'Vote on Account' is taken for two months for a sum equivalent to one, sixth of the estimated expenditure for the entire year under various demands for grants.

Budget Classification based on Themes

1. **Zero-based Budget:** Zero-based budgeting is different from the incremental (conventional) budgeting system in the sense that the former begins with a zero base, i.e., from scratch and are not based on previous trends/data. For example, if we are preparing the budget for any particular department or Ministry then all the expenses are calculated fresh rather than taking the previous year expenditure and just incrementing it by some percentage.
    - It ensures that the activities carried out are relevant for the accomplishment of objectives
    - Excessive and unnecessary expenditure on various activities is identified and eliminated
2. **Outcome Budget:** It reflects the endeavour of the Government to convert "Outlays" into "Outcomes" by planning expenditure, fixing appropriate targets and quantifying deliverables of each scheme. The "Outcome Budget" is an effort of the Government to be transparent and accountable to the people. Outcome budget is presented in the parliament.

    For example, suppose if government is budgeting Rs. 20,000 crores for the LPG subsidy for FY 2021-22 then under the outcome budget it may set a target that it is planning to distribute LPG cylinders to 9 crore households.
3. **Gender Budget:** Gender Budgeting includes gender sensitive formulation of legislation, policies, plans, programs, schemes, resource allocation, implementation, monitoring, audit and impact assessment of programs and schemes.

    Gender gaps persist in education, employment, entrepreneurship and public life opportunities and outcomes. Gender budgeting is a way for governments to promote equality through the budget process. Gender budget ensures that gender commitments are translated into budgetary commitments.

    Gender Budget Statement was first introduced in the Indian Budget in 2005-06. Government publishes a Gender Budget Statement annually along with the Union Budget. Gender budget has been allocated 10% of the overall budgetary resources.

4.2 Budget Procedure

The budget is presented in the parliament on the first working day of February at 11.00 am. The General Budget is presented in Lok Sabha by the finance minister and he/she makes a speech introducing the budget and after the speech it is presented in the Rajya Sabha. No discussion on Budget takes place on the day it is presented to the parliament.

The main budget documents presented to parliament comprise, besides the Finance Minister Budget Speech, of the following:

- Annual Financial Statement
- Demand for Grants
- Appropriation Bill
- Finance Bill

Budget is discussed in two stages – the general discussion followed by detailed discussion.

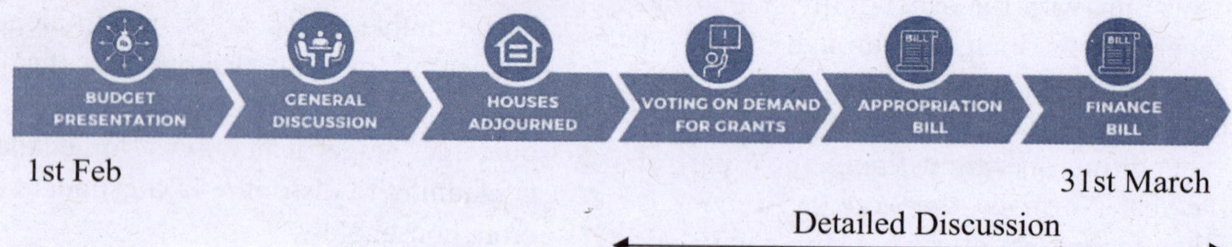

General Discussion

The general discussion on the Budget is held on the day subsequent to the presentation of the Budget by the finance minister. Discussion at this stage is confined to the general examination of the Budget and policies of taxation expressed during the budget speech. General discussion on the budget happens in both the houses of the parliament. After the general discussion is over, the houses are adjourned for a fixed number of days.

Detailed Discussion (Discussion on Demand for Grants)

During this period the demand for grants of various ministries/ departments are considered by the "Departmentally Related Standing Committees" (DRSC). (*There are 24 DRSCs and approximately 100 ministries. One DRSC needs to prepare reports on about 5 ministries' demands for grants*). These committees are required to make their reports to the house within the specified period without asking for more time. After the reports of the standing committees are presented to the house (Lok Sabha), the house proceeds to the discussion and voting on Demands for Grants, ministry wise. The time for discussion and voting of Demands for Grants is allocated by the speaker in consultation with the leader of the house. On the last day of the allocated days, the speaker puts all the outstanding demands to the vote of the house. This device is popularly known as "Guillotine". It concludes the discussion on demand for grants. In Rajya Sabha, there is only a General Discussion on the budget. It does not vote on the Demand for Grants.

[The demand for grants of Union Territories without Legislature is among the several demand for grants of the Centre and is approved as part of the Union budget. And the taxes from such Union territories are received under Consolidate Fund of India.

As per Article 113 of the Constitution, expenditure which is charged upon the Consolidated Fund of India shall not be submitted to the Vote of the Parliament, but discussion can happen in either House of the Parliament on any of those estimates. The estimates which relate to other (than charged) expenditure shall be submitted in the form of demands for grants to the Lok Sabha, and the Lok Sabha shall have the power to assent, or to refuse to assent, to any demand, or to assent to any demand subject to a reduction of the amount specified therein.]

Appropriation Bill

After the voting on Demand for Grants is over, Govt. introduces the Appropriation Bill as per Article 114 of the Constitution. The Appropriation Bill is intended to give authority to the Govt. to incur expenditure and meet grants from and out of the Consolidated Fund of India.

Finance Bill

The Finance Bill (Article 110) seeking to give effect to the Government's taxation proposals is introduced in the Lok Sabha immediately after the presentation of the General Budget on the same day but is taken up for consideration and passing after the Appropriation Bill is passed. *However certain provisions in the Bill related to levy and collection of fresh duties or variations in the existing duties come into effect immediately on the expiry of the day on which the Bill is introduced by virtue of a declaration under the Provisional Collection of Taxes Act 1931.* The Parliament has to pass the Finance Bill within 75 days of its introduction.

Appropriation and Finance Bills are Money Bills. These bills are sent to the Rajya Sabha for passing but it is on the Lok Sabha whether to accept any recommendations of the Rajya Sabha or not. Whether Lok Sabha accepts the recommendations of the Rajya Sabha or not the Bills are deemed to be passed by both the houses.

During the Budget, to change ***direct taxes****, amendment in the particular Act is required through the Finance Act. But in case of* ***indirect taxes*** *like "Central Excise", "Customs Duty", a ceiling rate is specified in the particular Act and if the Excise and Customs duty are within that ceiling rate then amendment in the particular Act is not required but if the duty has to be increased beyond the Ceiling rate, then amendment in that particular Act is required through the Finance Act. For amending GST rates, GST Council takes a decision and a gazette notification is issued.*

Supplementary Demand for Grants

If the amount authorized to be expended for a particular service for the current financial year is found to be insufficient for the purpose of that year or when a **need has arisen** during the current financial year for supplementary or additional expenditure upon some 'new service' not contemplated in the budget for that year then the President causes to be laid before both the Houses of Parliament another statement showing the estimated amount of that expenditure which is called "Supplementary Demand for Grants".

Demand for Excess Grants

If any money **has been spent** on any service during a financial year in excess of the amount granted for the service for that year, the President causes to be presented to Lok Sabha a demand for such excess (which is called "Demand for Excess Grants"). All cases involving such excesses are brought to the notice of Parliament by the CAG through a report on the Appropriation Accounts. The excesses are then examined by the Public Accounts Committee which makes recommendations regarding their regularisation in its report to the House.

*The "**Supplementary Demands for Grants**" are presented to and passed by the House **before** the end of the financial year while the "**Demands for Excess Grants**" are made after the expenditure has actually been incurred and **after** the financial year to which it relates has expired.*

4.3 Government Accounts

The Accounts of government of India are kept in three parts:

1. **Consolidated Fund of India (CFI):** All revenues received by the government by way of taxes whether direct or indirect and other receipts flowing to the government in connection with the conduct of government business like receipts from Railways, Post, transport, government PSUs etc. are credited into the CFI. Similarly, all loans raised by the government by issue of public notifications, treasury bills and loans obtained from foreign governments and international institutions are credited into this fund. All expenditures incurred by the government for the conduct of its business including repayment of internal and external debt and release of loans to States/ Union Territory governments for various purposes are debited against this fund and no amount can be withdrawn from the Fund without the authorization from the Parliament.
2. **Contingency Fund of India:** This fund is in the nature of an imprest (a fixed fund for a specific purpose) account and is kept at the disposal of the President of India (by the Secretary to the Government of India, Ministry of Finance, Department of Economic Affairs) to enable the government to meet unforeseen expenses pending authorization by the Parliament. The money is used to provide immediate relief to victims of natural calamities and also to implement any new policy decision taken by the Government pending its approval by the Parliament. In all such cases after the Parliament meets, a Bill is presented indicating the total expenditure to be incurred on the scheme/ project during the current financial year. After the Parliament votes the Bill, the money already spent out of the Contingency Fund is recouped/ withdrawn from the Consolidated Fund of India to ensure that the corpus of the Contingency Fund remains intact. The corpus of the fund is Rs. 30,000 crores and can be enhanced from time to time by the Parliament.
3. **Public Account of India:** All the public money received by the government other than those which are credited to the Consolidated Fund of India are accounted for Public Account. The receipts into the Public Account and disbursements out of it are not subject to vote by the Parliament. Receipts under this account mainly flow from the sale of Savings Certificates, contributions into General Provident Fund, Public Provident Fund, Security Deposits and Earnest Money Deposits (a kind of security deposits) received by the government. In respect of such deposits, the government is acting as a Banker or Trustee and refunds the money after the completion of the contract/ event.

State Governments has their own Consolidated Fund, Public Account and Contingency Fund (as mandated by the Constitution). Union Territory (with Legislative Assembly) has their own Consolidated Fund, Contingency Fund and Public Account as per "The Government of Union Territories Act, 1963". The Contingency Fund of Union Territories lies with their "Administrators" or "Lieutenant Governors".

4.4 Budget Classification

The article 112 specifies that the budget must distinguish the expenditures on revenue account from other expenditures (capital account). Therefore, the budget comprises of the Revenue Budget and Capital Budget.

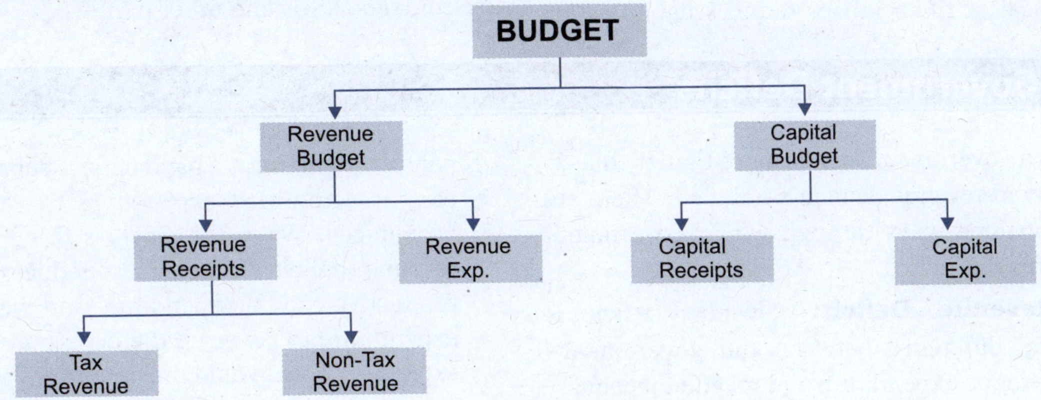

Revenue Receipts: Those receipts of the government which neither creates a liability for the government nor reduces the assets (physical or financial) of the government are called revenue receipts. Revenue receipts are non-redeemable i.e., they cannot be reclaimed from the government. Revenue receipts can be of two types.

- Tax Revenues consists of direct and indirect taxes of the central government.
- Non-Tax Revenue consists of interest receipts on account of loans given by central government, dividend and profits on investments made by the central government (i.e., PSUs), fees and fines and other receipts for services rendered by the government like passport fees etc. Cash grants-in-aid from foreign countries and international organisations are also part of the non-tax revenue.

Revenue Expenditure: Those expenses of the government which neither creates any asset (physical or financial) nor reduces any liabilities are called revenue expenditure. Revenue expenses relate to the expenses incurred for the normal functioning of the government departments and various services, interest payments on debt incurred by the central government and grants given to the state government and local bodies.

Capital Receipts: Those receipts of the government which either creates liability or reduces the assets (physical or financial) are called capital receipts. The main items of capital receipts are loans raised by the government from the public (market borrowings), borrowing by the government from the RBI, commercial banks and other financial institutions through the sale of government securities (treasury bills/ dated securities), loans received from foreign governments and international organizations, and recovery of loans previously granted by the central government. It also includes small savings schemes (Post office savings accounts,

National Savings Certificates etc.), Provident Funds and net receipts obtained from the sale of shares in PSUs (disinvestment).

Capital Expenditure: Those expenses of the government which either creates assets (physical or financial) or reduces liabilities are called capital expenditures. Capital expenditures include acquisition of land, building, machinery, equipment, purchase of shares by the government and loans and advances by the central government to state and union territory governments, PSUs and other parties.

4.5 Government Deficits

When a government spends more than it collects by way of revenue, it incurs a deficit. There are mainly three ways through which government captures this deficit.

1. **Revenue Deficit:** Revenue Deficit is the difference between the government's revenue expenditure and revenue receipts.

   Revenue Deficit = Revenue Expenditure – Revenue Receipts

   Revenue Deficit implies that government's current expenses are more than its current revenues and will have to use up the savings of other sectors of the economy to finance its consumption expenditure. Since a major part of the revenue expenditure (salary, pension, interest payments, subsidies etc.) is committed expenditure, it cannot be reduced. When the Govt. is faced with revenue deficit, it generally reduces the productive capital expenditure and welfare expenditure to cover up the excess revenue expenses. This would mean lower future growth and adverse welfare implications. Revenue Deficit is bad because it implies that Govt. is spending more on its current and day to day needs (which may not give return in future) than its current revenues.

2. **Fiscal Deficit:** It is the difference between the government's total expenditure (Revenue and Capital) and its total receipts (Revenue and Capital) except the borrowings.

Fiscal Deficit = Total Expenditure – Total Receipts except borrowing
= (Rev Exp. + Cap Exp.) – (Rev Rec. + Cap Rec. except borrowing)
= (Rev Exp. - Rev Rec.) + (Cap Exp. – Cap Rec. except borrowing)
= Revenue Deficit + Cap Exp. – Cap Rec. except borrowing
= Total borrowing
= Borrowing at home + borrowing from RBI + Borrowing from abroad

Let us understand fiscal deficit with an example.

Suppose, government's total expenditure = 17 lakh crore

and receipts = 13 lakh crore

Then government will have to borrow (17 lakh crore –13 lakh crore) 4 lakh crores to meet its expenditure. And this 4 lakhs crore is called the fiscal deficit. That is why fiscal deficit is also equal to the total borrowing i.e. 4 lakh crore.

But this 4 lakhs crore which government borrowed **is also part of capital receipt** for the government and it must be included in capital receipts. So, in actual sense, government's total receipts will become 17 lakh crores (i.e., 13 lakh crore + 4 lakh crore borrowing).

Hence, in the above example:

Fiscal Deficit = Total expenditure - total receipts **except borrowing**

Otherwise, the difference of total expenditure and total receipts will always be zero.

Fiscal deficit indicates the total borrowing of the government from all sources i.e. domestic borrowing plus borrowing from external sources. Domestic borrowing includes government's debt securities like Treasury Bills and Dated Securities. Commercial banks purchase these securities on a major scale to meet their SLR requirements. Other financial institutions and RBI also purchases these securities.

The fiscal deficit is a key variable in judging the financial health of the government sector and the stability of economy. It can be seen from above that revenue deficit is a part of fiscal deficit. A large share of revenue deficit in the fiscal deficit indicates that a large part of borrowing is being used to meet its consumption expenditure needs rather than investment.

3. **Primary Deficit:** A large part of the government's fiscal deficit is because it needs to pay interest on its previous accumulated debt. If we want to measure the government's deficit excluding the interest payment on the previous debt then it is called the primary deficit. The goal of measuring the primary deficit is to focus on present fiscal imbalances.

   Primary Deficit = Fiscal Deficit - Net interest liabilities

   So, primary deficit tells about the deficit in the government's budget excluding the interest liabilities on the government's accumulated debt.

'Effective revenue deficit' and 'effective capital expenditure'

The definition of the revenue expenditure is that it shall not create any physical or financial assets. But this creates a problem in accounts. There are several **grants** given by the Central Government to the States / UTs which comes under revenue expenditure for the central government but some of these grants create assets, which are owned by the State government and not by the Central government. Hence, for Central Government it is basically revenue expenditure but ultimately it is creating asset for the State government. For example, under the MGNREGA programme, some capital assets such as roads, ponds etc. are created, thus the grants for such expenditure shall not strictly fall in the revenue expenditure. Hence the central government also calculates 'effective revenue deficit' which excludes such grants that are used for creation of assets and 'effective capital expenditure' which adds such grants.

- Effective Revenue Deficit = Revenue Deficit – Grants given to states for creation of capital assets
- Effective Capital Expenditure = Capital Expenditure + Grants given to states for creation of capital assets.

Deficit financing is the budgetary situation where government expenditure is higher than its revenue. It is a practice adopted for financing the excess expenditure with outside resources by either printing of additional currency or through borrowing.

4.6 Fiscal Policy

(Fiscal means related to expenses and receipts of the Government). Fiscal policy is the means by which government adjusts its **spending levels** and **tax rates** to monitor and influence a nation's economy. It is a sister strategy to monetary policy. Fiscal policy and monetary policy are used in various combinations to direct a country's economic goals.

The main objectives of government's fiscal policy are:

- Economic Growth (Stabilisation of business cycles)
- Maintain high level of employment
- Control inflation
- Equitable distribution of wealth
- Welfare (subsidies, income support, health, education etc.)

The above are not priority wise and depending on the situation of the economy, Govt. keeps on changing its focus among these.

Fiscal Policy can be either Expansionary or Contractionary.

- **Expansionary fiscal policy:** In case of expansionary fiscal policy Govt. increases spending and reduces tax levels to increase the aggregate demand in the economy. For example, suppose an economy has slowed down, unemployment levels are up, consumer spending is down and businesses are not making substantial profits. A Govt. thus decides to fuel the economy's engine by decreasing tax levels (which will increase consumers disposable income) and increasing Govt. spending in the form of buying services from the market (i.e., building roads, infrastructure, schools etc.) By paying for such services, the government creates jobs and wages that are in turn pumped into the economy. Pumping money into the economy by decreasing tax level and increasing government spending is also known as **pump priming**. With more money in the economy and fewer taxes to pay, consumer demand for goods and services increases. This in turn rekindles businesses and turns the cycle around from stagnant to active.
- **Contractionary fiscal policy:** In case of contractionary fiscal policy, Govt. reduces spending and increases tax levels to suck the money out of economy and hence reduces the aggregate demand. For example, when the inflation in the economy is high, the economy may need a slowdown. In such a situation, the government can use its fiscal policy to decrease public spending and increase taxes to suck money out of the economy i.e., decrease the money circulation. This ultimately reduces the demand for goods and services in the economy as people have less money and lowers the inflation level.

Government's fiscal policy has big role in stabilizing the economy during business cycles. The two important phases of business cycles are boom and recession. A recession should not be allowed to grow into a deep recession. Similarly, a boom should not explode bigger. We may say that amplifying the business cycle is dangerous (growing boom and deepening recession). Practically fiscal policy responses using taxation and expenditure can go in two ways in response to the business cycle: Countercyclical and pro-cyclical.

A **counter-cyclical** fiscal policy refers to strategy by the government to counter boom or recession through fiscal measures. It works against the ongoing boom or recession trend; thus, trying to stabilize the economy. Understandably, countercyclical fiscal policy works in two different ways during these two phases. During the boom phase, countercyclical fiscal policy tries to reduce the aggregate demand by reducing government expenditure and increasing tax levels. During the recession phase, countercyclical fiscal policy raises aggregate demand by increasing expenditure and reducing the tax levels. So, a counter cyclical fiscal policy tends to cool down the economy when there is a boom and stimulate the economy when there is a slowdown.

Pro-cyclical is the opposite of countercyclical. Here, fiscal policy goes in line with the current mood of the business cycle i.e., amplifying them. For example, during the time of boom, government makes high expenditure and doesn't hike taxes. Thus, boom grows further. Such a policy is dangerous and brings instability in the economy. And during recession, government reduces the spending and increases the tax leading to further slowdown in the economy. This kind of fiscal policy is dangerous and brings instability in the economy.

The Economic Survey 2016-17 has acknowledged that India's fiscal stance has an in-built bias toward higher deficits, because spending rises pro-cyclically during growth surges (boom period), while revenue and spending are deployed counter-cyclically during slowdowns.

Business Cycle Fiscal Policy	Boom	Recession	Outcome
Pro-Cyclical	Expenditure increases Tax decreases	Expenditure decreases Tax increases	Deepens recessions and amplifies expansions, thereby increasing fluctuations in the business cycles
Counter Cyclical	Expenditure decreases Tax increases	Expenditure increases Tax decreases	Softens the recession and moderates the expansions, there-by decreasing fluctuations in the business cycle

Fiscal Consolidation policy: It is an effort by the Government to bring down fiscal deficit. It is an effort to reduce public debt, raise revenues and bring down wasteful expenses.

4.7 Perspectives on Deficit and Debt

One of the main criticisms of deficits is that they are inflationary. This is because when government increases spending or cut taxes, **aggregate demand increases**. Firms may not be able to supply/produce higher quantities that are being demanded at the ongoing prices, resulting in an increase in price. However, if there are unutilised resources in the economy and the output is held back by lack of demand then a higher fiscal deficit will be accompanied by higher demand and higher supply/output and therefore **it may not be inflationary.**

If the economy is in boom phase and the economic resources are fully utilized then if government incurs fiscal deficit, there is a decrease in private investment due to reduction in the amount of savings available to the private sector. This is because if the government decides to borrow from the private citizens by issuing bonds to finance deficits, these bonds (which are risk free) will compete with corporate bonds and other financial instruments for the available supply of funds. If people decide to buy government bonds, the funds remaining to be invested in private sector will be less. Thus, some private/corporate borrowers will get **"crowded out"** (displaced) of the financial markets as the government claims an increasing share of the economy's total savings.

Opposite of crowding out is "**crowding in**" where private investment increases as debt financed government spending increases. If in the economy there are unutilized resources or the economy is in slowdown/recession, then an increased government spending boosts the demand for goods which in turn increases the private sector demand for new output sources such as factories, equipment. Thus, the private sector crowds in (gets pulled in) to satisfy increasing consumer needs.

Do economies really need fiscal deficit?

Many economists including Lord Keynes had advocated the need for small fiscal deficits to boost economy specially in times of crisis. What it means is that, government should raise public investment by investing borrowed funds. The basic purpose of whole exercise is to accelerate the growth of the economy by government/ public intervention. Hence there is nothing fundamentally wrong with a fiscal deficit, provided the cost of intervention does not exceed the emanating benefits.

Also, if the government invests in infrastructure, future generations may be better off, provided the return on such investments is greater than the rate of interest. The actual debt can be paid off by the growth in output (and the resulting increase in tax resources). The debt should not then be considered burdensome. The growth in debt shall be judged by the growth of the economy as a whole.

The darker side of the story is, the borrowed funds, which always remain on tap have to be repaid. And pending repayment, these loans have to be serviced. **Ideally the return on investments on borrowed funds must be higher than the cost of borrowing.**

For example, if government borrows Rs. 100 at 10%, it must earn more than 10% on investment of Rs. 100. In that situation fiscal deficit will not pose any problem. However, the government spends money on all kinds of projects, including social sector schemes, where it is impossible to calculate rate of return at least in monetary terms. So, one will never know whether the borrowed funds are being invested wisely or not.

Findings from Previous Years Economic Surveys

- Debt sustainability depends on the "interest rate growth rate differential" (IRGD) i.e. the difference between the interest rate and the growth rate in the economy. Since the interest rate on debt paid by the Indian Government **has been less than** India's growth rate, in the Indian context, growth leads to debt sustainability but not necessarily vice-versa.

- As the IRGD is expected to be negative in the foreseeable future for India, a fiscal policy that provides an impetus to growth will lead to lower, not higher, debt to GDP ratio. This was the reason Economic Survey demonstrated counter-cyclical fiscal policy to enable growth during economic downturns like Covid-19.
- **In general, fiscal policy must be counter-cyclical** to smooth out economic cycles instead of exacerbating them. While counter-cyclical fiscal policy is necessary to smooth out economic cycles, it becomes critical during an economic crisis. This is because fiscal multipliers (the effect of Govt. expenditure on GDP growth) are greater during economic crisis.
- Most of the studies concur that fiscal policies are considerably more effective in recessions than in expansions.
- Studies have established that following a pro-cyclical fiscal stance leads to lower economic growth, higher volatility in output and higher levels of inflation. In contrast a counter-cyclical fiscal policy stance with policy actions against the cycle acts as a stabilizer by reducing output volatility and keeping growth on a steady path. It has also been established that industries have grown faster both in terms of output and pro ductivity in economies where fiscal policy has been more counter-cyclical.
- Evidence over the last two and a half decades demonstrates clearly that in India, higher GDP growth causes the ratio of debt-to-GDP to decline but not vice-versa.
- In India and other emerging market economies, evidence shows that the direction of **causality** between the two variables is: *higher growth leads to lower public debt as measured by their debt-to-GDP ratios but not vice-versa*. In contrast, when the GDP growth rate is low, no such causal relationship is reflected between growth and public debt. (This is because higher growth enables the IRGD to be negative and thereby ensuring debt sustainability).
- The phenomenon of crowding out of private investment is based on the notion that supply of savings in the economy is fixed. Therefore, higher fiscal spending may increase the demand for loanable funds and hence exert an upward pressure on interest rates, thereby discouraging private investment.
- However, for emerging economies such as India, an increase in public expenditure in areas that boost private sector's propensities to save and invest may enable private investment rather than crowding it out. In other words, in an economy that has unemployed resources, an increase in government spending increases the aggregate demand in the economy, which may induce the private sector to increase their investment in new machinery to cater to the increased demand, and hence put the unused resources to productive uses. This may have multiplier effects on aggregate demand, resulting in higher growth rates. In fact, if the public expenditure is directed to sectors where the fiscal multipliers are large – for instance for building infrastructure – such spending may significantly crowd in private investment as well.
- Recent research puts further doubt on the phenomenon of crowding out in rapidly growing economies by showing that the

supply of savings is not fixed but expands with income growth. In an economy operating below full capacity, the supply of savings may grow from greater government spending through demand creation and thereby greater employment. This is because, as highlighted by recent research, favourable demographics – in the form of a large population of working age – would enhance savings through meaningful jobs.

- While public investment is complementary to private investment in developing countries, the opposite holds true for developed countries. Whether an increase in Government expenditure for goods and services 'crowds out' domestic private investment, may depend upon how close the economy is to full employment. In India, there is no evidence of crowding out over the last three decades post liberalization.

Trends in Fiscal Deficit of Centre and States:

Central Govt. Fiscal Deficit

2017-18	2018-19	2019-20	2020-21	2021-22	2022-23	2023-24	2024-25	2025-26	2026-27
3.5%	3.4%	4.60%	9.20%	6.9%	6.4%	5.6%	4.8%	4.40%	4.30%

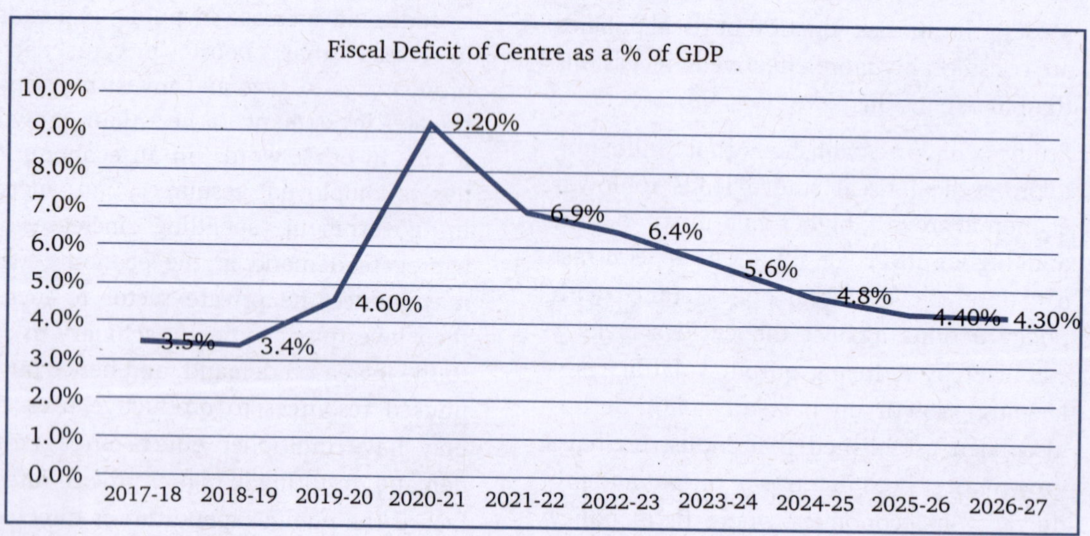

State Govt. Fiscal Deficit

2017-18	2018-19	2019-20	2020-21	2021-22	2022-23	2023-24	2024-25	2025-26
2.40%	2.50%	2.60%	4.70%	3.70%	3.40%	3.00%	3.30%	3.30%

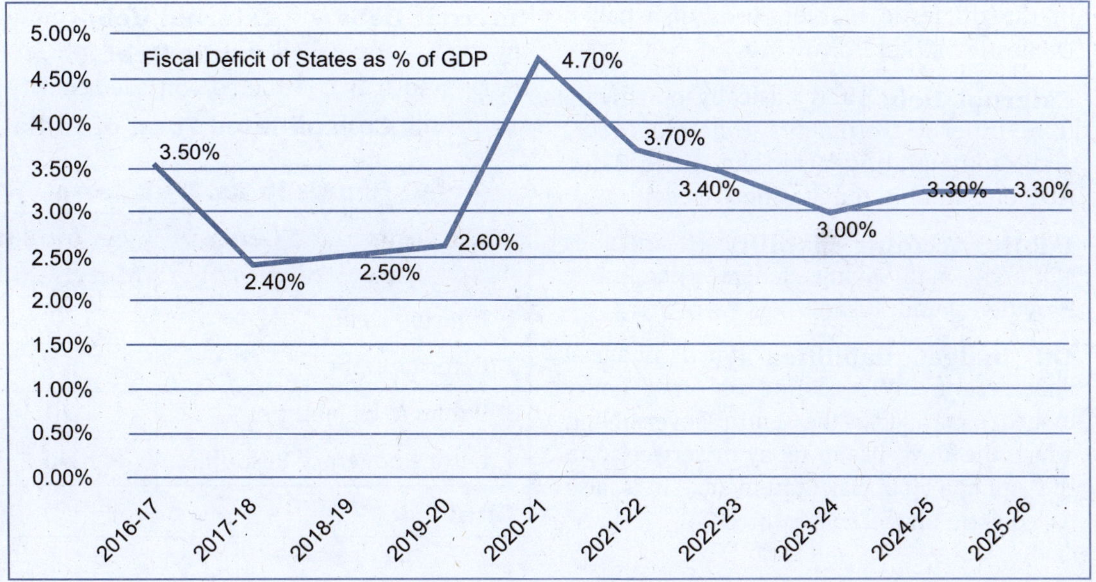

As per article 293 of Constitution, States need to take prior approval from the Centre for borrowing if:

- *States have taken debt from Centre and there are pending dues; or*
- *There is any outstanding loan on States with respect to which Central Govt. has given guarantee.*

But as almost every state has taken loan from the Centre and there are pending dues so they take permission from Centre before borrowing. If States are breaching their FRBM limits then they do not require Centre permission.

- For 2025-26, Rs. 2 lakh crore has been allotted for the 'Scheme of Financial Assistance to States for Capital Investment'. States can use these funds through this channel for capital expenditure and reforms.

Debt

Article 292 of the Constitution states that the government of India can borrow amounts specified by the Parliament from time to time. Article 293 of the Constitution mandates that the state governments in India can borrow only from internal sources. Thus, **the government of India incurs both internal and external debt while state governments incur only internal debt.** As per the recommendations of the 12th Finance Commission, access to external financing by the various **states** is facilitated by the Central Government which provides the **Sovereign guarantee for these borrowings**. From 1st April 2005 all General Category states borrow from multilateral and bilateral agencies (World Bank, ADB etc.) on a back-to-back basis viz. the interest cost and the risk emanating from currency and exchange rate fluctuations are passed on to states but **Central Government acts as a guarantor**(debt is basically in the name of Central Govt.)

Govt. of India (Central Govt.) Total Debt/ Liabilities = 1 + 2 + 3 + 4

1. **Internal Debt** [it is basically what Govt. of India borrows by issuing Debt Securities like Treasury Bills and Dated Securities

in the domestic market. It is also called Domestic Market Borrowings]

2. **External Debt** [It is basically borrowing from other Governments (bilateral debt) and Multilateral Agencies like World Bank, ADB etc. and FPI purchasing G-Secs]

3. **Public Account Liability** [It includes National Small Savings Schemes like Public Provident Fund, Kisan Vikas Patra etc.]

4. **Off budget liabilities** [Such financial liabilities of any corporate or other entity owned/controlled by the Central Government, which the Govt. has to repay or service from the Annual Financial Statement.] It is also called extra budgetary resources.

Internal Debt and **external debt** combined together is also called **Public Debt** (of Govt. of India) and it is contracted (on the security of) against the **Consolidated Fund of India**.

All figures in Rs. lakh crore	
Components of Central Govt. Debt	**As on 31st March 2026**
1. Internal Debt	170.3
2. External Debt	6.7
3. Public A/c Liabilities	20
4. Extra Budgetary Resources	Nil
Total	197

As on end March 2026, the total debt of Govt. of India was Rs. 197 lakh crore and out of this, public debt (internal + external) was Rs. 177 lakh crores which is around 90% of the total debt. In terms of GDP, the total central govt. debt is around 56% of GDP as on 31st March 2026.

Public debt in India is primarily contracted at fixed interest rates, with floating internal debt constituting only 1.7 per cent of GDP. The debt portfolio is, therefore, insulated from interest rate volatility, which also provides stability to interest payments.

The following chart represents Debt to GDP ratio of Centre and states for the last few years:

Debt/ GDP	2017-18	2018-19	2019-20	2020-21	2021-22	2022-23	2023-24	2024-25	2025-26	2026-27
Centre	46.0%	45.9%	47.80%	59.30%	57.0%	57.10%	57.80%	55.70%	56.1%	55.6%
State	25.1%	25.2%	26.30%	31.10%	28.7%	29.5%	28.20%	25.4%	–	–

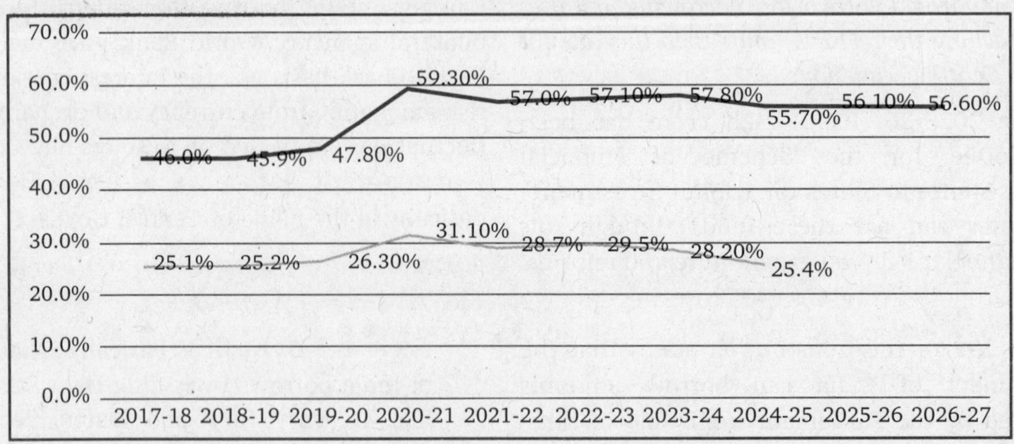

External Debt of India = External Debt of India refers to the debt owed to non-residents by the residents of the country (i.e., government and the private sector). As on Sept. 2025, external debt of India was $746 Billion (19.2% of GDP).

EXTERNAL DEBT OF INDIA (as on Sept. 2025) $746 billion = 19.2% of GDP	
"**Sovereign Debt**"	"**Non-Sovereign Debt**"
$155 billion (4% of GDP)	$591 billion (15.2% of GDP)
Sovereign Debt is also called Govt. of India (external) Debt *(State Govt. external debt is in the name of GoI only)* It includes • FPI/FII investments in G-securities • Loans under Bilateral Assistance • Loans under Multilateral Assistance	It includes • Commercial Borrowing • External Commercial Borrowing ECB plus FII investments in Indian corporate bonds • NRI Deposits

- India's external debt can also be classified as 'short-term' (18.4%) and long-term debt (81.6%).
- Commercial borrowings remained the largest component of external debt followed by non-resident deposits.
- Currency wise, India's external debt includes:
  - o US Dollar denominated (54.1%)
  - o Indian Rupee denominated (30.4%)
  - o And then some is Yen (6.5%), SDR (4.5%), Euro (3.6%).

  The Rupee denominated debt is basically FPIs/FIIs purchasing Indian Govt. bonds and Indian companies' bonds in Indian market and Masala bonds raised by Indian companies in abroad market and some NRI deposits in Indian rupees.
- Multilateral assistance includes loans from multilateral institutions such as International Bank for Reconstruction and Development (IBRD), International Development Agency (IDA) (IBRD and IDA are together called World Bank), International Fund for Agriculture Development (IFAD), Asian Development Bank (ADB), Organization of Petroleum Exporting Countries (OPEC) etc. Loan from IMF has been included under other govt. debt.
- Bilateral assistance includes loans from Japan, Germany, US, France, Russia
- Major portion of external debt is denominated in US dollars. Rest is in other currencies like Yen, Euro, Rupee (Masala bonds) etc. But all the external debt is **expressed** in US currency i.e., dollars. So, if 1 Euro has been raised as external debt and exchange rate is $1 = Euro 0.8, then external debt will become **$ 1.25** (1/0.8). Now if US dollar appreciated such that it becomes $1 = Euro 1, then the same external debt (of 1 Euro) will become **$ 1.** So, basically our W debt will decrease.

4.8 Monetization of Deficit and Deficit Financing

Before 1997, Govt. of India used to finance its deficit directly from RBI by issuing ad hoc Treasury Bills to RBI. So, Govt. used to issue bonds to RBI, which in return used to print currency and gives it to Govt., which used to create a debt on Govt. of India. This is called (direct) **monetization of deficit** from RBI and it's a primary market transaction between Govt. and RBI.

But this practice was stopped in 1997 by signing a historic agreement between Govt. of India and RBI and a scheme of 'Ways and Means Advance' (WMA) was started wherein govt. can take advances to accommodate temporary mismatches in the government's receipts and payments. So, basically **direct monetization of deficit was stopped since then (1997).**

And, it was also agreed that henceforth, the RBI would operate **only in the secondary market** through the Open Market Operation (OMO) route. The implied understanding also was that the RBI would use the OMO route not so much to support government borrowing but as a liquidity instrument to manage the balance between the policy objectives of supporting growth, checking inflation and preserving financial stability.

When govt. should go for direct monetisation?

Answer: When the banks do not have sufficient liquidity i.e., there is shortage of liquidity in the economy then if govt will try to borrow from banks then it will further deteriorate the liquidity situation and will result in increase in interest rate which will hamper the investments (for which govt is trying hard presently) in the economy and recovery may be slow. So, in this situation, govt can go for direct monetisation. BUT if banks are flush with liquidity, then first govt should try to borrow from banks.

Impact of "Monetization of Deficit"

- Helps in increasing aggregate demand in the economy thereby resulting in economic growth
- Results in increase in debt on Government thereby impacting overall macro-economic stability and may result in ratings downgrade
- Increases inflation due to increased money supply
- Increased money supply may result in depreciation of rupee which can lead to flight of capital from the country
- RBI can be seen as losing control over its monetary policy
- As such there is no issue if it is done once in exceptional circumstances but in India the problem is once it is done, then it will lure future governments of an easy route of financing their deficit

> ***"Deficit Financing":*** *It generally means that Govt. is having deficit (as expenses are more than receipts) which can be financed from different sources like from market borrowing or borrowing from abroad or there can also be the case that Govt may ask RBI to finance its deficit by printing more money i.e. monetization of deficit. (So, in deficit financing there can be various options to finance Govt.'s deficit and one of the options could be from RBI by printing cash i.e. monetization of deficit)*

4.9 Fiscal Responsibility and Budget Management (FRBM) Act 2003

India has a multi-party parliamentary system where electoral concerns play an important role in determining expenditure policies. In 2000, the fiscal situation of government of India had worsened and the Gross Fiscal Deficit reached to 6% of GDP. It was argued that, a legislative provision that is applicable to all governments - present and future - is likely to be effective in keeping the deficits under control. The government of India set up a committee (chaired by Dr. EAS Sharma) in 2000 to recommend draft legislation for fiscal prudence/ responsibility. Based on the recommendations of the committee, the government of India enacted the FRBM Act 2003 which became effective from July 2004.

The main objectives of the FRBM Act 2003 were:

- To ensure inter-generational equity
- Long term macroeconomic stability

The above two objectives were to be achieved broadly by

- Achieving sufficient revenue surplus
- Removing fiscal obstacles to monetary policy
- Effective debt management by limiting deficits and borrowing

Some of the important features of the FRBM Act 2003 are:

1. The central government shall

(a) take appropriate measures to limit the **fiscal deficit** up to **3% percent of GDP** by 31st March 2021

(b) endeavour to ensure that-

- ❖ The **general government debt** (equal to central govt. debt plus state govt. debt) does not exceed **60 per cent** of GDP by 2024-25
- ❖ The central government debt does not exceed 40 per cent of GDP by 2024-25

(c) not give additional guarantees (central government sometimes give guarantees for loans raised by State governments and PSUs) with respect to any loan on security of the Consolidated Fund of India in excess of 0.5 per cent of GDP in any financial year

(d) endeavour to ensure that the fiscal targets specified in (a) and (b) above are not exceeded after stipulated target dates

2. The central government shall prescribe the annual targets for reduction of fiscal deficit (in case it has crossed the above specified limit)

   Provided that exceeding the annual fiscal deficit target may be allowed on grounds of "*national security, act of war, national calamity, collapse of agriculture severely affecting farm output and incomes, structural reforms in the economy with unanticipated fiscal implications, decline in real output growth of a quarter by at least three per cent points below its average of the previous four quarters" (called escape clause)*

3. Any deviation from fiscal deficit target under the above clause (2) shall not exceed one half per cent (0.5%) of the GDP in a year.

4. The central government shall, in case of increase in real output growth of a quarter by at least three per cent points above its average of the previous four quarters, reduce the fiscal deficit by at least one-quarter per cent of the GDP in a year.

5. The central government **shall not borrow from the RBI** except by way of advances to meet temporary excess of cash disbursements over cash receipts.

6. Notwithstanding anything contained in clause 5 above, RBI may subscribe to the **primary issues** of the central government securities on grounds specified in clause 2 (**escape clause**)
7. Notwithstanding anything contained in clause 5 above, RBI may buy and sell central government securities in the secondary market.
8. Measures for fiscal transparency:

(a) The central government shall take suitable measures to ensure greater transparency in its fiscal operations in public interest and minimize as far as practicable, secrecy in the preparation of annual budget

(b) The central government at the time of presentation of the budget make such disclosures and, in such form, as may be prescribed

9. The finance minister shall review, on half-yearly basis, the trends in receipts and expenditure in relation to the budget and place before both Houses of Parliament the outcome of such reviews.
10. Except as provided under this Act, no deviation in meeting the obligations cast on the Central Government under this Act, **shall be permissible without approval** of **Parliament**.
11. The Central Government may entrust the CAG of India to review periodically as required, the compliance of the provisions of this Act and such reviews shall be laid on the table of both Houses of Parliament.
12. Central government shall lay, in each financial year, before both the houses of parliament, the following statements of fiscal policy along with the budget document:

(a) Medium Term Fiscal Policy Statement

(b) Fiscal Policy Strategy Statement

(c) Macroeconomic Framework Statement

(d) 'Medium-Term expenditure Framework Statement' should be laid in the session immediately following the session of the Parliament in which the budget has been presented)

Like Centre, every state has also fixed Fiscal deficit limit of 3% in their laws.

Due to the unprecedented Covid-19 crisis, Fiscal Deficit and Debt parameters deviated from the FRBM target levels. Accordingly, the FRBM Act should have been amended. But Government has not amended it till now as it admits that there are still potential unforeseen challenges. However, the Government would pursue a broad path of fiscal consolidation to attain a level of fiscal deficit lower than 4.5 per cent of GDP by FY 2025-26".

4.10 Strategic Disinvestment

In Disinvestment, the Govt. may sell its stakes (reduce its ownership) in a PSU/company to a buyer but the government may still retain its majority and management control. It may be done through listing of the PSU on the stock market (Initial Public Offering) or direct sale.

In the **Strategic sale** of a company, the transaction has two elements.

- Transfer of a block of shares to a strategic partner, and
- Transfer of management control to the strategic partner

The term "**Strategic Disinvestment**" means the sale of substantial portion of the Government share-holding of a central public sector enterprise (CPSE) of up to 50%, or such higher percentage (to the strategic partner) along with transfer of management control. *Strategic disinvestment is a way of privatisation.*

While Central Government is doing strategic disinvestment, other Government organizations (PSUs) or State Government are not allowed to bid/participate as it may continue the inherent inefficiencies of Government run firms.

Who decides for strategic disinvestment of PSUs?

As per the new policy (2019), Department of Investment and Public Asset Management (DIPAM) under the Ministry of Finance has been made the nodal department for the strategic disinvestment. DIPAM and NITI Aayog will now jointly identify PSUs for strategic disinvestment and then it is approved by CCEA.

Government has created an "**Alternative Mechanism**", which is an inter-Ministerial body to fasten the process of strategic disinvestment. It will decide the following:

- The quantum of shares to be transacted, mode of sale and final pricing of the transaction or lay down the principles/ guidelines for such pricing; and the selection of strategic partner/ buyer; terms and conditions of sale; and
- To decide on the proposals of Core Group of Secretaries on Disinvestment (CGD) with regard to the timing, price, the terms & conditions of sale, and any other related issue to the transaction.

This will facilitate quick decision-making and obviate the need for multiple instances of approval by CCEA for the same CPSE.

Purpose of Strategic Disinvestment

- The government has no business being in business. That is, the government's role is to facilitate a healthy business environment and the core competence of a government does not lie in selling fuel or steel at a profit.
- As governments spend more than they earn through taxes and other sources, additional income from the sale of stakes is always welcome especially for a developing economy as government needs to spend higher amounts on infrastructure to boost economic growth, along with its commitments on health and education.
- It is expected that the strategic buyer/ acquirer may bring in new management/ technology/investment for the growth of these companies and may use innovative methods for their development and may make these companies more profitable and create more value for its shareholders.

Purpose of disinvestment of profit-making PSUs

- Government may not want to remain in that business
- It gives revenue to government and helps in meeting fiscal deficit targets
- Even if a PSU is profitable, it may not be profitable because its efficiency. It can be profitable because it has a monopoly presence and private companies are not allowed in that sector. If government will privatize the PSU and allow other private companies then prices will come down and consumers will benefit.
- Example: Govt. of India in 1973 said that, in India only Govt will produce and sell coal through its PSU "Coal India Ltd. (CIL)". No private company can sell coal. All the blocks

were given to CIL and CIL extracts coal and supplies to govt and private power plants. The price is decided by govt. The question is how? Whatever is the cost of coal extraction, central govt. on top of it puts some profit margin and then it asks CIL to sell coal at that price. Now if the price is fixed on top of cost of production and no private player exists then the PSU will always be profitable. That is why CIL is one of the biggest coal company in the world, one of the most profitable coal company but quite inefficient.

Highlights of Disinvestment/Strategic Disinvestment Policy

Objectives

- Minimizing presence of Central Government Public Sector Enterprises including financial institutions and creating new investment space for private sector.
- Post disinvestment, economic growth of Central Public Sector Enterprises (CPSEs)/ financial institutions will be through infusion of private capital, technology and best management practices. Will contribute to economic growth and new jobs.
- Disinvestment proceeds to finance various social sector and developmental programmes of the government.

Policy features

- Policy covers existing CPSEs, Public Sector Banks and Public Sector Insurance Companies.
- Various sectors will be classified as strategic and non-strategic sectors.
- The strategic sectors classified are the following four:
  - Atomic energy, Space and Defence
  - Transport and Telecommunications
  - Power, Petroleum, Coal and other minerals
  - Banking, Insurance and financial services
- In strategic sectors, there will be bare minimum presence of the public sector enterprises. The remaining CPSEs in the strategic sector will be privatised or merged or subsidiarized with other CPSEs or closed.
- In non-strategic sectors, CPSEs will be privatised, otherwise shall be closed.

4.11 Fiscal Health Index (FHI)

The Fiscal Health Index (FHI) is a framework developed by NITI Aayog to assess the financial performance and financial stability of Indian states.

Objectives of Fiscal Health Index

- To provide a **comparative analysis of fiscal health** across Indian states through standardized metrics.
- To **identify areas of strength and concern** in states' fiscal management practices.
- To **promote transparency, accountability, and prudent fiscal management** through empirical assessment.

- To **assist policymakers in making informed decisions** aimed at enhancing fiscal sustainability and resilience.

FHI is based on a **comprehensive set of indicators** that are grouped into five broad categories:

1. **Revenue Generation and Mobilization:** Assessment of states' own revenue receipts, tax buoyancy, and non-tax revenue generation.
2. **Expenditure Management and Prioritization:** Evaluation of efficiency in expenditure allocation, prioritization of capital expenditure, and adherence to fiscal discipline.
3. **Debt Management:** Analysis of states' debt-to-GSDP ratios, interest payment burdens, and overall sustainability of debt portfolios.
4. **Fiscal Deficit Management:** Measurement of states' fiscal deficit as a percentage of Gross State Domestic Product (GSDP) and adherence to statutory limits.
5. **Overall Fiscal Sustainability:** Composite analysis of revenue, expenditure, deficit, and debt indicators to gauge long-term fiscal health.

Benefits of FHI

- **Informed policy decisions:** The index provides policymakers with insights into a government's fiscal health, helping them identify areas that require targeted reforms and strategic planning.
- **Promotes accountability:** By publicly ranking states, the index promotes transparency and incentivizes governments to adopt responsible fiscal management strategies.
- **Fosters competitive federalism:** When multiple states/jurisdictions are ranked, it encourages healthy competition to improve fiscal management and learn from top performers. This can lead to better outcomes for citizens.
- **Provides comparative analysis:** The index enables the benchmarking of a government's fiscal performance against its peers and best practices.

4.12 India's Tax System

Taxes can be classified in several ways:

1. One way is to classify them in progressive proportional and regressive way:

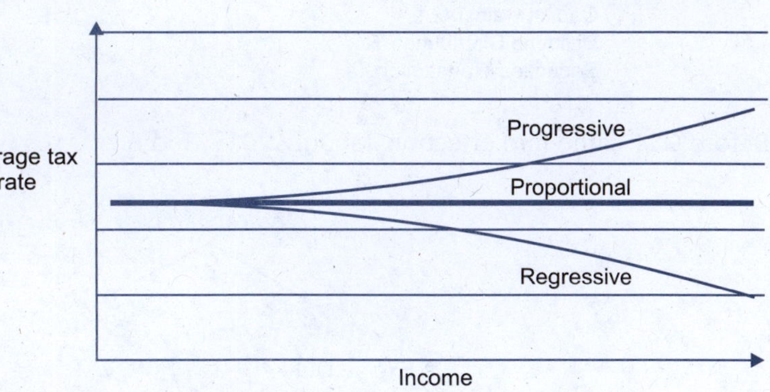

- Progressive Tax: Tax percentage increases with increase in income
- Proportional Tax: Tax percentage remains same/constant irrespective of income
- Regressive Tax: Tax percentage decreases with increase in income

2. Another way of classification is Specific tax and Ad-valorem tax:

❖ Specific tax is the tax which is fixed as per each unit of good or service rather than based on its value.

❖ Ad-valorem tax is levied as a percentage of value of the item it is imposed on, and not on the item's quantity, size, weight or other such factor.

3. Another way of classification is production and consumption-based tax. *(This classification is only for indirect taxes)*.

❖ Production tax (or origin-based tax) is levied where goods & services are produced.

❖ Consumption tax (or destination tax) are levied where goods & services are consumed.

4. Another way of classification is direct and indirect taxes:

❖ Direct taxes are those which are paid directly by an individual or organization to the imposing entity i.e., the government. For example, a taxpayer pays direct taxes to the government for different purposes like income tax, property tax etc.

❖ An indirect tax is a tax collected by an intermediary (such as a retail store) from the person who bears the ultimate economic burden of the tax (such as the consumer). For example, taxes levied on goods and services.

Following is the classification of the various taxes levied in India based on direct and indirect nature.

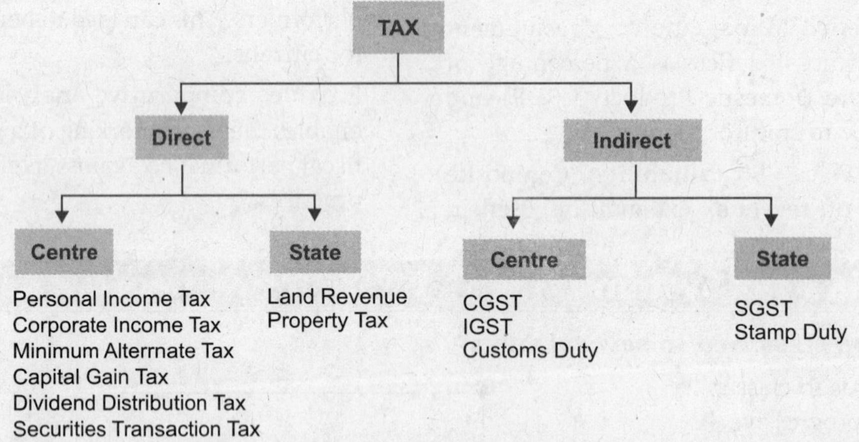

Before GST came into effect on 1st July 2017, Indirect taxes were classified in following way:

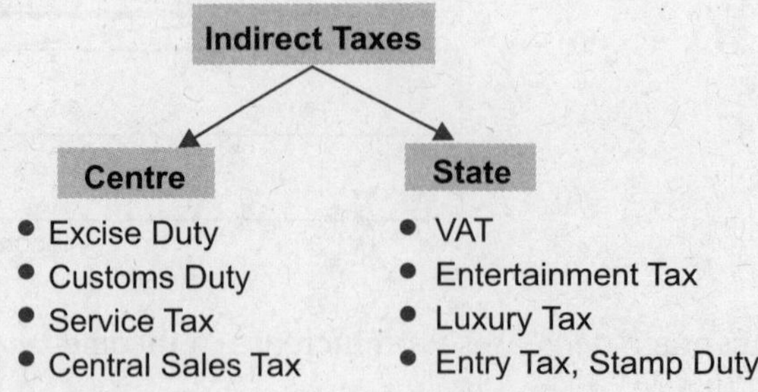

Central Government major taxes in FY 2024-25 were:

- Taxes on Income (Personal Income Tax): Rs. 12.57 lakh crore
- Corporate Income Tax: Rs. 9.8 lakh crore
- Goods and Services Tax: Rs. 10.6 lakh crore

Following are certain basic features of the above taxes: -

- **Personal income tax** is imposed by combining all sources of the individual's income like salary, rental income, interest income etc. Presently there are two tax regimes, new tax regime and old tax regime and individuals are free to choose either the old or new tax regime for tax payment but the new tax regime is the default one.

- **New Tax Regime:** In the new tax regime till Rs. 12 lakh income people will not have to pay any tax. But no exemptions/rebates are allowed in the new tax regime. If the income is more than Rs. 12 lakhs then the following slab will be applicable in the new tax regime:

Total income	Rate of tax
Upto Rs. 4,00,000	Nil
From Rs. 4,00,001 to Rs. 8,00,000	5 per cent
From Rs. 8,00,001 to Rs. 12,00,000	10 per cent
From Rs. 12,00,001 to Rs. 16,00,000	15 per cent
From Rs. 16,00,001 to Rs. 20,00,000	20 per cent
From Rs. 20,00,001 to Rs. 24,00,000	25 per cent
Above Rs. 24,00,000	30 per cent

A 'Standard Deduction' of Rs. 75000 is allowed for salaried employees. So, in case of salaried employees there is no tax till Rs. 12.75 lakh of annual income.

- In the old tax regime, till Rs. 5 lakh there is no tax. But individuals can claim exemptions related to savings under various schemes like PPF, NPS etc. up till certain limit. But if income is more than Rs. 5 lakhs then the following slab will be applicable:

Rs. 0 to 2.5 lakhs	Nil
Rs. 2.5 lakhs to 5 lakhs	5%
Rs. 5 lakhs to 10 lakhs	20%
Above Rs. 10 lakhs	30%

❖ **Corporate Income Tax (CIT)** is imposed on the profits of the corporates/ companies/ entities. All profit-making companies need to pay a flat rate of corporate income tax.

Presently two structures of CIT exist and the companies can opt anyone. If a company does not claim any tax exemptions, then it needs to pay 25.17% CIT, but if a company claims tax exemptions, then it needs to pay 34.94% as CIT.

Exemptions allowed		Exemptions not allowed	
CIT (standard rate)	= 30%	CIT (standard rate)	= 22%
Surcharge	= 12% (on 30%) = 3.6%	Surcharge	= 10% (on 22%) = 2.2%
CIT + Surcharge	= 33.6%	CIT + Surcharge	= 24.2%
Cess	= 4% (CIT + Surcharge) = 1.344%	Cess	= 4% (CIT+ Surcharge) = 0.97%
CIT + Surcharge + Cess	= 30% + 3.6% + 1.34%	CIT+ Surcharge+ Cess	= 22% +2.2% +0.97%
(CIT effective)	= **34.94%**	(CIT effective)	= **25.17%**

- **Minimum Alternate Tax (MAT):** At times it may happen that a taxpayer, being a company, may have generated income during the year, but by taking the advantage of various provisions of exemptions under the Income tax law (like depreciation, etc.), it may have reduced its tax liability or may not have paid any tax at all (zero tax companies). Due to increase in the number of zero taxpaying companies, MAT was introduced by the Finance Act, 1987. The objective of introduction of MAT was to bring into the tax net "zero tax companies" which in spite of having earned substantial book profits and having paid handsome dividends, do not pay any tax due to various tax concessions and incentives provided under the Income Tax Law.

  As per the concept of MAT, the tax liability of a company will be **higher** of the following i.e. (a) or (b):

(a) Tax liability of the company computed as per the normal provisions of the Income tax Law, i.e., tax computed on the taxable income of the company by applying the tax rate applicable. Tax computed in above manner can be termed as normal tax liability.

(b) Tax computed @ 15% (plus cess & surcharge) (17.16%) on book profit called the MAT.

Consider an example of a company named "XYZ Pvt. Ltd." for a particular year 2019-20:

Turnover/sales	= Rs. 1,00,00,000/-
Costs	= Rs. 60,00,000/-
(Booked) Profit	= Rs. 40,00,000/-
Exemptions/Rebates	= Rs. 25,00,000/-
Taxable Income	= Rs. 15,00,000/-

The tax liability of the company XYZ will be higher of:

(a) Normal tax liability = 34.94% of taxable income = 34.94% of Rs. 15,00,000/-
= Rs. 5,24,100/-

(b) MAT = 17.16% of Booked Profit = 17.16% of Rs. 40,00,000/- = Rs. 6,86,400/-

Thus, the tax liability of the company will be Rs. 6,86,400/- i.e., the company will have to pay MAT rather than the normal tax liability.

The companies claiming for the new tax rate of 25.17% CIT, would not be eligible for claiming tax exemptions/rebates and hence MAT will not be applicable on them. Those which will claim exemptions, the tax rate of 34.94% or MAT will be applicable.

- **Capital Gain Tax:** Capital gains tax is a tax on capital gains i.e., the gain/profit realized on the sale of an asset that was purchased at a cost amount that was lower than the amount realized on the sale. The most common capital gains are realized from the sale of shares/stocks, bonds, precious metals, artwork and property.
- Long term (holding period more than one year) Capital gain tax on equities is 12.5% and short term (holding period less than one year) capital gain tax is 20%.
- Long term (holding period more than 2 years) capital gain tax on real estate, gold and silver (physical or digital) is 12.5% and short-term gain is taxed at the applicable slab rates.
- **Dividend Distribution Tax (DDT):** Dividend is the distribution of a portion of company's profits/earnings to its owners/ shareholders. When a company announces dividends, it has to pay tax (DDT) on the dividend which is to be distributed to the owners and the owners also pay tax (as per their income tax slab) on the dividend received. DDT was abolished in the budget 2019-20 and dividend was made taxable in the hands of the shareholders.
- **Securities Transaction Tax (STT)** is a tax levied at the time of purchase and sale of securities like shares, bonds, debentures, mutual funds etc. listed on stock exchanges in India. The rate of STT differs based on the type of security traded and whether the transaction is a purchase or a sale. Purchaser and seller both pay STT. For example, while buying or selling an equity share purchaser and seller both need to pay 0.1% of share value as STT.
- **Land Revenue** is levied as per the different State Govt. Acts. Generally, the fixation of land revenue is done on the basis of classification of different types of land and cash value of the average yield of the land. Factors affecting productivity in value terms are taken into account. The land revenue tax is levied as Rs. per acre/hectare of land.
- **Property tax** in India is paid on "real property", which includes land and improvements on land, with the government appraising the monetary value of each such property and assessing the tax in proportion to its value. This tax amount is used to develop local amenities including road repairs, maintenance of parks and public schools, etc. Property tax varies from location to location and can be different in different cities and municipalities. Urban local bodies like municipal boards/ municipal corporations/ town area committees levy property tax under the relevant Acts.
- **All indirect taxes are regressive in nature.** Let us consider an example:

  Suppose a rich person (income 10 lacs) is purchasing bread worth Rs. 25 (including Rs. 5 tax). Then he is paying tax Rs 5. But if the same bread is purchased by a poor person whose income is Rs. 1 lac then he is also paying the same tax of Rs. 5.

  This means the poor person is paying higher tax percentage with respect to his income (Rs. 5/ Rs. 1,00,000 = .005%) and rich person is paying less tax percentage with respect to his income (Rs. 5/ Rs. 10,00,000 = .0005%). In that sense it is regressive.
- **Excise duty** was imposed on manufactured goods and was levied when the goods moved out of the factory area.

- **Customs duty** is imposed on export and import of goods.
- **Service Tax** was imposed on sale of services.
- **Central Sales Tax (CST)** was levied by the Centre on sale of goods from one state to another but the tax proceeds were collected and kept by the origin state, so it was also called origin-based tax.
- **Value Added Tax (VAT)** was imposed on the sale of goods within the state (Central government could not impose taxes on sale of goods within the state.) and it was imposed only on the value addition. In case of VAT, every entity in the value chain need to pay tax to the government according to their **value addition.**

Consider an example to understand VAT in a better way:

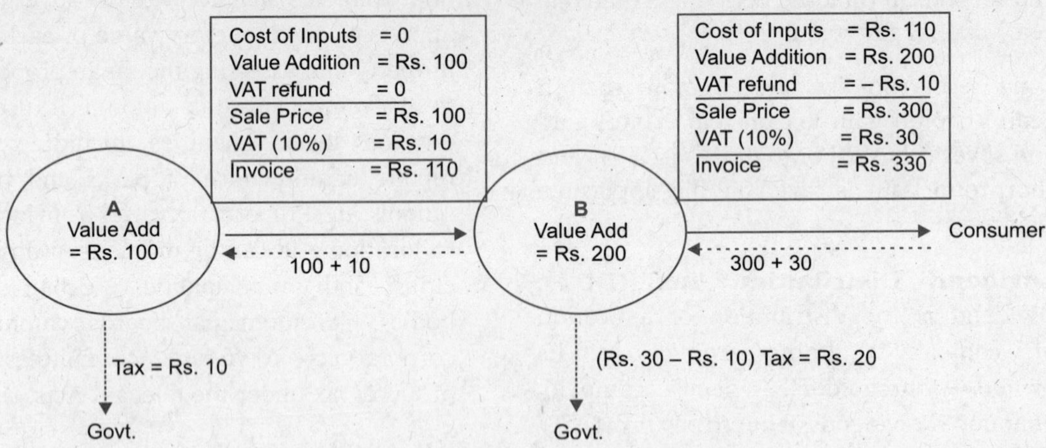

In the above example, A is doing value addition of Rs. 100 and selling the product to B in Rs. 110 and paying Rs. 10 as VAT to the government and B is doing value addi tion of Rs. 200 and is paying Rs. 20 VAT to the government. *Practically, B first pays the total VAT of Rs. 30 to the government on the total value addition of the product and when B shows the tax receipt of Rs. 10 (which B has paid to A on the purchase of inputs and A in turn has paid to the government) then the government credits/ refunds the Rs. 10 amount tax already paid by B to A on the purchase of inputs from A.* This is called **Input Tax Credit Mechanism** and it **prevents tax avoidance** because every entity in the value chain would ask for the tax receipt from the previous entity in the value chain to get credits of the taxes paid on the purchase of inputs.

- Entry Tax was a tax on the movement of goods from one state to another imposed by the state governments in India. It was levied by the recipient state to protect its tax base.
- Stamp Duty is a tax imposed on all legal property transactions. A physical stamp had to be attached to or impressed upon the document to denote that the stamp duty had been paid. Since it is imposed by states, the rate varies from state to state.

4.13 Goods and Services Tax (GST)

To understand GST, first we need to understand the basic problem under the indirect taxation system which was present before GST i.e., 1st July 2017. So, let us consider an example. Suppose the central excise duty is 12.5% and VAT rate is 10%.

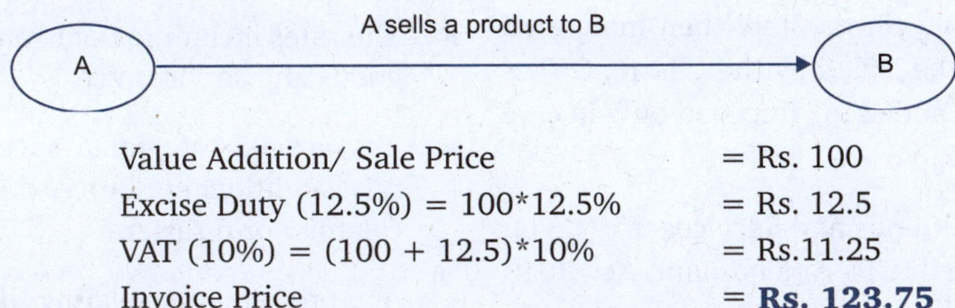

Value Addition/ Sale Price	= Rs. 100
Excise Duty (12.5%) = 100*12.5%	= Rs. 12.5
VAT (10%) = (100 + 12.5)*10%	= Rs.11.25
Invoice Price	= **Rs. 123.75**

So in the above example, VAT is being imposed even on excise duty, creating tax on tax and cascading effect and increasing the effective tax rate to 23.75%.

Till 30th June 2017, Central government used to impose its own indirect taxes like Service Tax, Excise Duty etc. and the State governments imposed their own indirect taxes like VAT, Entertainment Tax etc. So, when a producer used to produce a product then he used to pay Excise Duty to the Centre as well as VAT to the state which used to create tax on tax and when B used to sell the product to some other supplier it resulted in cascading effect and makes the product more costly in the market. Even in case of VAT, the credit was not available across the States. Further, different states had different VAT rates (1%, 4%, 12.5%, 20%) and gave exemptions on different category of products. Due to the above issues, effective tax used to be different in different states on the various goods and services and ultimately resulted in different prices of goods and services in different States. This fragmented the whole of India into a heterogeneous market affecting business and investment.

Goods and Services Tax (GST)

The introduction of GST across the nation is the most important indirect tax reform since independence. It has taken almost 16 years from the date of inception of the idea, formation of a task force, to passage in Parliament. It represents a Herculean, nationwide, multi-party consensus-building exercise and is the best example of the so called "cooperative federalism". It is an outcome of a grand bargain struck together by 29 States and seven UTs with the Central government. The States agreed to **give up** their right to impose sales tax on goods (VAT), and the Centre **gave up** its right to impose excise and services tax. In exchange they will each get a share of the unified GST collected nationally. The anticipated additional gains in efficiency, competitiveness, ease of doing business and overall tax collections are what drove this bargain.

GST has subsumed 17 Central and States indirect taxes viz. Central Excise Duty, Additional Excise Duty, Service Tax and State taxes like VAT, Entertainment tax, Entry tax, Purchase Tax, Luxury tax etc. which used to be imposed on sale of various goods and services. So, GST is one indirect tax on the supply of goods and services for the whole nation, which will make India one unified common market.

So now, when a product or service will be sold to the consumer across India, only one indirect tax will be imposed i.e. GST, which consists of Central GST (CGST) and States GST (SGST). And if a product is sold across State then Integrated GST (IGST) will be levied by the Centre. GST is basically a value added tax imposed only in case of value addition.

To introduce the Goods and Services tax (GST), the Constitution (101) Amendment Act 2016 was passed in September 2016. As per the Act, the Central Government has enacted Central GST (CGST) Act and every State Government has enacted State GST (SGST) Act in their respective States. Central Government has also enacted Integrated Goods and Services (IGST) Act which is applicable on interstate transactions and GST (Compensation to States) Act 2017 to compensate for the revenue shortfall of the States.

As per the Constitution (101st) Amendment Act 2016, GST council has been created which consists of the following: -

- The Union Finance Minister
- The Union Minister of State in charge of Revenue or Finance
- The Minister in charge of Finance or Taxation or any other Minister nominated by each State Government and UT with Assembly

The GST council makes recommendations to the Union and States regarding the following: -

- The taxes, cesses and surcharges which may be subsumed in GST
- Goods and services that may be exempted from GST
- Integrated Goods and Services Tax (IGST)
- The threshold limit of turnover below which goods & services may be exempted from GST
- The rates including floor rates with bands of goods and services tax
- Any special rate for a specified period, to raise additional resources during any natural calamity or disaster.
- Any other matter relating to the GST, as the Council may decide

Every decision of the GST council shall be taken at a meeting, by a majority of not less than three-fourths of the weighted votes of the members present and voting. The vote of the Central Government shall have a weightage of one-third and the vote of all the State Governments taken together shall have a weightage of two-thirds of the total votes cast.

Supreme Court Judgement [May 2022]

- *The recommendations of the GST Council are recommendatory in nature and not binding on the Union and States.*
- *The Parliament and State Legislatures posses' simultaneous power to legislate on GST.*
- *The recommendations of the GST Council are binding on the Government for only secondary/ subordinate legislations like changes in tax rates or framing of rules under CGST/SGST/ IGST but not for primary legislations. For primary legislations (like amendment in acts.... CGST/SGST), the recommendations have only persuasive value.*

Consider an example to understand GST in a better way:

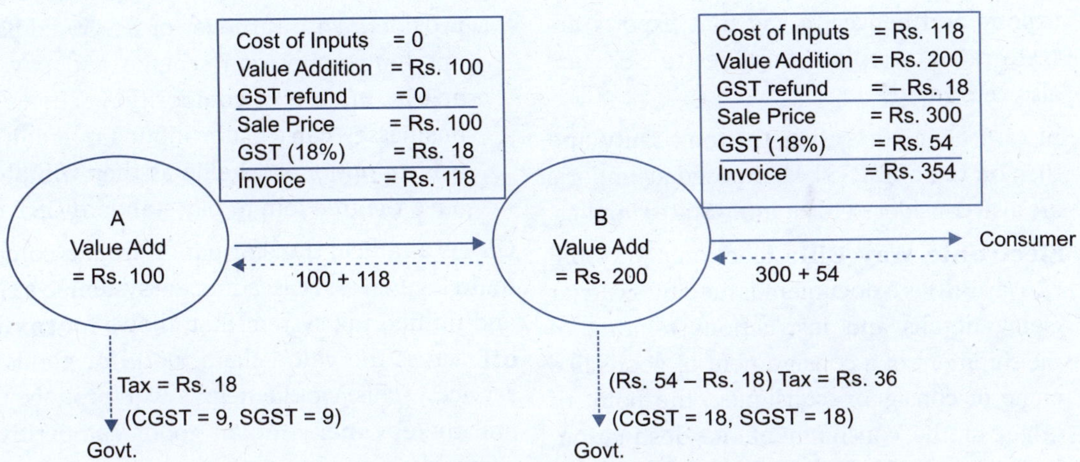

In the above example, A is doing value addition of Rs. 100 and selling the product to B in Rs. 118 and paying Rs. 18 GST to the government. B is doing value addition of Rs. 200 and is paying Rs. 36 GST to the government. *Since GST is a value added tax, so every entity in the value chain shall pay to the government tax only on their value addition.* Practically B shows the invoice of Rs. 354 to the government and pays a tax of Rs. 54 to the government but when it produces the tax receipt obtained from A to the government worth Rs. 18 then government credits/refunds Rs. 18 to B. This is called **Input Tax Credit Mechanism** as the taxes paid by B on the purchase of inputs from A i.e. Rs. 18 is credited by the government back to B.

Since there is only one tax i.e., GST and credits of input taxes paid at each stage is available in the subsequent stage of value addition **across India** (whereas in case of VAT input credit was available only within the State), hence it will prevent the dreaded cascading effect of taxes. This is the basic feature and advantage of GST.

Important aspects regarding implementation of GST:

- If A belong to one State (say UP) and B and the consumer belong to another State (say Bihar) then all the State GST i.e. Rs. 9 and Rs. 18 (=Rs. 27) will be passed on to the State where the product is being consumed by the consumer i.e., Bihar and the State where A belongs i.e. UP will not get any SGST. This is why GST is also called **consumption based and destination-based tax** as all the SGST is passed on to the consuming State i.e., Bihar.
- If A and B belong to different states then rather than GST, IGST will be levied by the Centre on the transaction between A and B which is again equal to the sum of CGST and SGST and ultimately distributed to the Centre and the consuming State equally.
- If B, rather than selling the product to the consumer in India, exports the products then IGST will be imposed as IGST is levied on inter-State supplies. The GST paid in the entire value chain and the IGST paid at

the border is refunded/credited back to the suppliers. So effectively there is no tax on exports and hence we say that exports are "zero rated" supplies. Supplies to SEZs are also zero rated.

- In case of imports, first Customs Duty and then on top of it IGST is imposed as imports are also considered to be Inter-State supplies.
- **Electronic Way Bill:** Electronic Way Bill (E-Way Bill) is a document issued by a carrier giving details and instructions relating to the shipment of a consignment of goods like name of consignor, consignee, the point of origin of the consignment, its destination, and route. **If the value of goods transported is more than worth Rs. 50,000/- then generation of e-way bill is mandatory.** E-Way Bill is basically a **compliance mechanism** wherein by way of a digital interface the person causing the movement of goods uploads the relevant information prior to the commencement of movement of goods and generates e-way bill on the GST portal. E-way bill is a mechanism to ensure that goods being transported comply with the GST Law and is an effective tool to track movement of goods and check tax evasion. The E-Way bill under the GST regime replaces the Way bill (which was a physical document) which was required under the VAT regime for the movement of goods.
- **Composition levy** is an alternative method of levy of tax designed for small businesses whose turnover is up to Rs. 1.5 crore. The objective of composition scheme is to bring simplicity and to reduce the compliance cost for the small businesses. Moreover, it is optional and the eligible person opting to pay tax under this scheme can pay tax at 1% flat rate, of his turnover, instead of paying tax at normal GST rate. Similarly, small service providers with turnover of Rs. 50 lakhs can opt for composition scheme and pay GST at 6%. In case of composition scheme, the businesses can't claim input tax credit and it is an optional scheme as they will always have the freedom to pay standard GST rate.

GST is a radical transformation from a complex, multi layered and cascading tax system to a single and unified tax system that allows for **tax set-off** across the value chain, both for goods and services. This would help lower product costs and thereby make Indian goods competitive in comparison to imports, increasing profitability of companies. GST will create an un-fragmented unified national market for goods and services, and will result in friendly tax structure over a common base of goods and services. There will be common rules and administration procedure across the nation. It will widen the tax base and simplify tax procedures bringing in clarity and transparency.

There are various benefits of GST which are summarized as under:

For business and industry

- Easy compliance: A robust and comprehensive IT system is the foundation of GST regime in India. Therefore, all tax payer services such as registrations, returns, payments, etc. are available to the taxpayers online which makes compliance easy and transparent. Under pre-GST regime, separate returns had to be filed for VAT to States and for Central Excise to Centre but now under GST only one return need to be filed.
- Uniformity of tax rates and structures: GST has ensured that indirect tax rates and structures are common across the

country, thereby reducing compliance cost and increasing certainty and ease of doing business. In other words, GST has made doing business in the country tax neutral, irrespective of the choice of place of doing business. Previously, every good faced an excise tax levied by the Centre and a state VAT. There were at least 8-10 rates of excise and 3-4 rates of state VATs. So, a structure of multiple rates (as much as 10 times X 4 times) has been reduced to a structure of 4 rates.

- Removal of cascading: A system of seamless tax-credits throughout the value-chain, and across boundaries of States, has ensured removal of cascading of taxes. This has improved competitiveness for the trade and industry
- Gain to manufacturers and exporters: The subsuming of major Central and State taxes in GST and complete set-off of taxes on input goods and services has reduced the cost of locally manufactured goods and services. This has increased the competitiveness of Indian goods and services in the international market and given boost to Indian exports.

For Central and State Governments

- Furthering cooperative federalism: Domestic indirect tax decisions to be taken jointly by the Centre and the states.
- Simple and easy to administer: Multiple indirect taxes at the Central and State levels have been subsumed under one GST. Backed with a robust end-to-end IT system, GST is simpler and easier to administer than all other indirect taxes of the Centre and State levied so far. With the elimination of the inter-state check posts (Entry Tax), GST has reduced the compliance scrutiny for inter-state movement of goods, which used to be a major source of concern.
- Better controls on leakage and reducing corruption: GST is self-policing in nature where invoice matching to claim input tax credit deters non-compliance and foster compliance.Previously invoice matching existed only for intra-state VAT transactions and not for excise and service taxes nor for imports. GST has resulted in better tax compliance through a robust IT infrastructure. Due to the seamless transfer of input tax credit from one stage to another in the chain of value addition, there is an in-built mechanism in the design of GST that has incentivized tax compliance by traders.
- Increase in tax base: As a lot of new agents, who were previously outside the tax net have sought GST registration, it has resulted in increasing in the tax base and tax buoyancy.
- Higher revenue efficiency: GST has decreased the cost of collection of tax revenues of the Government, and has led to higher revenue efficiency.

For the consumer

- Single and transparent tax proportionate to the value of goods and services: Due to multiple indirect taxes being levied by the Centre and State, with incomplete or no input tax credits available at progressive stages of value addition, the cost of most goods and services in the country used to be laden with many hidden taxes. Under GST regime, there is only one tax from the manufacturer to the consumer, leading to transparency (of taxes paid) to the final consumer.
- Relief in overall tax burden: Because of efficiency gains and prevention of leakages and removal of cascading effect, the overall tax burden on most commodities has come down and has benefited consumers.

GST has led to formalization of industry:

- The GST regime is particularly good at formalising areas where India's formal sector interacts with the informal industry through its input tax credit mechanisms. India's biggest companies across various industries have incentives to bring their informal supply chain into the formalised tax net to avail the benefits of input tax credit.
- For example, Textiles and clothing, that have historically paid little tax (whether in the form of duty or VAT) now have a formal GST rate and has little choice but to register, formalise and digitise their business. Previously, some parts of the value chain, especially fabrics, were outside the tax net, leading to informalization and evasion but now the textile and clothing sector is fully part of the GST tax net.

Next Generation GST Reforms [GST 2.0]

In a historic move to simplify the Goods and Services Tax (GST), GST Council in its 56th meeting reduced the GST structure from four slabs (5%, 12%, 18%, 28%) to two main rates—5% (merit rate) and 18% (standard rate) along with a 40% special rate for sin/ luxury goods. These changes came into effect from September 22, 2025. Following are various important points related to GST 2.0

- The principle behind the [GST 2.0] rate rationalisation exercise is to keep similar goods at the same rate to avoid issues of misclassification and disputes.
- Essentials like unbranded milk, unpacked grains, fresh fruits and vegetables, and core healthcare services remain at 0%.
- All dairy milk including UHT (ultra-high temperature) milk has been kept at 5% rate.
- Earlier bread was exempt while pizza bread, roti, porotta, paratha etc. attracted different rates. Now all Indian breads, by whatever name called have been exempted.
- Earlier, Paneer (Indian cottage cheese) other than pre-packaged and labelled form attracted nil rate. Now the pre-packaged paneer has also brought under nil rate. Since paneer (Indian cottage cheese) is mostly produced in small scale sector, so this measure is intended to promote Indian cottage cheese.
- Most of the processed food items GST rate has been reduced to 5%. For example, Namkeens, bhujia, mixture, Ice cream, fruit and vegetable juices, Sugar confectionery, pastry, cakes, biscuits, jams, fruit jellies etc.
- Pan masala, cigarettes, gutka, and other tobacco products are covered under the 40% GST rate. Deterrent rate on these products serves public health objectives while generating revenue from products with inelastic demand.
- Sweetened carbonated beverages, energy drinks, and other non-alcoholic beverages with added sugar or flavouring will also attract 40% GST rate. By raising tax rates on these goods and services consumed by younger demographics, GST aims to better harness India's demographic dividend.
- The GST rate on agriculture machinery/ equipment such as Tractors, sprinklers, drip irrigation system, Agricultural, horticultural or forestry machinery for soil preparation or cultivation; harvesting or threshing machinery, including straw or fodder balers; grass or hay mowers, other agricultural, horticultural, forestry, poultry-keeping or bee-keeping machinery, composting machines etc, which earlier attracted 12% GST, has now been reduced to 5%.

- All drugs/ medicines have been prescribed a concessional rate of GST of 5%, except those specified at nil rate. All medical devices, instruments, apparatus used in medical, surgical, dental and veterinary uses other than that are exempted specifically will also attract GST rate of 5%.
- The GST rate on small cars has been reduced to 18% and on mid-size and large cars and SUVs/MUVs, the GST rate will be 40%.
- The GST rate on renewable energy equipment/devices that were at 12% has been reduced to 5%.
- Individual life insurance policies including term, ULIP, and endowment plans and reinsurance services have been exempted (nil rate). Individual health insurance policies are also exempted.
- Passenger transportation services will be taxed at a merit rate of 5% with no input tax credit (ITC). However, service providers will have the option to charge a standard rate of 18%, which would allow them to claim full ITC.
- Travel by economy class (air travel) rate of GST is 5% otherwise 18%.
- Hotel accommodation services, where the value of supply is up to Rs. 7500 per unit per day, or equivalent, will be taxed at 5%.
- Betting, casinos, gambling, horse racing, lottery and online money gaming, GST rate of 40% will apply.
- Besides rate cuts, the GST Council approved procedural reforms through streamlined registration and return filing, provisional refund mechanisms especially for inverted duty claims and implementation of Goods and Services Tax Appellate Tribunal (GSTAT) to expedite appeal resolution and reduce litigation.

Challenges:

- Still, we have two rate GST structure (5% & 18%) and there is a special rate of 40% and certain items like gold and silver attract 3% GST rates. It is better than the previous 6/7 slab rates but still not the best form of GST rate. Experts say that eventually a single rate would simplify compliance, reduce classification disputes and make GST closer to the original vision of 'one nation one tax'.
- Alcohal, petroleum and energy products, electricity, land and real estate transactions are still outside the GST base and are taxed by the Centre and/ or states outside the GST. For example, keeping electricity out of GST undermines the competitiveness of Indian industry because taxes on power get embedded in manufacturer's costs and cannot be claimed back as input tax credits.
- Another closely connected issue is the GST threshold limit, which exempts businesses from registration for GST that has turnover of under 40 lakhs per year. These exemption limits are exploited to under report the sales figures by various business units.
- While GST 2.0 has resolved the Inverted Duty Structure (IDS) challenge for a large section of the value chain, items such as bicycle, tractor and some type of textiles continue to face inverted duty structure.
- Let us understand with example:

  Suppose there is a supply chain,

  $$A \rightarrow B \rightarrow \text{Consumer.}$$

  Now if the product which A sells to B has more GST rate say 18% and the product which B sells to the consumer has less GST rate say 5%, then we will say that the chain is having "inverted duty structure". Ideally the raw material should have less tax rate and final products should have more tax rate, but if this principle is not followed then it creates an inverted duty structure. This results in accumulation of unutilized input tax credit at (level of) B because in this case the tax paid by B to the Government may be less as compared to what B has paid on purchase of inputs. For example, even in GST 2.0, steel continues to attract 18% GST while final products like bicycles are in the 5% GST slab.

Remission of Duties or Taxes on Exported Products (RoDTEP)

Before GST, any taxes on import (customs duties) of inputs required to manufacture exported products were refunded through Merchandise Export of India Scheme (MEIS) by giving Duty Credit Scrips to exporters. This means if I export goods worth Rs. 100 crores then govt used to give me a paper (Duty Credit Scrip) worth Rs. 2 crore (some % of export value) which I could use to pay/adjust my customs duties on import of raw materials.

There were certain exemptions on domestic taxes also in case of exports.

But WTO said that the MEIS scheme is not compliant with the WTO trade rules (no need to go into it) and in 2020 it was replaced by Remission of Duties or Taxes on Exported Products (RoDTEP).

Under GST regime, Govt. exempts GST/IGST (taxes paid in case of domestic production and import of raw materials) in case of exports and this is called "exports are zero rated". Because first exporters pay GST/IGST (the standard rate) to the government and then they provide a proof to the government that it is a case of export (sold abroad) and the government reimburses the entire GST hence effectively no tax on exports.

However, certain products are outside GST and the taxes/duties/levies imposed on these products are still not refunded in case of exports even in the present GST regime. These taxes are VAT on fuel used in transportation, Mandi tax, taxes on electricity, petroleum products etc (which becomes embedded in the product price). Under the new RoDTEP scheme, these taxes will be refunded to exporters in their ledger accounts with Customs. The credits can be used to pay basic customs duty on imported goods/raw materials. The scheme is available for all kinds of exports from 1st Jan 2021.

4.14 Tax related Issues Across the Countries

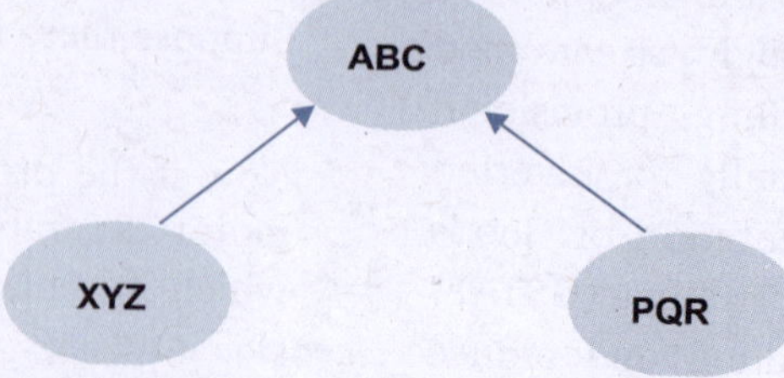

XYZ and PQR companies are owned by ABC. XYZ, PQR and ABC will be called related parties. And the directors/owners of these companies are also called **related parties**.

Any transaction happening between related parties are called **related/connected parties' transaction** and this transaction should happen at market price which is referred as '**Arm's Length Principle**'. The pricing of goods and services between related parties is called '**Transfer Pricing**' and it should follow 'arms-length principle'.

One of the disputed issues in taxation related to MNCs is the area of intra (group) company transactions or related party transactions.

Here, a parent company say in Japan may charge a convenient price from its subsidiary in India to minimise its tax payment in India. For example, suppose that Maruti Suzuki India has higher profit and has to pay higher tax to the Government of India. In this case, if Suzuki Japan charges a high price for a component it sold to Maruti, then profit of Maruti in India will come down and the tax payment of the company to GoI will also come down. On the other hand, the revenue/profit of Suzuki Japan will go up. Altogether, the Suzuki Motor Corporation (SMC) group improves its position; but GoI's tax revenue gets affected.

This is a strategy/manipulation to shift the profit from Maruti India to Suzuki Japan because the tax is favourable in Japan. This would be called "**Base Erosion and Profit Shifting" (BEPS)**. In recent times, MNCs are developing sophisticated and refined tax planning practices to avoid tax by shifting their incomes/profits to other countries, especially to tax havens. Such practices eroded the tax base.

To avoid such a manipulation, tax department of India pre-sets the price charged for different components between Maruti Suzuki India and Suzuki Japan. But this price should follow "**arm's length principle**" i.e., market based. An arm's length transaction refers to a business deal in which buyers and sellers act independently without one party influencing the other. These types of sales asserts that both parties act in their own self-interest and are not subject to pressure from the other party; furthermore, it assures others that there is no collusion between the buyer and seller.

At the beginning of the year, the price charged for intra company transactions will be determined in advance and will be kept for the coming five years or so. This price arrangement between Maruti and India's tax department is called **advance pricing agreement (APA)**.

An APA is a contract, usually for multiple years, between a taxpayer and at least one tax authority specifying the pricing method that the taxpayer will apply to its **related-company transactions**. These programmes are designed to help taxpayers voluntarily resolve actual or potential transfer pricing disputes in a proactive, cooperative manner, as an alternative to the traditional examination process. APAs gives certainty to taxpayers reduces disputes, enhance tax revenues and make the country an attractive destination for foreign investments. These agreements would be binding both on the taxpayer as well as the government. Similarly, they lower complaints and litigation costs.

Double Taxation Avoidance Agreement (DTAA)

DTAA is a tax treaty signed between India and another country (or any two/multiple countries) so that taxpayers can avoid paying double taxes on their income earned from the source country as well as the residence country.

For example, suppose a Foreign Portfolio Investor (FPI) registered in Mauritius purchased shares of an Indian listed company. Now when the FPI receives dividend (or if it sells shares then it may realize capital gain) then India may also impose tax on dividend (or capital gain tax) and when the FPI takes that income to Mauritius then Mauritius Govt. may also impose tax which results in Double Taxation. Now to avoid such double taxes (referred as tax benefits), India and Mauritius may sign Double Taxation Avoidance Agreement (DTAA).

Indian and Mauritius has actually signed DTAA. But, recently, DTAA between India and Mauritius has been amended to include **Principal Purpose Test (PPT)**. PPT means the tax benefits under the treaty will not be applicable if it is established that obtaining that duty benefit was the principal purpose of any transaction or arrangement. And this is in line with the global Base Erosion Profit Shifting (BEPS) framework.

In June 2019, India ratified the Multilateral Convention to Implement Tax Treaty Related Measures to Prevent Base Erosion and Profit Shifting (multilateral instruments (MLI)), which was signed by the finance minister in Paris in June 2017 on behalf of India, along with representatives of more than 65 countries. The MLI is a result of concerted work by the G20 countries to tackle the issue of base erosion and profit shifting, something that affects them all. The MLI will modify India's tax treaties to curb revenue loss through treaty abuse and base erosion and profit shifting strategies by ensuring that profits are taxed where substantive economic activities generating the profits are carried out. The MLI will be applied alongside existing tax treaties (such as Double Taxation Avoidance Agreement), modifying their application in order to implement the BEPS measures. The MLI came into force for India from October 1, 2019.

Global Minimum Corporate Tax (GMCT)

The Global Minimum Corporate Tax Framework has two-pillar package.

- **Pillar 1:**

  Issue: With the advent of information technology, it has become possible for a company resident outside India to earn revenues/profit from India without having a physical presence here. But these companies are not subject to tax in India as these companies do not book profit in India rather, they book profit in their home country. (*Govt. of India had put Equalization Levy on such companies but it has now been abolished*)

  Resolution Proposed:

  Pillar 1 will ensure a fairer distribution of profits and taxing rights among countries with respect to the largest Multi-National Enterprises (MNEs), including digital companies. It would re-allocate some taxing rights over MNEs from their home countries to the markets where they have business activities and earn profits, regardless of whether firms have a physical presence there.

- **Pillar 2:**

  Issue: Big Technology companies shift their profits to such countries where the corporate tax rate is less. The companies do not shift the actual business but mostly financial transactions are involved. As the competition among the countries is increasing, to attract more business/investment, countries also resort to reduction in corporate taxes. This has led to the loss of tax revenue to the home country government.

Resolution Proposed:

- ✓ Pillar 2 seeks to put a floor on competition over corporate income tax, through the introduction of a global minimum corporate tax (GMCT) rate (agreed to be 15%) that countries can use to protect their tax bases. Let us understand with an example:
- ✓ Suppose there is a company XYZ in the US where corporate tax is 20%, and the company shifts its business revenues to another country to avoid tax, say Mauritius where corporate tax is 5%. Now as per GMCT (which has been agreed at 15%) US Govt. will have the authority to collect tax from XYZ = 15%-5%= 10% which will be in addition to the 5% tax payable to Mauritius. This means that now if companies shift their business revenues to tax havens, then also, they will have to pay a minimum tax.
- ✓ If there is another company which is based in Mauritius, then that company can continue paying 5% tax. GMCT is applicable only on those companies which have shifted their business to tax havens where tax rate is less just to reduce/avoid their tax burden.

Bilateral Investment Treaties (BIT):

BITs are agreements between two Countries (States) for the reciprocal promotion and protection of investments in each other's territories by individuals and companies situated in either State. When countries enter into a BIT, both countries agree to provide protections for the other country's foreign investments that they would not otherwise have. A BIT provides major benefits for investors in another country, including national treatment, fair and equitable treatment, protection from expropriation and performance requirements for investments, and access to neutral dispute settlement (international arbitration) etc.

The first BIT was signed by India on March 14, 1994. Since then, the Government of India has signed BITs with more than 80 countries. Recently, India has terminated its bilateral investment treaties (BIT) with 57 countries. In Dec 2015, The Union Cabinet gave its approval for the revised Model Text for the Indian Bilateral Investment Treaty. The revised model BIT will be used for re-negotiation of existing BITs and negotiation of future BITs. The new model clarifies that it only covers investments that have a physical presence and substantial business activities in the territory of the host state. Foreign investors also claim that the new model BIT is protectionist in nature.

4.15 Direct Tax Reforms

There are around 7.5 crore direct taxpayers. They pay tax and file return (tax document). Taxpayers use various ways to avoid paying taxes and showing their income way below the actual income. So, government has set certain parameters to pick for assessment/ review of these cases. For example, those tax payers whose income is quite high (say 30 lakhs) but tax payment is very less supposing only 2 lakhs or suppose in any particular savings account more than Rs. 10 lakhs got deposited in a financial year etc.

Now suppose there are 5 lakh such cases, out of which Govt. may pick **randomly** 50,000 cases for review/assessment (as all cannot be reviewed because of resource constraint). So,

Govt. will send notice and you will have to give clarifications. And Govt. may scrutinize such cases in quite detail and if some wrong doings were found, you may be penalized.

1. **Faceless Assessment:** Earlier (before e-assessment scheme was launched), these cases were selected by tax officials and there used to be face to face meetings between tax officials and taxpayers and where taxpayers were used to be harassed. But now all such cases will be randomly picked by computer and no face-to-face grilling would happen but only through electronic mode of communication. So, this will improve transparency and efficiency, and governance and thus improves the quality of assessment and monitoring.
2. **Faceless Appeal:** In case a taxpayer files appeal against any assessment by the tax authority.
    - Appeals to be randomly allotted to any officer in the country
    - The identification of the officers deciding appeal will remain unknown
    - The tax payer will not be required to visit the income tax office or the officer
    - The appellate decision will be team-based and reviewed

    Income Tax Act 1961 has been amended to introduce faceless assessment & faceless appeal.
3. **Taxpayers' Charter** is a two-way document for the assessor (Govt.) and the assessee (taxpayer). Through this document, the government has committed the following to the taxpayers:
    - To provide fair, courteous, and reasonable treatment
    - Treat taxpayer as honest
    - To provide mechanism for appeal and review
    - To provide complete and accurate information
    - To provide timely decisions
    - To collect the correct amount of tax
    - To respect privacy of taxpayers
    - To maintain confidentiality
    - To hold its authorities accountable
    - To enable representative of choice
    - To provide mechanism to lodge complaint and provide a fair and just system
    - To publish service standards and report periodically
    - To reduce cost of compliance

    The Taxpayers' Charter also highlights the **obligations of the taxpayer**. These are as follows:
    - To be honest, informed and compliant
    - To keep accurate records
    - To know what your representative does on your behalf
    - To respond in time and to pay in time
4. **New Income Tax Act, 2025**

The New Income Tax Act 2025, has become effective since 1st April 2026, which has replaced the six-decade old Income Tax Act 1961.

The new Income Tax Act 2025 has made the language and implementation of the income tax legislation simpler for taxpayers. The new income-tax act does not have long sentences, provisos and explanations and marks a different way of engagement with citizens, with no aim to put any new tax burden. The new act is clear and direct in text with close to half of the present law, in terms of both chapters and words. It is simple to understand for taxpayers and tax administration, leading to tax certainty and reduced litigation.

4.16 Funds Transfer from Centre to States/UTs

Indian constitution has divided the taxation powers as well as the spending powers (and responsibilities) between the Union and the state governments. The subjects on which Union or State or both can levy taxes are defined in the Concurrent List of the constitution. Further, limited financial powers have been given to the local governments also as per 73rd and 74th amendments of the constitution.

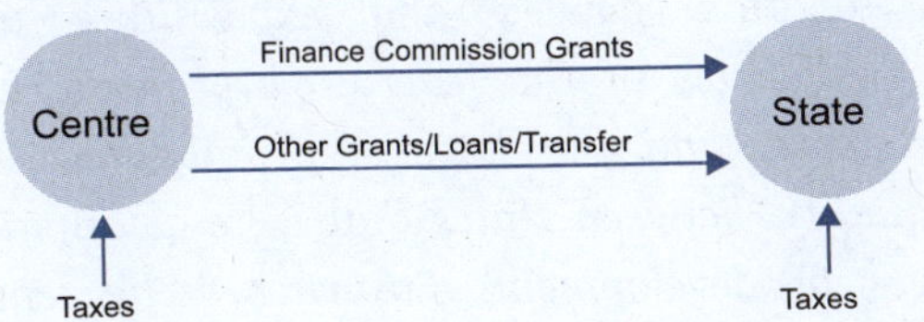

1. Finance Commission Grants

As per Article 280 of the Constitution, the President is required to appoint a Finance Commission after every five years (or such earlier tim e if President considers it necessary) which shall consist of a chairman and four other members appointed by the President. The Finance Commission is required to recommend to the President on the following matters.

- The distribution of the net proceeds of taxes to be shared between the centre and the states (vertical devolution) and the allocation of such proceeds among the states (horizontal devolution).
- The principles that should govern the grants-in-aid to the states by the Centre out of the Consolidated fund of India.
- The measures needed to augment the consolidated fund of a state to supplement the resources of the Panchayats and the Municipalities in the state on the basis of the recommendations made by the State Finance Commissions.
- Any other matter referred to it by the President in the interests of sound finance.

The **XVI Finance Commission** has recommended the following transfers for **2026-31**:

(i) As percentage share of central taxes (this is called *vertical devolution)*, which will be **41%** of the **divisible pool** of Central taxes and will be distributed among 28 States. This never becomes part of the Consolidated Fund of India and is **untied** grants which mean no restriction is imposed on States on how to spend.

(No UT either with or without Assembly gets this vertical devolution. UTs without their own Assembly are allocated funds by the Central Government from Budgetary Resources through demand for grants under Ministry of Home Affairs)

*The pool of tax resources of the Union Govt. to be shared with the States is called the "**Divisible Pool**" and it **excludes** the following items from the gross tax revenue:*

- *Cost of collection of taxes*
- *Cess and Surcharge*
- *Tax Revenue of the Union Territories without Assembly*
- *National Calamity Contingency Duty (NCCD)*

The parameters for distribution of taxes **among the states** *(horizontal distribution)* are:

- Income Distance (42.5%),
- Population (2011 Census) (17.5%),
- Demographic Performance (10%),
- State Area (10%),
- Forest and Ecology (10%),
- Contribution to GDP (10%)

(ii) As Grants-in-Aid (Article 275) in the form of (these are charged on Consolidated Fund of India and tied grants) following two types:

1. **Local Body Grants**

The 16th FC has recommended grants worth Rs 4.4 lakh cro re and Rs 3.6 lakh crore for rural and urban local bodies, respectively. These grants are divided into **basic** (80%) and **performance-based** (20%) components. Special Infrastructure Grants and Urbanisation Premium Grants have also been recommended for urban local bodies.

All local body grants will be made available upon fulfilment of three entry-level criteria: (i) constitution of the local bodies as per the Constitution, (ii) publication of provisional and audited accounts of the local bodies in the public domain, and (iii) timely constitution of the State Finance Commission.

Basic grants: 50% of the basic grant will be untied and the rest 50% will be tied to: (i) sanitation and solid waste management, and/or (ii) water management.

Performance grants: These grants for local bodies are further divided into state performance grants and local body performance grants. State performance grants will be made available upon meeting a minimum benchmark for transfers to local bodies from their own resources. Local body performance grants are linked to achievement of minimum targets specified by the Commission for own source revenue growth.

2. **Disaster Management Grants**

The Commission has recommended disaster management corpus of Rs 2,04,401 crores for State Disaster Relief and Management Funds (SDRF and SDMF). The cost-sharing pattern between the centre and states is recommended to be: (i) 90:10 for north-eastern and Himalayan states, and (ii) 75:25 for all other states. Centre's share in total will be Rs 1,55,916 crores.

The framers of the constitution were seeking to address the vertical imbalance between the taxation powers and expenditure and responsibilities of the federal government and the states, and the horizontal imbalance, or inequality, between states that were at different stages of development. Ensuring inclusiveness is, therefore, a key mandate of the Finance Commission. That means assigning weights to things like population, income distance between top ranked states and others, etc. It is not that best performing state will be allocated the highest share - even if delivery, execution and governance are better - rather, the effort will be to narrow the development gap between states.

2. Other Grants/Loans/Transfers

Various other transfers from Central Government to States are Special Assistance Grants, Additional Central Assistance (Grants and Loans), Assistance to States from National Disaster Response Fund (NDRF) etc.

Central Sector Schemes and Centrally Sponsored Schemes

Public Finance (Central) Division under Department of Expenditure, Ministry of Finance in consultation with the Budget Division, Department of Economic Affairs, Ministry of Finance communicates the outlays for both

Central Sector Schemes (CSs) and Centrally Sponsored Schemes (CSSs) over a Finance Commission cycle. The Public Finance (Central) Division is also responsible for preparation of outcome budgets for all Central Ministries/ Departments in consultation with the NITI Aayog. This output-outcome framework (outcome budget) is for all CSSs and CSs dealing with identified measurable outcomes in the relevant medium-term framework and physical and financial outputs are targeted on a year-to-year basis.

Under **Centrally Sponsored Schemes** (CSSs), a certain percentage of the funding is borne by the States in the ratio such as 50:50, 70:30, 75:25 or 90:10. It is implemented by the State Governments. Centrally Sponsored Schemes are formulated on subjects under the State List to encourage States to prioritise in areas that require more attention. Till 2013-14, Funds for CSS were routed through two channels, the consolidated fund of the States and directly to the State/ District Level Autonomous Bodies/Implementing Agencies. *(CSSs are a part of funds transfer to States/UTs)*. In 2014-15, direct transfers to State implementing agencies were discontinued and all transfers to States including for the CSS were routed through the Consolidated Funds of the States.

The Governing Council of NITI Aayog set up a sub-group of Chief Ministers on Rationalization of Centrally Sponsored Schemes (CSSs). The sub-group has recommended that the number of CSSs should not normally exceed 30. The sub-group recommended that the CSSs should be categorized into three categories:

- **Core Schemes:** Focus of CSSs should be on schemes that comprise the National Development Agenda where the Centre and States will work together in the spirit of Team India. Ex. Pradhan Mantri Gram Sadak Yojana
- **Core of the Core Schemes:** Those schemes which are for social protection and social inclusion should form the core of core and be the first charge on available funds for the National Development Agenda. Ex. MGNREGA
- **Optional Schemes:** The Schemes where States would be free to choose the ones they wish to implement. Funds for these schemes would be allocated to States by the Ministry of Finance as a lump sum.

Central Sector Schemes (CSs) are generally those that are implemented by a central agency and 100% funded by the centre on subjects within the union list. *(CSs are not part of funds transfer to States/UTs)*. For example, Namami Gange, Sagarmala, Pradhan Mantri Fasal Bima Yojana etc.

PREVIOUS YEARS' QUESTIONS

Prelim Questions

1. Which of the following statements appropriately describes the "fiscal stimulus"? **[2011]**

   (a) It is a massive investment by the government in manufacturing sector to ensure the supply of goods to meet the demand surge caused by rapid economic growth

   (b) It is an intense affirmative action of the Government to boost economic activity in the country

   (c) It is Government's intensive action on financial institutions to ensure disbursement of loans to agriculture and allied sectors to promote greater food production and contain food inflation

(d) It is an extreme affirmative action by the Government to pursue its policy of financial inclusion

2. Which of the following is **not** a feature of "Value Added Tax"? [2011]
   (a) It is a multi-point destination-based system of taxation
   (b) It is a tax levied on value addition at each stage of transaction in the production-distribution chain
   (c) It is a tax onfinal consumption of goods/services and must ultimately be borne by the consumer
   (d) It is basically a subject of the Central Government and the State Governments are only a facilitator for its successful implementation

3. Both Foreign Direct Investment (FDI) and Foreign Institutional Investor (FII) are related to investment in a country. Which of the following statements best represents an important difference between the two? [2011]
   (a) FII helps bring better management skills and technology, while FDI only brings in capital
   (b) FII helps in increasing capital availability in general, while FDI only targets specific sectors
   (c) FDI flows only into the secondary market, while FII targets primary market
   (d) FII is considered to be more stable than FDI

4. The authorization for the withdrawal of funds from the Consolidated Fund of India must come from [2011]
   (a) The President of India
   (b) The Parliament of India
   (c) The Prime Minister of India
   (d) he Union Finance Minister

5. All revenues received by the Union Government by way of taxes and other receipts for the conduct of Government business are credited to the [2011]
   (a) Contingency Fund of India
   (b) Public Account
   (c) Consolidated Fund of India
   (d) Deposits and Advances Fund

6. When the annual Union Budget is not passed by the Lok Sabha, [2011]
   (a) The Budget is modified and presented again
   (b) The Budget is referred to the Rajya Sabha for suggestions
   (c) The Union Finance Minister is asked to resign
   (d) The Prime Minister submits the resignation of Council of Ministers

7. Under which of the following circumstances may "capital gains" arise? [2012]
   (i) When there is an increase in the sales of a product
   (ii) When there is a natural increase in the value of the property owned
   (iii) When you purchase a painting and there is a growth in its value due to increase in its popularity

   Select the correct answer using the codes given below:
   (a) (i) only
   (b) (ii) & (iii) only
   (c) (ii) only
   (d) (i), (ii) & (iii)

8. The Reserve Bank of India acts as a banker's bank. This would imply which of the following? [2012]
   (i) Other banks retain their deposits with the RBI
   (ii) The RBI lends funds to the commercial banks in times of need
   (iii) The RBI advises the commercial banks on monetary matters

Select the correct answer using the codes given below:

(a) (ii) & (iii) only (b) (i) & (ii) only
(c) (i) & (iii) only (d) (i), (ii) & (iii)

9. Which of the following measures would result in an increase in the money supply in the economy? **[2012]**

(i) Purchase of government securities from the public by the Central Bank
(ii) Deposit of currency in commercial banks by the public
(iii) Borrowing by the government from the Central Bank
(iv) Sale of government securities to the public by the Central Bank

Select the correct answer using the codes given below:

(a) (i) only (b) (ii) & (iv) only
(c) (i) & (iii) only (d) (ii), (iii) & (iv) only

10. With reference to the Union Government, consider the following statements: **[2015]**

(i) The Department of Revenue is responsible for the preparation of Union Budget that is presented to the Parliament
(ii) No amount can be withdrawn from the Consolidated Fund of India without the authorization from the Parliament of India
(iii) All the disbursements made from Public Account also need the authorization from the Parliament of India

Which of the statements given above is/are correct?

(a) (i) & (ii) only (b) (ii) & (iii) only
(c) (ii) only (d) (i), (ii) & (iii)

11. Which of the following is/are included in the capital budget of the Government of India? **[2016]**

(i) Expenditure on acquisition of assets like roads, buildings, machinery, etc.
(ii) Loans received from foreign governments
(iii) Loans and advances granted to the States and Union Territories

Select the correct answer using the code given below.

(a) (i) only (b) (ii) & (iii) only
(c) (i) & (iii) only (d) (i), (ii) & (iii)

12. What is/are the most likely advantages of implementing 'Goods and Services Tax (GST)'? **[2017]**

(i) It will replace multiple taxes collected by multiple authorities and will thus create a single market in India.
(ii) It will drastically reduce the 'Current Account Deficit' of India and will enable it to increase its foreign exchange reserves.
(iii) It will enormously increase the growth and size of economy of India and will enable it to overtake China in the near future.

Select the correct answer using the code given below:

(a) (i) only (b) (ii) & (iii) only
(c) (i) & (iii) only (d) (i), (ii) & (iii)

13. Consider the following statements: **[2017]**

(i) Tax revenue as a percent of GDP of India has steadily increased in the last decade.
(ii) Fiscal deficit as a percent of GDP of India has steadily increased in the last decade.

Which of the statements given above is/are correct?

(a) (i) only
(b) (ii) only
(c) Both (i) & (ii) only
(d) Neither (i) & (ii)

14. Consider the following statements: **[2018]**

(i) The Fiscal Responsibility and Budget Management (FRBM) Review Committee Report has recommended a debt to GDP ratio of 60% for the general (combined) government by 2023, comprising 40% for the Central Government and 20% for the State Governments.

(ii) The Central Government has domestic liabilities of 21% of GDP as compared to that of 49% of GDP of the State Governments.

(iii) As per the Constitution of India, it is mandatory for a State to take the Central Government's consent for raising any loan if the former owes any outstanding liabilities to the latter.

Which of the statements given above is/are correct?

(a) (i) only (b) (ii) & (iii) only
(c) (i) & (iii) only (d) (i), (ii) & (iii)

15. Consider the following statements **[2019]**

(i) Most of India's external debt is owed by governmental entities.

(ii) All of India's external debt is denominated in US dollars.

Which of the statements given above is / are correct?

(a) (i) only (b) (ii) only
(c) Both (i) & (ii) (d) Neither (i) nor (ii)

16. Which one of the following effects of creation of black money in India has been the main cause of worry to the Government of India? **[2021]**

(a) Diversion of resources to the purchase of real estate and investment in luxury housing

(b) Investment in unproductive activities and purchase of precious stones, jewellery, gold, etc.

(c) Large donations to political parties and growth of regionalism

(d) Loss of revenue to the State Exchequer due to tax evasion

17. With reference to the expenditure made by an organization or a company, which of the following statements is/are correct? (Economy) **[2022]**

1. Acquiring new technology is capital expenditure.
2. Debt financing is considered capital expenditure, while equity financing is considered revenue expenditure.

Select the correct answer using the code given below:

(a) 1 only (b) 2 only
(c) Both 1 and 2 (d) Neither 1 nor 2

18. With reference to the Indian economy, consider the following statements: **[2022]**

1. A share of the household financial savings goes towards government borrowings.
2. Dated securities issued at market-related rates in auctions form a large component of internal debt:

Which of the above statements is/are correct?

(a) 1 only (b) 2 only
(c) Both 1 and 2 (d) Neither 1 nor 2

19. Consider the following: **[2023]**

1. Demographic performance
2. Forest and ecology
3. Governance reforms
4. Stable government
5. Tax and fiscal efforts

For the horizontal tax devolution, the Fifteenth Finance Commission used how many of the above as criteria other than population area and income distance?

(a) Only two (b) Only three
(c) Only four (d) All five

20. With reference to Union Budget, consider the following statements: [2024]

1. The Union Finance Minister on behalf of the Prime Minister lays the Annual Financial Statement before both the Houses of Parliament.
2. At the Union level, no demand for a grant can be made except on the recommendation of the President of India.

Which of the statements given above is/are correct?

(a) 1 only (b) 2 only
(c) Both 1 and 2 (d) Neither 1 nor 2

21. Suppose the revenue expenditure is ₹80,000 crores and the revenue receipts of the Government are 60,000 crores. The Government budget also shows borrowings of 10,000 crores and interest payments of 6,000 crores. Which of the following statements are correct? [2025]

1. Revenue deficit is 20,000 crores.

II. Fiscal deficit is 10,000 crores.

III. Primary deficit is 4,000 crores.

Select the correct answer using the code given below.

(a) I and II only (b) II and III only
(c) I and III only (d) I, II and III

22. A country's fiscal deficit stands at ₹50,000 ₹10,000 crores. It is receiving crores through non-debt creating capital receipts. The country's interest liabilities are 1,500 crores. What is the gross primary deficit? [2025]

(a) 48,500 crores (b) 51,500 crores
(c) 58,500 crores (d) None of the above

ANSWERS

1.(b)	2.(d)	3.(b)	4. (b)	5.(c)	6. (d)	7. (b)	8. (d)	9. (c)	10. (c)
11. (d)	12. (a)	13. (d)	14. (c)	15. (d)	16 (d)	17. (a)	18. (c)	19. (b)	20. (b)
21. (d)	22. (a)								

Main Questions

1. The public expenditure management is a challenge to the Government of India in the context of budget making during the post liberalization-period. Clarify it. [2019]
2. Enumerate the indirect taxes which have been subsumed in the GST in India. Also, comment on the revenue implications of the GST introduced in India since July 2017. [2019]
3. Explain the rationale behind the Goods and Services Tax (Compensation to States) Act of 2017. How has Covid-19 impacted the GST Compensation fund and created new federal tensions. [2020]
4. Distinguish between capital budget and Revenue Budget. Explain the component of both these budgets. [2021]
5. Explain how the Fiscal Health Index (FHI) can be used as a tool for assessing the fiscal performance of states in India. In what way would it encourage the states to adopt prudent and sustainable fiscal policies? [2025]

Land Reforms

5.1 Land Rights before Independence

In India, during the Mughal period (before 1765), zamindars or "revenue collectors" collected revenue on behalf of the Mughal Emperor, whose representatives or Diwan supervised their activities. The zamindar served as an intermediary who procured economic rent from the cultivator and after withholding a percentage for his own expenses, made available the rest, as revenue to the State. Under the Mughal system, the land itself belonged to State (People, Territory, Government and Sovereignty) and not to the zamindar, who could transfer only his right to collect rent. The Nawabs of Bengal ruled the area under the Mughal Empire through their feudal chiefs.

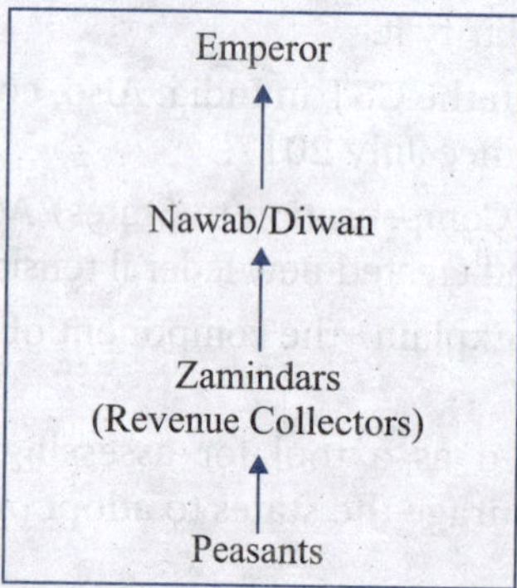

In India, the rule of the British East India Company commenced from 1757, after the battle of Plassey, in which the nawab of Bengal (Sirajudaulla) was defeated by the Company. The battle of Buxar consolidated the Company's power and forced Emperor Shah Alam II to surrender the Diwani Rights (the right to collect revenue) in 1765 in Bengal and Bihar (later the Company started exercising the Diwani Rights over Orissa also).

Warren Hastings, the first Governor General of Bengal (1772 – 1785)

Warren Hastings, the first Governor General, had introduced the Five-Year Settlement according to which the right of collection of land revenue was given to the highest bidder for five years on contract basis. But the problem with this system was that, at the time of auctions the new contractors, who had no experience of realization of the tax, used to make such a high bid, that they failed to deposit the amount of the bid in the royal treasury. This introduced instability in the Company's revenue at a time when the Company was hard pressed for money. Though the amount of land revenue was pushed high by zamindars and other speculators bidding against each other, the actual collection varied from year to year and seldom came up to official expectations. Moreover, neither the peasant nor the zamindar would do anything to improve cultivation when they did not know what the next year's assessment would be or who would be the next year's revenue collector.

Lord Cornwallis, Governor General of Bengal (1786 – 1793) and the Permanent Settlement of Revenue Administration:

Since the earlier system introduced by Hastings proved defective for the peasants and the Company both, Lord Cornwallis introduced the Permanent Settlement in Bengal, Bihar and Odisha in 1793 which continued in India till India achieved its freedom. Its chief aim was to impart stability to the revenue system. He did exhaustive survey of the past records and on the basis of past 10 years, he fixed how much revenue can be collected from the entire land and fixed the amount to be collected for future years.

Features

- Before the commencement of the tenure of Cornwallis, the landlords were not considered to be the owners of the land. By the permanent settlement, the landlords were accepted to be the owners of the land in place of peasants. The revenue began to be realized from the landlords instead of from the farmers.
- The Zamindars and revenue collectors were converted into landlords. They were not only to act as agents of the Government in collecting land revenue from the peasants but also to become the owners of the entire land in their zamindaris. Their right of ownership was made hereditary and transferable.

Ryotwari Settlement

The Ryotwari settlement was introduced by Thomas Munro and Alexander Reed in Bombay and Madras Presidencies in 1820. In these areas, there were no zamindars and Land revenue settlement was made directly with the peasants called Ryots, thus no intermediaries were involved.

Features:

- The land revenue demand was fixed by the state which was exorbitantly high.
- The cultivator or ryot was recognized as the owner of the land. Each peasant was given a "patta" by the government which was a piece of document confirming the ownership right of the ryot/peasant.
- While in theory, the ryotwari conferred rights on the actual landowners, in reality, the actual cultivator was often different from the owner.
- The ryotwari settlement was not made permanent and was revised periodically after 20 to 30 years.
- The Government retained the right to enhance land revenue at will.

Mahalwari System

Mahalwari system was a modified version of the zamindari settlement and was introduced in the Ganga valley, the North-West provinces, parts of Central India and the Punjab. The revenue settlement was to be made at the village (which were called estates or mahal) level i.e. the village collectively paid revenue to the state.

Common to all the systems in force was the fact that the British had unfairly distorted the land rights of the peasants in India. They had completed a scientific survey of land and recorded the rights of the owners in their revenue records, while leaving unrecorded the entitlements of the actual cultivators, sharecroppers, tenants, and lessees. During British rule, the owner's land could be attached and sold to collect revenue, and the purchaser could obtain sound title to the land.

5.2 Land Reforms Post-independence

"Land" is a state subject and the system of land records management varies from state to state, often even within a state, depending upon their historical evolution and local traditions. Several departments are involved in managing land records in most of the states, and the citizen has to approach three to four, or even more, agencies for complete land records, e.g., Revenue Department for textual records and mutations; Survey & Settlement (or Consolidation) Department for the maps; Registration Department for verification of encumbrances and registration of transfer, mortgage, etc.;the Panchayats (in some States, for mutation), and the municipal authorities (for urban land records), leading to waste of time, exposure to rent seeking, and harassment.

Land reform usually refers to redistribution of land from rich to poor. More broadly, it includes regulation of ownership, operation, leasing, sales, and inheritance of land. In an agrarian economy like India with great scarcity and unequal distribution of land, coupled with a large mass of below poverty line rural population, there are compelling economic and political arguments for land reform. At the time of independence, ownership of land was concentrated in the hands of a few. This led to the exploitation of the farmers and was a major hindrance towards the socio-economic development of the rural population. Equal distribution of land was therefore an area of focus of Independent India's government, and land reforms were seen as an important pillar of a strong and prosperous country. Not surprisingly, it received top priority on the policy agenda at the time of Independence. In the decades following independence, India passed a significant body of land reform legislation. The Constitution of 1949 left the adoption and implementation of land and tenancy reforms to state governments. This led to a lot of variation in the implementation of these reforms across states and over time.

Following are the major land reforms introduced in India after independence:

1. **Abolition of Intermediaries – zamindars, jaghirdars etc.**

   The main aim of the abolition of intermediaries was to bring the cultivator into direct relationship with the government. By 1949, zamindari abolition bills were introduced in a number of provinces with the report of UP Zamindari Abolition Committee acting as the initial model for many others. The zamindars in various parts of the country moved to courts and challenged the constitutionality of the law permitting zamindari abolition and raised issues like violation of right to property and unjustness of the compensations. The government responded by getting the constitutional amendments passed (first, fourth and seventeenth) and strengthening the hands of the State legislatures by making the question of violation of any fundamental right or insufficiency of compensation not permissible in the courts.

   Considering the entire process occurred in a democratic framework, with virtually no coercion or violence being used, it was completed in a remarkably short period and most of the provinces passed the zamindari abolition acts by 1956. This was partly because zamindar as a class had been isolated socially during the national movement itself as they were seen as part of the imperialist camp. The abolition of zamindari was quite successful and about two crore erstwhile tenants became landowners.

A major difficulty in implementing the zamindari abolition acts was the absence of adequate land records. The major weaknesses in the manner in which some of the clauses relating to zamindari abolition was implemented was that in various parts of the country, the zamindars were permitted to retain lands that were declared to be under their 'personal cultivation'. What constituted 'personal cultivation' was very loosely defined 'making it possible for not only those who tilled the soil, but also those who supervised the land personally or did so through a relative, or provided capital and credit to the land, to call themselves a cultivator. There was no limit on the size of the lands that could be declared to be under the 'personal cultivation' of the zamindars.

2. Tenancy Reforms

Under the Zamindari and ryotwari systems, tenancy cultivation had been quite common in India. There were broadly three categories of tenants:

- Occupancy tenants-enjoyed permanent and heritable rights on land. They had security of tenure and could claim compensation from the landlords for any improvement affected on the land.
- Tenants at will - did not have security of tenure, made to pay exorbitant rent to the landlords and could be evicted from the land whenever landlord so desired.
- The Sub tenants-were appointed by the occupancy tenants.

The tenancy reforms were introduced in 1950's and 60's and the main objectives of the reforms were:

- **To guarantee security of tenure to tenants** who had cultivated a piece of land continuously for a fixed number of years, say six years – met only with limited success.
- **To seek the reduction of rents paid by tenants** to a fair level which was generally considered to range between one-fourth to one-sixth of the value of the gross produce of the leased land – only the upper stratum of tenantry which had secured occupancy rights and was often indistinguishable from a landowner, was able to enforce the payment of legal rates of rent.
- **The tenant should gain the right to ownership of the lands he cultivated** subject to certain restrictions – achieved only partially.

Tenancy reforms introduced in many states led to the tenancy being pushed underground i.e., it continued in a concealed form. The tenants were now called 'farm servants' though they continued in exactly the same status. In the early years of land reform, tenants were often converted to sharecroppers, as surprisingly the latter were not treated as tenants and therefore were not protected under the existing tenancy legislation in some states as in UP. Only cash rent payers were treated as tenants and not those who paid fixed produce rents or those who paid a proportion of total produce as rent i.e. sharecroppers. Perhaps, what contributed most to the insecurity of tenants was the fact that most tenancies were oral and informal, i.e. they were not recorded and the tenants therefore could not benefit from the legislation in their favor.

3. **Ceilings on size of Landholdings and its distribution**

The land ceiling acts define the size of land that an individual/family can own. The main objective of the ceiling legislation was redistribution of the surplus land to the landless so that to make land distribution more equitable.

By early 1960's all the State governments had passed the land ceiling acts but till 1970 not a single acre was declared surplus in most of the large states. The ceiling limits fixed under the act varied from State to State. To bring uniformity across the states, a new land ceiling policy was evolved in 1971. In 1972, national guidelines were issued with ceiling limits as 10-18 acres for best land, 18-27 acres for second class land and for the rest with 27-54 acres with a slightly higher limit in the hilly and desert areas.

The ceiling reform met only with partial success as one of the major weaknesses of the Ceiling Legislations was that a large number of exemptions to the ceiling limits were permitted by for tea, coffee and rubber plantations, orchards, specialized farms operated by sugar factories and efficiently managed farms on which heavy investments had been made. A number of other factors such as exemptions for religious and charitable institutions, benami transfers, falsification of land deeds, judicial interventions, loopholes in ceiling laws, non-availability of land records, inefficient administration and lack of political-will etc. account for the failure of the land ceiling. Further, generally poor quality of surplus lands and lack of financial and institutional support to bring these lands under cultivation was also a major issue in the implementation of the ceiling reform.

Although land ceiling would result in impediment in achieving economies of scale in agriculture but it would create more uniform ownership of land. This will restrict monopolies by farmers who are basically businessmen as they produce and sell the surplus in the markets. More uniform distribution of land will result in more competition among the farmers (businessmen) which would ultimately result in lowering of prices of agricultural produce benefiting all the consumers of the country.

4. **Consolidation of land holdings:**

Consolidation of land holdings means bringing together the various small plots of land of a farmer scattered all over the village as one compact block, either through purchase or exchange of land with others. The average size of holdings in India is very small. The size of the holdings is decreasing but number of holdings is increasing over time. This is due to the inheritance laws because of which farms are being subdivided and fragmented with every passing generation. Subdivision and fragmentation of holdings results in several disadvantages such as wastage of land, difficulties in land management, difficulty in the adoption of new technology, disputes over boundaries, low productivity etc.

Legislation for compulsory consolidation of holdings was enacted in Bombay in 1947, in the Punjab in 1948 and in U.P. in 1953. Similar provisions were made in other provinces except Kerala and Madras. By 1964-65, a total area of 55 million acres was consolidated. Those who gained the most were the upper strata of the peasantry for whom it facilitated the shift to capitalist farming.

There were various obstacles to the speedy implementation of the consolidation programme. These were poor response from the cultivators due to the perceived advantage of having land in fragmented parcels in the event of floods and other natural calamities or acquisition, complicated process of land consolidation, wide variation in the quality of land, lack of enforcing machinery, lack of political will etc.

Impact of Land reforms

- Tenancy reforms, in total, led to more than one crore tenants getting ownership right in Assam, West Bengal, Kerala, Tamil Nadu and Gujarat.
- More than 10 lakh individuals became beneficiary (surplus land distributed to them) from the ceiling laws implemented in West Bengal.
- The landlords had no personal interest in the lands they owned and also did not take interest in investing on land improvement. But when the same land went into the hands of actual cultivators, they invested and multiplied the gains.
- Distribution of land to the actual cultivators provided an intangible incentive 'to convert the land into gold' which ultimately improved productivity of agriculture.
- It improved the social status of the landless and tenants.

5.3 Land Acquisition Act 2013

Introduction:

Under the Constitution of India, "land" falls under the state list while "**land acquisition**" comes under the **concurrent list** empowering the centre as well as the States to legislate on the matter. But the States have to frame their laws in conformity with the central legislations and in case of any conflict; the Central law prevails over the State's law.

The original Land Acquisition Act 1894 was a colonial legislation enacted by the British primarily to acquire private land to lay railway lines and for other such construction works. When India got its independence, this Act remained in force and was being used by the government although with few amendments till 31st December 2013. The following were the major issues with the Act:

- The Land Acquisition Act 1894, of late, was felt by all concerned that it did not adequately protect the interest of the land owners/persons interested in the land.
- The Act did not provide for rehabilitation of persons displaced from their land although by such compulsory acquisition, their livelihood gets affected.
- The compensation given to the landowners as per the 1894 Act used to be substantially less than the actual market value of the land.
- It did not meet the evolving requirements and gradually, the injustices caused by it began to generate resistance in the society, causing abandonment of several projects, including the Tata Motors' small car project at Singur.
- To say the least, the Act had become outdated (120 years old) and needed to be replaced by fair, reasonable and rational enactment in tune with the constitutional provisions, particularly, Article 300A of the Constitution.

When we adopted the Constitution after independence, the right to property was a fundamental right. In the year 1978, the 44th Constitutional Amendment **eliminated** the right to acquire, hold and dispose of property as a fundamental right (Article 31 was repealed and Article 19 was amended). However, in another part of the Constitution, Article 300(A) was inserted to affirm that no person shall be deprived of his property except by the authority of law. This power of compulsory acquisition is described by the term "eminent domain". It is the power the government has to obtain the property of an individual even without the person's full consent. This allows the government to seize land to be used in public enterprises such as roads; schools or utilities and the landowner gets compensated for the land at fair market value. Government uses this eminent domain power for all forceful acquisitions of land. So now, the right to property is just a constitutional or statutory right.

The Right to Fair Compensation and Transparency in Land Acquisition, Rehabilitation and Resettlement Act 2013 (shortly "LA Act 2013"): The LA Act 2013 was passed in September 2013 and came into force on 1st January 2014. The LA Act 2013 can be used for acquisition of land only for public purpose projects. The following category of projects comes under public purpose projects:

- Projects for strategic purposes relating to naval, military, air force including central paramilitary forces or any work vital to national security or projects of PSUs.
- Projects for infrastructure like railways, highways, roads, ports, power plants, industrial corridors, mining, agro-processing, warehousing.
- Government aided or administered educational and research institutions excluding private hospitals, private educational institutions and private hotels
- Projects for project affected families
- For residential purposes for the poor and landless etc.

Applicability

The LA Act 2013 applies in the following conditions:

- When the appropriate (Central or State) govt. acquires land for its own use, hold and control (including PSUs) for public purpose (no consent required).
- When the appropriate govt. acquires land for Public Private Partnership (PPP) projects (ownership of land lies with the government) for public purpose on the condition that prior consent of at least 70% of the affected families (owners of land) has been obtained.
- When the appropriate government acquires land for private companies for public purpose on the condition that prior consent of at least 80% of the affected families (owners of land) have been obtained.

Salient Features:

The following are some important features of the LA Act 2013:

(i) Compensation: It is equal to the Market Value of land and immovable property multiplied by a factor of 1 in case of urban land and multiplied by 2 in case of rural land. In case the land lies between urban and rural area then the multiplying factor will be between 1 and 2 depending on the distance of the project from the urban area.

In addition to the above, a "**Solatium**" (compensation for emotional attachment) equal to 100% of the above compensation shall also be given. So, the total compensation stands out to be twice the Market Value for urban area and four times the market value for rural area.

(ii) The Act prohibits acquisition of irrigated multi-cropped land other than under exceptional circumstances. This restriction does not apply to project which are linear in nature such as roads, irrigation canals, railways & power lines.

Multi-cropped irrigated land can be acquired in case of exceptional circumstances as demonstrable last resort and in that case, the Act empowers the State governments to fix the limits on the acquisition of multi-cropped land, acquisition of agricultural land and limits of private purchase.

(iii) Social Impact Assessment (SIA): Whenever the government intends to acquire land, it shall consult the Panchayat, Municipality as the case may be in the affected area and carry out an SIA study in consultation with them and it shall make available the report to the general public. The SIA report shall include the following:

- Whether the proposed acquisition serves public purpose
- Estimation of affected and displaced families
- Extent of land, houses, settlements and other common properties likely to be affected
- Whether the extent of land proposed for acquisition is the absolute bare-minimum
- Whether land acquisition at an alternate place has been considered and found not feasible
- Study of social impacts of the project, its cost and overall cost of the project vis-a-vis the benefits of the project

The process of obtaining ***consent*** *shall be carried out along with the SIA study.*

(iv) Rehabilitation and Resettlement (R&R): The project affected families shall be provided with the following in addition to the compensation mentioned in point (i) above:

- A job (where job is created) or onetime payment of five lakhs per affected family or monthly payment of Rs 2000 (linked to CPI) for 20 years
- One time "Resettlement Allowance" of Rs. 50,000/- for each affected family
- Each affected family shall get monthly subsistence allowance of Rs. 3000 for one year
- In case of displacement, if a house is lost, the person should be provided with constructed house

Comment: The new LA Act 2013 has sought to streamline the land acquisition procedure, bring about greater transparency and safeguard the rights of land owners to be compensated and rehabilitated. In setting out to achieve a balance between promoting industrial growth and ensuring the rights of landowners, the new LA Act 2013 slant towards the protection of land owner's rights. And getting the consent of 70% to 80% of the project affected families is really challenging in times of rising population density.

5.4 Model Agricultural Land Leasing Act 2016

Land leasing laws relating to rural agricultural land in Indian states were enacted during decades immediately following the independence. At the time, the abolition of Zamindari and redistribution of land to the tiller were the highest policy priorities. Top leadership of the day saw tenancy and sub-tenancy as integral to the feudal land arrangements that India had inherited from the British. Therefore, tenancy reform laws that various states adopted sought to not only transfer ownership rights to the tenant but also **either prohibited or heavily**

discouraged leasing and sub-leasing of land. However, politically influential landowners were successful in subverting the reform and till as late as 1992, ownership rights were transferred to the cultivator on just 4% of the cultivated land.

In trying to force the transfer of ownership to the cultivator, many States abolished tenancy altogether. But while resulting in minimal land transfer, the policy had the unintended consequence of ending any protection tenants might have had and forced future tenants underground. Some states allowed tenancy but imposed a ceiling on land rent at one-fourth to one-fifth of the produce. But since this rent fell well below the market rate, contracts became oral in these states, with the tenant paying closer to 50% of the produce in rent.

Many large states including Telengana, Bihar, Karnataka, Madhya Pradesh and Uttar Pradesh ban land leasing with exceptions granted to landowners among widows, minors, disabled and defence personnel. Some states including Punjab, Haryana, Gujarat, Maharashtra and Assam do not ban leasing but the tenant acquires a right to purchase the leased land from the owner after a specified period of tenancy. This provision too has the effect of making tenancy agreements oral, leaving the tenant vulnerable. Only the states of Andhra Pradesh, Tamil Nadu, Rajasthan and West Bengal have liberal tenancy laws with the last one limiting tenancy to sharecroppers. A large number of states among them Rajasthan and Tamil Nadu, which otherwise have liberal tenancy laws, do not recognize sharecroppers as tenants.

The original intent of the **restrictive** tenancy laws no longer holds any relevance. Today, these restrictions have detrimental effects on not only the tenant for whose protection the laws were originally enacted but also on the landowner and implementation of public policy. The tenant lacks the security of tenure that she would have if laws permitted her and the landowner to freely write transparent contracts. In turn, this discourages the tenant from making long-term investments in land and also leaves her feeling perpetually insecure about continuing to maintain cultivation rights. Furthermore, it deprives her of potential access to credit by virtue of being a cultivator. Landowner also feels a sense of insecurity when leasing land with many choosing to leave land fallow. The latter practice is becoming increasingly prevalent with landowners and their children seeking non-farm employment.

Keeping these things in mind, Central Government got a model act drafted on land leasing by an expert panel under the NITI Aayog in April 2016 and has forwarded it to States to implement it. It secures the rights of landowners while allowing tenant farmers access to facilities like insurance, credit and compensation for crop damage.

The idea behind the **model law** is to allow owners to lease out agricultural land to tenant farmers without any fear of losing it. This will incentivise tenants to make investment in improvement of land, landowner will also be able to lease land without fear of losing it to the tenant and the government will be able to implement its policies efficiently. It would allow unused land to be used productively, and enable tenant farmers to invest in the land and access credit and insurance. As per estimates, about 18% of land holdings and 13% cultivable area are managed by tenant farmers.

Important Features of the Model Act 2016

- The Model law allows that a person can take agricultural land on lease for cultivation (agriculture and allied activities)

- The model law enables tenant farmers and share croppers to avail bank credit, crop insurance and disaster relief benefits.
- The model law allows consolidation of farm land so that small plots of land that are economically unviable can be leased out *(using tractors and farm equipment is not economically viable for small plots of 2-3 acres)*. Large operational holdings will reduce the cost of cultivation and increase profitability of farming.
- The duration of the lease and the consideration amount will be decided mutually by the owner and the tenant.
- There will be no ceiling on the area of land that can be leased out or consolidated as the Government wants market forces to determine the size of operational holdings.
- Under the new law, land can also be leased out for allied activities like livestock or animal husbandry for a maximum period of five years.
- The Model Act proposes quicker litigation process in case of disputes, by suggesting recourse through criminal proceedings and special tribunals. The dispute settlement will be taken up at the level of the Gram Sabha, Panchayat and Tehsildar and are kept outside the jurisdiction of courts.

Current restrictions on land leasing have reduced the occupational mobility of landowners who want to take up employment outside agriculture but are forced to stick to their land due to the fear of losing it. Bans or restrictions on land leasing have led to 'concealed tenancy'—where agreements between landowner and tenant are informal or tenancy agreements are not recorded—due to which tenant farmers do not have any incentive to invest in land improvement. Lease farming has now become an economic necessity and not a symbol of feudalism, as it was thought before. The growth of an active land lease market would be helpful for the rural poor to get out of the poverty trap.

Few examples:

- China has already revised its land leasing laws, where farmers can lease out their land, even to corporate entities for cultivation for up to 30 years. Such a move can attract long term investments in high value crops.
- Andhra Pradesh and Kerala's have liberalized their restrictive land leasing laws, while fully protecting the land rights of the owners, and their innovative institutional experiences offer key lessons for policymakers at the centre.

Way Forward

One reason landowners fear leasing out their lands for long is the absence of tamper-proof land records with the revenue departments. If the Government digitise and geo-tag land records and link them with Aadhaar Card and the bank accounts of farmers, then this will create a centralised, transparent and easily assessable land records system which will go a long way in leasing out agricultural land.

5.5 Land Pooling Policy

- **Land Pooling** is a concept where small chunks of land owned by individuals are given to Land Pooling Agency for the development of infrastructure like roads, drainage, park etc. After the development of the land, the Agency redistributes the land after deducting some portion of land as compensation towards infrastructure development costs.
- Generally, the people who give their land get 60-70% of their land holdings back after infrastructure is developed on it. The people

are willing to surrender some part (30% to 40%) of their land for the development of infrastructure because they also benefit from the better infrastructure in the locality and because of development the 60% to 70% of the land which they get back has higher valuation.

- This is being done to overcome challenges that come with unavailability of land due to surge in land compensation cost after Right to Fair Compensation and Transparency in Land Acquisition, Rehabilitation and Resettlement Act, 2013 came in to force.
- In case of Delhi, the land pooling agency is the Delhi Development Authority (DDA), and it is urbanizing the villages and outskirts of Delhi and converting into a smart city. In this policy DDA is launching an online portal where you submit your land to DDA. If a person contributes land between 2-20 hectares, then he will get 48% developed land and Land owners offering more than 20 hectares will get 60% of it back.
- Gujarat and Maharashtra have already implemented this policy.
- **Land reforms to be done by States** Govt. of India, Ministry of Finance is nudging States to digitize their land records. States like Karnataka, Rajasthan, Madhya Pradesh, Uttar Pradesh, Kerala, Andhra Pradesh, Telangana and Gujarat have digitized their land records.
- This will help in creating Online "Mortgage Charge" on the Land which will help in better credit/loan delivery and it will also help in reducing loan frauds as now only those people will be able to take agriculture loan who are real farmers and own land.
- Creating "Mortgage Charge" means transfer of interest in the ownership of a property/land for the purpose of securing repayment of any debt.
- Now since land records will be digitized, so all this process will happen online. For example, earlier if a farmer wants loan, then he needs to provide his land records in the physical form and then banks need to authenticate this land paper (where there were chances of fraud) and required a lot of documents to be signed and then provide the loan. But now all this will happen online very fast with digitized land records.
- Assignment of a Unique Land Parcel Identification Number (ULPIN) or Bhu-Aadhaar for all rural lands.
- Digitisation of cadastral maps in rural areas.
- Digitizsation of land records using GIS mapping in urban areas.

PREVIOUS YEARS' QUESTIONS

Main Questions

1. How did land reforms in some parts of the country help to improve the socio-economic conditions of marginal and small farmers? **[2021]**
2. State the objectives and measures of land reforms in India. Discuss how land ceiling policy on land holding can be considered as an effective reform under economic criteria. **[2023]**
3. What were the factors responsible for the successful implementation of land reforms in some parts of the country? Elaborate. **[2024]**

6

Indian Economy (1947-2014)

6.1 Impact of British Rule on Indian Economy

The economic policies followed by the British led to the rapid transformation of India's economy into a colonial economy. There were certain basic features of the colonial structure which characterized the Indian economy before independence.

1. Colonialism led to the complex but complete integration of the Indian economy with the world capitalist system but in a subservient position. Since 1750's, India's economic interests were wholly subordinated to that of Britain. To suit British industry, a peculiar structure of production and international division of labour (by which Britain produced high technology, high productivity and capital-intensive goods while India did the opposite) was forced upon India. It produced and exported food stuffs and raw materials like cotton, jute, oilseeds, tobacco, minerals and imported manufactured products of British industry from biscuits and shoes to machinery, cars and railway engines.

2. A basic characteristic to the process of economic development is the size and utilization of economic surplus or savings generated in the economy for investment and expansion of the economy (net savings of the Indian economy from 1914 to 1946 was barely 3% of GNP). A very large part of the India's social surplus or savings was appropriated by the colonial state (for military expenditure and colonial administration) and indigenous landlords and moneylenders while only a very small part of it was spent on the development of agriculture, industry or social infrastructure or nation building activities such as education and healthcare. Tax system was regressive i.e. peasants were burdened with high tax while bureaucrats, landlords, merchants hardly paid any taxes. And then there was "**Drain**" that is the unilateral transfer to Britain of social surplus and potential investible capital by the colonial state and its officials from India.

3. India's policy was determined in Britain and in the interest of the British economy and British capitalist class. An important aspect of the underdevelopment of India was the denial of state support to industry and agriculture. This was contrary to what happened in nearly all capitalist countries which enjoyed active support in the early stages of development (protection of their infant industries by imposing heavy

import duty on the import of foreign manufacturers). The colonial state imposed free trade in India and refused to give tariff protection to Indian industries as Britain, Europe and US had done.

Accordingly, colonialism led to the complete backwardness and underdevelopment of the Indian economy. The situation of the economy at independence can be described as follows:

1. The agrarian structure which evolved during the British period was dominated by landlords, moneylenders, merchants and the colonial state who appropriated more than half of the total agricultural production and whose interests in agriculture was primarily confined to collecting land revenue and it spent very little to improve agriculture.
2. During the 19th century, there was a quick collapse of the Indian handicraft and artisanal industries largely because of two reasons: First, the competition from the cheaper imported manufacturers of Britain together with the policy of free trade imposed on India. And secondly, Britain and other European countries imposed high import duties on Indian goods. This led to the virtual closing of European markets to Indian manufacturers after 1820. The ruined artisans failed to find alternative employment and crowed into agriculture as tenants, share croppers and agricultural labourers which were followed by an extreme subdivision of land into small holdings and fragmentation.
3. Industrial development was confined to cotton, jute, coal and tea in the 19th century and to sugar, cement and paper in the 1930's. There had been some development in the iron and steel industry after 1907, but as late as 1946, cotton and jute textiles accounted for nearly 30% of all workers employed in factories. In 1950, India met about 90 percent of its needs of machine tools (machine for cutting and shaping metals) through imports.
4. A serious weakness of Indian industrial effort was the almost complete absence of heavy or capital goods industries, without which there can be no rapid and independent development of industries. In terms of production as well as employment, the modern industrial development of India was paltry compared with the other countries.
5. Foreign capital dominated the industrial and financial fields and controlled foreign trade. British firms dominated coal mining, jute industry, shipping, banking and insurance and tea and coffee plantations. Moreover, through their managing agencies, the British capitalist controlled many of the Indian owned companies.

So, at the eve of independence, our country inherited the colonial legacy of economic underdevelopment, gross poverty, illiteracy (84%), wide prevalence of diseases and stark social inequality. Colonialism resulted in the underdevelopment and pauperization of the people especially the peasantry and the artisans.

6.2 Economy After Independence

Once the British left India, there was a general consensus among the national leaders that India shall be built on the values of nationalism, secularism and democracy and the goals of rapid economic development which shall be within democratic political structure as political stability was must for greater economic development. But the structural distortions created by colonialism in the Indian economy and society made the future transition to self-sustained growth more difficult.

The leaders of independent India had to decide, among other things, the type of economic system most suitable for our nation, a system which would promote the welfare of all rather than a few. There are different types of economic systems and among them, socialism appealed to Jawaharlal Nehru the most. However, he was not in favour of the kind of socialism established in the former Soviet Union where all the means of production, i.e., all the factories and farms in the country, were owned by the government. There was no private property. It is not possible in a democracy like India for the government to change the ownership pattern of land and other properties of its citizens in the way that it was done in the former Soviet Union. Nehru, and many other leaders and thinkers of the newly independent India, sought an alternative to the extreme versions of capitalism and socialism. Basically, sympathising with the socialist outlook, they found the answer in an economic system which, in their view, combined the best features of socialism without its drawbacks. So, they tried to cut out a middle path for development which combines the virtues of individual freedom and liberty with that of equality, while avoiding the evils of both capitalism and socialism. In this view, India would be a socialist society with a strong public sector but also with private property and democracy; the government would plan for the economy with the private sector being encouraged to be part of the plan effort. The 'Industrial Policy Resolution' of 1948 and the Directive Principles of the Indian Constitution reflected this outlook. In 1950, the Planning Commission was set up with the Prime Minister as its Chairperson. The era of five-year plans had begun.

Industrial Policy Resolution (IPR) 1948

Independent India's first Industrial Policy Resolution was issued in April 1948. It emphasized to the economy of securing a continuous increase in production and its equitable distribution and pointed out that state must play of progressively active role in the development of industries. It marked the dawn of the mixed economy and outlined the role of the public and private sectors in India. The IPR 1948 classified the industries into broadly four categories based on whether government or private sector will play a major role in the establishment of these industries:

- **State Monopolies:** Manufacturing of arms and ammunitions, atomic energy and railway transport. These industries were under the exclusive monopoly of the Govt. of India.
- **Basic Industries:** Coal, iron and steel, ship building, aircraft manufacturing, telephone, telegraph and wireless and mineral oils. These industries were considered basic in nature for the development of the economy and were under the central government. But the existing private companies operating in these sectors were allowed to continue.
- **Regulated industries:** Automobiles, heavy machinery, chemicals, fertilizers, sugar, paper, cement, cotton, woollen textiles etc. Government would regulate (pricing, quantity of production etc.) these industries as they were important to the masses.

- **Private industries:** All other industries were left open to the private sector as well as cooperatives.

Hence, the main thrust of the IPR 1948 was to lay down the foundation of a mixed economy, in which both public and private enterprises would coexist and accelerate the pace of industrial development.

Planning in India

India's five-year plans did not spell out how much of each and every good and service is to be produced. This is neither possible nor necessary (the former Soviet Union tried to do this and failed). It is enough if the plan is specific about the sectors where it plays a commanding role, for instance, power generation and irrigation, while leaving the rest to the market. Planning Commission used to recommend funds for various developmental expenditures including schemes in every Five-Year Plan.

Objectives of Planning

- **Economic Growth:** It refers to increase in the country's capacity to produce the output of goods and services (GDP) within the country. It is necessary to produce more goods and services if the people of India are to enjoy a more rich and varied life.
- **Modernization:** To increase the production of goods and services the producers have to adopt new technology. Adoption of new technology is called modernisation. However, modernisation does not refer only to the use of new technology but also to changes in social outlook such as the recognition that women should have the same rights as men.
- **Self-Reliance:** A nation can promote economic growth and modernisation by using its own resources or by using resources imported from other nations. The first seven five-year plans gave importance to self-reliance which means avoiding imports of those goods which could be produced in India itself. This policy was considered a necessity in order to reduce our dependence on foreign countries, especially for food. It is understandable that people who were recently freed from foreign domination should give importance to self-reliance. Further, it was feared that dependence on imported food supplies, foreign technology and foreign capital may make India's sovereignty vulnerable to foreign interference in our policies.
- **Equity:** Growth, modernisation and self-reliance, by themselves, may not improve the kind of life which people are living. A country can have high growth, the most modern technology developed in the country itself, and also have most of its people living in poverty. It is important to ensure that the benefits of economic prosperity reach the poor sections as well instead of being enjoyed only by the rich. So, in addition to growth, modernisation and self-reliance, equity is also important. Every Indian should be able to meet his or her basic needs such as food, a decent house, education and health care and inequality in the distribution of wealth should be reduced.

Types of Planning

- **Imperative Planning:** This refers to centralized planning and implementation, as well as resource allocation. It is utilized by socialist countries, where the state has complete control over all aspects of planning.
- **Indicative Planning:** It proposes/indicates a set of broad principles and recommendations for achieving a set of objectives. The government provides full support to the

private sector but does not have control over it. Rather, it directs the private sector to implement the plan in particular areas.

India's plan documents not only specify the objectives to be attained in the five years of a plan but also what is to be achieved over a period of twenty years. This long-term plan is called '**perspective plan**'.

For the first eight Plans the emphasis was on a growing public sector with massive investments in basic and heavy industries, but since the launch of the Ninth Plan in 1997, the emphasis on the public sector became less pronounced and the planning shifted to more of ***indicative*** *in nature. After the 12th Five-Year Plan in 2012-17, Govt. did not bring any new plan and finally Planning Commission was abolished and NITI Aayog was established in January 2015.*

First Five-Year Plan (1951-56): The main focus of the first FY Plan was on the development of Agriculture. Many irrigation projects were initiated including Bhakra Dam and Hirakund Dam. Besides increasing food production, the other major emphasis of the plan was on the development of transport and communications, and the provision of social services.

In the 1950's, there was a considerable debate happening on what should be the model for economic development. There were two schools of thought; one is the **Bombay** and the other **Calcutta** school of thought on an appropriate theory of economic development for India. The Bombay school was driven by business, commercial and industrial interests, while the Calcutta school was driven by academic, technical, and welfare interests, but both schools contained seasoned professionals of each genre.

Calcutta School of thought

The Calcutta school of thought was propounded by Professor Prasanta Chandra Mahalanobis, of the Indian Statistical Institute. Professor Mahalanobis was a Cambridge educated physicist turned statistician turned economic planner. The core of the Calcutta school strategy was a move towards **capital-intensive and heavy industrialization, led by the public sector, to build the key industries and control the commanding heights of a new modern industrial economy for India**. The private sector would play a complementary role in the mixed economy. The Calcutta school was based on the setting-up of very large plants, in substantial state-owned enterprises, in sectors such as steel and heavy machinery. These capital-intensive facilities, employing few people, would deliver low returns over long gestation periods. But they would be used for the purposes of building machines that built other machines. Without these other machines which are the output of the important capital goods sector, downstream (and other consumer goods) industries could not be set up.

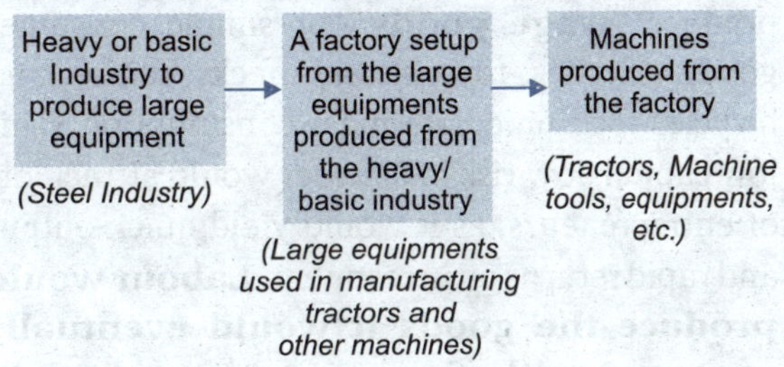

Certain types of big industries were treated as **basic** because they made possible the emergence of other industrial enterpri ses, whether basic or not. The approach represented a means for the government to influence the speed and direction of economic growth.

In this model, the capital good enters into the production of the consumer good and capital good both. As capital goods go into the production of both types of goods, a larger share of a given investment outlay allocated to the production of capital goods, if maintained indefinitely, would lead to greater final output, even of consumer goods, over time. In this capital goods model, the rise in overall output is postponed because there is a greater gestation lag between investment and the emergence of output. So, while a larger share of investment in consumer goods today may lead to a faster rate of growth of aggregate output initially, but this outcome is trumped in the longer term by a greater allocation to capital goods production to start with.

Bombay School of thought

In the 1950's there was an alternative vision to that of Calcutta school of thought or Mahalanobis model. It belonged to the Bombay Economists C. N. Vakil and P. R. Brahmanand. Its starting point was that India lacked financial capital but had plenty of cheap human labour. There was huge disguised unemployment in the countryside. The thing to do was to put these people into productive work at the lowest capital cost. They suggested that we employ the surplus labour to produce "**wage goods**", or simple consumer goods - clothes, toys, shoes, snacks, radios, and bicycles for immediate mass consumption. This low capital, low risk businesses would attract lots of entrepreneurs, as it would yield quick output and rapid returns on investment. **Labour would produce the goods it would eventually consume with the wages it earned in producing the goods. They were called wage goods because the wage earner would create the demand for the goods that he produced.** This Bombay strategy was exactly opposite to Mahalanobis's vision of huge state controlled, capital intensive industries such as steel plants, employing few people and delivering low returns over long gestation periods. The "wage goods" strategy would have pushed investments into agriculture, rural infrastructure, agriculture-based industries and simple consumer manufacturers for both the home and export markets. It would have meant postponing the ambitious projects in capital and heavy industry. We would have imported the capital goods in the near term, and the foreign exchange for their import would have been earned from the export of simple consumer items - the sort of products that Japan and the Asian tigers like Taiwan, South Korea started with. The result would have been high economic growth, high employment, rising exports and prosperity.

Other Plans/ Models

Sarvodaya Plan: The plan was drafted by Jayaprakash Narayan in 1950 and emphasised small and cotton industries alongside agriculture and suggested freedom from foreign technology. It also stressed upon land reforms.

Bombay Plan: Proposed by a group of industrialists including JRD Tata, GD Birla and others in 1944, it proposed presence of Govt. in the core sectors of economy without diminishing the role of private sector.

People's Plan: This plan was drafted by M. N. Roy in 1945 and gave greatest priority to agricultural production. It also emphasized on manufacture of consumer goods and development of communication and transport network.

Gandhian Plan: In 1944, Sriman Narayan Agarwal authored The Gandhian Plan, in which he emphasized the promotion of agriculture and village and cottage industries based on Gandhian economic ideas.

2nd Five Year Plan (1956 - 61)

The leading economists of India were supporting the Calcutta school of thought and ultimately this model got accepted for building the 2nd Five Year Plan document. This model was, among other things, an evocation of the old nationalist model of swadeshi, or self-reliance. The government shall develop the basic heavy industries for the manufacture of producer goods (capital goods) to strengthen the foundation of economic independence. And the household sector, village and cottage industries shall focus on the production of consumption goods. It was a two-pronged attack on the problem of breaking through India's static economy: the creation of a large machine-building industry as a basis for the expansion of secondary industries; and decentralized cottage industries to create jobs for India's army of unemployed." The latter was expected to produce consumer goods at a low cost and create employment with minimum social dislocation.

The essence of the model was shift in the pattern of industrial investment towards building up a domestic consumption goods sector. The strategy was in order to reach high standards in consumption; investment in building capacity in the production of capital goods is firstly needed for which the responsibility lies with the government. So, rapid development of heavy and capital goods industries was promoted in the public sector. Hydroelectric power projects, three steel plants at Bhillai, Durgapur and Rourkela were established, coal production increased and railway lines added.

In the 2nd Plan document, Mahalanobis put into practice the socialist ideas of investment in a large public sector (at the expense of the private sector), with emphasis on heavy industry (at the expense of consumer goods) and a focus on import substitution (at the expense of export promotion), besides other follies which were inspired by the USSR. This model continued in the 3rd Five Year Plan also till the death of Nehru.

Business Class view

The business class, who should have been the first to protest, was too timid. In the years after independence, people had been hard hit by inflation because of post-war dislocations and the partition of the country. As the prices of food rose, it was natural for the middle class to blame the usurious merchants and businessman, calling them "profiteers and black marketers." Hence the businessmen were defensive.

Industrial Policy Resolution (IPR) 1956:

In December 1954, the Parliament accepted the socialist pattern of society as the objective of social and economic policy. Industrial policy, as other policies, was therefore to be governed by these principles and direction. Hence the scope of public sector got widened.

Mahalanobis's thinking on the 2nd Plan was logically extended to the Industrial Policy Resolution in 1956, which reserved seventeen industries exclusively for the public sector. The reserved industries included iron and steel, mining, machine tool manufacture, and heavy electrical plants. The logic behind "reservations" was that these were industries of "basic strategic importance" and "required investment on a scale which only the state could provide". The industries were divided into Schedule A, B and C.

Result of the Mahalanobis Model

In the absence of serious opposition, the Calcutta vision won the day in the 1950s and 1960s. But it never did make sense to close an industry to the private sector - it was similar to discouraging entrepreneurship and competition. Even the industries which were allowed for private sector, there were creeping controls through the licensing system. The industrial licensing framework was formalized, under the Industries Development and Regulation (IDR) Act of 1951, to be the principal instrument for coordinating and controlling investments in industry. It controlled entry, expansion of capacity, technology, output mix, capacity, location and import content which infamously established 'License Raj' in India.

State supervision of development along planned lines, dividing activity between public and private sector, preventing rise of concentration and monopoly, protecting small industry, ensuring regional balance, canalizing resources according to planned priorities and targets etc. - all this involved the setting up of an elaborate and complicated system of controls and industrial licensing through the Industries Development and Regulation Act 1951. Further Balance of Payment (BoP) crisis and acute shortage of foreign exchange reserve that occurred in 1956-57, at the very start of second Plan led to the imposition of stringent import and foreign exchange controls.

The seeds of the Licence Quota rules and regulations were thus laid and in later years, it was found that it was not easy to dismantle a system that had acquired a vicious stranglehold over the Indian economy. The bureaucracy politician nexus and certain sections of business that were beneficiaries of the system restricted such a change.

The mixed economy ended in combining the worst features of both socialism and capitalism - the "controls" of socialism with the "monopolies and lobbies" of capitalism - and we got the worst of both the worlds. The "controls" suppressed growth by subduing the innovative energies of capitalism and the mixed economy did not deliver social justice and welfare, which at least the socialist countries did. Instead of delivering quality education and public health to the masses, it delivered subsidies, which usually went to the better off and led to **resource misallocation**.

Socialism was attractive to any sensitive person in the idealistic 1950's. The country had become free after two hundred years, and there was a sense of hope. The class with money and influence was small and came entirely from the upper castes. It had monopolized power and privilege and the few scarce facilities for education, health and infrastructure. It naturally wanted to preserve its privileges. The rest of the population had been left out in the cold. It was natural for the ordinary Indian to expect that Independent India (government) should intervene on behalf of the masses. The spirit of the times offered socialism as the answer.

The problem of the mixed economy was not of principle but of performance. It was a noble vision which led to the oppression by the State. Indians later learned from painful experience that the State does not necessarily work on behalf of the people. It works on behalf of itself - the politicians, bureaucrats, and the interests which directly supported them. State employees went on to become a powerful vested interest that was responsible to no one, and they often believed that they did not have to work.

There were certain flaws with our socialism.

- We adopted an inward-looking, import-substituting path rather than an outward looking, export-promoting route, and thus we did not participate in world trade and the prosperity that trade engendered in the post war era
- We set up a massive, inefficient, and monopolistic public sector to which we denied autonomy of working
- We overregulated private enterprises with the worst (case-by-case) controls in the world, which diminished competition in the home market
- We discouraged foreign capital and denied

ourselves the benefits of technology and world-class competition

- We pampered organized labour and that led to extremely low productivity

Ultimately, we paid a heavy price for our socialism. We did not trust our entrepreneurs and felt that only the State could assume the role to transform the country rapidly. We were mesmerized by the Soviet economic miracle and this led to a bias towards heavy industry and against agriculture and light consumer industry.

he strategy underlying the first three plans assumed that once the growth process gets established, the institutional changes would ensure that benefits of growth trickle down to the poor. But doubts were raised about the effectiveness of the '**trickle down**' approach and its ability to banish poverty. Further, the growth itself generated by the planned approach remained too weak to create adequate surpluses - a prerequisite for the 'trickle down' mechanism to work. Public sector did not live up to the expectations of generating surpluses to accelerate the pace of capital accumulation and help reduce inequality. Agricultural growth remained constrained by perverse institutional conditions. There was unchecked population growth in this period. Though the growth achieved in the first three Five Year Plans was not insignificant, yet it was not sufficient to meet the aims and objectives of development. These brought into view the weakness of economic strategy.

But Mahalanobis model led to capital deepening in India. It led to the increased base of capital goods industries like machine tools, heavy electricals, transportation equipment and the ultimate intermediate goods in the context of industrialization, namely, iron and steel.

The allocation of public expenditure on education at the time reveals a skewness towards higher education (the first IIT and IIM were started in the Nehru era) and a privileging of its technical segment. Not only was there insufficient emphasis on primary education, but there was also no evident assault on illiteracy among adults.

There is no trend increase or decrease in the incidence of poverty seen during this period. Rather there was a pattern of fluctuation, with the incidence of poverty falling in periods of good agricultural performance and rising in periods of poor performance.

Why did India build a large public sector after Independence?

With the benefit of hindsight, we can perhaps understand and interpret the actions of those policymakers. The key argument to have public sector companies occupying the 'commanding heights' of the economy perhaps lay in a 'big push' that was required to solve the coordination problem in economic development. The early industrialization required a large number of different elements of the economy to come about, and there was a coordination problem. The aluminium factory would not come about as the entrepreneur considering that project could not be convinced that another entrepreneur would surely build an aircraft factory, and vice versa. The big push by the government created a skeleton around which the market economy could get going in an incremental fashion. Key staff persons in most private banks have an employment history in public sector banks. Similarly, Hindustan Aeronautics Limited (HAL incubated aerospace knowledge in India, and Indian Drugs and Pharmaceuticals Limited (IDPL) alumni laid the foundations of the private Indian drugs industry.

6.3 Economic Situation after Nehru (1965 to 1991)

Two successive monsoon failures in 1965 and 1966 added to a burden on agriculture which was showing signs of stagnation. Rate of inflation rose to 12% from 1965 to 1968 and food prices rose to 20%. The two wars of 1962 (China) and 1965 (Pakistan) led to massive increase in defence expenditure which resulted in governments consolidated fiscal deficit of 7.3% of GDP in 1966-67. The balance of payment, fragile since 1956-57 deteriorated further, with foreign exchange reserve of about $340 million during 1964-65, enough to cover less than two months of imports.

It was at this most vulnerable time for the Indian economy (with high inflation, low foreign exchange balance, food stocks so low as to threaten famine conditions in some areas calling for large imports) that the US, the most important donor at that time decided to suspend its aid in response to the India Pakistan war (1965) and refused to renew the PL-480 agreement (it was a food aid programme by the US for its strategic and humanitarian concerns behind it) on a long-term basis.

The US, the World Bank and the IMF wanted India to

- Liberalize its trade and industrial controls
- Devalue the Rupee
- Adopt a new Agricultural Policy

Though there was considerable indigenous support for a new initiative in agriculture, there was plenty of suspicion about the first two measures. The rupee was nominally devalued to 36.5% and trade liberalization was initiated by Indira Gandhi in the mid 1960's but it got associated with the continuing recession in industry, inflation and failure of exports to pick up, all of which was at least partly caused due to exogenous (outside) factors such as major drought of 1966-67 and partly by the inadequate manner in which these policies were initiated. These policies were condemned before their long-term effect could be realized.

The perceived failure of the devaluation and liberalization of controls on trade and industry combined with the resentment at the "arm twisting" resorted to by the external agencies (World Bank & IMF) in favour of the policies, using India's economic vulnerability led to a reversal to the earlier policies of control and State intervention.

The post 1967 period, therefore, saw the launching of a series of radical economic policies which were to have long term effect on India's development effort. Some of these policies accentuated the shortcomings that had begun to emerge during the first phase of planning itself and others created new distortions.

- The major private commercial banks were nationalized in 1969.
- Monopoly and Restrictive Trade Practices Act (MRTP), severely restricting the activities of large business houses was passed in 1969
- A series of measures increasing government control and intervention were introduced
- Insurance was nationalized in 1972
- Coal industry was nationalized in 1973
- The Foreign Exchange and Regulation Act (FERA) was passed in 1973 putting numerous restrictions on foreign investment and the functioning of foreign companies in India, making India one of the most difficult destinations for foreign capital in the world. *(At the same time East Asian countries like South Korea, Hong Kong, Singapore, Taiwan were opening up their economy for foreign capital).*

- The government also decided to take over and run sick companies, such as a number of textile mills, rather than allow such loss-making companies to close down.

Higher Growth Phase of 1980's

From the early 1970s the importance of openness and light regulation had begun to receive prominence in global fora concerned with economic development.

When Indira Gandhi returned to power in 1980, she realigned herself politically with the organized private sector and dropped her previous rhetoric. The national government's attitude towards business went from being outright hostile to supportive. Indira Gandhi's switch was further reinforced, in a more explicit manner, by Rajiv Gandhi, following his rise to power in 1984.

The Rajiv Gandhi government (1984 - 89) introduced certain reforms in the second half of the 1980s like relaxation in the grant of licenses, reduction in import restrictions, introduction of export incentives which led India to a higher growth of over 5.5% of GDP in the 1980s and broke the 3.5% growth record of the **previous three decades called the "Hindu rate of Growth" (the term was coined by Prof. Raj Krishna).**

The below figure represents the savings, investment and growth rate of Indian economy in the 20th century.

	1900	↔	1950	↔	1965	↔	1980	↔	1990
GDP Growth		0.7%		3.5%		3.5%		5.5%	
Savings			3%		11%		20%		
Investment			5%		14%		22%		

Poverty

It is undeniable that poverty declined (percent) during the Indira Gandhi years, in fact the decline had commenced early in her tenure. The reason is the faster growth in agricultural production due to Green Revolution rather than anti-poverty interventions as it was too soon for poverty-reduction schemes of Indira Gandhi to have influenced the trajectory of growth.

There can be no better indication that the nature of growth matters for poverty reduction, in this case *where* in the economy growth is occurring. For about a decade and a half from the mid-1960s, while the growth of the economy slowed, agriculture grew faster as a result of the Green Revolution. The latter development was significant as the largest number of poor persons at that time were located in rural India.

Structural bottlenecks during the period 1950-1991

1. The License Raj

The purpose of licensing was:

- to create the planned pattern of investment
- to counteract monopoly and the concentration of wealth
- to maintain regional balance in locating industries
- to protect the interests of small-scale sproducers and encourage the entry of new entrepreneurs

- to encourage optimum scale of plants and advance technology

All these were good intentions, but the way the bureaucracy went about administrating the licensing system created a nightmare for the entrepreneur. Since the system was based on first come, first serve, "the bigger houses cornered a considerable amount of targeted capacity by putting in multiple and early applications for the same product. Thus, they could "foreclose capacity", without any intention of implementing the successful license application. Tragically, the system ended in thwarting competition, entrepreneurship, and growth, without achieving any of its social objectives. The endless delays in clearing applications discouraged the entry of efficient and honest entrants and rewarded wily, inefficient producers who could manipulate the system.

The administrative mechanisms for implementing the policies of the License Raj provided incentives to circumvent/bypass laws and regulations. Regulation was complex and it was implemented more with courage than with wisdom, covering industrial licensing, import and export regulations, price controls, capital issue controls, and the allocation of indigenously produced materials. It created large and powerful group of vested interests. **These comprised politicians, bureaucrats, and a large section of private industry**. The rigidity of the License Raj, where businessmen could not shape their firms' destinies, was perhaps one factor leading to the decline of India's share in global commerce.

In the mid-1970s, an assessment of the system noted that detailed controls put strain on the administrative machinery and delayed implementation. Yet, for political compulsion, the government led by Mrs. Indira Gandhi reinforced the controls system.

2. Monopolistic and Restrictive Trade Practices (MRTP) Act 1969

Indira Gandhi enacted the MRTP Act in 1969 and crippled the private industry for a generation. The MRTP Act turned out to be one of the most damaging in modern Indian history. Any business group with combined assets above Rs. 20 crores were declared a monopoly and effectively debarred from expanding its business after 1969. The Tatas, who used to control the largest industrial empire in India, made over a hundred proposals for new business projects or to expand existing ones over the twenty years period since the MRTP law but all of them were rejected. Thus, Indian firms lost numerous opportunities to derive **economies of scale**, and they never had a chance to launch their own industrial revolution. In the mid-1980's, Rajiv Gandhi's government raised the MRTP asset limit fivefold to Rs. 100 crore and finally in September 1991, the Narasimha Rao government scrapped this ridiculous law.

3. Reservation for Small Scale Industries

India's lack of manufacturing prowess might have resulted from the reservation policies made for small scale firms, and Indian industry was unable to reap the benefits of economies of scale. Small scale enterprises, which belong to organized and unorganized sectors both, were not able to bring in technology and capital and they did not have the professional management experience to run these enterprises. With limited capital, they were not able to achieve economies of scale and increase their productivity and efficiency. Small scale industries were recognized for its importance in providing employment to educated men as well as women in their homes. Thus, a concern with employment, and an anxiety about shortage of capital, led to initial reservations for small scale and cottage industries. The first formal definition of small-scale units was given in 1955 and in 1967, reservation of production of 47 items by the small-scale sector was introduced. By March 1987, the reservation had been extended to over 800 items. These items were produced by other countries through better technology and at a larger scale at a much lesser cost and they flooded our domestic market once we reduced the import duties afters 1991 reforms.

4. Import Substitution Industrialization (ISI)

The Import Substitution Industrialization (ISI) strategy adopted after independence based on heavy protection to indigenous industries was very effective in deepening and widening India's industrial base and giving the economy lot of freedom from foreign dependence. However, overtime the excessive protection through tariff (customs duty) and quota restrictions started leading to inefficiency and technological backwardness in Indian industry. India's inward oriented development path after independence **failed to make a timely shift** from the export pessimism inherent in the first three Five Year Plans. Basically, it failed to take advantage of the globalization process in which the East Asian countries like Singapore, South Korea, Taiwan, Hong Kong etc. participated.

While the reasons for adopting a centrally directed strategy of development were understandable against the background of colonial rule, it, however soon became clear that the actual results of this strategy were far below expectations. Instead of showing high growth, high public savings and a high degree of self-reliance, India was actually showing one of the lowest rates of growth in the developing world with a rising public deficit and a periodic balance of payment crises. Between 1950 and 1990, India's growth rate averaged less than 4 per cent per annum and this was at a time when the developing world and other least developed countries, showed a growth rate of over 5% per annum. An important assumption in the choice of post-independence development strategy was the generation of public savings, which could be used for higher and higher levels of investment. However, this did not happen, and the public sector-instead of being **a generator of savings** for the community's good- became, over time, **a consumer of community's savings**.

6.4 Economic Reforms of 1991 (LPG Reforms)

(Liberalization, Privatization and Globalization)

*(**Liberalization** means removal of state restrictions on private business activities; **Privatization** means transfer of business, industry or service from public to private ownership and control; and **Globalization** is the flow of goods, services, capital and labour across international borders)*

Chronology of Events

Dec 2, 1989 - Nov 10, 1990	*VP Singh (PM, Janata Dal) & Madhu Dandavate (FM)*
Nov 10, 1990 - June 21, 1991	*Chandra Sekhar (PM, Janata Dal) & Yashwant Sinha (FM)*

(Chandra Sekhar resigned on March 6, 1991 as Congress withdrew its support, but he remained in office as a caretaker till June 21, 1991 and his govt. was not given a chance to present the budget)

June 21, 1991 *PV Narasimha Rao (Sworn in as PM, Congress, (Colition))*

July 24, 1991 *Budget was presented by Dr. Manmohan Singh, FM*

Background

The Rajiv Gandhi government (1984-1989) introduced certain reforms in the second half of the 1980s to mitigate the rigours of the control regime **(the license Raj)** like relaxation in the grant of licenses, reduction in import restrictions, introduction of export incentives etc. However, these **changes were marginal, rather than fundamental in nature** amounting more to loosening controls and operating them more flexibly rather than a comprehensive shift away from regime of controls. But certainly, it led India to a higher growth of over 5.5% of GDP in the decade of 1980s and broke the 3.5% growth record of the previous three decades called the "**Hindu rate of Growth**".

While on one hand, the Indian economy in the eighties seemed to be doing quite well, on the other hand there were certain **long term structural weaknesses** building up in the system due to pervasive industrial control through the license raj, Monopolies and Restrictive Trade Practices Act (MRTP) 1969, Nationalization of banks and other industries, self-sufficiency and inward-looking trade policy and Import Substitution Industrialization (ISI).

In the second half of the s1980's, there was enormous deficit on the trade front as imports were nearly double that of exports (export earnings were only 55% of imports). By the late 80's, all this forced India to resort to **more and more short-term borrowings**. Until the early 80s, the government had managed the fiscal (revenue and expenditure) situation conservatively but began indulging in fiscal profligacy (recklessly wasting of money) by substantial borrowing to support various development programmes and keep growth going and which led to the problems in the late '80s and early '90s. This resulted in weak **macroeconomic fundamentals** (fiscal deficit of 8.4%, current account deficit of 3.1%, high inflation of 17% and high external debt etc. in 1990-91) and created a lot of pressure on the Balance of Payment (BoP) front.

The economic situation (January to July 1991) was vulnerable because of three reasons:

- Short term debt was about $6 billion, of which $2 billion was rolled over every 24 hours with overnight borrowings in international capital markets
- Outstanding NRI deposits of more than $10 billion began to be withdrawn rapidly
- By June 1991, foreign exchange reserves were down to a mere $1 billion that were not enough to finance imports even for a fortnight, let alone debt service payments

The Iraqi invasion of Kuwait in August 1990, leading to increase in oil prices (and import bill) and a fall in Indian exports to the Middle East or Gulf region partly contributed to the alarming foreign exchange situation. India's international credit rating (**Sovereign rating**) was sharply downgraded and it was becoming extremely difficult to raise credit (loan) abroad. In such a situation where, foreign lending had virtually dried up, the government was forced to pledge as collateral **67 tonnes of gold** to the Union Bank of Switzerland and Bank of England to raise over $600 million in between April to July 1991 to tide over its immediate transactions. **The country was at the edge of default** as India had to repay its short-term loans which it had raised from abroad. And this formidable economic challenge was juxtaposed with continuing political uncertainty *(see the chronology of events)*.

In the backdrop of this alarming situation, the economic reforms were introduced between June 21, 1991, when the PV Narasimha Rao govt. took over and July 24, 1991, when Dr. Manmohan Singh presented the budget. *(The blue print of the reforms was already there in the Budget which never got presented by Mr. Yashwant Sinha in March 1991 as the Congress did not allow the budget to be presented. And the credit for reforms goes to Narasimha Rao more than Manmohan Singh, for his deft political management as there was opposition to reforms from outside the government as well as inside)*

The economic reforms of 1991 were carried out mainly in three directions: -

1. We dismantled the complex regime of licenses, permits and controls.
2. We reversed the strong bias towards state ownership of means of production and proliferation of public sector enterprises in almost every sphere of economic activity.
3. We abandoned the inward-looking trade policy.

The main objective of the reforms was to integrate the Indian economy with the global economy through trade, investment and technology flows and for this purpose to create conditions which would give Indian entrepreneurs an environment broadly comparable to that in other developing countries and to do so within the span of four to five years.

Following lists down the details of the major reforms carried out in June-July 1991:

1. **Fiscal Stabilisation:** Fiscal stabilisation is an essential **precondition** for the success of economic reforms. A reduction in the Central Government's fiscal deficit was therefore critical for the reforms to take off which had reached to 8.4% in 1990-91. The following steps were taken to reduce the fiscal deficit.
   - Abolition of export subsidies in 1991-92 and the partial restructuring of fertilizer subsidy in 1992-93
   - Budget support to loss-making public-sector units in the form of government loans to cover their losses was progressively phased out
   - Certain development expenditure was restructured including expenditure on social and economic infrastructure
2. **Industrial Policy:** The most radical changes implemented in the reform package have been in the area of industrial policy. The system of pervasive industrial licensing (License Raj) prevalent earlier, which required government permission for new investments as well as for substantial expansion of existing capacity was abolished. Licensing is now required only for small list of industries primarily because of environmental and pollution considerations. The parallel but separate controls over investment and expansion by large industrial houses through the MRTP Act were also eliminated.

   The list of industries exclusively reserved for public sector was drastically pruned and many critical areas were opened for private sector like power generation, hydrocarbon (exploration, production and refining of oil & gas), air transport, telecommunication etc.

3. **De-licensing of items reserved for MSME Sector:** Since 1991, the ministry of Commerce and Industry was progressively de-licensing the items reserved for MSME sector through a forward-looking policy. Over the years since 1991, the list of items reserved for manufacturing by MSME sector was reduced from over 800 to nil by April 2015. The items which were reserved consisted of pickles & chutneys, mustard oil (except solvent extracted), groundnut oil wooden fixtures, exercise books and registers, wax candles, laundry soap, glass bangles, steel almirah, rolling shutters, steel chairs and tables, padlocks, stainless steel and aluminium utensils etc.

4. **Foreign Investment:** Before 1991, India's policy towards foreign investment was very selective and was widely perceived as being unfriendly. The percentage of ownership allowed to foreign investors was generally restricted to 40% except in certain high technology areas and foreign investment was generally discouraged in consumer goods sector unless supported by strong export commitments.

   The new policy was much more actively supportive of foreign investment in a wide range of activities. Permission is automatically granted for foreign equity investment up to 51% in a large list of 34 industries and for more than 51% Govt. approval was required.

   Various restrictions earlier applied on the operation of companies with foreign ownership of more than 40% were eliminated by replacing the Foreign Exchange Regulation Act (FERA) 1973 with Foreign Exchange Management Act (FEMA) 1999, and all companies incorporated in India were now treated alike, irrespective of the level of foreign ownership.

5. **Trade and Exchange Rat Policy:** The complex import control regime earlier applicable to imports of raw materials, other inputs, capital goods were virtually dismantled. Now all raw materials, other inputs required for production and capital goods can be freely imported except for a relatively small negative list. Import of certain consumer goods were allowed against special import licenses which were given to certain categories of exporters as incentives. The exclusion of consumer goods from trade liberalisation was a restrictive element in trade policy which the government promised will be gradually liberalized, but for all other sectors, quantitative restrictions on imports were largely eliminated. The removal of quantitative restrictions on imports was accompanied by a gradual lowering of customs duties.

   Before 1991, the Indian Rupee was converted into foreign currency on the basis of officially fixed exchange rate by RBI. In July 1991, rupee was devalued by about 24% (for alignment of the exchange rate with the market rate). And in March 1993, India moved to market-based exchange rate system (floating rate/managed float). Rupee was made fully convertible at current account. On capital account, rupee is still partially convertible.

6. **Tax Reforms:**
   - The maximum marginal rate of personal income tax was 56% in June 1991. This was reduced to 40%
   - Corporate income tax was reduced from 51.75% to 46% for public listed companies
   - Customs duty was considerably reduced from an average of around 200% to 65%

7. **Public Sector Reforms:** Reform of the public sector is a critical element in structural adjustment programmes all over the world and was also included on India's reform agenda. Instead of outright privatization, the government initiated a limited process of disinvestment of government ownership/ equity in public sector companies with government retaining 51% of the equity and management control.

   Public sector companies were given a clear-cut signal that in future their investment plans must be financed either by **internal resource generation (profit)** or **by resources raised from the capital market** - both alternatives being bound to encourage and reward efficiency and commercial orientation. The government announced that budgetary support to finance loss making PSU's will be phased out over three years. And this shall be supplemented with a policy for active restructuring of these units wherever it is possible to make them economically viable and with closure combined with adequate compensation for labour where it is not.

8. **Financial Sector Reforms:**
   - Banking Sector was opened up to private competition from new private banks and several new banking licenses were granted.
   - Transparency and supervision in trading practices in capital markets. SEBI (established in 1988 but given statutory powers in April 1992) was established as an independent statutory authority for regulating stock exchanges and supervising the major players in the capital markets.
   - Capital market was opened for portfolio investments and Indian companies were allowed to access international capital markets by issuing equity/ shares abroad through Global Depository Receipts (GDR).
   - The requirement of government permission of companies issuing capital as well as system of government control over the pricing of new equity by private companies was abolished with the repeal of the Capital Issues Control Act in May 1992.

(The aforementioned reforms implemented were necessitated by the macroeconomic compulsions but were also put as a precondition by the IMF and the World Bank for the additional financial assistance. And it is remarkable that even if the reform process was put in place by a Congress led government, the successive non-Congress governments have carried forward the reforms in a much bolder way).

The 1991 crisis compelled India to create a new framework in which the fundamental principle would be that **competition is the key to improving efficiency**. Therefore, there has been a common thread running through the various reform measures that have been implemented since 1991, which is to improve productivity by infusing competition.

Impact of reforms (short term) on various macroeconomic parameters:

- Inflation reduced from a peak of 17% in August 1991 to about 8.5% within 2.5 years
- Forex reserves increased from $1.2 billion in June 1991 to over $15 billion in 1994
- GDP growth increased from 1.1% in 1991-92 to 4% in 1992-93
- Fiscal deficit reduced from 8.4% in 1990-91 to 5.7% in 1992-93
- Exports more than doubled from 1990-91 to 1993-94

Impact of reforms on poverty reduction (long term)

Growth helps in reduction of poverty in two ways; first through the percolation (trickle down) effect and second through the ability to raise more resources on the part of the government to provide for increased social sector expenditures. Therefore, to make a dent in the poverty, a twofold strategy is needed:

- letting the economy grow fast, and
- focusing on targeted programmes to help the poor and disadvantaged

As we initiated the reforms in 1991, the Indian economy moved on a higher growth trajectory of 6.3%, which helped the government to raise more resources and it also pulled in a lot of population in the growth process. And this led to an accelerated reduction in poverty post in the post reform period.

The proportion of nationwide population living below the poverty line (as per the planning commission estimates) fell from 36% (40.7 cr) in 1993-94 to 27.5% (35.5 cr) in 2004-05. So, **there is evidence that the reforms augmented the growth process and have reduced the poverty in India.** And that is why, we moved away from the old socialist policies, with their deleterious effect on economic performance, as it had failed to deliver on poverty reduction and other social goals.

But despite all the reforms, a lot many Indians continue to remain poor and there are still 21.9% (26.9 cr) of the population below the poverty line as per the Tendulkar Committee estimate in 2011-12. They are not only poor but are also deprived of the basic amenities of which we have been talking since Independence and before that. Reforms will not become acceptable to the people of India until and unless we take care of them through direct government action and ensure that they are provided the basic amenities.

Reforms are the first important step towards raising the growth rate. But as our experience over the last few years shows, reforms alone are not enough. They must be supplemented by a proactive government which is focused on development and not distracted by other considerations. And it must be recognized that reforms are means and not ends in themselves. The essential objective of development is to eradicate poverty and improve the living conditions of the people.

Impact of reforms on the disparity between rich and poor (long term)

Data from the National Council of Applied Economic Research says that, the Gini coefficient in income (rural + urban) which was 0.52 in 2004-05, increased to 0.55 in 2011-12 *(higher the Gini coefficient higher the inequality)*. If we consider non-income indicators like the health and education then inequalities between the poor and rich have increased further after the reform period. So, the conclusion is that poverty declined faster but inequality increased in the post-reform period. But certain economists claim that we have not been able to establish direct relation between reforms and its impact on inequality.

Economic reforms should focus more on efficient delivery systems of public services. Many reckon that poor governance is the biggest constraint in achieving the aspirations of a new generation and reduction in poverty and inequality. A major institutional challenge is the accountability of service providers, particularly the **public sector**. Recent literature also focused on eradication of **corruption** for reduction in inequalities. Issues like electoral reforms, crony capitalism, election funding and corruption should be part of the reform agenda to reduce inequalities. Fiscal instruments like public investment in physical and social infrastructure can be used to reduce inequality.

For reducing inequality, some advocate measures such as redistribution of assets and wealth in favour of the poor via higher taxes for the rich. However, these may not be pragmatic solutions. The tax/GDP ratio has to be raised with a wider tax base rather than increasing the tax rate. The new generation wants equality of opportunity rather than redistributive measures.

Comment: The post reform period has been termed as jobless growth as we have not been able to create enough employment opportunities for the youth. India's most pressing challenge currently is to generate a large number of good jobs as it is the only sustainable solution for persistent poverty otherwise the demographic dividend could become a nightmare of unemployment and underemployment. The other major problem in India is the low growth in rural productivity, unlike China where rural entrepreneurship was the biggest growth driver for years. According to Raghuram Rajan (2014), India simply shifted resources to rural areas through transfer programmes (redistribution) like the guaranteed rural job scheme and minimum support price (MSP) for crops, without the concomitant rise in farm productivity which fuelled demand for goods and services and led to higher inflation.

A Comparison with China

China started its reforms in1978 (under the leadership of Deng Xiaoping) in Agriculture sector and then moved up to the industrial sector (Bottom-up approach). It dismantled the commune system (in case of commune system individuals forfeited their private plots to common ownership) in land holdings and established household responsibility system and by and large freed up the agricultural prices from controls. The real income of farsmers grew in double digits which increased the demand for manufactured products resulting in a manufacturing boom in China.

By making agriculture the starting point of market-oriented reforms, a sector which gave majority of the people their livelihood, China could ensure widespread distribution of gains and build consensus and political support for the continuation of reforms. Reform of incentives resulted in greater returns to farmers and in more efficient resource allocation, which in turn strengthened the domestic production base and made it more competitive. Besides, prosperity in agriculture favoured the development of a dynamic rural non-farm (RNF) sector, regarded as one of the main causes for rapid poverty reduction in China as it provided additional sources of income outside farming.

The rapid development of the RNF sector also encouraged the government to expand the scope of policy changes and put pressure on the urban economy to reform as well, since non-farm enterprises in rural areas had become more competitive than the state-owned enterprises (SOEs). Reforms of the SOEs, in turn, triggered macroeconomic reforms, opening up the economy further.

In Contrast, India liberalized the industrial and services sector in 1991 and it did not touch the agriculture sector where reforms are being introduced now (A Top-down approach). When in India, industrial/ manufacturing and services sector liberalized in 1991, most of the companies went into services and did not enter into manufacturing as major bottlenecks were present for the manufacturing sector like issues in land acquisition, costly transport, costly electricity, labour laws etc. As our rural economy remained week, the demand of manufactured products never came from this section and resulted in less and inefficient production and whatever was required we started importing from China as this period also coincided with WTO's free trade policies.

In 1978 China's per capita income was lower than India but now it is 5 times that of India.

6.5 Economy Jumped from Agriculture to Services

	Agriculture	Industry				Services
	Agriculture forestry, fishing	Mining & quarrying (2.6%)	Manufacturing (15%)	Const ruction (8%)	Electricity, gas, water supply (2.4%)	Trade, Hotel, Financial, defence etc.
% Share in GDP (2013-14)	18%	28%				54%
% Labour Force (2013-14)	*48%*	24%				28%
% Share in GDP (1947)	55%	15%				30%

As per NSO Classification

Primary Sector: Agriculture, Livestock, Forestry & Fishing and Mining & Quarrying

Secondary Sector: Manufacturing, Electricity, Gas, Water supply & Other Utility Services and Construction

Tertiary Sector: Trade, Hotels, Transport, Communication and Services related to Broadcasting, Financial, Real Estate & Professional Services and Public Administration, Defence & Other Services

Introduction: As we can see from the above table, the share of Agriculture in India's GDP was 55% at the time of independence while services sector constituted 30% and industrial sector a meagre 15%. In the last 67 years after independence (**till 2014**), Indian economy moved from a dominant agricultural sector to the services sector constituting 54% share in India's GDP. Generally, **the economies move from agriculture to industry (manufacturing) and then to services in their process of development** but India is an exception and shifted directly from agriculture to services while ignoring the industrial sector.

We will be able to understand why India ignored manufacturing only when we know what were the basic requirements of manufacturing sector and whether, we fulfilled those requirements in India or not. Manufacturing growth depends on the following basic factors:

- Availability of land (easier land acquisition processes)
- Better and cheaper transportation infrastructure like railway and roads
- Efficient ports for import of raw materials and export of finished goods
- 24×7 availability of cheap power
- Simple labour laws (easy to comply labour laws)
- Simplified tax system
- Simple procedures for getting clearances like environment, forest, water, power etc.

Now let us see whether the previous Governments in India fulfilled the above requirements in the last 67 years (till 2014) to the entrepreneurs/businessmen trying to enter into manufacturing sector or not.

1. **Availability of land (or easier land acquisition processes):** With very high population density and the second largest population, there is less availability of land per person. Further, complicated land acquisition procedures made it very difficult to acquire large tracts of land required for industrial purpose. A services industry may get established on a small piece of land or on a rented floor like software, IT, education, banking etc. but to establish a manufacturing industry thousands of acres of land is required. And till now, we have not been able to provide land easily to set up an enterprise.

2. **Better and cheaper transportation infrastructure like railway and roads:** Any manufacturing industry requires connectivity to source the raw materials and supply the finished products in the market. In India, we have not been able to provide better quality roads and the connectivity in the rural areas is still an issue. In case of railway, the freight/fare is one of the costliest among the world and we have not added the railway tracks as per the demand which has created a huge congestion leading to poor average speed and inordinate delays. All this makes Indian transportation system a costly and time-consuming affair which hurts the efficiency of our manufacturing enterprises making products costly and less competitive with other economies like China, Japan, South Korea, Taiwan etc.

3. **Efficient ports for import of raw materials and export of finished goods:** In India, majority of the export and import of goods traffic goes through the major ports under the Central government and are controlled and operated through trusts. These trusts have not been able to manage the ports efficiently, creating huge delays in export and import of goods and making the goods more costly in the export market. Due to this our manufacturing firms have not been able to globally compete and explore the world market leading to reduced share of manufacturing in GDP.

4. **24X7 availability of power:** Till now we have not been able to supply power all across the country 24×7 which is one of the basic requirements of a manufacturing enterprise. Every manufacturing firm requires uninterrupted and cheaper power supply to produce cost effective products. In many parts of UP and Bihar, several industries

got closed as government was not able to provide cheaper power. A service industry can run on a Diesel Generator set for an hour or two if there is hindrance in power supply but a manufacturing firm cannot.

5. **Simple labour laws (or easy to comply labour laws):** In India we had 44 central labour laws (now government has merged into four labour codes) and more than hundred State labour laws making it one of the most rigid labour markets all over the world. It is almost impossible for any manufacturing firm to comply will all the labour laws. Companies cannot fire a worker on its own and require government approval which is very difficult to come by, if they employ more than 100 labours. Service establishments are required to abide by only with few labour laws but for a manufacturing firm, a whole gamut of laws exist which deters entrepreneurs to venture out in manufacturing industry.

6. **Simplified tax system:** In India, we had one of the most complicated tax structures. Due to federal structure of taxation, both Centre and State levy and collect taxes leading to cascading effect and double taxation and in turn the products produced in India becomes costlier. Now it has been simplified through GST in 2017

7. **Simple procedures for getting approval/ clearances like environment, forest, water, power:** Most of the industries in the manufacturing sector require approvals from the government regarding environment and forest clearances. Since the industries also require very large amount of water and power supply, they need to take approval of the government which may not be required for a service industry. These approvals are difficult to get and time consuming because of red tapism and also there is no fix time frame provided by the government to grant these clearances

As the government in India was not able fulfil the above requirements in the years after independence and till now, we are still a laggard in the manufacturing sector.

But why services industry leapfrogged?

India has a huge entrepreneurial talent which was not able to showcase it as we followed a socialist model of development in the years after independence. As time passed the entrepreneurial energy got crippled with the burden of "license raj", MRTP Act, FERA and reservation of several industries for the government only.

The economic reforms of 1991 opened the product and capital markets. India changed its economic policy and opened the doors for foreign firms in India, allowed most of the sectors for private competition, removed license raj, reduced trade barriers etc. This period got coincided with the internet and telecom revolution **(a necessary ingredient for services)** in India and the vast entrepreneurial talent moved into the services sector propelling the growth of the Indian economy. But the major infrastructural bottlenecks and land and labour issues, in which reforms were must for manufacturing industry to flourish, remained as it is and prevented India from becoming a manufacturing hub like China.

6.6 Planning Commission and Five Year Plans

The Planning Commission, although no longer active, was an important feature of policymaking and governance in India. The Planning Commission was set up by a Resolution of the Government of India in March 1950. The prime objectives of the Government were to propel a rapid increase in the living standard of Indians by the productive exploitation of the country's resources, raising production and securing opportunities for everyone for employment in the service of society. The Planning Commission was assigned the responsibility of assessing all the resources of the country, enhancing scarce resources, drafting plans for the most productive and balanced usage of resources and ascertaining priorities. Pandit Nehru was the first Chairman of the Planning Commission.

The following were the functions of Planning Commission:

- To make an evaluation of the material, capital and human resources of the country, including technical employees, and investigate the possibilities of augmenting those related resources which are found to be deficient in relation to the nation's requirement.
- To devise a plan for the most effective and balanced utilisation of country's resources.
- To define the stages, on the basis of priority, in which the plan should be implemented and propose the allocation of resources for the due completion of each stage.
- To specify the factors that tends to retard economic development.
- To determine the conditions which need to be established for the triumphant execution of the plan within the incumbent socio-political situation of the country.
- To determine the nature of the mechanism required for securing the successful implementation of each stage of the plan in all its aspects.
- To evaluate from time to time the improvement achieved in the implementation of each stage of the plan and also recommend the adjustments of policy and measures which are deemed important for successful implementation of the plan.
- To make required recommendations from time to time regarding those things which are deemed necessary for facilitating the execution of these functions. Such recommendations can be related to the current economic conditions, current policies, measures or development programmes.

Five Year Plans

Although the planned economic development in India began in 1951 with the inception of First Five Year Plan, theoretical efforts had begun much earlier, even prior to the independence. Setting up of National Planning Committee by Indian National Congress in 1938, The Bombay Plan & Gandhian Plan in 1944, Peoples Plan in 1945 (by post war reconstruction Committee of Indian Trade Union), Sarvodaya Plan in 1950 by Jaiprakash Narayan were steps in this direction.

Five-Year Plans (FYPs) were centralized and integrated national economic programs. Joseph Stalin implemented the first FYP in the Soviet Union in the late 1920s. Most communist states and several capitalist countries subsequently adopted them. China and India both adopted the FYPs, although India discontinued in 2017 and China renamed its Eleventh FYP, from 2006 to 2010, a guideline, rather than a plan, to signify the central government's more hands-off approach to development.

After independence, India launched its First FYP in 1951, under socialist influence of first Prime Minister Jawaharlal Nehru. The process began with setting up of Planning Commission in March 1950 in pursuance of declared objectives of the Government to promote a rapid rise in the standard of living of the people by efficient exploitation of the resources of the country, increasing production and offering opportunities to all for employment in the service of the community. The Planning Commission was charged with the responsibility of making assessment of all resources of the country, augmenting deficient resources, formulating plans for the most effective and balanced utilisation of resources and determining priorities.

For the first eight Plans the emphasis was on a growing public sector with massive investments in basic and heavy industries, but since the launch of the Ninth Plan in 1997, the emphasis on the public sector became less pronounced and the thinking on planning in the country, in general, changed increasingly to indicative in nature.

FY PLAN	DESCRIPTION
First Plan (1951 - 56) Target Growth : 2.1 % Actual Growth 3.6 %	• It was based on **Harrod-Domar Model.** • Influx of refugees, severe food shortage & mounting inflation confronted the country at the onset of the first five-year Plan. • The Plan Focussed on agriculture, price stability, power and transport • It was a successful plan primarily because of good harvests in the last two years of the plan. Objectives of rehabilitation of refugees, food self-sufficiency & control of prices were more or less achieved.
Second Plan (1956 - 61) Target Growth: 4.5% Actual Growth: 4.3%	• Simple aggregative Harrod Domar Growth model was again used for overall projections and **the strategy for resource allocation to the various sectors was prepared by Prof. PC Mahalanobis**. (Plan is also called Mahalanobis Plan). • Second plan was conceived in an atmosphere of economic stability. It was felt agriculture could be accorded lower priority. • The Plan focussed on rapid industrialization- heavy & basic industries. Advocated huge imports through foreign loans. • The Industrial Policy 1956 was based on establishment of a socialistic pattern of society as the goal of economic policy. • Acute shortage of forex led to pruning of development targets, price rise was also seen (about 30%) vis-a-vis decline in the earlier Plan & the 2nd FYP was only moderately successful.

Third Plan (1961 - 66) Target Growth: 5.6% Actual Growth: 2.8%	• At its conception, it was felt that Indian economy has entered a "take-off stage". Therefore, its aim was to make India a **'self-reliant'** and **'self-generating'** economy. • Based on the experience of first two plans, agriculture was given top priority to support the exports and industry. • The Plan was thorough failure in reaching the targets due to unforeseen events - Chinese aggression (1962), Indo-Pak war (1965), severe drought 1965-66. Due to conflicts the approach during the later phase was shifted from development to defence & development.
Three Annual Plans (1966-69) euphemistically described as Plan holiday.	• Failure of Third Plan that of the devaluation of rupee (to boost exports) along with inflationary recession led to postponement of Fourth FYP. Three Annual Plans were introduced instead. Prevailing crisis in agriculture and serious food shortage necessitated the emphasis on agriculture during the Annual Plans. • During these plans a whole new agricultural strategy was implemented.Itinvolvingwide-spreaddistributionofhigh-yielding varieties of seeds, extensive use of fertilizers, exploitation of irrigation potential and soil conservation.
Fourth Plan (1969 - 74) Target Growth: 5.7% Actual Growth: 3.3%	• Refusal of supply of essential equipments and raw materials from the allies during Indo Pak war resulted in twin objectives of "**growth with stability**" and "**progressive achievement of self-reliance**" for the Fourth Plan. • Main emphasis was on growth rate of agriculture to enable other sectors to move forward. The plan was considered as a failure
Fifth Plan (1974-79) Target Growth: 4.4% Actual Growth: 4.8%	• The final Draft of fifth plan was prepared and launched by D.P. Dhar in the backdrop of economic crisis arising out of run-away inflation fuelled by hike in oil prices and failure of the Govt. takeover of the wholesale trade in wheat. • It proposed to achieve two main objectives: **'removal of poverty'** (Garibi Hatao) and **'attainment of self-reliance'** • Promotion of high rate of growth, better distribution of income and significant growth in the domestic rate of savings were seen as key instruments
Rolling Plan (1978 - 80)	• There were 2 Sixth Plans. Janta Govt. put forward a plan for 1978- 1983 emphasising on employment, in contrast to Nehru Model which the Govt criticised for concentration of power, widening inequality & for mounting poverty. However, the Govt. lasted only for two years. Congress Govt. returned to power in 1980 and launched a different plan.

Sixth Plan (1980 - 85) Target Growth: 5.2% Actual Growth: 5.7%	• The Plan focussed on **Increase in national income, modernization of technology, ensuring continuous decrease in poverty and unemployment**
Seventh Plan (1985 - 90) Target Growth: 5.0% Actual Growth: 6.0%	• The Plan aimed at accelerating food grain production, increasing employment opportunities & raising productivity with focus on 'food, work & productivity'. The plan was very successful.
Eighth Plan (1992 - 97) Target Growth 5.6 % Actual Growth 6.8%	• The eighth plan was postponed by two years because of political uncertainty at the Centre • Worsening Balance of Payment position, rising debt burden, widening budget deficits, recession in industry and inflation were the key issues during the launch of the plan. • The plan undertook drastic policy measures to combat the bad economic situation and to undertake an annual growth of 5.6% through introduction of fiscal & economic reforms including liberalisation under the Prime Minister Shri P V Narasimha Rao.
Ninth Plan (1997- 2002) Target Growth: 6.5% Actual Growth: 5.4%	• The Plan prepared under United Front Government focussed on "**Growth with Social Justice & Equality**". Ninth Plan aimed to depend predominantly on the private sector – Indian as well as foreign (FDI) & State was envisaged to increasingly play the role of facilitator & increasingly involve itself with social sector viz education, health etc and infrastructure where private sector participation was likely to be limited.
Tenth Plan (2002 - 2007) Target Growth 8 % Actual Growth 7.6 %	• **Recognising that economic growth can't be the only objective of national plan**, Tenth Plan had set 'monitorable targets' for few key indicators (11) of development besides 8 % growth target. The targets included reduction in gender gaps in literacy and wage rate, reduction in Infant & maternal mortality rates, improvement in literacy, access to potable drinking water cleaning of major polluted rivers, etc. Governance was considered as factor of development & agriculture was declared as prime moving force of the economy.
Eleventh Plan (2007 - 2012) Target Growth 9 % Actual Growth 8 %	• Eleventh Plan was aimed "**Towards Faster & More Inclusive Growth**" • India had emerged as one of the fastest growing economies by the end of the Tenth Plan. The savings and investment rates had increased, industrial sector had responded well to face competition in the global economy and foreign investors were keen to invest in India. But the growth was not perceived as sufficiently inclusive for many groups, specially SCs, STs & minorities as borne out by data on several dimensions like poverty, malnutrition, mortality, current daily employment etc.

Twelfth Plan (2012 - 2017) Target Growth 8% Actual Growth 6.5%	• The broad vision and aspirations which the Twelfth Plan sought to fulfil were reflected in the subtitle: '**Faster, Sustainable, and More Inclusive Growth'**. Inclusiveness is to be achieved through poverty reduction, promoting group equality and regional balance, reducing inequality, empowering people etc whereas sustainability includes ensuring environmental sustainability, development of human capital through improved health, education, skill development, nutrition, information technology etc and development of institutional capabilities, infrastructure like power telecommunication, roads, transport etc.

PREVIOUS YEARS' QUESTIONS

Prelim Questions

1. Which of the following has/have occurred in India after its liberalization of economic policies in 1991? **[2017]**

(i) Share of agriculture in GDP increase enormously.
(ii) Share of India's exports in world trade increased.
(iii) FDI inflows increased.
(iv) India's foreign exchange reserves increased enormously

Select the correct answer using the codes given below.

(a) (i) & (iv) only
(b) (ii), (iii) & (iv) only
(c) (ii) & (iii) only
(d) (i), (ii), (iii) & (iv)

2. With reference to the sectors of the Indian economy, consider the following pairs :

Economic activity	Sector
1. Storage of agricultural produce	Secondary
2. Dairy farm	Primary
3. Mineral exploration	Tertiary
4. Weaving cloth	Secondary

How many of the pairs given above are correctly matched? **[2024]**

(a) Only one (b) Only two
(c) Only three (d) All four

ANSWERS

1.(b) 2. (b)

Main Question

1. Normally countries shift from agriculture to industry and then later to services, but India shifted directly from agriculture to services. What are the reasons for the huge growth of services vis-à-vis industry in country? Can India become a developed country without a strong industrial base? **[2014]**

7 Indian Economy After 2014

7.1 NITI Aayog

Government of India, in keeping with its reform agenda, constituted the NITI Aayog to replace the Planning Commission. This was done in order to better serve the needs and aspirations of the people of India. An important evolutionary change from the past, NITI Aayog acts as the quintessential platform for the Government of India **to bring states to act together in national interest, and thereby fosters cooperative federalism**.

National Institution for Transforming India, also known as NITI Aayog, was formed via a resolution of the Union Cabinet on 1 January 2015. NITI Aayog is the premier **policy think tank** of the Government of India, providing directional and policy inputs. Apart from designing strategic and long-term policies and programmes for the Government of India, NITI Aayog also provides relevant technical advice to the Centre, states and UTs.

To evolve a shared vision of national development priorities, sectors and strategies with the active involvement of states, NITI Aayog works towards the following **objectives/functions**:

- To evolve a shared vision of national development priorities, sectors and strategies with the active involvement of States.
- To foster cooperative federalism through structured support initiatives and mechanisms with the States on a continuous basis, recognizing that strong States make a strong nation.
- To develop mechanisms to formulate credible plans **at the village level and aggregate these progressively at higher levels of government.**
- To ensure, on areas that are specifically referred to it, that the interests of national security are incorporated in economic strategy and policy.
- To pay special attention to the sections of our society that may be at risk of not benefiting adequately from economic progress.
- To design strategic and long-term policy and programme frameworks and initiatives, and monitor their progress and their efficacy. The lessons learnt through monitoring and feedback will be used for making innovative improvements, including necessary mid-course corrections.
- To provide advice and encourage partnerships between key stakeholders and national and international like-minded Think tanks, as well as educational and policy research institutions.

- To create a knowledge, innovation and entrepreneurial support system through a collaborative community of national and international experts, practitioners and other partners.
- To offer a platform for resolution of inter-sectoral and inter departmental issues in order to accelerate the implementation of the development agenda.
- To maintain a state-of-the-art Resource Centre, be a repository of research on good governance and best practices in sustainable and equitable development as well as help their dissemination to stake-holders.
- To actively monitor and evaluate the implementation of programmes and initiatives, including the identification of the needed resources so as to strengthen the probability of success and scope of delivery.
- To focus on technology upgradation and capacity building for implementation of programmes and initiatives.
- To undertake other activities as may be necessary in order to further the execution of the national development agenda, and the objectives mentioned above.

The **Governing Council of NITI Aayog** comprises the Prime Minister of India, Chief Ministers of all the States and Union Territories. It is the premier body tasked with evolving a shared vision of national development priorities, sectors and strategies with the active involvement of States in shaping the development narrative. The Governing Council presents a platform to discuss inter-sectoral, inter-departmental and federal issues in order to accelerate the implementation of the national development agenda, in the spirit of Ek Bharat, Shrestha Bharat.

The following are the various initiatives and programmes of NITI Aayog:

- Aspirational District Programme
- Poshan Abhiyan
- Atal Innovation Mission
- With emphasis on outcomes, NITI finalized indices to measure incremental annual outcomes in critical social sectors like health, education, water and Sustainable Development Goals (SDG). For example, Health Index, 'School Education Quality Index' (SEQI), 'SDG India Index', 'Digital Transformation Index' (DTI).

Difference between NITI Aayog and Planning Commission

- Planning Commission was an advisory body, and so is NITI Aayog. Main difference between Planning commission and NITI Aayog is that while the former had powers to allocate funds to ministries and states, this function is now of finance ministry.
- The role of states in the planning commission era was restricted. The states yearly needed to interact with the planning commission to get their annual plan approved. They had some limited function in the National Development Council.
- Since NITI Aayog has all chief ministers of states and administrators of UT in its Governing Council, it is obvious that states are expected to have greater role and say in planning/ implementation of policies.
- NITI Aayog has adopted a **bottom-up approach** in planning which is a noteworthy contrast to the Planning Commission's tradition of **top-down decision-making**.

7.2 Manufacturing

After India liberalized its economy in 1991, the services sector was among the fastest growing part of the economy, contributing significantly to GDP, economic growth, international trade and investment. Manufacturing contributed just 15 percent to India's GDP till 2014, compared to a 54 percent contribution by services. But the services sector employs **fairly skilled** people and **India's most abundant resource is unskilled labour**, that is why it has not been able to provide employment to the large unskilled Indian population. At present, 12 million people enter the Indian workforce each year. A substantial part of them is low skilled workers, many having migrated from rural India to the urban centres. The scale and nature of employment that is required to employ these people with limited skills and education can only be provided by low and semi-skilled manufacturing. While India is good at making complex things, which require skilled labour and frugal engineering (cars and automotive components), it is quite uncompetitive at low skilled manufacturing.

For manufacturing to take off in India, we must create hubs that are ecosystems for innovation, specialized skills and supply chains as it is difficult to make a country the size of India into a uniformly attractive manufacturing location. Even China started its manufacturing journey by creating a few oases in the form of four special economic zones which were remarkably easy places to manufacture in. Pune, Chennai, Bengaluru and Delhi are already emergent hubs but we must give incentives to attract the world's leading companies to establish global innovation and manufacturing centres in these hubs. India must stop tax terrorism, improve infrastructure, reform labour laws, invest in skills development, make it easier to acquire land, remove GST hurdles and fast track approvals. And through these measures, it can become a manufacturing powerhouse to gainfully employ its demographic dividend. With China's competitive advantage in manufacturing eroding (because of higher wages), India has the opportunity to take some share of global manufacturing away from China and fortunately we have two major natural advantages of a big labour pool and a large domestic market.

Challenges:

There is only one time-tested way for a country to get rich. **It moves farmers to factories and imports foreign manufacturing technology.** When surplus farmers are moved to cities their productivity soars. So far, no country has reached high levels of income by moving farmers to service jobs en-masse. This may be because manufacturing technologies are embodied in the products themselves and in the machines that are used to make the products, while service businesses get their productivity from organizational models, human capital and other intangibles that are harder for poor countries to imitate and tougher to grow quickly.

But the problem is that **manufacturing is shrinking. Although the total amount of physical stuff that humans make keeps expanding, the percent of our economic activity that we put into making physical goods keeps going down**. This is happening all across the globe, even in China. This may be partly because manufacturing has been a victim of its own success - **this sector has grown so productive that it is now pretty cheap to make all the stuff we need.** (And after all that is what happened in agriculture).

The main engine of global growth since 2002 has been the rapid industrialization of China. By channelling the vast savings of its population into capital investment, and by rapidly absorbing technology from advanced countries, China was able to carry out the most stupendous modernization in history, moving hundreds of millions of farmers from rural areas to cities. And that in turn also powered the growth of the countries like Brazil, Russia and many developing nations which exported oil, metal and other resources to the new workshop of the world. But now China has started slowing down.

Comparison with China

There is a risk in focusing on manufacturing and attempting to follow the export-led growth path that China followed.

- First, the slow growing advanced/ industrial countries will be much less likely to be able to absorb a substantial additional amount of imports in the foreseeable future and the world as a whole is unlikely to accommodate another export-led China.
- Second, industrial countries have been improving capital-intensive flexible manufacturing, so much so that some manufacturing activity is being re-shored (brought in their own countries). Emerging markets wanting to export manufacturing goods will have to compete with this.
- Third, when India pushes into manufacturing exports, it will have China to compete with. Export-led growth will not be as easy as it was for the Asian economies who took that path before us.

Accordingly, China might have been the last country to hop on board the industrialization train. And in that case, India, Africa, Latin America and the Middle East might get left behind and may not be able to catch up, as China did.

Comments:

As building things (manufacturing) becomes less important and doing things becomes more important to the global economy, **human capital will be more crucial than ever**. This requires enhancing the quality and spread of healthcare, nutrition and sanitation, better and more appropriate education and training for skill valued in the labour markets. So, while we should continue to push to improve infrastructure of the country but it may be even more important to focus on **education** (human capital).

Manufacturing or Services

India's most abundant resource is unskilled labour. But the services sector employs fairly skilled labour and if India wants that its growth is driven by services then it must focus on "Skilling India" aggressively. But skilling (which requires greater focus on education) will take time and a major portion of the present unskilled population can be left out. If we want our growth to be driven by manufacturing then we should start building the infrastructure that supports unskilled intensive manufacturing.

7.3 Make in India

Make in India

- Govt. of India launched the "Make in India" campaign in Sept. 2014 which is the first of its kind for the manufacturing sector as it addresses areas of regulation, infrastructure, skill development, technology, availability of finance, exit mechanism and other pertinent factors
- It contains a vast number of proposals including easier norms and rules designed to get foreign companies to set up shop and make the country a manufacturing powerhouse
- Since its launch, 'Make in India' initiative has made significant achievements and presently focuses on 27 sectors under Make in India 2.0. Department for Promotion of Industry and Internal Trade is coordinating action plans for manufacturing sectors (15), while Department of Commerce is coordinating service sectors (12).

The main targets under the scheme are:

- Increase in manufacturing sector growth to 12-14% per annum
- Increase in the share of manufacturing in country's GDP from 15% to 25% by 2025
- Create 100 million additional jobs by 2025 in manufacturing sector
- Increase in domestic value addition and technological depth in manufacturing
- Enhance the global competitiveness of the Indian manufacturing sector
- Create appropriate skill sets among rural migrants & urban poor for inclusive growth
- Ensure sustainability of growth, particularly with regard to environment

Challenges faced by the "Make in India" Initiative

- **Labour Productivity is low:** India's manufacturing sector's productivity is low and the skills of the labour force are insufficient. According to McKinsey's report, the Indian workers in the manufacturing sector are, on average, almost four to five times less productive than their counterparts in Thailand and China.
- **Investment from shell companies:** The major part of the FDI inflow is neither from foreign nor direct. Rather, it comes from Mauritius-based shell companies that are suspected to be investing black money from India.
- **The size of the industrial units is small** and therefore, it cannot attain the desired economies of scale. It also cannot invest in modern equipment and develop supply chains.
- **Complicated Labour laws:** The Indian labour laws were conceived during the independence period and are based on import-substitution and statist (state intervention and control) model of economic development which are not suited to the present time of highly competitive world. *(New labour laws have still not come into effect)*
- **Lack of Transportation:** Government has not been able to add enough railway track which can provide cheaper mode of transportation for goods in bulk across the country
- **Costly Electricity:** India lacks in providing cheaper and consistent electricity which is a must for a manufacturing enterprise

- **Delay in Land Acquisition:** The land acquisition process in India takes around 3 to 4 years as compared to two years in other emerging economies

Our Strategy for "Make in India"

While focusing on "Make in India", we should not follow export-led strategy that involves subsidizing exporters with cheap inputs as well as an undervalued exchange rate, simply because it is unlikely to be as effective at this juncture. And we should accept that, India is different from China and is developing at different time. Further, we should also not see "Make in India" as a strategy of import substitution through tariff barriers. This strategy has earlier not worked because it ended reducing domestic competition, making producers inefficient and increasing costs to consumers. Instead "Make in India" shall mean more openness, creating an environment that enables our firms to compete with the rest of the world and encourage foreign firms to create jobs in India.

Successful Examples of Make in India:

Electronics Manufacturing:

- India has become the second largest mobile phone producer in the world.
- In 2014-15, 26% of mobile phones sold in India were locally made, rising to 99.2% by December 2024.
- India's mobile phone exports surged from ₹1,566 crore in 2014-15 to ₹1.2 lakh crore in 2023-24, marking a 77-fold increase.

Manufacturing of railway coaches :

- A prime example is Vande Bharat trains, manufactured at the Integral Coach Factory in Chennai. These modern trainsets have not only transformed rail travesl in India, gaining immense popularity among passengers but also stand as a testament to India's self-reliance in railway manufacturing.

Defence Manufacturing:

- India is among top 5 military spenders and one of the emerging defence manufacturing hubs in the world. To support the growth of the defence sector and enhance manufacturing capacity in the sector, two **Defence Industrial Corridors** are being set up in India, one in Uttar Pradesh and the other in Tamil Nadu.

7.4 Smart Manufacturing: Industry 4.0

"Data is often referred to as the raw material of the twenty-first century."

First Industrial Revolution: 1765

The first industrial revolution began in Britain in the late 18th century, with the mechanisation of the textile industry. Tasks previously done laboriously by hand in hundreds of weavers' cottages were brought together in a single cotton mill, and the factory was born. It witnessed the emergence of mechanization, a process that replaced agriculture with industry as the foundations of the economic structure of society. Mass extraction of coal along with the invention of the **steam engine** created a new type of energy that thrusted forward all processes.

Second Industrial Revolution: 1870

Nearly a century later at the end of the 19th century, new technological advancements initiated the emergence of a new source of energy: **electricity, gas and oil**. As a result, the development of the **combustion engine** set out to use these new resources to their full potential. Methods of communication were also revolutionized with the invention of the telegraph and the telephone and so were transportation methods with the emergence of the automobile (Ford's mass production techniques) and the plane at the beginning of the 20th century.

Third Industrial Revolution: 1969

Nearly a century later, in the second half of the 20th century, a third industrial revolution appeared with the introduction **of electronics and information technology**. For industry, this revolution gave rise to the era of high-level automation in production, thanks to two major inventions: automatons (programmable logic controllers) and robots.

The first industrial revolution used ***water and steam to mechanize production****, the* ***second used electric energy to create mass production*** *and the* ***third used electronics and information technology to automate production****. Today,* ***a fourth industrial revolution is underway which builds upon the third revolution and the digital revolution*** *that has been taking place since the middle of the last century. This fourth revolution with exponential expansion is characterized by merging technology that blurs the lines between the physical, digital and biological spheres to completely uproot industries all over the world. The extent and depth of these changes are a sign of transformations to entire production, management and governance systems.*

Fourth Industrial Revolution (Industry 4.0): Present

With rapid development in the fields of information technology and hardware, the world is about to witness a fourth industrial revolution i.e., **Industry 4.0**, which is rooted in a new technological phenomenon - **digitalization**. This digitalization enables us to build a new virtual world from which we can steer the physical world.

While Industry 3.0 focussed on the automation of single machines and processes, Industry 4.0 concentrates on the end-to-end digitisation of all physical assets and their integration into digital ecosystems with value chain partners. Driven by the power of big data, high computing capacity, artificial intelligence and analytics, Industry 4.0 aims to completely digitise the manufacturing sector. Driven by the amalgamation of emerging technologies like advanced robotics and cyber-physical systems, it is making it possible the meeting of the real and virtual worlds.

Industry 4.0 is the next phase in bringing together conventional and modern technologies in manufacturing to create "smart factories". Such factories consist of machines (in the entire production chain) that are digitally connected and can learn from the large amount of data generated and then make autonomous decisions.

Challenges for the Labour Force (Industry 4.0 and Labour 1.0)

The shift in employment caused by adoption of industry 4.0 will be gradual but profound and existing jobs will require to be transformed with the aid of virtual reality and augmented reality. The existing workforce would require large scale re-skilling to adjust to the new reality as there is fundamental incompatibility of Industry 4.0 and our Labour Standards 1.0. There will be a need for massive up skilling as 'digital labour would become integral to most work profiles.

At the very core of Industry 4.0 is the fact that lifetime or permanent employment as we know it—that is becoming increasingly rare in even Industry 3.0—will more or less cease to exist with workers. Instead of finishing their education and then looking for a job as they do today, the labour force will continuously be retooling themselves depending upon what the market wants and what robots can't do better.

The maximum impact of the emergence of intelligent automation will be felt on the global industry of IT services and BPO workers. A technology research firm had predicted in 2015 that one in three jobs will be converted to software, robots and smart machines by 2025.

Industry 4.0 and India

Usually, physical systems in any industry go through a technology ladder — from electrification, automation to digitisation and then "smart factories". Most parts of the manufacturing sector in the country are still in the post-electrification rungs of the ladder. Similarly, the use of IT in manufacturing is dominated by embedded systems in machine units that operate independently of each other. The integration of physical systems on cyber platforms, too, is at a very nascent stage. Also, a huge number of MSMEs have just started to enter the automation phase.

To achieve the ambitious target of making India a global hub for manufacturing, design and innovation, and augmenting the share of manufacturing in GDP from the current 16% to 25% by 2025, the adoption of Industry 4.0 technologies becomes imperative to increase competitiveness and build efficient value chains. In its pursuit to foster best-in-class manufacturing infrastructure in India, the "Make in India" initiative is spearheading wider adoption of 'Industry 4.0'. Banking on India's strength in Information Technology and a large workforce of IT professionals, the transformative journey of manufacturing through Industry 4.0 has already begun in the country. Under the Government of India's 'Smart Cities Mission', the projects to build 100 smart cities across India are being touted as the forerunners of the Industry 4.0 environment.

General Electric (GE) has established a smart factory in Pune which can be termed as Industry 4.0. While most factories take weeks to switch over from one production line to another, GE has produced a multi-product factory that reduces this switchover time dramatically, as a result of which it can produce items as diverse as locomotive engines and wind turbine blades within days from the same factory. Designs coming in from engineers automatically get converted into 3D drawings that are fed into the machines—overhead cranes take parts from one machine to another while an optimising solution reconfigures the assembly line depending upon the need of the day; the latter, in turn, is decided by the fact that the factory's equipment 'talk' to one another over the internet and can take decisions based on what customers across the world want.

Future Strategy:

The biggest challenge that we face today is job creation. Traditional economic thinking for a country transitioning from low to medium-income is to focus on large-scale manufacturing and merchandise exports to the developed world as big job-creators. Japan, Korea, Taiwan, China - all followed this path. But that was before Industry 4.0 and growth of economic nationalism hit global manufacturing. Today, global merchandise trade is stagnating while services trade, especially digital services trade, is growing. Intra-Asia trade, among the region's developing countries, is growing more than two times faster than trade with the developed world. Manufacturing off-shoring by developed economies, driven by labour arbitrage, seems to have peaked and in-shoring by these countries is beginning to happen. Large manufacturing companies are not creating jobs as they replace people with machines, but, at the same time, the gig economy and MSMEs are creating more jobs. Finally, the potential for 'consumption of mass services' creating millions of service-jobs is growing from a combination of digital technologies, competition and good regulations that drives down the cost of services by anywhere from 3 to 10 times as we have seen in the telecom sector in India. So, in light of all these radical changes, the policy makers will have to bring in fresh and radical thinking on strategies for job creation.

7.5 Index of Industrial Production and Core Industries

The all-India Index of Industrial Production (IIP) is a composite indicator that measures the short-term changes in the volume of production of a basket of industrial products during a given period. The IIP data is compiled and published monthly by the National Statistical Office (NSO) and is released with a time lag of six wseeks.

The scope of the Index of Industrial Production (IIP) as recommended by the United Nations Statistical Office (UNSO) includes mining, manufacturing, construction, electricity, gas & water supply. But due to constraints of data availability, the IIP compiled in India has excluded construction, gas & water supply sectors.

Base Year 2011-12	Index of Industrial Production (IIP)		
	Mining	Manufacturing	Electricity
Weights	14.373	77.633	7.994

The eight core industries which comprises 40.27% of the weight of items included in the Index of Industrial production, is compiled and published monthly by Ministry of Commerce and Industry and comes with a time lag of one month. The base year for the index of the eight core industries is 2011-12 and it comprises of the following industries.

Core Industry	Crude Oil	Natural Gas	Refinery Products	Coal	Steel	Cement	Electricity	Fertilizers
Weights	8.98%	6.88%	28.04%	10.3%	17.9%	5.73%	19.85%	2.63%

7.6 Micro Small and Medium Enterprises (MSME)

Introduction

Economic development of a nation is closely associated with the growth of its industrial sector. Industrial sector is composed of Large, Medium, Small and Micro enterprises. While large industries help in the overall economic development of a nation, the contribution of MSMEs is quite significant in employment generation, industrial production and exports.

MSME industries have the advantage of labour intensiveness, low-cost technology, low capital/ investment, short gestation period and their strong forward and backward linkages with other sectors. The following are certain facts regarding MSMEs:

- MSMEs contribute 30% to India's GDP
- MSMEs contribute 40% to manufacturing GDP

- MSMEs contribute 45% to merchandise exports
- There are around 6 crore MSMEs employing more than 11 crore workers

MSME's role in Socio-economic Development

MSME sector has emerged as a highly vibrant and dynamic sector of the Indian economy over the last five decades. MSMEs not only play crucial role in providing large employment opportunities at comparatively lower capital cost than large industries but also help in industrialization of rural & backward areas, thereby, reducing regional imbalances, assuring equitable distribution of national income and wealth and leading to socio economic development of the country. **MSMEs don't compete with large scale industries** rather they **complement** them as **ancillary units** and play critical role in manufacturing value chains. They also play a key role in the development of economies with their effective, efficient, flexible and innovative entrepreneurial spirit.

The sector has huge potential in addressing the structural problems like unemployment, regional imbalances, unequal distribution of national income and wealth across the country but is fraught with various issues. **Following are the major challenges faced by the MSME sector:**

- Absence of adequate and timely banking finance
- Limited capital and knowledge
- Non-availability of suitable technology
- Low production capacity and not able to exploit economies of scale
- Ineffective marketing strategy
- Constraints on modernization & expansions
- Non availability of skilled labour at affordable cost
- Follow up with various government agencies to get payment and resolve problems

Role of government in the Promotion of MSME Sector:

The majorities of people living in rural areas draw their livelihood from agriculture and allied sectors. However, the growth and balanced development of other sectors such as industry and services is also necessary to sustain the growth of Indian economy in an inclusive manner. The socio-economic policies adopted by the Indian Govt. since the Industries (Development and Regulation) Act, 1951 have laid stress on MSMEs as a means to improve the country's economic conditions. The primary responsibility of promotion and development of MSMEs is of the State Governments. However, the Government of India, supplements the efforts of the State Governments through various initiatives. The role of the Ministry of Micro, Small and Medium Enterprises and its organizations is to assist the States in their efforts to encourage entrepreneurship, employment and livelihood opportunities and enhance the competitiveness of MSMEs in the changed economic scenario.

Following are some of the new initiatives undertaken by the Government of India for the promotion and development of MSMEs: -

- **Udyam Registration Number:** MSMEs can file one page registration form that would constitute a self- declaration format under which the MSME will self-certify its existence, bank account details, promoter/ owner's Aadhaar detail and other basic details, based on which MSMEs will be issued a unique identifier i.e. **"Udyam Registration Number"** which enable MSMEs to seek information and apply online about various services being offered by all Ministries and Departments.

- **Raising and Accelerating MSME Performance (RAMP):** The scheme aims at:
  - o Strengthening institutions and governance at the Centre and State level
  - o Improving Centre-State linkages and partnerships
  - o Improving access of MSMEs to market and credit,
  - o Technology upgradation
  - o Addressing issues of delayed payments
  - o Greening of MSMEs
- **ASPIRE:** Government has launched A Scheme for Promoting Innovation and Rural Entrepreneurs (ASPIRE) with the objective of setting up a network of technology centres and incubation centres to accelerate entrepreneurship and promote start-ups for innovation and entrepreneurship in rural and agriculture-based industries.
- **Employment Exchange:** Government of India has launched Employment Exchange for Industries to facilitate match making between prospective job seekers and employers
- Government has created a framework for revival and rehabilitation of MSMEs
- **Faster access to credit:** MSMEs are provided in-principle approval of working capital and term loan worth Rs. 1 lakh to Rs. 1 crore in 59 minutes.
- **Credit Guarantee:** To improve access to credit, Government provides credit guarantee cover to MSMEs.
- **Credit Card:** In the budget 2025-26, Government has announced to introduce customized credit cards with a Rs. 5 lakh limit for micro enterprises registered on Udyam portal.
- **CHAMPIONS:** In May, 2020, the GoI launched CHAMPIONS online platform to help and handhold the MSMEs. 'CHAMPIONS' stands for Creation and Harmonious Application of Modern Processes for Increasing the Output and National Strength. It is an ICT based technology system aimed at making the smaller units big by solving their grievances, encouraging, supporting, helping and handholding them throughout the business lifecycle. The platform facilitates a single window solution for all the needs of the MSMEs.
- As per the FY 2024-25 budget, Public Sector Banks have developed their inhouse capabilities to assess MSMEs for giving credit, moving away from external assessments. This will reduce financing cost for MSMEs. Presently, if an MSME wants to raise credit from a PSB then the MSME requires credit rating from an external Credit Rating Agency (CRA) and for that MSMEs need to pay to the CRA.

U K Sinha Committee and K V Kamath Committee *have recommended several reforms for MSMEs.*

Micro; Small and Medium Enterprises Development (MSMED) Act 2006

The MSMED Act was notified in 2006 to address policy issues affecting MSMEs as well as the coverage and investment ceiling of the sector. The Act seeks to facilitate the promotion and development of these enterprises as also enhances their competitiveness. It provides the first-ever legal framework for recognition of the concept of "enterprise" which comprises both **manufacturing and service entities**. As per the recent changes, the new classification/ definition of MSMEs is:

Classification	Micro	Small	Medium
Manufacturing & Services	Investment < Rs. 2.5 cr And Turnover < Rs. 10 cr	Investment < Rs. 25 cr And Turnover < Rs. 100 cr	Investment < Rs. 125 cr And Turnover < Rs. 500 cr

Further, the Turnover with respect to exports will not be counted in the limits of Turnover for any category of MSME units whether Micro, Small or Medium. This will help in bringing more units under MSME classification even if their exports are more.

Khadi and Village Industries Commission (KVIC)

KVIC is a statutory body established in 1956 as per "The Khadi and Village Industries Commission Act 1956".

Objective of KVIC

- The social objective of providing employment
- The economic objective of producing saleable articles
- The wider objective of creating self-reliance amongst the poor and building up of a strong rural community spirit

Functions of KVIC

- To plan and organise training of persons employed or desirous of seeking employment in khadi and village industries
- To build up reserves of raw materials and implements/tools and supply them to persons engaged or likely to be engaged in production of khadi or village industries
- To promote sale and marketing of khadi or products of village industries or handicrafts
- To encourage and promote research in the technology used in khadi and village industries
- To provide financial assistance to institutions or persons engaged in the development and operation of khadi or village industries and guide them through supply of designs, prototypes and other technical information
- To promote and encourage co-operative efforts among the manufacturers of khadi or persons engaged in village industries
- To ensure genuineness and to set up standards of quality and ensure that products of khadi and village industries do conform to the said standards
- To undertake studies of the problems/challenges faced by khadi or village industries
- *To establish and maintain separate organisations for the purpose of carrying out any or all of the above activities*

7.7 Production Linked Incentive Scheme (PLIS)

Govt. has launched PLI scheme for 13 sunrise sectors to create national manufacturing champions and generate employment and export opportunities.

Explanation of PLIS Scheme

If a company's sales of goods manufactured in India increases from a particular year (considered as base year) then the Company will get an incentive of 4% to 6% on incremental/ additional sales. For example, earlier a company was selling goods worth Rs. 1 lakh in a year and now its sales increased to Rs. 1.2 lakh. Then the company will get incentive of 4% on Rs. 20,000 = Rs. 800. The financial incentives are based on **additional sales, provided companies set up indigenous Greenfield/ brownfield investment.**

The various sectors are:

- Advance Chemistry Cell (ACC) Battery
- Electronic/Technology Products
- Automobiles & Auto Components
- Pharmaceuticals drugs
- Critical Key Starting materials/Drug Intermediaries and Active Pharma Ingredients
- Manufacturing of Medical Devices
- Telecom & Networking Products
- Textile Products: MMF segment and technical textiles
- Food Products
- High Efficiency Solar PV Modules
- White Goods (ACs & LED)
- Speciality Steel
- Mobile Manufacturing and Specified Electronic Components

7.8 Start-ups and Policy Enablers for Innovation

As per Ministry of Commerce & Industry (DPIIT), an entity shall be considered as a Startup:

- Up to a period of ten years from the date of its incorporation
- Turnover of the entity since its incorporation has not exceeded Rs. 200 crores in any FY
- The entity is working towards innovation, development or improvement of products or process or services, or if it is a scalable business model with a high potential of employment generation and wealth creation

A **'Deep Tech Startup'** means a 'Startup' with the following criteria:

- *Up to a period of twenty years from the date of its incorporation*
- *Turnover of the entity since its incorporation has not exceeded Rs. 300 crores in any FY*
- *It is working on producing a solution based on new knowledge/advancements within a scientific or engineering discipline or multiple disciplines, which is yet to be developed or is in the process of being developed;*
- *It has a high percentage of expenditure on research and development (R&D) activities as a percentage of revenue/funding;*
- *It owns or is in the process of creating significant novel intellectual property (IP) and taking steps to commercialize the same; and*
- *It is facing extended development timelines, long gestation periods, high capital and infrastructure requirements, and carrying large technical or scientific uncertainty.*

To facilitate the growth of startups, Govt. of India had announced the "Startup India, Stand-up India" initiative. The action plan is based on the three pillars "**Simplification and Handholding**", "**Funding Support and Incentives**", and "**Industry-Academia Partnership and Incubation**". Government has launched various schemes over the past few years to promote a culture of entrepreneurship, innovation and start-ups in the country:

- **Stand Up India:** It is aimed at promoting entrepreneurship and job creation at the grassroots level, especially keeping in mind the SCs/STs and women
- **Start Up India:** Aimed at promoting bank financing for startup ventures to boost entrepreneurship and encourage job creation. Rural India's version of Startup India has been named Deen Dayal Upadhyaya Swaniyojan Yojana
- **Atal Innovation Mission (AIM):** Govt's flagship initiative to promote a culture of innovation and entrepreneurship in the country. AIM's objective is to develop new programmes and policies for fostering innovation in different sectors of the economy, provide platform and collaboration opportunities for different stakeholders create awareness and create an umbrella structure to oversee innovation ecosystem of the country.
- **Chunauti:** Govt. of India (MeitY) launched Project "Chunauti" (challenge) - Next Generation Startup Challenge Contest to further boost startups and software products with special focus on Tier-II towns of India. It aims to identify around 300 startups working in identified areas and provide them seed fund of upto Rs. 25 Lakhs and other facilities.
- **Priority Sector Lending (PSL):** Startups have now been included under the priority sector lending rules of RBI for credit from banks
- **Tax exemption:** Startups can avail tax holiday for 3 consecutive financial years out of its first ten years since incorporation
- **State Rankings:** DPIIT provides ranking of States based on the various policy initiatives regarding promotion and support of startups
- Knowledge Involvement in Research Advancement through Nurturing **(KIRAN)** Scheme
- The **Biotechnology Ignition Grant (BIG)** scheme
- **Govt. Connect:** Dept. of Animal Husbandry & Dairying has conducted a grand challenge in association with Startup India to award top startups with Rs. 5 lakhs in 5 categories

With around 1.12 lakh startups registered and recognized by the Govt, India has the 3rd largest startup ecosystem in the world. Maharashtra, Karnataka and Delhi are the top three performers in terms of State-wise distribution of recognized startups in India.

7.9 National Policy for Skill Development and Entrepreneurship

- *Today, India is one of the youngest nations in the world with more than 62% of India's population is in the working age group of 15 to 59 years*
- *Our country presently faces a dual challenge of paucity of highly trained workforce, as well as non-employability of large sections of the conventionally educated youth, who possess little or no job skills.*

National Policy for Skill Development and Entrepreneurship 2015 supersedes the policy of 2009.

Vision

To create an ecosystem of empowerment by Skilling on a large Scale at Speed with high Standards and to promote a culture of innovation-based entrepreneurship which can generate wealth and employment so as to ensure Sustainable livelihoods for all citizens in the country.

Objective: to empower the individual, by enabling her/him to realize their full potential through a process of **lifelong learning** where competencies are accumulated via instruments such as credible certifications, credit accumulation and transfer, etc. As individuals grow, the society and nation also benefit from their productivity and growth.

Mission

- Create a demand for skilling across the country
- Correct and align skilling with required competencies
- Connect the supply of skilled human resources with sectoral demands
- Certify and assess in alignment with global and national standards

The objectives and targets under the Policy will be met in mission mode approach and for that National Skill Development Mission was launched on 15th July 2015 (**World Youth Skills Day 15th July**) to implement and coordinate all skilling efforts in the country towards the objectives laid down in the policy. The Mission is housed under the Ministry of Skill Development and Entrepreneurship (MSDE) and the key institutional mechanism for achieving the objectives of the Mission has been divided into a three-tier structure:

Central Level *(Governing Council, Steering Committee, Mission Directorate)*

State Level *(State Skill Development Missions, Steering Committee, Mission Directorate)*

District Level *(District Committees at functional level)*

Some initiatives of Govt. of India for Skilling:

- Pradhan Mantri Kaushal Vikas Yojana
- Pradhan Mantri Kaushal Kendra
- Jan Sikshan Sansthan
- Skill Acquisition and Knowledge Awareness for Livelihood Promotion **("SANKALP")**
- Aspirational Skilling Abhiyan
- National Apprenticeship Promotion Scheme **(NAPS)**
- Skill Strengthening for Industrial Value Enhancement **(STRIVE)**
- **PRIME:** Ministry of Electronics and Information Technology has partnered with NASSCOM to create an online platform to upskill IT professionals in emerging technologies such as AI, Blockchain, Cybersecurity, IoT etc. to increase their employability called **Future Skills PRIME** (Programme for Reskilling/Upskilling of IT Manpower for Employability).

- **ASEEM:** In an endeavour to improve the information flow and bridge the demand-supply gap in the skilled workforce market, the Ministry of Skill Development and Entrepreneurship on 10th July 2020 launched **'Aatamanirbhar Skilled Employee Employer Mapping (ASEEM)'** portal to help skilled people find sustainable livelihood opportunities. ASEEM is an AI-based digital platform to bridge demand-supply gap of skilled workforce across sectors. The portal will map details of workers based on regions and local industry demands.
- **DigiSaksham:** It is a digital skills programme to enhance the employability of youth by imparting digital skills that are required in an increasingly technology driven era. It is a joint initiative of Ministry of Labour with Microsoft India and is an extension of the Government's ongoing programs to support the youth from rural and semi-urban areas.

7.10 Land Banks and National Single Window System (NSWS)

Land Banks

- Govt. of India (DPIIT, Ministry of Commerce and Industry) is in the process of creating a **"National Land Bank Portal"** which will map around 5 lakh hectares of land, spread across various industrial belts and special economic zones.
- Building land banks allows Govt. to offer land to private investors right away, rather than having to wait for the lengthy process of land acquisition each time an investor wants land. Investors also get interested to know that the land is acquired and available, and that they won't run into political problems down the road.
- 21 States already have GIS enabled land banks which will be integrated with the National Land bank. State Governments have built land banks from private land, common land, forest land and if some land was acquired by a company but did not start the work, so govt takes the possession of the land and puts into land bank. (Land is a state subject and hence till now mostly states have created their own land banks). DPIIT is just creating a national portal which will integrate all the land banks across the country with other useful information for the investors and hence if a foreign investor is coming, he will not have to look for land in every state, rather he can check the 'National Land Bank Portal'. Investors will be able to locate the land and will have access to details of logistics, land & rail connectivity and even raw material supply which will make it easy for them to start a project.
- Central Govt. is planning to give a major boost to manufacturing which has stagnated at around 16% of GDP in the last three decades post liberalization of economy in 1991. DPIIT is also in the process of creating an **"Investment Clearance Cell"** (a kind of single window clearance), which will be one digital platform for investors to obtain all requisite central and state approvals in a time bound and hassle-free manner.

National Single Window System (NSWS)

- DPIIT has launched NSWS which is a digital platform for guidance of investors to identify and to apply for approvals as per their business requirements.
- It will remove the requirement of running to Govt. offices for approvals and registrations i.e., ease of doing business and ease of living
- NSWS would bring in transparency, accountability and responsiveness in the ecosystem and all information will be available on a single dashboard. An applicant dashboard would be there to apply, track and respond to queries.
- NSWS is envisioned to address information asymmetry, duplication of information submitted across platforms and authorities and inefficient tracking of approvals and registration faced by investors
- NSWS has been designed keeping the needs of entrepreneurs & investors at the centre
- The NSWS portal hosts approvals across different central departments and states.

7.11 E-Commerce

E-Commerce includes buying, selling, marketing or distribution of (i) goods, including digital products and (ii) services; through electronic network. Delivery of goods, including digital products, and services may be online or through traditional mode of physical delivery.

E-Commerce and Benefit to Exports

- Electronic commerce helps in minimizing costs of marketing, advertising
- E-Commerce provides opportunity to sellers or traders and consumers to communicate and connect beyond the limitations of geography and time
- It helps in improving outreach to new markets and consumers. Apparel, textile and jewellery exporters are few examples.
- E-commerce has helped in better value realization for exporters because of reduction in costs due to multiple intermediaries in the traditional set-up

E-Commerce and the MSME Sector

- E-commerce (marketplace) is an excellent platform for Indian MSMEs to grow, as it allows them to expand and scale up their reach by getting access to world market and enjoying a level playing field.
- It opens up a global market for product categories such as diamonds, gems and jewellery, finished leather goods, granite and marble, handloom products, and handicrafts, and allows small-scale industries in India to reach an international consumer base
- Digitization has ensured that many small industries, which were previously isolated, have now become a part of a larger economy.
- Amazon has partnered with Federation of Indian MSMEs to help MSMEs to tap into opportunities in the e-commerce sector and sell their products online.

E-Commerce and Inequality

- We are witnessing a new digital world. In this world, the presence of network effects means size begets size: be it an e-commerce platform, social media network or search engine. The presence of **'network effects'** means that in the era of data, the larger the firm, the greater the access to potential sources of data and greater the likelihood of its success.

- Greater access to data provides a greater digital capital to a corporation, granting it an advantage over its competitors. Without access to adequate data, MSMEs and start-ups remain at a disadvantage to develop a large number of innovative solutions.
- While people had hoped that the internet era would be a tool to minimize inequality and would give greater access to a larger number of sellers, benefit smaller sellers etc., reality has been somewhat different. While consumers have had access to benefits of increased competition by way of lower prices and greater variety, selling at loss and 'cash burning' and capital burning had anti-competitive consequences.
- A handful of companies today dominate the digital economy. They are successfully exploiting the significant **first mover's advantage** in the data-driven ecosystem. Once a certain scale is reached, it becomes virtually impossible for the 'second mover', on its own to, make an entry in this ecosystem.

E-commerce and WTO:

India has thus far **not been a party to negotiations on e-Commerce** at the multilateral level. These negotiations, under WTO, are intended to create binding obligations on all the WTO member countries regarding (among other things) permanently accepting the moratorium on imposing customs duties on electronic transmissions. By agreeing to the permanent moratorium (**India has agreed not to impose customs duty temporarily for the time being**), countries which have tariff schedules, which allow putting duties on these kinds of products, will give up these rights forever and lose revenues.

7.12 FDI in Retail

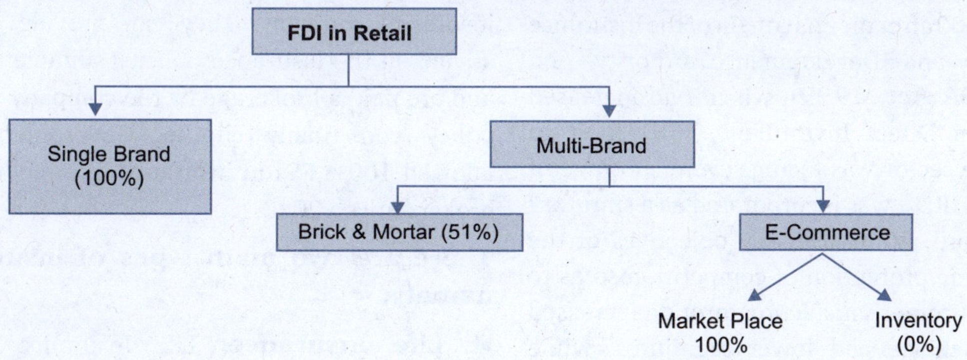

E-commerce companies can operate under two different models in India.

- The first is the **marketplace** model where the e-commerce firm simply acts as a platform that connects buyers and sellers. 100% FDI is allowed in e-commerce companies in this model.
- The second model is **inventory-based** where the inventory of goods sold on the portal is owned or controlled by the

e-commerce company. FDI is not allowed under this model.

What was happening earlier was that large e-commerce companies such as Amazon and Flipkart, while not owning inventory themselves, were providing a platform for their group companies such as CloudTail and WS Retail respectively. This was skewing the playing field, especially if these vendors enjoyed special incentives from the e-commerce firm, over others. These controlled or owned vendors may then be able to offer discounts to customers that competitors may not be able to match. Hence, Government in Dec 2019, made the following clarifications/changes in the FDI policy in e-commerce:

1. Vendors that have any stake owned by an e-commerce company cannot sell their products on that e-commerce company's portal.
2. Any vendor who purchases 25% or more of its inventory from an e-commerce group company will be considered to be controlled by that e-commerce group company and thereby barred from selling on its portal.
3. E-commerce marketplace entity will not mandate any seller to sell any product exclusively on its platform only
4. E-commerce firm will not be allowed to influence the price of a product sold on its portal by giving incentives to particular vendors.

7.13 FDI in Insurance

Insurance business was nationalized in 1972 with the passing of the General Insurance Business (Nationalisation) Act 1972 which became effective from 1st January, 1973.

The insurance sector was opened up for private sector in 2000 after the enactment of the Insurance Regulatory and Development Authority Act, 1999 (**IRDA Act, 1999**), which had increased the Foreign Direct Investment (FDI) limit to 26% as the sector was facing severe shortage of funds [The IRDA was incorporated as a statutory body in April, 2000. The key objectives of the IRDA include promotion of competition so as to enhance customer satisfaction through increased consumer choice and lower premiums, while ensuring the financial security of the insurance market].

Govt., in February 2015, raised the foreign investment ceiling in insurance sector from 26% to 49% under automatic route and then in 2021 it has again been increased to 74%. Budget 2025-26 has announced further increase of FDI cap to 100%.

Insurance Brokers represent the customers, and are licensed to give you policies from any insurance company. They can provide expert advice on the insurance policies suitable to you and are paid a brokerage by the company whose policy you finally choose. Government has allowed 100% FDI in insurance intermediaries/brokers in Feb 2020.

There are two main types of insurance namely:

- **Life insurance:** Life Insurance is an insurance coverage that pays out a certain amount of money to the insured or their specified beneficiaries upon a certain event such as death of the individual who is insured.

- **General (nonlife) insurance:** General insurance is an insurance policy that protects you against losses and damages other than those covered by life insurance such as fire, marine, motor, home, health etc.

> ❖ ***Insurance penetration*** *is measured as the percentage of insurance premium to GDP. Inf FY 2023-24, insurance penetration was 3.7%.*
>
> ❖ ***Insurance density*** *is measured as the ratio of premium in US $ to total population. Inf FY 2023-24 insurance density has increased to $95.*

Insurance Sector in India: The Indian insurance market is currently dominated by Life Insurance Corporation (PSU), which captures nearly 75% of the market. Raising the foreign investment limit to 49% is expected to generate inflows of $6-8 billion USD in the insurance sector that is looking for growth capital.

The Indian insurance industry has evolved significantly over the past decade or so, but the insurance penetration and insurance density levels are significantly lower than the developed as well as comparable developing countries. **The under-penetration is due to:**

- Lack of overall financial awareness,
- Lack of understanding of insurance products,
- Low perceived benefits,
- Propensity to purchase insurance based on reactive drivers such as insistence by financers, statutory requirements, etc.

Impact of the increased limit on Indian economy:

- Will attract more FDI/FPI and will lead to growth of insurance industry in India in the under insured markets resulting in creation of more jobs
- Foreign investors will bring in professional management, capital and new technology
- Will lead to increased competition in the Indian insurance market leading to new products, competitive quotes/premiums, improved services and better claim settlement ratio benefitting the common man
- Insurance sector has the capability to bring in long-term capital (through premiums) from the masses which can then be channelled into funding long gestation infrastructure projects

Earlier individuals were allowed to purchase health insurance policy only till the age of 65 years. Now, as per the recent amendment, IRDAI has allowed anyone regardless of age is eligible to buy a new health insurance policy.

> As per Ministry of Commerce and Industry FDI policy of 2022, FDI is **prohibited** in the following sectors:
>
> - Lottery business
> - Gambling and betting including casinos
> - Chit funds
> - Nidhi company
> - Trading in Transferable Development Rights (TDRs)
> - Real Estate Business or Construction of farm houses
> - Manufacturing of cigars, cheroots, cigarillos and cigarettes of tobacco or of tobacco substitutes
> - Railway operations and atomic energy

7.14 Atmanirbhar Bharat

Corona resulted in one of the biggest and most unprecedented crises that the world has ever seen. It impacted every country on the earth infecting more than 50 crores people and causing 62 lakhs deaths.

As a nation today we stand at a very crucial juncture. We have been hearing since the last century that the 21st century belongs to India. We have seen how the world was before Corona and the global systems in detail. When we look at these two periods from India's perspective, it seems that the 21st century is the century for India. This is not our dream, rather a responsibility for all of us. The state of the world today teaches us that a (**Atmanirbhar Bharat**) "**Self-reliant India**" is the only path.

But, today the meaning of the word self-reliance has changed in the global scenario. The debate on Human Centric Globalization versus Economy Centralized Globalization is on. India's fundamental thinking provides a ray of hope to the world. The culture and tradition of India speaks of self-reliance and the soul is ***VasudhaivaKutumbakam***.

India does not advocate self-centric arrangements when it comes to self-reliance. India's self-reliance is ingrained in the happiness, cooperation and peace of the world.

This is the culture which believes in the welfare of the world, for all the living creatures and the one which considers the whole world as a family. Its premise is **'माता भूमिः पुत्रो अहम पृथिव्यः'** (land is our mother and we are her son), the culture that considers the earth to be the mother. And when the Bharat Bhumi, becomes self-sufficient, it ensures the possibility of a prosperous world. India's progress has always been integral to the progress of the world.

India's goals and actions impact the global welfare. When India is free from open defecation, it has an impact on the image of the world. Be it TB, malnutrition, polio, India's campaigns have influenced the world. International Solar Alliance is India's gift against Global Warming. The initiative of International Yoga Day is India's gift to relieve stress. Indian medicines (including Covid-19 vaccine) have given a fresh lease of life to the people in different parts of the world.

These steps have brought laurels for India and it makes every Indian feel proud. The world is beginning to believe that India can do very well, so much good for the welfare of mankind can give.

The question is - how?

The answer to this question is – A Combined resolve of 135 crore citizens for a self-reliant India i.e., **Aatmanirbhar** Bharat. Today we have the resources, we have the power, and we have the best talent in the world. We will make the best products, will improve our quality further, make the supply chain more modern, we can do this and we will definitely do it.

And this magnificent building of self-reliant India will stand on 5 pillars:

- First Pillar is **Economy**, an economy that brings Quantum Jump rather than Incremental change.
- Second Pillar is **Infrastructure**, an infrastructure that became the identity of modern India.
- Third Pillar is Our **System**. A system that is driven by technology which can fulfill the

dreams of the 21st century; a system not based on the policy of the past century.

- Fourth Pillar is Our **Demography**. Our Vibrant Demography is our strength in the world's largest democracy, our source of energy for self-reliant India.
- The fifth pillar is Demand. The cycle of demand and supply chain in our economy, is the strength that needs to be harnessed to its full potential. In order to increase demand in the country and to meet this demand, every stake-holder in our supply chain needs to be empowered. We will strengthen our supply chain, our supply system built up with the smell of the soil and the sweat of our labourers.

But today's Aatmanirbhar **Bharat** is different as compared to the **self-sufficiency model** of development followed in the post-independence period in the following ways:

- In the post-independence period, we restricted our private sector and most of the industries were reserved for Govt. But today we are encouraging entrepreneurs and businesses and are disinvesting the PSUs and opening all the sectors for private businesses like coal, railway, defence, space etc.
- In the past we had **license raj** which required every industry to take govt. permission but today we are focusing more on ease of doing business and giving timely clearance.
- In the past we followed **import substitution** and isolationism and did not focus on exports but today we are willing to participate in the global supply chain and encouraging exports.
- Far from suggesting a centralised, top-down model directed from the "commanding heights" of the Planning Commission, the Aatma Nirbhar Bharat talks of freeing Indian entrepreneurship and innovation from bureaucratic hurdles. This is about decentralised localism that takes pride in local brands, emphasises resilience and flexibility, and encourages local capacity-building and indigenisation.
- In the post-independence period, we restricted foreign capital (FDI/FPI) and devoid ourselves of foreign technology, but today India is willing to attract foreign capital in every sector for 'Make in India'.
- We are supporting our MSME enterprises by providing them credit guarantee and other hand holding support rather than reserving products which could be produced only by MSMEs, which we did in the period before 1991. This will help our MSMEs to participate in the global supply chain and become competitive rather than making them inefficient.

In order to understand the intellectual underpinnings of **Atmanirbhar** Bharat, therefore, it is necessary to skip past the **socialist-era connotation of the termto an earlier era of thinkers like Swami Vivekananda.** Today's **"Aatmanirbhar Bharat"** reflects upon the idea of 'self-reliance' given by Swami Vivekananda in the second half of the 19th Century, which was about resilience, leveraging internal strengths, personal responsibility, and a sense of national mission. **Atmanirbhar** Bharat is not just a slogan but a vision with deep roots in India's intellectual tradition and it means standing up confidently in the world, and not about isolationism behind "narrow domestic walls".

In Indian culture, it is said that **'सर्वम आत्म वशं सुखम्'** i.e., what is in our control, is happiness. Self-reliance leads to happiness, satisfaction and empowerment. Our responsibility to make the 21st century, the century of India, will be fulfilled by the pledge of self-reliant India. This responsibility will only get energy from the life force of 130 crore citizens. This era of self-reliant India will be a new vow for every Indian as well as a new festival. Now we have to move forward with a new resolve and determination. When ethics are filled with duty, the culmination of diligence, the capital of skills, then who can stop India from becoming self-reliant? We can make India a self-reliant nation. We will make India self-reliant. And this we are planning to do by carrying forward the reforms which were introduced in 1991 in a much more aggressive way and introducing the reforms which were left untouched during that period for example, railway, coal, defence, aerospace, Electricity, Labour etc.

Post 2014, there has been a visible shift of focus towards the rural/agriculture and manufacturing sector. Government in the past few years have introduced several structural reforms like GST, IBC, Banking/Payment, Labour laws etc. and has allocated more budgetary resources for rural infrastructure as well as for general infrastructure like roads, railways, metros, airports, power etc. This has slowly started improving the overall efficiency of the economy, resulting in multiplier effect on economic growth and increasing the share of manufacturing in GDP.

2024-25	**Agriculture**	**Industry**				**Services**
	Agriculture forestry, fishing	Mining & quarrying (2%)	Manufacturing (16%)	Const ruction (8%)	Electricity, gas, water supply (3%)	Trade, Hotel, Financial, Defence etc.
% Share in GDP	17%	29%				54%
% Labour Force	*40%*	*28%*				32%

Five dynamic sifts that are underway in Indian Economy:

1. Fortunes shifting in favour of the farm sector
2. Changing energy mix in favour of renewable
3. Leveraging ICT and Start-ups to power growth
4. Shifts in supply/value chains both domestic and global
5. Infrastructure as the force multiplier

Addressing the 95th annual plenary session of the Indian Chamber of Commerce in Kolkata on 11th June 2020, our Prime Minister said that the time has come to take the Indian Economy from "Command and Control to Plug and Play".

"Command and Control": In the period from 1950 to 1990, the Central Govt. used to plan everything regarding how much production of major items (steel, cement, coal etc..) will be done, what should be the capacity of the plant, on which technology the plant will be based and accordingly government used decide almost everything from top to down. Decisions were not based on market forces of demand and supply rather were controlled/commanded by the Central Govt. This started easing out after 1991 LPG Reforms.

"Plug and Play": Plug and Play in literal sense is used to describe devices that work with a computer system as soon as they are connected. For example, a video card or hard drive may be a Plug and Play device, meaning the computer will recognize it as soon as it is installed.

But here our PM's interpretation regarding "Plug and Play" is that Government will provide all the supporting stuff/ policy support/ land and Infrastructure and the private businessmen will have to just set up their business and start activity without any red tape or bureaucratic hurdles/control.

Amrit Kaal

India has completed 75 years of independence and entered into the 'Amrit Kaal' [2022-2047]; the 25 year long lead up to India @100. Prime Minister has outlined five commitments for the next 25 years for India, called 'Panch Pran of Amrit Kaal'. These are:

1. Country should move ahead with a big resolve and that big resolution is of a developed India
2. Get rid of any signs of slavery
3. We should feel proud of our heritage and legacy
4. Unity and solidarity
5. Duties of citizens

PREVIOUS YEARS' QUESTIONS

Prelim Questions

1. With reference to foreign-owned e-commerce firms operating in India, which of the following statements is/are correct? **[2022]**

1. They can sell their own goods in addition to offering their platforms as market-places.
2. The degree to which they can own big sellers on their platforms is limited.

Select the correct answer using the code given below:

(a) 1 only (b) 2 only
(c) Both 1 and 2 (d) Neither 1 nor 2

2. Consider the following statements with reference to India: **[2023]**

1. According to the Micro, Small and Medium Enterprises Development (MSMED) Act, 2006, the 'medium enterprises are those with and machinery between is crore and 25 crores.
2. All bank loans to the Micro, Small and Medium Enterprises quality under the priority sector.

Which of the statements given above is/are correct?

(a) 1 only (b) 2 only
(c) Both 1 and 2 (d) Neither 1 nor 2

3. Consider the following statements: **[2023]**

Statement-I: India accounts for 32% of global export of goods.

Statement-II: Many local companies and some foreign companies operating in India have taken advantage of India's Production-linked Incentive' scheme.

Which one of the following is correct in respect of the above statements?

(a) Both Statement-I and Statement-II are correct and Statement-ll is the correct explanation for Statement-I.

(b) Both Statement-I and Statement-II are correct and Statement-l is not the correct explanation for Statement-I.

(c) Statement-I is correct but Statement-II is incorrect.

(d) Statement-I is incorrect but Statement-II is correct.

ANSWERS

1.(b) 2. (b) 3. (d)

Main Question

1. Faster economic growth requires increased share of the manufacturing sector in GDP, particularly of MSMEs. Comment on the present policies of the government in this regard **[2023]**
2. What is the status of digitalization in the Indian economy? Examine the problems faced in this regard and suggest improvements **[2023]**
3. Discuss the rationale of the Production Linked Incentive (PLI) scheme. What are its achievements? In what way can the functioning and outcomes of the scheme be improved? **[2025]**

8 Inclusive Growth and Issues

8.1 Inclusive Growth

The 'inclusive growth' as a strategy of economic development received attention owing to a rising concern that the benefits of economic growth have not been equitably shared. Inclusive growth basically means making sure everyone is included in growth, regardless of their economic class, gender, sex, disability and religion. Inclusive growth is economic growth that creates opportunity for all segments of the population and distributes the dividends of increased prosperity to every section of the society. The Eleventh Plan defines inclusive growth to be "a growth process which yields broad-based benefits and ensures equality of opportunity for all", it stands for "equitable development" or "growth with social justice". This concept expands upon traditional economic growth models to include focus on the equity of health, human capital, environmental quality, social protection, and food security.

Growth is inclusive when:

- It takes place in the sectors **in which the poor work** (e.g., agriculture);
- Occurs in places **where the poor live** (e.g., undeveloped areas with few resources);
- Uses the factors of production **that the poor possess** (e.g., unskilled labour); and
- Reduces the prices of consumption items **that the poor consume** (e.g. food, fuel and clothing)

The "equality of opportunity" and "participation in growth by all" with a special focus on the most vulnerable people of the society is the very basis of inclusive growth.

Inclusive growth as the literal meaning of the two words refers to both the pace and the pattern of economic growth. The literature on the subject draws fine distinction between direct income redistribution or shared growth and inclusive growth. The inclusive growth approach takes a **longer-term perspective** as the focus is **on productive employment** rather than on direct income redistribution, as a means of increasing incomes for excluded groups. In the short run, governments could use income distribution schemes to reduce the negative impacts on the poor of policies intended to jump start growth, but transfer schemes cannot be an answer in the long run and can be problematic also in the short run. In poor countries such schemes can impose significant burdens on already stretched budgets, and it is theoretically impossible to reduce poverty through redistribution. Inclusive growth is, therefore, supposed to be inherently sustainable as distinct from income distribution schemes. While income distribution schemes can allow people, to benefit from economic growth in the short run, inclusive growth allows people to "contribute to and benefit from economic growth" in a sustainable manner for long term.

The inclusiveness involves four attributes. **They are opportunity, capability, access and security.** The opportunity attribute focuses on generating more and more opportunities to the people and focuses on increasing their income. The capability attribute concentrates on providing the means for people to create or enhance their capabilities in order to exploit available opportunities. The Access attribute focuses on providing the means to bring opportunities and capabilities together. The security attribute provides the means for people to protect themselves against a temporary or permanent loss of livelihood. Together inclusive growth is a process in which economic growth is measured by a sustained expansion in GDP which contributes to an enlargement of the scale and scope of all four dimensions.

Rapid and sustained poverty reduction requires inclusive growth that allows people to contribute to and benefit from economic growth. Rapid pace of growth is unquestionably necessary for substantial poverty reduction, but for this growth to be sustainable in the long run, it should be broad-based across sectors, and inclusive of the large part of the country's labour force.

Apart from addressing the issue of inequality, the inclusive growth may also make the poverty reduction efforts more effective by explicitly creating productive economic opportunities for the poor and vulnerable sections of the society. The inclusive growth by encompassing the hitherto excluded population can bring in several other benefits as well to the economy. The concept "Inclusion" should be seen as a process of including the excluded as agents whose participation is essential in the very design of the development process, and not simply as welfare targets of development programmes.

Features of Inclusive Growth (as per World Bank)

- Inclusive growth focuses on economic growth which is a necessary and crucial condition for poverty reduction. Inclusive growth adopts a long-term perspective and is concerned with sustained growth.
  (a) For growth to be sustained in the long run, it must be broad-based across sectors. Issues of structural transformation for economic diversification therefore take a front stage.
  (b) It must also be inclusive of the large part of the country's labour force, where inclusiveness refers to equality of opportunity in terms of access to markets, resources and unbiased regulatory environment for businesses and individuals.
- Inclusive growth focuses on both the pace and pattern of growth. How growth is generated is critical for accelerating poverty reduction, and any inclusive growth strategies must be tailored to country-specific circumstances.
- Inclusive growth focuses on productive employment rather than income redistribution. Hence the focus is not only on employment growth but also on productivity growth.
- Inclusive growth has not only the firm, but also the individual as the subject of analysis.
- Inclusive growth is in line with the absolute definition of pro-poor growth, not the relative one.

(Under the absolute definition, growth is considered to be pro-poor as long as poor people benefit in absolute terms, as reflected in some agreed measure of poverty. In contrast, in the

relative definition, growth is "pro-poor" if and only if the incomes of poor people grow faster than those of the population as a whole, i.e., inequality declines.)

- Inclusive growth is not defined in terms of specific targets such as employment generation or income distribution. These are potential outcomes, not specific goals.
- Inclusive growth is typically fuelled by market-driven sources of growth with the government playing a facilitating role.

Need for Inclusive Growth in India

Economic liberalization which began in the early 1990's has accelerated India's growth rate to 6% in the 1990's and about 7% to 8% in later decades from the meagre 3.5% growth achieved in the first three decades after independence. During this period India transformed itself from an agricultural economy to a services economy. Services now form 54% of the Indian economy. The growth and development of the Information Technology and Information Technology enabled services have had a significant role in changing the face of the economy. And India has become the fastest growing among the big economies.

However, this high growth continues to bypass a large section of people. A large majority of Indians living in the villages; women, children, backward castes and classes and other minorities have been excluded from India's growth story. Exclusion continued in terms of low agriculture growth, low quality employment growth, low human development, rural-urban divides, gender and social inequalities, and regional disparities etc. The sectoral, social and spatial inequalities have raised questions about welfare approaches of government planning, and emphasized the role of the private sector in addressing development issues in the country. Employment generation, social and developmental infrastructure, health-care and rural diversification are some of the major concerns. Due to faulty approaches and often politically motivated policies, growth has generated inequalities. It is imperative for the planners and policy-makers to make growth inclusive through adoption of pragmatic policies. The journey towards balancing the outcome of economic growth involves many challenges. The dominant challenges include the imperative of maintaining the acceleration of economic growth without compromising on human development and sustainability.

Inclusive growth has become the buzzword in policy-spheres with recent phenomenon of rapid growth with characteristic patterns of exclusion. The Government aimed at promoting 'inclusive growth' as it recognized that high national income growth alone did not address the challenge of employment promotion, poverty reduction and balanced regional development or improving human development. Inclusive growth is necessary for sustainable development and equitable distribution of wealth and prosperity.

Achieving inclusive growth is the biggest challenge in a country like India. In a democratic country like India, bringing the 60% people living in rural India into the mainstream is the biggest concern. The challenge is to take the levels of growth to all section of the society and to all parts of the country. The best way to achieve inclusive growth is through developing people's skills. According to former Prime Minister Manmohan Singh, the key components of inclusive growth strategy include a sharp increase in investment in rural areas, rural infrastructure and agriculture, increase in credit for farmers, increase in rural employment through a unique social safety net and a sharp increase in public spending on education and health care.

For a developing country like India, the need for inclusive growth is vital to achieve the overall progress of the country. **Following are the major concerns for developing countries**

like India to achieve the inclusive growth:

- Lack of quality primary education
- Lack of health facilities
- Lack of skilling
- Regional disparities
- Huge informal sector
- Corruption in provision of public services at the lower level of government
- Subsidies/freebies crowding out capital expenditure

The increase in number of incidents such as theft, murder, naxalism is a direct result of the economic exclusion and the unfulfilled aspirations of the bottom billion. These aspirations of the bottom billion cannot be wished away. If India is unable to address these aspirations, the "demographic dividend" will become a demographic nightmare. This mammoth task cannot be done by government alone. Industry and civil society must partner with government to drive inclusive growth. Cognizant of income disparities and growing aspirations of the people, the government has been working to address these through programmes like MGNREGA and Aadhar. Civil society has contributed with design and governance oversight. But the greatest lever for driving inclusion is jobs.

While it is quite evident that inclusive growth is imperative for achieving the equity objective, what is, perhaps, not so obvious is, why inclusive growth is now considered essential even to sustain the growth momentum. Majority of the population living in rural areas is often identified with the agriculture sector. **However, it is the unorganised non-farm sector that is increasingly absorbing most of the labour force**. This sector has huge potential for growth once there is sufficient investment in infrastructure ensuring linkage to markets and easier access to assets and skills. Infusion of appropriate technology, skills, and easier access to credit, especially start-up capital, apart from facilitating market development, can make this segment an expanding base for self-sustaining employment and wealth generation and also foster a culture of creative and competitive industry. Entrepreneurial development has to be encouraged by having an enabling competitive environment and easy availability of finance for newer projects and enterprises. In Prof. C. K. Prahalad's words, "If we stop thinking of the poor as victims or as a burden, and start recognising them as resilient and creative entrepreneurs and value conscious consumers, a whole world of opportunity will open up."

8.2 Poverty Estimation in India

Growth is not the sole objective of economic policy. It is necessary to ensure that the benefits of growth accrue to all sections of the society. Eradication of poverty is thus an important objective. Human beings need a certain minimum consumption of food and non-food items to survive. However, the perception regarding what constitutes poverty varies over time and across countries. Nevertheless, there is need for a measure of poverty. Only then, it will be possible to evaluate how the economy is performing in terms of providing a certain minimum standard of living to all its citizens. Measurement of Poverty has, therefore, important policy implications.

In India we have had a long history of studies on measurement of poverty. There are broadly two approaches to it.

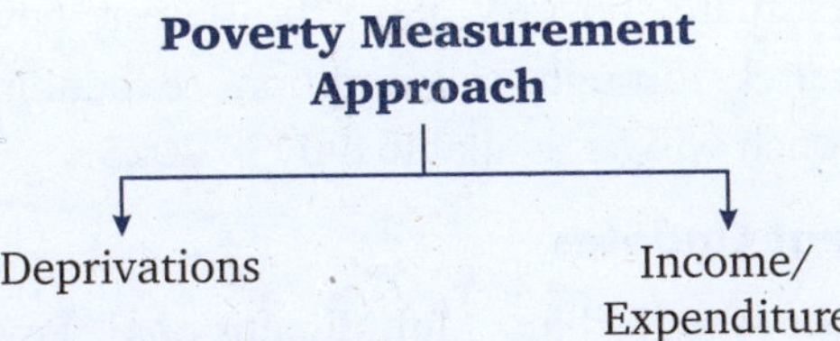

Some analysts focus on deprivations but there are many problems associated with this approach including difficulties in measurability and aggregation across indicators. For example, access to safe drinking water cannot be aggregated with indicators such as child mortality.

In the minds of most people, being rich or poor is associated with levels of income. The various non-income indicators of poverty are in fact reflections of inadequate income. Defining poverty in terms of income or in the absence of such data in terms of expenditure seems most appropriate, and it is this method which is followed in most countries including India.

So, poverty is looked at in terms of certain minimum consumption expenditure per person or preferably per household. Any household failing to meet this level of consumption expenditure can be treated as a poor household. This minimum level of consumption expenditure can be derived, in turn, in terms of minimum expenditure on food and non-food items. Minimum food consumption is related to fulfilling certain nutritional standards but the estimation of minimum non-food consumption is more difficult.

How has Poverty been Estimated in India?

Since the time of Dadabhai Naoroji's 1901 book 'Poverty and Un-British Rule in India, poverty has been estimated using a monetary measure. The official data on poverty used to be made available to the public by the Planning Commission. It used to be estimated on the basis of consumption expenditure data collected by the National Sample Survey Organization (NSSO). The idea was to arrive at an amount of money that is considered necessary to either eat a subsistence diet or to achieve a minimum standard of living.

Since data on income was difficult to collect, India used regular (five-yearly) consumption expenditure surveys which showed how much people were spending on consumption of food and non-food items. Based on this data, several expert committees - led by DT Lakdawala (1993), Suresh Tendulkar (2009), and C Rangrajan (2014) - drew a 'poverty line'. The line is the level of consumption expenditure (in Rupees) that divides those who are poor from those who are not.

The following are the poverty estimates by various groups:

	1973-74	**1993-94**	**2004-05**	**2009-10**	**2011-12**	**2009-10**	**2011-12**
	Lakdawala			**Tendulkar**		**Rangarajan**	
Rural	56.4%	37.3%	28.3%	33.8%	25.7%	39.6%	30.9%
Urban	49.0%	32.4%	25.7%	20.9%	13.7%	35.1%	26.4%
All India	**54.9%**	**36.0%**	**27.5%**	**29.8%**	**21.9%**	**38.2%**	**29.5%**
Absolute	32 cr	32 cr	30.2 cr	35.5 cr	27 cr	45.5 cr	36.3 cr

As per the Tendulkar report, if people are spending less than Rs. 27 per day in rural area and Rs. 33 per day in urban area, then they will be considered BPL and arrived at a cut off of **21.9% of the population as BPL in 2011-12**. However, this amount was such low that it immediately faced a backlash from all section of media and society and the government appointed another committee under C. Rangarajan to review the poverty estimation methodology. Rangarajan committee raised these limits to Rs. 32 per day in rural area and Rs. 47, per day in urban area, and worked out poverty line of **29.5% in 2011-12**.

Defining a poverty line has always been a controversial issue in India. The new NDA government which came in 2014 has not accepted any of the above Rangarajan and Tendulkar committee estimates on the poverty line but has informally supported the Tendulkar committee estimates.

India's last official poverty statistics (based on consumption expenditure) are from 2011-12 based on Tendulkar/Rangarajan Committees report. Since then, poverty estimates have not been published as Government junked the consumption expenditure survey of 2017-18 done by National Sample Survey (NSS) under 75th round. That survey showed a decline in rural consumption and, as such, pointed to an increase in poverty. (This may be because of the impact of GST and Demonetization).

The 79th round of National Sample Survey (NSS) was again on Household Consumption Expenditure which has already been completed (1st July 2022 to 30th June 2023). And NSS has again started the 80th round on Household Consumption Expenditure (HSCE) from August 2023 to July 2024. The back-to-back two consecutive years of household consumption expenditure data will be better and more accurate to estimate poverty. So, the latest poverty estimates through consumption (expenditure) approach will be available only in 2025.

Recent Updates

As per the Indian Multidimensional Poverty Index (MPI) [NITI Aayog report based on National Family Health Survey], poverty has reduced to 15% in 2019-21.

As per the Global Multidimensional Poverty Index (MPI), [published jointly by the United Nations Development Programme (UNDP) and the Oxford Poverty and Human Development Initiative (OPHI)], poverty has reduced to 15.5% in 2022.

India's MPI is not exactly the same as Global MPI. For instance, India's MPI has 12 variables, while the Global MPI has 10. The two additional variables in India's MPI are maternal health and bank account.

But Multidimensional poverty estimates which focus on deprivations based on education, health and standard of living are different from Consumption based poverty estimates.

The World Bank defines extreme poverty as people living on less than $3.0 per day (in PPP exchange rate, which is around $1=Rs. 20). As per the World Bank report published in April 2025, 5.3% of Indians were living under extreme poverty in 2022-23.

Identification of Poor for Various Government Schemes

Presently, in India, identification of poor is done by the State Governments based on information from Below Poverty Line (BPL) censuses of which the latest is the Socio-Economic Caste Census 2011 (SECC 2011).

The SECC Census was conducted by the States / UTs simultaneously for rural and urban areas under the technical and financial support from the Government of India. It captured data on households - individual particulars, housing, deprivation, employment, income, assets/ amenities, and landownership. SECC 2011 captured data on socio economic status of 17.97 crore rural households and 6.51 crore of urban households.

The SECC 2011 ranked households in three categories:

- **Automatically Excluded:** Households meeting exclusion criteria - any of the 13 assets and income-based parameters (for example one parameter is 'a household member govt. employee') are automatically excluded from welfare benefits;
- **Automatically Included:** Households satisfying inclusion criteria – any one of the 5 acute social destitution parameters (households without shelter, destitute living on alms, manual scavenger families, primitive tribal groups, bonded labours) are automatically included for welfare benefits;
- **Others:** "Others" are ranked on the basis of 7 indicators of deprivation and would, resources permitting be eligible for welfare benefits.

Unlike BPL Censuses, SECC-2011 allows for the first time to track the **deprivation** of households and address gaps effectively **with focus on multi-dimensionality of poverty**. Being outside the Census Act, it provides a rare opportunity to know the specific deprivation of each household. The **Sumit Bose Committee** (2017) recommended using SECC 2011 data to identify beneficiaries for all centrally sponsored, central and state government schemes as far as possible.

The Government has used SECC data for identification of beneficiary households while implementing its social welfare programmes including Pradhan Mantri Aawas Yojana-Gramin, Deendayal Antyodaya Yojana-National Rural Livelihood Mission, Pradhan Mantri Jan Arogya Yojana-Ayushman Bharat, Pradhan Mantri Sahaj Bijli Har Ghar Yojana, and Pradhan Mantri Ujjwala Yojana. It is also being used by several state governments to implement National Food Security Act.

Use of SECC data in the implementation of Government programmes allows for evidence based developmental interventions. With the use of SECC data, the programme specific priority list is generated keeping in view the fiscal space of the welfare programme for targeting specific pro-poor interventions. The selection of beneficiaries gets validated through Gram Sabhas, while identity is established through Aadhaar wherever legally allowed. This leads to selection of right beneficiaries and minimizes duplication and fraud. This has substantially enhanced the effectiveness of government's efforts to tackle multi-dimensional poverty, going beyond income or expenditure-based poverty.

National Sample Survey (NSS)

The National Sample Survey (NSS) is a national socioeconomic survey conducted in **annual rounds** with a cycle of **rotating topics**. For example, the purpose of the 71st round of the National Sample Survey (NSS) conducted in 2014 was to develop indicators on health and education. The purpose of the 68th round (July 2011 – June 2012) and 75th round (July 2017 – June 2018) of Natio nal Sample Survey was household consumption expenditure.

The household Consumption Expenditure Survey (CES) generally comes after every five years (quinquennial) during these annual rounds of NSS.

The NSS Consumer Expenditure Survey (CES) generates estimates of household Monthly Per Capita Consumer Expenditure (MPCE) and the distribution of households and persons over the MPCE classes. It is designed to collect information regarding expenditure on consumption of goods and services (food and non-food) consumed by households. The results, after release, are also used for rebasing of the GDP and other macro-economic indicators.

The 79th (2022 to 2023) and 80th (2023 to 2024) Round of NSS is again on household consumption expenditure (HCES). This HCES has also collected data on items received free from the Government's welfare programmes.

The below figure represents how low economic growth and low levels of health and education results in poverty trap:

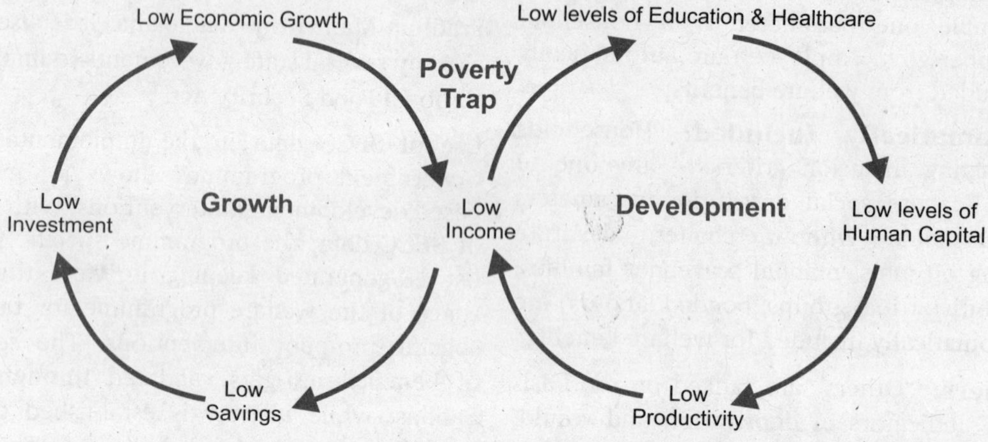

Since independence, Government's approach towards poverty reduction is in three dimensions.

1. Growth oriented [Since First Five-Year Plan]
2. Poverty alleviation Programs [Since Third Five Year Plans]
3. Providing basic minimum amenities [Since Fifth Five Year Plan]

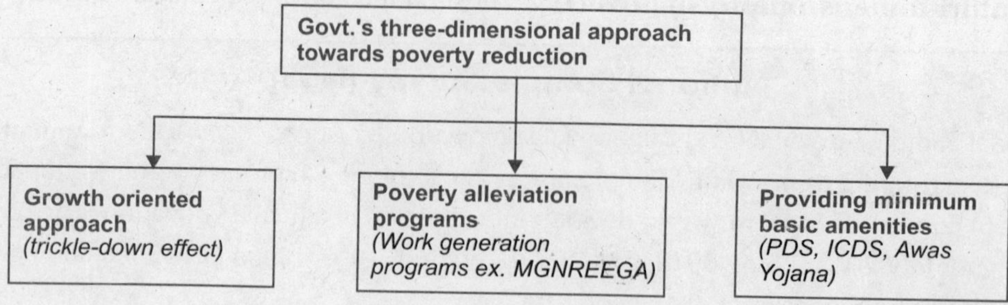

8.3 Inequality in India

Spectacular economic growth over the past three and half decades has made India a global economic powerhouse. Between 1990 and 2025, India's economy grew at a rate of around 7% at constant prices, making it a $4.0 Trillion economy. The Indian economy is now the third largest in the world by purchasing power parity after China and the United States and fourth largest in nominal terms after Germany, China and United States. The surging economic growth has improved living conditions of its citizens, but these improvements were not uniformly distributed among India's diverse population.

Income and wealth inequality reached historically high levels in India since the 1980s when economic and trade liberalisation began in the country, with the top one percent of the population accounting for 22.5% of the national income in 2022-23. In terms of wealth, the top 1% of India's population owns nearly 40 % of its wealth.

The Gini coefficient is one of the important variables used to examine trends in inequality across income, wealth and consumption. As per the data analysed from several sources including national level surveys and tax records, following is the trend in Gini coefficient of consumption, income and wealth which shows that inequality in income and wealth is much higher than that of consumption in India.

Gini Coefficient	Gini - Consumption	Gini - Income	Gini - Wealth
2011-12	0.288	0.6	0.74
2022-23	0.255	0.61	0.75

Inequality in India declined in the post-independence period for three and a half decades since 1950, but since we introduced the reforms in 1991, it has increased. The reasons for the same could be found in a famous paper of 1955 by **Simon Kuznets**, where he has argued that in the early period of economic growth, distribution of income tends to worsen i.e., inequality increases, and that only after reaching a certain level of economic development an improvement in the distribution of income occurs.

One of the main reasons of increase in inequality in the post reform period is that when the economy was opened in 1991, the people having financial and educational resources grabbed up the opportunities created by opening of the economy and were able to multiply their wealth and income in a much faster way as compared to the poor people who lacked these resources. But once the government (tax) resources will increase from the expanding economy and the government spends these resources in the human capital then in future the inequality may decline. Human capital can be understood as a person's endowment derived from education and robust health. When a population is more or less equally endowed with human capital then the returns to labour would be relatively equal compared to the country in which the distribution of human capital is unequal (pyramidical), which has been the case for India till now. Government is still spending a lot on subsidies rather than health and education which will ultimately provide equalisation of opportunities.

Why consumption inequality is less and has declined over the past few years?

(As per a recent report of World Bank, India has one of the lowest levels of inequality, but that is in consumption terms)

Inequality in consumption will always be lower than inequality in wealth or income. A poorer household will spend a majority of its income on the necessities of life, and will have very little savings. If its income doubles, consumption spending will not double since the household will now be able to save some amount of its income; its consumption levels will not rise in the same proportion as their incomes. Thus, consumption inequality will always be less than income or wealth inequality.

As incomes rise, assuming that there is no fall in the real incomes of the poor, the consumption of the poor would rise in a greater proportion than middle and upper classes, who would be able to save much more out of their rising incomes. The higher income of upper classes would allow for greater levels of savings, which can then be transformed in greater levels of wealth.

Consumption inequality can reduce even when income and wealth inequality rise; all these outcomes characterize Indian economy today. What is of significance is the extreme concentration of income and wealth that have accompanied (economic) growth in India today, making it one of the most unequal economies in the world, an outcome that has consequences for future growth prospects of the economy.

Many economists reckon that poor governance is the biggest constraint in achieving the aspirations of a new generation and reduction in poverty and inequality in India. A major institutional challenge is the accountability of service providers, particularly the public sector. Recent literature also focused on eradication of corruption for reduction in inequalities. Issues like electoral reforms, crony capitalism, election funding and corruption should be part of the reform agenda to reduce inequalities and the economic reforms should focus more on efficient delivery systems of public services. Fiscal instruments like public investment in physical and social infrastructure can be used to reduce inequality. For reducing inequality, some advocate measures such as redistribution of assets and wealth in favour of the poor via higher taxes for the rich. However, these may not be pragmatic solutions. The tax/GDP ratio has to be raised with a wider tax base rather than increasing the tax rate. The new and aspiring India wants equality of opportunity rather than redistributive measures.

As we initiated the reforms in 1991, the Indian economy moved on a higher growth trajectory of 6.3%, which helped the government to raise more resources and it also pulled in a lot of population in the growth process. The proportion of nationwide population living below the poverty line (as per the planning commission estimates) fell from 36% (40.7 cr) in 1993-94 to 27.5% (35.5 cr) in 2004-05 and 21.9% (26.9 cr) in 2011-12. (As per some reports it is 15% in 2020-21) Growth helps in reduction of poverty in two ways; first through the percolation (trickle down) effect and second through the ability to raise more resources on the part of the government to provide for increased social sector expenditures.

While economic growth is absolutely crucial in raising living standards of India's vast population, the distributional effects of economic growth, as measured by income distribution, play a significant role in determining the long-term development trends and socio-economic well-being of the citizens. India is one the richest countries in the world, and yet, the average Indian is relatively poor as a result of highly-skewed income distribution. Economic inequality can adversely exacerbate a range of social problems, including inter-group relations and conflict, social cohesion and violent crime. Inequality hurts not only the poor but everyone with increased crime and increased workplace accidents.

Findings from Previous Years Economic Survey

- By examining the correlation of inequality and per-capita income with a range of socio economic indicators, including health, education, life expectancy, infant mortality, birth and death rates, fertility rates, crime, drug usage and mental health, the Survey highlights that both economic growth (as reflected in the income per capita) and inequality have similar relationships with socio-economic indicators (for example birth and fertility rates both decline with increase in inequality and growth). Thus, unlike in advanced economies, in India economic growth and inequality converge in terms of their effects on socio-economic indicators (and hence there is an absence of a trade-off between economic growth and inequality).
- Furthermore, economic growth has a far greater impact on poverty alleviation than inequality. Therefore, given India's stage of development and knowing that our growth potential is high (and absolute level of poverty is also high), India must continue to focus on economic growth to lift the poor out of poverty by expanding the overall pie. Note that this policy focus does not imply that redistributive objectives are unimportant, but that redistribution is only feasible in a developing economy if the size of the economic pie grows.

8.4 Demographic Dividend

- Total Fertility Rate (TFR) is defined as the total number of children that would be born to each woman if she were to live to the end of her child-bearing years.
- Replacement level fertility (RLF) is the level of fertility at which a population exactly replaces itself from one generation to the next. Ideally it should be 2.0 but generally it is 2.1 all over the world as we cannot expect all the female children will survive till the child bearing ages.
- As per the latest National Family Health Survey (NFHS), India's TFR has declined to 2.0 which is below the replacement level fertility. But still there will be positive population growth in the next two decades due to:
  - (a) Population momentum (it occurs because it is not only the number of children per woman that determine population growth, but also the number of women in reproductive age which is more for India.), and
  - (b) Continued rise in life expectancy
- Population growth in India has been slowing in recent decades from an annual growth rate of 2.5% during 1971-81 to around 1% in 2020s.
- The share of India's young (i.e., 0-19 years) population has started declining and is projected to drop to 25 percent by 2041. On the other hand, the share of elderly (60 years and above) population is rising and will increase to 16 percent by 2041.
- India's working age (20-59) population will continue to increase through 2041. India's demographic dividend will peak around

2041, when share of working-age (20-59 years) population to non-working age population is expected to hit a maximum of 1.43 (WA/NWA = 59%/41% = 1.43).

[In Economic Survey 2018-19, an analysis has been done regarding working age people where working age has been considered 20+ because now a lot of people are entering in the job market after attaining the age of 19. Legally working age may be 14+ but practically it has increased over the years due to education.]

India's Population	Young Age (0-19) *(Has started declining)*	Working Age (20-59) *(Is still increasing)*	Old Age (60+) *(Has started increasing)*
2011	41%	50.4%	8.6%
2041	25%	59%	16%

Demographic Dividend is an episode of higher economic growth driven by changes in the age structure of the population ***(it is the additional growth due to demographic factors alone).*** The specific variable driving the demographic dividend is the ratio of the working age (WA) population (20-59) to non-working age (NWA) population. Both the level and the growth of the WA/NWA ratio have a positive impact on economic activity.

India's demographic cycle is about 10-30 years behind that of the other countries like China, Korea, Brazil etc. indicating that the next few decades present an opportunity for India to catch up to their per capita income levels. This does not mean that the demographic dividend will turn negative thereafter, rather positive impact will slow down.

A distinctive feature in India is the large heterogeneity among the States in their demographic profile evolution. There is a clear divide between peninsular India (West Bengal, Karnataka, Kerala, Tamil Nadu and Andhra Pradesh) where WA/NWA population ratio will peak early as compared to the hinterland States (Madhya Pradesh, Rajasthan, Uttar Pradesh and Bihar). The divide in the WA/NWA ratio of the peninsular India and the hinterland States is because of the difference in their levels of Total Fertility Rate (the average number of children that a woman would have over her childbearing years). So demographically, there are two India's, with different policy concerns: a soon-to-begin ageing India where the elderly and their needs will require greater attention: and a young India where providing education, skills, and employment opportunities must be the focus. Of course, heterogeneity within India offers the advantage of addressing some of these concerns via greater labour mobility, which would in effect reduce this demographic imbalance.

8.5 Labour Laws in India

Employment Data (2024-25)

Total labour force = 65 crore
Employed = 61 crore
Formal = 9 crore (13%)
Informal = 52 crore (87%)

As per the Constitution of India, labour is a concurrent subject. Central government has merged the earlier 29 labour laws into four new labour codes. These four labour codes have come into effect since Nov. 2025.

1. The Code on Wages, 2019

It has replaced (repealed) four previous acts viz: Payment of Wages Act, 1936, Minimum Wages Act, 1948, Payment of Bonus Act, 1965, Equal Remuneration Act, 1976.

- A **statutory** concept of **'Floor Wage'** introduced which will be applicable on all the workers either organized or unorganized sector. Neither Central nor State agencies can reduce the minimum wage below the 'Floor Wage' for any kind of employment.
- The code provides that there would be a review/ revision of minimum wages at intervals not exceeding five years. Further, the rate of wages for overtime work shall not be less than twice the rate for normal wages. MGNREGA wages have been kept outside the purview of Code on Wages.
- Method of fixation of minimum wage rates simplified. Factors to be taken into account are types of skills and geographical location as against the earlier system of wage being fixed employment-wise.
- In case the employee is removed, dismissed, retrenched, resigns or becomes unemployed due to closure of an establishment, the wages are required to be paid within two working days.
- The provisions of the previous Minimum Wages Act and the Payment of Wages Act used to apply only to workers drawing wages below a particular ceiling and working in scheduled employments only. However, under the Code, the minimum wages and the payment of wages provisions cover all establishments, employees and employers.
- The definition of "wages" includes basic pay, dearness allowance and retaining allowance. It specifically excludes components such as statutory bonus, utilities (light, water, medical etc.), conveyance allowance, house rent allowance, overtime allowance etc. The specified exclusions however may not exceed 50% of the total remuneration. This is aimed at ensuring that companies do not adopt compensation structures which result in wages being reduced below 50% of total compensation.
- All employees whose wages do not exceed a specific monthly amount (to be notified by the central or state government) will be entitled to an annual bonus. Bonus is payable on higher of minimum wage or the wage ceiling fixed by the appropriate government for payment of bonus. Minimum bonus prescribed under the Code is 8.33 percent and the maximum bonus payable is 20 percent of the wages.
- The cut-off date for salary disbursement has been advanced to the 7th of the subsequent month.

2. The Occupational Safety, Health and Working Conditions Code, 2020

It has replaced (repealed) 13 previous acts including The Factories Act 1948.

- The code deals with the duties of the employer in respect of workplace safety and working conditions, and makes issue of employment letter a must for all employees, a move that will promote formalisation of employment.
- The code specifies leave and working hours (which is limited at 8 hours, and any overtime requires workers' consent and wages have to be doubled), requires health and safety norms including adequate lighting and ventilation and other welfare facilities such as separate toilets for male, female and transgender employees.

- A manufacturing unit will be defined as a factory if it employs 20 workers (and uses electricity) or 40 workers (without using electric power)
- The State government may, in public interest, exempt any new industrial establishment from "all or any of the provisions" of the Codes in the interest of increased economic activity and employment generation.
- Employment of women has been allowed in all establishments for all types of works and in the night shift, subject to their consent and requires employers to provide adequate safeguards. This will promote gender equality.

3. The Code on Social Security, 2020

It has replaced (repealed) 9 previous Acts.

- The Code proposes social security benefits to all employees and workers in the country (around 56 crores) including those in the **unorganized sector** leading to universalization of social security.
- To cater to emerging new forms of employment, new definitions like of aggregator, gig worker, platform worker have been introduced. A small contribution from aggregator between one to two per cent of turnover subject to limit of five per cent payable to gig and platform workers has been introduced.
- "Social Security Fund" will be created to fund social security schemes for extending benefits like death and accident insurance, maternity benefit and pension cover to all of the 90% (basically informal) of the countries over 50 crore workforce who do not till now come under any sort of social security cover.
- Scheme will be framed for unorganized workers, gig workers, platform workers and even those self-employed and the members of their families for providing benefits. Establishments will be allowed to join Employees' Provident Fund Organization (EPFO) and Employees' State Insurance Corporation (ESIC) on voluntary basis even if they have fewer workers (less than 20 in case they use electricity or less than 40 in case they do not use electricity).
- EPFOs coverage would be applicable on all establishments having 20 workers. Earlier it was applicable only on establishments included in the relevant Schedule.

4. The Industrial Relations Code, 2020

The new Act replaces the following previous acts (some provisions will be repealed as and when the code comes into effect and some provisions may be repealed in future):

- *The Trade Unions Act, 1926*
- *The Industrial Employment Act, 1946*
- *The Industrial Disputes Act, 1947*

- A much larger segment of firms – those with workers up to **300** (as against 100 earlier) will be able to resort to closure and retrenchment/ lay off without prior government permission. And the state governments are authorized to increase these 300 thresholds just by a **notification**.
- Companies having more than 300 workers need to apply for approval to lay off any worker, but if authorities do not respond to their request, then it will be **deemed approved**.
- The Central or State government may, in public interest, **exempt** any (existing or new) industrial establishment from "all or any of the provisions" of the Codes for a specified period.

- The Code **prohibits** the employment of **contract workers** in any core activity, and specifically permits employment in a specified list of non-core activities including canteen, security and sanitation services.
- **Fixed Term Employment** has been made applicable for all industries which will help those businesses that witness seasonal spurt/change in activities.
- Requirement of mandatory **14-day notice** for strikes and lockouts will now apply to all units which was earlier for just public utility firms.
- Definition of strike has been amended to include 'mass **casual leave**' within its ambit. Concerted casual leave on a certain day by 50% or more workers will be treated as a strike.
- Proliferation of Trade Unions will be curbed, as only those unions with support of more than **51% of the workers** on the muster roll of the unit concerned will have the right to negotiate the terms with the management.
- Encourages resolution of disputes through negotiation.

Arguments in Favour of Labour Laws

- The new labour codes were the demand of the changing time and changing requirements as some of the labour laws dates back to pre-independence period. It balances the labour welfare and industry welfare.
- Will simplify the labour laws and ensure a conducive environment for doing business which will immensely help the country in brining much needed economic growth and will help in employment generation.
- Will promote investment and will create harmonious industrial relations in the country.
- As a relaxation to small enterprises, the Occupational Safety Code (which prescribes safety standards and maximum work hours) exempts small establishments from its purview.
- Labour issue is in the Concurrent list of the Constitution and therefore states have been given the flexibility to make changes in the labour laws as they wish to attract companies for investment. Many essential features which were present in the previous laws are no longer specified in the new labour Codes but have been delegated to be prescribed by the government through Rules (for example retrenchment threshold, social security schemes, safety standards etc.)
- The labour reform was two decades in the making. It drastically reduces complexity and internal contradictions, increases flexibility & modernizes regulations on safety/working conditions.

Criticism

- Tilted in favour of the employers and would adversely affect industrial peace
- Bargaining power of the worker has been diluted
- The power given to States to exempt provisions of the codes can have serious implications on workers' rights and safety

Key Points/highlights of Labour Laws

- Gives industries flexibility in doing business and hiring & firing
- Make industrial strikes difficult while promoting fixed term employment
- Reduces influence of trade unions
- Reduction of cost & complexity in compliance
- Lead to formalization of jobs resulting in increase in wages to employees

- Universalization of minimum wages and making it statutory rights
- Universalization of social security by expanding benefits to informal sector workers

8.6 Different Types of Employment

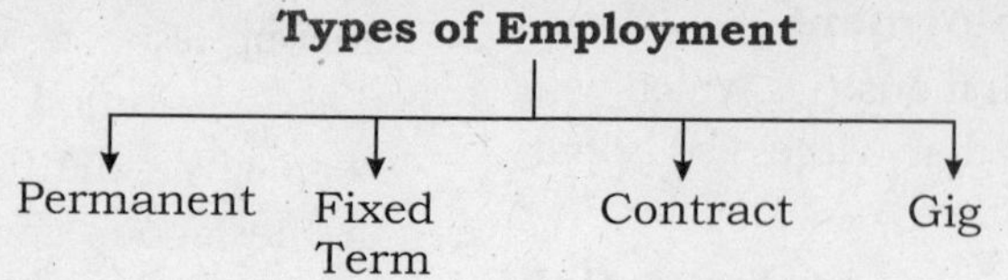

1. Permanent Employee

A permanent employee is a worker who has been hired for indefinite employment contract with a company and there is no set end date. Permanent employees typically receive a full range of benefits, such as health insurance, paid time off, and retirement plans. They are generally expected to work regular hours and are entitled to job security and certain legal protections. They are on the payroll of the company.

2. Fixed Term Employment

Fixed Term Employment is a contract in which an enterprise hires a labour for a specific period of time or a specific task (ex. a project) and the payment is fixed in advance and is not altered till the term expires. Such contracts are not given for routine jobs and are usually given out for jobs which are temporary in nature. After the term expires the worker will leave the job and there is no case of firing of worker and he gets all the benefits of regular/permanent workers. Fixed term employees are on the payroll of the company.

Positives of Fixed Term Employment

- Industries will have the flexibility in employment and will lead to more job creation in the formal sector
- Industries can hire workers for a fixed term directly without going through the contractor
- As per the newly enacted Labour Codes, fixed term employment workers should get wages and allowances equal to that of permanent worker
- The fixed term employment worker will be eligible for all statutory benefits like PF, gratuity, medical insurance which are available to a permanent worker proportionately according to the period of service

Negatives of Fixed Term Employment

Due to the introduction of "fixed term employment", there is a risk that companies may convert even their permanent/regular workers into "Fixed Term Employment" as there is no issue of hiring and firing of the "fixed term" workers. The fixed term workers will have to automatically leave after the term or task is over and if the company wants them to stay for more, then the companies can always extend their term.

3. Contract Worker

Contract Workers are hired through an external agency i.e., contractor (basically the contractor has a pool of labours which they provide to the companies on contract basis for non-core activities), and the company pays compensation to the contractor/agency which then forwards the payment to the contract labourers. But in-between, the contractor deducts a hefty amount and do not pass all the benefits provided by the companies to the contract workers. In case of contract labour, the labour is not on the "payroll"/employee of the company but is of the employee of the contractor.

4. Gig Worker

Workers who perform work or participates in a work arrangement and earns from such activities outside of traditional employer-employee relationship are called gig workers. Gig workers can further be classified as **platform** and **non-platform** workers.

Platform gig workers operate through digital platform or online software apps. An example for platform (gig) worker is 'Uber' cab driver. Here consumers are purchasing transport services from the cab driver by using 'Uber' as a platform. So, 'Uber' platform is connecting consumers with cab drivers. Consumers are not purchasing travel services from 'Uber' and 'Uber' is just getting some commission (%) from what the consumers pay to the cab driver.

Non-platform gig workers work part-time or full-time in traditional sectors as casual wage workers or own-account workers. An example for non-platform (gig) worker would be a freelance educator teaching in an institute. In this arrangement, students will purchase the course from the institute and not from the educator. Institute is purchasing educator's services and producing educational services and then selling it to the students. Students are not directly purchasing the course from the educator through any platform. In this case the educator may be a permanent employee of the institute or is teaching based on per hour contract. So, if the educator is teaching based on per hour on a temporary contract, then he/she will be a gig-worker and he/she will not be on the payroll of the company and also not get any social security benefit by the employer. Other example of non-platform gig workers are domestic workers (maids), construction workers.

8.7 Migrant Labour

According to the 2011 census, there are 5.6 crore migrant labourers from the States of Uttar Pradesh, Bihar, Jharkand, Rajasthan and Madhya Pradesh traversing state borders for informal contract work in more developed parts of the country. Though there is no official data available, it is estimated that currently there are at least 10 crore migrant labourers, accounting for 10% of India's GDP.

The following are issues faced by migrant labour

- They are treated as second-class citizens
- Lack of proper accommodation, low standard of living, low wages, inaccessibility to state given services due to lack of identity proof and other documents
- Usually unable to speak the lingua franca of where they migrate to, rarely represented by any union or social movement, they are easily harassed by employers, government institutions and by other workers
- This vulnerability makes them more easily controlled, cheap and dispensable
- Unlike farmers, who benefit from several government schemes and labourers in rural areas who benefit from MNREGA — migrant labourers receive no formal govt. support.

In order to protect the interests of migrant labourers and avoid their exploitation, the

Inter-State Migrant Workmen (Regulation of Employment and Conditions of Service) Act, was passed in 1979 which has now been replaced by The Occupational Safety, Health and Working Conditions Code, 2020. The following are the various features/benefits for migrant labourers incorporated in the new Code, 2020:

- An inter-state migrant worker has been defined as who is employed in an establishment in another state and whose wages does not exceed Rs. 18,000/month or any higher amount notified by the Central Government.
- The Central Government and the State Governments shall maintain the database/ record for inter-State migrant workers
- It shall be the responsibility of the contractor or the employer to ensure suitable conditions of work for the inter-state migrant worker
- Extend all benefits to the inter-state migrant worker which is available to any other worker regarding provident fund, insurance, medical check-up etc.
- The employer shall pay, to every inter-state migrant worker, in every year a lump sum amount of fare to and for journey to his native place from the place of his employment
- The government shall make scheme to provide an option to the inter-State migrant worker for availing benefits of PDS either in his native state or where he is employed

8.8 Employees' Provident Fund Organization (EPFO)

Employee Provident Fund Organization (EPFO) is a statutory body established under the Employees' Provident Fund and Miscellaneous Provisions Act, 1952 and is under the administrative control of the Ministry of Labour and Employment, Govt. of India. EPFO provides two schemes:

1. Employee Provident Fund (EPF)
2. Employee Pension Scheme (EPS).

Employees Provident Fund (EPF) Scheme

- Employees Provident Fund (EPF) is a scheme under the Employees' Provident Funds and Miscellaneous Provisions Act, 1952 and is regulated under the purview of EPFO. Basically, it is a social security scheme.
- If an establishment (factory or service industry) has more than 20 workers then it is mandatory to get registered with EPFO. But all the employees working in such a registered (with EPFO) establishment don't need to subscribe to the EPF scheme. Only those workers whose salary is up to Rs. 15000 need to contributes 12% of his/her basic salary (including dearness allowance) into this scheme and the same amount is also contributed by the employer. For other employees earning more than Rs. 15000, it is voluntary.

Employees' Pension Scheme (EPS) 1995

- The Employees' Provident Funds and Miscellaneous Provisions Act, 1952 originally did not provide for any pension scheme. In 1995, through an amendment, a scheme was formulated for employees' pension (existing and new EPF members), wherein the pension fund was to comprise a deposit of 8.33 per cent of the employers' contribution to be made towards provident fund (EPF) corpus.
- Both the employee and the employer contribute 12 per cent of the employee's

basic salary and dearness allowance to the EPF. The employee's entire part goes to EPF, while the 12 per cent contribution made by the employer is split as 3.67 per cent contribution to EPF and 8.33 per cent contribution to EPS. Apart from this, the Government of India contributes 1.16 per cent as well for an employee's pension. Employees do not contribute to the pension scheme.

- EPF Pension which is technically known as EPS (Employees' Pension Scheme), is a social security scheme provided by EPFO. The scheme makes provisions for employees working in the organized sector for a pension after their retirement at the age of 58 years.

8.9 National/New Pension System (NPS)

- National Pension System (NPS) is a pension cum investment scheme launched by Government of India to provide old age security to Citizens of India. The Scheme is administered and regulated by Pension Fund Regulatory and Development Authority (PFRDA) set up under PFRDA Act, 2013. National Pension System Trust (NPST) established by PFRDA is the registered owner of all assets under NPS.
- NPS is broadly classified into two categories:

1. Government Sector

(a) **Central Government:** The Central Government had introduced the National Pension System (NPS) with effect from January 1, 2004 (**except for armed forces**). All the employees of Central Autonomous Bodies (CABs) who have joined on or after the above-mentioned date are also covered under Government sector of NPS. Central Government/CABs employee contributes towards pension from monthly salary along with matching contribution from the employer. NPS is **mandatory** for Central Govt. and CAB employees.

Govt. employees make a monthly contribution at the rate of 10% of their salary and a matching contribution is paid by the Central Govt. For central Govt. employees, the **employer's** contribution rate has been enhanced to **14%** w.e.f. 01.04.2019.

(b) **State Government:** Any state government and its autonomous bodies **can** also adopt NPS. State Government/State Autonomous Bodies employees also contribute towards pension from monthly salary along with matching contribution from the employer. *(West Bengal & Tamil Nadu have not joined and now Rajasthan & Chhattisgarh have decided to walk out)*

2. Private Sector

(a) Corporates: Companies **can** adopt NPS for their employees with contribution rates as per the employment conditions.

(b) All citizens of India: Any individual (aged between **18 - 70** years) not being covered by any of the above sectors has been allowed to join NPS on **voluntary** basis from May 01, 2009.

- NRIs have also been allowed to open NPS account.
- There are tax benefits under NPS but no need to go into such details.
- NPS account can be opened only in individual capacity and not jointly.

Following is a comparison between the New Pension Scheme (NPS) and the Old Pension Scheme (OPS):

New Pension Scheme (NPS)	Old Pension Scheme (OPS)
• In NPS, those employed by the government contribute 10 percent of their salary (basic plus dearness allowance), while their employers contribute 14 percent.	• In the OPS, upon retirement, employees receive 50 percent of their last drawn salary (basic plus dearness allowance) or their average earnings in the last ten months of service, whichever is more advantageous to them.
• Private sector employees can also participate in the NPS voluntarily and their employer contributions is optional.	• A ten-year service requirement should be met by the employee.
• At the time of retirement, employees are required to purchase an annuity plan for a monthly pension with a minimum of 40% of the accumulated corpus. The employee can withdraw the remaining corpus (60%) as a lump sum.	• Under OPS, employees are not required to contribute anything to th eir pensions.
• With NPS, the customer has much greater flexibility and has a greater sense of control over her fate as the customers can choose fund managers as well as they can decide the percentage of funds invested in equity and debt.	• OPS was a major incentive for taking government employment as there was guarantee of a pension post-retirement without any contribution.
• Under NPS, whatever is the fund value at the time of maturity, you can withdraw max. 60% one time (lump sum) and for rest 40% you need to purchase annuity. The 60% lump sum amount is exempt from tax. The 40% fund is also exempt from tax when you get but the annuity income which you get yearly (from annuity purchase) is taxable as per the income tax slab rate.	• OPS became unsustainable for governments due to rise in life expectancy. • Under OPS, monthly pension is taxable as per the income tax slab rate. • On demise of the person, 50% of the pension will be paid to family member/spouse

Unified Pension Scheme (UPS)

The salient features of the UPS are:

- Assured pension: 50% of the average basic pay drawn over the last 12 months prior to superannuation for a minimum qualifying service of 25 years. This pay is to be proportionate for lesser service period up to a minimum of 10 years of service.

- In case of UPS, employer/government contribution is 18.5% of basic pay plus dearness allowance and employee contribution is 10% of basic pay plus dearness allowance.
- Assured family pension: @60% of pension of the employee immediately before her/his demise.
- Assured minimum pension: @10,000 per month on superannuation after minimum 10 years of service.
- Inflation indexation: on assured pension, on assured family pension and assured minimum pension. This means that the pension will keep on increasing as per inflation and it (Dearness Relief) will be based on All India Consumer Price Index for Industrial Workers (AICPI-IW) as in case of service employees.
- Lump sum payment at superannuation in addition to gratuity - 1/10th of monthly emoluments (pay + DA) as on the date of superannuation for every completed six months of service this payment will not reduce the quantum of assured pension.
- The new scheme (UPS) is applicable from April 1, 2025. It will affect 23 lakh Central Govt. Employees, and States may also join it benefiting around 60 lakh state Govt. employees. Employees can choose either UPS or NPS.

The main difference between OPS, NPS and UPS is OPS does not require any contribution from employee and offers assured pension while NPS and UPS require employee contribution. While NPS does not offer any assured pension (rather depends on market value of the contribution), UPS does offer assured pension.

8.10 Informal and Formal Economy

There is variation in definitions of the unorganized/informal and organized/formal sector which attempt to draw boundaries in these two sectors based on differences in features such as legal status, employment size, organizational form and technology. But in general, the informal/unorganized sector is defined as that part of the economy which is neither registered nor taxed nor monitored by any form of government or sometimes having less than 10 workers.

Over the years, in India, the number of enterprises belonging to informal or unorganized category have retained a position of considerable importance in terms of employment (more than 85% of the total labour force of 64 crore is employed in informal sector) and they have contributed more than 30% to the total output/GDP of India. The sub-sectors that account for a dominant share of informal sector employment are manufacturing, construction and trade (wholesale and retail). A substantial segment of the unorganized sector are 'own account enterprises' (OAEs) or those that employ no hired labour on a regular basis and are typically 'household units' located in household premises or units without a fixed location such as activities undertaken by street vendors or in mobile markets.

Competitive pressure in the Indian manufacturing sector increased as a consequence of the reforms undertaken in the early 1990s that abolished licensing requirements for most industries and the liberalization of international trade and foreign investment. The regulation of labour markets, however, was left largely untouched and constitutes an important difference between the formal and informal sector. Pressure to cut costs and increase flexibility, together with strict labour laws affecting only formal enterprises, form clear incentives for formal enterprises to subcontract activities to the informal sector and thus pushing more and more people in the informal sectors. The absence of employment opportunities in the formal sector explains the reason for a large informal economy. Since Indian agriculture does not provide the required opportunity, people find something to do in the non-agricultural informal economy, with much lower incomes.

A large informal economy exists because low wages allow it to compete with the formal sector in a host of non-agricultural activities varying through manufacturing, construction and trade. Another reason for the proliferation of unorganized units and informal employment could be the many areas where the informal sector is not only not in competition with the formal sector, but actually services its requirements and in the process low wages in the informal economy help sustains profit in the formal sector.

The formal sector firms are **much more productive** when compared to their informal counterparts. The reason for lower productivity of informal units is lack of financial resources, technical expertise, professional management etc. which results in low wages in informal sectors. This hinders the overall progress of the labours as they are not able to upgrade their skills and are stuck in the same kind of task for their lifetime and remain destitute. If we really want that the condition of the poor improves and we could achieve inclusive growth then they must be brought into the formal employment.

8.11 Unemployment and its Types

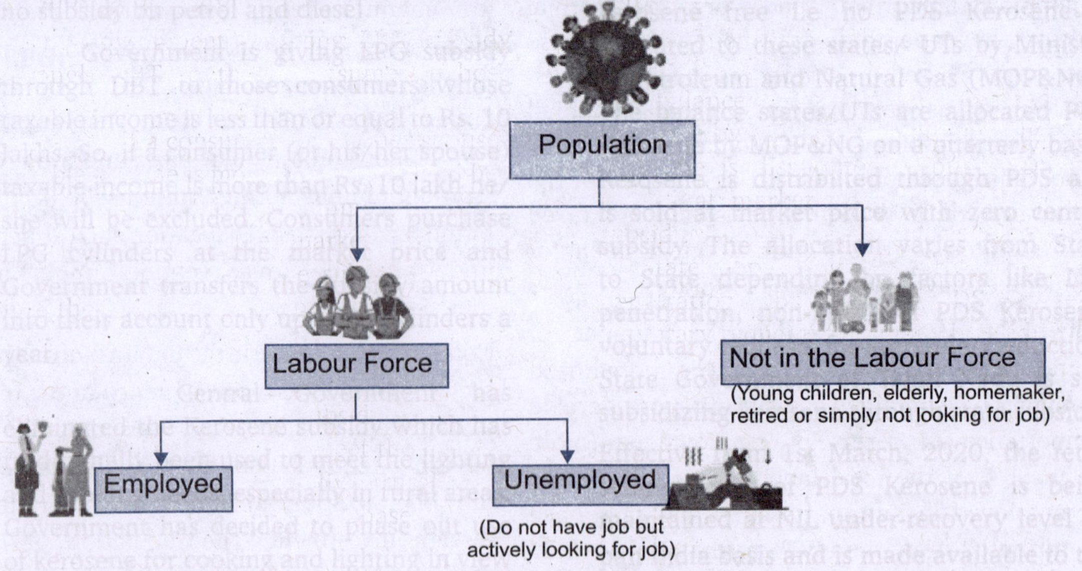

The whole population of the country can be categorized into "labour force" and "not in the labour force". Not in the labour force means that population who cannot do job like children and elderly or who are keeping house or any other person who is not interested in doing any job. Labour force means that population who is either employed or who is unemployed i.e., not employed but actively looking for job.

Economists define unemployed person as one who is not able to get employment of even one hour in half a day. Unemployment is referred as the percentage of number of unemployed people to that of the labour force.

$$\text{Unemployment\%} = \frac{\text{Unemployed people}}{\text{Labour Force}} \times 100\%$$

There are various sources of data on unemployment:

- Reports of Census of India
- Periodic Labour Force Survey (PLFS) done by National Statistical Office (NSO)
- Directorate General of Employment and Training Data of registration with Employment Exchanges (under Ministry of Labour and Employment)

Different Types of Unemployment

1. **Structural Unemployment:** A longer lasting form of unemployment caused by fundamental shifts in the economy. Structural unemployment occurs for a number of reasons – workers lacking the requisite job skills, change in government policy or change in technology, or they may live far from regions where jobs are available but are unable to move there or simply unwilling to work because existing wage levels are too low. So, while jobs are available, there is a serious mismatch between what companies need and what workers can offer.

   Structural unemployment exists when there are jobs available and people willing to do work, but there are not a sufficient number of people qualified to fill the vacant jobs. In other words, employers can neither find enough workers nor can workers find jobs for which they are qualified. Structural unemployment often occurs when the demand for specific types of labour changes as the economy changes.

   Example: Earlier people used hand looms to make textiles. Many weavers were engaged in making cloth through the use of these hand looms. The Industrial Revolution came along, and machines were created that could weave the cloth without the use of a skilled weaver. All of a sudden, weavers were out of work, and their skills didn't match the needs of the marketplace.

2. **Cyclical Unemployment:** This type of unemployment occurs because of the cyclical trends in the business cycle. When business cycles are at their peak, cyclical unemployment will be low because economic activity is high. When the economic output (GDP) falls, the business cycle is at low and cyclical unemployment will rise. Cyclical unemployment arises because the overall demand for labour declines due to business cycle downturns.

3. **Frictional Unemployment:** This kind of unemployment arises due to people moving between jobs, career or location or people entering and exiting the labour force or workers and employers having inconsistent or incomplete information. Many people first leave job and then they try to find a new job according to their choice and this process takes some time to apply for new

jobs and for employers to make a selection and hence they remain unemployed for this transition period. That is why frictional unemployment is also called as transitional unemployment and it is always present in the economy. Frictional unemployment can occur even when an economy is at **full employment**– where anyone who is willing to work at the prevailing wages is, in fact, employed.

4. **Seasonal Unemployment:** Seasonal unemployment occurs when people are unemployed at certain times of the year, because they work in industries where they are not needed all year round. Examples of industries where demand, production and employment are seasonal include tourism and leisure, farming, sugar factory etc.

5. **Disguised Unemployment:** Disguised unemployment exists where part of the labour force is either left without work or is working in a redundant manner. Under this kind of unemployment, the overall productivity of labour is very less and marginal productivity of labour is zero. Disguised/hidden unemployment exists frequently in developing countries whose large populations create a surplus in the labour force. In India, agriculture sector is facing this kind of unemployment.

6. **Open Unemployment:** In many cities, you might find people standing in some select areas looking for people to employ them for that day's work. Some go to factories and offices and give their bio-data ask for a job but stay home when there is no work. Some go to employment exchanges and register themselves for vacancies notified through employment exchanges. Open unemployment is a situation in which all those who, owing to lack of work, are not working but either seek work through employment exchanges, intermediaries, friends or relatives or by making applications to prospective employers or express their willingness or availability for work under the prevailing condition of work and remunerations. This kind of unemployment is clearly visible in the society.

Unemployment data is captured through Periodic Labour force Survey (PLFS) by National Statistical Office (NSO). NSO captures the unemployment data in two ways:

- **Current Weekly Status (CWS):**
  The estimate of unemployed in current weekly status gives an average picture of unemployment in a short period of 7 days preceding the date of survey. According to the current weekly status approach, a person is considered as unemployed in a week if he/she did not work even for 1 hour during the week but sought or was available for work at least for 1 hour during the week.

- **Usual Status:**
  The estimate of the labour force in the usual status includes the persons who either worked or were seeking/available for work for a relatively long part of the 365 days preceding the date of survey. For example, if a person reports as having worked and/or sought/available for work for a total of seven months then he is part of labour force and if out of these seven months he was working only for two months and reported seeking/available for work for remaining five months, then h/she will be classified as 'Unemployed' on the usual principal status basis.

8.12 Underemployment

Underemployment is a situation in which a worker is employed, but not in the desired capacity, whether in terms of compensation, skill level, experience, education or their availability. While not technically unemployed, the underemployed are often competing for available jobs. Underemployed workers can be divided into several categories. The most common type of underemployed workers is listed below:

- Skilled workers in low-paying jobs
- Skilled workers in low-skill jobs
- Part-time workers preferring full-time hour job

Underemployment is a social problem that affects job growth, poverty level, economic growth and emotional health of underemployed workers. Underemployment is a vicious cycle in which each effect is linked to the next. For instance, underemployed workers generally have less disposable income which creates a tendency to spend less, which impacts economic growth, poverty levels and underemployed worker's emotional outlook.

Since long, we are facing the crisis of jobless growth in India, but the bigger challenge that presently the country faces is "underemployment" rather than unemployment. A possible reason may be because the Indian entrepreneurs' tendency to invest only in capital-intensive businesses or those requiring high-level skills. The successful industries in India has tended to be capital-intensive or skilled-labour intensive as the Indian entrepreneurs have ventured mainly in those industries that require high-end of technological or capital deployment. And these sectors did not create well-paid jobs for those at the bottom of the pyramid. While Indian firms have succeeded in sectors such as automobiles, software, telecom, finance and engineering; investments in clothing, light manufacturing or food processing, where jobs could be aplenty for people with less or no skills, have been abysmal. This is the reason why the transition in India of taking the workforce out of agriculture towards industry and services is the slowest in the world. Govt. as well as private sector has just not done a good job of "creating jobs with over 90% of our workforce in the informal/unorganized sector", where productivity is low and jobs are clearly not well-paid.

While the growth in the last three decades was good enough, we have not seen a transformation in the workforce because not enough well-paid jobs were being created for those who could migrate from agriculture. Rampant underemployment is a serious problem in India which has resulted in lower productivity and the government and Industry Associations must take it on a war footing.

In China, wages have been rising over 10 per cent a year for more than a decade and currently they are 2-3 times the wages in India on an average. Wages in China will continue to rise much faster than they will rise in India. Lot of labour-intensive firms are moving out of China and India ought to be the natural destination for them.

8.13 PLFS and AQEES

Periodic Labour Force Survey (PLFS)

Employment and Unemployment Surveys (EUS) conducted by NSSO were the primary source of labour market data at National and State level in India. Regular EUS were conducted quinquennially (after every five years) since 1972. Considering the importance of availability of labour force data at more frequent intervals, National Statistics Office (NSO) under Ministry of Statistics and Programme Implementation is conducting PLFS to produce annual statistics of employment and unemployment characteristics for both rural and urban areas, along with quarterly estimates for urban areas. The first annual report based on the data collected in PLFS during July 2017- June 2018 was published in May 2019.

PLFS survey provides monthly and quarterly estimates of various labour force indicators like Labour Force Participation Rate (LFPR), Worker Population Ratio (WPR) and Unemployment Rate (UR) for the country. The monthly report publishes the various indicators at the all-India level while the quarterly report publishes the various indicators at the state and country level both. An annual report is also released.

All-India Quarterly Establishment-Based Employment Survey (AQEES)

AQEES has been started by Labour Bureau (Ministry of Labour and Employment) to provide quarterly updates about the employment and related variables of establishments, in both organized and unorganized segments of nine selected sectors. These sectors altogether account for majority of the total employment in the non-farm establishments. These nine selected sectors are Manufacturing, Construction, Trade, Transport, Education, Health, Accommodation and Restaurant, IT/ BPO and Financial Services.

There are two components under AQEES:

- Quarterly Employment Survey (QES): This is in respect of establishments employing 10 or more workers (mostly constituting the 'organized' segment)
- Area Frame Establishment Survey (AFES): This is to build up a frame in respect of establishments employing 9 or less workers (mostly the 'unorganized' segment)

✓ The first report of the **QES** covering the period April to June 2021 was released in Sept. 2021. The following are the major highlights from the report of the first round of QES:

- Nearly 90% of the establishments have been estimated to work with less than 100 workers
- The over-all participation of female workers stood at 29 percent

✓ AFES field work has recently commenced.

AQEES (QES and AFES) will provide employment scenario from demand side at regular intervals which was required for policy planning. **Economic Censuses** are establishment based (demand side) but have been conducted at irregular intervals and do not cover all types of establishments. Economic Census has been conducted in years 1977, 1980, 1990, 1998, 2005, 2013-14 and 2020. Results of the 7th Economic Census [2020] is yet to appear in the public domain.

8.14 Sustainable Development Goals (SDG)

Sustainable development is development that meets the needs of the present without compromising the ability of future generations **to meet their own needs**. The concept of sustainable development can be interpreted in many different ways, but at its core is an approach to development that looks to balance different, and often competing, needs against an awareness of the **environmental**, **social** and **economic** limitations we face as a society.

Focus of sustainable development is not only on environment. It's also about ensuring a strong, healthy and just society. This means meeting the diverse needs of all people in existing and future communities, promoting personal well-being, social cohesion and inclusion, and creating equal opportunity.

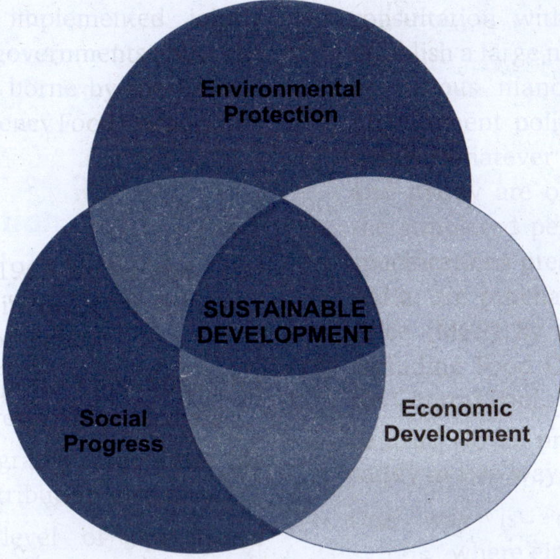

The Sustainable Development Goals (SDGs), also known as the Global Goals, were adopted by all United Nations Member States in 2015 as a universal call to action to end poverty, protect the planet and ensure that all people enjoy peace and prosperity by 2030.

The 17 SDGs are integrated that is, they recognize that action in one area will affect outcomes in others, and that development must balance social, economic and environmental sustainability.

Through the pledge to Leave No One Behind, countries have committed to fast-track progress for those furthest behind first. That is why the SDGs are designed to bring the world to several life-changing 'zeros', including zero poverty, hunger, AIDS and discrimination against women and girls.

Everyone is needed to reach these ambitious targets. The creativity, knowhow, technology and financial resources from all of society are necessary to achieve the SDGs in every context. As the lead UN development agency, UNDP support countries in achieving the SDGs. **The following are the 17 SDGs**:

- Eliminate Poverty
- Erase Hunger
- Establish Good Health and Well-Being
- Provide Quality Education
- Enforce Gender Equality
- Improve Clean Water and Sanitation
- Affordable and Clean Energy
- Create Decent Work and Economic Growth
- Increase Industry, Innovation, and Infrastructure
- Reduce Inequality
- Mobilize Sustainable Cities and Communities
- Influence Responsible Consumption and Production
- Organize Climate Action
- Develop Life Below Water
- Advance Life on Land
- Guarantee Peace, Justice, and Strong Institutions
- Build Partnerships for the Goals

Several initiatives have been taken at both the national and the sub national level to mainstream the SDGs into the policies, schemes and programmes of the Government. India has been taking several proactive climate actions to fulfil its obligations "on the basis of equality and in accordance with their common but differentiated responsibilities and respective capabilities". As mandated in the UNFCCC and its Paris Agreement, the climate actions of the developing countries would have to be supported by finance flows from the developed to the developing countries. The **Nationally Determined Contribution** (NDC) submitted by the country has been formulated keeping in mind the developmental imperatives of the country and is on a "best effort basis".

We need to strive for equity across nations and within a nation, and equity across and within the generations. The COVID-19 pandemic and the iniquitous impact of the consequent lockdown reemphasizes the fact that sustainable development is the only way forward.

Localisation of SDGs is crucial to any strategy aimed at achieving the goals under the 2030Agenda. Essentially, localising SDGs involves the process of adapting, planning, implementing and monitoring the SDGs from national to local levels by relevant institutions and stakeholders. In terms of engagement and collaboration of institutions, it is consequential how the Centre, State and Local Governments work together to achieve the SDGs at the national level; and how SDGs provide a framework for sub-national and local policy, planning and action for realization of the SDG targets at local levels. To accelerate SDG achievements, the country has adopted the approach of cooperative and competitive federalism which is based on Centre-State collaboration in nation building and healthy competition among the States in various development outcomes. The SDG India Index and Dashboard, designed and developed by NITI Aayog, is the principal tool to measure and monitor SDG performance at the national and sub-national levels. The states are institutionally empowered and positioned to achieve the SDGs with the support of the Central Government and allied institutions. Hence, the States are the key actors in the process of localisation of SDGs with the Central Government playing an enabling role.

States and UTs have created discrete institutional structures for implementation of SDGs in their own specific contexts. Several states have also created nodal mechanisms within every department and at the district levels to make coordination, convergence and data management more precise and predictable. Figure (A&B) below shows the institutional set up for SDG localisation.

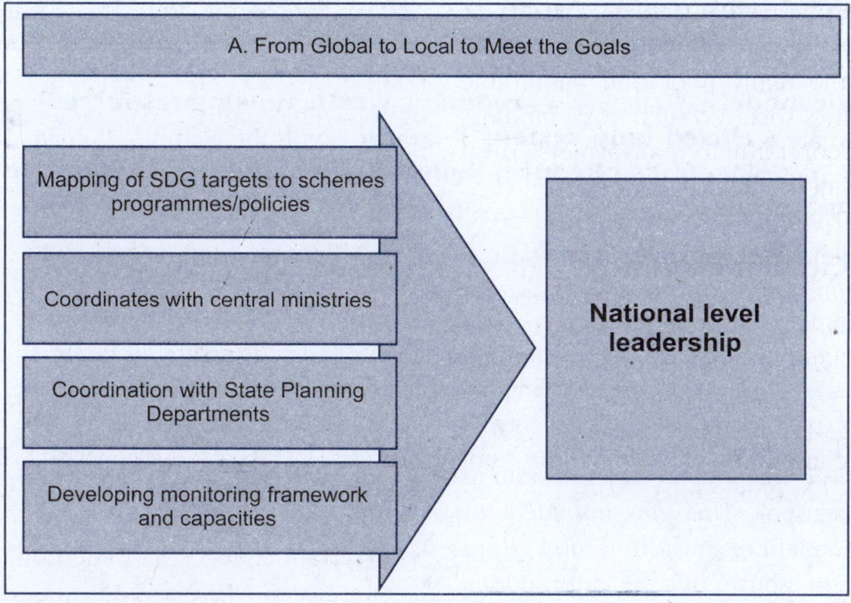

Source : NITI Aayog

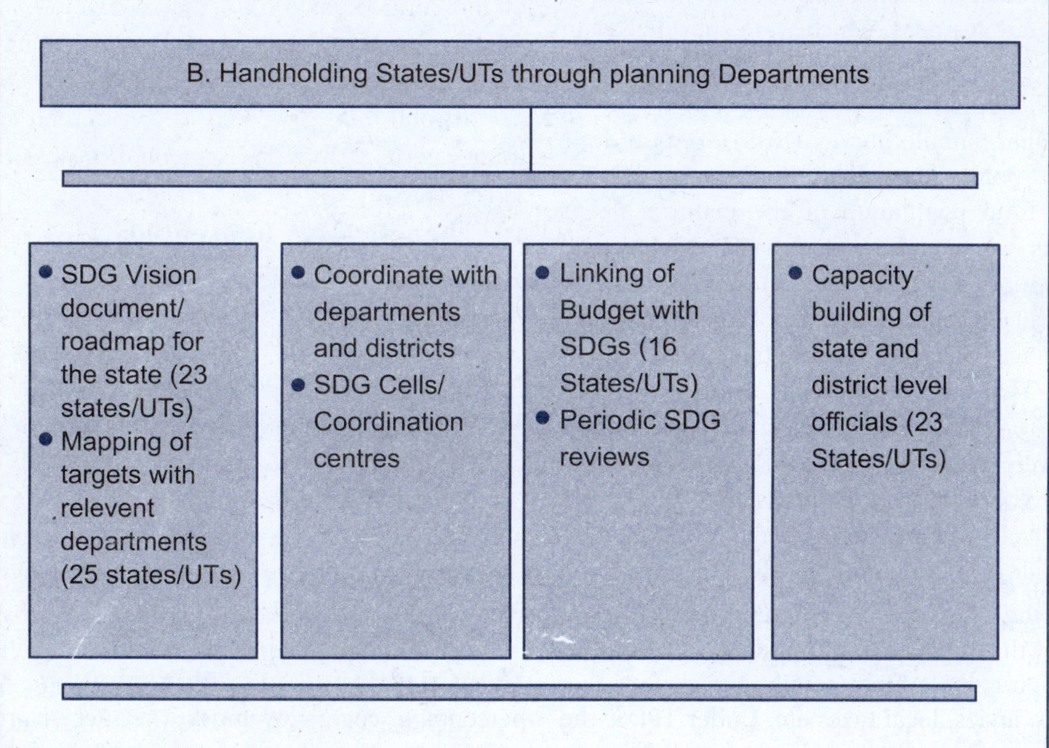

8.15 Circular Economy

It is an **economic model** that emphasises **reducing waste, reusing resources**, and **recycling materials** to create a **closed-loop system**, contrasting with the traditional linear **take-make-dispose** model. It includes **6 R's - Reduce, Reuse, Recycle, Refurbishment, Recover, and Repairing of materials**.

Example of Circular Economy

A practical example of a circular economy is the electronics industry's approach to smartphone production. Companies now focus on designing devices for easy disassembly, enabling the recovery of valuable materials like rare earth elements and metals present in it. Used phones are refurbished or recycled to extract components, reducing e-waste and conserving resources. This closed-loop system not only minimises environmental impact but also lowers production costs and supports sustainable consumption patterns.

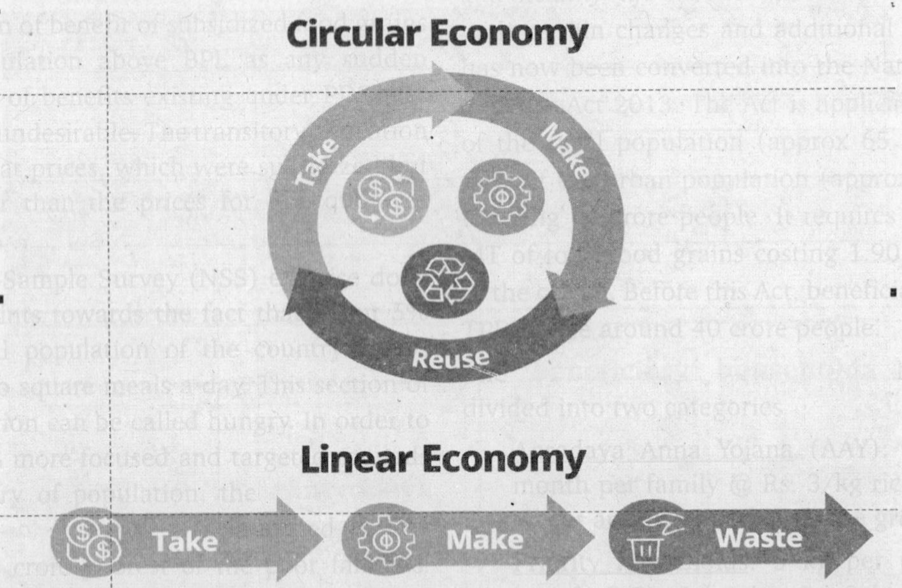

Need for Circular Economy

- With only 2% of the world's landmass and 4% of freshwater resources, a linear economy model of **'Take-Make-Dispose'** would constrain India's manufacturing sector and, consequently, the overall economy. Therefore, it is essential to recognize and revolutionize the material flow in the manufacturing process and shift towards a circular economy, which provides multipronged economic and ecological benefits.
- Rapid urbanisation, population growth, and changing consumption patterns have overwhelmed existing waste management systems, leading to environmental pollution, overflowing landfills, degradation of water resources and public health risks.

- Circular economy focuses on minimising waste while maximising utilisation and calls for a production model aiming to retain the most value to create a system that promotes sustainability, longevity, reuse, and recycling.
- Circular economy can lead to the emergence of more sustainable production and consumption patterns, thus providing opportunities for developed and developing countries to achieve economic growth and inclusive and sustainable industrial development in line with the 2030 Agenda for Sustainable Development.

India's Initiatives to Promote Circular Economy

- Plastic Waste Management Rules 2022
- E-Waste Management Rules 2022
- Battery Waste Management Rules 2022
- These rules set out targets regarding waste disposal standards for manufacturers, producers, importers, and bulk consumers, along with enabling transactions among stakeholders for **Extended Producer Responsibility (EPR)** certificates. EPR means it is the responsibility of the producer of electrical or electronic equipment for meeting recycling targets only through registered recyclers of E-Waste to ensure environmentally sound management of such waste.
- Construction and Demolition Waste Management Rules 2025
- Metals Recycling Policy

Challenges in Achieving Circular Economy

- Lack of efficient recycling technologies
- High initial costs and investment needs
- Regulatory and policy barriers
- Supply chain complexities and collaboration
- Complex product design and material variability

Comment

The key to an ***aatmanirbhar Bharat*** is sustainable growth. The need of the hour is a development model that leads to the optimum utilization of resources. With a growing population, rapid urbanization, climate change and environmental pollution, India must move towards a **circular economy**.

8.16 Socio Economic Indicators

1. Lorenz Curve and Gini Coefficient

Lorenz curve was developed by Max O Lorenz in 1905 for representing inequality of the wealth distribution of a country or province. The Lorenz curve is used to show what percentage of a nation's residents possess what percentage of that nation's wealth. While the Lorenz curve is most often used to represent economic inequality, it can be used to represent inequality in any system.

Consider the below figure where the X axis represents the percentage of households in the economy and Y axis represents the % of income that these households possess. The further away the Lorenz curve from the ideal line, represented by the diagonal, the higher the level of inequality it represents.

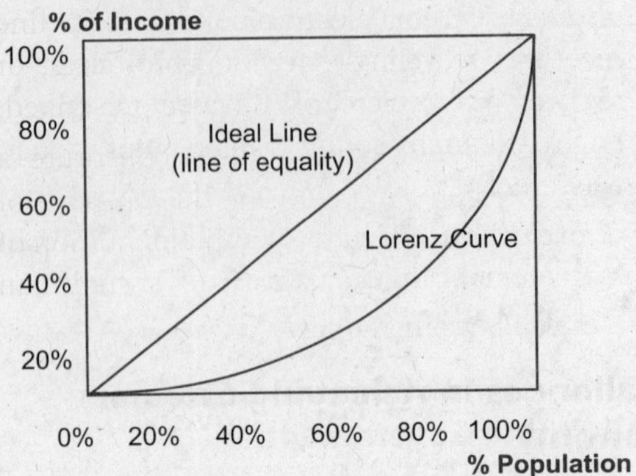

The Gini index is a measurement of the income distribution of a country's residents. This number, which ranges between 0 and 1 and is based on residents' net income helps define the gap between the rich and the poor, with 0 representing perfect equality and 1 representing perfect inequality. It is typically expressed as a percentage, referred to as the Gini coefficient.

Gini Coefficient

$$= \frac{\text{Area between the ideal line and Lorenz curve}}{\text{Total area under the ideal line}}$$

2. Kuznets Curve

The Kuznets curve is a hypothetical curve that graphs economic inequality against per capita income over the course of economic development. In the 1950s and 1960s, Simon Kuznets hypothesized that as an economy develops, market forces first increase then decrease the overall economic inequality of the society, which is illustrated by the inverted U-shape of the Kuznets curve. For instance, the hypothesis holds that in the early development of an economy, new investment opportunities increase for those who already have the capital to invest. These new investment opportunities mean that those who already hold the wealth have the opportunity to increase that wealth. Conversely, with the influx of inexpensive rural labour to the cities keeps wages down for the working class thus widening the income gap and escalating economic inequality.

The Kuznets curve implies that as a society industrializes, the centre of the economy shifts from rural areas to the cities as rural labourers such as farmers begin to migrate seeking better-paying jobs. This migration, however, results in a large rural-urban income gap and rural populations decrease as urban populations increase. But according to Kuznets' hypothesis, that same **economic inequality is expected to decrease when a certain level of average income is reached** and the processes associated with industrialization, such as democratization and the development of a welfare state, take hold.

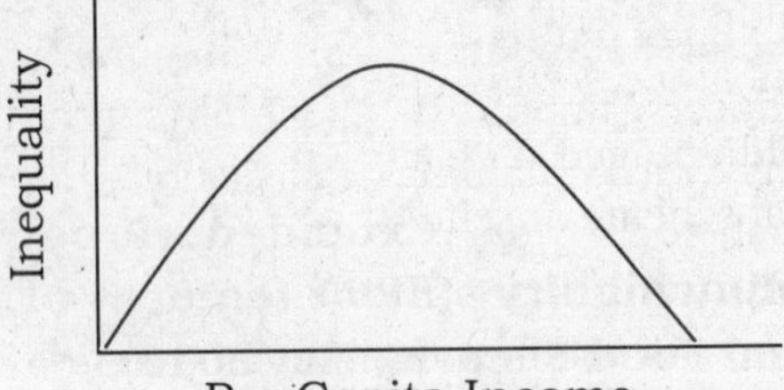

The **environmental Kuznets** curve suggests that economic development initially leads to deterioration in the environment, but after a certain level of economic growth, a society begins to improve its relationship with the environment and levels of environmental degradation reduces. It is also a U shape curve.

3. Human Development Index

The Human Development Index (HDI) was developed by Mahbub-ul-Huq and Amartya Sen. As per UNDP, HDI is a summary measure of average achievement in key dimensions of human development: a long and healthy life, being knowledgeable and have a decent standard of living. HDI is a composite index of the following three parameters:.

- Standard of Living, measured by gross national income per capita
- Health, measured by life expectancy at birth
- Education, measured by expected years of schooling for a child and mean of years of schooling for adults aged 25 years and more

All the three parameters are separately calculated on a scale of 0 to 1 and then the HDI is derived from the geometric mean of normalized indices for each of the three dimensions.

United Nations Development Programme (UNDP) publishes its annual report called "Human Development Report" (HDR), which captures the HDI. Since 2010, the HDR also includes Inequality-adjusted HDI, Gender Inequality Index (GII) and Multi-Dimensional Poverty Index (MPI).

The Inequality-adjusted Human Development Index (IHDI) is computed as a geometric mean of inequality-adjusted dimensional indices. The IHDI uses the same three dimensions as the HDI. The IHDI accounts for inequalities in HDI dimensions by "discounting" each dimension's average value according to its level of inequality. The IHDI value equals the HDI value when there is no inequality across people but falls below the HDI value as inequality rises. In this sense, the IHDI measures the level of human development when inequality is accounted for.

PREVIOUS YEARS' QUESTIONS

Prelim Questions

1. Which of the following can aid in furthering the Government's objective of inclusive growth?

(i) Promoting Self-Help Groups **[2011]**

(ii) Promoting Micro, Small and Medium Enterprises

(iii) Implementing the Right to Education Act

Select the correct answer using the codes given below:

(a) (i) only (b) (i) & (ii) only
(c) (ii) & (iii) only (d) (i), (ii) & (iii)

2. In a given year in India, official poverty lines are higher in some States than in others because **[2019]**

(a) poverty rates vary from State to State

(b) price levels vary from State to State

(c) Gross State Product varies from State to State

(d) quality of public distribution varies from State to State

3. Consider the following statements **[2025]**

Statement I: Circular economy reduces the emissions of greenhouse gases.

Statement II: Circular economy reduces the use of raw materials as inputs.

Statement III: Circular economy reduces wastage in the production process.

Which one of the following is correct in respect of the above statements?

(a) Both Statement II and Statement III are correct and both of them explain Statement I

(b) Both Statement II and Statement III are correct but only one of them explains Statement I

(c) Only one of the Statements II and III is correct and that explains Statement I

(d) Neither Statement II nor Statement III is correct

ANSWERS

1. (d), 2. (b), 3. (a)

Main Questions

1. It is argued that the strategy of inclusive growth is intended to meet the objectives of inclusiveness and sustainability together. Comment on this statement. **[2019]**
2. Explain intra-generational and inter-generational issues of equity from the perspective of inclusive growth and sustainable development. **[2020]**
3. Is inclusive growth possible under market economy? State the significance of financial inclusion in achieving economic growth in India. **[2022]**
4. "Economic growth in the recent past has been led by increase in labour productivity". Explain this statement. Suggest the growth pattern that will lead to creation of more jobs without compromising labour productivity. **[2022]**
5. Most of the unemployment in India is structural in nature. Examine the methodology adopted to compute unemployment in the country and suggest improvements. **[2023]**
6. Distinguish between 'care economy' and 'monetized economy'. How can care economy be brought into monetized economy through women empowerment? **[2023]**
7. Examine the pattern and trend of public expenditure on social services in the post-reforms period in India. To what extent this has been in consonance with achieving the objective of inclusive growth? **[2024]**
8. Discuss the merits and demerits of the four 'Labour Codes' in the context of labour market reforms in India. What has been the progress so far in this regard? **[2024]**
9. Distinguish between the Human Development Index (HDI) and the Inequality-adjusted Human Development Index (IHDI) with special reference to India. Why is the IHDI considered a better indicator of inclusive growth? **[2025]**

◈◈◈

9 Subsidies

9.1 Introduction

Subsidies are measured as costs incurred by the government through budgetary resources for the provision of goods which are not classified as **"public goods"**. Public Goods has the following two characteristics:

- Non rival: Consumption by somebody does not reduce the availability of that good for others
- Non excludable: No feasible way of excluding anyone from enjoying the benefits of that good

For example, police services, border security services, etc. are public goods.

Subsidies can be classified based in various ways:

I		II		III		IV	
Consumer	Producer	Direct	Indirect	Explicit	Implicit	Social	Economic
Benefit provided to consumers Ex: LPG	Benefit provided to producers Ex: MSP to farmers	Direct payment in cash Ex: LPG	Providing goods and services below market price & govt. procurement in excess of market price Ex: Fertilizer	Specified in the budget document or through budgetary resources Ex: PDS	By providing subsidized public services and are not provided in budget Ex: Railway	Subsidy given for social services Ex: Health	Subsidy given for economic services Ex: Power

The various subsidies given by Central government are: health, education, housing, social welfare and nutrition, urban development, water supply and sanitation, welfare of SCs, STs, agriculture and allied activities etc.

Major Explicit Subsidies of Central Government

Rs. Crore	Food	Fertilizer	Fuel	Interest	Total
2025-26	Rs. 2.28 lakh cr	Rs. 1.86 lakh cr	Rs. 0.15 lakh cr	Rs. 0.25 lakh cr	**Rs. 4.54 lakh cr**
2026-27	Rs. 2.28 lakh cr	Rs. 1.71 lakh cr	Rs. 0.12 lakh cr	Rs. 0.27 lakh cr	**Rs. 4.38 lakh cr**

9.2 Different Ways of Disbursing/implementing Subsidies

Economic growth has historically been good for the poor, both directly because it raises incomes, and indirectly, because it gives the State resources to provide public services and social safety nets that the poor need. Government uses these resources to help the poor by giving various kinds of subsidies which has formed an important part of the anti-poverty discourse in India and the government's own policy initiatives.

Since independence government is giving 'price subsidies' to the poor. From 2014 onwards, with the help of Jan Dhan Account, Aadhar and Mobile (JAM), Government started shifting to 'DBT' for various kinds of subsidies. From 2019, it has also started giving 'Income Support' to farmers. So, support/subsides to the poor can be given in three ways viz. price subsidies, Direct Benefit Transfer (DBT) and Income Support.

9.2.1 Price Subsidies

Though price subsidies have helped the poor households fight inflation and price volatility but price subsidies have not transformed the living standards of the poor.

The following are various issues associated with **price subsidies:**

1. Price subsidies are often regressive:

Regressive means a rich household benefit more from the price subsidy than a poor household. As various state governments give subsidy on electricity, and since richer households consume more electricity than poor, it means richer households are enjoying more subsidy than the poor. The same stands true for water and LPG cylinders as the consumption by relatively rich households is more as compared to poor.

2. Price subsidies distort markets in a way that ultimately hurts the poor:

In a market economy, prices play a key role in allocating scarce resources to different sectors. The government provides subsidies for wheat and rice by purchasing it at Minimum Support Prices. Due to the guaranteed procurement of these crops, farmers are not willing to grow non-MSP supported crops such as pulses, oilseeds, onions etc leading to under cultivation of these crops. The resultant supply demand mismatch raises prices of non-MSP supported crops and makes them more volatile. This contributes to food price inflation that disproportionately hurts poor households who tend to have uncertain income streams and lack the assets to weather economic shocks.

3. Leakages undermine the effectiveness of price/product subsidies:

Price subsidies are prone to leakages and wastes a lot of government resources which could otherwise be used for other welfare programmes. Consider the example of fertilizer subsidy which is provided by selling the fertilizers at below the market price. The price of subsidized Urea in the domestic market is around Rs. 5/kg and in the international market is around Rs. 20/kg. Now the agencies involved in selling urea in the domestic market, divert the Urea in the neighbouring countries of Nepal & Bangladesh (rather than selling to the intended beneficiaries) where they fetch international price and they also recover the difference of Rs 15/kg (Rs. 20/kg - Rs. 5/kg) as subsidy from the government. In the same way some Urea is also sold to chemical companies in India which uses it as inputs to make other products. *(Now Government has introduced Aadhar based authentication for purchase of Urea).*

9.2.2 Direct Benefit Transfer (DBT)

In case of DBT, Govt. allows people to purchase/ sale products from/in the market and it directly transfers the money in their account. The following are important features of DBT:

1. Cash transfers increases the effectiveness of anti-poverty programmes by reducing the number of government departments and costs involved in the distribution process.
2. When government transfers the cash in the beneficiaries Aadhaar linked bank account and he/ she purchase the product at market price then it removes the possibility of leakages and diversion.
3. Cash transfers frees up the prices of various goods and services bought and sold in the market which then perform their role of efficiently allocating resources in the economy and boosting long run growth.

By implementing DBT in LPG subsidy, government has been able to save more than Rs. 10,000 core a year.

9.2.3 Income Support

The most important feature of income support is that, the poor don't need to purchase/sell specific items to get this kind of support. Government transfers certain amount to the public and they will be free to decide what to do with that money. This is not the case with price subsidies and DBT where the beneficiary needs to purchase/ sale the specific item to get the benefit of subsidy. Because of this feature, income support does not distort the market. Income support can be given to a class of population (for example PM-KISAN is given to farmers) or it may be extended to the entire population, in such case it is called Universal Basic Income (UBI).

Universal Basic Income (UBI) is a radical and compelling paradigm shift in thinking about both social justice and a productive economy. It could be to the twenty first century what civil and political rights were to the twentieth. It is premised on the idea that a just society needs to guarantee to each individual a minimum income which they can count on, and which provides the necessary material foundation for a life with access to basic goods and a life of dignity. A universal basic income is, like many rights, unconditional and universal: it requires that every person should have a right to a basic income to cover their needs, just by virtue of being citizens. UBI has the following characteristics:

- **Periodic:** Paid at regular intervals and not as a onetime grant
- **Cash Payment:** It is paid in appropriate medium a llowing those who receive it to decide what they spend it on. It is therefore not paid in kind or in vouchers dedicated to a specific use.
- **Individual:** It is paid on an individual basis and not to household
- **Universal:** It is paid to all without means test
- **Unconditional:** It is paid without a requirement to work or to demonstrate willingness-to-work

There are certain misconceptions/arguments against UBI

- Whether UBI reduces the incentive to work? The levels at which UBI is likely to be pegged are going to be minimal guarantees at best; they are unlikely to crowd incentives to work.

- Moral Hazard: Would a UBI reduce labour supply? Another argument against UBI is the moral hazard i.e., free money makes people lazy and they drop out of the labour market.
- Would UBI promote vice (temptation goods)? Detractors of UBI argue that, as a cash transfer programme, this policy will promote spending on social evils such as alcohol, tobacco etc.

UBI shall not be framed as a transfer payment from the rich to the poor. The idea of UBI is that we have a right to a minimum income, merely by virtue of being citizens. It is the acknowledgment of the economy as a common project. This right requires that the basic economic structure be configured in a way that every individual gets a basic income.

Difference between Price Subsidy, DBT and Income Support

Price Subsidy	DBT	Income Support
• Regressive • Distortive • Leakage	• Regressive • Distortive • No leakage	• Not regressive • Not distortive • No leakage

9.3 Fuel Subsidies

Fuel Subsidies earlier used to be given on four items viz. LPG, Kerosene, Petrol, Diesel.

1. **Petrol and Diesel:** Petrol and Diesel prices were deregulated in 2002 and are being sold at the market prices and there is no subsidy on petrol and diesel.
2. **LPG:** Government is giving LPG subsidy through DBT to those consumers whose taxable income is less than or equal to Rs. 10 lakhs. So, if a consumer (or his/her spouse) taxable income is more than Rs. 10 lakh he/she will be excluded. Consumers purchase LPG cylinders at the market price and Government transfers the subsidy amount into their account only up to 12 cylinders a year.
3. **Kerosene:** Central Government has eliminated the Kerosene subsidy which has traditionally been used to meet the lighting and cooking needs, especially in rural areas. Government has decided to phase out use of kerosene for cooking and lighting in view of the increasing coverage of electricity for lighting needs and LPG as a clean cooking fuel. Post Saubhagya (Pradhan Mantri Sahaj bijli har ghar yojana) and Ujjwala Yojana the use of kerosene is steadily going down.

Out of 37 states/UTs, 11 states/UTs are kerosene free i.e no PDS Kerosene is allocated to these states/ UTs by Ministry of Petroleum and Natural Gas (MOP&NG). The balance states/UTs are allocated PDS Kerosene by MOP&NG on a quarterly basis. Kerosene is distributed through PDS and is sold at market price with zero central subsidy. The allocation varies from State to State depending on factors like LPG penetration, non-lifting of PDS Kerosene, voluntary requests for surrender/reduction. State Government of Tamil Nadu is still subsidizing kerosene through state subsidy.

Effective from 1st March, 2020, the retail selling price of PDS Kerosene is being maintained at NIL under-recovery level on pan India basis and is made available to the states at market prices.

9.4 Fertilizer Subsidies

The four major fertilizers consumed in India are Urea, Diammonium Phosphate (DAP), Muriate of Potash (MoP) and Complex Fertilizers. Urea prices are regulated/fixed by the Govt, but the prices of DAP, MoP and Complex Fertilizers have been deregulated (market driven).

Fertilizers provides three major nutrients which increase agriculture yields. The optimal N:P:K ratio varies across soil types but is generally around 4:2:1.

With the objective of sustainable agricultural growth, Government of India is providing subsidized fertilizers to the farmers since 1970's. The subsidized fertilizers such as urea (N), DAP (P) and MOP (K)earlier used to be sold under the **Retention Pricing Scheme (RPS).** Under this scheme fertilizer manufactures used to get fix return of 12% on their investments and used to sell the fertilizer at the govt. notified price. This had two major drawbacks: -

- The manufacturers need to submit their audited costs to the government based on which government used to reimburse them the net cost plus 12% return on investment. This motivated the companies to inflate their costs and increased the scope of corruption.
- There was no motivation for the manufactures to reduce their costs and become efficient as they used to get all the cost adjusted/ reimbursed from the government.

But now there are separate mechanism for Urea subsidy and DAP & MOP subsidy.

Urea Subsidy

Under the "**new urea policy 2015**":

- Government implemented the pooling of gas for urea from 1st July 2015 onwards. Under this policy the domestic gas is pooled with imported Re-gasified Liquified Natural Gas (R-LNG) to provide natural gas at uniform delivered price to all-Natural Gas grid connected urea manufacturing plants for the purpose of manufacturing of urea.
- All the gas-based urea plants have been placed in three categories based on group specific energy norms *(how much gas is required to produce a particular quantity of urea)*. Urea plants falling in same category will be getting the same amount of subsidy per KG as fixed by the government (based on normative cost of each group plants), no matter what is their actual cost of production. This will force plants to become more efficient as the subsidy will be same for each plant within a group and a plant being more efficient or having lesser cost of production will be more profitable.

Following are some of the benefits of "New Urea Policy 2015":

- The policy is expected to maximize indigenous urea production with additional production of around 2 MT annually which will reduce import dependency in urea sector.
- It will promote energy efficiency in urea units because of group based norms which will ultimately reduce the subsidy burden on the government.
- Savings in energy will reduce the carbon-footprint and would thus be more environment friendly.
- Urea units would adopt best available technology in the world and will become globally more competitive.

From May 2015, Government of India has made it mandatory for all indigenous urea manufacturers (and importers of urea too) to produce 100% **neem coated urea**, so that farmers are benefitted. Neem coated urea is required less in quantity with same plot size and gives higher crop yields. Underground water contamination due to leaching of urea also gets reduced with neem coating since nitrogen in the neem coated urea gets released to plants very slowly. Neem coated urea is not fit for industrial use, so chances of its illegal diversion to industries will also be lesser. Farmers pay an additional price of only Rs.14/- per bag of neem coated urea.

Issues with Urea Subsidy: Presently Govt. **intervenes** in the production and distribution of urea in the following ways:

- Govt. sets a controlled Maximum Retail Price (MRP) at which urea must be sold to the farmers which is Rs. 5.36/kg (45 kg/ bag) excluding tax (imported/ international price is approximately Rs. 30/kg).
- Government provides subsidy to urea plants based on the difference between the MRP and cost of production (group-based norms) and is paid to the fertilizer company.
- Due to the limited availability of domestic gas, urea players mostly depend on costly imported gas for production. And only three companies are allowed to import urea into India (*canalisation*).
- About half of the movement of fertilizer is directed i.e., the government tells manufacturers and importers how much to import and where to sell their urea.

Thus, nearly all the actors - consumers, producers, importers, and distributors are controlled by the government. The movement plan for urea is given by the government every month to urea suppliers, to ensure its timely and adequate availability, in all parts of the country which means that the central **government controls the fertilizer supply chain**. This has led to distortions feeding upon each other and together creating an environment leading to leakage, less availability for small farmers, under-pricing leading to inefficient consumption.

Nano Urea

Liquid Nano Urea has been developed and Patented by IFFCO. IFFCO Nano Urea is the only Nano fertilizer approved by the Government of India and included in the Fertilizer Control Order (FCO). To ensure adequate availability of right quality of fertilizers at right time and at right price to farmers, Fertilizer was declared as an Essential Commodity and Fertilizer Control Order (FCO) was promulgated under Section 3 of Essential Commodities Act,1955 to regulate, trade, price, quality and distribution of fertilizers in the country.

- Application of 1 bottle (half litre) of Nano Urea can effectively replace at least 1 bag of Urea (45 kg).
- Presently there is no subsidy on Nano Urea.
- When sprayed on leaves, Nano Urea easily enters through stomata and other openings and is assimilated by the plant cells. It is easily distributed through the phloem from source to sink inside the plant as per its need.
- Liquid Nano Urea contains 4% nitrogen by volume and comes in the form of nanoparticle.
- Its efficiency is 85%-90% as compared to 25% for conventional urea.
- Unutilized nitrogen is stored in the plant vacuole and is slowly released for proper growth and development of the plant.

- Small size (20-50 nm) of Nano Urea increases its availability to crop by more than 80%.

DAP (P) and MOP (K) and Complex Fertilizers (NPK) [Nutrient Based Subsidy]

The subsidy regime in DAP and MOP fertilizers is called Nutrient Based Subsidy (NBS) which is in effect since 2010. Under this regime, the producers and importers of DAP and MOP fertilizers receive subsidy based on the amount of nutrient (N, P & K) present in a given amount of fertilizer. Per kg of subsidies on DAP and MOP fertilizers are hence fixed by the government every year and they do not vary with the market prices. The market prices (at which farmers purchase) of these fertilizers are deregulated (but are adjusted with fixed nutrient subsidy given by the government) i.e., manufacturers are free to decide the market price at which they want to sell. This means that the producers and importers are free to sell these fertilizers at any price but since they receive a fixed subsidy from the government and due to competition in the market, they reduce the market price in proportion to the subsidy. The government involvement in DAP and MOP fertilizers is limited to paying producers and importers a fixed nutrient-based subsidy which works out to be roughly 35 percent of the cost of production.

The department of fertilizer has fixed the subsidies for the various nutrients for the year 2020-21 at the following rates: nitrogen (N) at Rs 18.78 per kg, Phosphorus (P) at Rs 14.88 per kg, Potash (K) at Rs 10.11 per kg and Sulphur (S) at Rs. 2.37 per kg. DAP contains higher proportion of phosphorus and MOP contains higher proportion of Potassium but these fertilizers also contain in some proportion other nutrients i.e., N, P, K and S. Based on the proportion of nutrients present in the fertilizers, the per Kg subsidy on DAP and MoP can be calculated. The fertiliser companies are required to print Maximum Retail Price (MRP) along with applicable subsidy on the fertilizer bags clearly. Any sale above the printed MRP is punishable under the Essential Commodities Act. The MRP for DAP is currently hovering at Rs. 24000/tonne and for MOP it is Rs. 16000/tonne approximately and it stands deregulated.

Nano DAP

- IFFCO Nano DAP is an efficient source of available nitrogen (N) and phosphorus (P_2O_5) for all the crops and helps in correcting the Nitrogen & Phosphorus deficiencies in standing crops.
- Nano DAP formulation contains Nitrogen (8.0% N w/v) and Phosphorus (16.0 % P_2O_5 w/v). Nano DAP (Liquid) has advantage in terms of surface area to volume as its particle size is less than 100 Nanometre (nm). This unique property enables it to enter easily inside the seed surface or through stomata and other plant openings.
- Nano DAP (Liquid) is indigenous and non-subsidised fertiliser.
- Nutrient use efficiency is more than 90 percent under optimum field conditions.

DBT in Fertilizer

In January 2018, Government implemented DBT facility for fertilizer subsidies in all the States and Union Territories (UTs). The DBT model in fertilizers is different from the conventional system of DBT being implemented in LPG. Under DBT system in fertilizer subsidies, the farmers/beneficiaries will continue to receive Urea at statutory subsidised prices (Rs. 5.36/kg) and P & K fertilizers at subsidized prices in the market. The fertilizer companies which earlier used to receive subsidy on receipt of fertilizers at the district level, will now get subsidy only after the fertilizers are sold to farmers/ beneficiaries by the retailers through Point of

Sale (PoS) machines (linked to the Department of Fertilizers' e-Urvarak DBT portal) through biometric authentication by Aadhar Card or Voter ID Card or Kisan Credit Card.

Government has done a study to implement Direct Cash Transfer, DCT (which is basically the DBT being implemented in case of LPG) where farmers will be purchasing the fertilizers at the market price and govt. will be transferring the cash amount in the farmers account. But most of the farmers do not want this mechanism of DCT, as the farmers will have to pay upfront market price which may be quite high and they will have to wait for the government money in their account which is generally delayed and in some cases it has not come. To remove this problem of upfront payment of market price by farmers, government is planning to create e-wallet account for every farmer and transfer the money before the sowing season in the e-wallet of every farmer and upon the actual purchase by farmers it will be adjusted and carry forwarded to next year.

Proposed Reforms in Fertilizer Sector

- Transfer Rs. 5000 to Rs. 6000 per farmer annually in lieu of fertilizer subsidies
- Become self-reliant in Fertilizer Production
- Implement NBS model for Urea also
- Develop alternative sources of nutrient for plants i.e., non-chemical fertilizers
- Improve fertilizer efficiency through need-based use. For example, Nano Urea developed by IFFCO

Recently, Ministry of Chemicals and Fertilizers, Govt. of India has launched two important schemes:

1. Pradan Mantri Kisan Samruddhi Kendras (PMKSK)

PM inaugurated 600 Pradan Mantri Kisan Samruddhi Kendras under the Ministry of Chemicals & Fertilisers. Under the scheme, the retail fertiliser shops in the country will be converted into PMKSK in a phased manner. PMKSK will cater to a wide variety of needs of the farmers and provide:

- Agri-inputs (fertilisers, seeds, implements),
- Testing facilities for soil, seeds, and fertilisers;
- Generate awareness among farmers;
- Provide information regarding various government schemes and
- Ensure regular capacity building of retailers at block/district level outlets.
- PMKSKs are not merely sales centres for fertiliser but a mechanism for establishing a deep bond with the farmers of the country.
- More than 3.3 lakh retail fertiliser shops are planned to be converted into PMKSK.

2. Pradhan Mantri Bhartiya Jan Urvarak Pariyojana - One Nation One Fertiliser (ONOF)

- Under ONOF companies are allowed to display their name, brand, logo and other relevant product information only on one-third space of their bags.
- On the remaining two-thirds space, the "Bharat" brand and Pradhanmantri Bharatiya Jan Urvarak Pariyojana logo will have to be shown.
- The single brand name for UREA, DAP, MOP and Complex Fertilizers (NPK) etc. would be BHARAT UREA, BHARAT DAP, BHARAT MOP and BHARAT NPK etc. respectively for all Fertiliser Companies, State Trading Entities (STEs) and Fertiliser Marketing Entities (FMEs).
- It will bring about uniformity in fertiliser brands across the country
- The farmer will get rid of all kinds of confusion about the quality of the fertiliser and its availability.

3. PM Programme for Restoration, Awareness Generation, Nourishment and Amelioration of Mother – Earth (PM-PRANAM)

- Centre would incentivise those States which would adopt alternative fertilizers (like Nano-Fertilizers and Bio-Fertilizers) with the subsidy that was saved by reducing the use of chemical fertilizers
- For example, if a State was using 10 lakh tonnes of conventional fertilizers and reduces its consumption by three lakh tonnes, then the subsidy saving would be around Rs. 3,000 crores. Out of that subsidy savings, the Centre will give 50% of it to that State Government

9.5 Food Subsidy

Food subsidy is being implemented jointly by Central and State governments but the major financial burden is borne by the Central government through its agency Food Corporation of India (FCI).

9.5.1 Food Corporation of India(FCI)

The FCI was set up in 1965 under the Food Corporation's Act 1964, in order to fulfil the following objectives of food policy.

- Effective price support operations for safeguarding the interests of the farmers
- Distribution of food grains throughout the country for public distribution system
- Maintaining safety level of operational and buffer stocks of food grains to ensure national food security

Since its inception, FCI has played a significant role in India's success in transforming the crisis management-oriented food security into a stable security system. FCI ensures effective market intervention thereby keeping the prices under check.

To achieve its objectives, FCI carries out the following functions:

1. **Procurement:** To facilitate the procurement of food grains (wheat and paddy), FCI and various state agencies in consultation with the State governments establish a large number of purchase centres at various mandis and key points. The procurement policy is **open ended**. That means, whatever (without any limit) wheat and paddy are offered by farmers, within the stipulated period & conforming to the specifications prescribed by Government of India, are purchased at Minimum Support Price (MSP) by the Government agencies including Food Corporation of India (FCI) for Central Pool.

   Central Govt. procures wheat and rice/ paddy in two ways:

   - One way is "Centralized Procurement System" where either FCI procures or it asks States to procure and hand over the stock to FCI and FCI pays for it. And then FCI stores and distributes under NFSA.
   - The second is "Decentralized Procurement System" where Centre has asked States to procure, store and distribute under NFSA and other welfare schemes and Centre (FCI) pays to States.

2. **Storage and Contract:** FCI provides scientific storage facility for the million tonnes of food grains procured by it. In order to provide easy physical access in deficit, remote and inaccessible areas, the FCI has

a network of storage depots strategically located all over India. These depots include silos, godowns and an indigenous method called Cover and Plinth (CAP).

Construction of godowns has been undertaken in PPP mode in 24 states under Private Entrepreneurs Guarantee (PEG) Scheme through the private sector as well as the Central Warehousing Corporation (CWC) and the State Warehousing Corporation (SWC).

The Government of India has also approved action plan with construction of steel silos in the country for a capacity of 100 LMT in public private partnership (PPP) mode with a view to modernize storage infrastructure and improve shelf life of stored food grains.

3. **Moving and Transportation:** The food grains are procured from the surplus states and transported to the deficit states of north-east and southern states. The food grain surplus is confined to the northern states and transportation involves long distance throughout the country. Stocks procured in the market and purchase centres is first collected in the nearest depots and from there dispatched to the recipient states in limited time.

4. **Buffer Stocks:** FCI maintains buffer stock (central pool) for the following purposes:
   - To feed the Targeted Public Distribution System (TPDS) and other schemes
   - To ensure food security during the periods when production is short of normal demand during bad agricultural years
   - To stabilize prices during production shortfall through open market sales

The FCI is mandated to keep approximately 25 Million Tonnes (MT) of buffer stock (wheat and rice combined) in **central pool** including strategic reserve of 2 MT of rice and 3 MT of wheat. But on an average FCI holds more than double the mandated stock leading to huge storage cost and wastage. The reason being FCI is bound to procure all the stock which the farmers are bringing in the mandis but only a limited amount is required to be distributed under National Food Security Act. The FCI also sells the food grains in the domestic market as well as exports it too from the central pool.

There has been a paradigm shift on food (cereal) front between the time when FCI was created and today. India has moved from being a food scarce country to a food surplus country with a substantial increase in production and has emerged as a net exporter of cereals. The Government policies of assured procurement and distribution gave the right incentives to increase production at that time. But the current food grain economy is, however, riddled with various economic inefficiencies in procurement, storage, transportation and distribution. The farmers are deriving their signals, not from the demand patterns in the market but from the Government policies of procurement and distribution policies for grains.

These policies, therefore, need to move on now to incentivize diversification and environmentally sustainable production. The farmers need to be empowered through direct investment subsidies and cash transfers, which are crop neutral and do not interfere with the cropping decisions of the farmers.

Minimum Support Price (MSP): The rate announced by GoI at which purchases are made from the farmers by GoI and State governments and their agencies for the central pool. The MSP is same for the entire country and there is no limit for procurement in terms of volume/ quantity provided that stock satisfies Fair Average Quality (FAQ).

Central Issue Price (CIP): The price at which food grains (wheat and rice) are issued to the State governments/ UTs from the central pool at uniform prices for distribution under Targeted Public Distribution System (TPDS)/NFSA. CIP is fixed by Department of Food and Public Distribution, Ministry of Consumer Affairs, Food and Public Distribution.

Economic Cost: The cost incurred by the central government by way of procurement (at MSP), storage, transportation and distribution (to the nearest depot).

Consumer Subsidy: The difference between the economic cost and Central Issue Price (CIP) is called the consumer subsidy and is borne by the central government.

In addition to the above, the FCI maintains large buffer stocks of food grains (for future exigencies) which entails a substantial carrying/storage cost and is termed as buffer subsidy. Consumer subsidy and the buffer subsidy together add up to the total food subsidy of Govt. of India.

9.5.2 Public Distribution System (PDS)

The concept of Public Distribution System (PDS) in the country evolved during the 2nd World War (1942) due to the shortage of food grains and the government intervention in the distribution of food started with certain essential commodities. During the critical food shortage of 1960's (China war 1962, Pakistan war 1965, two draughts of 1965, 1966) PDS focussed on distribution of food grains mainly in urban areas. In light of green revolution, as the national agricultural production grew, the outreach of PDS was extended to tribal blocks and areas of high incidence of poverty in the 1970's and 1980's.

PDS has evolved as a system of management of scarcity and for distribution of food grains at affordable prices. Over the years and with every lap of five-year planning, it has become an important part of government's policy for management of food economy in the country. **PDS is incremental in nature** and is not intended to make available the entire requirement of any of the commodities distributed under it to a household or a section of the society. Under PDS, commodities distributed mainly are wheat, rice, sugar and kerosene but some states also distribute pulses, edible oils, iodized salt, spices etc.

PDS till 1992, was a general entitlement scheme for all consumers without any specific target. Revamped PDS was launched in June 1992 in 1775 blocks throughout the country. RPDS was launched with a view to strengthen and streamline the PDS as well as to improve its reach in the far flung, hilly, remote and inaccessible areas where a substantial section of the poor live.

Targeted Public Distribution System (TPDS) In June 1997, Govt. of India launched the TPDS with focus on the poor. Under the TPDS, States were required to formulate and implement fool proof arrangements for identification of the poor for delivery of food grains and for its distribution in a transparent and accountable manner at the Fair Price Shop (FPS) level.

The scheme when introduced was intended to benefit 6 crore poor families. To work out the population below the poverty line under the TPDS, it was decided to adopt a methodology used by the expert group set up by planning commission under the chairmanship of Prof. Lakdawala. Guidelines were issued in which states were advised to identify the BPL families by involving the Gram Panchayats and Nagar Palikas. While doing so, the thrust would be to include the really poor and vulnerable sections of the society such as landless agricultural labourers, marginal farmers, rural artisans/ craftsmen such as potters, weavers, blacksmiths, carpenters etc. in the rural areas and slum dwellers and persons earning their livelihood on daily basis in the informal sector like potters, ricksha-pullers, cart pullers, fruit and flower sellers on the pavement etc. in urban areas.

The quantum of food grains in excess of the requirement of BPL was provided to the state as "Transitory Allocation". This was intended for continuation of benefit of subsidized food grains to the population above BPL as any sudden withdrawal of benefits existing under PDS was considered undesirable. The transitory allocation was issued at prices, which were subsidized but were higher than the prices for BPL quota of food grains.

A National Sample Survey (NSS) exercise done in 2000 points towards the fact that about 5% of the total population of the country sleeps without two square meals a day. This section of the population can be called hungry. In order to make TPDS more focused and targeted towards this category of population, the **"Antyodaya Anna Yojana" (AAY)** was launched in Dec 2000 for 1 crore poorest of the poor families. They were to be provided 35 Kg per month per family of wheat and rice at Rs. 2/kg and 3/kg respectively. Later on, this scheme was expanded to include 1.5 crore more families.

Under the TPDS scheme, the end retail price is fixed by the States/ UTs after taking into account margins for wholesalers/ retailers, transportation charges, levies, local taxes etc. Under TPDS, the states were requested to issue food grains at a difference of not more than 50 paise per Kg over and above the Central Issue Price (CIP) for distribution to BPL families. For AAY, the end retail price was to be retained at CIP i.e., Rs. 2/kg for wheat and Rs. 3/kg for rice. There was no restriction on APL and other welfare schemes under TPDS and were to be issued at end retail price above CIP as decided by the State.

9.5.3 National Food Security Act (NFSA) 2013

(Food security is defined as "when all people, at all times, have physical and economic access to sufficient, safe and nutritious food that meets their dietary needs and food preferences for an active, and healthy life"). The earlier TPDS scheme, with certain changes and additional incentives, has now been converted into the National Food Security Act 2013. The Act is applicable to 75% of the rural population (approx 65 crore) and 50% of the urban population (approx 19 crore) totalling 84 crore people. It requires around 60 MT of total food grains costing 1.90 lakh crore to the centre. Before this Act, beneficiaries under TPDS were around 40 crore people.

The **beneficiary households** have been divided into two categories.

- Antodaya Anna Yojana (AAY): 35 kg per month per family @ Rs. 3/kg rice, Rs. 2/kg wheat and Rs. 1 per kg coarse grains.
- Priority households: 5 kg per person per month @ Rs. 3/kg rice, Rs. 2/kg wheat and Rs. 1 per kg coarse grains.

[*Starting from* 1st *January* 2023, *Central Government has started providing the foodgrains (rice, wheat and coarse grains) for free at zero prices under NFSA* 2013]

Identification of Households: The percentage coverage under the Act in rural and urban areas for each State shall, subject to the cap of 75% rural population and 50%

urban population, be determined by the Central Government and the total number of persons to be covered in such rural and urban areas of the State shall be calculated on the basis of the population estimates as per the census of which the relevant figures have been published.

The State government shall, within the persons determined above, identify:

- The households to be covered under the Antyodaya Anna Yojana in accordance with the guidelines applicable to the said scheme.
- The remaining households as priority households in accordance with such guidelines as the State government may specify.

The Act provides additional benefits to:

- Pregnant women and lactating mothers: Free meal during pregnancy and up to six months after child birth through Aanganwadi and Rs. 6000 in instalments
- Children aged 6 months to 6 years: Free meal at local Aanganwadi
- Children aged 6 years to 14 years: Mid-day meal scheme at school

The following are salient features of the National Food Security Act 2013:

1. Women Empowerment:

- The eldest woman who is not less than 18 years of age, in every eligible household, shall be the head of the household for the purpose of ration cards.
- When no woman above 18 but a female less than 18, a male member (eldest) shall get the ration card and at attaining the age of 18, the female shall get the ration card.

2. Grievance Redressal Mechanism:

- Every State government shall put in place an internal grievance redressal mechanism which may include call centres, help line numbers, designation of nodal officers, or such other mechanism as may be prescribed.
- Every State government shall constitute a State Food Commission for the purpose of monitoring and review of implementation of this Act which shall consist of a chairman and five other members.

3. Obligations of Central Government and State Government:

- State governments shall take delivery of food grains from the designated depots of the Central government in the respective State by paying the FCI the Central Issue Price (CIP) i.e., Rs. 3/kg rice, Rs. 2/kg wheat and Rs. 1/kg coarse grains, organize intra State allocations for delivery of the allocated food grains through their authorized agencies at the door step of each FPS and ensure actual delivery or supply of the food grains to the entitled persons at the above-mentioned prices.
- Central govt. shall provide the assistance to the State government in meeting the expenditure incurred by it towards intra-state movement, handling of food grains and margins (profit) paid to Fair Price Shop (FPS) dealers in accordance with the norms and manner as may be prescribed by the Central govt.

4. Miscellaneous Provisions:

- The provisions of this Act shall not preclude the Central government or the State government from continuing or formulating other food-based welfare schemes.
- State government may continue with or may formulate food or nutrition-based plans or schemes providing for benefits higher than the benefits provided under this Act, from its own resources.

- The Central government or the State government as the case may be shall be liable for a claim by any person entitled under this Act, except in the case of war, flood, drought, fire, cyclone, earthquake affecting the regular supply of food grains or meals to such person under this Act.
- The Central government, the State government and the local authorities, shall for the purpose of advancing food and nutritional security strive to progressively ensure livelihood security to farmers by way of remunerative prices, access to inputs, credit, irrigation, power, crop insurance etc.

One Nation one Ration Card (ONORC):

- For the nation-wide portability of the ration cards under the National Food Security Act, 2013, the Central Govt. has introduced ONORC plan. The ONORC scheme is aimed at enabling migrant workers and their family members to buy subsidized ration from any fair price shop anywhere in the country under the NFSA.
- ONORC allows migrant beneficiaries to claim either full or part foodgrains from any Fair Price Shop (FPS) in the country whereas the family members back home, if any, can claim the balance foodgrains on the same ration card.
- Earlier, NFSA beneficiaries were not able to access their PDS benefits outside the jurisdiction of the specific fair price shop to which they have been assigned. The Govt. envisioned the ONORC to give them access to benefits from any fair price shop.
- ONORC is based on technology that involves details of beneficiaries' ration card, Aadhaar number, and electronic Points of Sale (ePoS).

9.6 Shanta Kumar Committee Recommendations

Government of India (GOI) set up a High-Level Committee (**HLC**) in August 2014 with Shanta Kumar as the Chairman to suggest restructuring or unbundling of FCI with a view to improving its operational efficiency and financial management. The committee submitted its recommendations in 2015. Following are the major recommendations:

Procurement

- FCI hand over all procurement operations of wheat, paddy and rice to states that have gained sufficient experience in this regard and have created reasonable infrastructure for procurement. FCI will accept only the surplus (after deducting the needs of the states under NFSA) from these state governments to be moved to deficit states.

PDS and NFSA

- HLC recommends to have a relook at the current coverage of 67 percent of population as it is on much higher side, and should be brought down to around 40 percent, which will comfortably cover BPL families and some even above that.
- 5kg grain per person to priority households is actually making BPL households worse off, who used to get 7kg/person under the TPDS. So, HLC recommends that they be given 7kg/person. On central issue prices, HLC recommends while Antyodya households can be given grains at Rs 3/2/1/kg for the time being, but pricing for priority households must be linked to MSP, say 50 percent of MSP. Else, HLC feels that this

NFSA will put undue financial burden on the exchequer, and investments in agriculture and food space may suffer.

- HLC recommends gradual introduction of cash transfers in PDS.

Stocking and Movement

- FCI should outsource its stocking operations to various agencies such as Central Warehousing Corporation, State Warehousing Corporation, Private Sector.
- Many of FCI's old conventional storages that have existed for long number of years can be converted to silos with the help of private sector and other stocking agencies. Better mechanization is needed in all silos as well as conventional storages.
- Movement of grains needs to be gradually containerized which will help reduce transit losses, and have faster turn-around-time by having more mechanized facilities at railway sidings.

Buffer Stocking and Liquidation Policy

- A transparent liquidation policy is the need of hour, which should automatically kick-in when FCI is faced with surplus stocks than buffer norms. Greater flexibility to FCI with business orientation to operate in open market sale scheme (OMSS) and export markets is needed.

Labour

- FCI engages large number of workers (loaders) to get the job of loading/unloading done smoothly and in time which results in very high cost for the government. FCI should put these depots on priority for mechanization so that reliance on departmental labour reduces.

Direct subsidy to farmers

- Since the whole system of food management operates within the ambit of providing food security at a national as well as at household level, it must be realized that farmers need due incentives to raise productivity and overall food production in the country. The committee recommends that farmers should be given direct cash subsidy (of about Rs 7000/ha) and fertilizer sector can then be deregulated.

End to end computerization

- Total end to end computerization of the entire food management system, starting from procurement from farmers, to stocking, movement and finally distribution through TPDS.

New face of FCI

- The new face of FCI will be akin to an agency for innovations in Food Management System with a primary focus to create competition in every segment of foodgrain supply chain, from procurement to stocking to movement and finally distribution in TPDS, so that overall costs of the system are substantially reduced, leakages plugged, and it serves larger number of farmers and consumers.

PREVIOUS YEARS' QUESTIONS

Prelim Questions

1. With reference to the provisions made under the National Food Security Act, 2013 consider the following statements: **[2018]**
   (i) The families coming under the category of 'below poverty line (BPL)' only are eligible to receive subsidised grains.
   (ii) The eldest woman in a household, of age 18 years or above, shall be the head of the household for the purpose of issuance of a ration card.
   (iii) Pregnant women and lactating mothers are entitled to a take-home ration' of 1600 calories per day during pregnancy and for six months thereafter.

   Which of the statements given above is/are correct?

   (a) (i) & (ii) only (b) (ii) only
   (c) (i) & (iii) only (d) (iii) only

2. The economic cost of food grains to the Food Corporation of India is Minimum Support Price and bonus (if any) paid to the farmers plus **[2019]**
   (a) transportation cost only
   (b) interest cost only
   (c) procurement incidentals and distribution cost
   (d) procurement incidentals and charges for godowns

3. With reference to chemical fertilizers in India, consider the following statements: **[2020]**
   1. At present, the retail price of chemical fertilizers is market driven and not administered by the Government
   2. Ammonia, which an input of urea, is produced from Natural gas
   3. Sulphur, which is a raw material for phosphoric acid fertilizer, is a by-product of oil refineries

   Which of the following statements given above is/are correct?

   (a) 1 only (b) 2 and 3 only
   (c) 2 only (d) 1, 2 and 3

ANSWERS

1. (b) 2. (c) 3. (b)

Main Questions

1. What are the salient features of the National Food Security Act, 2013? How has the Food Security Bill helped in eliminating hunger and malnutrition in India? **[2021]**
2. What are the major challenges of Public Distribution System (PDS) in India? How can it be made effective and transparent? **[2022]**
3. Elucidate the importance of buffer stocks for stabilizing agricultural prices in India. What are the challenges associated with the storage of buffer stocks? Discuss. **[2024]**

◈◈◈

10 Agriculture: Part-I

10.1 Introduction

Facts:

Farmer Category	No. of Holdings (Crore)	% of Holdings	Area (Crore ha)
Marginal (0-1 ha)	10.03	67.59	3.80
Small (1-2 ha)	2.58	18.81	3.64
Semi Medium (2-4 ha)	1.40	9.34	3.72
Medium (4-10 ha)	0.56	3.72	3.14
Large (above 10 ha)	0.08	0.54	1.42
Total	**14.65**	**100.00**	**15.78**

In the absence of an estimate of the number of farmers in the country, the number of land holdings (14.65 crore) is taken as its proxy.

- Agricultural/Cultivable land = 15.78 crore (157.8 million) hectare
- Number of farmers = 14.65 crore (146.5 million)
- Average land holding per farmer = 1.08 ha (15.78/14.65)
- Area under irrigation = Approx. 50%
- Small and marginal farmers are 86% which operate on 47% of the total agri-area
- 73.2% of rural women are engaged in farming activities but only 12.8% own landholdings

Following chart represents agriculture (and allied) sector real GDP growth rate in the last few years.

2016-17	2017-18	2018-19	2019-20	2020-21	2021-22	2022-23	2023-24	2024-25	2025-26
6.8%	6.6%	2.10%	6.2%	4.10%	3.50%	4.00%	2.70%	4.60%	3.10%

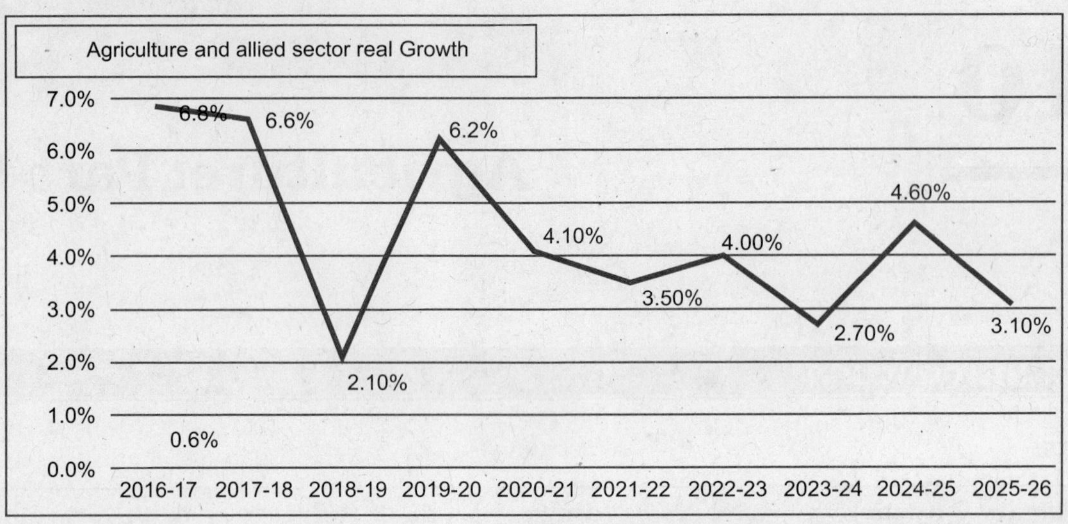

10.2 Agriculture in India: A Brief History

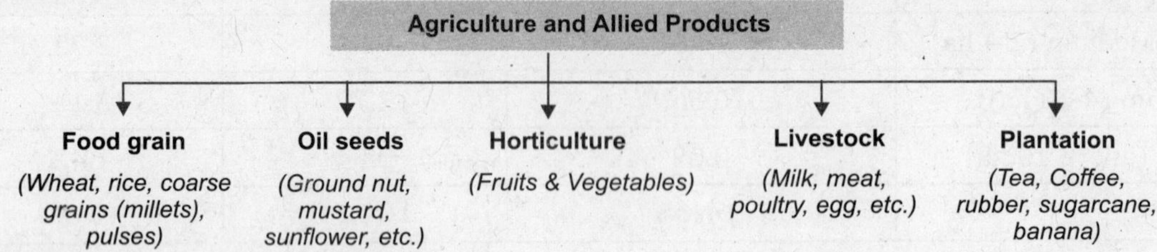

Agriculture is the most important sector of Indian economy from the perspective of poverty alleviation and employment generation and contribution to nation's GDP. The share of agriculture in national GDP has been declining from over 50% in 1950-51 to 16% in 2019-20. In 1950-51, agriculture provided 70% employment which has now decreased to around 42%. Hence the growth of Indian agriculture can be considered necessary condition for 'inclusive growth'. A report published by the World Bank says that *"Growth in agriculture is critical for any economy as research has revealed that GDP growth originating in agriculture is at least twice as effective in reducing poverty as GDP growth originating outside agriculture".*

Between 1951 and 1966 food grain production rose at a rate of 2.8% per annum, a rate that failed to keep up with the consumption demand of the rising population which was growing at more than 2 percent per annum. Thus, from the mid 1950's, India began to rely on imports of food grains to feed its growing population. In 1956, India signed the agreement of Public Law (PL) 480 with the United States to receive food aid, mostly in the form of wheat.

Because of the two wars (with China in 1962 and Pakistan in 1965), India was not able to channelize its resources in rural investments and the two consecutive droughts (1965 and 1966) plunged the country into an unprecedented food crisis, with food grain production and yield declining by 19% and 17% respectively in 1966. To avoid massive starvation, food grain imports were increased. Against the backdrop of the cold war, food aid was used to "twist the arms" of recipient countries to seek compliance and India fell prey to this policy when on one occasion, the US shipments were abruptly stopped for 48 hours at the height of drought. Indian leaders then realized the high level of political risk inherent in relying on foreign sources for food security and resolved to achieve self-sufficiency in food grain production.

Green Revolution

The Green Revolution refers to the renovation of agricultural practices beginning in Mexico in the 1940's. The beginning of Green Revolution is attributed to Norman Borlaug, an American scientist interested in agriculture. In the 1940's he began conducting research in Mexico and developed new disease resistance high yielding varieties of wheat. Because of its success, green revolution technologies spread worldwide in 1950's and 1960's.

The introduction of High Yielding Variety (HYV) of seeds, fertilizers, pesticides, better irrigation facilities, mechanized equipment and modern agricultural techniques is collectively known as **Green Revolution**. The idea of green revolution was to use technology to increase food output and the introduction of more western type of farming techniques. M.S. Swaminathan is known as the **"Father of Green Revolution in India"**.

Green Revolution in India can be divided in three phases:

- **Phase I (1966 - 72):** In 1966, India ordered the import of 18,000 Tonnes of HYV seeds of wheat that were distributed in the highly irrigated areas of Punjab, Haryana and western Uttar Pradesh.
- **Phase II (1973 - 80):** The extension of HYV technology from wheat to rice, favoured by the growth of tube wells (private as well as govt.) spread the green revolution to new areas in eastern UP, Andhra Pradesh, coastal areas of Karnataka and Tamil Nadu.
- **Phase III (1981 - 90):** The green revolution spread to the erstwhile low growth areas of eastern region of West Bengal, Bihar, Assam and Odisha.

Due to the Green Revolution, the production of food grains increased from 74 MT in 1966-67 to 105 MT in 1971-72 and in that year, India became self-sufficient with grain imports declining to nearly zero.

Year	1950-51	1966-67	1971-72	2000-01	2013-14	2024-25
Food Grain (MT)	51	74	105	197	265	**353**

*Food grain includes wheat, rice, coarse grains and pulses

Some Facts:

- *Production of foodgrains (2024-25) in MT*

  Rice: 150 MT

  Wheat: 118 MT

  Coarse Grains: 59 MT

  Pulses: 26 MT
- *Horticulture production in 2024-25 is around 368 MT*
- *India is the largest producer of milk contributing 24% of global milk production*
- *India is the largest producer (25% of global production) and consumer of pulses in the world*

- *India is the second largest producer of rice, wheat, sugarcane and fruits and vegetables*
- *India is the largest exporter of rice and second largest exporter of beef and cotton*
- *In FY 2024-25, Indian agri-exports were $51.9 billion against imports of $38.5 billion. This is nothing short of a wonder for a country which used to be dependent on US imports for its cereals in mid-1960's.*

White Revolution

Dr. Verghese Kurien, also known as the milkman of India, came to Anand in 1949 to start his professional career. While working at Anand in a Govt. creamery, he found that poor and illiterate farmers were being used by the distributors of milk. Though their products were of superior quality but Indian farmers were being exploited. First of all, they were not paid well for the milk and secondly, they were not allowed to sell the milk directly to the vendors. While working, Kurien got inspired by the leader Tribhuvandas Patel who was working on the cooperative movement against this exploitation. Kurien along with Patel started working on cooperatives in the Kheda district of Gujarat. This led to the establishment of "Amul" in 1949, also known as KDCMPUL (Kaira District Cooperative Milk Producer's Union Ltd.) and used to supply milk and other dairy products but did not have proper supply chain. When initiated, it had two co-operative societies and 247 liters of milk.

Amul was working on cooperative scheme and it got so popular that it received government's attention. To inaugurate the new cattle-feed plant of Amul, the then Prime Minister Mr. Lal Bahadur Shastri was invited to Anand in 1964. He was so impressed with the entire process that he asked Dr Kurien to replicate the same model across the country as this model was helping the farmers to improve their economic condition. To fulfil this objective, the National Dairy Development Board (NDDB) in the year 1965 was formed and Dr Kurien was made in charge of this board.

At that time demand for milk was growing and crossed its supply but financing was the biggest problem. In 1969 NDDB approached World Bank and got approved loan for the operation that later on known as **Operation Flood to replicate the working of Anand project across India.** The main objectives of Operation Flood were:

- Increase milk production ("a flood of milk")
- Augment rural incomes
- Reasonable prices for consumers

The business model of "operation flood" was based on three tier structure:

Village Society: The milk producers at the village level form village dairy cooperative society (DCS). Any producer can become a DCS member by buying a share and committing to sell milk only to the society. Each DCS has a milk collection center where members take milk every day. Each member's milk is tested for quality with payments based on the percentage of fat and SNF. At the end of each year, a portion of the DCS profits is used to pay each member a patronage bonus based on the quantity of milk procured.

The District Union: A District Cooperative Milk Producers' Union is owned by dairy cooperative societies. The Union buys all the societies' milk, then processes and markets fluid milk and products. Most Unions also provide a range of inputs and services to DCSs and their members: feed, veterinary care, artificial insemination to sustain the growth of milk production and the cooperatives' business. Union staff train and provide consulting services to support DCS leaders and staff.

The State Federation: The District Cooperative milk producers' unions in a state form, a State Federation, which is responsible for marketing the fluid milk and products of member unions. Some federations also manufacture feed and support other union activities.

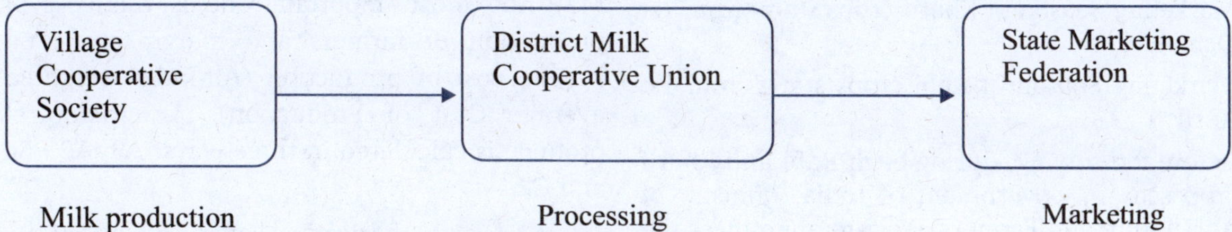

Milk production Processing Marketing

Milk is collected at the village dairy society, obtained and processed at the district milk union, and marketed at the state milk federation.

Achievements of the White Revolution:

- The phenomenal growth of milk production in India – from 20 million MT to 100 million MT in a span of just 40 years – has been made possible only because of the dairy cooperative movement. This has propelled India to emerge as the largest milk producing country in the world today (210 MT in 2020-21).
- The dairy cooperative movement has spread across the length and breadth of the country, covering more than 125,000 villages of 180 Districts in 22 States.

Pink Revolution

Pink revolution refers to the **modernization of meat and poultry processing sector**. Modernization refers to the specialization, mechanization and standardization of processes in the meat industry. Technological up gradation and industrialization are necessary for Indian entities to keep up with global standards. Also, adoption and development of mass production capabilities will help the industry be more productive. There is especially immense scope for development of the domestic market. A sizable number of Indians still prefer to buy meat at the local shop or from the wet market instead of standardized packaged meat. Additionally, in light of the increasing threat of zoonotic diseases, it is important for India to maintain or build top notch facilities so that exports from India do not get banned by other countries.

In a report titled the 'Indian Meat Industry Perspective', the UN Food and Agriculture Organization (FAO) outlined four steps that should be taken if India's food industry is to successfully go pink. These recommended steps were:

- setting up state of the art meat processing plants;
- developing technologies to raise male buffalo calves for meat production;
- increasing the number of farmers rearing buffalo under contractual farming; and
- establishing disease-free zones for rearing animals.

India has already become quite rosy and meat production has been steadily growing over the past decade. According to the United States Department of Agriculture (USDA) Foreign Agricultural Service, India became the largest exporter of buffalo meat in 2012, exporting approximately 1.5 million metric tons of beef. The largest importers of Indian meat are primarily countries in the Middle East and South East Asia.

10.3 Minimum Support Price (MSP)

Agriculture Crop Year: 1st July - 30th June

Marketing Season of Kharif crops starts from 1st October

Marketing Season of Rabi crops starts from 1st April

Before the sowing, during each Rabi and Kharif crop season, Government of India, Ministry of Agriculture and Farmers' Welfare announces the Minimum Support Prices (MSP) for procurement based on the recommendation of the Commission for Agricultural Costs and Prices (CACP) under Ministry of Agriculture and Farmers' Welfare and upon approval of the Cabinet Committee on Economic Affairs (CCEA).

MSP does not have any legal backing till now and farmers can't demand it as a legal right. It is just government policy and an administrative decision to purchase some food grains at MSP. And govt can't even force private players to procure at MSP.

CACP, which recommends MSP, is again not a statutory body and it is just an office attached to Ministry of Agriculture. CACP just recommends MSP but the decision on fixing and even not fixing and its implementation (i.e., procurement at MSP) lies with the Govt.

CACP takes into account the following factors to recommend MSP to the dept. of Agriculture

- Cost of production and margin (profit) to farmers
- Demand and supply
- Price trends in the market both domestic and international
- Inter crop price parity
- Terms of trade between agriculture and non-agriculture products
- Likely implication of MSP on consumers of that product

Among several criteria for recommending the MSP, the most important one is the cost of production of farmers and margin/profit on it. The cost of production (All-India weighted average Cost of Production) of agricultural produce is calculated in three ways: A2, A2+FL and C2.

- A2 costs basically cover all paid-out expenses, both in cash and in kind, incurred by farmers on seeds, fertilizers, chemicals, hired labour, fuel, irrigation, machinery, etc.
- A2+FL cover actual paid-out costs plus an imputed value of unpaid family labour.
- C2costs are more comprehensive, accounting for the rentals and interest forgone on owned land and fixed capital assets respectively, on top of A2+FL.

Finance Minister, while presenting the budget of 2018-19 announced that, the Government will be offering MSP of at least 50 percent over cost of production (A2 + FL).MSP is same all across India for a particular crop.

As of now, CACP recommends MSPs of 23 commodities, which comprise of:

- 7 cereals (paddy, wheat, maize, sorghum, pearl millet, barley and ragi),
- 5 pulses (gram, tur, moong, urad, lentil),
- 7 oilseeds (groundnut, rapeseed-mustard, soyabean, seasmum, sunflower, safflower, nigerseed), and
- 4 commercial crops (copra, sugarcane, cotton and raw jute).

But in addition to the above 23 crops, the MSPs of 'toria' and 'de-husked coconut' are fixed on the basis of the MSPs of rapeseed/mustard and copra respectively.

So, although CACP recommends MSP of 23 crops but MSP is declared for 25 crops including Sugarcane for which it is called Fair and Remunerative Price (FRP).

For sugarcane, Ministry of Consumer Affairs, Food and Public Distribution recommend Fair and Remunerative Price (FRP), while some States announces their own State Advised Price (SAP). SAP/FRP is the price at which mill owners are bound to purchase sugarcane from the farmers and it is done through 'Sugarcane Control Order 1966' under the Essential Commodities Act 1955.

There are two separate things, one is declaration/announcing of MSP and the other is procurement of food grains at MSP by Govt. Agencies. The purpose of announcing MSP is not that Govt. is going to purchase all the crops under MSP, rather its purpose is that the farmers should get that minimum price. And if the mandi/private markets prices are above MSP then the Govt.'s purpose is already achieved and Govt. may not procure crops from farmers and the farmers will also be not willing to sell to govt. at MSP.

Minimum Support Price (MSP)

Kharif Crops		Rabi Crops	
1	Paddy	15	Wheat
2	Jowar	16	Barley
3	Bajra	17	Gram
4	Ragi	18	Lentil (Masur)
5	Maize	19	Rapeseed/ Mustard
6	Tur (Arhar)	20	Safflower
7	Moong	21	Toria
8	Urad	**Other Crops**	
9	Groundnut	22	Copra
10	Sunflower Seed	23	De-husked Coconut
11	Soyabeen	24	Jute
12	Sesamum	25	Sugarcane *(Fair & Remunerative Price)*
13	Nigerseed		
14	Cotton		

Even though MSP is declared for 25 crops, Govt. procures mostly wheat and rice and that too mostly from Punjab, Haryana and few other states like Western UP, MP. Some other crops which are procured are Cotton by Cotton Corporation of India, pulses for buffer stock and sugarcane by sugar mills.

Issues with MSP:

- Cost-plus pricing of MSPs is risky in that it entirely ignores the demand side, i.e., demand-supply, domestic and international price trends, terms of trade, inter-crop price parity, etc. It is apparent from history and experience that higher MSPs don't necessarily fetch better value to the farmers, nor prevents distressing surpluses and price crashes rather it causes deficits and surpluses.
- MSP becomes the base price and cause inflation.
- MSP based procurement creates distortions in market affecting not just prices, but cropping patterns, deteriorations in soil quality, water tables, and so on.
- There are other spill over too, the most serious being deterring fresh, private investments in the sector—investors are attracted by freeing markets, not by restricting free play.

[It is practically not possible for Govt. to procure all the crops at MSP all over India. If Govt will procure all the 25 crops at MSP from all over India (which will be a huge financial burden and practically not possible) then the farmers who are cultivating Fruits, Vegetables, livestock which consists of almost 50% of the value and for which there does not exist any MSP, then these farmers will also shift to those 25 crops. And all the diversification of crops that Govt is trying will go for a toss. It will also lead to huge corruption in the procurement process which is already there in MSP procurement of wheat and rice.

And if govt will procure only few crops at MSP in some regions then all the farmers in that region will move only to those few crops and you know what problem Punjab and Haryana is facing. There is possible chance of desertification of the land because of huge water extraction, pesticides, fertilizers and same cropping pattern of wheat and rice.

The best way is to give the farmers' income support (PM-KISAN) and remove the subsidies and ask them to produce as per the market demand. This will resolve the problem in terms of diversification of crops, environment, soil degradation problem and water problem will also get resolved.]

[What are the subsidies given to agriculture sector in India?

Answer: Farmers in India are provided support on both the input and output side of agriculture. On the input side, an average Indian farmer receives subsidies on fertilisers, seeds, farm machinery and equipment, electricity etc. On the output side, MSP and logistics subsidies are offered. However, small and marginal farmers are able to get only a small amount of these subsidies.]

MSP of Minor Forest Produce (MFP)

"Mechanism for marketing of Minor Forest Produce (MFP) through Minimum Support Price (MSP) and Development of Value Chain for MFP" is a Centrally Sponsored Scheme (CSS), under ministry of Tribal Affairs. The scheme has been started with the objective of providing fair price to MFP gatherers and enhance their income level and ensure sustainable harvesting of MFPs.

The Minimum Support Price (MSP) for Minor Forest Product (MFP) is reviewed/revised once in every three years by the Pricing Cell under the Ministry of Tribal Affairs.

Tribal Cooperative Marketing Development Federation of India (TRIFED) acts as the Central Nodal Agency for implementation and monitoring of the scheme through State level implementing agencies. State designated agencies undertakes procurement (generally in case, market price falls below MSP) of notified MFPs directly from MFP gatherers (individual or collectives) at haats notified procurement centres at grass root level at prefixed Minimum Support Price and ensure full & timely on the spot payment to MFP gatherers. Central government provides financial support in the ratio 75:25 (Centre: State) for procurement, infrastructure creation, storage capacity, processing units for these MFPs.

The MSP declared by Govt. of India shall be reference MSP for fixing MSP and State government shall have latitude of 10% of MSP declared by Govt. of India i.e., State can fix MSP up to 10% higher or lower than MSP declared by Govt. of India.

10.4 PM – AASHA

Giving a major boost to the pro-farmer initiatives of the Government and in keeping with its commitment and dedication for the Annadata, the Union Cabinet approved a new Umbrella Scheme prdhan Mantri Annadata Aay Sanrakshan Abhiyan' (PM-AASHA) in September 2018. The Scheme is aimed at ensuring remunerative prices to the farmers for their produce as announced in the Union Budget for 2019. The Umbrella Scheme includes the mechanism of ensuring remunerative prices to the farmers and is comprised of three sub schemes:

- Price Support Scheme (PSS): In Price Support Scheme (PSS), physical procurement of pulses, oilseeds and Copra will be done by Central Nodal Agencies with proactive role of State governments. It is also decided that in addition to NAFED, Food Cooperation of India (FCI) will take up PSS operations in states /districts. The procurement expenditure and losses due to procurement will be borne by Central Government as per norms.
- Price Deficiency Payment Scheme (PDPS): Under Price Deficiency Payment Scheme this scheme (PDPS), it is proposed to cover all oilseeds for which MSP is notified. In this direct payment of the difference between the MSP and the selling/modal price will be made to pre-registered farmers selling his produce in the notified market yard through a transparent auction process. All payment will be done directly into registered bank account of the farmer. This scheme does not involve any physical procurement of crops as farmers are paid the difference between MSP price and Sale/modal price on disposal in notified market. The support of central government for PDPS will be given as per norms.
- Pilot of Private Procurement & Stockist Scheme (PPSS): A private agency shall procure the commodity at MSP in the notified markets during the notified period from the registered farmers in consonance with the PPSS Guidelines, whenever the prices in the market fall below the notified MSP and whenever authorized by the state/ UT government to enter the market and maximum service charges up to 15% of the notified MSP will be payable.

10.5 PM – KISAN

- Pradhan Mantri Kisan Samman Nidhi (PM-KISAN) scheme is effective from 1.12.2018
- It is a Central Sector scheme with 100% funding from Government of India
- Under the Scheme an income support of Rs.6000/- per year is provided to all eligible farmer families across the country in three equal instalments of Rs.2000/- every four months
- Definition of family for the Scheme is husband, wife and minor children
- The entire responsibility of identification of beneficiary farmer families rests with the State / UT Governments
- Some farmers have been excluded from this scheme for example, employees of central and state government, PSU employees, pensioners etc.

- The fund is directly transferred to the bank accounts of the beneficiaries
- For enrolment, the farmer is required to approach the local patwari / revenue officer / Nodal Officer (PM-Kisan) nominated by the State Government
- The Common Service Centres (CSCs) have also been authorized to do registration of the farmers for the Scheme upon payment of fees

PM-Kisan scheme may have some impact on inflation since the cash would lead to spends on consumer staples, and other goods, but this is likely to be far less inflationary than other schemes/subsidies like MSP, and input subsidies. More important, it will not distort the market as this support is not linked to production of any particular crop or not linked to production at all. Whether a farmer produces any agricultural output or not he will still get the benefit. Till such time the government is able to free agriculture markets and carry out other reforms to limit the role of middlemen, this is probably the best strategy to alleviate farm distress.

10.6 Agriculture Extension Services

Extension services, also called rural advisory services constitute a key input for improving the productivity in agriculture by providing timely advisory services to farmers to adopt best practices, technology, meet with contingencies, market information etc. In India, there are multiple agencies offering agricultural extension/advisory services.

- The Department of Agriculture and Cooperation (DAC), along with NABARD, has introduced a scheme for establishment of agri-clinics / agri-business centres / ventures by the agricultural graduates.
- The ICAR is also associated in agriculture extension activities through Krishi Vigyan Kendras (KVKs) and the Institute Village Linkage Programme (IVLP) all over the country.
- FPOs, NGOs and the corporate sector

National Mission on Agricultural Extension & Technology (NMAET), launched during the 12th plan period, consists of 4 Sub Missions:

1. **Sub Mission on Agricultural Extension (SMAE):** Adoption of quality seeds is the most cost-effective means for increasing agricultural production and productivity. Agri Clinics, Agri business centres, Kisan Call Centres will be used for providing extension services.
2. **Sub-Mission on Seed and Planting Material (SMSP):** The Sub-Mission will cover the entire gamut of seed chain from nucleus seed to supply to farmers for sowing. SMSP also envisages strengthening of Protection of Plant Varieties and Farmers' Rights Authority (PPV&FRA) in order to put in place an effective system for protection of plant varieties, rights of farmers and plant breeders and to encourage development of new varieties of plants.
3. **Sub Mission on Agricultural Mechanization (SMAM):** There is a strong co-relation between farm power availability and agricultural productivity. Therefore, Sub-Mission on Agricultural Mechanization focuses on farm mechanization. The Sub-Mission will mainly cater to the needs of

the small and marginal farmers and to the regions where availability of farm power is low to offset the adverse economies of scale and high cost of individual ownership through institutional arrangements such as **Custom Hiring Centres**, mechanization of selected villages, subsidy for procurement of machines & equipment, etc.

4. **Sub Mission on Plant Protection and Plant Quarantine (SMPP):** The mission envisages increase in agricultural production by keeping the crop disease free using scientific and environment friendly techniques through promotion of Integrated Pest Management.

What are 'Custom Hiring Centres (CHC)'?

CHCs are basically a unit comprising a set of costly, advance and bigger farm machinery, implements and equipment (used for tillage, sowing, planting, harvesting, reaping, threshing, plant protection, inter cultivation and residue management) meant for custom hiring by farmers on rental basis who could not afford to purchase the high-end agriculture machineries and equipment. Govt. through SMAM is providing funds/subsidy to rural level entrepreneurs, SHGs etc. to set up CHCs. Under the SMAM scheme, subsidy is being provided by Govt. @ of 40% of the project cost to individual farmers up to a cap of Rs.60 lakh and 80% to the group of farmers up to a project cost of Rs. 10 lakhs for setting up Custom Hiring Centres.

The common threads running across all 4 Sub-Missions in NMAET are Extension and Technology. Therefore, while 4 separate Sub-Missions are proposed for administrative convenience, these are inextricably linked to each other at the field level and most components thereof have to be disseminated among farmers and other stakeholders through a strong extension network. Agricultural extension and technology have to go hand in hand and that is the genesis of the National Mission on Agricultural Extension and Technology.

The aim of the Mission is to restructure & strengthen agricultural extension to enable delivery of appropriate technology and improved agronomic practices to the farmers. This is envisaged to be achieved by a judicious mix of extensive physical outreach & interactive methods of information dissemination, use of ICT, popularisation of modern and appropriate technologies, capacity building and institution strengthening to promote mechanisation, availability of quality seeds, plant protection etc. and encourage the aggregation of farmers into Interest Groups to form Farmer Producer Organizations (FPOs).

As per Economic Survey 2019-20, farm mechanization in India is only about 40 per cent as compared to about 60 per cent in China and around 75 per cent in Brazil.

10.7 Krishi Vigyan Kendras (KVK)

In India, the role of science and technology in agriculture is pertinent to not only ensure food security of the country, but also to provide farmers a competitive edge and to maintain affordability of the food items for the public at large. To realize their true potential, farmers must have access to the state-of-the-art technologies, necessary inputs and related information. In this context, the Government of India through Indian Council for Agricultural Research (ICAR) has established a large network of over 700 Krishi Vigyan Kendras (KVKs) across the country with an aim to conduct technology assessment and refinement, knowledge dissemination and provide critical input support for the farmers with a multidisciplinary approach.

KVKs provide various types of farm support to the agricultural sector:

- They play a vital role in conducting on farm testing to demonstrate location specific agricultural technologies. KVKs conduct demonstrations to prove the potential of various crops at farmers' fields.
- They also conduct need-based training programmes for the benefit of farmers, farm women and rural youths.
- KVKs are creating awareness about improved agricultural technologies through large number of extension programmes.
- Critical and quality inputs like seeds, planting materials, organic products, bio-fertilizers and livestock, piglet and poultry strains are produced by the KVKs and made available to the farmers.

The KVKs are evolving as the future grass root level institutions for empowering the farming community. KVKs have made dent and has become part of decentralized planning and implementation instrument to achieve desired level of growth in agriculture and allied sector. The linking of 3.37 lakh common service centres (CSCs) with 721 KVKs has tremendously enhanced outreach of the KVKs and provided demand driven services and information to farmers.

10.8 Farmers Producer Organization (FPO)

- Indian agriculture is dominated by marginal and small farmers, who suffer serious disadvantage in terms of scale, uneconomic lot for marketing and price risk. Small sized farmers are also disadvantaged in terms of bargaining power in various transactions in the input and output markets. These handicaps can be overcome by organizing farmers under some institutional mechanism like the farmers producers' organizations (FPOs).
- FPOs can be a company, a cooperative society, Trust or any other form of legal entity which provides for sharing of profits/ benefits among the farmers. Ownership control is always with the members/ farmers and management is through the representatives of the members. The main aim of an FPO is to ensure better income for the farmers through an organization of their own.
- FPOs enable member farmers to reap the benefits of economies of scale in purchase of inputs, processing and marketing of their produce and can also provide access to timely and adequate credit facilities and linkages to market.
- Small Farmers Agribusiness Consortium (SFAC), National Co-operative Development Corporation (NCDC) and NABARD are promoting and helping in establishment of FPOs.
- SFAC is running Equity Grant Fund (EGF) Scheme, under which it is providing equity equal to the amount of shareholders/farmers equity in the FPO subject to cap of Rs. 10 lacs.
- In order to ensure access of FPOs to credit from mainstream Banks and Financial Institutions, a Credit Guarantee Fund (CGF) has been established by NABARD and NCDC

which will provide suitable credit guarantee cover to accelerate flow of institutional credit to FPOs by minimizing the risk of financial institutions for granting loan to FPOs so as to improve their financial ability to execute better business plans leading to increased profits.

- NABARD provides loan to FPO members without any collateral for contribution towards share capital up to a cap of Rs. 25000 per member. NABARD also provides credit support for business operations of FPOs. NABARD also provides technical, managerial and financial support for hand-holding, capacity building and market intervention efforts of the FPO.
- SFAC and NABARD provide training to top management of FPOs to enable them to function effectively. Further, Indian Council of Agricultural Research (ICAR) is providing technical support to FPOs through Krishi Vigyan Kendras (KVKs).
- There is some minimum number of member requirements to form an FPO depending on the legal form of PO (cooperative/company/Trust). Studies have shown that an FPO will require about 700 to 1000 active producers/farmers as members for sustainable operation.
- The primary producers have skill and expertise in producing. However, they generally need support for marketing of what they produce. The FPO will basically bridge this gap. The FPO will take over the responsibility of any one or more activities in the value chain of the produce right from procurement of raw material to delivery of the final product at the ultimate consumers' doorstep. In brief, the PO could undertake the following activities:

Procurement of inputs, disseminating market information, dissemination of technology and innovations, facilitating finance for inputs, aggregation and storage of produce, primary processing like drying, cleaning and grading, brand building, packaging, labelling and standardization, quality control, Marketing to institutional buyers, participation in commodity exchanges and exports

- An FPO will support the farmers in getting more income by undertaking any/many/all of the activities above. By aggregating the demand for inputs, the FPO can buy in bulk, thus procuring at cheaper price compared to individual purchase. Besides, by transporting in bulk, cost of transportation is reduced. Thus, reducing the overall cost of production. Similarly, the PO may aggregate the produce of all members and market in bulk, thus, fetching better price per unit of produce. The PO can also provide market information to the producers to enable them hold on to their produce till the market price become favourable. All these interventions will result in more income to the primary producers.
- Income derived by an FPO through agricultural activities is treated as agricultural income and is **exempted from taxation**.
- Presently there are more than 7000 FPOs registered and functioning. *(Example: Potato papadmaking by Kashi Vishwanath Farmer Producer Company Limited, Varanasi)*
- Government of India has launched a new Central Sector Scheme titled "Formation and Promotion of 10,000 FPOs" with a clear strategy and committed resources to form and promote 10,000 new FPOs in the country with budgetary provision of Rs 6865 crore.

Issues in Agriculture Credit

Cheaper credit has always helped in booming of any sector. But in case of agriculture even if Government is providing subsidy on agriculture credit to farmers, it is not helping the 86% small and marginal farmers and their income is stagnating. Every year Govt. sets a target for agriculture credit in the budget. For the FY 2024-25, Govt. has set a target of Rs. 22 lakh crores (through the private sector) but the question is where all this agriculture credit is going. The following issues have been observed:

- 86% of Small and marginal farmers are getting only 15% of the subsidized institutional loan from banks and cooperatives while big farmers are getting 79% of the subsidized loan
- The share of institutional credit is rising with increase in land holdings and the bulk of the agriculture credit is grabbed by big farmers and diverted to agriculture business companies
- Despite increase in agriculture credit, 95% of the tractors and other agriculture equipments are being financed indirectly through NBFCs
- RBI has set the target of 18% credit to agriculture sector (out of total 40% to priority sector) and within this 8% to small and marginal farmers, but these are being diverted and leaked to big farmers and companies.

All this shows the diversion of agriculture credit for non-agriculture purpose. One reason for this diversion is that subsidized credit disbursed at a 4% to 7% rate of interest is being refinanced to small farmers and in the open markets at a rate of interest of up to 36%. The way forward to the above issues is:

- Give small and marginal farmers income support on per hectare basis or per farmer rather than subsidized credit. In most of the States land record are getting digitized so it can be a easy for Government to provide support on per hectare basis
- Provide agriculture credit through FPOs of small farmers

10.9 Marketing of Agricultural Produce

10.9.1 Agriculture Produce and Marketing Committee (APMC) Acts

Agricultural Markets in most parts of the country are established and regulated under the State APMC Acts. The whole geographical area in a State is divided into various market areas/ mandis wherein each market is managed by a Market Committee constituted by the State Government. Once a particular area is declared a market area and falls under the jurisdiction of a Market Committee, no person or agency is allowed freely to carry on wholesale marketing activities outside the market. The Act states that the **first sale** of agricultural commodities produced in the region such as cereals, pulses, edible oilseed, fruits and vegetables and even chicken, goat, sheep, sugar, fish etc. can be conducted only under the aegis of the APMC through the commission agents licensed by the APMCs setup under the Act. The wholesalers, retail traders (retail chains like reliance fresh etc) or food processing companies cannot purchase the farm output directly from the farmers, rather they need to purchase from these established mandis and the farmers also need to sell their produce in these mandis.

Salient features of APMC Act

- For a trader to operate in a Mandi, he has to get a license for which he must have a shop or warehouse in the Mandi ;
- The price of the farmers' produce shall be discovered through auctioning so that farmers get a good price of their produce.

The following are the various issues with the APMC acts:

- The wholesalers, retail traders (retail chains like reliance fresh etc.) or food processing companies cannot purchase the farm output directly from the farmers, rather they need to purchase from these established mandis and the farmers also need to sell their produce in these mandis.
- Different States levy different mandi charges which create market distortion. These mandi charges at the first level of trading have significant cascading effects on the prices as the commodity passes through the supply chain.
- Mandis located across a State are not integrated and there are substantial transaction costs for moving the produce from one mandi to another within a State. Separate licenses for each mandi are required for trading in different mandis within a State.

How APMC Act has exploited the farmers and consumers

- Getting a license involves paying bribes and leads to corruption.
- Auctioning does not take place and even if it happens, the traders in these mandis form a cartel and collectively keep the prices low ultimately hurting the farmers. During the peak season when the traders buy from farmers at low prices, they don't reduce the prices to final consumers and during the lean season when consumer prices are high, traders don't pass it to farmers.

10.9.2 Electronic - National Agriculture Market (e-NAM)

National Agricultural Market is not entirely a new concept but **it is an online platform** with physical markets or mandis at the backend. NAM is not a parallel marketing structure but rather an instrument to create **a national network of physical mandis** which can be accessed online. NAM seeks to leverage the physical infrastructure of mandis through an online trading portal, enabling buyers situated even outside the State to participate in trading at the local level. NAM provides a pan-India electronic trading portal which connects selected APMC mandis to create a Unified National Market for agricultural commodities. The scheme is being implemented through Small Farmers Agribusiness Consortium (SFAC), which is an autonomous organization under Dept. of Agriculture and Cooperation (DAC).

NAM was launched in April 2016 by Govt. of India, Ministry of Agriculture, and the plan is to connect all the 2500 APMC mandis across India through e-NAM out of which 1500 have already joined the platform.

In e-NAM sale, traders from all over India could bid and whoever quotes highest price, the farmer can sell his produce to that trader (it may be inter-state). Then farmer will receive the payment in his account and then only the trader can take the physical produce. Transportation charge will be on trader's account. Even if a farmer wants to sell his produce online through e-NAM, he needs to take his produce in APMC mandi or FPO collection centre or WDRA registered warehouses (actually these have been integrated with e-NAM platform).

Govt is working on the modalities so that farmers will be able to sell their produce online sitting at their home through their mobile with their physical produce at home, but it may take a year or more.

The following are some of the important features/benefits of NAM:

- NAM increases the choice for a farmer after he brings his produce to a mandi. He can sell his produce to the local traders (present in the physical mandi) or he can sell the produce to traders on the electronic platform sitting in other States.
- The gradual integration of all major mandis into the NAM e-platform would ensure common procedures for issue of licenses, levy of fee and movement of produce. Over the next 3-5 years volume of business will significantly increase creating greater competition and better price discovery and resulting in major benefits through higher returns to farmers, lower transaction costs for buyers and stable prices and availability to consumers.
- NAM will facilitate the emergence of integrated value chains in major agricultural commodities across the country and help promote scientific storage and movement of agricultural goods.
- Respective APMC mandis will have to ensure quality standards of agricultural goods sold through the e-platform. NAM envisages harmonization of quality standards of agricultural produce and provisions of quality testing infrastructure in every market to enable informed bidding by buyers.
- Logistics services has also been integrated with e-NAM for transporting the agri produce and there are various other services which are also being integrated like QC services, transportation & delivery services, sorting/grading services, packaging services, insurance, trade finance, warehouses etc. through the e-NAM platform.

Challenges:

- The major challenge of the electronic portal is in making traders to move online who have been transacting physically and dealing in cash since long.
- Another challenge lies in knowing the quality of produce as the farmers and traders may be in different mandis/places. Govt. is setting up quality labs so that when the farmers bring their produce in mandi, a quality certificate is generated which is uploaded online and the traders sitting in another mandi can access the quality certificate. Still, the traders want to verify quality physically.
- Another major challenge is the storage capacity in the mandis as farmers still needs to bring their produce in the mandi and it takes time for traders in other mandi to take this produce.
- First the traders need to make payment online then afterward they will be eligible to take the produce from the mandi.
- Since the e-NAM project was launched in April 2016, less than 5% of the wholesale trade in farm commodities has shifted online and as far as inter-mandi/inter-state e-NAM trade is concerned, it has remained a non-starter.

10.9.3 [Model] Agri Produce and Livestock Marketing Act 2017

Central Government brought a **model** law "Agricultural Produce and Livestock Marketing (Promotion and Facilitation) Act 2017" on 25th

April 2017. The law seeks to liberalize the trade in agri-products and livestock and will thereby help in doubling the farmers' income by 2023. The new model law replaces the earlier model law proposed by the centre in 2003 which the states were not keen to adopt.

The following are some of the important features of the model Act:

- The law proposes private wholesale markets, direct sale by farmers to bulk buyers (presently the States restrict bulk buying directly from the farmers) and promotion of electronic trading.
- The law also allows godowns, warehouses and cold storages to act as regulated markets. Currently a regulated market is available per 462 sq km while ideally there should be one every 5 sq. km. So, the goal is to increase the avenues where a farmer can sell the produce which will in turn increase competition among buyers and lead to better farm gate prices for the farmers.
- The law proposes to have a single licence and single point of levy of market fee/ mandi charges at the State level and then gradually move towards a single licence and single point of levy of market fee at the national level. The idea is to remove disincentives for farmers and traders to trade across the country. *(Presently a trader requires separate licenses for trading in each mandi and the mandi charges are levied several times if the produce moves through several markets)* The law also proposes a cap on levy of market fees at 2% of sale price for fruits and vegetables and 1% for food grains.
- Other proposals in the model Act include promotion of national market for agriculture produce through provisioning of inter-State trading licence, grading and standardisation and quality certification, rationalisation of market fee and commission charges, provision for special commodity market yard and promotion of e-trading to increase transparency.

Impact/Benefit

- The Centre's decision to issue a new model law liberalising marketing of farm produce is a long overdue measure that will not only give farmers a better deal but will also help consumers with more stable prices of food items.
- Bringing down intra State and inter State barriers to free movement of agriculture and livestock produce is also essential to transform India into one common market.

Comment: The key to the success of the Act lies in efficient adoption and implementation by State Govt's of this Act as it is a state subject and this law is not binding on the States.

10.10 Contract Farming

Introduction

Contract farming can be defined as agricultural production carried out according to an agreement between a buyer and farmers, which establishes conditions for the production and marketing of a farm product or products. Typically, the farmer agrees to provide agreed quantities of a specific agricultural product. These should meet the quality standards of the purchaser and be supplied at the time determined by the purchaser. In turn, the buyer commits to purchase the product and, in some cases, to support production through, for example, the supply of farm inputs, land preparation and the provision of technical advice.

Advantages

Both partners engaged in contract farming can benefit.

- Farmers have a guaranteed market outlet, reduce their uncertainty regarding prices and often are supplied with loans in kind, through the provision of farming inputs such as seeds and fertilizers.
- Purchasing firms benefit from having a guaranteed supply of agricultural products that meet their specifications regarding quality, quantity and timing of delivery.

Issues

As with any other form of contractual relationship, there are also potential disadvantages and risks associated with contract farming.

- If the terms of the contract are not respected by one of the contracting parties, then the affected party stands to lose. Common contractual problems include farmer sales to a different buyer (side selling or extra-contractual marketing), a company's refusal to buy products at the agreed prices, or the downgrading of produce quality by the company.
- A frequent criticism of contract farming arrangements is the uneven nature of the business relationship between farmers and their buyers. Buying firms, who are invariably more powerful than farmers, may use their bargaining clout to their short-term financial advantage, although in the long run this would be counterproductive as farmers would cease to supply them.

These problems notwithstanding, the balance between advantages and disadvantages for both firms and farmers seems to be on the positive side. Contractual arrangements are more and more frequently being used in agriculture worldwide.

In 2003, Central government had proposed a **Model** Agricultural Produce and Marketing Committee (APMC) Act to the States which had clear provisions for contract farming, which allowed buyers and sellers to transact without routing through mandis. Yet, contract farming has not been promoted or has become popular to the extent expected. Even in States that adopted the model marketing Act and allowed direct transactions between organized private sector and producers/farmers, contract farming has been minimal.

Contract farming in India have some major success stories. For example, in poultry it has been widely successful, but in numerous other commodities contract farming has not taken off or has failed. **The roadblocks for contract farming relate to both demand as well as supply side of the market.**

- **On the supply side,** the most important constraint has been the scale of farm produce. Most Indian farmers are marginal and small (86% land holdings are less than 2 hectares). All states except Punjab, have less than one-hectare average size. With such small holding, the marketable surplus of individual farmer has turned out to be extremely small. Buyers have no incentive for contract farming with a large number of small and marginal farmers due to high transactions (ex. costs related to negotiation) and marketing costs (ex. cost of collecting produce). Further the problem is heterogeneity in quality of produce with a large number of small farmers who can't be monitored for quality and safety. If contract farming is to succeed, we have to consolidate farmers through farmer producer organizations (FPOs) and self-help groups as a precursor to firm-farm coordination.

- **On the demand side,** we allowed the big foreign retail chains like Amazon, Tesco to invest in India only recently (FDI in food retail was opened only in 2016). These retail chains have an efficient supply chain and a successful business model running in other countries. If these companies will come in India, they will bring in technology and expertise which will definitely create a demand for the direct sourcing of farm produce from the farmers.

[Model] Contract Farming Act 2018

Government of India in May 2018 drafted the **Model Agriculture Produce and Livestock Contract Farming and Services (Promotion & Facilitation) Act, 2018** and asked States to implement the same. *(The Model Agricultural Produce and Livestock Marketing (Promotion and Facilitation) Act, 2017* ***left out*** *all provisions relating to* ***contract farming*** *and paved the way for drafting an* ***exclusive model law*** *on the subject of contract farming.)*

The following are the salient features of the Model Contract Farming Act 2018:

- Setting up of an appropriate and unbiased state level agency called "Contract Farming (Development and Promotion) Authority" to carry out the assigned mandates under the provisions of contract farming and popularize it among the stakeholders.
- Constitution of a "Registering and Agreement Recording Committee" at district/block/taluka level for registration of contract farming sponsor (buyer) and recording of contract, so as to implement effectively contract farming.
- No rights, title ownership or possession to be transferred or alienated or vested in the contract farming sponsor.
- Enables production support, including extension services to the contracting farmers or group of farmers through supply of quality inputs, scientific agronomic package of practices, technology, managerial skills and necessary credit.
- Promoting Farmer Producer Organization (FPOs) / Farmer Producer Companies (FPCs) to mobilize small and marginal farmers to benefit from scales of economy in production and post-production activities.
- Ensuring buying of entire pre-agreed quantity (of a specified quality) of one or more of agricultural produce, livestock or its product of contract farming producer as per the contract
- Making provision to guide the contracting parties to fix pre-agreed price and also to decide sale-purchase price in case of violent movement (upswing or downswing) of market price vis-à-vis pre-agreed price as a win-win framework.
- Providing Contract Farming Facilitation Group (CFFG) at village /panchayat level to take quick and need based decision relating to production and post production activities of contracted agricultural produce, livestock and/or its product.
- Caters to a dispute settlement mechanism at the lowest level for quick disposal of disputes arising out of the breach of contract or contravention of any provision of the Act.

The 1966 **Green Revolution** in agriculture is not considered as "**Market reforms**". This is because Green revolution was supported by **huge Govt. led subsidies** like MSP, fertilizer, electricity, water etc. So, all the inputs were provided free of cost and the produce was purchased by Govt. at higher than Market price (MSP). So, it was Govt. led boom and not market reforms. But Govt led support is not sustainable and govt. cannot support this for long for such a huge country, and now it has become unsustainable for the Govt. to keep this support in terms of MSP and subsidies. So, Govt. of India has recommended 'MODEL' acts to States like 'Agricultural land leasing Act 2016', 'Agricultural Produce and Livestock Marketing Act 2017' and 'Contract Farming Act 2018, and now it is up to the States to implement it.

10.11 Agriculture Based Clusters

- Agriculture in the twenty-first century is reinventing itself as a new global business reshaped by globalization, standardization, high-value production, massive growth in demand, retail and packaging innovations, and a ramp up in efficiency. Faced with constant productivity and market pressures, the "new agriculture" needs new tools to enhance its competitiveness and innovation capacity. One of these tools is the promotion of agriculture-based clusters.
- A cluster can be defined as the geographical concentration of industries which gain advantages through co-location. Agriculture Clusters (ACs) are simply a concentration of producers, agro-industries, traders and other private and public actors engaged in the same industry and inter-connecting and building value networks, either formally or informally, when addressing common challenges and pursuing common opportunities.
- Agriculture clusters is based on creation of **"value networks"** which is the aggregation of:
    - **Horizontal relationships** among producers, which take the form of producer groups, self-help groups or farmers producers' organization (FPOs)
    - **Vertical relationships** among suppliers of raw materials/production inputs, agricultural producers, processors and exporters, branded buyers and retailers
- Agriculture Clusters (ACs) seem to generate a number of advantages for small producers and agribusiness firms, from agglomeration economies to improving access to local and global markets, to higher value-added production. Consequently, ACs raise the competitive advantage of farmers and agribusiness firms as they increase their current productivity and their innovative capacity.
- Clusters promotes "co-opetition" (a balance between competition and cooperation)
- ACs constitutes an important tool for the economic and social development of a given territory. They can have positive impacts on income enhancement, employment generation and well-being of workers and entrepreneurs of the cluster and, more generally, they offer great potential for improving the local economy.

Challenges for Agriclusters

- Presence of large number of small and marginal farmers (86%)

- Regulatory hurdles like APMCs and land leasing
- How to better meet consumer demands at the same time increase efficiency and productivity
- The need to introduce market driven innovation and new technologies
- Increasingly stringent environmental regulations

Example of Agro based clusters

- Jute based industries in the rural parts of west Bengal
- Bamboo and organic food-based processing facilities in North-east
- Mega Food Parks in Punjab, Uttarakhand and few other states are an example of agro-based clusters as it connects farmers, suppliers, food-processors and retail chains in an-agricultural setting

10.12 Digital Agriculture Mission

Key objectives of the Digital Agriculture Mission are:

- To create a robust and holistic farmer-centric digital ecosystem in the country
- To improve transparency and efficiency in the implementation of government initiatives
- To support the government in making informed policy decisions
- To promote public and private innovation and partnerships, encouraging Agri techs in India's digital economy

Digital Agriculture Mission comprises of two foundational pillars:

1. **Agri Stack**

   Agri Stack is envisaged as a digital public good like "Aadhar" for efficient and effective service delivery to the farmers. It will be built in a 'federated architecture' as a collaborative project between the various agencies of the Central and State Governments and the UTs. It consists of three foundational registries or databases in the agriculture sector, i.e.:

   - Farmers registry

     It is a dynamic, accurate, and verified database of farmers created and managed by the States/ UTs. It will provide comprehensive and useful data on farmers comprising authenticated demographic details, land holdings, family details, crops sown, soil health, livestock owned, fisheries assets, and other vocations.

   - Village land maps registry

     Geo-referenced Village Maps are required for conducting digital crop surveys. Geo-referenced village maps will enable trustful ground truth data collection and mapping of the data points at the land parcel level during the Digital Crop Survey exercise, geography-based crop advisory system, etc.

   - Crop Sown Registry

     A Digital Crop Survey (DCS) System will be established to collect crop - sown details through a mobile interface, ensuring data is captured directly from the field. This database will provide accurate, real-time crop area information for every agricultural plot, aiming to replace traditional survey methods like Girdawari. The DCS system will also enhance remote sensing capabilities for seamless crop area mapping, reducing the need to conduct surveys in the future.

2. **Krishi Decision Support System (Krishi-DSS)**

   Krishi-DSS integrates and standardizes geospatial and non-geospatial data, including satellite, weather, soil, crop signatures, reservoir, groundwater data, and government scheme information. Krishi-DSS offers crop maps, soil maps, automated yield estimation models, drought/flood monitoring systems, etc., which support the government's evidence-based decision-making and facilitate innovative solutions by research institutions and the agritech industry. This Krishi-DSS platform is aligned with the government's National Geo-Spatial policy. The information available on Krishi-DSS would support crop map generation for identifying crop sown patterns and crop diversification, drought/flood monitoring, and technology/model-based yield assessment for settling crop insurance claims by farmers.

Benefits of Digital Agriculture Mission

- Better decision making for farmers
- Improved crop yield and productivity
- Efficient resource management
- Improved service delivery for farmers
- Optimized value chains

Challenges associated with Digital Agriculture Mission

- Low digital literacy among farmers
- Inadequate infrastructure (lower internet penetration)
- Fragmented land holdings
- Lack of standardized data
- Diverse agro-climatic zones and farming practices make it challenging to develop one-size-fits-all digital solutions

10.13 National Mission on Edible Oil

The Mission is being implemented over a seven-year period, from 2024-25 to 2030-31. The mission focuses on

1. Enhancing the production of key primary oilseed crops such as Rapeseed-Mustard, Groundnut, Soybean, Sunflower, and Sesamum
2. Increasing collection and extraction efficiency from secondary sources like Cottonseed, Rice Bran, and Tree Borne Oils
3. Targets to increase domestic edible oil production to 25.45 million tonnes by 2030-31 meeting around 72% of our projected domestic requirement. This will be achieved by promoting adoption of high-yielding high oil content seed varieties, extending cultivation into rice fallow areas, and promoting intercropping.
4. Over 600 Value Chain Clusters will be developed across 347 unique districts which will be managed by value chain partners such as FPOs, cooperatives, and public or private entities
5. The Mission will harness ongoing development of high-quality seeds by using cutting-edge global technologies such as genome editing.
6. The Mission aims to significantly enhance domestic oilseed production, advancing the goal of Atmanirbharta (self-reliance) in edible oils, thereby reducing import

dependency and conserving valuable foreign exchange while boosting farmers' incomes.

7. It will also accrue significant environmental benefits in the form of low water usage and improved soil health and making productive use of crop fallow areas.

Presently the country is heavily reliant on imports which account for 57% of its domestic demand for edible oils.

10.14 Pradhan Mantri Fasal Bima Yojana (PMFBY)

"Pradhan Mantri Fasal Bima Yojana" (PMFBY) is being implemented from Kharif season of 2016. The following are the salient features of the PMFBY scheme: -

- Only one premium rate for each season for all food grains, oilseeds and pulses - removing all variations in rates across crops and districts within a season. Kharif - 2% and Rabi - 1.5%. For horticulture and cotton crops, the premium may go up to 5%
- So, farmers premium is fixed while Government (Centre and States equally) bears the remaining financial burden of the premium
- The farmers get full insurance cover. There will be no capping of the sum insured, and hence claim amounts will not be cut or reduced
- For the first time, post-harvest losses arising out of cyclones and unseasonal rains have also been covered nationally
- For the first time, emphasis has been given to mobile and satellite technology to facilitate accurate assessment and quick settlement of claims

Coverage of Crops:

- Food crops (Cereals, Millets and Pulses),
- Oilseeds
- Commercial / Horticultural crops

Coverage of Risks:

Following stages of the crop and risks leading to crop loss are covered under the scheme.

- **Prevented Sowing/ Planting Risk:** Insured area is prevented from sowing/ planting due to deficit rainfall or adverse seasonal conditions
- **Standing Crop (Sowing to Harvesting) :** Comprehensive risk insurance is provided to cover yield losses due to non- preventable risks, viz. Drought, Dry spells, Flood, Inundation, Pests and Diseases, Landslides, Natural Fire and Lightening, Storm, Hailstorm, Cyclone, Typhoon, Tempest, Hurricane and Tornado.
- **Post-Harvest Losses:** Coverage is available only up to a maximum period of two weeks from harvesting for those crops which are allowed to dry in cut and spread condition in the field after harvesting against specific perils of cyclone and cyclonic rains and unseasonal rains.
- **Localized Calamities:** Loss/damage resulting from occurrence of identified localized risks of hailstorm, landslide, and Inundation affecting isolated farms in notified areas.

Losses arising out of war and nuclear risks, malicious damage and other preventable risks shall be excluded. The scheme is optional.

Use of Technology for Crop Insurance:

Drone technology can be used for crop insurance which is experiencing explosive growth. Drones are low-cost, can fly at low heights and capture images in all resolutions needed to assess crop damage. They are even better than satellites and remote sensing when it comes to avoiding cloud cover and have higher frequency images. Low-cost satellites called doves, can also be useful in crop monitoring. They have good resolution, fly on low orbit and are able to collect data from anywhere on earth. With these technologies, monitoring and assessing crop damage will become much easier, faster and cost effective.

Implementation of the Scheme:

The 'Unit of Insurance' for a crop during a season is decided by the State. For major crops, the Unit of Insurance shall ordinarily be Village/Village Panchayat level and for minor crops may be at a higher level so that the requisite number of crop cutting experiments could be conducted during the notified crop season. The Threshold Yield for a crop in an Insurance Unit shall be based on average yield of last seven years and based on that, Insurance protection shall be given to all the insured farmers in that Insurance Unit. The sum-insured for the farmers will be up to the Threshold Yield X MSP or gate price of the insured crop

State Govt. would invite all the empanelled insurance companies to quote their premium rates for the notified crops in the notified insurance unit area, Threshold Yields, Sum Insured etc. as indicated by the State for the season. The company quoting the minimum insurance premium will be selected and there will be only one company for every district.

To assess the damage/loss, State has to conduct requisite number of Crop Cutting Experiments (CCEs) at the level of notified insurance unit area for all the notified crops and the yield data will be submitted to insurance company within the prescribed time limit (within a month of harvest). Insurance Agency shall process the claims liability assessed and approve the claims. The claim amount along with particulars will be released to the individual Nodal Banks. The Banks at the grass-root level, in turn, shall credit the accounts of the individual farmers and display the particulars of beneficiaries on their notice board. The Banks shall provide individual farmer wise details claim credit details to Insurance Agency and shall be incorporated in the centralised data repository.

The scheme is doing well and coverage has increased to around 40% of the farmers (around 5.5 crore farmers every year on an average). But, some incidents were reported like states not paying their part of the premium subsidy on time and the delay in settlement of claims to farmers and insurance companies making huge profits.

Under PMFBY, if the insurance company charges premium of 40% then farmers pay 2% (fixed for kharif crop) and the rest 38% premium is shared by Centre and State equally means centre will pay 19% and State also 19%. And in case premium charged by insurance company increases then Farmers burden always remain fixed at 2% and Centre and States equally share the burden.

But in **Feb 2020**, Central Govt. announced that centre will comply with above formula only if the premium is max 30% but if the premium increases beyond 30% say 35% then Centre will pay only 14% (which is the premium burden of Centre in case of premium charged by company is 30%), farmers will have to pay 2% and States will have to pay 14% + 5%. That means whatever is the extra burden beyond 30%, will be borne by States. This 30% cap is for unirrigated area. For irrigated area it is 25%.

10.15 Increasing Farmers' Income

Growth in agricultural output does not translate into a proportionate growth in farmers' income because of the **price factor**. The experience shows that in some cases, growth in output brings similar increase in farmers' income but in many cases farmers' income did not grow much with increase in output. Farmers' welfare is more linked to farmers' income (Output X Price) rather than the agricultural output.

As far as agriculture is concerned, our political and bureaucratic system has always been more tonnage-centric than farmer-centric. We are happy and satisfied when production goes up, but did not care whether farmers have gained from it. That is the reason why Central Government changed the name of Ministry of Agriculture to Ministry of Agriculture and Farmers Welfare in 2015.

To increase the farmers' income, strong measures are needed to harness all possible sources of growth in farmers' income within as well as outside agriculture sector. ***Dalwai Committee in 2018 recommended the following seven points to increase farmers income:***

1. **Improvement in productivity of crops:** Productivity of most of the crops in the country is low and there is considerable scope to raise it. Except wheat, productivity of other crops in the country is below world average and much lower than agriculturally advanced countries. Even, within the country there is large variation in yield across states which are due to variation in access to irrigation. Enhancing access to irrigation and technological advancement are the most potent instruments to raise agricultural productivity and production in the country.
2. **Improvement in livestock productivity:** The livestock plays an important role in the economy of farmers. The farmers in India maintain mixed farming system i.e. a combination of crop and livestock where the output of one enterprise becomes the input of another enterprise thereby realize the resource efficiency. Driven by the structural changes in agriculture and food consumption pattern, the growth of this sector has to match the rising demand reflected in increasing share of these items in consumption expenditure.
3. **Increase in cropping intensity:** India has two main crop growing seasons namely kharif and rabi, which make it possible to cultivate two crops a year on the same piece of land. With availability of irrigation and new technologies it has become possible to raise short duration crops after the main kharif and rabi season. Land use statistics show that the second crop is taken only on 39 percent of net sown area. This implies that more than 60 percent agricultural land in the country remains unused for half of the productive period. Lack of access to water (less than 50% of cultivable land is under irrigation) to meet crop requirement is said to be the main reason for low crop intensity.
4. **Resource use efficiency or saving in cost of production:** The improvement in Total Factor Productivity (TFP) is an

important source of output growth which directly contributes to cost savings and thus increase in farmers' income. TFP accounts for effects in total output growth relative to the growth in total inputs used in production. TFP growth represents effect of technological change, skill, infra, etc.

5. **Diversification towards high value crops:** Diversification towards high value crops (HVC) offers great scope to improve farmers' income. The staple crops (cereals, pulses, oilseeds) occupy 77 percent of gross cropped area but contribute only 41 percent of total output of the crop sector. Interestingly, almost the same value of output is contributed by HVC (fruits, vegetables, fibre, spices, sugarcane) which just occupy 19 percent of the gross cropped area.

6. **Improvement in terms of trade for farmers:** To arrive at the change in real income of farmers, we need to adjust the current income of the farmers with an appropriate inflation index. If the inflation in the economy is higher than the farm produce prices then actually it reduces the real income of farmers. And when prices received by farmers for agricultural produce rise faster than the inflation, it adds to the real income, even without an increase in the volume of output.

7. **Shifting cultivators from farm to non-farm occupations:** Approximately 43% of the labour force is involved in agricultural activities contributing just 17% of the GDP. This shows over-dependence of workforce on agriculture with significant underemployment. This also reveals large difference in per worker productivity between agriculture and non-agriculture sectors. Thus, income of farmers can be improved substantially by shifting workforce away from agriculture to non-farm activities like agro-processing, food processing, tourism, leather, footwear, pottery, crafts, handlooms etc. as the available farm income will be distributed to a lesser number of workforce.

The neglect of required reforms in the agriculture sector has created wide disparity between agriculture sector and non-agriculture sectors. Till 1990-91, the growth rates in the two sectors moved in tandem and show very close correlation. **As the LPG reforms progressed, the growth trajectories diverged**. **Growth rate in the non-agriculture sector accelerated from below 6% towards more than 8% for most of the period**. **However, agriculture sector moved on cyclical path around long term trend of 3%.** It emerges from this comparison that in the absence of market reforms in agriculture sector, the agriculture growth remained low and the sector could not keep pace with the growth in the non-agriculture sector.

Doubling of farmers' income will require not only interventions to develop the agricultural sector but it also requires strong linkages with manufacturing and service sectors to transform the 'agricultural units to agricultural enterprises. Thus, it is not an isolated game that would transform the face of Indian agriculture; rather, it will need putting all forces together for the holistic development and to provide it more modern and professional orientation to this sector.

10.16 Agriculture Export Policy 2018

In order to provide an impetus to agricultural exports, the Government came out with a comprehensive "Agriculture Export Policy" in 2018 aimed at doubling the agricultural exports and integrating Indian farmers and agricultural products with the global value chains. The Agriculture Export Policy has the following vision: *"Harness export potential of Indian agriculture, through suitable policy instruments, to make India global power in agriculture and raise farmers' income."*

Objectives of the Agriculture Export Policy were as under:

- To double agricultural exports from $ 30+ Billion (2017-18) to $ 60+ Billion by 2022 and reach $ 100 Billion in the next few years thereafter, with a stable trade policy regime
- To diversify our export basket, destinations and boost high value and value-added agricultural exports including focus on perishables
- To promote novel, indigenous, organic, ethnic, traditional and non-traditional Agri products exports
- To provide an institutional mechanism for pursuing market access, tackling barriers and deal with sanitary and phyto-sanitary issues
- To strive to double India's share in world agri exports by integrating with global value chain at the earliest
- Enable farmers to get benefit of export opportunities in overseas market

Although agriculture export fell short of the target, but the recommendations of the policy are relevant for the exam.

Key Recommendations:

1. **Stable Trade Policy Regime:** Given the domestic price and production volatility of certain agricultural commodities, there has been a tendency to utilize trade policy as an instrument to attain short-term goals of taming inflation, providing price support to farmers and protecting the domestic industry. Such circumstantial measures are often product and sector specific, for instance, the ad-hoc ban or imposition of minimum export prices (MEP) for onion and non-Basmati rice exports. Such measures require constant fine tuning **and keep the market anxious**. India is seen as a source of high-quality agricultural products in many developing nations, ASEAN economies and changes in export regime on ground of domestic price fluctuations, religious and social belief can have long-term repercussions. While these decisions may serve the immediate purpose of maintaining domestic price equilibrium, they end up distorting India's image in international trade as a long term and reliable supplier. It is imperative to frame a stable and predictable policy with limited State interference to send a positive signal to the international market.

Thus, the policy aims to provide a policy assurance that **the processed agricultural products and all kinds of organic products will not be brought under the ambit of any kind of export restriction** (viz. MEP, export duty, export ban, etc.) even though the primary agricultural products which are essential from food security perspective or non-organic agricultural products is brought under some kind of export restrictions.

2. **Infrastructure and Logistics:** Presence of robust infrastructure remains a critical component of a strong agricultural value chain. This involves pre-harvest and post-harvest handling facilities, storage & distribution, processing facilities, roads and world class exit point infrastructure at ports facilitating swift trade. Given their perishable nature and stringent import standards, efficient and time-sensitive handling is extremely vital to agricultural commodities. Identifying strategically important clusters, creating inland transportation links alongside dedicated agri infrastructure at ports with 24x7 customs clearance for perishables will therefore go a long way in boosting trade exponentially. **It is often pointed out that expenses towards logistics handling in India are about 14 to 15% of the cost of exports. Benchmarked against 8 to 9% in some of the developed economies**, the savings on account of improved logistics can make Indian agricultural exports significantly competitive in the global market place.

3. **Cluster Development:** Exporting horticultural products requires significant volumes of high-quality produce of the same variety with standard parameters matching import demands. Small landholding pattern and low farmer awareness in India has often meant limited volumes of different varieties of multiple crops with little or no standardization. **Export oriented cluster development across States** will be key to ensuring surplus produce with standard physical and quality parameters which meet export demands.

4. **Promoting Value Added Exports:** India's export basket is dominated by products with little or no processing or value addition**. Industry estimates also suggest a significant quantity of our exports head to countries which conduct limited value addition and re-export it.** There is a huge demand for processed products in the global market. Only a limited range of products (mango pulp, puree, by-products of oil crops, soya meal, cakes and few ready to eat products) and single processed products such as Sugar, tea, edible oils, coffee and essential oils are exported from India. India can look at exports of a whole range of value- added fruits and vegetables, Ready to eat products, Pickles, soups and sauces, Dairy products, processed livestock, Aquaculture products, textile products, etc.

5. **Ease of Doing Business:** There has been a consistent demand from exporters across sectors for a dedicated platform to access trade and market related information. There is a portal on Trade Analytics which provides the trends for different commodities in different markets. Similarly, APEDA (Agricultural and Processed Food Exports Development Authority) and MPEDA (Marine Products Export Development Authority) run agri exchange portal and fish exchange portal respectively to provide market intelligence to their stakeholders. India Trade portal provides information relating to tariff scenarios in FTA and non-FTA situations, the SPS (Sanitary and phytosanitary) notifications and also provides a window for Indian

Embassies to offer market leads. Thus, relevant information on market intelligence is scattered in different web pages. There is a need to develop an integrated online portal for real time updates relating to tariff, non-tariff, documentation, pesticide & chemical MRL notifications. This portal will facilitate exporters to make well-informed decisions related to markets, pricing, hedging and SPS notifications. The portal may also include a grievance redressal mechanism allowing exporters to flag off market related issues and challenges.

Exporters reveal that lengthy and cumbersome documentation and operational procedures at ports are a constant challenge. They have often recommended to implement 24 x 7 single window clearance of perishables imports and exports at key ports across the nation. It is equally important to station more quarantine officers at strategically important ports.

6. **SPS and TBT (Technical Barriers to Trade) Response Mechanism:** It is common knowledge that issues relating to market access go on for months, sometimes years before countries allow market access for products. Apart from tariff barriers, which have been declining over the years on account of Free Trade Agreements & Regional Trade Agreements, the Non-Tariff Barriers (NTBs) and stringent quality/ phyto-sanitary standards are becoming the norm for restricting/ preventing market access. It is necessary to respond to rapid alerts and warnings and to ensure that the concerns/ problem areas percolate to the producers/ processors and exporters. In the absence of a response mechanism, the likelihood of temporary restriction/ ban looms large and sometimes it may take years to lift the ban. (e.g., ban on fruits and vegetables to EU, ban on green chilly to Saudi Arab, etc).

7. **Developing Sea Protocol:** Developing Sea protocols for perishables must be taken on priority for long distance markets. Export of perishables requires special storage, transportation and handling at desired temperatures. Time is a major constraint and air freight proves costly for exporters. However, India's export of fresh produce can grow exponentially if sea protocols are established across exportable varieties of shortlisted commodities. **A sea protocol will indicate at what maturity level harvesting can be done for transportation by sea** This exercise has to be carried out in partnership with shipping lines, reefer service providers, Indian Council of Agriculture Research and APEDA. Philippines and Ecuador are a classic case in point – both countries were successful in developing sea protocols for exporting bananas for 40 and 24 days of sea journey respectively. Philippines has been shipping Bananas to the Middle East which takes around 18 days while India has only been able to ship produce around 2-4 days transit period. Thus, developing sea protocol will go a long way in promoting trade.

8. **Conformity Assessment:** Many importing countries do not recognize India's export inspection and control processes. The lack of recognition of Indian testing procedures and conformity standards proves costly to exporters and therefore farmers. Many times, this means multiplicity and duplication of tests by various laboratories across the country, Spices, organic food, Basmati products have been most affected by this. Equally, the government must make concerted efforts during bilateral discussions for mutual recognition of ethnic and organic products and standards.

10.17 A comparison of Indian Agriculture with China (2018-19)

Comparison	India	China
Agricultural Land	158 million hectares	120 million hectares
Irrigation Cover	48%	41%
Agriculture Output	$ 540 billion (17%)	$ 1400 billion (7%)
Expenditure on agriculture R&D and extension	$1.5 billion	$ 7.8 billion
Fertilizer consumption	166 kg/ha	503 kg/ha
Labour Force in Agriculture	40%	25%

- Both have adopted modern technologies in agriculture, starting with high yield variety (HYV) seeds, in the mid-1960s, increasing irrigation cover and using more chemical fertilisers to produce more food from limited land.
- China started procuring at support prices from its farmers which resulted in huge stocks and it incurred large expenditure. Having burnt their fingers, China stopped price support scheme for corn and has started reducing support prices for wheat and rice. But India has kept on increasing the procurement at MSP.
- China has combined its major input subsidies in a single scheme, which allows **direct payment to farmers on per hectare basis and has spent $20.7 billion for this purpose in 2018-19. This gives the farmers freedom to produce any crop rather than incentivising them to produce specific crops.** Inputs are priced at market prices giving right signals to farmers to use resources optimally. India, on the other hand, spent only 3 billion dollars under its direct income scheme, PM-KISAN in 2018-19, but the country has spent $27 billion on heavily subsidising fertilisers, power, irrigation, insurance and credit. This leads to large inefficiency in their use and also creates environmental problems. It may be better for India to also consolidate all its input subsidies and give them directly to farmers on per hectare basis and free up prices from all controls. This would go a long way to spur efficiency and productivity in Indian agriculture.
- China's productivity in most crops is 50 to 100 per cent higher than India's.

PREVIOUS YEARS' QUESTIONS

Prelim Questions

1. The Fair and Remunerative Price (RFP) of sugarcane is approved by the **[2015]**
   (a) Cabinet Committee on Economic Affairs
   (b) Commission for Agricultural Costs and Prices
   (c) Directorate of Marketing and Inspection, Ministry of Agriculture
   (d) Agricultural Produce Marketing Committee

2. In India, markets in agricultural products are regulated under the **[2015]**
   (a) Essential Commodities Act, 1955
   (b) Agricultural Produce Market Committee Act enacted by States
   (c) Agricultural Produce (Grading and Marking) Act, 1937
   (d) Food Products Order, 1956 and Meat and Food Products Order, 1973

3. With reference to 'Pradhan Mantri Fasal Bima Yojana', consider the following statements: **[2016]**
   (i) Under this scheme, farmers will have to pay a uniform premium of two percent for any crop they cultivate in any season of the year.
   (ii) This scheme covers post-harvest losses arising out of cyclones and unseasonal rains
   Which of the statements given above is/are correct?
   (a) (i) only (b) (ii) only
   (c) Both (i) & (ii) (d) Neither (i) nor (ii)

4. Consider the following statements: **[2017]**
   The nation-wide 'Soil Health Card Scheme' aims at
   (i) Expanding the cultivable area under irrigation.
   (ii) Enabling the banks to assess the quantum of loans to be granted to farmers on the basis of soil quality.
   (iii) Checking the overuse of fertilizers in farmlands.
   Which of the above statements is/are correct?
   (a) (i) & (ii) only (b) (iii) only
   (c) (ii) & (iii) only (d) (i), (ii) & (iii)

5. What is/are the advantage/advantages of implementing the 'National Agriculture Market' scheme? **[2017]**
   (i) It is a pan-India electronic trading portal for agricultural commodities.
   (ii) It provides the farmers access to nationwide market, with prices commensurate with the quality of their produce.
   Select the correct answer using the code given below:
   (a) (i) only (b) (ii) only
   (c) Both (i) & (ii) (d) Neither (i) nor (ii)

6. In India, which of the following can be considered as public investment in agriculture? **[2020]**
   (i) Fixing Minimum Support Price for agriculture produce of all crops
   (ii) Computerization of Primary Agricultural Credit Societies
   (iii) Social Capital Development
   (iv) Free electricity supply to farmers
   (v) Waiver of agricultural loan by the banking system
   (vi) Setting up of cold storage facilities by the governments

Select the correct answer using the code given below:

(a) (i), (ii) and (v) only

(b) (i), (iii), (iv) and (v) only

(c) (ii), (iii) and (vi) only

(d) (i), (ii), (iii), (iv), (v) and (vi)

7. Which of the following factors/policies were affecting the price of rice in India in the recent past? **[2020]**

1. Minimum Support Pric
2. Government's trading
3. Government's stockpiling
4. Consumer subsidies

Select the correct answer using the code given below:

(a) 1, 2 and 4 only (b) 1, 3 and 4 only

(c) and 3 only (d) 1, 2, 3 and 4

8. Consider the following statements: **[2023]**

1. India has more arable area than China.
2. The proportion of irrigated area is more in India as compared to China.
3. The average productivity per hectare in Indian agriculture is higher than that in China.

How many of the above statements are correct?

(a) Only one (b) Only two

(c) All three (d) None

9. Which one of the following best describes the concept of 'Small Farmer Large Field'? **[2023]**

(a) Resettlement of a large number of people, uprooted from their countries due to war, by giving them a large cultivable land which they cultivate collectively and share the produce

(b) Many marginal farmers in an area organize themselves into groups and synchronize and harmonize selected agricultural operations

(c) Many marginal farmers in an area together make a contract with a corporate body and surrender their land to the corporate body for a fixed term for which the corporate body makes a payment of agreed amount to the farmers

(d) A company extends loans, technical knowledge and material inputs to a number of small farmers in an area so that they produce the agricultural commodity required by the company for its manufacturing process and commercial production

ANSWERS

1.(a) 2. (b) 3. (b) 4. (b) 5. (c) 6. (c) 7. (d) 8. (b) 9. (b)

Main Questions

1. What do u mean by Minimum Support Price (MSP)? How will MSP rescue the farmers from the low-income trap? **[2018]**

2. What are the main constraints in transport and marketing of agricultural produce in India? **[2020]**

3. How does e-technology help farmers in production and marketing of agricultural produce? Explain it. **[2023]**

4. What are the causes of persistent high food inflation in India? Comment on the effectiveness of the monetary policy of the RBI to control this type of inflation. **[2024]**

11

Agriculture: Part-II

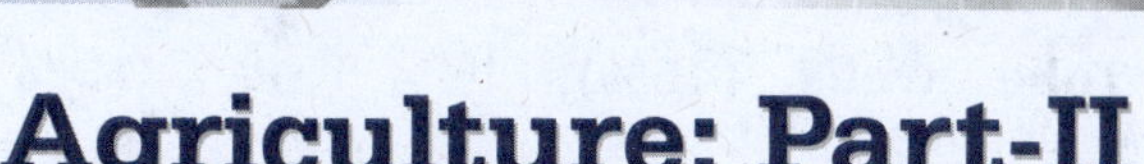

11.1 Irrigation in India

Introduction

Agriculture is the nerve of any country as it is needed for survival of living beings. For growing crops, irrigation is major process. Irrigation is described as the artificial application of water to the land or soil (whereas rain-fed farming is the natural application of water to the soil through direct rainfall.). It is the substitute or supplement of rainwater with another source of water. It is used in dry areas and during periods of insufficient rainfall. It is considered as basic infrastructure and vital input required for agricultural production.

Sources of Irrigation

1. **Canals (24%):** Canals are most important source of irrigation from the period of 1950s and 60s, but in the 1970s, they yielded first place to wells and tube wells and now constitute the second most important source of irrigation in India. Canals are most effective techniques of irrigation in areas of low-level relief, deep fertile soils, perennial source of water and extensive command area. Therefore, the main concentration of canal irrigation is in the northern plain of India, especially the areas comprising Uttar Pradesh, Haryana and Punjab.

   Canals are constructed by putting some form of barrage across the river which flows throughout the year and diverting its water by means of a canal to the agricultural fields, both far and near. Canals are also constructed by pumping water out of the river through big electric pumps.

   Indira Gandhi Canal is the longest canal in India and the largest irrigation project in the world. It is 649 Km long and starts from the Harike Barrage at Harike, a few kilometers below the confluence of the Satluj and Beas rivers in the Indian state of Punjab and terminates in the Thar Desert in the north west of Rajasthan State by flowing through Haryana. The canal is one of the projects of Green Revolution in India and also runs through The Great Thar Desert.

2. **Wells (17%):** Wells provide the most widely distributed source of irrigation in India. A well is a hole dug in the ground to obtain the subsoil water. An ordinary well is about 3-5 metres deep but deeper wells up to 15 metres are also dug. Well irrigation is more popular in those regions where ground water is in ample and where there are few canals for ex. eastern UP, Bihar etc. Some or the other type of lift is always required for using the well water for irrigation whereas old methods like mot are still practised

widely in many areas, power driven pumps have become exceedingly popular in most part.

3. **Tube wells (46%):** Tube wells are common in areas where the water table is rather deep, say, over 15 metres. The sub-soil water is exploited through deep well pumping. Indo-Gangetic valley and in certain coastal deltaic areas tube well is common.

4. **Tanks (12% irrigation):** A tank acts as an irrigation storage system which is developed by constructing a small bund of earth or stones built across a stream. The water impounded by the bund is used for irrigation and for other purposes. Some tanks are built partly as dugouts and partly by enclosing bunds. Tanks are of varying size but most of the tanks are of small size and are built by individual farmers or groups of farmers. Tank irrigation is more suitable in the peninsular plateau area such as Andhra Pradesh (Including Telangana) and Tamil Nadu. In these States tanks are formed through natural depression by building earthen embankments. There we have hard rocks and non-porous which hold water for long. Andhra Pradesh including Telangana is the largest state of tank irrigation which has about 29 per cent of tank irrigated area of India. Odisha and Karnataka also have some tank irrigation.

Techniques of Irrigation

1. Surface/flood irrigation

- **Basin:** Basin irrigation is the most common form of surface irrigation, particularly in regions with layouts of small fields. If a field is level in all directions, is encompassed by a dyke/embankment to prevent runoff, and provides an undirected flow of water onto the field, it is herein called a basin. A basin is typically square in shape but exists in all sorts of irregular and rectangular configurations. It may be furrowed or corrugated, have raised beds for the benefit of certain crops, but as long as the inflow is undirected and uncontrolled into these field modifications, it remains a basin. It is suited for paddy, wheat crops.

- **Furrow:** Furrow irrigation is conducted by creating small parallel channels along the field length in the direction of predominant slope. Water is applied to the top end of each furrow and flows down the field under the influence of gravity. Water may be supplied using gated pipe, siphon and head ditch. The speed of water movement is determined by many factors such as slope, surface roughness and furrow shape but most importantly by the inflow rate and soil infiltration rate. The spacing between adjacent furrows is governed by the crop species, common spacings typically range from 0.75 to 2 metres. The crop is planted on the ridge between furrows. It is suited for crops such as cotton, sugarcane and fruits and vegetables.

- **Bay/border:** Border strip or bay irrigation could be considered as a hybrid of level basin and furrow irrigation. The field is divided into a number of bays or strips, each bay is separated by raised earth check banks (borders). The bays are typically longer and narrower compared to basin irrigation and are orientated to align lengthwise with the slope of the field. Typical bay dimensions are between 10-70m wide and 100-700m long. The water is applied to the top end of the bay, which is usually constructed to facilitate free-flowing conditions at the downstream end. One common use of this technique includes the irrigation of pasture for dairy production generally used for large farms.

2. Micro Irrigation (Drip/Trickle/Sprinkler/Localized)

Drip irrigation involves dripping water onto the soil at very low rates (2-20 litres/hour) from a system of small diameter plastic pipes fitted with outlets called emitters or drippers. **Water is applied close to plants so that only part of the soil in which the roots grow is wetted**, unlike surface and sprinkler irrigation, which involves wetting the whole soil profile. With drip irrigation water, applications are more frequent (usually every 1-3 days) than with other methods and this provides a very favourable high moisture level in the soil in which plants can flourish.

Drip irrigation is most suitable for row crops (vegetables, soft fruits like grapes), tree and vine crops where one or more emitters can be provided for each plant. Generally, only high value crops are considered because of the high capital costs of installing a drip system.

Drip irrigation is adaptable to any farmable slope. Normally the crop would be planted along contour lines and the water supply pipes (laterals) would be laid along the contour also. This is done to minimize changes in emitter discharge as a result of land elevation changes.

Drip irrigation is suitable for most soils. On clay soils water must be applied slowly to avoid surface water ponding and runoff. On sandy soils higher emitter discharge rates will be needed to ensure adequate lateral wetting of the soil.

Bamboo Irrigation (a kind of drip irrigation): In Meghalaya and some north-eastern states, an ingenious system of tapping of stream and Springwater by using bamboo pipes to irrigate plantations is widely prevalent. It is so perfected that about 18-20 litres of water entering the bamboo pipe system per minute gets transported over several hundred metres and finally gets reduced to 20-80 drops per minute at the site of the plant. The tribal farmers of Khasi and Jaintia hills use the 200-year-old system.

The bamboo drip irrigation system is normally used to irrigate the betel leaf or black pepper crops planted in arecanut orchards or in mixed orchards. Bamboo pipes are used to divert perennial springs on the hilltops to the lower reaches by gravity. The channel sections, made of bamboo, divert and convey water to the plot site where it is distributed without leakage into branches, again made and laid out with different forms of bamboo pipes. Manipulating the intake pipe positions also controls the flow of water into the lateral pipes. Reduced channel sections and diversion units are used at the last stage of water application. The last channel section enables the water to be dropped near the roots of the plant.

Sprinkler Irrigation

Sprinkler irrigation is a method of applying irrigation water which is similar to natural rainfall. Water is distributed through a system of pipes usually by pumping. It is then sprayed into the air through sprinklers so that it breaks up into small water drops which fall to the ground. The pump supply system, sprinklers and operating conditions must be designed to enable a uniform application of water. Sprinklers are buried in the ground along with their supporting plumbing, although above ground and moving sprinklers are also common.

- Sprinkler irrigation is often used **when the land is uneven and thus, not suitable for surface irrigation.** This method is better than surface irrigation in that less water is wasted and water is distributed more evenly. Pipes fitted with sprinklers are laid over or along the field. The sprinklers have rotating heads, which spray water over the crops.
- Sprinklers are **best suited to sandy soils with high infiltration rates** although they are adaptable to most soils. Sprinkler irrigation is suited for most row, field and tree crops and water can be sprayed over or under the crop canopy.

Challenges faced by Indian Irrigation System

- Deterioration of irrigation infrastructure: Many of India's irrigation system like dams and canals are decades old and are poorly maintained resulting in inefficiencies and water wastage. Dams and canals are silted, clogging and inadequate water distribution

- Inefficient water use: Subsidy on electricity for pumping of water for agricultural purposes encourages farmers to over extract groundwater resulting in depletion of aquifers especially in Punjab and Haryana
- High Costs of modern irrigation system: Drip and sprinkler irrigation are effective in saving water but have high initial costs. This makes it difficult for small and marginal farmers to adopt these technologies
- Climate change: Climate change is increasing the frequency of extreme weather events such as floods and droughts, which disrupt traditional irrigation practices

Measures taken by the government for efficient irrigation management

- National Mission for sustainable agriculture
- Pradhan Mantri Krishi Sichai Yojana
- Jal Shakti Abhiyan
- Command Area Development and Water Management

11.2 Farming System and Cropping Pattern in India

Agriculture is an age-old economic activity in our country. Over these years, cultivation methods have changed significantly depending upon the characteristics of physical environment, technological know-how and socio-cultural practices. Farming varies from subsistence to commercial type. At present, in different parts of India, **the following farming systems are practised.**

- Primitive Subsistence Farming: This type of farming is still practised in few pockets of India. Primitive subsistence agriculture is practised on small patches of land with the help of primitive tools like hoe, dao and digging sticks, and family/community labour. This type of farming depends upon monsoon, natural fertility of the soil and suitability of other environmental conditions to the crops grown. Farmers clear a patch of land and produce cereals and other food crops to sustain their family. When the soil fertility decreases, the farmers shift and clear a fresh patch of land for cultivation. This type of shifting allows Nature to replenish the fertility of the soil through natural processes; land productivity in this type of agriculture is low as the farmer does not use fertilisers or other modern inputs.
- Intensive Subsistence Farming: This type of farming is practised in areas of high population pressure on land. It is labour intensive farming, where high doses of biochemical inputs and irrigation are used for obtaining higher production. Though the 'right of inheritance' leading to the division of land among successive generations has rendered land-holding size uneconomical, the farmers continue to take maximum output from the limited land in the absence of alternative source of livelihood. Thus, there is enormous pressure on agricultural land.
- Commercial Farming: The main characteristic of this type of farming is the use of higher doses of modern inputs, e.g., high yielding variety (HYV) seeds, chemical fertilisers, insecticides and pesticides in order to obtain higher productivity. The degree of commercialisation of agriculture varies from one region to another. For example, rice is a commercial crop in Haryana and Punjab, but in Odisha, it is a subsistence crop.

Plantation is also a type of commercial farming. In this type of farming, a single crop is grown on a large area. The plantation has an interface of agriculture and industry. Plantations cover large tracts of land, using capital intensive inputs, with the help of migrant labourers. All the produce is used as raw material in respective industries. In India, tea, coffee, rubber, sugarcane etc. are important plantation crops. Since the production is mainly for market, a well-developed network of transport and communication connecting the plantation areas, processing industries and markets plays an important role in the development of plantations.

Cropping pattern is defined as how crops are distributed in time and space. **Cropping system** comprises all cropping patterns grown on the farm and their interaction with farm resources, other household enterprises and the physical, biological, technological and sociological factors or environments.

India has three cropping seasons — rabi, kharif and zaid (the summer months between rabi and kharif). Depending on the terrain, topography, slope, temperature, amount and reliability of rainfall, soils and availability of water for irrigation, the cropping patterns vary from region to region. Following are different types of **cropping pattern** followed in India:

- **Monocropping or Monoculture:** In this system, only one crop is grown on farm land year after year. For ex., Wheat, corn in areas where irrigation facility is not available.
- **Multiple Cropping:** The growing of more than one crop on the same land in one year. There are different types of multiple cropping:
    - o **Inter Cropping:** Growing of two or more crops simultaneously **in alternate rows** or otherwise in the same area, where there is significant amount of inter crop competition. Pigeon pea planted with sorghum.
    - o **Mixed Cropping:** Cultivation of two or more than two crops simultaneously, on the same piece of land **without any definite row pattern or fixed ratio**. Wheat and mustard crops in northern India.
    - o **Sequential Cropping:** Growing of two or more crops in quick succession on the same piece of land in a farming year. The sowing of the succeeding crop and harvesting of the preceding crop may be done simultaneously or in a quick succession e.g. Just after the harvest of Maize, Potato is sown and just after digging of potato, Chili is sown. Rice-wheat in Northern India, Rice-Rice in Assam and West Bengal and coastal regions of Andhra, Tamil Nadu. Soya bean-wheat in Maharashtra, MP and Rajasthan. Rice-Pulses in Chhattisgarh, Odisha and Bihar.
    - o **Relay Cropping:** Relay planting is inter-sowing of seeds/seedlings of the succeeding crop before harvesting the preceding/maturing crop. Generally, second crop is planted after the first crop has reached its reproductive stage of growth e.g., Potato is planted before the harvest of Maize and Radish is sown before harvesting of Potato.
- **Crop Rotation:** Crop Rotation means changing the type of crops grown in the field each season or each year (or changing from crops to fallow). For example, planting maize one year, and beans the next.
- **Ratooning:** One of the important methods of intensive cropping, allowing the stubbles of the original crop to strike again after harvesting and to raise another crop.

- **Mixed Farming:** A system of farming on a particular farm which includes crop production, raising livestock, poultry, fisheries, bee keeping etc. to sustain and satisfy as many needs of the farmer as possible. The objective is subsistence while higher profitability without altering ecological balance is important in farming system.

11.3 Food Systems

Food systems (FS) encompass the entire range of actors and their interlinked value-adding activities involved in the production, aggregation, processing, distribution, consumption and disposal of food products that originate from agriculture, forestry or fisheries, and parts of the broader economic, societal and natural environments in which they are embedded.

The food system is composed of sub-systems (e.g., farming system, waste management system, input supply system, etc.) and interacts with other key systems (e.g., energy system, trade system, health system, etc.). Therefore, a structural change in the food system might originate from a change in another system; for example, a policy promoting more biofuel in the energy system will have a significant impact on the food system.

A sustainable food system (SFS) is a food system that delivers food security and nutrition for all in such a way that the economic, social and environmental bases to generate food security and nutrition for future generations are not compromised.

- **Economic sustainability:** It should generate benefits, or economic value-added, for all categories of stakeholders: wages for workers, taxes for governments, profits for enterprises, and food supply improvements for consumers.
- **Social Sustainability:** A food system is considered sustainable when there is equity in the distribution of the economic value-added, taking into account vulnerable groups categorized by gender, age, race and so on. Food system activities need to contribute to the advancement of important socio-cultural outcomes, such as nutrition and health.
- **Environmental sustainability:**

  Sustainability is determined by ensuring that the impacts of food system activities on the surrounding natural environment are neutral or positive, taking into consideration biodiversity, water, soil, animal and plant health, the carbon footprint, the water footprint, food loss and waste, and toxicity.

A sustainable food system lies at the heart of the United Nations' Sustainable Development Goals (SDGs). Adopted in 2015, the SDGs call for major transformations in agriculture and food systems in order to end hunger, achieve food security and improve nutrition by 2030.

11.4 Animal Husbandry

India's livestock sector is one of the largest in the world comprising 4.5% of total GDP of India and 30% of agricultural GDP in 2022-23. The livestock sector has been growing faster than many other sectors of agriculture and is the engine of growth for Indian agriculture.

The livestock plays an important role in the rural economy. The farmers in India maintain mixed farming system i.e., a combination of crop and livestock where the output of one enterprise becomes the input of another enterprise thereby realizing the resource efficiency. Livestock rearing is a key livelihood and risk mitigation strategy for small and marginal farmers, particularly across the rain-fed regions of India. The livestock serve the farmers in many different ways as follows:

1. Income: Livestock is a source of subsidiary income for many families in India especially the resource poor who maintain few heads of animals. Cows and buffaloes if in milk will provide regular income to the livestock farmers through sale of milk. Animals also serve as sources of income during emergencies to meet exigencies like marriages, treatment of sick persons, children education, repair of houses etc. The animals also serve as assets which provide economic security to the owners.
2. Employment: A large number of people in India being less literate and unskilled depend upon agriculture for their livelihoods. But agriculture being seasonal in nature could provide employment for a maximum of 180 days in a year. The land less and less land people depend upon livestock for utilizing their labour during lean agricultural season.
3. Food: The livestock products such as milk, meat and eggs are an important source of animal protein to the members of the livestock owners.
4. Social security: The animals offer social security to the owners in terms of their status in the society. The families especially the landless which own animals are better placed than those who do not. Gifting of animals during marriages is a very common phenomenon in different parts of the country. Rearing of animals is a part of the Indian culture. Animals are used for various socio religious functions. Cows for house warming ceremonies; Bulls and Cows are worshipped during various religious functions.
5. Draft/Draught: The bullocks are the back bone of Indian agriculture. The farmers especially the marginal and small depend upon bullocks for ploughing, carting and transport of both inputs and outputs.
6. Dung: In rural areas dung is used for several purposes which include fuel (dung cakes), fertilizer (farm yard manure), and plastering material (poor man's cement).

Driven by the structural changes in agriculture and food consumption pattern, the utility of livestock has been undergoing a steady transformation. The non-food functions of livestock are becoming weaker. Importance of livestock as source of 'draught power' has declined considerably due to mechanization of agriculture operations and declining farm size. Use of dung manure is increasingly being replaced by chemical fertilizers. On the other hand, their importance as a source of quality and nutritional food has increased. Sustained income and economic growth, a fast-growing urban population, burgeoning middle-income class, changing lifestyles, increasing proportion of women in workforce, improvements in transportation and storage practices and rising of supermarkets especially in cities and towns are fuelling rapid increase in consumption of animal food products.

The following are some of the important aspects of animal rearing:

- In the rural sector, livestock wealth is much more equitably distributed than wealth associated with land. Thus, when we think of the goal of inclusive growth, we should not forget that from equity and livelihood perspectives, livestock rearing must be at the centre of the stage in poverty alleviation programmes.
- Livestock rearing at the household level is

largely a women-led activity, and therefore income from livestock rearing and decisions related to management of livestock within the household are primarily taken by women. Interventions in India have demonstrated that support for livestock rearing has contributed significantly to the empowerment of women and an increasing role in decision making at both the household and village level.

- Livestock rearing, particularly in the rain-fed regions of the country, is also emerging as a key risk mitigation strategy for the poorest. They face increasingly uncertain and erratic weather conditions which negatively impact crop productivity and wage labour in the agriculture sector.

Although livestock products make important contributions to food security and poverty reduction for many low-income rural families, the policy and institutional framework has failed to serve the needs of these poorest households.

Following are the major challenges faced by the livestock sector:

- Inadequate testing and treatment facilities for veterinary diseases mostly in rural areas where more than 95% of the livestock is concentrated
- Failure to connect small holder livestock keepers to better paying markets
- Lack of insurance and credit facilities
- Livestock producers, including traditional pastoralists and smallholders, have become victims of natural resource degradation impacting animal productivity

As per the revised provisions of the livestock health and disease control programme, there is a major focus on establishment and strengthening of Veterinary services – Mobile Veterinary Units (MVU). MUVs will plug the challenges posed by the limitations of stationary hospitals by providing veterinary diagnostics and treatments facilities at a farmers' doorstep for ailments, diseases, or any other emergency veterinary conditions.

11.5 National Livestock Mission

(Share of Livestock in the overall GDP is around 4.5%)

The Department of Animal Husbandry & Dairying, Government of India is implementing the scheme of National Livestock Mission since the financial year 2014-15. In view of the present need of the sector the NLM scheme has been revised and realigned from FY 2021-22. The revised scheme of National Livestock Mission (NLM) aims towards employment generation, entrepreneurship development, increase in per animal productivity and thus targeting increased production of meat, goat milk, egg and wool under the umbrella scheme Development Programme. The excess production will help in the export earnings after meeting the domestic demands. The concept of NLM Scheme is to develop the entrepreneur in order to create the forward and backward linkage for the produce available at the unorganized sector and to link with the organized sector.

Mission Objectives

The NLM intends to achieve the following objectives:

- Employment generation through entrepreneurship development in small ruminant, poultry and piggery sector & Fodder sector.

- Increase of per animal productivity through breed improvement.
- Increase in production of meat, egg, goat milk, wool and fodder.
- Increasing availability of fodder and feed to substantially reduce the demand – through strengthening the fodder seed supply chain and availability of certified fodder seeds.
- Encouraging establishment of fodder processing units to reduce the demand supply gap.
- Promoting risk management measures including livestock insurance for farmers.
- Promoting applied research in prioritized areas of poultry, sheep, goat, feed and fodder.
- Capacity building of state functionaries and livestock owners through strengthened extension machinery to provide quality extension service to farmers.
- Promoting skill-based training and dissemination of technologies for reducing cost of production, and improving production of livestock sector.

The realigned National Livestock Mission has following three Sub-Missions:

- Sub-mission on Breed Development of Livestock and Poultry
- Sub-mission on Feed and Fodder Development
- Sub Mission on Innovation and Extension

11.6 Mission for Integrated Development of Horticulture (MIDH)

Mission for Integrated Development of Horticulture (MIDH) is a Centrally Sponsored Scheme for the holistic growth of the horticulture sector covering fruits, vegetables, root & tuber crops, mushrooms, spices, flowers, aromatic plants, coconut, cashew, cocoa and bamboo.

Salient Features

- Under MIDH, Government of India (GOI) contributes 60% of total outlay for developmental programmes in the states and 40% share are contributed by State Governments. In the case of North Eastern States and Himalayan States, GOI contributes 90%.
- In case of National Horticulture Board (NHB), Coconut Development Board (CDB), Central Institute for Horticulture (CIH), Nagaland and the National Level Agencies (NLA), GOI contributes 100%.
- MIDH also provides technical advice and administrative support to State Governments/ State Horticulture Missions (SHMs) for the Saffron Mission and other horticulture related activities like Rashtriya Krishi Vikas Yojana (RKVY).
- The strategy of the MIDH is on production of quality seeds and planting material, production enhancement through productivity improvement measures along with support for creation of infrastructure to reduce post-harvest losses and improved marketing of produce with active participation of all stake holders, particularly farmer groups and FPOs.

11.7 National Bamboo Mission

The National Bamboo Mission envisages promoting holistic growth of bamboo sector by adopting **area-based**, **regionally differentiated strategy** and to increase the area under bamboo cultivation and marketing. Under the Mission, steps have been taken to increase the availability of quality planting material by supporting the setting up of new nurseries and strengthening of existing ones. To address forward integration, the Mission is taking steps to strengthen marketing of bamboo products, especially those of handicraft items.

Objectives:

- To increase the area under bamboo plantation in non-forest Government and private lands to supplement farm income and contribute towards resilience to climate change as well as availability of quality raw material requirement of industries.
- The bamboo plantations will be promoted predominantly in farmers' fields, homesteads, community lands, arable wastelands, and along irrigation canals, water bodies etc.
- To improve post-harvest management through establishment of innovative primary processing units near the source of production, primary treatment and seasoning plants, preservation technologies and market infrastructure.
- To promote product development keeping in view market demand, by assisting R&D, entrepreneurship & business models at micro, small and medium levels and feed bigger industry.
- To rejuvenate the under developed bamboo industry in India.
- To promote skill development, capacity building, awareness generation for development of bamboo sector from production to market demand.
- To realign efforts so as to reduce dependency on import of bamboo and bamboo products by way of improved productivity and suitability of domestic raw material for industry, so as to enhance income of the primary producers.

67% of the Bamboo in India is grown in North East States and Govt. is providing support/subsidy for establishment of Bamboo based clusters in North Eastern States.

11.8 Genetically Modified (GM) Crops

GM crops are plants whose DNA (a molecule that encodes the Genetic Information) has been modified using Genetic Engineering. The following are some benefits of GM crops:

- More nutritional value
- Resistance to bacteria, virus and other components that can damage the plant
- Longer shelf life
- Less costly GM foods and higher yields

The Genetic Engineering Appraisal Committee (GEAC) is the apex body for regulating GM crops, in the Ministry of Environment and Forest under the Environment Protections Act 1986.

At present, the government allows commercial production of **only one GM crop which is BT cotton** and is allowed since 2002. Though **BT Brinjal** has passed its field trials, it was n ot allowed to go for commercial production and a moratorium is placed since 2010, amid strong protest by civil society groups. There is a lobby that strongly opposes the use of GM foods, they claim that certain GM foods can trigger allergic reactions in humans (cotton pickers) and may also be of toxic in nature.

Government regulation regarding BT cotton seed pricing:

In India, Monsanto Mahyco Biotech (India) Ltd. (a joint venture between Mahyco Seeds Ltd and Monsanto), licensed its patented Bollgard II cotton seed technology to 50 seed companies in exchange for a royalty fee. More than 90% of the cotton grown in India used this technology.

In March 2016, the government cut the price of genetically modified Bollgard II cotton seeds to Rs.800 per 450g packet from Rs.830 - Rs.1000 earlier and slashed royalty (trait) fees by 74% from Rs. 163 to Rs. 43 to bring uniformity in pricing of Bt cotton seeds across the country. The government said that the order to regulate the Bt Cotton seed prices has been issued to safeguard the interests of the farming community under section 3 of the "Essential Commodities Act 1955".

The industry lobby of R&D firms slammed the government's decision as "it violates the principle of free market economics. They said that the decision has been taken for short term populist measures which will be detrimental in the long run as companies may have to **reconsider** their investments in seed-based R&D in the country. This sends a bad signal internationally that we're fairly arbitrary. We have the power to regulate patents, no doubt, but it should be open, transparent and based on robust methodology for a concrete, legitimate purpose".

In one of the cases before the Delhi High Court, involving Monsanto and Nuziveedu (seed company) and the other with the Protection of Plant Variety and Farmers Rights (PPVFR) Authority, the Govt. has submitted that the Indian Patents Act 1970 (Section 3(j)) excludes patenting of seeds, plants and their varieties and the patent granted to Monsanto is not legal. Whereas, Monsanto argues that it is not patenting ***Bt cotton seeds*** *but the* ***genes*** *in them (when you buy a software on a CD, the copyright is for the software even though it is made available via the CD), the Govt. is arguing that under PPVFR Act 2001, once a gene is inserted into the seed it is a plant* ***'variety'*** *and hence not patentable under the Indian Patent Act 1970. That is, even if a patent is valid, it becomes invalid the moment the gene is put into a seed and cross-pollinated to create new hybrids.*

The Delhi High court in April 2018 ruled in favour of Nuziveedu and PPVFR Authority by declaring Monsanto's Bollgard and Bollgard-II patent illegal and has allowed Monsanto to move to Supreme Court. Supreme Court in **January 2019**, gave judgement in favour of Monsanto, and **restored the BT Cotton patent in India till its validity is decided finally by the High Court.** SC sent it back to the lower court for a full trial by evidence considering the complexities involved in the case. But whether Monsanto will benefit or not is still not clear because the prices of BT cotton seeds are still government regulated under Essential Commodities Act 1955.

GM Mustard

- In Oct. 2022, The Genetic Engineering Appraisal Committee (GEAC) constituted under Environment (Protection) Act, 1986 has recommended the environmental release of the genetically modified (GM) mustard variety DMH (Dhara Mustard Hybrid)-11, paving the way for the commercialisation of the country's first GM food crop.
- But GEAC nod is not the final approval for commercial release but a step forward. It remains to be seen if the Central Government will accept the GEAC's recommendations or not.

- While giving the nod, the GEAC has said that simultaneous field studies will have to be conducted with ICAR on the effect of GM mustard on honeybees and other pollinators
- DMH-11 has been shown to deliver 30 per cent higher yields than existing varieties. The average yield of existing mustard varieties is around 1,000-1,200 kilograms per hectare, while the global average is over 2,000-2,200 kgs.

Environmental activists and the Swadeshi Jagran Manch, an affiliate of the RSS, have opposed the move and urged the government to not give a final nod as there are several issues and concerns like:

1. Studies have shown a strong correlation between growth of GM crops, the herbicides they promote and the diseases such as acute kidney injury, diabetes, Alzheimer's and cancer in the past 20 years in US. (17 of the 20 most developed countries including Japan, Russia, Israel and most Europe refuse to grow GM crops).
2. The GM crops are said to be herbicide tolerant (i.e., one can use the herbicide to remove the herbs/weeds in GM crops). But it promotes constant exposure to a single herbicide to which the weeds eventually become resistant. And to control these weeds, desperate farmers increase the use of these herbicides manifold which is very hazardous to human health.
3. The GM mustard, if introduced in India, will affect every Indian who consumes mustard in any form, as he will consume the herbicide residues in it; the millions of poor women who depend on weeding to support their family who will be displaced; the bee keepers whose honey will be contaminated; farmers whose yields will fall eventually as bees die out; and the Indian nation, which will find that it has lost its seed diversity and the international competitive advantage of its non-GM mustard and honey.
4. Our small and marginalized farmers (86%) will not be able to afford the high cost of cultivation of GM (Mustard) crops and it will further push them into poverty.

Protection of Plant Varieties and Farmers Rights (PPVFR) Act 2001

The Act provides for the establishment of an effective system for protection of plant varieties, the rights of farmers and plant breeders and to encourage the development of new varieties of plants. Following are the rights granted to breeders and farmers under the PPVFR Act:

Breeders' Rights

- A breeder can be a person or group of persons or a farmer or group of farmers or any institution which has bred, evolved or developed any plant variety. And the breeder (or his successor, his agent or licensee) of the protected variety will have the right to produce, sell, market, distribute, export and import such variety.

Farmers' Rights

- A farmer who is engaged in the conservation of genetic resources of land races and wild relatives of economic plants and their improvement through selection and preservation shall be entitled in the prescribed manner for the recognition and reward from the Gene Fund, provided that material so selected and preserved has been used as donors of genes in varieties registrable under this Act.
- A farmer shall be deemed to be entitled to save, use, sow resow, exchange, share or sell his farm produce including seed of a variety protected under this Act in the same manner as he was entitled before the coming into force

of this Act, provided that the farmer shall not be entitled to sell branded (packaged) seed of a variety protected under this Act

National Gene Fund

The Central Government shall constitute a National Gene Fund:

- The Breeder will have to pay royalty (on the basis of benefit gained by such breeder/agent) which will go to the National Gene Fund
- If someone gives a claim that the genetic material possessed by him was used in the development of the seed variety by the breeder then the claimant will get "benefit sharing" from the National Gene Fund. The amount of the "benefit sharing" to a variety will have to be deposited by the breeder of such variety to the National Gene Fund. ("benefit sharing", in relation to a variety, means such proportion of the benefit accruing to a breeder of such variety for which a claimant shall be entitled as per the authority).

11.9 Organic Farming

Introduction

Organic farming is a form of agriculture that relies on techniques such as crop rotation, green manure, and biological pest control. It is a method of farming system which primarily aims at cultivating the land and raising crops in such a way, as to keep the soil alive and in good health by use of **organic wastes** and other **biological materials** along with beneficial microbes (**bio fertilizers**) to release nutrients to crops for increased sustainable production in an eco-friendly pollution free environment. This is a method of farming that works at grass root level preserving the reproductive and regenerative capacity of the soil, good plant nutrition and sound soil management, produces nutritious food rich in vitality which has resistance to diseases.

Among all the states, **Madhya Pradesh** has covered largest area under organic certification followed by Himachal Pradesh and Rajasthan. **Sikkim is the first truly Organic state of India in January 2016**, as declared by PM Narendra Modi. Organic products produced in India includes all varieties of food products namely Sugarcane, Oil Seeds, Cereals & Millets, Cotton, Pulses, Medicinal Plants, Tea, Fruits, Spices, Dry Fruits, Vegetables, Coffee, cotton fibre etc.

Organic Products and Certification:

Once used to refer to a natural, balanced and eco-friendly system of farming, the definition of 'organic' has become a lot more specific in recent years. With the rules governing certification of organic food becoming more stringent, the term is used solely to refer to foods produced without using chemical pesticides, fertilisers or genetically modified raw materials and processed without using chemical additives or other synthetic substances. The definition also extends to meat, poultry and dairy products produced without using antibiotics or artificial growth hormones. While this is the generic, universally accepted understanding of organic food, the exact definition varies from country to country.

Food Safety and Standards Authority of India (FSSAI) regulates organic foods in India. FSSAI in Nov 2017 published regulations on organic food which regulates manufacture, sale, distribution and import of organic food in India.

As a consequence, any food to be sold as 'organic' in India will have to be certified under either of the two prevailing systems. The two systems are National Programme for Organic Production (**NPOP**) and the Participatory Guarantee System for India (**PGS-India**).

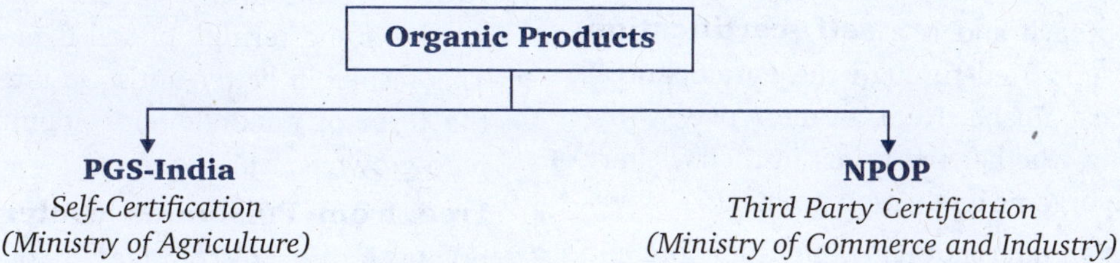

Both the programmes (NPOP and PGS-India) are independent of each other and products certified under one system cannot be processed or labeled under another system. While NPOP certified products can be traded in export and in domestic market including imports, PGS-India certified products can be traded only in domestic market.

Apart from operationalising these regulations, FSSAI has also developed a unified logo for organic food (either certified under NPOP or PGS India) from India called 'Jaivik Bharat' as an identity mark to distinguish organic products from non-organic ones. All products labelled as organic shall be required to be certified either under NPOP or PGS-India and shall bear logo of Jaivik Bharat (FSSAI organic food logo) along with the concerned certification programme (PGS-India or NPOP) logo. The organic regulations allow import of organic food into India without being re-certified in India if the organic standards of the exporting country have been recognised as equivalent to NPOP.

NPOP: The National Programme for Organic Production (NPOP) is a third-party certification programme, run by the ministry of commerce and industries since 2001, which lays down the norms governing the production of organic food. The guidelines have a sweeping scope and cover even the smallest details. These norms need to be followed by the farmers and enterprises who are involved in the production of organic fruits, vegetables, grains and process and packaging. For instance, for a honey manufacturing enterprise to be certified, everything from bee box to farmer's land on which the bee box is kept, to farms within a 5 km radius of the bee box, all have to meet organic standards.

While the NPOP lays down the guidelines, central bodies such as National Accreditation Board (NAB) and Agricultural & Processed Food Products Export Development Authority (APEDA) accredit the certifying bodies that carry out inspections and grant organic status to individual farmers and enterprises after verification of their farms, storages and processing units. Apart from a number of private certifying bodies like Indian Organic Certification Agency (INDOCERT), Natural Organic Certification Pvt. Ltd., the Central government agency FSSAI and State government bodies such as Uttarakhand State Organic Certification Agency also issue certification for organic products. Indian organic products duly certified by the accredited certification bodies of India are accepted by the importing countries.

PGS-India: PGS-India is implemented by Ministry of Agriculture through the National Centre for Organic Farming. Unlike the top-down approach of NPOP, PGS-India involves a peer-review approach and is a **self -certification process** supported through the Paramparagat Krishi Vikash Yojana. Here, farmers play a role in certifying whether the farms in their vicinity adhered to organic cultivation practices.

The PGS is an internationally applicable organic quality assurance system [like ISO 9000] implemented and controlled by the committed organic farmer-producers through active participation, along with the consumers, in the process based on verifiable trust. It is not an "inspection raj" certification system but, rather, one that is based on personal integrity and peer pressure. Integrity is honesty when no one is looking over your shoulder to see what you are doing. The farmer pledges that the production process is free from manufactured chemicals [fertilizers, insecticides, herbicides, hormones, etc] and lives by his word of honour. The "Local Group" of five or more organic farmers is the fulcrum of the self-regulatory support system of PGS. The quality assurance standards are harmonized by the PGS Organic Council, which permits the use of its PGS label on a product as a mark of quality.

Advantages of Organic farming/ products:

Organic farming is inherent farming technique in India. Since ancient times, best practices of farming include methods such as crop rotation and natural compost which boosts crop health and increases soil fertility. With rise in use of chemical fertilizers, pesticides and insecticides, crop quality as well as soil fertility has reduced a great deal. Organic farming has the potential to reverse these changes. Following are the various benefits of organic products from consumption point of view:

- **Increased Nutrition content in food:** Organic farming practice ensures that nutrition and fertility of soil is maintained. This results in better nutrition retention, in the form of minerals and vitamins in the food grown as well.
- **Free from Poisonous content:** Since organic farming discourages use of chemical products such as pesticides and fertilizers, toxic content absorbed by crop is also very less. This results in toxin free food and reduces health issues caused due to these toxins.
- **Better and Original taste:** Organic food have better nutrition quotient and thus they even taste better. If processed food has been prepared organically, then they are also free of preservatives and thus taste is more similar to that of freshly prepared food.
- **Longer storage life:** Organic plants have greater metabolic and structural integrity in their cellular structure than non-organic grown crops. This enables storage of organic food for a longer time.

Scope of Organic Farming in India

The scientific way of agricultural production (Green Revolution) by use of excessive fertilizers and pesticides is perceived as creating several health related and environmental problems. It is contaminating the vegetables and food grains and causing health related issues and lifestyle diseases. Organic farming can be used to revive traditional farming practices and methods to save the soil and agricultural produce from contamination caused by the chemical inputs.

It is a proven fact that productivity of organic cultivation will be lower and that more organic resources will be required to ensure there is no substantial decline in productivity. Hence, organic farmers will be forced to sell their produces at premium prices which will be unbearable to the common man.

Organic farming may not be practical for large scale cultivation essential for feeding a country with a population of 140 crore people. So, India will have to take a balanced approach that makes a judicious blend of organic methods and science & technology both.

Following are the various challenges faced by organic farming/products in India:

- First, the supply chain is underdeveloped and small and mid-sized farmers located in hilly regions and tribal belts find it extremely difficult to access the market. There is a shortage of pack houses and refrigerated vehicles, which leads to spoilage. Organic products have to be stored separately from conventional products to avoid cross-contamination and the existing supply chain does not often provide that facility.
- Second, while the government is subsidising farmers under the Participatory Guarantee System (PGS) for India, these farmers are not allowed to export. In fact, the APEDA has made it mandatory to have a third-party certification for exports.
- Third, as a farmer converts his/her land from conventional chemical-based farming to organic farming, there is a risk of loss in yield due to the withdrawal of chemical inputs and high-yielding varieties of seeds. A number of countries have carefully designed subsidies to compensate for the yield loss during the conversion period. However, in India, there is no such subsidy.
- Fourth, there is a serious shortage of good quality organic inputs, which increases the risk of loss of yield. The available organic fertilizers are much below the required quantity and there is a shortage of good quality organic seeds also.
- The fifth and the biggest challenge is, there are many brands available which offer organic products, but all are not strictly compliant to govt. guidelines and the question arises that among the ocean of organic brands available, which brand is authentic?

11.10 Zero Budget Natural Farming (ZBNF)

- Natural farming is a system where the laws of nature are applied to agricultural practices. This method works along with the natural biodiversity of each farmed area, encouraging the complexity of living organisms, both plants, and animals that shape each particular ecosystem to thrive along with food plants.
- ZBNF is based on stimulation of microbial activity in the soil which is to be achieved by applying bacterial culture made by fermenting cow dung and urine.
- The neo-liberalizationof the Indian economy led to a deep agrarian crisis that is making small scale farming an unviable vocation. Privatized seeds, inputs, and markets are inaccessible and expensive for peasants. Indian farmers increasingly find themselves in a vicious cycle of debt, because of the high production costs, high interest rates for credit, the volatile market prices of crops, the rising costs of fossil fuel-based inputs, and private seeds. Debt is a problem for

farmers of all sizes in India. Under such conditions, 'zero budget' farming promises to end a reliance on loans and drastically cut production costs, ending the debt cycle for desperate farmers.

- The word 'budget' refers to credit and expenses, thus the phrase 'Zero Budget' means without using any credit, and without spending any money on purchased inputs. 'Natural farming' means farming *with* Nature and *without* chemicals.

Features of Zero Budget Natural Farming (ZBNF):

- The premise of ZBNF is that soil has all the nutrients plants need. To make these nutrients available to plants, we need the intermediation of microorganisms. For this, "four wheels of ZBNF" have been suggested:
  - **Bijamrit** is the microbial coating of seeds with formulations of cow urine and cow dung
  - **Jivamrit** is the enhancement of soil microbes using an inoculum of cow dung, cow urine, and jaggery
  - **Mulching** is the covering of soil with crops or crop residues which creates humus and encourages the growth of friendly microorganisms
  - **Waaphasa** is the building up of soil humus to increase soil aeration
- According to ZBNF principles, plants get 98% of their supply of nutrients from the air, water, and sunlight. And the remaining 2% can be fulfilled by good quality soil with plenty of friendly microorganisms. (Just like in forests and natural systems)
- The system requires cow dung and cow urine obtained from Indian breed cow only. Desi cow is apparently the purest as far as the microbial content of cow dung, and urine goes.
- In ZBNF, multi-cropping is encouraged over single crop method.

Example: Surat Model of Natural Farming

(In connection with 75 years of Independence i.e., Amrit Kaal, 75 farmers in every Panchayat in Surat district are adopting Natural Farming.)

Challenges faced by ZBNF

- Less yield
- Availability of livestock for urine and dung
- Farmers aren't equipped with appropriate training to make the shift towards ZBNF

Similarities between Organic Farming and ZBNF:

- Organic and natural farming both systems discourage farmers from using any chemical fertilizers, pesticides on plants and in all agricultural practices.
- Both farming methods encourage farmers to use local breeds of seeds, and native varieties of vegetables, grains, pulses and other crops.
- Both farming methods promote nonchemical and homemade pest control methods.

Differences between Organic Farming and ZBNF:

- In organic farming, organic fertilizers and manures like compost, vermicompost, cow dung manure, etc. are used and added to farmlands from external sources. While in natural farming, neither chemical nor organic fertilizers are added to the soil. In fact, no external fertilizers are added to soil or given to plants whatsoever. In natural farming, decomposition of organic matter by microbes and earthworms is encouraged right on the soil surface itself, which gradually adds nutrition in the soil, over the period.

- Organic farming requires basic agro practices like ploughing, tilling, mixing of manures, weeding, etc. to be performed. While in natural farming there is no ploughing, no tilling of soil and no fertilizers, and no weeding is done just the way it would be in natural ecosystems.
- Organic farming is still expensive due to the requirement of bulk manures, and it has an ecological impact on surrounding environments; whereas, natural agriculture is an extremely low-cost farming method, completely moulding with local biodiversity.

11.11 Integrated Farming System (IFS)

Integrated Farming System (IFS) is an innovative approach wherein solo agriculture systems are integrated with livestock, aquaculture, forestry, or other inter-related set of enterprises to multiply gains and reduce input cost. Waste from one enterprise becomes an input for other, thus cost is reduced, production is increased and the ultimate income gets multiplied. The integration of various enterprises not only supplement the income of the farmers but also help in increasing the family labour employment and mitigating risk and is **best suited for small-sized farms** with limited resources.

Presently, the farmers concentrate mainly on crop production which is subjected to a high degree of uncertainty in income and inefficient resource utilization by the farmers. In this context, it is imperative to evolve suitable strategy for augmenting the income of a farm by adopting integrated farming system.

The following are the advantages of the IFS:

- Reduced production cost of components through input recycling from the by-products of allied enterprises and optimal utilization of resources. For example, poultry droppings are used as a feedstock for fish. Another example is, cattle dung mixed with crop residues and farm waste can be converted into nutrient-rich vermi-compost.
- Sustainable soil fertility and productivity through organic waste recycling and is resilient and adaptive to climate variability.
- Integrated farming will help in environmental protection through effective recycling of waste from animal activities like piggery, poultry and pigeon rearing and will help in water conservation too.
- Integration of allied activities will result in the availability of nutritious food enriched with protein, carbohydrate, fat, minerals and vitamins
- Regular stable income through the products like egg, milk, mushroom, vegetables, honey and silkworm cocoons from the linked activities in integrated farming
- A judicious mix of agricultural enterprises like dairy, poultry, piggery, fishery, sericulture etc. suited to the given agro-climatic conditions and socio-economic status of the farmers would bring prosperity in the farming.
- IFS approach has multiple objectives of sustainability, food security, farmer security and poverty reduction. And there can be different IFS models, depending on agro-climatic zones like rice-fish-poultry model, pig/poultry-fish-vegetable model, rice-fish-vegetable model etc.

Figure: Integrated Farming System

Due to the above advantages, Ministry of Agriculture and Farmers' Welfare has laid major emphasis on IFS while planning for doubling farmers' income by 2022.

The Indian Council of Agricultural Research (ICAR) has developed 60 location specific, cost effective, eco-friendly, socially acceptable multi-enterprise IFS models in farmers' participatory mode to reduce risk in farming, enhance farm productivity/profitability and secure livelihoods of resource poor small and marginal farmers. Although these models are highly location specific, but choice of a model varies from place to place and even farmer to farmer in the same area. Net return from an IFS also varies depending on the selected model, characteristics of soil, input of resources etc.

Bio-intensive cropping systems having higher productivity potential for different agro-climatic zones have been included in the crop production guide /package of practices of respective states. These models are also being disseminated to small and marginal farmers through the nation-wide chain of ICAR Krishi Vigyan Kendras (KVKs).

11.12 Agroecology

Agroecology is farming that centres on food production that makes the best use of nature's goods and services while not damaging these resources. Farming thrives when it works with local ecosystems, for example, improving soil and plant quality through available biomass and biodiversity, rather than battling nature with chemical inputs.

Agroecology is an integrated approach that simultaneously applies ecological and social concepts and principles to the design and management of food and agricultural systems. **It seeks to optimize the interactions between plants, animals, humans and the environment** while taking into consideration the social aspects that need to be addressed for a sustainable and fair food system.

Worldwide, scientists, grassroots organizations, NGOs, consumers, universities, and public agencies are working with farmers to construct sustainable and nutritious food systems based in agroecology.

Present System of Agriculture not Sustainable

The present system of farming has resulted in the threat to food systems and bio-diversity. As a result of industrial farming, friendly insects are no longer part of the agricultural landscape, water pollution is rampant, depleted soils are commonplace and plunging groundwater tables have become the norm. The opportunity cost incurred from investing only in industrial methods of agriculture is one that has been borne largely by the farming community and the natural systems.

There are now unprecedented opportunities to advance agroecology globally as corporate food system has negative impacts on people's health, the environment, and the well-being of family farmers. **Agroecology is recognized as both a mitigation and adaptation strategy for climate change** Consumers are increasingly demanding healthier food and a closer connection to food producers. Social movements around the globe – many with significant leadership by women's and indigenous organizations – are campaigning for a healthy food system built on an environmental and human rights ethos. The demand for agroecology is rising.

What makes agroecology distinct?

Agroecology is fundamentally different from other approaches to sustainable development. It is based on bottom-up and territorial processes, helping to deliver contextualised solutions to local problems. Agroecological innovations are based on the co-creation of knowledge, combining science with the traditional, practical and local knowledge of producers. By enhancing their autonomy and adaptive capacity, agroecology empowers producers and communities as key agents of change.

Rather than tweaking the practices of unsustainable agricultural systems, agroecology seeks to transform food and agricultural systems, addressing the root causes of problems in an integrated way and providing holistic and long-term solutions. This includes an explicit focus on social and economic dimensions of food systems. Agroecology places a strong focus on the rights of women, youth and indigenous peoples.

Benefits:

We presently have a subsidy-based agricultural system where farm inputs are firmly in the hands of corporations and their elite networks. Agroecology-based farming is not regressive, but rather a technology of the future with a traditional idiom. Agroecology has the following benefits:

- enhances fertile landscapes,
- increases yields,
- restores soil health and biodiversity,
- promotes climate resilience and
- improves farmers' well-being

11.13 Conservation Agriculture

Conservation Agriculture (CA) is defined as a sustainable agriculture production system comprising a set of farming practices adapted to the requirements of crops and local conditions of each region, whose farming and soil management techniques protect the soil from erosion and degradation, improve its quality and biodiversity, and contribute to the preservation of the natural resources, water and air, while optimizing yields.

This novel resource conservation practice encompasses **no or minimum soil disturbance, providing a vegetative soil cover through crop residues or other cover crops, and crop rotations for achieving higher productivity** and reducing adverse environmental impacts. Conservation Agriculture is based on three core principles:

- Minimum soil disturbance (No tillage or reduced tillage)
- Maintenance of permanent soil covers
- Cropping system diversity, crop rotations

Advantages of Conservation Agriculture (CA):

- CA based crop management practices not only enhance crop productivity but also reduces cost of production
- Improvement of resource use efficiency through residue decomposition, increased recycling and availability of plant nutrients
- Protection of organic matter and soil and water conservation

- Reduction in greenhouse gas emissions

Challenges in Adopting Conservation Agriculture:

- Development, standardization and adoption of farm technology/machinery for seeding with minimum soil disturbance, developing crop harvesting and management systems
- Lack of knowledge about the potential of CA to agricultural leaders, extension agents and farmers
- CA has to be mainstreamed in relevant ministries, departments or institutions and supported by adequate provision of material, human and financial resources to ensure that farmers receive effective and timely support from well trained and motivated extension staff.

A paradigm shift has become a necessity in view of widespread problems of resource degradation, which accompanied the past strategies to enhance production with little concern for resource integrity. **Integrating concerns of productivity, resource conservation and soil quality and the environment is now fundamental to sustained productivity growth for which conservation agriculture is the solution.**

Some distinguishing features of conventional and conservation agriculture are as follows:

Conventional Agriculture	Conservation Agriculture
Cultivating land using science and technology to dominate nature	Least interference with natural processes
Excessive mechanical tillage and soil erosion	No-till or drastically reduced tillage (biological tillage)
Residue burning or removal	Surface retention of residues (permanently covered)
Use of ex-situ composts	Use of in-situ organic/composts
Mono cropping, less efficient rotations	Diversified and more efficient rotations

11.14 Protected Cultivation

- Protected cultivation is the most contemporary approach to produce, mainly, horticulture crops qualitatively and quantitatively and has spread extensively the world over in the last few decades. It is also known as Controlled Environment Agriculture (CEA) and is highly productive, encourages water and land conservation as well as protects the environment.
- The technology involves cultivation of horticulture crops in a controlled environment wherein factors like the temperature, humidity, light, soil, water, fertilisers etc. are manipulated as per the requirement of the crop to attain the maximum produce as well as allow a regular supply of them even during off-season.
- Crops grown in the poly houses are protected from intense heat, bright sunlight, strong winds, hailstones and cold waves. Every factor influencing a crop can be controlled in a poly house. High tech poly houses even have heating systems as well as soil heating systems to purify the soil of unwanted viruses, bacteria etc.
- Protected cultivation of high-value horticultural crops have great potential to

enhance income especially of small farmers in India which can help them to produce more crops each year from their land, particularly during off-season when the prices are higher.

Objectives of Protected Cultivation

- To create a favourable environment for the sustained growth of crop, so as to realise its maximum potential even in adverse climatic conditions.
- Protection of plants from abiotic stress (physical or by non-living organism) such as temperature, excess/deficit water, hot and cold waves, and biotic factors such as pest and disease incidences, etc.
- Efficient water use with minimum weed infestation.
- Enhancing productivity per unit area.
- Minimising the use of pesticides in crop production.
- Promotion of high value, quality horticultural produce.
- Year-round and off-season production of flower, vegetable or fruit crops.
- Production of disease-free and genetically better transplants.

There can be different Types of Protected Cultivation

1. Greenhouse/ Polyhouse

Polyhouse or a greenhouse is a house or a structure made of translucent material like glass or polyethylene where the plants grow and develop under controlled climatic conditions. A greenhouse is a glass house whose interiors become warm when exposed to sunbeams as the house stops the greenhouse gas to leave. So, when it is cold outside, the temperature inside is survival friendly and warm for the plants.

There can be different structures of Polyhouses/Greenhouse:

(a) Semi-circular: It is a framed structure covered with UV stabilized (absorbs UV radiation and prevents damage) plastic films in which crops are grown under partially or controlled environment conditions. It warms up during the day via penetration of the sun's rays which heat the plants, soil and structure. This heat is given up gradually throughout the night.

(b) Walk-in tunnels: These are covered with UV film, suitable for all types of crops; flowers and vegetables.

(c) Plastic tunnel: These are miniature structures producing greenhouse like effect. Facilitates entrapment of carbon dioxide thereby enhancing the photosynthetic activity. It protects plants from harsh climatic conditions such as rain, wind, hail snow etc. These are mainly used for raising nursery.

2. Shade Nets:

A Shade net house is a structure enclosed by agro nets or any other woven material to allow required sunlight, moisture and air to pass through the gaps. Shade net house are considered as one of the major technologies to provide development of healthy grafts/ seedlings & hardening for various horticultural crops irrespective of climatic conditions.

3. Plastic mulching:

Covering the soil around the plant with plastic film to conserve the soil moisture that prevents weed growth and regulate soil temperature.

Advantages of protected cultivation:

- Better quality of produce
- Higher productivity
- Efficient use of resources
- Better insect and disease control and reduced use of pesticides
- Production of exotic/non-native & off-season vegetables & for raising quality seedlings

Challenges to protected cultivation

- High cost of initial infrastructure (capital cost)
- Non-availability of skilled human power and lack of technical knowledge
- Requires close supervision and monitoring.
- Repair and maintenance are major hurdles.
- Requires assured marketing, since the investment of resources like time, effort and finances, is expected to be very high.

Ministry of Agriculture and Farmers' Welfare is providing various investment (project cost) subsidies for the creation of different structures like polyhouses, shadenet etc. through various schemes like Mission for Integrated Development of Horticulture, National Horticulture Mission, Horticulture mission for North East & Himalayan States.

11.15 Permaculture

"Permaculture, originally **'Permanent Agriculture'**, is often viewed as a set of gardening techniques, but it has in fact developed into a whole design philosophy and for some people a philosophy for life. Its central theme is the creation of human systems which provide for human needs, but using many natural elements and drawing inspiration from natural ecosystems. Its goals and priorities coincide with what many people see as the core requirements for sustainability." Following are some important points related to permaculture:

- Permaculture is an innovative framework for creating sustainable ways of living.
- It is a practical method of developing ecologically harmonious, efficient and productive systems that can be used by anyone, anywhere.
- Permaculture tackles how to grow food, build houses and create communities, and minimise environmental impact at the same time.
- By thinking carefully about the way we use our resources - food, energy, shelter and other material and non-material needs - it is possible to get much more out of life by using less using permaculture. We can be more productive for less effort, reaping benefits for our environment and ourselves, for now and for generations to come.
- The essence of permaculture is the design of an ecologically sound way of living - in our households, gardens, communities and businesses. It is created by cooperating with nature and caring for the earth and its people.

Permaculture principles are being constantly developed and refined by people throughout the world in very different climates and cultural circumstances.

11.16 Use of Technology in Agriculture

The agriculture industry has radically transformed over the past 50 years. Advances in machinery have expanded the scale, speed, and productivity of farm equipment, leading to more efficient cultivation of more land. Seed, irrigation, and fertilizers also have vastly improved, helping farmers increase yields. Now, agriculture is in the early days of yet another revolution, at the heart of which lie data and connectivity. Artificial intelligence, analytics, connected sensors, Internet of Things (IoT) and other emerging technologies could further increase yields, improve the efficiency of water and other inputs, and build sustainability and resilience across crop cultivation and animal husbandry.

Application of Technology in Agriculture:

- Artificial Intelligence can be used with historic weather data to predict the best time for sowing of seeds. With the help of historic data from the farms, AI can predict other stages of the farming process such as when to irrigate the field and apply fertilizers etc. to get the maximum yield with least input cost.
- Farmers are also using AI to create seasonal forecasting models to improve agricultural accuracy and increase productivity. These models are able to predict upcoming weather patterns months ahead to assist decisions of farmers.

- IoT-led devices with remote sensors can be placed at farms to record crop, soil, humidity, and weather conditions in real-time and the data collected by the device is harnessed using AI and ML to generate farm-specific, crop-specific, and crop-stage-specific intelligence that can be delivered to farmers through app/messages. Farmers can use these insights and predictions to plan their irrigation management, pest and disease management, fertilizer, fungicide and pesticide application or make any other adjustments needed to create optimal growth conditions for crops.
- Farmers over irrigate because they have no definitive way to assess the amount of water (or other inputs) needed in the crop's life cycle. The soil may look dry on top, but it retains water at the root zone. As a result, agriculture is fast depleting India's largest natural resource i.e., water which can be protected using technology.
- In addition to ground data, farmers are also taking to the sky to monitor the farm. By using drone technology with AI enabled cameras, agricultural farmers and pest control companies can virtually walk every crop and provide nearly full-time monitoring to look for irregular crop degradation, pests, disease spots or dead soil. A farmer can then collect data from a specific crop area and stop the spread of disease. Unmanned drones are able to cover far more land in much less time than humans on foot allowing for large farms to be monitored more frequently.
- The volume of data collected through technologies like farm machinery, drone imagery and crop analytics is too abundant for humans to process. Farmers and agricultural technology workers are turning to AI to help analyze data points, thus enhancing the value derived from these data sources.
- With the implementation of AI, farmers can analyze weather conditions, temperature, water usage and soil conditions collected from their farm to make informed decisions on business choices like determining the most feasible crop choices that year or which hybrid seeds decreased waste. Big data analysis also determines optimized irrigation, helps reduce greenhouse gas emissions, and pinpoints the exact soil, light, food and water requirements necessary for propagation.
- Blue River Technology is working with Facebook AI and machine learning to create camera-enabled machines that use image recognition technology to label weeds at point of contact and immediately remove or spray them.
- Microsoft has developed an AI-sowing app for farmers in India. The tech giant is using AI and historic weather data to predict the best time for sowing seeds and other stages of the farming process, and pass on that information to farmers via SMS which has resulted in 30% increase in yields.
- **Precision Farming:** Precision farming is an approach where inputs are utilized in precise amounts and accurate way to get increased average yields, compared to traditional cultivation techniques. It is information and technology-based farm management system which identifies analyses and manages variability in fields by conducting crop production practices at the right place and time and in the right way, for optimum profitability, sustainability and protection of the land resource. In India, one major problem is the small field size. More than 58 per cent of operational holdings in the country have size less than one hectare (ha).

- **Precision Farming** uses AI technology to aid in detecting diseases in plants, pests and poor plant nutrition on farms. AI sensors can detect and target weeds while deciding which herbicides to apply within the right buffer - preventing over application of herbicides and excessive toxins that find their way in our food.
- **Precision Farming** can be very helpful for horticulture crops. Horticulture crops are high input and high output crops which require continuous monitoring and active management of soil nutrients, pests, and diseases. That is where most farmers face problems.
- **Resolving Labour Challenge:** With less people entering the farming profession, most farms are facing the challenge of a workforce shortage. One solution to help with this shortage of workers is AI agriculture bots. These bots augment the human labor workforce and are used in various forms. These bots can harvest crops at a higher volume and faster pace than human laborers, more accurately identify and eliminate weeds, and reduce costs for farms by having a round the clock labor force. Chatbots are also helping farmers to answer a variety of questions and provide advice and recommendations on specific farm problems.

Smart Farming

- Smart Farming represents the application of modern Information and Communication Technologies (ICT) into agriculture. Smart farming employs hardware (IoT) and software (SaaS i.e. Software as a service) to capture the data and give actionable insights to manage all the operations on the farm, both pre and post-harvest. The data is organized, accessible all the time and on every aspect of finance and field operations that can be monitored from anywhere in the world.
- IoT (Internet of Things) in agriculture involves sensors, drones and robots connected through internet which function automatically and semi automatically performing operations and gathering data aimed at increasing efficiency and predictability.
- **Semi-automatic robots** with arms can detect weeds and spray pesticides in the affected plants, saving up the plants as well as overall pesticide costs. These robots can also be used in harvesting and lifting. Heavy farming vehicles can also be navigated from the comfort of homes through phone screens to perform tasks and GPS can track their positions at every time.
- **Drones** equipped with sensors and cameras are used for imaging, mapping and surveying the farms. They can be remotely controlled or they can fly automatically through software-controlled flight plans in their embedded systems, working in coordination with sensors and GPS. From the drone data, insights can be drawn regarding crop health, irrigation, spraying, planting, soil and field, plant counting and yield prediction and much more.
- IoT based remote sensing utilizes sensors placed along the farms like weather stations for gathering data which is transmitted to analytical tool for analysis. They monitor the crops for changes in light, humidity, temperature, shape and size. The data collected by sensors in terms of humidity, temperature, moisture precipitation and dew detection helps in determining the weather pattern in farms so that cultivation is done for suitable crops.
- **Computer imaging** involves the use of sensor cameras installed at different corners of the farm or drones equipped with cameras to produce images which undergo digital

image processing. The images are used for quality control, disease detection, sorting and grading yield and irrigation monitoring through Image processing combined with machine learning which uses images from database to compare with images of crops to determine the size, shape, color and growth therefore controlling the quality.

Traditional Farming	Smart Farming
• Same set of practices for cultivation of a crop throughout the region.	• Each farm is analyzed to see the suitable crops and water requirements for optimization.
• Geo-tagging and zone detection not possible.	• Satellite imagery detects the different zones in farms.
• Application of fertilizers and pesticides throughout the field.	• Early detection and application at the affected region only, saving costs.
• No way to predict weather.	• Weather analysis and prediction.
• Traditional irrigation method is used to irrigate the field wasting a lot of water resources.	• Drip irrigation system with smart IoT enabled sensors track moisture level and apply the water effectively where needed.

- **Advantags**
  - Higher crop productivity
  - Decreased use of water, fertilizers and pesticides which reduces production cost
  - Greater efficiency and lower agricultural product prices
  - Reduced impact on natural ecosystems
  - Less runoff of chemicals into rivers and groundwater
- **Challenges:**
  - High Cost
  - Lack of technical expertise knowledge and technology
  - Not applicable or difficult/costly for small land holdings
  - Heterogeneity of cropping systems

PREVIOUS YEARS' QUESTIONS

Prelim Questions

1. Consider the following statement: **[2024]**

Statement-I: India does not import apples from the United States of America.

Statement-II: In India, the law prohibits the import of Genetically Modified food without the approval of the competent authority.

Which one of the following is correct in respect of the above statements?

(a) Both Statement-I and Statement-II are correct and Statement-II explains Statement-I

(b) Both Statement-I and Statement-II are correct, but Statement-II does not explain Statement-I

(c) Statement-I is correct, but Statement-II is incorrect

(d) Statement-I is incorrect, but Statement-II is correct

ANSWER

1.(d)

Main Questions

1. How has the emphasis on certain crops brought about changes in cropping patterns in recent past? Elaborate the emphasis on millets production and consumption. [2018]
2. Sikkim is the first 'Organic State' in India. What are the ecological and economical benefits of Organic State? [2018]
3. Assess the role of National Horticulture Mission (NHM) in boosting the production, productivity and income of horticulture farms. How far has it succeeded in increasing the income of farmers? [2018]
4. How fare is Integrated Farming System (IFS) helpful in sustaining agricultural production? [2019]
5. What are the major factors responsible for making rice-wheat system a success? In spite of this success how has this system become bane in India? [2020]
6. What are the present challenges before crop diversification? How do emerging technologies provide the opportunity for crop diversification? [2021]
7. How and to what extent would micro-irrigation help in solving India's water crisis? [2021]
8. What is Integrated Farming System? How is it helpful to small and marginal farmers in India? [2022]
9. Explain the changes in cropping pattern in India in the context of changes in consumption pattern and marketing conditions. [2023]
10. What are the major challenges faced by Indian irrigation system in recent times? State the measures taken by the government for efficient irrigation management. [2024]
11. Explain the factors influencing the decision of the farmers on the selection of high value crops in India. [2025]

◈◈◈

12

Supply Chain and Food Processing Industry

12.1 Supply Chain: An Introduction

A supply chain is a system of organisations, people, activities, information and resources involved in moving a product or service from supplier to customer. Supply chain activities transform natural resources, raw materials and components into a finished product that is delivered to the end customer.

Supply chain management is an integrating function with primary responsibility for linking major business functions and business processes within and across companies into a cohesive and high performing business model. It includes all the logistics management activities, manufacturing processes and operations, channel partners which can be suppliers, intermediaries, third party service providers and customers. Supply chain management requires coordination of processes and activities with and across marketing, sales, product design, finance and information technology. Within an organization, such as a manufacturer, the supply chain includes all functions involved in receiving and filling a customer request.

Example:

Consider a customer walking into a 'Big Bazaar' store to purchase a detergent. The supply chain begins with the customer and their need for detergent. The next stage of this supply chain is the 'Big Bazaar' retail store that the customer visits. Big Bazaar stocks its shelves using inventory that may have been supplied from a finished goods warehouse that Big Bazaar manages or from the wholesaler/distributor. The wholesaler in turn is stocked by the manufacturer (Hindustan Unilever Ltd.). The HUL plant receives raw material from a variety of suppliers who may themselves have been supplied by lower tier suppliers.

The arrow indicates the direction of movement of products from the supplier to the customer and is referred as the **forward direction**. And the direction opposite to the forward direction is referred as the **backward direction**.

A supply chain is dynamic and involves the constant flow of information, product and funds between different stages. The information regarding availability, pricing and funds flow is also a part of supply chain. So, a typical supply chain may involve:

- Customers
- Retailers
- Wholesalers/Distributors
- Manufacturer
- Raw material supplier

Upstream Stage: The upstream stage of the production process involves searching for and extracting raw materials. The upstream part of the production process does not do anything with the material itself such as processing the material.

Downstream Stage: The downstream stage in the production process involves processing the materials collected during the upstream stage into finished products. The downstream stage further includes the actual sale of that product also.

Upstream and downstream are business terms applicable to the production process that exist within several industries. Earlier these terms were basically used for oil and gas and metals industries but now a day's these terms are used across all the industries. **Upstream and downstream terms depend on the point of reference.** For example, in the above case, with reference to the wholesaler, the manufacturer and raw material supplier belongs to upstream sector and the retailer will belong to downstream sector.

Vertical and Horizontal Integration:

Consider an example from the power sector:

Coal Mine ⟶ Power Generation (Tata Power) ⟶ Transmission & Distribution ⟶ Customer

Tata power was in power generation business while it was procuring coal from some other coal mining company and it was selling its power to the government distribution company in Delhi. Since Tata Power deals regularly with the Coal Company for procurement of coal and it also deals with Distribution Company to sell its power, Tata Power gets considerable experience of the **coal mining sector** and **transmission and distribution sector**.

If Tata Power acquires a coal mine company or starts a new business in coal mining sector then it is called **backward integration**. When Tata Power acquires a transmission & distribution company or starts a new business in transmission and distribution sector then it is called **forward integration**. **And either forward or backward integration is called "Vertical Integration".**

But when Tata Power acquires another company in the same sector of power generation like "Reliance Power" to increase its market share then it is called "**Horizontal Integration**".

12.2 Food Processing Industry

Introduction:

India is one of the world's largest producers as well as consumer of food products, with the sector playing an important role in contributing to the development of the country. Food and food products are the largest consumption category in India, with a market size of $250 billion.

Food processing is a **sunrise industry** in India and is increasingly seen as a potential source for driving the rural economy as it brings about synergy between the consumer, industry and agriculture. A well-developed food processing industry is expected to increase farm gate prices, reduce wastages, ensure value addition, promote crop diversification, generate employment opportunities as well as export earnings. Major industries constituting the food processing sector are grain milling, sugar, edible oils, beverages, fruits & vegetables processing, meat and poultry, dairy products, chocolates, confectionery, soya-based products, mineral water & high protein food.

Facts of Food Processing Industry in India:

Annual growth rate of around 10%

Contributes 9% to manufacturing GDP

Food Processing	Unorganized	Organized
No. of Enterprises	25,00,000	40,000
Value Addition	28%	72%
Investment in Plant & M/c	7%	93%
Employment	74%	26%

Location: In India, majority of the food processing industries are concentrated in the coastal states of Andhra, Karnataka, Kerala, Maharashtra, Gujarat and West Bengal and in non-coastal states of UP and Punjab. India has a strategic geographical location and proximity to food importing nations which favour it in terms of exporting processed foods. Exports of food items have been rising steadily, the main export destinations being Middle East and South East Asia.

Government's Policy: Following are some of the major initiatives taken by the government of India which will lead to the future growth of the food processing industry:

- 100% FDI is permitted under the automatic route in food processing industries
- 100% FDI is allowed in multi-brand retail through government approval route for trading, including through e-commerce in respect of food products sourced from Indian farmers or manufactured or produced in India.
- RBI has classified loan to food & agro-based processing units and Cold Chain under agriculture activities for Priority Sector Lending (PSL)
- Many food processing sectors like pickles etc. that were earlier reserved for small scale industries under the reserved list till 2015 have now been de-reserved

Scope and Growth drivers: India possesses large arable land resources of 160 million hectares with 127 agro climatic zones and has 46 of the 60 soil types in the world. **It is the largest producer of milk and second largest producer of fruits and vegetables.** With liberalisation of the economy and the growth of organised retail, the Indian retail market has become more attractive for global players. With a large agricultural resource base, abundant livestock and cost competitiveness, India is fast emerging as a sourcing hub of processed foods. The following are some of the **major growth drivers** for the Indian food processing Industry:

- With favourable economic & cultural transformation, shift in attitudes & lifestyles, consumers are experimenting with different cuisines, tastes and new brands.

- Forty percent of the population will be living in urban areas by 2030 and this urbanisation will shift the consumption towards packaged and ready-to-eat foods.
- Demand for processed food rising with growing disposable income, urbanising young population, growing middle-class, and nuclear families.
- The large population base and distinct consumer segments support customised offerings/ new categories and brands within each segment.
- Changing lifestyle and increase in awareness and concern for wellness and health has increased the expenditure on health and nutritional food like high protein, low fat, wholegrain and organic food.

Job creation:

There is a sizable presence of small-scale industries in the food processing sector which points to the sector's role in employment generation. Food processing industry is one of the major employment intensive segments and can play a major role in encouraging the movement of labour from agriculture to manufacturing, thereby removing the problem of disguised unemployment and increasing the productivity of labour and wages. By 2024, food processing sector is expected to employ 9 million people in India.

Challenges in food processing industry:

Many of the problems faced by the food processing units arise primarily on account of the perishable nature of raw material, seasonal nature of their operation and low scale of operation. With a sizable number of units in micro and small-scale segment, these enterprises are embroiled in a vicious circle of low level of invested capital, inadequate access to credit, high cost of credit, lower return & profitability and lower investible surplus. So, the challenges for the food processing sector are diverse and demanding, and need to be addressed on several fronts to derive maximum market benefits. Some of the major challenges are: -

1. **Inadequate Infrastructure Facilities:** Inadequate support infrastructure is the biggest bottleneck in expanding the food processing sector, in terms of both investment and export includes: long and fragmented supply chain, inadequate cold storage and warehousing facilities, road, rail and port infrastructure. Also, lack of modern logistics infrastructure such as logistics parks, integrated cold chain solutions, last mile connectivity, dependence on road over rail, customized transportation, technology adoption (barcodes, RFID) are some of the lacunae that exist in supply chain and logistics sector. In India, the road and railway transportation infrastructure are very poor, slow and costly which creates problem in transporting the fruits and vegetables from the hinterland to the urban centres and makes the products costly to the end consumers. The wastage of food from the farm before it reaches the consumers is estimated to be about 25%, because of inadequate cold chain and logistics infrastructure.
2. **Lack of technology and applied research:** Though central institutes, like Central Food Technological Research Institute (CFTRI), Central Institute of Post-Harvest Engineering (CIPHET), selected IITs and IIMs and State Agricultural universities offer specialized courses on food technology and also undertake applied research but most of the R&D institutions have not been able to develop innovative products, processing and machinery of global stature

as reflected in India's share in global trade. The key reasons for this are segregation of academics from applied research, inadequate industry interface, low commercial orientation and lack of collaborative efforts with global peers. Technology is still being imported for establishment of large-scale export-oriented units for production of items like banana paste, concentrates of various fruit juices, sorting, cleaning, washing, waxing and packaging of raw fruits and vegetables.

3. **Lack of skilled manpower:** Many positive developments in the food processing sector in the past few years have resulted in the apprehension about the emerging skill shortages due to mismatch between the demand for specific skills and available supply. Of late, shortage of skilled and semi-skilled workers has emerged as a critical factor impacting the competitiveness of Indian food industry. Many organizations in this industry are dissatisfied with the skills of the available trained manpower and their ability to use appropriate and modern tools, equipment, and technologies specific to their job.

4. **Lack of organized retail**

The above is a general flow diagram for an Indian market for the sale of fruits and vegetable from the farmer to the end customer. The farmer supplies its fresh fruits and vegetables to the local traders or aggregators who in turn supply to the wholesale mandi present in that area. The retailers then buy out these fruits and vegetables from the wholesale mandis and supply it to the end consumers. The supply chain is quite lengthy and big corporate retailers are missing from the scene (more than 95% of the retail market is captured by small/unorganized retailers). Entry of corporate retailers will lead to creation of more cold storage facilities and selling of processed items, which has not been done till now by small retailers.

5. **Competitiveness:** India despite being one of the major producers of agri-commodities, the level of food processing and value addition continues to remain low impacting our competitiveness & export performance and income of farmers.

6. **Inadequate linkage** of processors, exporters and bulk purchasers with farmers resulting in mismatch between the requirements of industry and supply of agri-produce by the farmers. The problem is often compounded by legal provisions relating to restrictions on commodity storage and movement.

7. **Regulations:** The food supply chain is highly regulated through APMC acts by the State governments. Retailers and food processing units are not allowed to buy directly from farmers resulting in higher input costs.

8. **Regulatory Clearances:** Multiple clearances are required for setting up of food processing units. The small processors are also required to go through the same processes as is applicable to larger units. Availing permission for Change in Land Use (CLU), environmental clearance, water and power connections are not only time consuming but costly also.

12.3 Essential Commodities Act 1955

Introduction:

While India is a market economy where prices are ostensibly decided by demand and supply, ECA empowers the Centre to intervene in the market to protect consumer interests. This Act empowers the Central Govt. and under the delegated powers, the State Governments/UT Administrations to regulate **production, distribution, pricing** and other aspects of trading in respect of the commodities declared as essential in order to make them available to consumers at fair prices.

The list of items under the Act includes drugs, fertilisers, foodstuffs, petroleum and petroleum products, hank yarn, raw jute and seeds of food crops/fruits/vegetables, [Food crops including Sugarcane and Sugar are also regulated through this act]. There is no specific definition of essential commodities in the Act, which says that "essential commodity" means a commodity specified in the Schedule of the Act. The Centre [in consultation with State Governments] can include new commodities as and when the need arises and takes them off the list/Schedule once the situation improves.

How it works:

If the Centre finds that a certain commodity is in short supply and its price is spiking, it can notify **stock-holding limits** on it for a specified period. The States act on this notification to specify limits and take steps to ensure that these are adhered to. Anybody trading or dealing in a commodity, be it wholesalers, retailers or even importers are prevented from stockpiling it beyond a certain quantity.

A State can, however, choose not to impose any restrictions. But once it does, traders have to immediately sell into the market any stocks held beyond the mandated quantity. This improves supplies and brings down prices. As not all shopkeepers and traders comply, State agencies conduct raids to get everyone to toe the line and the errant are punished. The excess stocks are auctioned or sold through fair price shops.

Pros:

- The ECA gives consumers protection against irrational spikes in prices of essential commodities. The Government has invoked the Act several times to ensure adequate supplies. It cracks down on hoarders and black-marketeers of such commodities.

Cons:

- Given that almost all crops are seasonal, ensuring round-the-clock supply requires adequate build-up of stocks during the season. So, it may not always be possible to differentiate between genuine stock build-up and speculative hoarding.
- Also, there can be genuine shortages triggered by weather-related disruptions in which case prices will move up. So, if prices are always monitored, farmers may have no incentive to farm.

- With too-frequent stock limits, traders also may have no reason to invest in better storage infrastructure.
- Also, food processing industries need to maintain large stocks to run their operations smoothly. Stock limits curtail their operations. In such a situation, large scale private investments are unlikely to flow into food processing and cold storage facilities.

Without the ECA the common man would be at the mercy of opportunistic traders and shopkeepers. It empowers the government to control prices **directly**. But it hurts investment in storage infrastructure in the country.

This Act was enacted at a time when India was facing scarcity in food production and was dependent on import of foodstuffs and there was a need to prevent hoarding and black marketing. But now the situation has changed and we have moved from an era of food scarcity to become a major exporter of agri-commodities.

12.4 Supply Chain Schemes

12.4.1 Price Stabilization Fund (PSF)

- The Price Stabilization Fund (PSF) was set up in 2014-15 under the Department of Consumer Affairs to help regulate the price volatility of important agri-horticultural commodities like onion, potatoes and pulses.
- The scheme provides for maintaining a strategic buffer of aforementioned commodities for subsequent calibrated release to moderate price volatility and discourages hoarding and unscrupulous speculation.
- For building such stock, the scheme promotes direct purchase from the farmers/ farmers' association at farm gate/Mandi.
- Under PSF, Govt. provides budgetary support (interest free loan) for working capital and other incidental expenses for procurement and distribution of agri-horticultural commodities.
- The intervention is expected to regulate price volatility through procurement (by State/UT Government and Central agencies/ Central PSUs/Cooperative organisations like NAFED, NCCF) of selected produce, maintenance of buffer stocks and regulated release into the market.
- Apart from domestic procurement from farmers/wholesale mandis, import may also be undertaken with support from the Fund.
- Earlier Potato, Onion, Pulses were included under the PSF scheme which NAFED and NCCF used to procure from farmers (at harvest time) and release in the (retail) market if the prices used to increase. Now, NAFED and NCCF will also purchase wheat and rice from Food Corporation of India (FCI) and release it in the retail market (under Bharat Atta, Bharat Rice brand).

12.4.2 SAMPADA

(Scheme for Agro-Marine Processing and Development of Agro-processing clusters)

The objective of SAMPADA scheme is to supplement agriculture, modernize processing (of marine and agri-produce) and decrease agri-waste.

SAMPADA is an **umbrella** scheme of Govt. of India. Following are the sub-schemes and important features of SAMPADA scheme:

- Integrated Cold Chain and Value Addition Infrastructure Scheme
- Food Safety and Quality Assurance Scheme
- Creation/ Expansion of Food Processing and Preservation Capacities Scheme
- Creation of Infrastructure Development for Agro Processing Cluster Scheme
- Food Safety and Quality Assurance Scheme
- Research & Development
- Skill Development
- Operation Greens Scheme

1. Long term interventions
   - Enhancing value realisation of farmers by targeted interventions to strengthen production clusters and FPOs, and linking the farmers with the market.
   - Reduction in post-harvest losses by creation of farm gate infrastructure, development of suitable agri-logistics, creation of appropriate storage capacity linking consumption centres.
   - Increase in food processing capacities and value addition in value chain by creating firm linkages with identified production clusters.
2. Short term interventions
   - The objective of the Scheme is to protect the growers of eligible crops from making distress sale and to reduce post-harvest losses. Subsidy is provided for transportation and hiring of storage facilities for fruits and vegetables. Example: *Ministry of Food Processing Industries gives subsidy (50%) on transportation of notified fruits and vegetables through 'Kisan Rail' trains. Kisan Rail helps in transporting the produce of farmers to different parts of the country at a nominal cost (subsidized by Govt).*

Benefits:

- The implementation of SAMPADA will result in creation of modern infrastructure with efficient supply chain management from farm gate to retail outlet
- It will not only provide a big boost to the growth of food processing sector in the country but also help in providing better prices to farmers and is a big step towards doubling of farmers' income
- It will create huge employment opportunities especially in the rural areas
- It will also help in reducing wastage of agricultural produce, increasing the processing level, availability of safe and convenient processed foods at affordable price to consumers and enhancing the export of the processed foods

12.4.3 PM Matsya Sampada Yojana (PMMSY)

Fisheries constitute 1.2% of National GDP and 7.28% of Agriculture GDP.

The PMMSY is implemented as an umbrella scheme (under dept. of fisheries) with two separate Components namely (a) Central Sector Scheme (CS) and (b) Centrally Sponsored Scheme (CSS). The scheme will bring about **Blue Revolution** through sustainable and responsible development of fisheries sector in India. Under the scheme Central govt. is funding some percentage of the project cost (investments in plants and machinery) up to a certain limit.

Salient features of the Scheme are:

- The scheme intends to address critical gaps in fish production and productivity

- Harnessing of fisheries potential in a sustainable, responsible, inclusive, equitable manner
- Developing Marine, inland fisheries and aquaculture
- Enhancing of fish production and productivity through expansion, intensification, diversification and productive utilization of land and water
- Modernizing and strengthening of value chain - post-harvest management and quality improvement
- Development of infrastructure - fishing harbours, cold chains, markets etc.
- Doubling fishers and fish farmers' incomes and generation of employment
- Enhancing contribution to Agriculture GVA and exports
- Social, physical and economic security for fishers and fish farmers
- Robust fisheries management and regulatory framework
- Govt. will register "Sagar Mitra" to provide fisheries extension services and will encourage formation of Fish Farmers Producer Organizations to help achieve its goals

India is the second largest fish producing country, contributing 8 percent to the global fish production. The fish production in 2024-25 was 19.7 MT comprising of marine fish production of 4.5 MT and 15.2 MT from Aquaculture and Inland fishing. Challenges faced, to a certain extent, include increasing availability of quality seed, cold chain, meeting requirements of infrastructure and post-harvest infrastructure.

12.4.4 Formalization of Micro Food Processing Enterprises Scheme

The unorganized food processing sector in the country comprising nearly 25 lakh food processing enterprises are unorganized and unregistered. Nearly 66% of these units are located in rural areas and about 80% of them are family-based enterprises. This sector faces a number of challenges including the inability of the entrepreneurs to access credit, high cost of institutional credit, lack of access to modern technology and inability to integrate with the food supply chain and compliance with the health and safety standards. To address these challenges, government has launched an all India Centrally Sponsored Scheme.

The aim of the scheme is:

- To modernize and enhance the competitiveness of the existing individual micro enterprises and ensure their transition to formal sector.
- To support FPOs/ SHGs/ Cooperatives for delivery of package of services, creation of common infrastructure along the value chain, ensure backward & forward linkages, branding & marketing, etc.

Salient features of the scheme:

- The expenditure is shared in 60:40 ratio between Central and State Governments and will be implemented over a period of five years from 2020-21 to 2024-25 with an outlay of Rs 10,000 crores and will cover of 2,00,000 enterprises
- Cluster approach and focus on perishables
- Existing Individual micro food processing units desirous of upgradation of their unit

can avail credit-linked subsidy@35% of the eligible project cost with a maximum ceiling of Rs.10 lakhs per unit

- Additionally, FPOs/ SHGs/ producer cooperatives would be provided credit linked grant of 35% for capital investment and common infrastructure along the value chain.
- Handholding support for farm level upgradation plan, DPR preparation, Skill training, obtaining bank credit, FSSAI/ local body license, Udyog Aadhaar etc.
- Support to SHGs/ FPOs/ Co-operatives in brand building and marketing for the micro-enterprises.
- The Scheme adopts One District One Product (ODODP) approach to reap benefit of scale in terms of procurement of inputs, availing common services and marketing of products. The States would identify food product for a district keeping in view the existing clusters and availability of raw material. The ODOP product could be a perishable produce-based product or cereal based products or a food product widely produced in a district and their allied sectors.
- The Scheme also place focus on waste to wealth products, minor forest products and Aspirational Districts.

12.5 Warehouse Receipts

A warehouse receipt is a document which proves ownership of a given commodity that is stored in a recognised location, like a warehouse or a godown. Whether it's for bars of steel or sacks of grain, warehouse receipts are used as proof to show which party owns a given commodity, alongside specific details of the products being stored. Primarily a proof-of-ownership document, a warehouse receipt is also used by warehouse operators themselves, as evidence that a commodity of a specified quantity and quality has been secured and is being safeguarded at their premises.

Negotiable warehouse receipts (NWRs) allow transfer of ownership of a commodity stored in a warehouse without having to deliver the physical commodity.

Government of India enacted the Warehousing (Development & Regulation) Act 2007 under which it has constituted the Warehousing Development and Regulatory Authority (WDRA) under Ministry of Consumer Affairs, Food and Public Distribution for the implementation of the provisions of the Act. The main objectives of the Act are to make provisions for the development and regulation of warehouses, negotiability of warehouse receipts and related matters.

Any person commencing or carrying on the warehousing business and intending to issue Negotiable Warehouse Receipts (NWRs) has to get the warehouse registered with the Warehousing Development & Regulatory Authority (WDRA). The WDRA checks the warehouse on various parameters like, whether the construction has been according to norms, does it have trained staff, is it equipped with modern pest control and fumigation facilities, its security, fire-fighting and goods weighing facilities etc. and then WDRA issues a booklet containing the NWRs. The warehouse then issues these receipts to customers (farmers and people who have stored their produce in the godowns). As these receipts are recognised by the government, banks can easily grant loans against them. The farmer gets an officially recognised receipt against which he can take loan from bank for further farming activities or alternatively sell his produce to a third person by endorsing the receipt, without even taking physical possession.

As per the Act, as on January 2021 WDRA has notified 119 agricultural commodities and 26 horticulture commodities for issuing NWRs.

In 2017, Govt. launched the Electronic Negotiable Warehouse Receipts (e-NWRs). e-NWRs would have no chances of any tempering, mutilation, fudging, loss or damage and with no possibility of any multiple financing. Hence, these NWRs will not only facilitate an easy pledge/collateral financing (Warehouse Receipt Finance) by banks and other financial institutions but also smooth trading on various trading centres like commodity exchanges, electronic National Agriculture Markets (e-NAM) and other electronic platforms (Since April 2020, Govt. has allowed e-NWRs to be sold on e-NAM platform). These e-NWRs will save expenditure in logistics as the stocks could be traded through multiple buyers without physical movement and can be even split for partial transfer or withdrawal. It will revolutionise the marketing of agricultural commodities and help farmers realize better price for their produce.

Use of Blockchain Technology in Warehouse Receipt Finance

"**Whrrl**" is a start-up which provides "blockchain platform" for warehouse receipt financing and it has now on boarded Maharashtra State Coop bank as a lender on this platform. Earlier, the loan process for farmers used to take 7-15 days with a lot of documentation and verifications but now "**Whrrl**" allows the transfer of the loan amount to farmers in just five minutes in a secure and transparent way. Whrrl's solution combines **blockchain** along with **IoT** and Smart Contracts to make it easier for farmers to get loans against any commodity lying in the warehouse without any guarantors. For the banks, it becomes a risk-free lending process and brings transparency into the system.

12.6 FSS Act 2006 and FSSAI

Introduction:

The subject of "adulteration of foodstuffs and the production, supply and distribution of foodstuffs" comes under concurrent list.

The various Central Acts like Prevention of Food Adulteration Act, 1954, Fruit Products Order 1955, Meat Food Products Order 1973, Vegetable Oil Products (Control) Order, 1947, Edible Oils Packaging (Regulation) Order 1988, De-Oiled Meal and Edible Flour (Control) Order, 1967, Milk and Milk Products Order, 1992 etc. were repealed after the enactment of Food Safety and Standards (FSS) Act 2006.

The Act establishes a single reference point for all matters relating to food safety and standards, by moving from multi-level, multi-departmental control to a single line of command. For the above purpose, the Act establishes an independent statutory authority - the Food Safety and Standards Authority of India (FSSAI) with head office at Delhi. FSSAI along with respective State Food Safety Authorities shall enforce the various provisions of the Act.

Accordingly, various state governments have set up their own agencies for food and drug administration to implement the provisions under the Act. For example:

- *As per section 30 of the Act, every State government shall appoint 'Commissioner of Food Safety' for efficient implementation of food safety and standards as laid down under the Act.*
- *As per section 94 of the Act, any State government can make rules to carry out the functions under the Act with the previous approval of FSSAI and the rules shall be passed by the state legislature.*

Functions of Food Safety and Standards Authority of India (FSSAI) as per the Act:

Ministry of Health & Family Welfare is the Administrative Ministry for the implementation of FSS Act. FSSAI has been mandated by the Act for performing the following functions:

- Framing of regulations to lay down the standards & guidelines for food articles and specifying appropriate system of enforcing these standards
- Laying down mechanisms & guidelines for certification of laboratories and other bodies engaged in certification of food safety management system
- Collection of data regarding food consumption, contaminants in food, identification of emerging risks and introduction of rapid alert system
- Creating an information network across the country so that the public, consumers, local bodies etc. receive rapid, reliable and objective information about food safety
- Provide training programmes for persons who are involved or intend to get involved in food businesses
- Contribute to the development of international technical standards for food, sanitary and phyto-sanitary standards

PREVIOUS YEARS' QUESTIONS

Prelim Questions

1. Consider the following statements **[2018]**

(i) The Food Safety and Standards Act, 2006 replaced the Prevention of Food Adulteration Act, 1954.

(ii) The Food Safety and Standards Authority of India (FSSAI) is under the charge of Director General of Health Services in the Union Ministry of Health and Family Welfare.

Which of the statements given above is/are correct?

(a) (i) only

(b) (ii) only

(c) Both (i) & (ii)

(d) Neither (i) nor (ii)

2. With reference to organic farming in India, consider the following statements: **[2018]**

(i) The National Programme for Organic Production' (NPOP) is operated under the guidelines and directions of the Union Ministry of Rural Development.

(ii) The Agricultural and Processed Food Products Export Development Authority' (APEDA) functions as the Secretariat for the implementation of NPOP.

(iii) Sikkim has become India's first fully organic State.

Which of the statements given above is/are correct?

(a) (i) & (ii) only (b) (ii) & (iii) only

(c) (iii) only (d) (i), (ii) & (iii)

ANSWERS

1. (a), 2. (b)

Main Questions

1. Examine the role of supermarkets in supply chain management of fruits, vegetables and food items. How do they eliminate number of intermediaries? **[2018]**
2. Elaborate the policy taken by the Government of India to meet the challenges of the food processing sector. **[2019]**
3. What are the challenges and opportunities of food processing sector in the country? How can income of the farmers be substantially increased by encouraging food processing? **[2020]**
4. Elaborate the scope and significance of the food processing industry in India. **[2022]**
5. What are the main bottlenecks in upstream and downstream process of marketing of agricultural products in India? **[2022]**
6. Elaborate the scope and significance of supply chain management of agricultural commodities in India. **[2025]**
7. Examine the scope of the food processing industries in India. Elaborate the measures taken by the government in the food processing industries for generating employment opportunities. **[2025]**

13 International Organizations

13.1 Bretton Woods Conference (United Nations Monetary and Financial Conference)

In July 1944, the representatives of 44 Allied Nations met at the Mount Washington Hotel situated in Bretton Woods, New Hampshire, United States to regulate the international monetary and financial order after the 2nd World War. During the inter-war period (1st and 2nd World War), the financial system had been chaotic due to the collapse of the gold standard, the Great Depression and the rise of protectionism. It was decided that the conference should do away with the economic evils - the competitive devaluation and destructive impediments to trade which preceded the 2nd World War. Hence, the conference proposed the following:

1. **Creation of an International Trade Organization** (ITO) to establish rules and regulations for international trade.
2. **Creation of International Bank for Reconstruction and Development** (IBRD) to help in the reconstruction of nations devastated by the 2nd World War.
3. **Creation of International Monetary Fund** (IMF) to monitor exchange rates and lend reserve currencies to nations with trade deficits.

13.2 General Agreement on Tariffs and Trade (GATT) 1947

Regarding the first agenda, it was decided that ITO will be created at a UN conference on Trade and Employment scheduled to happen in Havana, Cuba in 1947. Meanwhile 15 countries (out of the 44 countries that were part of the Bretton Woods conference) had begun talks in Dec 1945 to reduce and bind customs tariffs to promote trade. They wanted to give an early boost to trade and liberalization and to begin to correct the legacy of protectionist measures which remained in place from the early 1930's.

The first round of negotiations resulted in a package of trade rules and 45,000 tariff concessions affecting $10 billion of trade. The group had expanded to 23 countries by the time the deal was signed on 30th Oct 1947 in Geneva. The tariff concessions came into effect by 1st Jan 1948 through a "**Protocol of Provisional Application**" and hence the new "General Agreements on Tariffs and Trade" was born with 23 founding members.

The 23 countries were also part of the larger group negotiating the ITO charter. The

Havana conference began on 2nd Nov 1947, less than a month after GATT was signed. The ITO charter was finally agreed in March 1948 but **ratification in some National legislatures proved impossible.** The most serious opposition was in the US Congress (there were differences between US and European nations related to sovereignty as EU wanted judicial powers to ITO which US thought could lead to sovereignty issues) and in 1950, the US government announced that it would not seek congressional ratification of the Havana charter and the ITO was effectively dead.

Rounds of negotiations and package:

Any multilateral issue cannot be negotiated and concluded in a single sitting at one time. Generally, they take various sittings to resolve the complex issues and that is why GATT negotiations happen through rounds of discussions. GATT rounds also offer a package approach (a set of issues) to trade negotiations that can sometimes be more fruitful than negotiations on a single issue. Agreements can be easier to reach through trade-offs if it consists of a package so that if a member compromises on one issue to reach a deal then other members can also make a trade off on other issues to reach a final deal on the package and conclude the discussions. Hence, any GATT round (of discussions) starts when there are a set (package) of issues and the place at which the first meeting of that round takes place is assigned the name of that round. For example, the eighth round of GATT negotiations started in 1986 and its first meeting was in Uruguay, hence the eighth round is also called the Uruguay round.

Uruguay/ Eighth Round (Sept 1986 - April 1994)

Apart from the normal talks on trade in goods, this round of talk extended the trading system into several new areas notably trade in services and intellectual property rights and to reform the trade in sensitive sectors of agriculture and all the original articles of GATT were up for review during this round. There was also the agenda for creation of a new institution, to streamline the Dispute Settlement System and the Trade Policy Review Mechanism which provided for the first comprehensive, systematic and regular reviews of national trade policies and practices of GATT members.

The Uruguay Round of negotiation was concluded in 1994 and a deal was signed on April 15 by ministers participating from 123 countries at a meeting in Marrakesh, Morocco. **The following were the main agreements signed during the Uruguay round.**

- Agreement establishing the WTO (WTO Agreement)
- Updated General Agreement on Tariffs and Trade (GATT) 1994
- General Agreement on Trade in Services (GATS)
- Trade Related Aspects of Intellectual Property Rights (TRIPS)
- Trade Policy Review Mechanism
- Dispute Settlement
- Agreement on Agriculture

All these Agreements were negotiated during the Uruguay round and signed on 15th April 1994 and came into effect on 1st Jan 1995. There were around total 60 agreements signed. The Marrakesh Agreement included commitments to reopen negotiations on agriculture and services at the turn of the century which began in early 2000 and were incorporated into the Doha Development Agenda in late 2001. Intellectual property rights were also to be considered in post Uruguay round agenda.

Free Trade Agreements (FTA): A free trade agreement is a preferential arrangement in which members reduce tariffs on trade among themselves, while maintaining their own tariff rates for trade with non-members.

Customs Union (CU): A customs union is a free trade agreement **(FTA)** in which members apply a common external tariff (CET) schedule to imports from non-members.

Common Market (CM): A common market is a customs union **(CU)** where movement of factors of production is relatively free amongst member countries.

Economic Union (EU): An economic union is a common market **(CM)** where member countries coordinate macro-economic and exchange rate policies.

13.3 WTO Agreements

WTO Agreements

Agreement Establishing WTO		
Goods	**Services**	**Intellectual Property**
GATT *(1994)*	**GATS**	**TRIPS**
Other goods Agreements And Annexure	Services Annexure	
Countries schedules of commitments	Countries schedules of commitments	
Dispute Settlement		
Trade Policy Review Mechanism		

These agreements are often called the WTO's trade rules and the WTO is often described as "rules-based", a system based on rules. But it is important to remember that the rules are actually agreements that governments negotiated.

Reasons for creation of WTO:

- GATT was provisional and at the time of GATT's creation, ITO was expected to manage the international trade and GATT was expected to be included in the charter of ITO
- Trade in services was not covered by GATT rules and was becoming major part of world trade and was of considerable interest to more and more countries
- Changes in the world economy and globalization
- Procedures for settling disputes existed under GATT, but it had no fixed timetables, rulings were easier to block and many cases dragged on for a long time

The following are some of the important features regarding WTO

- It is a place where member governments go to try sort out the trade problems
- The bulk of the WTO's current work comes from the Uruguay round and earlier negotiations under GATT
- WTO is born out of negotiations and everything WTO does is the result of negotiations
- WTO consists of a set of agreements, negotiated and signed by the bulk of the world trading nations. These documents provide the legal ground rules for international commerce. They are essentially contracts,

binding governments to keep their trade policies within agreed limits

- The goal of WTO is to help producers of goods and services, exporters and importers conduct their business, while allowing the Govt.'s to meet social and environmental objectives
- The overriding purpose of WTO is to help trade flow as freely as possible so long as there are no undesirable side effects, as this is important for economic development/wellbeing
- It also ensures that individuals, companies and governments known what the trade rules are around the world and give them the confidence that there will be no sudden change of policy. In other words, rules have to be transparent and predictable
- Presently WTO has 166 members

13.4 Principles of WTO Trade

WTO agreements are lengthy and complex because they are legal texts covering a wide range of activities. They deal with agriculture, textiles, clothing, banking, telecommunications, government purchase, industrial standards, products and safety, food sanitation regulations, intellectual property and much more. But a number of simple fundamental principles run throughout all these documents. These principles are the foundation of the multilateral trading system.

Following are the principles.

1. Trade without discrimination:

- Most Favoured Nation (MFN): Under WTO agreements, countries cannot normally discriminate between their trading partners. In general MFN means that every time a country lowers a trade barrier (import duties) or opens up a market or gives some country a special favour, it has to do so for the same goods or services from all its trading partners - whether rich or poor, weak or strong. Certain exceptions are allowed in case of developing countries or if a product is traded unfairly from a country but only under strict conditions.

However, exceptions allowed to this rule include the following:

a. Free Trade Agreements (FTA): WTO member countries are allowed to sign free trade agreements but WTO says that whatever benefits are offered to the FTA partners, the same should be passed on to all WTO member countries progressively *(no time limit specified)*.

b. Security Clause: India accorded the MFN status to Pakistan in 1996 as per India's commitments as a member of the WTO. But after the attack in Pulwama, in Feb 2019 India withdrew MFN status making use of a '**security exception**' clause in the GATT.

   This is because Article 21(b)(iii) of GATT states that "*Nothing in this Agreement shall be construed to prevent any contracting party (including India in this case) from taking any action which it considers necessary for the protection of its essential security interests taken in time of war or other emergency in international relations.*"

c. Special and Differential Treatment given to developing/poor nations. Under the **Generalized System of Preferences**

(GSP), developed countries offer non-reciprocal preferential treatment (such as zero or low duties on imports) to products originating in developing countries. Preference-giving countries unilaterally determine which countries and which products are included in their schemes.

- National Treatment (NT): It says that imported and locally produced goods should be treated equally after the foreign goods have entered into the domestic markets. The same should apply to foreign and domestic services and to foreign and local trademarks, copyrights and patents. National Treatment only applies once a product, service or item of intellectual property has entered the market. Therefore, charging customs duty on an import is not a violation of National Treatment even if locally produced goods/ products are not charged an equivalent tax.

2. Free Trade (gradually through negotiation)

Lowering trade barriers is one of the most obvious means of encouraging trade. The barriers are Tariffs (customs duties) and Quotas (quantitative restrictions). Opening markets can be beneficial but it requires adjustments. The WTO agreements allow countries to introduce changes gradually through "progressive liberalization". Developing countries are usually given longer time to fulfil their obligations. As a result of negotiations, by the mid 1990's industrial countries tariff rates on industrial goods had fallen steadily to less than 4%.

3. Binding and enforceable commitments:

In the WTO, when countries agree to open their markets for goods or services, they bind their commitments. For goods these bindings amount to **ceilings** on customs tariffs rate. A country cannot increase its ceiling rates (bindings) without negotiating with its trading partners which could mean compensating them for loss of trade.

4. Transparency:

WTO members are required to publish their trade regulations and to make sure decisions affecting trade are notified to other WTO members and to the WTO secretariat itself. The WTO also has a trade policy review mechanism which periodically reviews the laws and regulations of a WTO member country.

5. Single Undertaking:

All WTO agreements are held together as a single undertaking. This means that member countries cannot selectively choose which agreement they will join. The WTO and all of its agreements is a single package that member states must join on all or nothing basis.

The WTO has a tradition of making decisions not by voting but by consensus. This allows all members to ensure their interests are properly considered even though, on occasion, they may decide to join a consensus in the overall interests of the multilateral trading system. Where consensus is not possible, the WTO agreement allows for voting — a vote being won with a majority of the votes cast and on the basis of "one country, one vote".

13.5 Agreements Under GATT

The following are some of the important agreements under GATT:

13.5.1 Sanitary and Phytosanitary (SPS) Measures

The Agreement on the Application of Sanitary and Phytosanitary Measures (the "**SPS Agreement**") entered into force with the establishment of the World Trade Organization on 1 January 1995. The Agreement on the Application of Sanitary and Phytosanitary Measures ensures that food is traded safely across international borders and that animal and plant pests or diseases are not spread through trade means. The SPS Agreement sets out the basic rules for food safety for humans and animal and plant health standards.

The Agreement allows countries to set their own standards. But it also says regulations must be based on science. They should be applied only to the extent necessary to protect human, animal or plant life or health. And they should not arbitrarily or unjustifiably discriminate between countries where identical or similar conditions prevail.

The agreement allows countries to use different standards and different methods of inspecting products. Member countries are encouraged to use international standards, guidelines and recommendations where they exist. However, members may use measures which result in higher standards if there is scientific justification. They can also set higher standards based on appropriate assessment of risks so long as the approach is consistent, not arbitrary.

All countries maintain measures to ensure that food is safe for consumers, and to prevent the spread of pests or diseases among animals and plants. These sanitary and phytosanitary measures can take many forms, such as requiring products to come from a disease-free area, inspection of products, specific treatment or processing of products, setting of allowable maximum levels of pesticide residues or permitted use of only certain additives in food. Sanitary (human and animal health) and phytosanitary (plant health) measures apply to domestically produced food or local animal and plant diseases, as well as to products coming from other countries.

13.5.2 Agreement on Agriculture (AoA)

The main objective of this agreement is to discipline and reduce domestic support (subsidies) given to agriculture while at the same time giving freedom to the member countries in designing their domestic agricultural policies with respect to their specific needs.

The nature of the domestic support (subsidy) given by a government can be broadly divided into two categories:

- Support with no or minimal distortive effect on trade ("Green Box")

(exempted/ allowed under WTO)

- Support that distorts trade ("Amber Box")

(restricted/not allowed under WTO)

WTO classifies all the domestic support into **three categories**. *The above two categories and a third one which is basically distorting in nature but the distortion in trade is less in value and hence WTO allows/exempts it.*

Domestic Supoport

allowed under WTO	allowed under WTO	restricted under WTO
1. Green Box	**2. Other exempted measures**	**3. Amber Box**
R&D support, infra support like irrigation, electricity, expenses related to accumulation & holding of public stocks for food security, domestic food aid to the section of population in need and any direct payment to producers which is not linked to production.	Development Measures : Investment related subsidies, agriculture input subsidies to low-income farmers. Blue Box : payments made on fixed areas or number of livestock. Production is required to receive the payment but actual payment not linked to production. De-minimis Support (explained below)	Any support which does not fall in the 1st or 2nd category is subject to reduction of commitments. The WTO members should try to reduce this type of support

Total Aggregate Measurement of Support (AMS) and De-minimis level:

Every member country is required to calculate their aggregate measurement of support like price support, input subsidies, interest subsidies etc. Price support is calculated by multiplying the quantity of production with the difference between the administered price (in India it is Minimum Support Price) and the external reference price (world market price). In similar way any kind of support (fertilizer subsidy and others) is calculated by the difference of administered price and the market price. For a developing country if the total **AMS is less than 10%** of the value of the production then there is no penalty and comes under "**De-minimis support**" under point 2 above, but if it is more than 10% then it will come under point 3 above and the countries must try to bring it under 10% (for a developed country this cap is 5%).

"India's apprehension is that its total AMS may exceed 10% of the permitted cap." And there is also an obligation that all members of WTO must notify the Committee on Agriculture (in WTO), the extent of their domestic support measures under Green Box, other exempt measures, Blue Box and non-exempt support and their AMS calculations.

Peace Clause: During Bali Conference (Dec 2013), the member countries agreed to a "peace clause" which refers to a time period during which the member countries would refrain from seeking penalty against countries which still breach the 10% domestic support (total AMS) cap. The 'peace clause' said that no country would be legally barred from food security programmes (in case of India it is procurement by FCI at MSP and its distribution through

PDS) even if the subsidy breached the limits (10%) specified in the WTO Agreement on Agriculture. The "peace clause" was an **interim measure** which prevents any WTO member from challenging any developing country for crossing the 10% subsidy cap. It was expected to be in force for four years until Dec. 2017 and after that it would expire. The members had agreed to work on a permanent solution to reach an agreement by Dec. 2017. *Countries including India feared that the "peace clause" would expire by Dec. 2017 and if a permanent solution is not reached by then, then their subsidy programme may be challenged by other WTO members.*

But India bargained hard in further negotiations and now the temporary peace clause has been replaced with an open-ended statement - "until a permanent solution to the issue of public stockholding and agricultural subsidies is arrived at, no member country can challenge other members for crossing the 10% subsidy cap". So now, there is no time limit within which we have to restrict our subsidies below 10%. But this is applicable only for those subsidies which were prevalent at that time and not for new subsidies.

*[**Just for info**: As per the WTO norms, countries are not allowed to export foodgrains from public stockholdings as they are procured at regulated/ subsidized rates and there is subsidy in storage also.]*

13.5.3 Information Technology Agreement (ITA)

Production of electronic products in India goes back to the 1960s when public sector enterprises were tasked with responsibility of producing computing devices. Consumer electronics took roots in the following decade and a fledgling industry was in place by the time the policies of economic liberalization were introduced in 1991.

In the early phase of import liberalization, the electronics sector was largely kept out of this exercise, but the situation changed drastically after India, in 1996, joined the Information Technology Agreement (ITA), a plurilateral agreement under the WTO. When the ITA became effective on 1st July 1997, only 29 members had acceded to the agreement. (As of now the number of participants has grown to 82, representing about 97 per cent of world trade in IT products). ITA covers a large number of high technology products, including computers, telecommunication equipment, semiconductors, semiconductor manufacturing and testing equipment, software, scientific instruments, as well as most of the parts and accessories of these products.

The ITA requires each participant to eliminate and bind customs duties at zero for all products specified in the Agreement.

Accordingly, India agreed to eliminate import duties on 217 IT products by 2005. Consequently, India's average import duties on IT products came down from 66.4% in the pre-ITA phase to 37.8% in 1997 to below 12% in 2001, before the tariffs were completely eliminated on 1st January 2005.

The rationale for India's accession to ITA seems difficult to understand as India was a minor player in the global market for ITA products. India's exports of IT products were the lowest among the 29 original signatories to the ITA between 1997 to 2003. In sharp contrast, China had become the third largest exporters of IT products in 2003, and with Hong Kong taken together, they were the largest exporters of IT products from 2003 onwards. India's experience with the ITA has been most discouraging, which almost wiped out the IT industry from India. The real gainer from that agreement has been China which raised its global market share from 2% to 14% between 2000-2011.

In light of the new technological developments, some WTO members considered that the current product coverage of the ITA should be expanded (which will be called ITA–II) to include new generation semi-conductors, semi-conductor manufacturing equipment, optical lenses, GPS navigation equipment, and medical equipment such as magnetic resonance imaging products and ultra-sonic scanning apparatus.

But Government of India has decided not to participate in the ITA expansion (ITA-II) negotiations for the time being. This is because the Government wants to build a sound manufacturing environment in the field of Electronics and Information Technology and this is the time for India to incubate our industry rather than expose it to undue pressures of competition.

Recently Inda has increased tariffs on mobile phones and some other IT related products, and several countries have taken this issue to the WTO. But India has explained that the IT goods in question do not fall under ITA. It had all along maintained that IT and telecom technologies have evolved with new applications and equipment which were neither existent nor even conceived at the time of signing the ITA-I in Dec. 1996, at the WTO's first trade Ministerial Conference in Singapore.

13.5.4 Trade Related Investment Measures (TRIMS)

The Agreement on TRIMs of the WTO is based on the belief that **there is strong connection between trade and investment. Restrictive measures on investment are trade distorting.** Several restrictive measures on investment are prohibiting trade and hence are not allowable. According to the TRIMs provision, countries should not adopt the *investment measures* which restrict and distort trade.

Investment measures are those steps used traditionally against foreign investment by host countries. Here, the TRIMs instruct that WTO members may not apply any measure that discriminates against foreign investment that violates basic WTO principles (like the MFN and National Treatment). WTO gives a list of **prohibited investment measures** under TRIMs like:

- local content requirement
- export obligation
- quantitative restrictions on imports or exports
- domestic employment
- technology transfer requirement etc.

Few exemptions to developing countries are also provided under TRIMs. The Committee on TRIMs monitors the operation and implementation of the TRIMs Agreement and offers consultation for member countries.

The objective of TRIMs is to ensure fair treatment of investment in all member countries. As per the TRIMs Agreement, members are required to notify the WTO Council for Trade in Goods of their existing TRIMs that are inconsistent with the agreement.

TRIMS agreement applies only to measures that affect trade in **goods**. The General Agreement on Trade in Services (**GATS**) **addresses foreign investment in services as one of four modes of supply of services.**

13.6 General Agreement on Trade in Services (GATS)

Negotiated in the Uruguay round (and came into effect on 1st Jan 1995), it was developed in response to the huge growth of the services economy over the past few years. Services represent the fastest growing sector of the global economy and account for two third of global output, one third of global employment and nearly 20% of global trade. The following are salient features of GATS.

- GATS does not require any service to be deregulated or privatized.
- Government services are specially carved out of the agreement and are defined in the agreement as those that are not supplied commercially and do not compete with other suppliers. These services are not subject to GATS disciplines and commitments on market access and National Treatment do not apply to them.
- But GATS says government should regulate services reasonably, objectively and impartially.
- GATS says government must publish all relevant laws and regulations and set up enquiry points within their bureaucracies. Foreign companies and governments can then use these enquiry points to obtain information about regulations in any service sector.
- GATT says each government has the right to decide which sectors it wants to open to foreign companies and to what extent. The Uruguay round was only the beginning for GATS, which requires more negotiations which began in early 2000 and is now part of the Doha Development Agenda. The goal is to take liberalization process further by increasing the level of commitment in schedules.

13.7 Intellectual Property Rights (IPR)

Most of the value of new medicines and high technology product lies in the amount of invention, innovation, research, design and testing involved. Films, music recordings, books, computer software and on-line services are bought and sold because of the information and creativity they contain, not usually because of the plastic, metal or paper used to make them.

Creators can be given the right to prevent others from using their inventions, designs or other creations and to use that right to negotiate payment in return for others using them. These are "Intellectual Property Rights". These rights motivate the people for new innovations and research. These rights can take various forms.

- Books, paintings and films come under copyright
- New inventions can be patented
- Brand names and product logos can be registered as trademarks

Intellectual property rights are the rights given to persons over the creations of their minds. They usually give the creator an exclusive right over the use of his/her creation for a certain period of time. IPRs strike a balance between the long-term benefits and possible short-term costs to the society. In the short term (during the protection period) the products become costlier due to the payment of royalty to the owner. But society benefits in the long term when intellectual property protection encourages creation and invention, especially when the period of protection expires and created inventions enter the public domain.

In India, the IPRs come under Department for Promotion of Industry and Internal Trade, Ministry of Commerce & Industry. The following are various intellectual property rights:

(i) Copyright: Copyrights protect the "expression of ideas". Artistic works are generally considered to be expressions of ideas – books, paintings, songs, movies, and computer programs are examples of copyrights. Copyright will not protect the process through which a particular work was created or the use of information within it (instructions, etc.).

Cookbooks are often used to illustrate the difference between the "expression of an idea" and the "idea" itself. Cookbooks cannot be reproduced without permission because they are an "expression of ideas" (the recipes). However, people can still follow the recipes in the cookbook because they are replicating the "ideas" contained in the literary work. If the recipes were protected by a patent, users would need permission to follow them, since patents protect particular "ideas" from being used without authorization.

Copyrights occur automatically. You don't need to get it registered with the government authority. In India, copyrights are protected through "Copyright Act 1957". For literary, dramatic, musical or artistic work published within the lifetime of the author, the copyright shall subsist until 60 years from the beginning of the calendar year next following the year in which the author dies. In the case of a cinematograph film or sound recording, copyright shall subsist until sixty years from the beginning of the calendar year next following the year in which the film or the sound recording is published.

The rights in copyright vary according to the class of work. Some copyrights can be given on hire basis or it can be sold also. For example, cinematograph film, sound recording, computer programs etc. can be sold.

(ii) Patents: A patent is a right, granted by the government, to exclude others from making, using, or selling your invention. Patents protect inventions such as new processes, machines, or chemicals. The central idea is that patents protect "ideas", not just "expressions" of them. The main effect of patents is to give their holders the right to challenge any use of the invention by a third party.

Patents must be registered. If you invent something and fail to register it, another person who independently invents or discovers your invention can patent it. The term of the patent is generally for 20 years from the date of filing of the application of the patent. In India, patents are protected through "Indian Patent Act 1970".

"Ever greening of Patents" is referred to the practice whereby pharmaceutical firms extend the patent over products that are about to expire by doing minor reformulations or other iterations of the drug, without necessarily increasing the therapeutic efficacy. Ever greening delays the entry of generic drugs in the market. The decision to prevent ever greening of patents would help in maintaining an affordable and accessible supply of generic medicines in India.

The patent owner may give permission to, or license, other parties to use the invention on mutually agreed terms. The owner may also sell the right to the invention to someone else, who will then become the new owner of the patent.

(iii) Trademarks: Trademark is typically a name, word, phrase, logo, symbol, design, image or a combination of these elements. A trademark is a sign that you can use to distinguish your business' goods or services from those of other traders. Through a registered trade mark, you can protect your brand (or "mark") by restricting other people from using its name or logo. The registration of a trademark is for a period of ten years and can be renewed. So, once acquired, a trade mark can last indefinitely.

Trademark owner can be an individual, business organization or any legal entity. In India, trademarks are protected through "The Trade Marks Act 1999". Trademarks can be assigned/transferred from one party to another party also.

(iv) Trade Secrets: Broadly speaking, any confidential business information which provides an enterprise a competitive edge may be considered a trade secret. Trade secrets encompass manufacturing or industrial secrets and commercial secrets. The unauthorized use of such information by persons other than the holder is regarded as an unfair practice and a violation of the trade secret.

The subject matter of trade secrets is usually defined in broad terms and includes sales methods, distribution methods, consumer profiles, advertising strategies, lists of suppliers and clients, and manufacturing processes. While a final determination of what information constitutes a trade secret will depend on the circumstances of each individual case, clearly unfair practices in respect of secret information include industrial or commercial espionage, breach of contract and breach of confidence.

Contrary to patents, trade secrets are protected without registration, that is, trade secrets are protected without any procedural formalities. Consequently, a trade secret can be protected for an unlimited period of time. As per the TRIPS, the following are prerequisites for a trade secret.

- The information must be secret (i.e. it is not generally known among, or readily accessible to, circles that normally deal with the kind of information in question).
- It must have commercial value because it is a secret.
- It must have been subject to reasonable steps by the rightful holder of the information to keep it secret (e.g., through confidentiality agreements).

Trade secrets can be sold and licensed.

(v) Geographical Indication (GI): A geographical indication is a sign used on products that have a specific geographical origin and possess qualities or a **reputation that are due to that origin.** In order to function as a GI, a sign must identify a product as originating in a given place. In addition, the qualities, characteristics or reputation of the product should be essentially due to the place of origin. Since the qualities depend on the geographical place of production, there is a clear link between the product and its original place of production. The right to use a protected geographical indication belongs to producers in the geographical area defined, who comply with the specific conditions of production for the product.

However, a protected geographical indication does not enable the holder to prevent someone from making a product using the same techniques as those set out in the standards for that indication. Protection for a geographical indication is usually obtained by acquiring a right over the sign that constitutes the indication. The registration of a geographical indication shall be for a period of ten years, but may be renewed from time to time. The Controller-General of Patents, Designs and Trade Marks appointed under the Trade Marks Act, 1999, shall be the Registrar of Geographical Indications.

India, as a member of the World Trade Organization (WTO), enacted the Geographical Indications of Goods (Registration & Protection) Act, 1999 and has come into force with effect from 15th September 2003.

Recent Geographical Indications (GIs) in India (2023-2024) include Banaras Thandai, Assam Bihu Dhol, Nagri Dubraj rice, and Kandhamal Haladi. Other notable additions are Ladakh Wood Carving, Manadurai pottery, Kumbam grapes, Mithila Makhana, and the unique Similipal Kai Chutney.

(vi) Industrial Designs: In a legal sense, an industrial design constitutes the ornamental or aesthetic aspect of an article. An industrial design may consist of three-dimensional features, such as the shape of an article, or two-dimensional features, such as patterns, lines or colour.

The industrial design recognizes the creation of new and original features of new shape, configuration, surface pattern, ornamentations and composition of lines or colours applied to articles which in the finished state appeal to and are judged solely by the eye.

Industrial designs are applied to a wide variety of products of industry and handicraft items: from packages and containers to furnishing and household goods, from lighting equipment to jewelry, and from electronic devices to textiles. Industrial designs may also be relevant to graphic symbols and graphical user interfaces (GUI). Industrial Designs in India are protected under the Design Act 2000.

In most countries, an industrial design needs to be registered in order to be protected under industrial design law as a "registered design". In some countries, industrial designs are protected under patent law as "design patents".

The Controller General of Patents, Designs and Trade Marks under Department for Promotion of Industry and Internal Trade, Ministry of Commerce and Industry shall be the "Controller of Designs" for the Design Act 2000. Once a design is registered, the Controller of Designs will grant a certificate of registration to the proprietor of design. Once a design is registered, the registered proprietor of the design shall have copyright in the design during ten years from the date of registration.

13.8 Trade Related Aspects of Intellectual Property Rights (TRIPS)

Negotiated during the Uruguay round, TRIPS came into effect on 1st Jan 1995 and the deadline for complying with TRIPS obligations for India (a developing country) was January 1st 2005.

Accordingly, The Patents Act, 1970 (of India) was amended twice in 2002 and 2005 to make it fully TRIPS compliant by 2005. Through the Patents (Amendment) Act of 2002, the provisions related to **compulsory license** which was there in the 1970 Act was substituted with a completely new one (section 84). And by the Patents (Amendment) Act, 2005 ***product* patents** were allowed to be granted for drugs, which were not allowed under the 1970 Act. As per the 1970 Act only *process* patenting was allowed which means patenting of the method of manufacturing a product.

Ideas and knowledge are becoming an important part of trade. Accordingly, WTO's TRIPS establishes minimum level of protection that each member country has to give to the intellectual property of fellow WTO members.

The following are some of the important features of TRIPS.

1. Protection of IPR: It ensures that adequate standards of protection exist in all member countries for the various intellectual property rights. The starting point for TRIPS is the obligations of the main international agreements of the World Intellectual Property Organization (WIPO) that existed before the WTO was created.
    - Paris Convention for protection of Industrial Property (Patents, Industrial Designs)
    - Berne Convention for the protection of literary and artistic works (copyrights)

Some areas were not covered by the above conventions. And in some cases, the standards of protection prescribed were thought inadequate. So, the TRIPS agreement added a significant number of new or higher standards for the protection of the IPRs.

2. Enforcement (tough and fair): Just having intellectual property laws is not enough. They have to be enforced. The agreement says governments have to ensure that intellectual property rights can be enforced under their laws, and that the penalties for infringement are tough enough to deter further violations. The procedure must be fair and equitable. They should not entail unreasonable time limits or unwarranted delays.

3. Technology Transfer: Developing countries in particular see technology transfer as part of the bargain in which they have agreed to protect intellectual property rights. The TRIPS agreement includes a number of provisions on this. Like, it requires developed country governments to provide incentives to their companies to transfer technologies to least developed countries.

13.9 Generic Drugs and Compulsory Licenses

Generic Drugs: A generic drug is a medication that has exactly the same **active ingredient** as the brand name drug and yields the same therapeutic effect. It is the same in dosing, safety, strength, quality, the way it works, the way it is taken, and the way it should be used. Generic drugs do not need to contain the same **inactive ingredients** as the brand name product, say colour or taste can be different.

However, a generic drug is generally marketed after the brand name drug's patent has expired, which may take up to 20 years. So, during the protection period of 20 years, the patent owner tries to recover its cost which it has spent on research and development and the drug is quite costly during this time as it is produced only by the patent owner under its brand name and others can't manufacture and sell. After the protection period is over, any company can sell the generic versions of the drug and there is fierce competition which ultimately reduces the price of the drug.

But the (Indian Patent Act 1970) patent laws provide a remedy to the high price issue of branded drugs in the form of licenses to the generic manufacturers even during the protection period of 20 years. This remedy is available in the form of voluntary and compulsory licensing of the drug.

1. Voluntary License: Under this arrangement, a patent holder may give license (on its own) to the third party to manufacture, import and distribute **generic versions** of the pharmaceutical product and much more. The licensee of the patent will act as an agent of the company. The terms in a voluntary license may set price ranges, royalty from the distribution of the sales etc. [There is no legal provision given under Patent Act 1970 as this license access is done through mutual contractual agreement.]

2. Compulsory License: If the patent owner is exploiting its monopoly position and not manufacturing and supplying the branded drugs in the market or if the drug is not being made available at a reasonably affordable price in the market, then government can give compulsory licenses in two ways:

a) If a manufacturer himself approaches the government that he can produce the drug **(generic versions)** at a very cheap price, but only after the negotiation between patent owner and manufacturer has failed for voluntary license. [Section 84 of Patent Act 1970]

b) In case of National emergency (pandemic like Covid-19) or extreme urgency, Govt. can give notification that it will give compulsory licenses to any manufacturer who wants to manufacture **generic versions** of the drug with such terms and conditions. [Section 92 of Patent Act 1970]

But in both the cases of compulsory license mentioned above, the manufacturer (the compulsory license holder) will have to pay royalty to the patent owner as decided by the Government.

If a government authority has granted patent to someone (person or entity) in its own country then WTO's TRIPS agreement says that each other member country (government) will have to give protection to the patent right of the fellow member. But WTO also provides a reasonable restriction on the rights of the patent holder under certain circumstances. This restriction is provided by allowing other member countries to enact provisions for granting Compulsory Licenses to prevent the abuse of patent right and member countries have been given freedom to determine the grounds for granting Compulsory Licenses. *Compulsory licensing means that the government allows someone else to produce the patented product or process without the consent of the patent owner.*

13.10 WTO – Doha Development Agenda

The Doha Round (also known as 'Doha Development Agenda') is the latest round of trade negotiations in the WTO. The Round was officially launched at the WTO's Fourth Ministerial Conference in Doha, Qatar, in November 2001. The original deadline to conclude the negotiations was 1st January 2005 but was missed and since then several deadlines have been missed and it is still not concluded. Its aim is to achieve major reform of the international trading system through the introduction of lower trade barriers and revised trade rules with a special focus to improve the trading prospects of developing countries. The work programme covers about 20 areas of trade including agriculture, services, intellectual property rights, trade facilitation etc. but the main agenda (of Doha round) is the centrality of 'development' (improving the trading prospects of the developing nations by providing them special and differential treatment) in the multilateral trading system. Following are some of the issues which are being discussed and debated in WTO's Ministerial Conference.

1. Fisheries Subsidies:

- WTO members have forged an 'Agreement on Fisheries Subsidies' which sets new global rules to curb harmful subsidies and protect global fish stocks.
- The agreement prohibits support for illegal, unreported and unregulated (IUU) fishing.
- It bans support for fishing in overfished stocks.
- And it takes a first but significant step forward to curb subsidies for overcapacity and overfishing by ending subsidies for fishing on the unregulated high seas

- For a period of 2 years from the date of entry into force of this Agreement, subsidies granted or maintained by developing country Members, including LDC Members, up to and within the Exclusive Economic Zones (EEZ) shall be exempt from actions
- A Member shall exercise due restraint in raising matters involving an LDC Member
- Developing country members including LDC members shall be provided targeted technical assistance for the purpose of implementation of the various measures in the agreement. For this a voluntary WTO funding mechanism shall be established in cooperation with relevant international organizations such as the Food and Agriculture Organization of the United Nations (FAO) and International Fund for Agricultural Development. (A WTO Fish Fund has been established)
- The Agreement came into effect on 15th September 2025, but India has still not signed the Agreement.
- *WTO is nudging for more and more members to formally accept the Agreement.*

2. Work Programme on e-Commerce:

Members agreed to maintain the current practice of not imposing customs duties on electronic transmissions until the next (14th) Ministerial Conference or till 31st March 2026. Some countries, particularly from the developed world, are demanding a 'permanent moratorium' on imposing duties on electronic transmissions. **India is against such a move** and has put pre conditions for extension of such a moratorium. The 'moratorium', which was included in the 1998 'Declaration on Global E-commerce,' at the trade body's second Ministerial Conference, stated that "member countries will continue their current practice of not imposing customs duties on electronic transmission". This moratorium — which is 'temporary' in nature — gets extended at every biennial MC.

WTO has agreed to continue the work under the Work Programme on e-Commerce since based on the existing mandate. *(India is against any attempt by developed countries to push for negotiations on setting global rules on e-commerce, as domestic rules on e-commerce are in a flux. And at present, India's e-commerce entities lack the strength to compete with giants in China and the developed countries).*

3. Food Insecurity:

- WTO resolved to cooperate with a view to ensuring enhanced productivity and production, trade, availability and accessibility and affordability of food for those who need it, especially in humanitarian emergencies.
- The World Food Programme (WFP) for humanitarian food purchases have been exempted from export restrictions.

4. WTO Reforms:

WTO members have agreed to undertake a comprehensive review of the WTO's functions in order to ensure the organization is capable of responding more effectively to the challenges facing the multilateral trading system.

Increasing protectionism, inadequate members in the Appellate Tribunal for dispute resolution, increasing number of Regional Trade Agreements (RTAs) and Free Trade Agreements (FTAs) etc. have resulted in member countries questioning the efficacy of WTO as an institution meant to ensure free trade and promote multilateralism. In the ongoing discussions on WTO reforms, India's proposal seeks to re-affirm the importance of development and promote inclusive growth. The broad elements of India's proposal include:

- Preserving the core values of the Multilateral Trading System;

- Resolving the impasse in the Dispute Settlement System;
- Safeguarding development concerns; and
- Transparency and Notifications.

13.11 Free Trade Agreements (FTAs)

A Free Trade Agreement (FTA) is a preferential arrangement in which members reduce tariffs on trade among themselves, while maintaining their own tariff for trade with non-members. Around the world, FTAs have been proliferating, especially since the establishment of the WTO in 1995. Till 2014, –India mainly focused on partnering with other Asian countries, and more in goods than in services. In addition to its long-standing commitment to multilateralism under WTO agreements and in line with global trends, India has made use of FTAs as a key component of its trade and foreign policy, especially from 2003-04 onwards.

India has bilateral FTAs with Sri Lanka, Afghanistan, Thailand, Singapore, Bhutan, Nepal, Korea, Malaysia and Japan and regional trade agreements, the South Asian Free Trade Agreement (SAFTA, 2004) and India - ASEAN Agreement (2010).

Impact of these FTAs on trade:

Trade flows between countries are directly proportional to the size (GDP) of the two countries and inversely proportional to the distance between them. Distance is a proxy for all trade costs between countries, including not just transport costs, but also those related to language, currency, policy etc.

India's FTAs have increased trade with FTA countries more than would have happened otherwise. But increased trade has been more on the import than export side, most likely because India maintains relatively high tariffs and hence had larger tariff reductions than its FTA partners after signing the FTAs.

Post 2014 Strategy in FTAs: With tectonic shifts happening in global politics, multilateralism has taken a backseat. Accordingly, India has calibrated its trade strategy more towards bilateral agreements and that too with developed nations. Earlier India mostly focussed on signing FTAs with Asian economies which were more competitive than India in the same set of industries. But India changed this strategy post 2014, and now it is looking to sign bilateral agreements with those countries where there is a complementarity. India has recently signed bilateral agreements with UAE, Australia, UK, Oman, EFTA (Iceland, Liechtenstein, Norway, and Switzerland) and is at different stages in finalizing the trade agreements with Canada, USA, Israel and European Union.

- **India-UAE** Comprehensive Economic Partnership Agreement (CEPA) covers different areas like trade in goods and services, rules of origin, customs procedures, government procurement, IPRs, e-commerce. Both the countries have removed tariffs on 80% of products. The FTA will give zero duty access to 90% of India's exports to UAE. The FTA will benefit a number of labour-oriented businesses like gems, jewellery, textiles, leather footwear, sports goods, engineering goods and pharmaceuticals. *It came into effect in May 2022.*
- **India-Australia** Economic Cooperation and Trade Agreement (ECTA) covers areas like Trade in Goods, Rules of Origin, Trade in Services, Technical Barriers to Trade (TBT), Sanitary and Phytosanitary (SPS) measures, Dispute Settlement, Movement of Natural Persons, Telecom, Customs Procedures,

Pharmaceutical products, and Cooperation in other Areas. India will benefit from preferential market access provided by Australia on 100% of its tariff lines. On the other hand, India will be offering preferential access to Australia on over 70% of its tariff lines. In services, India and Australia both have offered market access and Most Favoured Nation in different sub-sectors.

It came into effect in Dec. 2022.

- **India-EFTA trade deal:** India signed Trade and Economic Partnership Agreement (TEPA) with the European Free Trade Association (EFTA) which includes four countries namely Iceland, Liechtenstein, Norway, and Switzerland. It is an innovative and well-balanced pact that covers two-way trade in goods and services as well as bilateral investments. Under the agreement, the four-member EFTA has committed $100 billion in investments in India over 15 years and the tariffs between both blocs are expected to reduce. India has consistent trade deficit with EFTA members. India imports Gold and other items while it exports chemicals, semi-precious stones etc. to EFTA members. Became effective in October 2025.
- **India-UK Comprehensive Economic and Trade Agreement (CETA):** Presently the bilateral trade between the two countries stand at nearly USD 56 billion, with a joint goal to double this figure by 2030. CETA secures unprecedented duty-free access for 99% of India's exports to the UK, covering nearly the entire trade basket. This is expected to open new opportunities for labour-intensive industries such as textiles, marine products, leather, footwear, sports goods, toys, and gems and jewellery, alongside fast-growing sectors like engineering goods, auto components, and organic chemicals.
- The services sector, a strong driver of India's economy, will also see wide-ranging benefits. The agreement provides greater market access in IT and IT-enabled services, financial and legal services, professional and educational services, and digital trade. Indian professionals, including those deployed by companies to work in UK across all services sectors, professionals deployed on contracts such as architects, engineers, chefs, yoga instructors, and musicians, will benefit from simplified visa procedures and liberalised entry categories, making it easier for talent to work in the UK. To become effective by April 2026.

Following are the WTO compliant measures for protection of the domestic industry: -

➢ ***Anti-Dumping Duty*** *When goods are exported by a country (say A) to another country (say B) at a lower price as compared to the prevailing price in the country A, then this is called dumping. And to stop this, country B is allowed to put extra duty/tariff (other than its normal customs/ import duty) on imports coming from country A. This extra tariff is called "Anti-Dumping Duty".*

Anti-dumping is a measure to rectify the situation arising out of the dumping of goods and its trade distortive effect. Thus, the purpose of anti-dumping duty is to rectify the trade distortive effect of dumping and re-establish fair trade. The use of anti-dumping measure as an instrument of fair competition is permitted by the WTO. In fact, anti-dumping is an instrument for ensuring fair trade and is not a measure of protection per se for the domestic industry. It provides relief to the domestic industry against the injury caused by dumping and is country specific.

➢ ***Countervailing Duty*** *When a government is giving subsidies to its exporters then the importing country can put extra tariff/duty (other than its normal customs/import duty) on those products entering into their market. This extra duty is called "Countervailing Duty". It is also called anti-subsidy duty and is country specific.*

➢ ***Safeguard Duty*** *is applied when there is a surge in imports of a particular product irrespective of a particular country/ies. Safeguard duty is a WTO compliant temporary measure that is brought in for a certain time frame to avert any damage to a country's domestic industry from cheap imports.*

➢ ***Non-Tariff Barriers (NTBs):*** *Trade barriers can be in the form of tariffs (import duty) or non-tariff. Modern Free Trade Agreements reduce tariffs (import duty) but impose various types of Non-tariff Barriers (NTBs). NTBs often come in the form of regulations, standards, testing, certifications etc. Various examples of NTBs are:*

- *Import licensing*
- *Rules for the valuation of goods at the customs*
- *Pre-shipment inspections (further checks on imports) that are aimed at protecting human, animal or plant health and the environment*
- *Rules of origin*
- *Quantitative restrictions*

13.12 International Monetary Fund (IMF) and World Bank

The following is a comparison between the World Bank and IMF:

World Bank	IMF
Objective:	Objective:
• Reconstruction of war affected countries (achieved) • To promote development to raise standard of living in developing countries (& LDC also) • To eliminate poverty • To promote investment in developing countries by providing finance, technical assistance (related to development programmes, environment and infrastructure) and guarantees	• To promote international monetary cooperation (facilitate payments transactions) • To assist member countries to overcome Balance of Payment problems • To ensure exchange rate stability • To ensure balanced international trade • To minimize restrictions on convertibility of currencies • Surveillance (it reviews economic policies of member countries and assess risks especially financial risks)

	• Provides technical assistance like training to officials, related to banking, finance, BoP • Policy advice to governments and Central Banks based on analysis of economic trends and cross-country experiences.
Source of Funds:	Source of Funds:

• Share capital (subscribed by member countries based on share in GDP)	• Quota (subscribed by member countries) (main source of funds)
	  ○ 25% in Gold or foreign currency
	  ○ 75% in Domestic currency

• Issuance of bonds in international financial markets (main source of funds)	• Borrowings from specific countries
Lending	Lending
• Usually long term loans of 25 to 30 years to developing and LDC countries • Usually concessional loans without condition • Lends for both policy reforms and projects	• Usually conditional short-term loans to all member countries to reform those things which resulted in crisis • Usually non concessional loans • Lends for only policy reforms and not for specific projects
Votes: Votes = Basic votes + 1 vote for each Share (1 share = $ One lakh) *Basic votes are equally allotted to all member countries*	Votes: Votes = Basic votes + 1 vote for each Quota of SDR one lakh *Basic votes are equally allotted to all member countries*
Organizational Structure All powers of the Bank are vested with the Board of Governors, which is the highest decision-making body under whom there is Board of Directors, while the Bank is headed by the President.	Organizational Structure All powers of IMF are vested with the Board of Governors, which is the highest decision-making body under whom there is Board of Directors, while the IMF is headed by the Managing Director.
It is a convention that President is always from the US. Every member country appoints a governor (Fin. minister) and an alternate governor (RBI governor). Board of governors usually meet once in a year.	*It is a convention that Managing Director is always from Europe. Every member country appoints a governor (Fin. minister) and an alternate governor (RBI governor). Board of governors usually meet once in a year.*

Reports: • World development report • International Debt Statistics • Ease of doing business report • Global Economic Prospects Headquartered in Washington DC, 189 members	Reports: • World Economic Outlook • Global financial stability report • Fiscal Monitor Headquartered in Washington DC, 191 members
Reforms proposed by India (developing countries perspective) in IMF/ World Bank	
• Appointment of President/MD should be open to all, merit based and transparent • Staff diversity should be increased • Basic votes should be increased • Resources should be increased • Double majority voting in case of major decisions (once a major decision is taken based on voting rights, half of the members should also approve it)	

IMF and World Bank are called Bretton Wood twins and the World Bank membership is conditional only if a country is member of IMF it can get World Bank membership (there can be exceptions).

International Monetary Fund (IMF)

IMF was established in 1944. When a country joins the IMF, it is assigned a **Quota** which is based on the country's four parameters:

- GDP (50%),
- openness (30%),
- economic variability (fluctuations in current and capital account, 15%),
- international reserves (5%)

Quotas are denominated in Special Drawing Rights (SDRs), the IMF's unit of account.

A member's quota subscription determines the maximum amount of financial resources the member is obliged to provide to the IMF. A member must pay its subscription in full upon joining IMF: up to 25% must be paid in SDRs or widely accepted currencies (US dollar, Euro, Yen, Pound, Yuan) while the rest 75% is paid in the member's own currency. Quota is supposed to be reviewed after every five years.

The amount of financing a member can obtain from the IMF is also based on its quota. For example, a member can borrow up to 145 percent of its quota annually and 435 percent cumulatively. However, access may be higher in exceptional circumstances. IMF grants loans only to member countries. Unlike development banks, the IMF does not lend for specific projects.

Quota is used to determine the following:

1. Subscription (maximum amount of financial resources that a member is obligated to provide to the IMF),
2. Voting power/rights in IMF decision making,
3. Member country's share of SDR allocations (acts as debt on member country)

4. Borrowing capacity (financial assistance a member may obtain from the IMF)

Reserve Tranche Position (RTP): That proportion of the Quota which the IMF member country can designate for its own use. The reserve tranche portion of the quota can be accessed by the member nation anytime at its own discretion (and is not under an immediate obligation to repay those funds to the IMF), whereas the rest of the member's quota is typically inaccessible. Member nation reserve tranche are typically 25% of the members' quota and is **accounted among the country's foreign exchange reserve.**

Foreign Exchange Reserve of a Country = Foreign Currency Assets + Gold + SDR + RTP

(RTP = Reserve Tranche Position)

Special Drawing Rights (SDR):

The SDR is an international reserve asset, created by the IMF in 1969 to supplement its member countries' official reserves in the context of the Bretton Woods fixed exchange rate system. The value of the SDR was initially defined as equivalent to 0.888671 grams of fine gold—which, at the time, was also equivalent to one U.S. dollar. After the collapse of the Bretton Woods system in 1973, the SDR was redefined as a basket of currencies. Currently, the SDR basket consists of the U.S. dollar, euro, Japanese yen, pound sterling and the Chinese Renminbi (RMB)/Yuan.

1 SDR = 0.434 US Dollar + 0.293 Euro + 0.123 Yuan + 0.076 Yen + 0.074 Pound

The IMF allocates SDRs to its members in proportion to their standing in the organization, which is largely based on their share of the global economy. The first allocation was done in 1970-72. As of 23rd August 2021, total around 660.7 billion SDRs have been created (456 billion new SDRs were created in Aug 2021 to increase global liquidity out of which India was allocated 12.57 billion SDRs) and allocated to members. India's share in SDR allocation (quota) is 2.75% and voting power in IMF is 2.63%.

SDRs can be exchanged for freely usable currencies (US dollar, Euro, Yen, Pound, Yuan). There are no notes and coins denominated in SDRs i.e., it is not present in hard currency and is thus called paper gold or notional currency. And SDRs cannot be held by private entities. But the SDR does play a role as an interest-bearing international reserve asset. The allocation of SDRs boosts its member countries' official reserves. While SDRs cannot be used to purchase goods and services directly, countries can exchange them among themselves. Once the SDRs have been added to a member country's official reserves, the country can exchange its SDRs for hard currencies, such as US dollars, Yen, Pound, Yen, Yuan through voluntary trading arrangements with other IMF member countries. If a member purchases SDRs and its holdings rise above its allocation, it earns interest on the excess. Conversely if it sells SDRs and holds fewer SDRs than allocated, it pays interest on the shortfall.

The various financing facilities provided by IMF are:

- Extended Fund Facility
- Stand-by Arrangements
- Precautionary and Liquidity Line
- Flexible Credit Line
- Stand-by Credit Facility
- Extended Credit Facility
- Rapid Credit Facility
- Rapid Financing Instrument

India and IMF

- India is a founder member of IMF
- RBI adopted Special Data Dissemination Standards (SDDS) of IMF
- As per our commitment, India adopted current account convertibility in 1994
- Methodology of National Income Accounting was changed (to Market Prices) in 2015
- IMF's regional training institute is in Delhi to provide training to government officials
- India is a net lender to IMF

World Bank

The World Bank includes two institutions IBRD and IDA:

International Bank for Reconstruction and Development (IBRD)

- IBRD was established in 1944 as one of the Bretton Wood Institutions to help Europe rebuild after World War II.
- But as Europe rapidly rebuilt its economies, IBRD shifted its focus towards middle income and credit worthy poorer countries to promote sustainable, equitable and job creating growth, reduce poverty and address issues of regional and global importance.
- IBRD was established to function as self-sustaining business and provide loans and advice to middle income and creditworthy poor countries. Its resources are used exclusively for the benefit of the members.
- IBRD raises most of its funds from the world financial/capital markets. The IBRD borrows at an attractive rate on the capital markets because of its AAA rating that it has had since 1959.

International Development Association (IDA)

- IDA was established in 1960 to help the world's poorest countries and it complements the World Bank's original lending arm - IBRD.
- IDA aims to reduce poverty by providing interest free loans called credits and grants for programmes that boost economic growth, reduce inequalities and improve people's living conditions. It provides finance for the development of areas in the members territories.
- IDA is one of the largest sources of assistance for the world's 82 poorest countries, 40 of which are in Africa.
- IDA is funded largely by contributions from the governments of its member countries. Additional funds come from IBRD and International Finance Corporation (IFC).
- Together, IBRD and IDA make up the World Bank. The voting power of the member countries in the World Bank is based on the economic size (GDP) in addition to their contribution to the IDA. World Bank gives loan to member countries/Govt. and private agencies in the member countries.

The **World Bank Group** consists of five organizations viz. IBRD, IDA, IFC, MIGA & ICSID.

International Finance Corporation (IFC)

The International Finance Corporation (IFC) is the largest global development institution **focused**

exclusively on the private sector. It helps developing countries achieve sustainable growth by financing investment, mobilizing capital in international financial markets, and providing advisory services to businesses and governments.

The Multilateral Investment Guarantee Agency (MIGA)

MIGA was created in 1988 to promote **foreign direct investment** into developing countries to support economic growth, reduce poverty, and improve people's lives. MIGA fulfils this mandate by offering **political risk insurance (guarantees) to private investors.**

The International Centre for Settlement of Investment Disputes (ICSID)

ICSID provides international facilities for conciliation and arbitration of investment disputes between **private investors and foreign countries**.

13.13 Asian Infrastructure and Investment Bank (AIIB)

- Established in 2016 and headquartered in Beijing, the Asian Infrastructure Investment Bank (AIIB) is a multilateral financial institution founded to bring countries together to address the daunting infrastructure needs across Asia.
- AIIB offers sovereign (Govt.) and non-sovereign (private) financing for sound and sustainable projects in energy and power, transportation and telecommunications, rural infrastructure and agriculture development, water supply and sanitation, environmental protection, and urban development and logistics.
- According to the Articles of Agreement of AIIB, the Bank will *"provide or facilitate financing to any member, or any agency, instrumentality or political subdivision thereof, or any entity or enterprise operating in the territory of a member, as well as to international or regional agencies or entities concerned with economic development of the Asia region."*
- Membership in AIIB shall be open to members of the International Bank for Reconstruction and Development (IBRD) or the Asian Development Bank (ADB).
- All powers of the Bank are vested with the Board of Governors, which is the highest decision-making body under whom there is Board of Directors, while the Bank is headed by the President. China has the highest voting power of 26.5% in the Bank while India has 7.6% voting power. More than 100 countries have joined AIIB.

13.14 New Development Bank (NDB)/ BRICS Bank

- The New Development Bank was established in 2015 with its headquarter in Shanghai. It is a multilateral development bank established by Brazil, Russia, India, China and South Africa
- The Bank finances infrastructure and sustainable development projects in BRICS and other emerging economies and developing countries.
- The Bank supports public or private projects through loans, guarantees, equity participation and other financial instruments.

- It complements the efforts of multilateral and regional financial institutions toward global growth and development.
- The Bank also provides technical assistance for projects to be supported by the NDB and engage in information, cultural and personnel exchanges with the purpose of contributing to the achievement of environmental and social sustainability.
- All powers of the Bank are vested with the Board of Governors, which is the highest decision-making body under whom there is Board of Directors, while the Bank is headed by the President.
- The Bank's Agreement specify that all members of the United Nations could be members of the bank, however the share of the BRICS nations can never be less than 55% of voting power.
- The Bank shall have an initial subscribed capital of US$ 50 billion which shall be equally distributed amongst the founding members (i.e., each member will have $10 billion of subscribed capital). The voting power of each (five) member shall be equal its subscribed shares in the capital stock of the Bank (each share value is equal to $ 1,00,000).

PREVIOUS YEARS' QUESTIONS

Prelim Questions

1. The terms 'Agreement on Agriculture', 'Agreement on the Application of Sanitary and Phytosanitary Measures' and 'Peace Clause' appear in the news frequently in the context of the affairs of the: **[2017]**

(a) Food and Agriculture Organization
(b) United Nations Framework Conference on Climate Change
(c) World Trade Organization
(d) United Nations Environment Programme

2. "Gold Tranche" (Reserve Tranche) refers to **[2020]**

(a) A loan system of the World Bank
(b) one of the operations of a Central Bank
(c) A credit system granted by WTO to its members
(d) A credit system granted by IMF to its members

3. With reference to Trade-Related Investment Measures (TRIMS), which of the following statements is/are correct? **[2020]**

1. Quantitative restrictions on imports by foreign investors are prohibited
2. They apply to investment measures related to trade in both goods and services
3. They are not concerned with the regulation of foreign investment

Select the correct answer using the code given below:

(a) 1 and 2 only
(b) 2 only
(c) 1 and 3 only
(d) 1, 2 and 3

4. "Rapid Financing Instrument" and "Rapid Credit Facility" are related to the provisions of lending by which one of the following? **[2022]**

(a) Asian Development Bank
(b) International Monetary Fund
(c) United Nations Environment Programme Finance Initiative
(d) World Bank

5. Consider the following statements in respect of the International Bank for Reconstruction (IBRD) : and Development **[2025]**

I. It provides loans and guarantees to middle income countries.

II. It works single-handedly to help developing countries to reduce poverty.

III. It was established to help Europe rebuild after the World War II.

Which of the statements given above are correct?

(a) I and II only (b) II and III only

(c) I and III only (d) I, II and III

ANSWERS

1. (c) 2. (d) 3. (c) 4. (b) 5. (c)

Main Questions

1. Food Subsidy Bill is expected to eliminate hunger and malnutrition in India. Critically discuss various apprehensions in its effective implementation along with the concerns it has generated in WTO. **[2013]**

2. What are the direct and indirect subsidies provided to farm sector in India? Discuss the issue raised by the World Trade Organization (WTO) in relation to agricultural subsidies. **[2023]**

3. What are the challenges before the Indian economy when the world is moving away from free trade and multilateralism to protectionism and bilateralism? How can these challenges be met? **[2025]**

14

Infrastructure and Investment Models

14.1 Infrastructure Development: An Introduction

Since independence government took the full responsibility of providing the entire infrastructure like roads, railways, ports, airports, power etc. But due to its capital-intensive nature and financial and human resource constraint, government in post 1991 (LPG reforms) period moved on to seek the help of the private sector to fill the huge infrastructure gap in the country. Infrastructure in the economy can be built on the following three models:

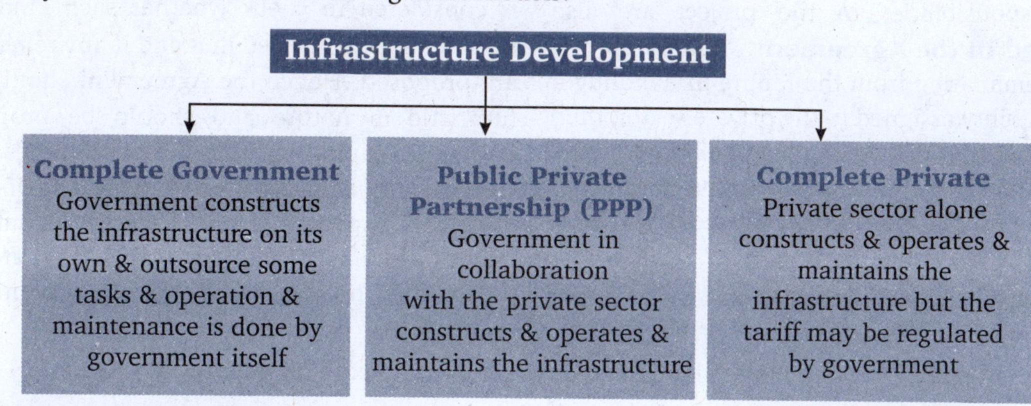

14.2 Public Private Partnership (PPP)

Public Private Partnership (PPP) is a way to **execute and maintain** a project (generally an infrastructure project) for delivering of goods and services through ***collaboration*** of government (public) and private sector. This collaboration is the defining characteristic of PPP model as certain kinds of collaboration may be considered PPP route and others may not be PPP. For example, when a government entity is building a road project and has procured construction material from a private company for construction of the road then this kind of collaboration is not considered as PPP. *Only those projects can be considered to be implemented through PPP route where the private sector is involved in at least operation and maintenance of the infrastructure project during its life.*

Whenever government decides that a certain project has to be implemented through PPP route then it selects a private partner through transparent competitive bidding. Once the private partner is selected for the project, the government entity signs an "**Agreement/ Contract Agreement/ Concession Agreement**" with the selected private entity. This Agreement basically defines the kind of **collaboration** between government entity and the private entity detailing in what will be the **roles and responsibilities** of the private sector and the government sector during the entire life of the project. When the roles and responsibilities are not handled properly then comes the **risk**. So, all the risks emanating from the failure in properly handling the roles and responsibilities in the project are also **detailed in the Agreement**. Accordingly, if a risk is emanating from the failure in handling a responsibility assigned to the private sector, then the cost of that risk will have to be borne by the private sector and if it is happening because of the government then the government will bear the cost of that risk.

Now the question arises that in any standard PPP project what roles and responsibilities government should handle and what should be given to the private entity. So firstly, all the roles and responsibilities of a project are listed and corresponding risks are also identified emanating from the failure of those roles and responsibilities. Those roles and responsibilities in which private party is more **efficient** in handling are assigned to the private party and those in which government is more capable are assigned to the government. In this way, all the roles and responsibilities and risks emanating from the project, and who will handle it are defined in the Agreement for the life of the project and the Agreement becomes the **guiding document** for the project for its entire life. If any dispute arises in future, then that Agreement is considered to check whether such kinds of disputes are mentioned in it and if any remedies are proposed. Hence the Agreement should be futuristic in nature and should be properly designed keeping in mind the possibilities and scenarios that may arise in future. And if that document is poorly designed then it becomes a major hurdle in the implementation of that PPP project and the project may get stuck in future.

The risks in a PPP project are also shared between the government and the private sector.

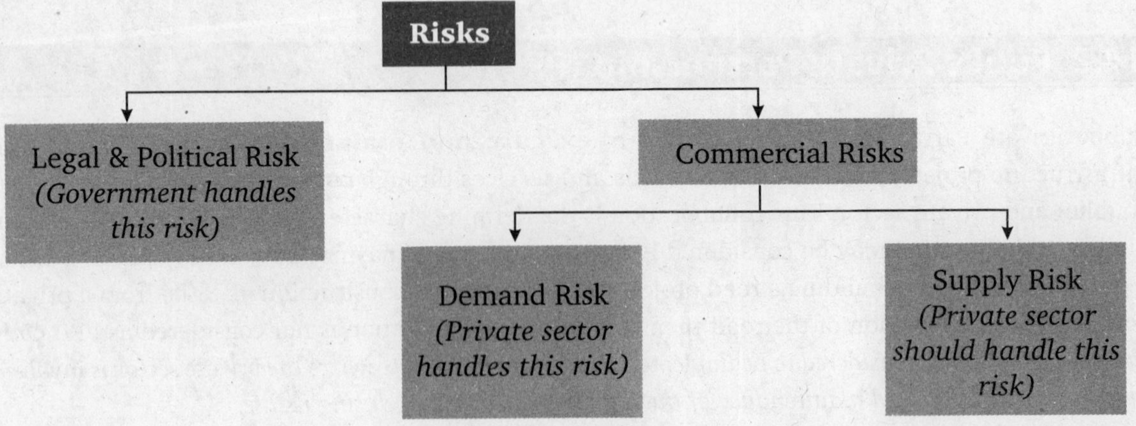

In a typical PPP project, generally government shall be responsible for getting all the clearances like environment, forest, water, power and land acquisition and the private party shall be responsible for construction and maintenance of the project. Any political risks like nationalization of a project, government abandoning the project in between, war or social unrest shall be taken care of by the government and the private party shall take care of design and construction quality and maintenance facilities. If a particular PPP project is not having enough demand (like very few people using airport facilities) then government may provide some kind of demand guarantee i.e., if number of people using the airport falls less than a specified number then Govt. shall bear the risk or compensate the private party.

There is currently no clear/standard definition of what constitutes a PPP. **The following are various definitions of PPP provided by different agencies:**

1. PPP is defined as an agreement between the government and one or more private partners according to which private partners deliver the service in such a manner that the service delivery objectives of the government are aligned with the profit objectives of the private partners and where the effectiveness of the alignment depends on a sufficient transfer of risk to the private partners. (OECD)
2. PPP refers to arrangements where the private sector supplies the infrastructure assets and services that traditionally have been provided by the government. (IMF)
3. PPPs are a generic term for the relationships formed between the private sector and public bodies often with the aim of introducing private sector resources and/ or expertise in order to help provide and deliver public sector assets and services. (EIB)
4. A project or a contract between a government or statutory entity on the one side and a private sector company on the other side, for delivering an infrastructure service on payment of user charges. (Dept. of Economic Affairs, Ministry of Finance, GoI)

The following are the various stages of a project executed through PPP route:

1. **Identification Stage:** It covers strategy planning, **broad viability of the project**, and identification of the key risk factors for the project, value for money analysis, PPP suitability checks and internal clearances to proceed with PPP development.
2. **Development Stage:** It covers detailed studies and investigations relating to technical, market analysis, and financial, legal aspects with the assistance from advisors/ consultants wherever required. The output of the project development activities, to the extent feasible, would be made available to the potential bidders during the bid process (in the next stage). It will also include project structuring, preparation of contractual documents and **obtaining of various project clearances and approvals.**
3. **Procurement Stage: Broadly it will cover selection of the successful bidder and award of the PPP contract.** Transparent, accountable, non-discriminatory, competitive and timely procurement processes would be followed so as to encourage maximum participation by private sector and to imbibe public confidence in the procedure.

   The bid documents used for procurement/ **selection** of private sector entities may comprise one or more of expressions of interest, request for qualifications, and request for proposals. Technical proposals would be invited, depending on the complexity of a project, to assess the ability of the private entity of their appreciation of the desired outcomes. Financial proposals would ideally be in the form of a single parameter.

4. **Contract Management Stage: It covers project implementation and monitoring over the life of the project.** Contract management is not a passive reporting exercise: it is an active process that involves a wide range of skills. Projects are not static; conditions change and the capability of the public authority at the interface with the private sector party is therefore crucial. The contract manager needs to be empowered to take action responsively and effectively which calls for effective and efficient governance processes and people with the right mix of skills including project management, commercial expertise and negotiation skills.

Role of PPP in Infrastructure Development

The PPPs were introduced in early 1990s which redefined the roles of public and private sectors in public service delivery. PPP basically fills a space between fully government and fully private way of executing and maintaining a project. Generally, a Special Purpose Vehicle (a company to execute a specific project) is formed to execute and maintain such a project.

Infrastructure projects are very capital intensive and require huge funds for their execution. Governments of various countries introduced PPPs because they had the potential of bringing in private finance to public service delivery and private players could deliver the services more efficiently i.e., **at least cost with better quality (more value for money)**. Many governments experienced the pressure of fiscal deficits and increasing public debt burdens by the mid-1990s and they found the private finance more attractive, especially for large infrastructure projects.

The private sector in India is quite large and possesses huge financial and technical resources. The private sector can very well **complement** the government sector in execution and delivery of large infrastructure projects through Public Private Partnership. In a country which is debt ridden and which has budget constraints, the private sector can play a pivotal role with its huge financial resources. But private participation in the process of infrastructure development through PPP is fraught with various hurdles and challenges. While private telecom services is a success story in India, the PPP constitutes a miniscule share in overall infrastructure building despite initiation of various policy adjustments and sector-specific reform programmes.

Stable macroeconomic framework, sound regulatory structure, timely resolving of disputes, investor friendly policies, sustainable project revenues, transparency and consistency of policies, effective regulation and liberalization of labour laws, and good corporate governance are the basic requirements, which defines the success of the PPP model. As we lack in providing the above environment, the status of the PPP in the infrastructure development in India, is not encouraging.

Challenges in the existing PPP framework in India:

Many infrastructure projects are today financially stressed, accounting for almost a third of stressed assets (NPAs) in banks. New projects are not able to attract sponsors as in recent PPP bids and banks are unwilling to lend. This current state of the PPP model is due to the poorly designed frameworks listed below:

1. Existing contracts focus more on fiscal (government revenues) benefits than on efficient service provision. For example, in port and airport contracts, the bidder offering the **highest share of revenue** to the government is selected. To win the bids, the private party quotes very aggressive which puts strain on private party finances and affects the quality of service provided to the users.
2. **Neglecting of the principles of allocating risk to the entity best able to manage it**. Instead, unmanageable risks for example traffic risk in highways (railways & ports), even though largely unaffected by their actions, are transferred to private parties.
3. Of late the government has started shifting its own responsibilities such as land acquisition, environmental and forest clearances etc. in various projects to the private parties. This has led to abandoning of the project in between by the private party if it is not able to get the clearances done. This creates disputes between the government and private entity and the project suffers huge delays.
4. There is no existing structure for **renegotiation** of projects in case of a failure. If a bureaucrat restructures a project, there are no rewards; instead, it may lead to investigation for graft. So, in such cases of failed projects, bureaucrats naturally avoid renegotiation and the project suffers long delays and court cases.
5. Certain bidders are involved in **reckless bidding** (very aggressive in quoting prices) as they know that the government will come to their rescue in case the project faces financial distress (for example Tata Ultra Mega Power Project in Gujarat). For such cases the government shall allow the projects to fail to enforce market discipline and warn future bidders of reckless bidding.

Reforms suggested:

- Developing a robust bond market for infrastructure companies
- Speedy resolution of infrastructure disputes
- Optimal risk sharing through better and balanced PPP contracts
- Sanctity and enforceability of contracts

14.3 Investment Models in Infrastructure

1. Engineering Procurement Construction (EPC) Contracts:

EPC is a prominent form of contracting agreement in the construction industry. The engineering and construction contractor will carry out the detailed engineering design of the project, procure all the equipment and materials necessary, and then construct to deliver a functioning facility or asset to their clients. Companies that deliver EPC Projects are commonly referred to as EPC Contractors. The Project Owner or client to the EPC Contractors will normally have a presence in the EPC Contractors offices during the execution of the EPC Contract. The Client places what can be termed a Project Management Team or PMT to overlook the EPC Contractor.

2. Cost-Plus Model

In the cost-plus pricing model, the purchaser agrees to pay the production price of the good plus a fixed percentage to the seller for profit. A cost-plus contract fully reimburses a contractor for the cost of materials and then adds additional money to arrive at the total cost of the job. Cost-plus pricing is often used in government contracts, and has been criticized as promoting wasteful expenditures in the form of direct and indirect costs. These costs are converted to per-unit costs for the product; then a predetermined percentage of these costs are added to provide a profit margin. This model is used when it is difficult to know the total cost of the project in advance. The main disadvantage of this model is **it provides an incentive for inefficiency to companies**, encouraging them to raise costs.

3. BOT/BOOT/DBFOT etc.

- BOT (Build Operate Transfer): In the BOT framework, the government delegates to a private sector entity to build infrastructure and to operate and maintain these facilities for a certain period. So, private party builds the project, operates and maintains it and then transfers the project to the government authority at the end of the contract period.
- BOOT (Build Own Operate Transfer): Private party builds the project, owns it and operates and maintains it for the contract period and then transfers the project to the government at the end of the contract period. This model is preferred by the private entities as compared to the BOT model because in this model the ownership of the infrastructure asset/facility is with the private entity which makes it easier for them to arrange finance from banks as the infrastructure asset acts as collateral.
- DBFOT (Design Build Finance Operate and Transfer): Private party takes the entire responsibility of designing the project, building, financing, operations and management and then transfer to the government at the end of the project life cycle.

4. Special Purpose Vehicles (SPV)

The name SPV is given to an entity which is formed for a single, well-defined and particular purpose. Technically, an SPV is a company and it has to adhere to all the rules and regulations laid down in the Companies Act.

The company, as distinguished from an SPV, may be called a general-purpose vehicle. A company may do many things which are mentioned in the memorandum of association (MoA) or permitted by the Companies Act. An SPV may also do the same, but its scope of operation is limited and focused to a particular project. If it is not so, the SPV should better be called a company.

Like a company, an SPV must have promoter(s) or sponsor(s). Usually, a sponsoring corporation hives off assets or activities from the rest of the company into an SPV. This isolation of assets is important for providing comfort to investors. The assets or activities are distanced from the parent company; hence the performance of the new entity (SPV) will not be affected by the ups and downs of the originating entity. The SPV will be subject to fewer risks and thus provide greater comfort to the lenders.

14.4 Road Sector

India has a total road network of 63.4 lakh km, including National highway (NH) network of 146,195 km. National highway network forms the arterial backbone of road transport network as even though it comprises only 2% of total road network yet it carries about 40% of the overall road freight/cargo traffic. In the recent times there has been a shift from project-based national highways to corridor-based approach, which aims to create advanced industrial cities along the highways, positioning them as major manufacturing and investment hubs. For example, an Electronics Manufacturing Cluster (EMC) is being developed along the Yamuna Expressway in Gautam Buddha Nagar, UP.

In India, Central and State Governments build road projects mainly on the following three models:

(i) Engineering Procurement and Construction (EPC): The government gives the contract only to build the road to a private contractor based on submission of the tender by the party **at the lowest cost**. Private party builds the road and hands it over to the government who then maintains the road. *(It is not a PPP model)*

(ii) BOT - Toll: The private party is selected to build, maintain and operate the road based on the party submitting the tender for maximum sharing of toll revenue to the government. In case the revenue from toll is expected to be not enough to cover the cost of the project then the government gives one-time support in terms of upfront grant called Viability Gap Funding (VGF) and the private party is selected based on who asks for **minimum VGF**. All the traffic and commercial risk lies with the private party and the private party is dependent on toll for its revenues. *(It is a PPP model)*

(iii) BOT - Annuity: The private party is selected to build, maintain and operate the road project based on the party submitting the tender asking for minimum annual payment from the government for the entire term of the contract. The private party recovers all the cost of construction and maintenance of the project **from the government** and there is no traffic and commercial risk to the private party. Toll collection right will be of the government and it may or may not collect toll. *(It is a PPP model)*

The major drawback of the annuity model is, the private party bears almost the entire cost of the project during the initial construction period but it receives payment from the government in equal annual instalments and it takes a long time for the private party to recover cost and become profitable. And because of this the private parties were becoming reluctant to participate under the Annuity model. Hence, central government approved a **fourth** model for the road sector in **January 2016**.

(iv) Hybrid Annuity Model: It is a mix of Annuity and EPC model. 40% of the bid project cost shall be payable by the government to the private party during the construction period (generally 2-3 years) linked to the physical progress of the project. Rest 60% of the cost will be paid annually by the government (to the bidder asking for lowest annual payment) after the completion of construction i.e., during the operation and maintenance period. The benefit of hybrid annuity is that, while the private partner continues to bear the construction and maintenance risks as in Toll and Annuity projects, it is required only to partly bear the financing risk. *(It is a PPP model)*

NHAI has recently started awarding the already constructed EPC road projects to private companies on Toll – Operate – Transfer (**TOT**) model.

(v) TOT model: Under this model, bidder quoting the maximum upfront amount (to be given to NHAI) wins the bid. The successful bidder will be responsible to collect the toll for the lease period (generally for 30 years) and will operate and maintain the road. NHAI is giving the **public-funded already constructed highway projects** through the TOT model to mobilise funds for new highway construction by transferring these **operational projects** on a long-term lease basis to domestic and foreign investors. NHAI uses the upfront receivables exclusively for funding construction of other highways. *(It is a PPP model)*

The *Delhi-Noida Direct* (DND) Flyway is one of the first PPP project based on Build Own Operate Transfer (BOOT) model. The expressway was opened to public in 2001.

Bharatmala Pariyojana:

The largest highway construction programme was launched under "National Highway Development Programme (NHDP)" in 1998 by the then Prime Minister Atal Bihari Vajpayee. NHDP spread across phase - I to phase - VII and had an aggregate length of 55,792 Kms. A large part has been completed and the rest will be subsumed under Bharatmala Pariyojana.

Bharatmala Pariyojana is a new umbrella program for the highways sector that focuses on optimizing efficiency of freight and passenger movement across the country by bridging critical infrastructure gaps through effective interventions like:

- development of Economic Corridors
- Inter Corridors and Feeder Routes
- National Corridor Efficiency Improvement
- Border and International connectivity roads
- Coastal and Port connectivity roads
- Green-field expressways

The project is implemented through National Highway Authority of India, National Highways and Infrastructure Development Corporation Limited (NHIDCL), Ministry of Road, Transport and Highways and State PWDs.

As per the National Transport Development Policy Committee Report, road transport is approx. handling 69% and 90% of the countrywide freight and passenger traffic, respectively.

14.5 Railways

14.5.1 Engine of Future Economic Growth

Since its inception, the Indian Railways has served to integrate the fragmented markets and thereby, stimulating the emergence of a modern market economy. It connects industrial production centers with markets and sources of raw materials and facilitates industrial development. It provides rapid, reliable and cost-effective bulk transportation to the energy sector, to move coal from the coal fields to power plants and petroleum products from refineries to consumption centers. It links agricultural production centers with distant markets and thus acts as the backbone of transportation needs of the various sectors. It also links places, enabling large-scale, rapid and low-cost movement of people across the length and breadth of the country. In the process, the Indian Railways has become a symbol of national integration.

The Indian Railways contributes to India's economic development, accounting for about one per cent of the National Income. It accounts for six per cent of the total employment in the organized sector directly and an additional 2.5 per cent indirectly through its dependent organizations. The Indian Railways, with nearly 63,000 route kilometers fulfils the country's transport needs, particularly, in respect of long-distance passenger and goods traffic.

Thus, Indian Railway has played a major role in the socio-economic development of the country but due to lack of capacity addition, congestion, poor services and weak financial health the share of railways in the country's GDP has declined to around 1% in recent years. But it has the potential to increase the growth of the economy by 2-3% if the country's railway network is pumped with massive investment to boost the connectivity.

Within the overall freight/cargo transportation in the country, transportation through railways has slipped to 32% from above 60% level in the post-independence period. Simultaneously, the freight transportation through roads has increased to around 66%. But with the recent reforms proposed and faster execution, railway has the potential to increase its freight share and add 2-3% points to the growth of the economy.

Rail Route to higher growth:

Increase in public infrastructure investment like railway, affects the economy in two ways:

- In the short run, it boosts aggregate demand and crowds in (pulls in) private investment due to the complementary nature of infrastructure services
- In the long run, a supply side effect also kicks in as the infrastructure-built feeds into the productive capacity of the economy

Railways are found to possess strong **backward linkages** (i.e., when we develop railway, it requires iron and steel as well as engineers therefore these industries will also develop with the growth of railways). Increasing investment in railway by Rs. 1 would increase output by Rs 3.3. This large multiplier has been increasing over time and the effect is greatest on the manufacturing sector i.e., it will be good for "Make in India" also.

Further there are sectors where railway services are input to production i.e., **forward linkages** (with the development of railways other industries like power plant, tourism will also get developed where railways is used as input). A Rs. 1 push in railways will increase the output of other sectors by about Rs. 2.5. This forward linkage effect has declined over time but this is largely due to the capacity constraint in the railways which has led to reliance on other modes of transport mainly road.

Combining forward and backward linkage effects suggests a very large multiplier (over 5) of investment in railways i.e., Rs. 1 increase in railways investment would increase economy wide output (GDP) by Rs. 5.

Also, rail transportation has a number of favourable characteristics as compared to road transportation. It is six times more energy-efficient than road and three times more economical. The social costs in terms of environmental damage or degradation are significantly lower in case of rail transport.

Foreign Investment in Railway up to 100%

100% FDI is allowed under automatic route in railway infrastructure but not in train operations and safety.

Railways are a capital intensive (i.e., huge amount of funds are required for development) sector and its growth depends heavily on availability of funds for investment in rail infrastructure. Currently, internal revenue sources (profit generated from Indian railway) and government funding through budget are insufficient to meet the capital requirement of the cash strapped rail sector. Increased foreign investment cap of 100% in building and maintenance of rail infrastructure will help in bringing the required capital for the highly congested rail infrastructure.

Bibek Debroy Committee Report on Railway Reforms

Railway is going through its biggest reform since independence as proposed by "Bibek Debroy Committee". The Indian Railway will be separated into two:

- Railway Infrastructure Corporation (RIC), and
- Indian Railway Trains (IRT)

As Indian Railway Trains (IRTs) are public service provider of railway transport services, there will be private trains also running on the infrastructure provided by RIC. So basically, on RIC infra, both Govt trains (IRTs) and private trains will run.

Since both govt. and private trains will be running, it will require a "Regulatory Body", whose role will not be merely to set tariffs, but also ensure fair competition (such as access to track) between IRTs (govt trains) and private train operators. The Railway ministry will set up broad policy and the regulatory body will implement the principles of competition determined by the policy and the present Railway Board will become a corporate Board for just the IRTs.

*The share of transport sector in Gross Value Addition (GVA) for 2022-23 was about 4.8% of which the share of road transport is the largest at 3.5%, followed by the share of the **Railways (0.9%)**, air transport (0.2%) and water transport (0.06%).*

The GoI has allowed the private players to operate in the Railways sector through the PPP mode under the "New India New Railway" initiative.

14.5.2 High Speed Rail (HSR)/ Bullet Trains in India

The average speed of Mail and Express trains is just 55 km/h, while freight trains run at an average of 30 km/h. Most of the main train routes runs at over 100% capacity leading to delays and accidents. The IR presently is highly constrained by capacity (and not by the demand).

Per capita mobility in India is lower than most of the developed countries. Driven by increase in population, GDP, income level and urbanization, intercity passenger travel demand is expected to leapfrog in the coming years.

Introduction:

The High-Speed Rail (HSR) System comprises of the infrastructure system, rolling stock (locomotives, wagons used on a railway) and operating conditions. Globally high-speed trains differ in their technology, infrastructure, rolling stock and achievable speeds. Currently, high speed rails can achieve speeds ranging from 200 kmph to 350 kmph depending on the technology and infrastructure.

The Union Budget 2026-27, presented on February 1, 2026, announced the development of 7 new high-speed rail (bullet train) corridors, aimed at enhancing connectivity between major economic, industrial, and cultural hubs.

- Mumbai-Pune
- Pune-Hyderabad
- Hyderabad-Bengaluru
- Hyderabad-Chennai
- Chennai-Bengaluru
- Delhi-Varanasi
- Varanasi-Siliguri

The Indian Railways' vision 2020 envisages a two-pronged approach to bring high speed rail in the country.

- The first strategy involves using **conventional** technology to increase the speed on segregated existing passenger corridors on trunk/ main routes, from the existing 80-100km/hr to 160-200 km/hr. (Vande Bharat one of the examples)

- The second approach involves identifying viable intercity routes to build new advanced high-speed corridors for speeds up to 350 km/hr (HSR).

Advantages of HSR:

- HSR is more time efficient as compared to air travel for distances below 800 km, if the access and exit to airports is considered. HSR also delivers multiple benefits including: revitalizing cities, encouraging high density real estate development along corridors, boosting the development potential of smaller cities along the corridor, providing employment access and choice to workers through better connectivity, linking cities into integrated economic regions and enhancing tourism.
- HSR transports more passengers per unit of energy compared to all other modes like air bus and private car. Hence it will offer a friendly environment, electrified railway with minimal environment damage,
- HSR can provide an opportunity to develop domestic manufacturing capacity for wagons and allied infrastructure. Railway modernization and HSR, in particular, are technology and capital intensive. The domestic manufacturing of rail and its components can promote innovation, opportunities for technology transfer and demand for industry – in particular, steel industry from manufacture of wagons and allied infrastructure.
- HSR creates opportunities for regional economic development by improving connectivity between large urban centres, as well as other small and medium cities along the corridors, and generates socio-economic benefits by improving access to employment, health, education and time savings. The ability of HSR to link small and medium cities can lead to a more geographically balanced development compared to air transport where only select few cities benefit.

Criticism

- HSR trains run at loss in every single country where they operate currently, despite the fact that tickets on these trains are often priced higher than an air ticket. For a country where majority of the population finds even Rajdhani fares beyond its reach, the number of people using the fancy HSR would be very limited and it could prove to be a white elephant.
- Some experts believe that India's current tracks can be improved to run trains at around 200 kmph, so why HSR, which will arguably soak in the entire budget of the Indian railways, which badly needs to upgrade and modernize its creaking infrastructure as well as add new lines to improve connectivity with the remote parts of the country, which remain cut off even over 70 years after the independence.

Comment: India has the fourth-largest rail network in the world. Considering the size, scale of operations and technology, it is appropriate that the railways build its first HSR line to move forward on the technology learning curve. Constructing HSR lines in the country should be seen as a nation-building exercise rather than a standalone project justified only on transport demand. *"India cannot remain blind to the technological advancements made across the world".*

Upfront investments for developing high speed rail corridors are high; however, the sustainability benefits are diffused and occur over a longer time frame. Therefore, investments for HSR would have to be viewed comprehensively for the long-term development benefits they generate. Given the large demand for intercity transport and increasing future incomes, the presence of several high-density corridors makes a strong case in India's intercity transport transition.

14.5.3 Dedicated Freight Corridors (DFCs)

It is the largest rail infrastructure project being built in independent India. Ministry of Railways has established a 100% subsidiary, "Dedicated Freight Corridor Corporation of India Ltd. (DFCCIL)", a Special Purpose Vehicle (SPV) for planning, development, mobilization of financial resources and construction, maintenance and operation of the eastern and western DFCs. The project has become operational. Following are the important features of Eastern and Western DFCs:

- DFCCIL is owning and operating the assets.
- Ministry of Railway is running trains on these tracks and paying **"access charge"** to DFCCIL. DFCCIL will also get access charge from other goods train run by private players in futures.
- There will be centralized control of operations on the DFC and double stacking containers will be running along these corridors.
- The operation and maintenance cost is expected to be half on DFC as compared with present IR network.
- DFCCIL will run freight trains at the maximum speed of 100 km/per hour as against the current maximum speed of 75 kmph on Indian Railway tracks whereas the average speed of freight trains will also be increased from existing speed of 26 kmph on Indian Railways lines to **70 kmph on DFC**.
- 70% of the goods train running on IR tracks will shift to DFC and will decongest the existing tracks for more passenger trains
- Government is building multimodal logistics park along the corridors to provide complete transport solutions to the customers.

Eastern Corridor: Ludhiana – Mugalsarai-Sonnagar-Kolkata (1835 Km)

(Ludhihana-Mugalsarai section debt funding by World Bank

Mugalsarai-Sonnagar section funded by Ministry of Railway

Sonnagar-Kolkatta section through PPP Model)

Western Corridor: Delhi – Rewari – Vadodara – Mumbai (1483 Km)

(funded by Japan)

PPP (investment/business model) in Dedicated Freight Corridor:

When a section of the railway line or DFC is built on PPP model then all the clearances and land acquisition is done by Indian railway (IR) and design, build, construction & maintenance of the track is done by the private player. Freight is collected by the Indian Railway (IR) and 50% of the freight of that section is given by IR to the private party. The private party is selected through tendering process. If 50% of the freight (which is going to the private party) is not expected to cover the full construction and maintenance cost then the private party will ask for Viability Gap Funding (VGF) from IR and that private party which asks for minimum funding will be selected. If 50% of the freight is expected to cover the full construction and maintenance cost then that private party will be selected which will give the maximum one time premium (funds) to the IR.

14.5.4 Development of Railway Stations

Ministry of Railways has launched Amrit Bharat Station Scheme for the development of stations on Indian Railways. Around 1309 Stations have been identified for development under this scheme. The various models are:

- Engineering Procurement Construction (EPC) model: Govt. does everything from planning to getting clearances as well as it operates and maintains the railway station. Only the construction part is done by a private developer/contractor. New Delhi, Mumbai and Ahmedabad railway stations have been planned to develop under this model.
- Public Private Partnership (PPP) model: Under this model, Government plans the project, gets statutory clearances and then a developer is chosen to upgrade/ modernize the railway station as well as to **operate and maintain** it. Habibganj, in the suburbs of Bhopal, is the country's first railway station redeveloped on PPP model.
- Non-EPC model (for example cost plus or fixed return on investment etc.)

14.5.5 Rail Development Authority (RDA)

The Government in April 2017, initiated a major reform in the railways by approving the setting up of Rail Development Authority (RDA) which will act as the regulator for the railway sector. It is envisaged that RDA will comprise of a Chairman and three other Members which shall make recommendations to the Government for appropriate consideration/decision.

Why RDA?

Since long it was being suggested that for the purpose of orderly development of infrastructure-enabling competition and protection of customer interest, it was important to have a regulation mechanism which is independent of the service provider i.e. the Ministry of Railway. The need for a regulatory authority had become acute over the years with railway ministers refusing to raise passenger fares, thus leading to freight revenue subsidising passenger traffic more and more, and consequently adding to the costs of industry. It was then felt that if an independent regulator handed down a revision of fares and freight rates which the railways had no option but to accept, then that would take the political sting out of the decision.

The RDA will act within the parameters of the Railway Act, 1989, and undertake the following broad **functions**:

- Recommend tariff, frame principles for social service obligation and guidelines for track access charge
- Ensure fair play and level playing field for stakeholder investment, make suggestions regarding policies for private investment, ensure reasonable safeguards to investors and resolve dispute regarding future concession agreements
- Set efficiency and performance standards
- Suggest measures for absorption of new technologies and human resource development
- Disseminate information, benchmarking of service standards against international norms and ensuring global best practices

- Provide a framework for non-discriminatory open access to the dedicated freight corridor infrastructure.
- Monitor policies on public-private partnerships

Comment: The RDA will help the government take appropriate decisions on important policy and operational issues, including pricing of services commensurate with costs, suggest measures for enhancement of non-fare revenue, ensure protection of consumer interests, promote competition, encourage market development, create positive environment for investment and promote efficient resource allocation. RDA would provide transparency to passenger and freight tariff determination and protect consumer interest by ensuring quality of service and cost optimisation.

14.6 Airports

The Airports Authority of India (AAI) was established in 1995 under the provision of Airport Authority of India Act 1994 for management of airports in India by a single authority. AAI under the Ministry of Civil Aviation is responsible for creating, upgrading, maintaining and managing civil aviation infrastructure both on the ground and air space in India. AAI manages/owns a total of 148 airports out of which some airports it has given to private parties to build, operate & maintain and some only for operation and maintenance purpose.

AAI Act was amended in 2003 to provide legal framework for airport privatization. Airport Economic Regulatory Authority (AERA) was established as a statutory body in 2009 under the Airports Economic Regulatory Authority of India Act, 2008 with its head office at Delhi.

AERA regulates the various tariffs at the Major airports *(those airports which handle more than 35 lakh passengers annually are termed as major airport)* while the tariffs at the non-major airports are regulated by the Directorate General of Civil Aviation (DGCA) under Ministry of Civil Aviation.

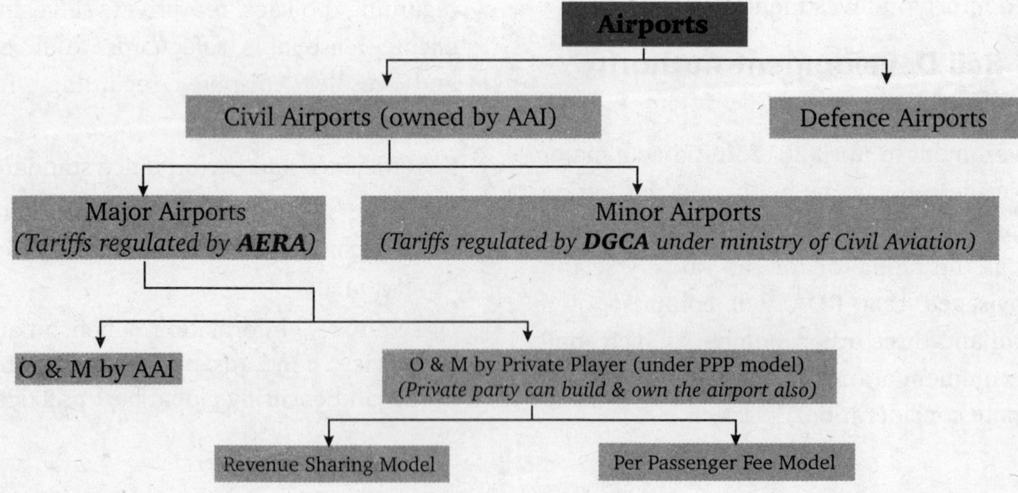

PPP in airports

The source of revenue for AAI in its airports is landing charges, parking charges, passenger service fee, cargo handling, advertising, rentals etc and with these revenues AAI operates and manages the various airports and builds new airports. Earlier AAI used to operate and maintain all the airports and used to collect these revenues. But from 2005-06, Govt. of India has started giving the operations and management responsibility of some airports to private operators. The private parties are given the responsibilities to make new investments in the airport infrastructure facilities and to operate and maintain the airport.

The first two airports were given on revenue sharing model (the private party quoting maximum revenue share) are Delhi and Mumbai to GMR and GVK respectively.

Case Study of Delhi Airport:

In September 2003, the Cabinet approved the restructuring of Delhi and Mumbai airports through the Joint Venture mode. In pursuance of this decision, after selection of the JV partner, AAI incorporated a subsidiary company viz. M/S Delhi International Airport Pvt. Ltd (DIAL), and subsequently sold 74% of the shares of DIAL to GMR (GMR had quoted the maximum revenue sharing of 45.99% to the government). On 4 April 2006, AAI signed an Operation Management Development Agreement (PPP Agreement) with DIAL. AAI handed over IGI airport, Delhi to DIAL on 3 May 2006 on 'as is where is' basis and granted DIAL the exclusive right to undertake functions of operations, maintenance, development, design, construction, modernization, finance and management of the Airport. On 26 April 2006 Government of India signed another agreement with DIAL viz State Support Agreement (SSA). The agreement laid down conditions and nature of support to be provided by Government of India, along with the mutual responsibilities and obligations between Government and DIAL.

The structure of the project is as following:

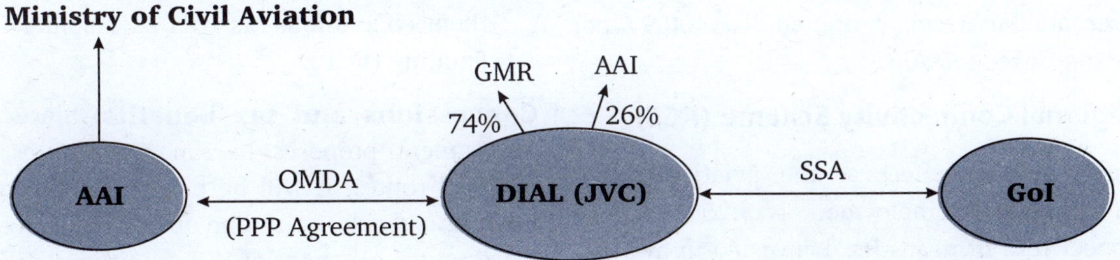

DIAL: Delhi International Airport Limited

JVC: Joint Venture Company

OMDA: Operation Management Development Agreement

SSA: State Support Agreement

To understand the revenue sharing model, let us take an example for a year say, 2021-22:

Revenue of DIAL = Rs. 5000 crore

Revenue shared with GoI = Rs. 2300 crore *(45.99%)*

Revenue left with DIAL = Rs. 2700 crore

Cost of DIAL = Rs. 1700 crore

Profit of DIAL = Rs. 1000 crore

Out of Rs. 1000 crore, GMR will get Rs. 740 crore profit and AAI will get Rs. 260 crore of profit by virtue of being the shareholder of DIAL. This model is revenue sharing (rather than profit sharing) because the private operator is sharing revenues with government. Anybody who owns DIAL is bound to get the profit by virtue of being the owner.

Later on, Ministry of Civil Aviation also awarded the airports of Bangalore and Hyderabad on the revenue sharing model through Public Private Partnership.

But for airports like Chennai, Kolkata, Lucknow, Jaipur, Ahmedabad and Guwahati, AAI itself modernized some of the airports and gave it to the private parties (in the year 2019) on PPP model for **operation and maintenance** of these airports. That private party which promised to give maximum **'per passenger fee' to the Government was selected.** Recently the 'NOIDA International Airport Private Limited' was also bid out on the same model to Zurich International where it offered Rs. 400.97 per passenger fee to AAI.

Regional Connectivity Scheme (RCS)

The multiplier effect of the aviation sector on output and employment is 3.25 and 6.10 respectively. It means Rs. 1 invested in aviation sector would increase output in the economy by Rs. 3.25 and one job created in aviation sector will lead to creation of 6.10 jobs in the other sectors in the economy. Thus, the growth in the aviation sector will have a large impact in terms of investment and employment creation in the economy.

Accordingly, Government of India launched the UDAN (UdeDesh ka AamNagarik)/ RCS scheme in April 2017. The objective of the RCS is to make flying affordable for the masses, to promote tourism, increase employment and promote balanced regional growth. The scheme intends to put on the aviation map, India's smaller cities and towns, which were till now uneconomical for commercial airlines to fly.

Integral to the scheme is the development of the 450 odd airports/ airstrips in the country which has immense potential but is lying dormant and construction of new airports. The civil aviation ministry with the assistance of state governments wants to develop "no frills" airports, at an indicative cost of Rs. 50-100 crore each.

The government has a two-pronged strategy for the implementation of the RCS:

- First, in order to stimulate demand on untapped routes, it has proposed capping fares at Rs. 2500 (for 50% of the seats) for a one-hour journey of around 500 Km.
- Second, to make the scheme lucrative for airlines, the government plans to provide them concessions, as well as Viability Gap Funding (VGF).

Concessions and tax benefits: Since the government proposes to cap the airfares on the RCS routes, it will be paying viability gap funding (subsidy) to airline operators plying on these routes. Payment of VGF to airlines will be made from the 'regional connectivity fund' to be established by the contribution of the Centre and the State in the ratio of 80:20. (Central Govt. will contribute to the VGF by charging a levy of up to Rs. 8500 on each departing flight of normal domestic airlines). The central and state govt. also proposes to give various tax and non-tax concessions to bring down the operational expenses of carriers and provide security and fire service free of cost.

Selection of the airline operator: It is up to the states whether they want to join the scheme or not. Once a state seeks the inclusion of an airport under the RCS' ambit, various **routes** would be offered for competitive bidding. The selection of operators on a particular RCS route is based on the bidder asking for the minimum VGF and will be operational for three years from the date of starting operations in a specific UDAN route. There will be only one operator operating the flights on a particular RCS route.

Under the RCS scheme, 619 routes connecting 88 airports, including two water aerodromes and 13 heliports have been operationalized so far.

14.7 Industrial Corridors

Background

- Industrial/Economic corridors connect economic agents along a defined geography on the foundation of an efficient transport system. They provide important connections between various economic nodes/hubs.
- Industrial corridors constitute world class infrastructure such as high-speed transportation (rail, road) network, ports, modern airports, special economic regions/ industrial areas, logistic parks/transhipment hubs, knowledge parks focused on feeding industrial needs, complementary infrastructure such as townships/ real estate, and other urban infrastructure along with enabling policy framework.
- Industrial Corridors recognize the inter-dependence of various sectors of the economy and offer effective integration between industry and infrastructure leading to overall economic and social development.
- Apart from the development of infrastructure, long-term advantages to business and industry along the corridor include benefits arising from smooth access to the industrial production units, decreased transportation and communications costs, improved delivery time and reduction in inventory cost.
- The strategy of an industrial corridor is thus intended to develop a sound industrial base, served by world-class competitive infrastructure as a prerequisite for attracting investments into export-oriented industries and manufacturing.
- With the above benefits in mind, Government of India has identified, planned and launched five industrial corridors: -
  - Delhi-Mumbai Industrial Corridor (DMIC)
  - Bangalore-Mumbai Economic Corridor (BMEC)
  - Chennai-Bangalore Industrial Corridor (CBIC)
  - Vishakhapatnam-Chennai Industrial Corridor (VCIC)
  - Amritsar-Kolkata Industrial Corridor (AKIC)
- GoI has adopted the strategy of developing integrated industrial/economic corridors in partnership with State Govts for boosting industrial development.
- A National Industrial Corridor Development Authority (NICDA) is being established to converge and integrate the development of all industrial corridors. These industrial corridors will provide an impetus to industrialization and planned urbanization. In each of these corridors, manufacturing will be a key economic driver and these projects are critical for the success of 'Make in

India' in raising the share of manufacturing in India's GDP from 16% to 25% by 2025.

- Along these corridors, the development of 100 Smart Cities has also been envisaged which are being developed to integrate the new workforce that will power manufacturing along the industrial corridors and to decongest India's urban housing scenario.
- These industrial corridors will also derive synergies with the 14 coastal economic zones (CEZs) planned along the coastal districts. The proposed industrial clusters under Sagarmala have been mapped to these industrial corridors: -
  - The leather clusters proposed in Muzaffarpur and Kolkata could fall on the AKIC and leather clusters in Perambur could fall on the twin corridors of CBIC and VCIC
  - Electronics cluster proposed in northern Maharashtra could fall on DMIC at JNPT node

14.8 Multi-Modal Logistics Park

'Logistics' means Transportation & handling of goods between points of production and consumption, storage, value addition and allied services. The logistics infrastructure comprises of nodes and connections, like ports, stations, Multimodal Logistics Parks, warehouses, and other business premises, connected by roads, railways, shipping, inland waterways, air routes, pipelines, etc., that are used by a wide range of carriers. The functionality of logistics includes processing the orders received from the customers, inventory planning and management, packaging, warehousing and transportation.

Multimodal transport refers to the transport of goods from one point to another via more than one mode of transport. Multimodal Logistics can be viewed as the chain that interconnects different links or modes of transport – air, sea, and land into one complete process that ensures an efficient and cost-effective door-to-door movement of goods under the responsibility of a **single transport operator**, known as a Multimodal Transport Operator (MTO), on one contract/transport document.

Multimodal Logistics Park (MMLP) provide all types of transportation facilities at a place for the end user or defined as a rail, road, ship, airplane based inter-modal traffic handling facilitation complex comprising container terminals, bulk cargo terminals, warehouses, banking and office space and facilities for mechanized handling, sorting/grading, cold chain, aggregation / desegregations etc. to handle freight traffic. The key components of a Multimodal Logistics Park are warehousing, transport and value-added services. The concept of multimodal logistics parks is relatively new in India.

Introduction:

The transport and logistics sector are fundamental to the development of a country. In India, since the 1990s, the transportation infrastructure has undergone a significant change. In a study by McKinsey, transport was identified as one of the most capital-intensive sectors in India, needing huge investments over the next several decades to sustain rapid urbanisation and growth of the Indian cities. Since freight (goods transported in bulk) forms an important part of the transport, the role of logistics and freight assumes importance.

In India, the logistics service providers are small players, mainly belonging to the unorganized sector. Even among the organized logistics players, few have offerings across multiple modes (air, water, rail and road) and services (transportation, warehousing and value-added services such as packaging, cold chain and customs clearance). This increases the cost of logistics in India with an unfavourable model mix. **Logistics account for 18% of the total product cost in India**, as against 8-12% in China and 12% in Europe. Thus, the focus needs to be given to 'integrated transport solutions' in preference to individual 'transportation' and 'distribution' services.

Why Multi Modal Logistics Parks?

Multi Modal Logistics Parks are the way forward for reducing logistics costs in India. They are expected to bring down logistics costs by serving four functionalities - Freight aggregation and distribution, Multi Modal freight transportation, Storage and Warehousing with modern, mechanized warehousing space satisfying the special requirements of different commodity groups and value-added services such as customs clearance with bonded storage yards, warehousing management services, etc.

Developing a network of multimodal logistics parks to act as logistics hubs will address the issues of unfavourable modal mix, inefficient fleet mix and an underdeveloped material handling infrastructure. Logistics parks are expected to help transition from the current situation **of point-to-point freight movement to an ideal situation of hub and spoke model** of freight movement as depicted in the figure below.

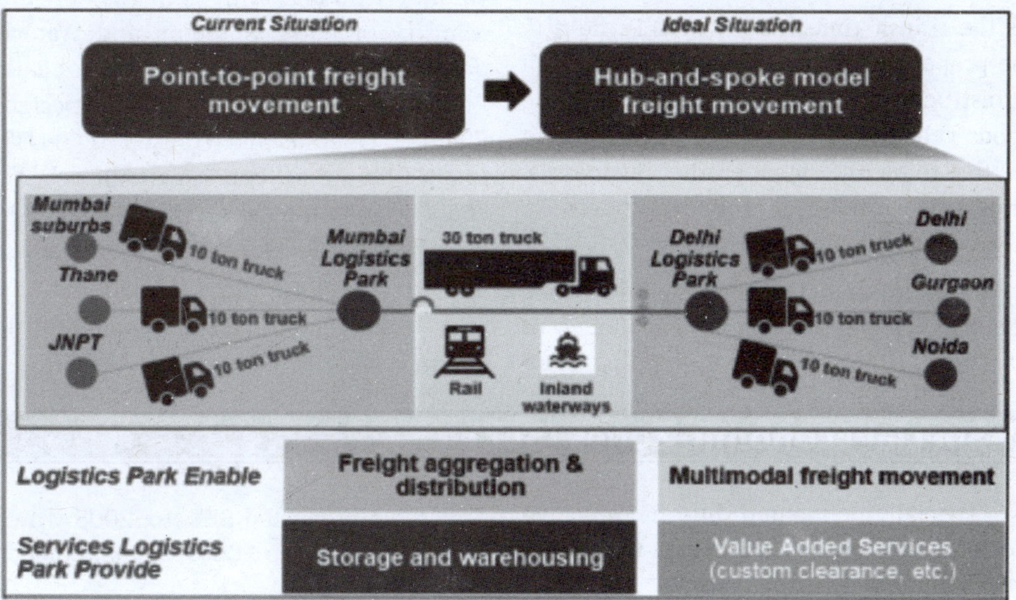

In the above figure, Mumbai and Delhi MMLP will act as centres for aggregation and disaggregation. In the absence of a MMLP, the freight (transport of cargo) from Thane/JNPT/Mumbai suburbs would have moved separately in smaller trucks to Delhi/Gurgaon/NOIDA.

Due to the presence of MMLPs in the outskirts of Mumbai and Delhi, first the cargo from the production areas nearby JNPT/Thane/Mumbai suburbs will be 'aggregated' in the Mumbai MMLP and then on a bigger truck/railway it will be transported to Delhi MMLP where it will be disaggregated and then move to Gurgaon/ NOIDA in smaller trucks.

Advantages of Multi Modal Logistics Park (MMLPs)

- MMLPs help in reducing transportation costs by using the right mode for the movement of goods.
- Since MMLPs help in reducing the transit time of the goods, it helps in reducing the inventory cost both for logistics operators as well as for the ultimate user of the transport mode.
- As the transit time is less, MMLPs help in the proper utilization of the assets like rail infrastructure, roads, warehouses etc. and the goods vehicles and the other infrastructure are free to be used for the other businesses. Thus, the per unit cost of the transportation of goods is reduced considerably.
- It helps in the optimal modal choice and balanced growth of all the modes of transport.

Challenges in logistics:

- Indian logistics market suffers from higher costs due to poor quality of road and rail infrastructure
- Large number of small and unorganised players exist in road transportation, with no industry consolidation and hence lack economies of scale
- Rail freight tariffs in India are among the highest in the world
- Rail freight lacks reliability and is deficient in terms of quality of operations, speed, and customer orientation
- There are inadequacies in gateway and hinterland connectivity of air freight and ports through rail and road
- There are inefficiencies and delays in loading and unloading of vessels at the ports

Ministry of Road, Transport and Highways (MoRTH) along with Ministry of Railways, Ministry of Ports, Shipping and Waterways is developing 35 Multi Modal Logistics Park under Public Private Partnership (PPP) on Design, Build, Finance, Operate and Transfer (DBFOT) mode under Bharatmala and Sagarmala schemes. The country's first international multimodal logistics park is being developed in Jogighopa, Assam. It is being developed by the National Highways and Infrastructure Development Corporation Limited (NHIDCL).

14.9 Special Economic Zones (SEZ)

SEZ is a specially delineated duty-free enclave treated as a **deemed foreign territory** within a country for the purpose of trade operations, duties and tariffs with special rules for facilitating foreign direct investment leading to exports.

Introduction:

Government enacted SEZ Act 2005 which came into force from Feb 2006.The main objectives of the SEZ Act are:

- generation of additional economic activity
- promotion of exports of goods and services;
- promotion of investment from domestic and foreign sources;

- creation of employment opportunities;
- development of infrastructure facilities;

The SEZ Rules provide for:

- Simplified procedures for development, operation, and maintenance of the SEZ and for setting up units and conducting business in SEZs;
- Single window clearance for setting up of an SEZ;
- Single window clearance for setting up a unit in a Special Economic Zone;
- Single Window clearance on matters relating to Central as well as State Governments;
- Simplified compliance procedures and documentation with an emphasis on self-certification

Any private or foreign entity and Central and State Government or its Agencies can set up SEZs in India.

Goods and services going into the SEZ area from Domestic Tariff Area (Any area that lies outside the SEZ and the custom bonded zone in India is known as DTA) shall be treated as ***exports*** *and goods coming from the SEZ area into DTA shall be treated as if these are being* ***imported****. SEZ units shall be a positive Net Foreign exchange Earner. Net Foreign Exchange Earning shall be calculated cumulatively for a period of five years from the commencement of production.*

Incentives offered to SEZ Units:

- 100% Income Tax exemption on export income for SEZ units under the Income Tax Act for first 5 years, 50% for next 5 years thereafter and 50% of the ploughed back export profit for next 5 years.
- Single window clearance for Central and State level approvals.
- Duty free import/domestic procurement of goods for development, operation and maintenance of SEZ units
- Supplies into SEZs are zero rated under the new GST law (i.e. no GST will be levied when the goods are purchased by SEZs from the DTA area)

Challenges:

India's SEZ experience has been disappointing till date. CAG in its report on SEZs stated that: "Considering the significant shortfalls in achievement of the intended socio-economic objectives by all the sectors of SEZs, there is an urgent need for the government to review the factors hindering the growth of non-operational and under-performing zones".The following are the various challenges faced by the SEZs:

- Unutilized land in SEZs. Lack of flexibility to utilise land in SEZs for different sectors
- Existence of multiple models of economic zones such as SEZ, Coastal Economic Zone, Delhi-Mumbai Industrial Corridor, National Investment and Manufacturing Zone, Food Parks and Textile Parks
- The domestic sales of SEZs face a disadvantage as they have to pay full customs duty, as compared to the lower rates with the ASEAN countries due to Free Trade Agreement
- Domestic firms are required to pay in foreign exchange for services rendered by a SEZ unit. However, this norm is not applicable for sale of **goods**, for which payments could be made in the rupee terms.
- Government's flip-flop policy on various tax exemptions on SEZs

Govt. in the budget 2022-23 has announced that "The Special Economic Zones Act" will be replaced with a new legislation that will enable the states to become partners in 'Development of Enterprise and Service Hubs (DESH)'.

14.10 SAGARMALA, CEZ and Ports

Sagarmala Project

Background:

Freight Transportation cost comparison through different modes:

road : rail : ship = 18 : 6 : 1

Waterways is the cheapest mode of transportation, then railway and then road.

Maritime logistics has been an important component of the Indian economy, accounting for 90% of EXIM (export & import) trade by volume. Coastal and inland waterway transportation is energy efficient, eco-friendly and reduces logistics costs for domestic freight but inadequate focus on its development has skewed the **modal mix** of transport in India with a disproportionately high share of roadways.

The Sagarmala Programme, launched in March 2015, is the flagship initiative of the Ministry of Ports, Shipping, and Waterways, aimed at revolutionizing India's maritime sector. With a 7,500 km coastline, 14,500 km of potentially navigable waterways, and a strategic position on key global trade routes, India holds immense potential for port-led economic growth. Sagarmala aims to streamline logistics, reduce costs, and enhance international trade competitiveness by shifting from traditional, infrastructure-heavy transport to efficient coastal and waterway networks. The program focuses on port modernization, industrial growth, job creation, and sustainable coastal development, ensuring minimal infrastructure investment while maximizing economic impact.

The Sagarmala Programme is a key pillar of the Maritime Amrit Kaal Vision 2047 (MAKV), driving India's ambition to become a global leader in maritime affairs. Building on Maritime India Vision 2030, MAKV sets ambitious targets, including 4 million GRT of shipbuilding capacity and 10 billion metric tons of port handling annually, aiming to position India among the top five shipbuilding nations by 2047.

MAKV outlines over 300 strategic initiatives to develop world-class ports, expand coastal and inland waterways, and promote a sustainable Blue Economy. As a core enabler, Sagarmala plays a transformative role in enhancing logistics, infrastructure, and shipping, accelerating India's maritime growth by 2047.

Objectives of the Sagarmala Program:

- Reduce logistics cost for EXIM and domestic trade with minimal infrastructure investment
- Lower logistics cost of bulk commodities by locating industries close to coast
- Create jobs and develop skills in ports and maritime sector
- Enhanced domestic waterways (inland and coastal) in the multi-modal transport

Components of the Sagarmala Program:

The overall set of projects under Sagarmala programme have been divided under five pillars:

1. **Port modernization and new port development**

   This focuses on upgrading existing ports and constructing new ones to enhance capacity and efficiency. It involves addressing bottlenecks and introducing modernization, mechanization, and computerization in port operations.

2. **Port connectivity enhancement**

   This component aims to improve connectivity between ports and the hinterland, optimizing both time and cost of cargo transportation. It includes the development of multi-modal logistics solutions, such as inland waterways and coastal shipping, to ensure seamless movement of goods.

3. **Port led industrialization**

   The initiative encourages the creation of industrial clusters near ports, promoting economic growth and reducing logistics costs. These clusters attract industries that benefit from efficient transportation and proximity to ports.

4. **Coastal community development**

   This focuses on the sustainable development of coastal communities by providing skill development and livelihood generation opportunities. It includes initiatives supporting fisheries, coastal tourism, and enhancing the well-being of the local population.

5. **Coastal shipping and inland waterways transport**

   This component promotes the use of coastal and inland waterways for cargo transportation, reducing dependence on road and rail networks. It is an environmentally friendly mode of transport that helps alleviate congestion on roads and railways.

Funding mechanism:

- Public Private Partnership (PPP)
- Internal and Extra Budgetary Resources (IEBR)
- Grants-in-aid
- Equity

Impact:

The **Sagarmala Programme** is transforming India's maritime sector by driving port-led economic growth, infrastructure modernization, and global trade competitiveness. With **839 projects** worth **₹5.5 lakh crore**, it has delivered remarkable outcomes, including **118% growth** in coastal shipping, a **700%** surge in inland waterway cargo movement, and **nine Indian ports ranking** among the **world's top 100**.

Sagarmala 2.0

The **Government of India** is advancing the **Sagarmala Programme** with **Sagarmala 2.0,** focusing on **shipbuilding, repair, recycling, and port modernization** to enhance India's maritime competitiveness.

With a budgetary support of **₹40,000 crore**, the initiative **aims to leverage investments of** ₹12 **lakh crore** over the next decade, driving **infrastructure development, coastal economic growth, and job creation**. Aligning with the vision of a Viksit Bharat and Atmanirbhar Bharat by 2047, **Sagarmala 2.0** will accelerate port-led development and strengthen India's position as a global maritime leader.

Coastal Economic Zones (CEZs), a part of Sagarmala Project

The CEZs are spatial economic regions comprising a group of coastal districts or districts with a strong port linkage. Each CEZ could be in the immediate hinterland of ports, in a radius of 100 Km with a sizable domestic market along with export potential. Within each CEZ, there will be multiple industrial clusters, each with distinct and separate land banks and a minimum size based on analysis of economies of scale for a given industry. These are bounded land parcels that could actually house industrial units and requisite infrastructure.

Fourteen CEZs have been identified along the coastline of the country. Leveraging the port ecosystem, these CEZs will provide the geographical boundary within which port-led industrialization will be developed.

Ports

(A port is like a railway station at which there are a number of Terminals like platforms at railway stations. The ships come at a Terminal of a port and load/unload the cargo like the trains come at a platform and passengers get on/off the train)

There are 13 Major Ports (defined as those owned/controlled by Central government) and around 187 Minor Ports (either owned by State government or private parties) in the country.

Ministry of Shipping, Government of India issued guidelines for PPP in 1996 to bring in new private players in the Major Ports sector. The objective was to attract private investment as well as to improve efficiency, productivity, quality of service and bring in competitiveness in port services in India. The private players were invited to build and operate the additional new Terminals in the existing Major Ports.

The source of revenue for a port operator is the charges that it collects from the ships which come and load/ unload their cargo at the ports. The main features of PPP guidelines were:

- That private player is selected which quotes the maximum share of revenue that it will share with the central government
- The period of contract is 30 years for which the private player will build and operate the Terminal and after that it will handover that terminal to the government
- Build Operate Transfer (BOT) and Build Own Operate Transfer (BOOT) models are followed for award of PPP projects

The first PPP in Major Ports was for the Jawaharlal Nehru Port Trust (JNPT) in Mumbai. Bids were invited to build a new Terminal at JNPT on Build Operate Transfer (BOT) model for 30 years contract. M/s P & O Ports, Australia won the bid but later it was acquired by DP World. DP World formed a new company Nhava Sheva International Container Terminal (NSICT), the Special Purpose Vehicle (SPV) to build and operate the Terminal. The Terminal became operational in 1999.

Now, in 2021, **Major Port Authorities Act 2021** was enacted (by repealing Major Port Trust Act 1963) to provide for the regulation, operation and planning of major ports in India. Following are the important features of the Act:

- Major port authority will be established for each major port
- The administration, control, management of major ports will be vested upon the boards of Major Port Authorities
- The board can sign PPP agreements with private players (concessionaire)
- **Revenue share** or other such financial model can be used
- Concessionaire (private developer) shall fix the tariff based on market conditions

In budget 2021-22, Govt. has proposed that it will give the management and operation of the Major ports to private players under PPP model.

A point that needs to be kept in mind is that after 1991, only new/additional terminals at major ports were given to private players on PPP model. But now (as proposed in budget 2021-22), Govt. is planning to give the entire (major) port to PPP player for operations and management through the Major Port Authorities Act 2021.

14.11 Coal, Coal Mines Act 2015 and MMDR Act 2015

Introduction:

In the federal structure of India, the "*Regulation of mines and mineral development*" falls under the Union List. Accordingly, the Central Government frames rules and regulation regarding the development and extraction of minerals but it has entrusted the respective state governments with mining related activities except in case of Coal, Petroleum & Natural gas and atomic minerals.

The State Governments are the owners of minerals located within the boundary of the State concerned and have the authority to collect "taxes/ royalty" on mineral rights. The Central Government is the owner of the minerals underlying the ocean within the territorial waters or the Exclusive Economic Zone of India. The State Governments grant the mineral concessions/rights for all the minerals located within the boundary of the State, under provisions of the Mines and Minerals (Development and Regulation) Act, 1957 (MMDR Act 1957) by taking prior permission of Central Government.

MMDR Act 1957 *applies to all minerals including coal and special provisions have been enacted for coal sector through* ***Coal Mines Act 2015***.

Background:

With the passing of the Coal Mines (Nationalization) Act 1973, the private companies were debarred from mining of coal and Coal India Ltd (CIL) which is a PSU got the monopoly for mining of coal.

However, through amendments, private companies and PSUs were allowed for captive mining which means coal blocks can be given to these companies only for specific end-use projects and they cannot sell the coal in the open market. The coal blocks were allocated for captive mining based on recommendation and there was no mechanism of bidding because of which there was 'Coalgate' scam and this process was ultimately stopped on the intervention of Supreme Court in 2014.

Coal Mines (Special Provisions) Act 2015:

The salient features of the Act are:

- The allocation of coal mines shall be done through (electronic) auction in a transparent manner. In case of a government company the allotment may be made without auction.
- The restriction of end-use captive mining has been removed (except in certain cases) and the companies can sell the coal in the market which they have won through the auction process.
- Govt. will auction coal for commercial mining as well as captive mining. Commercial mining means, the company who wins the bid will be free to sell the coal in the open market as well as export it. Under captive mining, Govt. auctions the coal mines for different sectors like steel/power etc and the winners of the bid can use that coal only for their specific projects in that sector.
- The proceeds/money coming from the auction process will be disbursed to the respective state governments.

Impact of the reforms/changes on Economy:

- This is the most ambitious reform of the coal sector since its nationalization in 1973

- This move will bring efficiency and competition in coal production, attract investments and best-in-class technology including for 'safe and efficient mining', and help create more direct and indirect jobs in the sector
- The new law gives highest priority to transparency, ease of doing business and ensures that natural resources are used for national development
- As the entire revenue from the auction of coal mines for sale of coal would accrue to the coal bearing States, this methodology shall incentivize them with increased revenues which can be utilized for the growth and development of backward areas (in the states of West Bengal, Odisha, Jharkhand, Chattisgarh) and their inhabitants including tribals
- Till now we used to spend billions of dollars of our foreign exchange reserves every year for import of coal even if our country is endowed with the fourth largest coal reserves. The volume growth and cost reduction from commercial coal mining will reduce imports and help in keeping import prices in check.
- This reform will lead to industry consolidation and rise of large vertically-integrated energy companies with interests in coal mining, power generation, transmission and distribution to retail supply.
- The utilities and manufacturing sector too will benefit from lower energy costs.

Govt. has started auctioning coal blocks for ***commercial mining*** *on* ***revenue sharing basis*** *which means that the company quoting maximum share of the revenue to the Govt. will be selected.*

Mines and Minerals (Development & Regulation) Act 1957:

The salient features of the Act (as per recent amendments) are:

- The Mining Leases is granted by the respective State Governments through auctions by competitive bidding including electronic auction, thereby bringing in greater transparency and removal of discretion.
- Earlier the government used to get only Royalty/taxes from the companies involved in mining. But now the companies will also be paying the amount (on per tonne basis) committed during the auction process to win the bid besides royalty which means that the Government will get an increased share from the mining sector.
- The Mining Leases will be granted for a period of 50 years and there would be no renewal as against the old practice of granting lease for 30 yrs and then renewing it.
- To check on illegal mining, penal provisions have been made stringent and higher penalties and jail terms have been provided. Further, a provision has been made for constitution of special courts by the state governments for fast-track trial of cases related to illegal mining.
- Central government has been given powers to intervene where state governments do not pass orders within prescribed timelines. This will eliminate delay.
- The Act provides for the creation of District Mineral Foundation (DMF) by the state governments in the districts where mining takes place. This is for the benefit of the persons in districts affected by mining related operations.

14.12 Power Sector

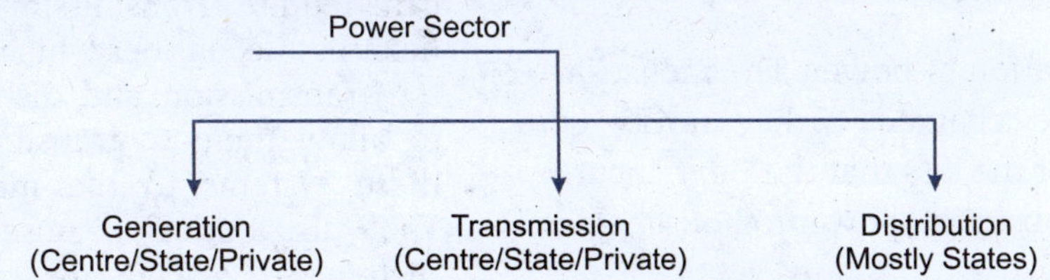

Generation Capacity from various sources as on 31.10.2025

Coal	Gas	Nuclear	Renewable	**Total**
44.5%	4%	1.7%	49.8%	**100%** **505 GW**

Renewable generation capacity breakup as on 31.10.2025

Solar	Large Hydro	Small Hydro	Wind	Others	**Total**
25.6%	10%	1%	10.6%	2.6%	**49.8%**

(Small Hydro Projects are of less than 25 MW capacity. Small hydro and large hydro both comes under renewable energy).

Introduction:

Over the past few years and specifically in the last two years, India has made impressive progress in overall power generation capacity but the same is not true for the power distribution sector. Now, a paradoxical situation has arisen, on one hand state distribution companies (DISCOMs) lack the means/finances to buy power from power generating units leading to severe power cuts and blackouts on the other hand surplus power is available in the hands of power generators due to which power generators are running at less than full capacity. This poor state of State DISCOMs is because of the inability of successive State governments to implement crucial reforms.

So, in power sector, the major problem lies with the distribution of electricity. A distribution company's main function is to procure power from the power generators and its distribution to the consumers. In the past Govt. has announced several schemes like UDAY etc. but it has not resulted in any structural reform in the DISCOMs. The following are the major issues in the distribution sector:

- Mostly the DISCOMs are state PSUs, in which there is interference from the State Govt. and they lack professional way working.
- The distribution infrastructure is in poor condition and PSUs lack capital and technology to upgrade this infrastructure.
- Inability to increase electricity tariffs due to Government control leads to financial constraints in improving the distribution infrastructure.
- Being under the control of state governments, DISCOMs have served as tools of populism

year after year. One example is free and subsidized power to farmers and other consumers.

- Cross subsidization of power. The industrial consumers are charged higher tariffs to compensate for the loss that the Govt. incurs in providing subsidized power to households and farmers.
- Presently the Aggregate Technical and Commercial (AT&C) losses are around 15%–18% in most of the DISCOMs leading to huge financial burden on DISCOMs.

In India, the electricity sector (generation, transmission, distribution, trading) is governed by the Electricity Act 2003. The following are the various reforms/changes which have been suggested in the Electricity Act 2003 through the Electricity Amendment Bill 2021:

Electricity Amendment Bill 2021

- Delicense the power distribution sector and allow private DISCOMs
- Strengthening of Appellate Tribunal for electricity to fasten resolution of long pending disputes
- Direct Benefit Transfer (DBT) of electricity subsidies targeting the poor
- Establishment of a Universal Obligation Fund to meet any deficits in cross subsidy
- Increase penalty for DISCOMs that fail to meet Renewable Purchase Obligations (RPOs)

"Making one India" in Power Sector (Open Access):

- Electricity Act 2003 puts in place a regime where electricity generators and consumers could choose the entity to or from whom they want to sell or purchase power. To achieve this, the Act provides for **non-discriminatory open access**, which means that a generator or a consumer can require transmission or distribution licensees i.e. entities which own and operate the transmission and distribution systems, to allow them to transfer power through these systems to the intended recipient. The distribution licensee cannot deny such access except for technical reasons. The Act provides that the state regulatory commissions should allow open access subject to payment of Cross Subsidy (CS) surcharge.
- *(Indian industrial/commercial consumers have been paying a higher tariff for the electricity they consume. This is in order to ensure that domestic and agricultural consumers receive power at a more affordable rate. This is known as cross-subsidy and has continued under the Act. When a commercial consumer decides to purchase power from an independent generator and not from the distribution licensee in that area, then that distribution licensee loses the cross-subsidy amount. The CS Surcharge is imposed on the commercial consumers to ensure that distribution licensee does not pass on this additional amount to the domestic & agricultural consumers, which can result in steep rise in the cost of power).*
- The Act provides for progressive reduction and elimination of CS surcharges to make open access viable leading to a single market price i.e., "Making one India". Power Exchanges were set up in 2008 to operationalize the open access policy and create a national electricity market where price discovery occurs through competitive bidding. But the increase in cross subsidy and additional surcharges for purchasing electricity from power exchanges, have acted as significant barriers for one market.

Till now Open Access is allowed to industrial customers (> 1 MW) and not to households.

Renewable Energy

- Fossil fuels are the world's biggest energy source but burning them produces heat-trapping greenhouse gases that contribute to global warming. As environmental degradation hurts the poor more than others, India is committed to make the development process as green as possible.
- Govt. of India has announced its intent to achieve 50% of its energy requirement through non-fossil fuels i.e., renewables by 2030 at COP26.
- Due to its renewed focus on renewable energy, the tariffs on electricity generated from the renewable sources have come down in the last few years. The following is the average power tariffs from various power sources. This is the tariff for generation and feeding into the transmission line at a particular point:

✓ Solar = Rs. 2/unit - Rs. 2.5/unit
✓ Wind = Rs. 2.5/unit - Rs. 3/unit
✓ Thermal = Rs. 3/unit - 3.5/unit
✓ Hydro = Rs. 5/unit - Rs. 6/unit
✓ Nuclear = Rs. 3/unit - Rs. 4/unit

Renewable Energy Certificates (RECs)

- Once a Renewable Power Generator/ provider has fed the energy generated into the electricity grid, he receives REC (which can then be sold on the open market as an energy commodity).
- RECs are a market-based instrument which certifies that the bearer (holder of REC) owns one megawatt-hour (MWh) of electricity generated from a renewable energy resource.
- RECs are proof that energy has been generated from renewable sources such as solar or wind power etc.
- When someone purchases RECs, renewable energy is generated on his/her behalf.
- RECs can go by many names, including Green tag, Tradable Renewable Certificates (TRCs), Renewable Electricity Certificates, or Renewable Energy Credits.
- To provide a fillip to the ambitious renewable energy target, obligations have been imposed on entities like power distribution companies, captive power plants (who establish power plants for their own consumption) and other large electricity consumers to purchase energy from renewable sources.
- These obligations called Renewable Purchase Obligations (RPOs) provide for either purchase of renewable energy certificates (RECs) from Indian Energy Exchange (IEX)/ Power Exchange of India (PXIL) or purchase of renewable power from the National Load Dispatch Centre (NLDC) by obligated entities.
- These RPOs are the backbone of India's renewable energy programme. Ministry of Power in consultation with ministry of New and Renewable Energy sets the target of RPOs (uniformly) for all States/UTs.

14.13 Oil and Gas Sector

Old regime of oil and gas:

Govt. of India opened up hydrocarbon (oil & gas) exploration and production sector in the country to the private players in 1991. Initially small and medium size blocks were offered to private players and since 1997-98 onwards, bigger blocks were being offered as per the New Exploration and Licensing Policy (NELP). NELP was based on profit sharing model under which the contractor committing the maximum profit share to the Government used to get selected for exploration and extraction of the block. The NELP policy was in existence for 18 years and then Government in 2016 brought a new **Hydrocarbon Exploration and Licensing Policy (HELP)**. The following are its key features: -

- There is uniform licensing system which will cover all hydrocarbons, i.e., oil, gas, coal bed methane etc. under a single license and policy framework.
- An 'Open Acreage Licensing Policy' (OALP) is implemented whereby a bidder may apply to the Govt. seeking exploration of any block not already covered by exploration. The Govt. will examine the proposal and if it is suitable for award, Govt. will call for competitive bids after obtaining necessary environmental and other clearances. This will enable a faster coverage of the available geographical area.
- Contracts will be based on "**revenue sharing**" model. Bidders will be required to quote % of revenue share to the Govt. in their bids which will be a key parameter for selecting the winning bid. In this model the operator will have to share the revenue with the government from the first year of production notwithstanding the operator is making a profit or loss. This model does not require auditing of costs incurred by the operator but is riskier for investors as it requires sharing of the revenues with the government from the first year itself before the operators have recovered their costs and even if they are making losses.
- The contractor will have **freedom for pricing and marketing of gas** produced in the domestic market on arm's length basis.
- In order to incentivize offshore exploration/ production which involves higher risks and costs, a graded system of reduced royalty will be applicable. For shallow water royalty will be 7.5%, for deep water 5% and for ultra-deep-water royalty will be 2%.

India is the ***third largest*** *energy consumer in the world after USA and China. However, India's oil production is one of the lowest among the major economies of the world and has been declining over a period of time.*

Presently, Energy Consumption per Capita in India is just 30% of the world average.

Kirit Parikh Committee Recommendations on Gas Pricing:

The mandate of the panel was to suggest a regime that would help raise domestic production to help meet the goal of 15% of energy coming from gas by 2030 and at the same time, provide fair price to consumers. The committee has looked at the pricing of gas from two sources:

1. The first set is the legacy or old fields (also called APM gas) which were given to ONGC and OIL on a nomination basis without any condition of sharing profits and therefore the government controls its price. The gas primarily goes to city gas distribution, fertilizer production and power plant.

Recommendation: Link it to imported crude oil price with a floor ($4MMBTU) and ceiling price ($6.5 MMBTU) till some time and then complete pricing freedom starting January 1, 2027.

1. The second set is for the ones that are in difficult geology like deep-water, ultra-deep water, and high pressure-high temperature.

Recommendation: Such producers have marketing and pricing freedom which is constrained by an upper bound fixed by the government. The committee has suggested continuing with the cap for three years and giving total pricing freedom from January 1, 2026, by removing the cap.

14.14 Smart Cities and AMRUT

1. Smart City

There is no universally accepted definition of smart city and its conceptualization varies from city to city and country to country depending on the level of development, willingness to change and reform, resources and aspirations of the city residents. To any city dweller in India, the picture of a smart city contains a wish list of infrastructure and services that describes his and her level of aspiration. Accordingly, a smart city provides quality of life and employment and investment opportunities and can be represented by the four pillars of the urban ecosystem: -

- Institutional infrastructure (e-governance, law & order, safety and security, banking/ financial institutions etc.)
- Physical infrastructure (public transport, power & water supply, drainage system etc.)
- Social infrastructure (education, healthcare, housing etc.)
- Economic infrastructure (job creation, livelihood activities etc.)

Financing of Smart Cities:

The Smart City Mission is operated as a Centrally Sponsored Scheme (CSS) where Central Government contribution is matched by States and Urban Local Bodies (ULB). But these funds meet only a part of the project cost. Balance funds are expected to be mobilized from:

- States/ULBs own resources from collection of user fees, land monetization, loans etc
- Additional resources transferred through Fourteenth Finance Commission
- Innovative finance mechanisms such as municipal bonds
- Borrowings from financial institutions, including bilateral and multilateral institutions
- Private sector through PPPs

Smart Cities are implemented through the establishment of Special Purpose Vehicle (SPV) at the city level. The SPV plans, appraises, approve, release funds, implement, manage, operate, monitor and evaluate the Smart City development projects. Each smart city has a SPV which is headed by a full time CEO and have nominees of Central Government, State Government and ULB on its Board. The SPV is a limited company incorporated under the Companies Act, 2013 at the city-level, in which the State/UT and the ULB are the promoters having 50 : 50 equity shareholdings. The private sector or financial institutions could be considered for taking equity stake in the SPV, provided the shareholding pattern of 50:50 of the State/UT and the ULB is maintained and the State/UT and the ULB together have majority shareholding and control of the SPV.

For the proper functioning of SPV, the States/ULBs shall ensure that:

- ➢ Dedicated and substantial revenue stream is made available to the SPV so as to make it self-sustainable and the SPV shall also be able to raise revenue from the market
- ➢ Government contribution for Smart City is used only to create infrastructure

The execution of projects may be done through joint ventures, subsidiaries, public-private partnership (PPP), turnkey contracts (the entire work is given as a contract to a third party), etc suitably combined with revenue sources.

Smart Cities adopt "**area-based development**" approach i.e., develop areas step by step. Three models of area-based development:

- City improvement (retrofitting),
- City renewal (redevelopment)
- City extension (greenfield development)

Smart Cities, Economic and Inclusive growth

- ➢ In India, the urban population is currently 40% (58 crores) of the total population (145 crores) and it contributes over 60% of India's GDP. It is projected that in the next 15 years urban population will touch 80 crores and will contribute nearly 75% of the national GDP. Accordingly, cities are referred to as the engines of economic growth.
- ➢ Smart cities with their better infrastructure and services attract investments and industries leading to agglomeration of economies (benefits that firms obtain by locating near each other) and generation of employment opportunities.
- ➢ Smart cities will transform the existing city areas, including slums, into better planned ones, thereby improving liveability of the whole city and it will also develop new areas around cities in order to accommodate the expanding population in urban areas.
- ➢ Application of smart solutions will enable cities to use technology, information and data to improve infrastructure and services both. Comprehensive development in this way will improve quality of life, create employment, enhance incomes for all, especially the poor and the disadvantaged, leading to inclusive cities.
- ➢ It is said that people owning their houses are more satisfied and have greater motivation in their life to work hard.
- ➢ The "Housing for All" scheme which plans "to provide 2 crore houses by 2022" to the poor and marginalized section will lead to better living standards for the poor and economic growth.

2. Atal Mission for Rejuvenation and Urban Transformation (AMRUT)

AMRUT scheme plans to ensure basic infrastructure services in urban areas relating to water supply, sewerage and septage management, drainage, pedestrian, non-motorized and public transport facilities, development of green spaces and parks to improve the quality of life for all. The scheme plans to transform urban living conditions through infrastructure up gradation. Implementation of this Mission is linked to promotion of urban reforms such as e-governance, capacity building, constitution of professional municipal cadre, devolving funds and functions to urban local bodies, review of building bye-laws, improvement in assessment and collection of municipal taxes, credit rating of urban local bodies, energy and water audit and citizen-centric urban planning and eventually laying a foundation **to enable cities and towns to grow into smart cities**. In AMRUT, States have been made equal partners in planning and implementation of projects, thus actualizing the spirit of cooperative federalism. Under this Centrally Sponsored Scheme (CSS), government has selected **500 cities** for up-gradation. AMRUT 2.0 has expanded the coverage of the scheme to all statutory towns and cities.

Smart Cities Mission and AMRUT were simultaneously launched and are interlinked. AMRUT adopts a project approach to ensure basic infrastructure services in 500 cities and towns while Smart Cities Mission adopts an area-based development approach (develop areas step-by-step) to promote 100 cities that provide core infrastructure and then adding on layers of smartness.

AMRUT follows a "**project-based**" approach focussing on:

- Water Supply
- Sewerage and septage management
- Storm Water Drainage to reduce flooding
- Non-motorized Urban Transport
- Green space/parks

14.15 InvITs and REITs and NIIF

InvITs and REITS

- Infrastructure Investment Trust (InvITs) and 'Real estate investment trust' (REITS) are trusts registered under the Indian Trusts Act, 1882 and regulated by SEBI.
- These trusts manage funds/ corpus which are invested in infrastructure and real estate property. InvITs invests in infrastructure projects in general while REITS are specifically into real estate projects. They both function in same manner.
- InvITs/REITS are mutual fund like institutions that enable investment into the infrastructure and real estate sector by pooling small sums of money from multitude of individual investors, financial institutions and companies.
- Most middle-class investors presently do not invest in commercial real estate and infrastructure projects because of the big size of investment. This entry barrier is removed through REITs as it makes the expensive real estate sector accessible to the middle-class investor.
- InvITs/REITS will help the infrastructure and real estate industry as the developers of infrastructure and real estate projects will be able to sell their property to InvITs/REITs and move on to execution of new projects.
- When investors invest in InvITs/REITS then this money is invested in different infrastructure and real estate projects. These InvITs/REITS are listed on stock exchanges and traded.
- There are certain restrictions on InvITs/REITS such as 80% of the asset value of InvITs/REITS should be into revenue generating projects and rest can be in under-construction projects.
- The regular revenue generated from the rentals/tolls or from the sale of project assets will come to InvITs/REITS which will then be returned as dividend to investors.

The following is a general structure of InvITs/REITs.

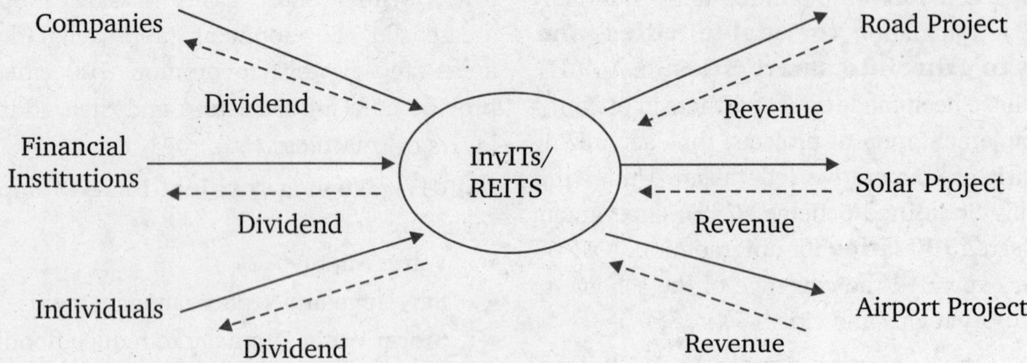

National Investment and Infrastructure Fund (NIIF)

Government established NIIF in 2015 with the aim to attract investment from both domestic and international sources for funding commercially viable Greenfield, Brownfield and stalled projects in infrastructure sector. NIIF has been formed as a trust and is registered with SEBI under Category II of Alternative Investment Fund *(for tax benefit)*. It is basically a quasi-sovereign wealth fund as government holds only 49% ownership.

NIIF will get funds from:

- Overseas sovereign/quasi-sovereign/ multilateral/bilateral investors through equity. Cash rich central PSU, provident funds, insurance funds can also invest in NIIF over and above Govt. of India share.
- Market borrowings (debt).

NIIF will invest in:

- Infrastructure projects through equity and debt both; and
- Non-Banking Financial Companies (NBFCs) and Financial Institutions (FIs) involved in infrastructure financing through equity.

14.16 National Monetization Pipeline (NMP 2.0)

Asset Monetization involves creation of new sources of revenue by unlocking of value of hitherto unutilized or underutilized public assets. Many public sector assets are sub-optimally utilized and could be appropriately monetized to create greater financial leverage and value for the companies and of the equity that the government has invested in them.

NMP 2.0 shall broadly follow the concept of asset monetisation as laid out in NMP 1.0. Asset monetisation shall comprise elements such as transfer of assets for a limited period, divestment of portions of listed entities to unlock additional capital, securitisation of cash flows or strategic commercial auctions. The following are the important features of NMP 2.0

- NMP 2.0 is aligned with the mission of achieving Viksit Bharat through accelerated infrastructure development and that the NMP has the potential to fuel India's growth momentum.
- The NMP 2.0 estimates aggregate monetisation potential of ₹16.72 lakh crore

- The various sectors under NMP 2.0 are highways (including ropeways), railways, power, petroleum and natural gas, civil aviation, ports, warehousing and storage, urban infrastructure, coal, mines, telecom and tourism.
- Proceeds from asset monetisation projects are allocated to four different heads depending on the implementing agency of the project, as well as the project's mode of monetisation.
  - o Consolidated Fund of India: Any type of Government revenue from a monetisation project that is implemented by a Central Ministry (for example, revenue share, premium, lease rental, royalty) shall flow to Consolidated Fund of India.
  - o PSU/Port Authorities allocation: Proceeds from monetisation activities undertaken by PSUs shall accrue to the concerned PSU (similar norm shall be followed for Major Port Authorities).
  - o State Consolidated Fund: Certain projects under NMP 2.0 are expected to generate revenues to the State Governments, especially those belonging to the mines and coal sectors (royalty payments). These proceeds shall accrue to State Consolidated Fund.
  - o Direct investment (private): This head shall record the investment by the private sector in monetisation projects that involve construction and/or major maintenance components.
- NMP 2.0 enables recycling of productive public assets, thereby unlocking resources for reinvestment in new projects and capital expenditure. This approach facilitates efficient mobilisation of funds for capital expenditure in public assets while minimising budgetary outgo of the Government.
- The NMP 2.0 pipeline has been developed by NITI Aayog, in consultation with infrastructure line ministries
- The strategic objective of the program is to unlock. the value of investments in brownfield public sector assets by tapping institutional and long-term patient capital, which can thereafter be leveraged for further public investments.
- Asset Monetization needs to be viewed not just as a funding mechanism, but as an overall paradigm shift in infrastructure operations, augmentation and maintenance considering private sector's resource efficiencies and its ability to dynamically adapt to the evolving global and economic reality.
- The end objective of this initiative is to enable 'Infrastructure Creation through Monetization' wherein the public and private sector collaborate, each excelling in their core areas of competence, so as to deliver socio-economic growth and quality of life to the country's citizens.
- Real time monitoring will be undertaken through the asset monetization dashboard

Challenges of NMP

- Lack of identifiable revenue streams in various assets
- Level of capacity utilization in gas and petroleum pipeline networks
- Dispute resolution mechanism
- Regulated tariffs in power sector assets
- Low interest among investors in National Highways below four lanes

Examples of Asset Monetization:

- Giving an asset (let us say Dedicated Freight Corridor) of a PSU/GoI to a Private Operator for Operation and Maintenance for a contract period (say 30 years) in return of one-time money

- Giving the already constructed NHAI roads to Private Parties on TOT (Toll Operate Transfer) model for a certain period in return for one time money
- Giving the Airports to Private Operators for a certain period in return of some lump sum payment
- Giving the Transmission Assets of PGCIL, Oil & Gas pipelines of GAIL, IOCL, HPCL to private operators in return for some lump sum payment for certain contract period.

There are certain misconceptions that once the infrastructure asset is monetized, tariffs will increase. But this may not be true as the tariffs will be regulated and capped with inflation in the Concession/ Agreement itself.

14.17 PM Gati Shakti

- It is the National Master Plan for infrastructure development and multi-modal connectivity (connecting various modes of transport like road, rail, airway, shipping etc.) which signals a paradigm shift in our approach to development planning.
- Gati Shakti is a digital platform which will bring several Ministries including Railways and Roadways together for integrated planning and coordinated implementation and execution of infrastructure connectivity projects. It will be a game changer in inter-ministerial and inter-departmental cooperation in infrastructure planning.
- Gati-Shakti will incorporate the infrastructure schemes of various Ministries and State Governments like Bharatmala, Sagarmala, inland waterways, dry/land ports, UDAN etc. Economic Zones like textile clusters, pharmaceutical clusters, defence corridors, electronic parks, industrial corridors, fishing clusters, agri zones will be covered to improve connectivity & make Indian businesses more competitive.
- The portal will offer 200 layers of geospatial data, including on existing infrastructure such as roads, highways, railways, and toll plazas, as well as geographic information about forests, rivers and district boundaries to aid in planning and obtaining clearances. It will also offer satellite imagery for monitoring of projects.
- The portal will also allow various government departments to track, in real time and at one centralised place, the progress of various projects, especially those with multi-sectoral and multi-regional impact. The objective is to ensure that "each and every department now have visibility of each other's activities providing critical data while planning and execution of projects in a comprehensive manner".
- The portal will help state governments give commitments to investors regarding timeframes for the creation of infrastructure.
- A project monitoring group under the DPIIT will monitor the progress of key projects in real time, and report any inter-ministerial issues to an empowered group of ministers, who will then aim to resolve these.
- Gati-Shakti portal would help reduce the human intervention required as ministries will be in constant touch, and projects will be reviewed by the project monitoring group in real time.

- The portal will also highlight all the clearances any new project would need, based on its location — and allow stakeholders to apply for these clearances from the relevant authority directly on the portal.
- Ordinarily, we may see one tunnel being made for roads and another for railways; however, such a platform would allow the ministries to coordinate, and create one large tunnel which may serve both purposes, saving the taxpayer thousands of crores.
- If a railway line is being built, the Ministry of Road Transport may immediately give clearance for an overpass, and the Power Ministry can begin projects to ensure that trains can immediately have access to power on completion of the tracks.
- It will leverage technology extensively including spatial planning tools with ISRO imagery to generate real time dashboard.
- Due to the wide gap between macro planning and micro implementation problems of lack of coordination, lack of advance information, thinking and working in silos has led to hampered construction and wastage of budget. Gati Shakti will address this as working on the basis of the master plan will lead to optimum utilisation of resources.
- The logistics cost in India is presently 13% of GDP which is quite high as compared to around 8% in developed countries. This has hurt India's competitiveness in exports. The Gati-Shakti plan will bring down the logistics costs.

14.18 National Logistics Policy 2022

The vision of the National Logistics Policy is to develop a technologically enabled, integrated, cost-efficient, resilient, sustainable and trusted logistics ecosystem in the country for accelerated and inclusive growth.

The policy aspires to:

- Reduce the cost of logistics in India to be comparable to global benchmarks (in single digit) by 2030
- Endeavour to be among top 25 countries by 2030 in the Logistics Performance Index ranking, and
- Create data driven decision support mechanism for an efficient logistics ecosystem.

The Policy will be implemented through a Comprehensive Logistics Action Plan (CLAP). The interventions proposed under the CLAP are divided into eight key action areas:

1. Integrated Digital Logistics Systems
2. Standardisation of physical assets and benchmarking service quality standards
3. Logistics Human Resources Development and Capacity Building
4. State Engagement
5. EXIM (Export-Import) Logistics
6. Service Improvement framework
7. Sectoral Plan for Efficient Logistics
8. Facilitation of Development of Logistics Parks

National Logistics Policy would bring down logistics costs, give a fillip to international trade, help in making India 'atmanirbhar' or self-reliant, usher in prosperity in the nation and present new opportunities to our startups. The policy would be highly beneficial to the farmers of the country, helping them to take their produce to the markets at a faster pace and reduce wastage and delay which would bring down prices in the economy.

Along with PM Gati Shakti National Master Plan, the National Logistics Policy is the logical next step which will provide a comprehensive agenda for development of entire logistics ecosystem.

Unified Logistics Interface Platform (ULIP) has been developed as an integrated portal in which information about the location of goods can be obtained on a real-time basis with considerable ease and it will help bring all digital services in the transport sector to a single portal.

PREVIOUS YEARS' QUESTIONS

Prelim Questions

1. Consider the following statements: **[2019]**

(i) Coal sector was nationalized by the Government of India under Indira Gandhi

(ii) Now, coal blocks are allocated on lottery basis

(iii) Till recently, India imported coal to meet the shortage of domestic supply, but now India is self-sufficient in coal production.

Which of the following statements given above is/are correct?

(a) (i) only (b) (ii) & (iii) only

(c) (iii) only (d) (i), (ii) & (iii)

2. Consider the following pairs: **[2023]**

Port	Well known as
1. Kamrajar Port	First major port in India registered as a company
2. Mundra Port	Largest privately owned port in India
3. Visakhapatnam Port	Largest container port in India

How many of the above pairs are correctly matched?

(a) Only one pair

(b) Only two pairs

(c) All three pairs

(d) None of the pairs

ANSWERS

1.(a), 2. (b)

Main Questions

1. Explain the meaning of investment in an economy in terms of capital formation. Discuss the factors to be considered while designing a concession agreement between a public entity and a private entity. **[2020]**

2. "Investment in Infrastructure is essential for more rapid and inclusive economic growth." Discuss in the light of India's experience. **[2021]**

3. Why is Public Private Partnership (PPP) required in infrastructural projects? Examine the role of PPP model in the redevelopment of Railway Stations in India. **[2022]**
4. Do you think India will meet 50 percent of its energy needs from renewable energy by 2030? Justify your answer. How will the shift of subsidies from fossil fuels to renewables help achieve the above objective? Explain. **[2022]**
5. What is the need for expanding the regional air connectivity in India? In this context, discuss the Government's UDAN scheme and its achievements. **[2024]**

Budget and Economic Survey

(Most of the budget and economic survey information have been included in the book in respective topics. The following is just additional information from budget and economic survey which does not relate to any specific chapter)

15.1 Budget (2026-27) Highlights

(Budget is based on nominal figures)

Central Finances	**2025-26**	**2026-27**
Total Expenditure Budget	Rs. 49.7 lakh cr	Rs. 53.5 lakh cr
• Revenue Expenditure	Rs. 38.6 lakh cr	Rs. 41.3 lakh cr
• Capital Expenditure	Rs. 11.1 lakh cr	Rs. 12.2 lakh cr
Total Receipts	Rs. 49.7 lakh cr	Rs. 53.5 lakh cr
• Revenue Receipts	Rs. 33.4 lakh cr	Rs. 35.3 lakh cr
• Capital Receipts	Rs. 16.3 lakh cr	Rs. 18.2 lakh cr
o Non-Debt Capital Receipts	Rs. 0.7 lakh cr	Rs. 1.2 lakh cr
o Debt Capital Receipts	Rs. 15.6 lakh cr	Rs. 17.0 lakh cr
Fiscal Deficit	4.4% (15.6 lakh cr)	4.3% (17.0 lakh cr)
Revenue Deficit	1.5% (5.3 lakh cr)	1.5% (5.9 lakh cr)
Effective Rev Deficit	0.6%	0.3 %
Primary Deficit	0.8%	0.7%
Nominal GDP	Rs. 357 lakh cr	Rs. 393 lakh cr
Nominal Growth	10%	
Gross Tax Revenue (Centre)	Rs. 40.8 lakh crore	Rs. 44 lakh crore
Tax to GDP (Centre)	11.4% (Rs.40.8 lcr/Rs.357 lcr)	11.2% (Rs.44 lcr/Rs.393 lcr)

Budget focuses on accelerating economic growth by intervening in the following six sectors:

1. Scale up manufacturing in strategic and frontier sectors:
   - ❑ Hi-Tech Tool Rooms will be established by CPSEs at 2 locations as digitally enabled automated service bureaus that locally design, test, and manufacture high-precision components at scale and at lower cost.
   - ❑ Scheme for Container Manufacturing to create a globally competitive container manufacturing ecosystem, with a budgetary allocation of ₹10,000 crore over a 5-year period.
   - ❑ Mega Textile Parks in challenge mode.
   - ❑ National Fibre Scheme for self-reliance in natural fibres such as silk, wool and jute, man-made fibres, and new-age fibres
   - ❑ To enhance domestic chemical production and reduce import-dependency, Govt. will launch a Scheme to support States in establishing 3 dedicated Chemical Parks, through challenge route, on a cluster-based plug-and-play model.
   - ❑ A Scheme for Rare Earth Permanent Magnets was launched in November 2025.
     [The total financial outlay of the scheme is Rs.7280 crore, comprising a sales-linked incentives of Rs. 6450 crore on REPM sales for five (5) years and capital subsidy of Rs.750 crore for setting up an aggregate of 6,000 MTPA of REPM manufacturing facilities. The scheme envisions allocating the total capacity to five beneficiaries through a global competitive bidding process. Each beneficiary will be allotted up to 1,200 MTPA of capacity.]
   - ❑ We now propose to support the mineral-rich States of Odisha, Kerala, Andhra Pradesh and Tamil Nadu to establish dedicated Rare Earth Corridors to promote mining, processing, research and manufacturing.

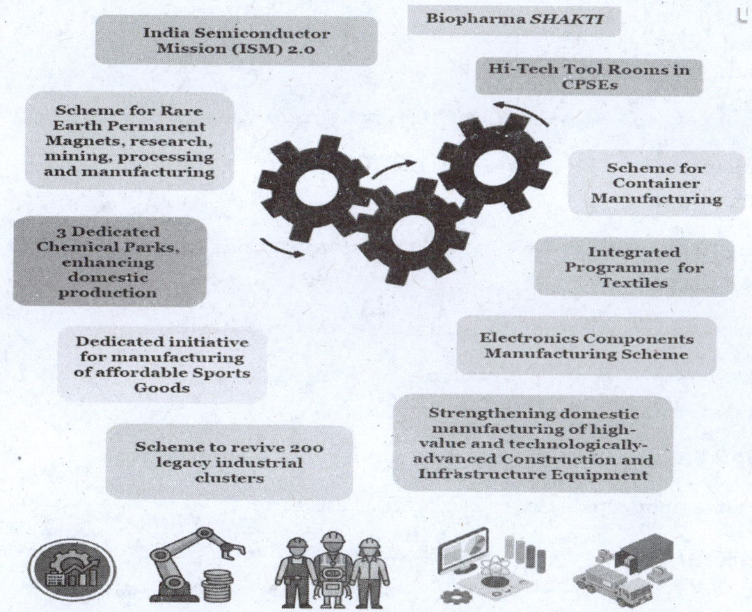

2. Legacy Industrial Clusters

A scheme will be proposed to revive 200 legacy industrial clusters to improve their cost competitiveness and efficiency through infrastructure and technology upgradation

3. Creating Champion MSMEs

Equity Support

- Dedicated ₹10,000 crore **SME Growth Fund.**
- Top up the Self-Reliant India Fund (2021) with ₹2,000 crore.

Professional Support

Government to facilitate Professional Institutions to develop 'Corporate Mitras' especially in Tier-II and Tier-III towns, to help MSMEs meet compliance requirements at affordable costs.

Liquidity Support through TReDS

- Mandate TReDS as the transaction settlement platform for all purchases from MSMEs by CPSEs, serving as a benchmark for other corporates.
- Introduce a credit guarantee support mechanism through CGTMSE for invoice discounting on the TReDS platform.
- Linking GeM with TReDS to encourage cheaper and quicker financing.
- TReDS receivables as asset-backed securities, to develop a secondary market and enhance liquidity and settlement of transactions.

4. Infrastructure

- **Setting up Infrastructure Risk Guarantee Fund** to provide prudently calibrated partial credit guarantees to lenders.
- Recycling of **real estate assets of CPSEs through the setting up of dedicated REITs.**
- Establishment of new **Dedicated Freight Corridors** connecting Dankuni in the East, to Surat in the West.
- Operationalising **20 new National Waterways** connecting mineral rich areas, industrial centres and ports.
- Setting up of ship repair ecosystem catering to inland waterways.
- Launch a **Coastal Cargo Promotion Scheme** to increase the share of inland waterways and coastal shipping from 6% to 12% by 2047.
- Launching a **Seaplane VGF Scheme** to indigenise manufacturing.
- ₹2 lakh crore support to states under **SASCI Scheme.**
- **Purvodaya: Development of Integrated East Coast Industrial Corridor.**

5. Long Term Energy Security

- ❑ Scheme to adopt Carbon Capture Utilization and Storage (CCUS) with an outlay of ₹20,000 crore.
- ❑ Exemption of BCD on import of sodium antimonate for use in manufacture of solar glass.
- ❑ Exemption of BCD on import of capital goods required for the processing of critical minerals in India.

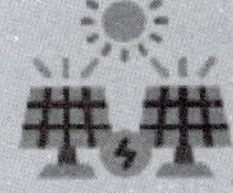

- ❑ Extending exemption of BCD to capital goods used for the manufacture of Lithium-Ion Cells for batteries to be used in battery energy storage systems.
- ❑ Extension of the existing basic customs duty exemption on imports of goods required for Nuclear Power Projects till the year 2035 and expand it for all nuclear plants irrespective of their capacity.
- ❑ Exclusion of entire value of biogas in Central Excise duty payable on biogas blended CNG.

6. City Economic Regions

- Cities are India's engines of growth, innovation and opportunities. Budget proposes Rs. 5000 crore scheme for city led urban development providing fiscal support for Tier-2 and Tier-3 cities along with temple towns.
- The scheme will be in challenge mode with a reform cum results based financing mechanism.

- ❖ **Amplifying the potential of cities to** deliver the economic power of agglomerations.
- ❖ Focus on Tier II, Tier III cities, and temple-towns.
- ❖ **'Growth Connectors' - 7 High-Speed Rail corridors** between cities - Mumbai-Pune, Pune-Hyderabad, Hyderabad-Bengaluru, Hyderabad-Chennai, Chennai-Bengaluru, Delhi-Varanasi, Varanasi-Siliguri - Environmentally sustainable passenger systems.

Budget also focuses on the following sectors:

Increasing Farmers' Income

- The focus of the budget is more on the allied sectors of agriculture rather than core crops with special emphasis on high value plantation crops such as coconut, cocoa, cashew and sandalwood and also on fisheries.
- To scale up availability of veterinary professionals by more than 20,000, budget has proposed a scheme for establishment of veterinary and para-vet colleges, veterinary hospitals, diagnostic laboratories and breeding facilities in the private sector.

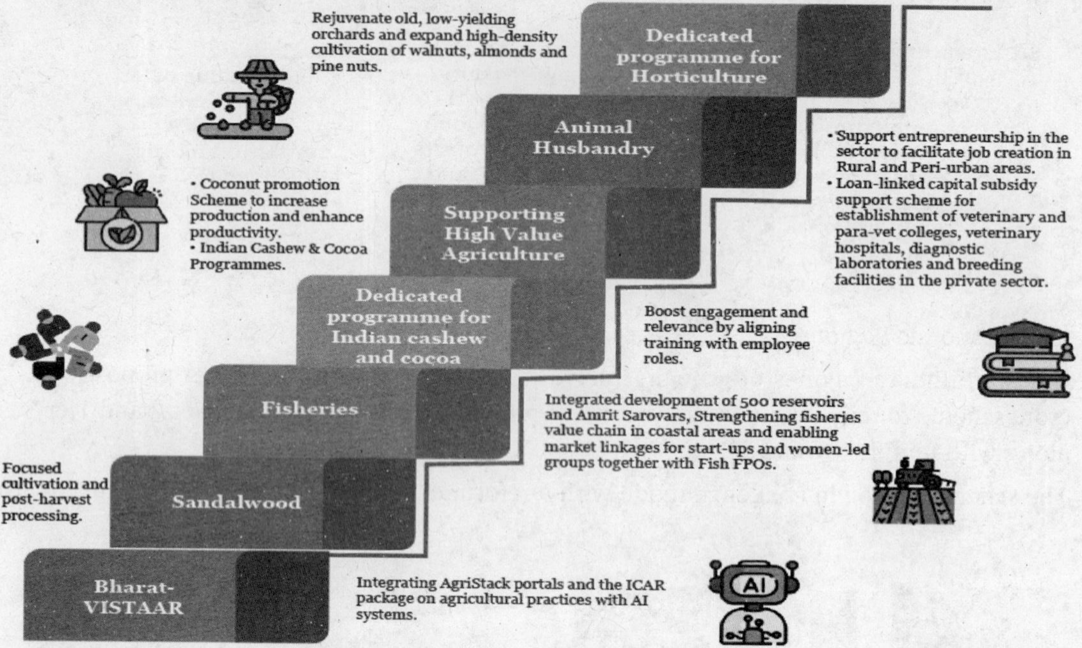

Data Centres

- Tax holiday to any foreign company till 2047 who provides cloud services globally using data center services in India.

Financial Sector

- Setting up of High-Level Committee on Banking for Viksit Bharat to align with India's next growth phase.
- Restructuring Power Finance Corporation (PFC) and Rural Electrification Corporation (REC). (These are Govt. NBFCs)

Simplification of Taxes

- Income Tax Act 2025 will become effective from 1st April 2026.

- The aim of the new Act is to make the language and implementation of the income tax legislation simpler for taxpayers. The new Act is clear and direct in text with close to half of the previous law, in terms of both chapters and words. It is simple to understand for taxpayers and tax administration, leading to tax certainty and reduced litigation.
- Securities transaction tax has been increased on future and options
    - Futures to 0.05% from earlier 0.02%
    - Options premium and exercise of options to 0.15% from earlier rate of 0.1% & 0.125% respectively
- Personal Income tax and Corporate Income tax has remained unchanged.
- Capital gains tax has been left unchanged
    - Long term capital gain tax on equity, valuable metals and real estate – 12.5%
    - Short term capital gain tax on equity – 20% and on valuable metals and real estate as per income tax slab

Taxes on buyback of shares

- Under the current provisions, consideration received by shareholders on a company's buyback of shares is treated as dividend income and taxed as per applicable personal income tax slabs.
- Under the proposed amendment, buyback consideration will be chargeable entirely under the head capital gains.
- This is mainly for minority shareholders i.e. retail and non-promotor shareholders.

Indirect taxes: Customs duty rationalization

- Exemption on parts, components and engines for manufacturing aircrafts.
- Exemption for goods for nuclear power projects.
- Exemption on capital goods for manufacture of lithium-ion cells for batteries of Battery Energy Storage Systems.
- Exemption on capital goods for processing of critical minerals.
- Sodium antimonate imported for solar glass manufacture.
- Monazite which is a key raw material for high performance permanent magnets for EVs.
- Customs duty is being exempted on 17 drugs/ medicines for treatment of cancer.
- Duty free personal imports of drugs/ medicines and food for 7 more rare diseases.
- Customs duty is being exempted on critical and cost-intensive components used in the manufacture of microwave ovens.

Capital Expenditure

- Capex has been increased from Rs. 11.1 lakh crore (2025-26) to Rs. 12.2 lakh crore (3.1% of GDP) in the budget 2026-27. This capex is only of Central Govt., but Central Govt. gives grants to States for capex under various schemes which effectively increases the capex.

- So, effective capex has been increased from Rs. 14 lakh crores in 2025-26 to Rs. 17.1 lakh crore (4.4% of GDP) in 2026-27.

Fiscal Consolidation

- The Central Government will target reaching a debt-to-GDP ratio of 50±1 percent by 2030-31.
- The debt-to-GDP ratio is estimated to be 55.6 percent of GDP in BE 2026-27, compared to 56.1 percent of GDP in RE 2025-26.

In RE 2025-26, the fiscal deficit has been estimated at par with BE of 2025-26 at 4.4 percent of GDP. In line with the new fiscal prudence path of debt consolidation, the fiscal deficit in BE 2026-27 is estimated to be 4.3 percent of GDP.

15.2 Economic Survey 2025-26

- The cumulative impact of policy reforms over recent years have lifted the economy's medium-term growth potential closer to 7 per cent. With domestic drivers playing a dominant role and macroeconomic stability well anchored, the balance of risks around growth remains broadly even. Taking these considerations together, the Economic Survey projects real GDP growth in FY27 in the range of 6.8 to 7.2 per cent. The outlook, therefore, is one of steady growth amid global uncertainty, requiring caution, but not pessimism.
- Over the past decade, changes in the Net International Investment Position (NIIP) have shaped the world's external wealth landscape. In CY 2024, Germany overtook Japan to become the world's largest creditor nation for the first time in 34 years, reflecting its sustained current account surpluses and strong trade performance. This position was maintained in Q2 CY 2025, with Germany and China emerging as the two largest creditor economies, followed closely by Japan, with a NIIP of USD 3.6 trillion. At the other end of the spectrum, the US remained the world's largest debtor, with a NIIP of USD 26.1 trillion at Q2 CY 2025, followed by Brazil, France and Spain. India ranked as the 11th largest debtor globally, with a negative NIIP of USD 0.3 trillion as of Q2 CY 2025.

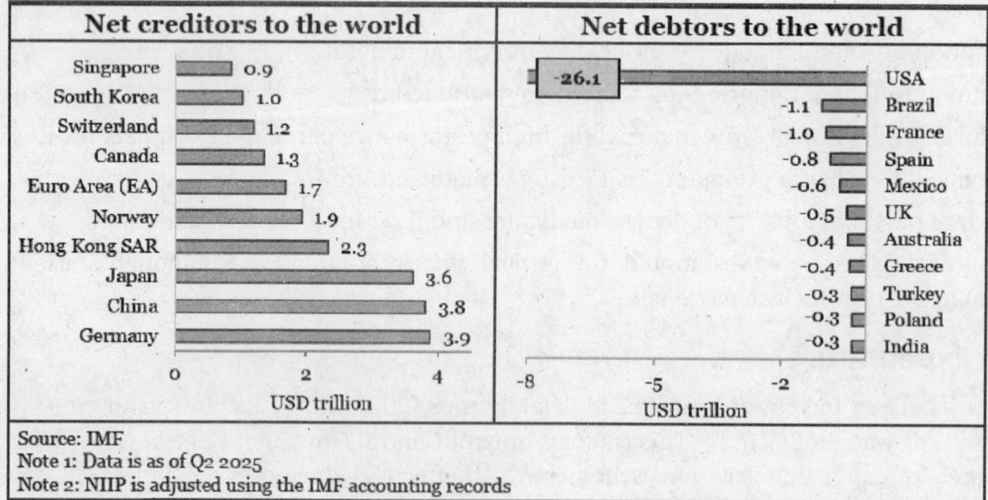

Source: IMF
Note 1: Data is as of Q2 2025
Note 2: NIIP is adjusted using the IMF accounting records

- A fundamental reordering of the global economic landscape is shaping India's external sector outlook. Trade, investment and capital flows are increasingly influenced by geopolitical alignments, industrial policy and strategic considerations, implying that the external environment is likely to remain volatile and less supportive than during the earlier phase of hyper-globalisation. For emerging market economies, this shift entails greater competition for capital, slower expansion of global trade volumes and heightened sensitivity of external flows to policy and geopolitical developments.
- India's external sector remains strong, with deepening global integration driven by robust exports, resilient services trade, and expanding trade networks. This reflects increased competitiveness, diversification, and adaptability to global demand. Services exports lead, while non-petroleum merchandise exports hit record levels, showcasing growth in high-value manufacturing and knowledge trade. This strength is supported by healthy foreign exchange reserves and a moderate external debt profile.
- Manufacturing export capability does not emerge overnight. Its foundations are scale, reliability, and integration built over time through disciplined capability building. Integration refers to embedding Indian firms into global value chains as well as embedding global production systems within India.
- Global trade is increasingly concentrated around a relatively small set of multinational production networks. This reinforces the importance of attracting such firms to India, not merely as sources of capital, but as anchors of export capability and currency strength.
- The state's role in this vision is demanding. It must be firm in enforcing discipline, flexible in adapting rules, and fair in allocating support. Firmness ensures that protection does not become entitlement. Flexibility allows policy to respond to feedback rather than assumptions. Fairness preserves legitimacy and prevents capture. Balancing these attributes is difficult, but not optional. States that fail on any one dimension either stifle initiative, entrench inefficiency, or provoke backlash.
- India's comparative advantage in the AI era does not lie in replicating frontier scale model development, although valuable process knowledge can be gained from the current efforts already underway. The country's strengths lie in application-led innovation, the productive use of domestic data, human capital depth, and the ability of public institutions to coordinate distributed efforts. A bottom-up strategy anchored in open and interoperable systems, sector-specific models, and shared physical and digital infrastructure offers a more credible pathway to value creation than a narrow pursuit of scale for its own sake.

16

Terminology

(Most of the terms have been included/defined in respective topics in the book. The following are miscellaneous/additional terms which does not relate to any specific chapter)

- **Absolute poverty:** It refers to a set standard which does not change over time *(inflation being taken care of)*. To calculate the absolute poverty, we estimate minimum physical items required for a subsistence level of living and then it is converted into monetary terms at market price level. An income-related example of absolute poverty would be "persons living on less than Rs. X per day".
- **Agglomeration Economy:** A localized economy in which a large number of companies, services, and industries exist in close proximity to one another and benefit from the cost reductions and gains in efficiency that result from this proximity.
- **Algorithmic trading:** Also called automated trading, black-box trading, or algo-trading uses a computer program that follows a defined set of instructions (an algorithm) to place a trade. The defined sets of instructions are based on timing, price, quantity, or any mathematical model. Apart from profit opportunities for the trader, algo-trading renders markets more liquid and trading more systematic by ruling out the impact of human emotions on trading activities.
- **Alternative Investment Fund (AIF):** Alternative Investment Fund means any fund established or incorporated in India (and regulated by SEBI) which is a privately pooled investment vehicle which collects funds from sophisticated investors, whether Indian or foreign, for investing it in accordance with a defined investment policy for the benefit of its investors.
- **Anchor investor:** Anchor investor is concept launched by SEBI in 2009. Anchor investors are institutional investors (not individual) who are invited to subscribe/purchase the shares before the IPO opens so that it popularizes the issue and increases the confidence of the other investors and improves the demand of the share.
- **Angel Investor:** An angel investor is a person who invests in highly risky companies, typically before those companies have any revenue or profits. Angel investors are often among an entrepreneur's family and friends and invest in small start-ups and entrepreneurs and provide more favourable terms. Angel investors are focused on helping start-ups take their first steps, rather than the possible profit they may get from the business. Fund-raising with angel investors is typically done more casually, using networking and crowd funding platforms. Essentially, angel investors are

the opposite of venture capitalists. Angel investors typically use their own money, unlike venture capitalists who takes care of pooled money from many other investors and place them in a strategically managed fund. Angel Investment in India is regulated by SEBI under Alternative Investment Funds (AIF).

- **Asset Liability Mismatch:** When a Bank borrows for 5 years and lends it for 10 years, that means the Bank will have to pay their liability after 5 years but the loan which it has given (asset for bank) will come only after 10 years. So, there is a mismatch in tenure of assets and liabilities of the bank and the bank may have to arrange funds from other sources after 5 years. So, banks and other financial institutions like NBFCs may face this kind challenge which is called asset liability mismatch.
- **Balance Sheet Recession:** A balance sheet recession is a type of economic recession that occurs when high levels of debt of either (or all) one of the sectors viz. Private sector, Household or Government causes them to focus on savings by paying down debt rather than spending or investing, causing economic growth to slow or decline. Covid-19 can end us in balance sheet recession.
- **Bilateral Netting:** A bilateral netting agreement enables two counterparties in a financial contract to offset claims against each other to determine a single net payment obligation due from one counterparty to the other.
- **Bail-in and bail-out:** A bail-in is rescuing a financial institution on the brink of failure by making its creditors and depositors take a loss on their holdings/deposits. A bail-in is the opposite of a bail-out, which involves the rescue of an institution/ financial institution by external parties, typically government using taxpayer's money.
- **Cash Deposit Ratio:** Cash-deposit ratio of banks is the ratio of cash in hands (i.e. in banks) and balances (deposits) with the RBI as percentage of aggregate (demand & time) deposits with the bank.
- **Cash flow-based lending:** Cash flow means the regular income which a business generates from its operations. Generally, banks give loan based on how much collateral someone is willing to keep or what are the assets of the company. This collateral/ asset acts as security for the loan given. Cash flow-based lending means that banks while giving loan should not seek collateral rather than they should look for whether the business is generating enough regular income (cashflow) so that the business is able to repay the loan. In this way the banks will be able to give more loans and credit/ GDP ratio can be improved. In cash flow lending, a financial institution grants a loan that is backed by the recipient's past and future cash flows that they anticipate they will receive in the future.
- **Circular Economy:** A circular economy is an industrial system that is restorative or regenerative by intention and design. It replaces the end-of-life concept with restoration, shifts towards the use of renewable energy, eliminates the use of toxic chemicals, which impair reuse and return to the biosphere, and aims for the elimination of waste through the superior design of materials, products, systems and business models.
- **Core Inflation:** It is a measure of headline inflation excluding volatile components i.e. food and fuel items.

- **Creeping Inflation:** When the rise in prices is very slow (less than 3% per annum) like that of a snail or creeper, it is called creeping inflation. Such an increase in prices is regarded safe and essential for economic growth.
- **Cross-Retaliation:** Under the traditional retaliation process, a WTO member can enforce a ruling of the Dispute Settlement Body (DSB) by suspending trade concessions enjoyed by the non-compliant member in the same sector. However, the WTO members who are economically more powerful are not likely to be harmed by the suspension of trade concessions in goods or services by substantially less powerful members. In solution to the above problem 'cross-retaliation' is proposed and adopted by the Dispute Settlement Mechanism. Under cross retaliation the complainant member country can suspend the intellectual property rights of the non-complaint nation. 'Cross-retaliation' has better potential for compliance by the defaulting countries and specifically developed countries, as it creates deterrence among the developed Countries regarding the protection of Intellectual property rights.
- **Cross-Subsidization:** Cross subsidization is the practice of funding one product with the profits generated by a different product.
- **Crowd funding:** Crowd funding or marketplace financing refers to a method of funding a project or new venture through small amounts of money raised from a large number of people, typically through a portal (internet/social media) acting as an intermediary. Crowd funding makes use of the easy accessibility of vast networks of people through social media and crowd funding websites to bring investors and entrepreneurs together. Crowd funding has the potential to increase entrepreneurship by expanding the pool of investors from whom funds can be raised beyond the traditional circle of owners.
- **Debt Overhang:** It refers to a debt burden so large that an entity cannot take on additional debt to finance future projects. A debt overhang serves to dissuade current investment, since all earnings from new projects would only go in repayment of debt.
- **Debt Restructuring:** Debt restructuring is a process used by companies facing cash flow problems or financial distress to avoid the risk of default. It can be carried out by reducing the interest rates on loans or by extending the payment term. It can also involve a bond haircut where the company may negotiate to write off (reduce/remove/extinguish) certain portion of interest or principal due to the investors. It can also include a debt for equity/share swap which means that company's creditors may agree to cancel some or all of the debt in exchange for equity/shares in the company. Restructuring debt can be a win-win for both entities as the company avoids bankruptcy and the lenders typically receive more than what they would through a bankruptcy proceeding.
- **Debt Trap:** It is a situation in which it becomes difficult or impossible to repay the debt, typically because high interest payments prevent repayment of the principal. It leads to the borrower into a cycle of re-borrowing, or rolling over, their loan payments.
- **Deleverage** means reducing the debt (by selling assets). A leveraged company means a company having huge debt/loan on its balance sheet.
- **Digital Banking Units (DBUs):** DBUs are physical banking units that will provide services without requiring paper. The products and services in these DBUs will be provided in two modes, namely, self-service and assisted modes, with self-service mode being available on 24*7*365 basis. The banks are also free to engage the services

of digital business facilitators and business correspondents to expand the footprint of the DBUs. In Oct. 2022, Scheduled Commercial Banks launched 75 DBUs in 75 districts.

- **Duty credit scrip:** It is an important export promotion incentive provided by the government to exporters in which government gives tax incentives to the exporters. The government gives a receipt/ paper to the exporter worth some percentage (2% to 5%) of the export value. This paper then exporter uses to adjust against tax payment, for example import duty on raw materials used for exports or other taxes on manufacturing processes.
- **Economies of Scale:** These are the cost advantages that enterprises obtain due to their scale/size of operation. Basically, when the size of a factory increases, the per unit cost decreases.
- **Employment Elasticity (of growth):** It is a measure of percentage change in **employment** associated with 1 percentage point change in economic growth. An employment elasticity of 0.01 implies that with every 1 percentage point growth in GDP, employment increases by just .01 percent. Employment elasticity is falling consistently from 0.4 in 1990s to 0.2 in 2014 and then 0.1 now.
- **Ever-greening of Loans:** It is a practice whereby banks extend even more loans to debt-laden companies to help them repay previous loans.
- **Financial repression:** It occurs when governments implement policies to channel to themselves funds that in a deregulated market environment would go elsewhere.
- **Fiscal Drag:** It is a situation where income growth or inflation moves taxpayers into higher tax brackets. This in effect increases government tax revenue without actually increasing tax rates. The increase in taxes reduces aggregate demand and consumer spending because a larger share of the people's income now goes into taxes, which leads to deflationary pressures or drag on the economy. Fiscal drag is an automatic fiscal stabilizer as it controls a rapidly expanding economy from overheating.
- **Fiscal dominance:** Fiscal dominance occurs when central banks use their monetary powers to support the prices of government securities and to keep interest rates at low levels to reduce the costs of servicing sovereign/government debt. Fiscal dominance implies that Fiscal considerations limit the scope for an independent and prudent monetary policy.
- **Fiscal Slippage:** It refers to the missing of fiscal targets like expenditure, receipts, deficit etc. in the country's budget.
- **Force Majeure:** Force Majeure is a French phrase that means a 'superior force'. The law relating to Force Majeure is embodied under Sections 32 and 56 of the Indian Contract Act, 1872. It is a contractual provision agreed upon between parties. The occurrence of a force majeure event protects a party from liability for its failure to perform a contractual obligation. Typically, force majeure events include an Act of God or natural disasters, war or war-like situations, epidemics, pandemics, etc. The intention of a force majeure clause is to save the performing party from the consequences of something over which it has no control. Force Majeure is an exception to what would otherwise amount to a breach of contract. This term is generally used in commercial contracts.
- **Forward Guidance:** It refers to the communication from a central bank about the state of the economy and likely future course of monetary policy.

- **Gig-Economy:** A labour market characterized by the prevalence of short-term contracts or freelance work as opposed to permanent jobs.
- **Hard Currency:** It refers to money that is issued by a nation that is seen as politically and economically stable. Hard currencies are widely accepted around the world as a form of payment for goods and services and is expected to remain relatively stable.
- **Headcount Ratio:** It is the proportion of population that lives below the poverty line.
- **Headline Inflation:** It measures price inflation arising due to all types of commodities in the economy.
- **Hot Money:** It refers to the currency which quickly and regularly moves between financial markets in search of higher short-term interest rates. Hot money continuously shifts from countries with low interest rates to those with higher rates. These financial transfers affect the exchange rate and impact a country's balance of payment.
- **Inflation Premium:** The higher return that investors demand in exchange for investing in a long-term security where inflation has a greater potential to reduce the real return.
- **Insurance density:** It is measured as the ratio of premium (in US dollar) to the total population.
- **Insurance penetration:** It is measured as the percentage of insurance premium to GDP.
- **Inter-connected lending** refers to a situation where the promoter/owner of the bank is also a borrower and, as such, it is possible for a promoter to channel the depositors' money into their own group companies.
- **Invisible Hand:** This phrase was introduced by 'Adam Smith' in his book 'The Wealth of Nations'. It is a metaphor for the unseen forces (of demand and supply) that move the free market economy. Through individual self-interest and freedom of production as well as consumption, the best interest of society, as a whole are fulfilled.
- **Investment multiplier:** It is the ratio of change in output (GDP) to change in Investment. For Example, if as a result of investment of Rs. 100 crores, the GDP increases by Rs. 300 crores then investment multiplier is equal to 3. This means that if the investment multiplier is more, we can achieve higher growth in output (GDP) with less investment.
- **Labour Force:** No. of employed persons plus no. of unemployed persons.
- **Labour Force Participation Rate (LFPR):** Labour Force Participation Rate is defined as the percentage of population in the labour force. (labour force/population)
- **Laffer Curve:** Laffer curve was developed by Arthur Laffer to show the relationship between tax rates and the amount of tax revenue collected by the government. With increase in tax rate, first the tax revenue increases and at certain tax rate, the tax revenue is maximum and after that, the tax revenue starts declining.
- **Letter of credit:** It is a letter from bank guaranteeing that a buyer's payment to a seller will be received on time and for the correct amount. In the event that the buyer is unable to make payment on the purchase, the bank will be required to cover the full or remaining amount of the purchase. Actually, in case of trade, when a seller sells something then the buyer makes payment generally after 15/30 days. But to secure his payment, the seller asks for "letter of credit" from the buyer, which it provides from a Bank. And the Bank gives letter of credit because the bank trusts the buyer and the buyers are

doing banking with the bank for long and the bank may also ask some margin/security from the buyer to provide the letter of credit.

- **Letter of Undertaking:** In international banking system, it is a provision of bank guarantee, under which an Indian bank allows its customer (say for importing something from a foreign country) to raise money from another Indian bank's foreign branch in the form of a short-term credit.
- **Line of credit:** It is a pre-set amount of money that a bank has agreed to lend you. You can draw from the line of credit when you need it, up to the maximum amount. You'll pay interest only on the amount you borrow.
- **Leverage Ratio:** It is the proportion of debt that a company has as compared to its equity/shareholders capital.
- **Liquidity Coverage Ratio (LCR):** The LCR is calculated by dividing institution (Banks/NBFCs) high-quality liquid assets (for example cash, govt. securities, securities issued or guaranteed by foreign governments etc.) by its total net cash flows, over a 30-day period. In background of IL&FS and HDFL crisis, RBI on 24th May 2019 proposed introducing LCR for large NBFCs to help tackle liquidity issues in the sector. NBFCs will have to maintain minimum high-quality liquid assets of 50% of total net cash outflows over the following 30 calendar days starting from Dec 1, 2020. Suppose a bank's expected cash outflow/spending for the next 30 days is Rs. 150 and cash inflow is expected to be Rs. 50, which means net cash outflow for next 30-day period is Rs. 100. In such a case if bank is holding cash and govt. securities (which are called High Quality Liquid Assets) of Rs. 60, then LCR = (High Quality Liquid Asset)/ (Banks Net cash outflow for 30-day period) = Rs. 60/ Rs. 100 = 60%.
- **Market distortion:** It is an economic scenario that occurs when there is an intervention in a given market by a governing body. The intervention may take the form of price ceilings, price floors, tax or subsidies or any other kind of restriction related to quantity etc. Market distortions create market failures, which is not an economically ideal situation. Market distortions are often a by-product of government policies that aim to protect and raise the general well-being of all market participants.
- **Market Failure:** It is the economic situation defined by an inefficient distribution of goods and services in the free market. In market failure, the individual incentives for rational behaviour do not lead to rational outcomes for the group. Public goods are examples of market failure.
- **Minimum Export Price (MEP):** It is the price below which exports are not permitted. It is imposed to curb the price rise and prevent disruptions in domestic supply.
- **Minimum Import Price (MIP):** It is the price below which imports are not allowed. It is imposed to curb imports and protect domestic producers.
- **Monetary Transmission:** Itis the pass-through of RBI's policy actions to the economy at large in terms of asset prices and general economic conditions.
- **Mutual Fund:** It is a type of financial vehicle made up of a pool of money collected from many investors to invest in securities like stocks, bonds, money market instruments, and other assets. Mutual funds are operated by professional money managers, who allocate the fund's assets and attempt to produce capital gains or income for the fund's investors. Mutual funds give small or individual investors access to professionally managed portfolios of equities, bonds, and other securities. Each shareholder, therefore, participates proportionally in the gains or losses of the fund.

- **National Small Savings Funds (NSSF):** A fund established in 1999 under Public Account of India. The receipts under various small savings schemes like Public Provident Fund (PPF), Post office deposit schemes, Sukanya Samridhi Scheme etc. goes into this fund.
- **Negative Consensus:** Under the Dispute Settlement Body of WTO, the decision of WTO panel can be rejected only by a negative consensus i.e. all member-countries present have to turn down the ruling.
- **Non-Convertible Debentures (NCD):** Non-convertible debentures (NCDs) are financial instruments that are issued by companies to raise medium to long-term capital. NCDs are debt instruments with a fixed tenure and people who invest in these receive regular interest at a certain rate. Some debentures can be converted into shares after a certain point in time. This is done at the discretion of the owner. However, this is not possible in the case of NCDs. That's why they are known as non-convertible. NCDs can be secured or unsecured both. They are listed on the stock exchanges.
- **Non-Tariff Barriers:** These are trade barriers that restrict the import or export of goods through means other than tariffs. WTO identifies various non-tariff barriers to trade, including import licensing, pre-shipment inspections, rules of origin, custom delayers, and other mechanisms that prevent or restrict trade.
- **Open Access (electricity):** Open access is the non-discriminatory use of transmission and distribution infrastructure of the licensees (the company which has provided such infrastructure) by consumers (with demand greater than or equal to 1MW) for procuring electricity from the source of their choice.
- **Openness (of an economy):** It is measured as exports plus imports of goods and services of a country as a percentage of its GDP.
- **Operating Ratio:** A company's operating expenses as a percentage of revenue/sales. The operating ratio shows how efficient a company's management is at keeping costs low while generating revenue or sales. If this ratio is decreasing that means company is becoming more efficient.
- **Overdraft:** It is a short-term credit facility from a lending institution that is granted when an account reaches zero. The overdraft allows the account holder to continue withdrawing money even when the account has no funds in it or has insufficient funds to cover the amount of the withdrawal. **Cash credit** is similar to overdraft but is commonly offered to businesses rather than to individual consumers and generally involves some form of collateral. **Overdraft** is generally offered to retail customers and is attached to a bank savings account.
- **Overhead Capital:** Overhead capital can be divided into economic overhead capital and social overhead capital. Economic overhead capital refers to such things as roads, railways, power transmission systems etc.; and social overhead capital is investment in such activities as education, health, police, fire, etc.
- **Overheating of Economy:** An overheating economy is an economy that is expanding at an unsustainable rate. The two main signs of an overheating economy are firstly rising rates of inflation; and secondly an unemployment rate that is below the normal rate for an economy.
- **Poverty:** It is a state or condition in which a person or community lacks the financial resources and essentials to enjoy a minimum standard of life and well-being that's considered acceptable in society.
- **Poverty Gap:** Poverty gap is the ratio by which the mean income of the poor falls below the poverty line. Poverty gap is used to reflect the intensity of poverty.

- **Provisioning:** When a bank gives loan, then, they need to set aside (keep in reserve and can't lend) certain funds for the safety of the depositors. This is called provisioning against loan and is expressed as a percentage of loan given. For normal/standard loans the provisioning requirement may be very less but for loans which have turned NPAs, the provisioning requirement may be very high. If RBI says provisioning is 1% that means if a bank gives loan of Rs. 100 then it needs to keep Rs. 1 in a separate reserve fund.
- **Public float:** The percentage of shares that are traded on the stock exchange are called 'Public float' and the investors holding these shares are called 'Public investors.' Rest of the shares are locked and are not traded and held by promotors, employees, Government etc. During 'Initial Public Offering (IPO)', minimum requirement of public float is 10% and within three years the public float should be 25%. Promoters should hold at least 20% shares.
- **Pump priming:** It is the action taken to stimulate an economy, usually during a recessionary period, through government spending and tax reductions. The term pump priming is derived from the operation of older pumps - a suction valve had to be primed with water so that the pump would function properly.
- **Relative poverty:** It refers to a standard which is defined in terms of the society in which an individual lives and which therefore changes over time. An income-related example would be "persons living on less than X% of average Indian income".
- **Revenue Neutral Tax Rate (GST):** Any change in the tax reforms may result in a deficit in the amount of revenue collected by the country. Therefore, there must be a method through which the change in this system does not affect the collections by the government. Revenue Neutral Rate or RNR as commonly known is the tax rate which ensures that the revenue collected by new tax regime is same as that collected by the previous one. The new tax rates are designed according to the Revenue Neutral Rate.
- **Reverse Charge Mechanism (under GST):** It is a mechanism where the recipient of the goods or services is liable to pay/deposit GST instead of the supplier. Generally, we see in the GST that the supplier charges the GST from the buyer and then he deposits the GST with Govt. But in certain cases (exceptions), it is the Buyer/Recipient who needs to deposit the GST with Govt. and of course he bears the burden of tax too.
- **Refinance:** Refinance means replacing an existing loan with a new loan that pays off the debt of the old loan. A refinance occurs when an individual or business revises the interest rate, payment schedule, and terms of a previous credit agreement. Debtors will often choose to refinance a loan agreement when the interest rate environment has substantially changed, causing potential savings on debt payments from a new agreement. A refinance involves the re-evaluation of a person or business's credit terms and credit status.
- **Regulatory Forbearance:** Forbearance means tolerance. Regulatory forbearance is the action of refraining from exercising a legal right, especially enforcing the payment of a debt by the regulator. So, regulatory forbearance occurs when a regulatory body is showing tolerance and not very strict in enforcing rules/regulations and giving a lot of relaxations.
- **Rollover loan/credit facility:** It is a type of loan which is automatically renewed when it is not repaid in full within a predefined loan term. Instead of entering into default, as would be the case with other types of

loans, the debt is simply carried over to a new loan. The terms and conditions of the new loan may be different to those of the original loan.

- **Round Tripping (of FDI):** Money from a country (example India) flow to a foreign country (Mauritius) and comes back as foreign direct investment (FDI) to India. This may happen because of more liberal tax rates in Mauritius or to send black money out of India and then returned to India as FDI.
- **Shell Company:** There is no clear definition of what shell company is in the Companies Act, or any other Act. But typically, shell companies include multiple layers of companies (subsidiaries) that have been created for the purpose of diverting money or for money laundering. Most shell companies do not manufacture any product or deal in any product or render any service. They are mostly used to make financial transactions without any real economic activity. Generally, these companies hold assets only on paper and not in reality. These types of corporations are not all necessarily illegal, but they are sometimes used illegitimately, such as to disguise business ownership from law enforcement agencies or the public.
- **Subsidiary Company:** A subsidiary company also called Daughter Company is a company owned and controlled (more than 50%) by another company. The owning company is called a parent company or sometimes a holding company.
- **Securitization:** Securitization is the process of pooling and repackaging of financial assets (like loans given) into marketable securities that can be sold to investors. For example, an NBFC has given loan to different companies. Now these different loan papers are an asset for NBFC. Suppose the loan papers are of Rs. 100 crores. Now, one lakh shares have been created out of this asset worth Rs. 100 each and these shares can be sold to different people. NBFCs will get immediate liquidity/money and the share price will vary depending on whether the loan is being repaid properly or not. If the companies to whom NBFC gave loan are not returning the principal or interest, the price of security/share will fall. *Banks/NBFCs can sell these loan papers directly ("Direct Assignment" with certain restrictions) or they can also create security ("Securitization") out of this loan paper and sell, both routes are adopted when they want liquidity.*
- **Sovereign Wealth Fund (SWF) :** It is a State (govt.) owned investment fund or entity that is commonly established from export surpluses, fiscal surpluses, proceeds from privatization etc. Countries generally create SWFs to diversify their revenue streams. For ex., UAE relies on oil exports for its wealth. Hence, it devotes a portion of its reserves to an SWF that invests in diversified assets that can act as a shield against oil-related risks.
- **Sweat Equity:** Owners or employees work in companies like cash-strapped startups at salaries below the market rate in return for a stake (shares) in the company, which they hope to profit from when the business eventually becomes profitable or sold out. This is called sweat equity i.e., getting shares in the company in return for their effort rather than purchasing shares by paying money.
- **Systemic Change:** Systemic change means that change has to be fundamental and affects how the whole system functions. Systemic change can mean gradual institutional reforms, but those reforms must be based on and aimed at a transformation of the fundamental qualities and principles of the system itself. Systemic change is a

change that pervades all part of the system rather than just one part.

- **Venture Capital:** It is a form of private equity and a type of financing that investors provide to start-up companies and small businesses that are believed to have long-term growth potential. Venture capital generally comes from well-off investors, investment banks and any other financial institutions.
- **Skewflation:** Skewflation means the skewness of inflation among different sectors of the economy i.e., some sectors are facing huge inflation, some none and some deflation.
- **Stagflation:** It is an exception to the general theory of inflation and growth. Generally, when economic growth is less (due to less demand) then inflation is also less. But if there is supply side issues like disruption in supply chain, labour protests, factories lockdown etc. then inflation increases (cost push inflation) and economy slows down. So, in stagflation growth is less but inflation and unemployment are high. It was triggered first in 1973 by the OPEC's fourfold increase in oil prices which raised all prices, thus slowing down economic growth.
- **Stimulus:** A stimulus is an attempt by policymakers to kickstart a sluggish economy through a package of measures. In case of fiscal stimulus, the Government increases its spending and or slashes tax rates to put more money in the hands of consumers to stimulate the economy. A monetary stimulus will see the central bank expanding money supply or reducing the cost of money (interest rates), to spur consumer spending.
- **Stock/Share Warrant:** It is a document issued by the company to the investor that gives the warrant holder (investor) a right to subscribe equity shares of the company at a predetermined price on or after a pre-determined time period. The warrant holder is given a right but not an obligation to subscribe equity shares. If the warrant holder does not exercise his option to subscribe to equity shares, then the initial amount (some percent of the total amount paid by the warrant holder to purchase the warrant) paid stands forfeited.
- **Tariff rate quotas (TRQs):** TRQs allow a pre-determined quantity of a product to be imported at lower import duty rates (in-quota duty) than the duty rate normally applicable to that product.
- **Tax Base:** Tax base is defined as the total value of the financial streams or assets on which tax can be imposed by the government. For example, in case of income tax, the tax base is all the income that can be taxed by the government (taxable income). If the minimum amount/threshold of the income on which tax is imposed is lowered, this will automatically increase (widen) the tax base; if it is raised, the tax base will be narrowed. In case of service tax, tax base is the value of services on which service tax is imposed. For example, if CCD sells tea/coffee worth Rs. 10 crore and of course it collects service tax/GST on 10 crores, so tax base will be Rs. 10 crores. In case of property tax, tax base is the value of property on which property tax is imposed. Because the size of the tax base influences the taxable revenues that are available to a government, the size and growth of the tax base is crucial to the planning efforts of any government.
- **Tax Buoyancy:** Tax buoyancy is an indicator to measure efficiency and responsiveness of revenue mobilization in response to growth in the GDP or National Income. It is measured as a ratio of growth in Tax Revenue to the growth in nominal GDP *(i.e., ratio of percentage change in tax*

revenue to percentage change in nominal GDP). Tax buoyancy greater than one is good for economy.

- **Tax Elasticity:** The tax elasticity measures the responsiveness of tax revenue to changes in tax rate and is defined as the ratio of percentage change in tax revenue to percentage change in tax rate.
- **Tax Expenditure:** Tax expenditure refers to the revenues foregone as a result of various exemptions and concessions given by the government. These exemptions are given for certain specific sectors to promote growth and to industries located in difficult areas and promoting balanced regional growth.
- **Terms of Trade (ToT):** It is the ratio of export price index to import price index. If a country is exporting only apples (price Rs. 120/kg) and importing only oranges (price Rs. 40/kg), then the terms of trade (TOT) is simply the ratio of price of apples to the price of oranges i.e. Rs. 120/ Rs. 40 = 3. So, TOT is a measure of how much imports an economy can get for a unit of exported goods which in this example is 3 times.
- **Trickle-down effect:** When the income of the big corporations and rich people increase then they invest/spend this income in the economy which ultimately reaches to the poor people at the bottom of the pyramid. When the poor people get income then they spend (their wages) to drive demand and economic growth. Trickle-down economics is a theory that claims benefits for the wealthy trickle down to everyone else. These benefits are tax cuts on businesses, high-income earners, capital gains, and dividends. Trickle-down theory is more specific. It says targeted tax cuts on rich people/corporations work better than general tax reduction across the board.
- **Velocity of Money:** Velocity refers to the number of times the available money stock may roll over or change hands to finance transactions equivalent of nominal GDP. It is derived as 'Nominal GDP'/Money Supply.
- **Walking Inflation:** When prices rise moderately and the annual inflation rate is in single digit (3% - 10%), it is called walking or trotting inflation. Inflation at this rate is a warning signal for the government to control it before it turns high.
- **Wage Inflation:** A general increase in the prices of goods that is preceded by and results from an increase in wages.
- **Withholding tax (WHT):** A withholding tax, or a retention tax, is an income tax to be paid to the government by the payer of the income rather than by the recipient of the income. The tax is thus withheld or deducted from the income due to the recipient. WHT is similar to Tax Deducted at Source (TDS) but is applicable for payments to non-residents i.e. foreign transactions.
- **Zombie (firms):** Zombies are typically identified using the interest coverage ratio which is the ratio of a firm's profit before interest and tax payment to its total interest expense. Firms with interest coverage ratio lower than one are unable to meet their interest obligations from their income and are categorized as zombies.

◈◈◈